Sint patrike be gan
ne to preche aboute þe
yere of oure lorde cc̄c̄
c̄c̄ iiii and as he pre
ched the passion of ie
n crist to the kynge of scotlonde he
stode before hym and lened vpon his
bordone that he helde in his honde
and his was perauenture vpon the
fote of the kynge and the point of
the bordon persed the kynges fote
and thanne the kynge wende that
the holy bisshop hadde done it we
tyngly and other weyes he myght
not receiue the faithe but yef he suf
fered so for ihu crist and therfor he
suffered it paciently, and thanne at
the laste the holy man conceiued thị
thinge that was al abasshed and
thanne anone he heled the kynge
by his praiers, and he gate to that
prouince that no venemous beste
myght liue ther ynne, and yet he
gate more that the trees and the
lether of that contre bene holsom
ayenst venyme ¶ Ther was a
man that hadde stole a shepe fro

British Library, MS Egerton 876, f.68ra.

GILTE LEGENDE

VOLUME 1

EDITED BY

RICHARD HAMER
with the assistance of Vida Russell

Published for
THE EARLY ENGLISH TEXT SOCIETY
by the
OXFORD UNIVERSITY PRESS
2006

OXFORD

UNIVERSITY PRESS

Great Clarendon Street, Oxford OX2 6DP

Oxford University Press is a department of the University of Oxford.
It furthers the University's objective of excellence in research, scholarship,
and education by publishing worldwide in

Oxford New York

Auckland Cape Town Dar es Salaam Hong Kong Karachi
Kuala Lumpur Madrid Melbourne Mexico City Nairobi
New Delhi Shanghai Taipei Toronto

With offices in

Argentina Austria Brazil Chile Czech Republic France Greece
Guatemala Hungary Italy Japan Poland Portugal Singapore
South Korea Switzerland Thailand Turkey Ukraine Vietnam

Oxford is a registered trade mark of Oxford University Press
in the UK and in certain other countries

Published in the United States
by Oxford University Press Inc., New York

British Library Cataloguing in Publication Data

Data available

Library of Congress Cataloging in Publication Data

Data applied for

ISBN 0-19-920577-9   978-0-19-920577-6

1 3 5 7 9 10 8 6 4 2

Typeset by Anne Joshua, Oxford
Printed in Great Britain
on acid-free paper by
The Cromwell Press, Trowbridge, Wiltshire

PREFACE TO VOLUMES 1 AND 2

This edition of *Gilte Legende* will be published as two volumes of text followed by a third consisting of general introduction, explanatory notes, select glossary and indexes.

A fuller list of acknowledgements will precede volume 3, but we wish at this stage to express our thanks to the librarians and staff of the manuscript room at the British Library, Duke Humfrey's Library at the Bodleian in Oxford, Lambeth Palace Library, Gloucester Cathedral Library, the Library of Trinity College Dublin, Cambridge University Library, and the Bibliothèque Nationale in Paris for assistance on our visits and for supplying photographic reproductions; to the librarians of Corpus Christi College Cambridge, Trinity College Cambridge, Durham University Library, the Lilly Library in Bloomington, Indiana, the Beinecke Rare Books Library at Yale University, the Bibliothèque Municipale in Rennes, and to Professor Toshiyuki Takamiya for supplying photographic reproductions; to all the above for permission to make use of manuscripts in their care and possession in the preparation of this edition; and to the Trustees of the British Library and the Dean and Chapter of Gloucester Cathedral for permission to include plates of reproductions from their manuscripts.

CONTENTS OF VOLUME 1

CONTENTS

PLATES IN VOLUME I

British Library, MS Egerton 876, f. 68^r frontispiece
reproduced by permission of the Trustees of the British Library
Gloucester Cathedral Library, MS 12, f. 75^r facing p. xiv
reproduced by permission of the Dean and Chapter of Gloucester Cathedral

SIGLA FOR VOLUME 1

A1 London, British Library, MS Additional 11565
A2 London, British Library, MS Additional 35298
D Oxford, Bodleian Library, MS Douce 372
Du Durham, University Library, MS Cosin V.ii.14
E London, British Library, MS Egerton 876
G Gloucester, Cathedral Library, MS 12
H1 London, British Library, MS Harley 630
H2 London, British Library, MS Harley 4775
K Cambridge, Corpus Christi College, MS 142
L London, Lambeth Palace Library, MS 72
M Tokyo, Professor Toshiyuki Takamiya Collection, MS 45/23
  & Bloomington, Indiana, Lilly Library, Poole MS 98/58
P2 Paris, Bibliothèque Nationale, MS fr. 244–5
S Rennes, Bibliothèque Municipale, MS 266
T1 Dublin, Trinity College, MS 319
T2 Cambridge, Trinity College, MS O. 9. 1
W William, *Passio Sancti Albani* in *Acta Sanctorum* Jun.
  V. 129–38

EDITORIAL PROCEDURES

THE TEXT

Gilte Legende (GiL) is a close translation, with a few additions and omissions, of Jean de Vignay's *Légende Dorée* (LgD), which in turn is a close translation of Jacobus de Voragine's *Legenda Aurea* (LgA). A colophon to MS D says that it was translated from French by 'a synfulle wrecche' (hereafter s.w.) in 1438. The main differences of content are the addition in GiL of lives of St Malchus and St Alban and chapters on the Conception of the Virgin Mary, Adam and Eve, and the Five Wiles of Pharaoh, the omission of Resurrection, the Virgin of Antioch, St Stephen pope and the Beheading of St John the Baptist, part-substitution of different versions for the Nativity of St John the Baptist and St Catherine, accidental duplication of St Cecilia, and the transfer of Advent from the beginning to near the end.

Explanatory notes in volume 3 will consist largely of citations from the French and Latin sources to show accidental and intentional variations between them and *Gilte Legende*. It will be seen that s.w. had to some extent referred to a copy of the Latin as well as the French.

The most recent edition of LgA is by G. P. Maggioni (2000), and of LgD by B. Dunn-Lardeau (1997); the latter was edited from an early printed edition which had been revised from the Latin, and therefore does not always precisely represent the French source of GiL, but the readings from the earliest extant manuscript of LgD are supplied in the critical apparatus. There are reliable modern translations of LgA, into English by W. G. Ryan (1993), French by J.-B. M. Roze (1902), and German by R. Benz (1915–1921), but these were made from the edition of LgA by Th. Graesse (1845 etc.), which, being based on an early printed edition, differs to some extent from Maggioni's text, and is in some respects closer to the version used by Vignay for the LgD. (Full details of these editions and translations are given in the bibliography in volume 3.)

Gilte Legende is more or less complete in MSS A1, A2, D, E, H1, H2 and L; G consists of the first half; also some chapters are found singly or in groups in other manuscripts. This edition is based on

MS E, and, when that is defective, on other manuscripts as indicated at the beginning of each chapter, usually G in volume 1 and H1 in volume 2. The five manuscripts whose text is closest to the original divide into two branches, EH1 and GDH2, of which E and G are the most accurate. H1 contains numerous corrections in several hands, some of them demonstrably taken from the other branch. D, which lacks many scattered leaves, is less accurate and has a tendency to minor paraphrase; H2 is a close and careful copy of D. A1, and to a greater extent A2, are characterised by minor paraphrases and expansions, some of them shared; both at the beginning of GiL primarily belong to the EH1 branch, but by the end have transferred, at different stages, to the other. L also has a certain amount of minor paraphrase, and basically had an exemplar not far remote from E; but it also had access, perhaps through corrections in its exemplar, to a copy closer to the original translation than any other surviving manuscript.

The aim is to re-construct as nearly as possible s.w.'s text, but in the spelling of the base manuscript and with modern punctuation, capitalisation, word–division and paragraph division. Therefore translation errors, whether directly attributable to s.w. or inherited from LgD, are allowed to stand, with the correct French or Latin version supplied in the explanatory notes in volume 3. In a few places this results in a meaningless text explicable only by reference to the notes. When it cannot be decided whether s.w. or an early copyist was responsible for an error, s.w. has been given the benefit of the doubt, and the text emended.

Emendations are printed within square brackets [ ], letters or words illegible or missing because of damage appear in angle brackets ⟨ ⟩, and marginal and interlinear corrections are enclosed in primes ` ´.

Abbreviations are expanded silently according to the usual conventions and following the normal practice of the scribe, such as for final curls or bars representing plurals. A prominent upward curl on -r, frequent in H1, is given as -e. *Ihu* is expanded to *Ihesu*, *Ihc* to *Ihesus*. Various abbreviated forms of *Capitulum* in the rubrics have not been expanded, nor has *et c.* in the text.

Many curls and strokes of uncertain significance are ignored, including superscript curves over final *p/pp* on such words as *bishop(p)* and *worship(p)*, and the downward flourish which is frequent on *-dd* , as *hadd*, and sometimes found on words ending in single *-d*, such as *and*, which also appears occasionally as *ande*.

Macrons over medial and final indeterminate *u/n* are ignored, the letter being assumed to be *n*, thus *prison* rather than *prisoun*. There is usually a bar through final *-ll*, but this is not always visible because placed across the bottom of the loops, and a bar through the loop of final *-h* is standard in hand A of MS E, and occasional in hand B; all these bars have been ignored, except for instances of the definite article spelt *th* with barred *h*, and *nobl* with barred *l*, on both of which final *e* is supplied..

Letters made up of minims can cause difficulties; *n* and *u* are often indistinguishable, and can appear to be the opposite of what is intended, though this is usually obvious from context. Unfamiliar names are a frequent source of uncertainty, sometimes leading to spellings with medial *v* for original *n* (*e.g. Clyvy* for *Cluny*). Similarly *ni* and *m* are sometimes interchanged and hard to distinguish, and it is, for example, impossible to tell whether E hand B writes *Mateins* or *Matenis* for 'Matins'.

A particular problem arises in the words *denien* and *deuien*, with overlapping sense. For reasons explained in the note to 2 Nicholas l. 34, it seems that s.w. translated forms of French *devier* into the appropriate form of *deuien/devien*, though subsequent scribes probably often took the medial *u* as *n*. Here *u* is given in the text, and uncertain cases are notified in the apparatus.

Many place and personal names had already become garbled in the French copy used by s.w., and others suffered further at the hands of the English scribes. In most cases the names are given in the form in which they appear in the base manuscript, unless other manuscripts suggest s.w. had used a better spelling, in which case the text is emended to that.

In H1 and G, yogh and zed are identical in form and have been transcribed according to their phonetic significance.

Both E hands usually spell *nought* as *not*, and this has been retained in the text.

Several manuscripts, including E, spell forms of 'live' and 'liver' (one who lives) and 'believe' and 'believer' indiscriminately with *i/y* or *e*, as *leue, lyue etc.*, and when this results in ambiguity it is clarified in the explanatory notes.

Forms of 'throw' sometimes appear in E with *d* for *th*. Such spellings, which are not recorded in the *Middle English Dictionary*, have been emended.

The scribes are generally casual about including superscript *e* or *te* to indicate ordinal numerals; such omissions have been left un-emended.

Punctuation in the manuscripts is light, especially in E, which not infrequently begins new sentences without indication. On the other hand H1 marks large numbers of new paragraphs, sometimes inappropriately in mid-sentence. Manuscript punctuation is mentioned in the apparatus only if it indicates a scribal misreading of the text. In line with the tendencies of E, editorial modernised punctuation of the text has also been kept relatively light.

APPARATUS

The critical apparatus has been limited for the most part to variants from one manuscript on each branch of the stemma, H1 and G for preference. For these two manuscripts, variants are comprehensively recorded , subject to the general exclusions listed below. When G is not available, which includes the whole of volume 2, variants are supplied either from D, which lacks a large number of scattered leaves, or from H2, a close copy of D. Variants from other manuscripts are supplied in passages near the beginning and end of GiL, where some main manuscripts are defective. The apparatus is given in full from all manuscripts for two long chapters, 84 Paul, apostle in vol. 1 and 155 All Saints in vol. 2. Variants from manuscripts containing one or a few chapters are recorded; but for T1, most of which is a close copy of H1, they are given only for 2 Nicholas and 84 Paul. When K and L are both running, in view of their close relationship (they were written by the same scribe) variants from both are recorded. The numerous corrections in H1 are recorded in the apparatus, but the hands of the correctors, some of which are distinctive, are not distinguished. Variants are generally given in the order EH1T1GDH2A1A2T2LK; except that any manuscript being used as temporary base is placed first in the list.

Excluded from the apparatus are spellings and almost all morphological and syntactical variants, unless they could have an effect on meaning, as are synonyms of shared etymology: *after/afterward, benefite/benifice, comenden/commaunden, conable/covenable, corone/crowne, cristen/cristenid, delites/delices, eche/euerych, exaumple/ensaumple, ferre/ferther, hele/helthe, helen/hillen, kerchef/keverchef, lownesse/lowelinesse, middel/middes, noblesse/nobleness, partie/parte,*

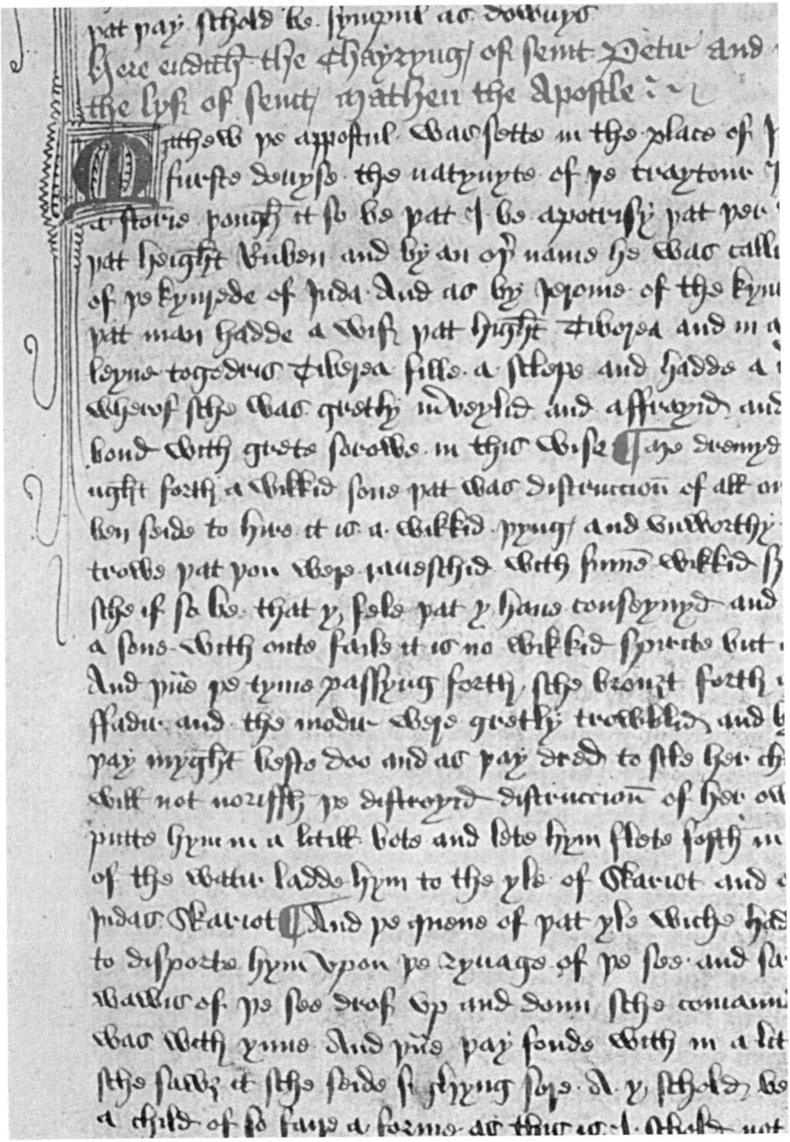

Gloucester Cathedral Library, MS12, f.75r.

proposen/purposen, restabliss(h)ed/restabled, riches/richesse(s, sacrifie/ sacrifice, sepulcre/sepulture, sympilnesse/simplesse, soune/sounde, thanks/thankingges, turment/turnament; likewise prefixes with no semantic significance: *before/afore/tofore, (en)closed, (a)downe, (en)dured, (be)falle, (de)faute, (en)haunsed, (be)hedid, (be)hight, (be)leue, (de)parte, (a)rose, (e)scape, (as)semblaunt, (be)sege, (de)spended,* and many others.

D and its copy H2 contain a high rate of minor paraphrase, such as frequent addition of *than* after *and*, substitution of names or descriptive nouns for pronouns, addition or omission of demonstratives and articles *that, the, this, etc.,* or substitution of one for another, transposition of words and phrases, variation of preposition and conjunction, use of adjectival form for adverbial, and many others. Where these manuscripts are used in volume 1, the variants are recorded in some detail, as for G. The contrast in the number of variants in DH2 and G can be seen by comparing the apparatus in 79 Alban pp. 376–98, from which G is missing, with pp. 399 to end when G has re-appeared. In volume 2, variants in D and H2 of most of the above mentioned types are excluded, though substitutions of names or nouns for pronouns are noted.

Only the most significant variants in the rubrics have been recorded, and general differences, such as omission of the first clause beginning *Here endeth* by L, omission of chapter numbers by H1, and frequent non-insertion of the rubric in the space provided in G, are not recorded. Most manuscripts sometimes indicate the beginning of miracles and other short narratives within a chapter by *Narracio* or *Miraculum*, and these have been ignored.

The intention being to reproduce as nearly as possible s.w.'s work, emendations based on readings from other manuscripts have in almost all cases been confirmed by reference to the French and Latin sources. Where a changed reading is common to all or almost all manuscripts, what s.w. wrote can usually be decided by reference to LgD, or to the Latin sources in 79 Alban and 66 Malchus, and sometimes this is confirmed by MS L, which in parts contains correct readings where all other manuscripts are wrong, and which must have had some access to an English copy closer to the original than any of the extant manuscripts. In the former cases the source reading is supplied in the apparatus, in the latter L is recorded as the source of the lemma (although readings from L are not otherwise generally recorded). In such cases the spelling of the lemma may not be that of L.

The following abbreviations are used in the apparatus: *del.* deleted, *illeg.* illegible, *ins.* inserted, *om.* omitted, *punct.* punctuated or punctuation, *subp.* subpuncted, *trs.* transposed. / in lemmata indicates the point of a transposition, and in a variant the end of a line; // signifies the end of a column or page. *so* is used to mean 'the same as the immediately preceding lemma or variant,' but excluding any insertion the preceding variant may itself consist of or contain.

GILTE LEGENDE

| Here biginnyth the meroure and the liuynge of holie martres and of
seintis that suffriden here in her liuis grete peyne and passioune in
encresinge her ioie in the blisse of heuen, to excite and stere symple
lettrid men and women to encrese in vertue bi the offten redinge and
hiringe of this boke. For bi hiringe mannes bileuinge is mooste stablid 5
and istrengthid. Whos names ben rehersid sewynge in this table
ymarkid with this noumbrarie, I. ij. iij. and so forth.

[*The table of chapters follows, ending on f. 2ᵛ; then on f. 3ʳ :*]

This book is compiled of the lyues of seyntes, callid yn
Latyn *Legenda Aurea*. First bygynnyth the lyff of Saynt
Andrewe.

| Seint Andrewe and othir of þe dissipullis weren callid þre tymys of Gf. 1r
oure Lord. Furste he callid hem to the knowlache of hym, so as
whanne Seint Andrewe dwellid with Seint Iohn þe Baptist his maystir 10
and anoþir dissipul with hym, he hurde how Seint Iohn seide: 'Loo
here þe lambe of God.' He come with anoþir dissipul and schewid
where Ihesu Crist dwellid, and b⟨o⟩de with hym all þat day. And
þanne Andrewe fonde his brothir Symond and brouȝt hym to Ihesu
Crist. Thanne þe day folowyng þay wente aȝen to her crafte for to 15
fisshe. And aftir þis he callid hem secondely to his frendschip, so as it
fill on a day þat þe pepul wente to Ihesu Crist bisidis þe stanke of
Genazareth, the wiche is callid þe See of Galile, [and] oure Lord
Ihesu Crist entrid into þe schippe of Petir and of Andrewe, [and] ther
was ⟨t⟩aken grete multitude of fisshis, and at þat tyme he callid Iamys 20
and Iohn ⟨þ⟩at weren in anoþir schippe, and þay come to hym and
folowid hym awhile, ⟨a⟩nd sithe þay wente aȝen to her propur placis.
The þridde tyme he callid hem laste of alle to be his dissiplis, in a
tyme as oure Lord Ihesu Crist walk⟨i⟩d bisidis þe ryuere of þe see he

GH2A1A2; G has an excision causing gaps from 31 *And* to 50 *Andrewe* and from 75
schold to 93 *in*, and has lost a few letters on the left-hand margin of f. 1a; H2 is rubbed and
partly illegible from 19 *entrid* to 64 *laddris;* H1 starts at 85 *yong* and breaks off after 166
concours; E starts at 102 *Andrewe*, but as the first column is largely illegible it is not used as
base till 129 *And truli*; A1 is rubbed and largely illegible from 172 *blessid* to 192 *veyne* and 209
slombre to 229 *plente of*, and from 239 *saide* to 249 *weddid* has lost some words and letters at
the left of the column.   1–7 *Only in* H2   *Rubric*] Here bygynneth the life of seyntes
and this boke is called yn latyn Legenda Sanctorum. Of the whiche first bygynneth the life
of Seint Andrewe the Apostle A1, Here begynneth the boke of þe lyfe of seyntes callid in
Latyn Legenda Sanctorum. Of þe whiche begynnyth first þe lyfe of Seynt Andrew⟨e þe⟩
Apostle A2   9 hym] hem A1   15 crafte] craftes A1   18 and] *om.* GA1
19 and²] *om.* G   22 sithe] aftir A1

25 callid hem fro her fisshyng and seide: 'Comyth aftir me and y schal
make ȝou fisshers of [men].' þanne anoon þay lefte schippe and nettis
and all þat þay hadde and folowid hym, [and] aftir þay dwellid stille
with hym and wente no more to her propur howsis.

[Seint Andrewe and oþir dissiplis he callid to be apostlis, so þat
30 aftir þe ascencioun of oure Lord þe apostlis were departid.] Seint
Andrewe was in Sithie and Mathewe in Morgundie. ⟨And þe pepul⟩
of þat cuntre refusid vttirly þe prechyng of Seint Mathewe, and p⟨utte
oute hi⟩s eyen and bonde hym faste and caste hym into a foule priso⟨n.
And in þis mene tym⟩e þe aungel of oure Lord apperid to Seint
H₂ f. 3rb Andrewe ⟨and comaundid hym to⟩ goo to Seint Mathewe | into
36 Morgundie. And he answerd that he coude not the way. Than the
aungel bad hym go the way toward the see, and whan he come thedir
he shuld entir into the first ship that he founde theer. And than anoon
gladli he fulfillid the wil and the commaundement of God and come to
40 the cite bi the aungel of God that lad hym, for he had alway good
wynde. And whan he come he fonde [the] prisoun dor open wherin
Seint Mathewe lay fast bounde. And whan he sagh hym, anone he
wepte bitterly and worshipid God and thankid hym an hundred tyme
that he wold send hym to conforth his brother. And than oure Lorde
45 bi his gret miraculis restored aȝeen his eyen which the wikked synful
men had drawen oute.

And than Mathewe partid fro thens and come into Antiochie, and
Seint Andrewe abode stil in Morgundie, and whan this wrecchid
peeple had perceyued that Seynt Mathewe was goone, in gret wrathe
G f.1^v thei took Seint Andrewe | and bonden his hondis bihynde hym and
51 drowȝ hym þoruȝ þe toun þat his bl⟨ode⟩ ranne as stremys fro hym.
Ȝit he prayid to oure Lord Ihesu Crist for hem and conuertid hem.
And fro þens he wente into Antioche. And whanne men sa[ye] þat
Seint Mathewe hadde recoueryd his siȝt by þe preyere of Seint
55 Andrewe, it is not like to be so, for it is to suppose þat þe apostul was
not so febul of faith but þat he myȝt liȝtly haue gete þat Seint
Andrewe gate so liȝtl⟨y⟩ to hym of God.

In a tyme þer come a nobul ȝong man to dwelle with Seint Andrewe
aȝens all his [frendys] wille, and for dispite þ⟨erof⟩ his kynne sette fire
60 in the hous where þis ȝong man dwellid with Sein⟨t⟩ Andrewe. And as

26 men] mennys soulis G   27 and³] *om.* GA1   aftir] *add* þat G   28 her] *add*
owne G   29–30 Seint . . . departid] *om.* G   37 the way] *om.* A1   39 the wil and]
om. A1   41 the] ther H₂   43 an hundred tyme] humbly A1   46 men] man A1
53 saye] sawȝ G   55 like to be] *om.* A1   suppose] be supposed A1   59 frendys]
kynnys G

þe flame encresid an heigh, þe ȝong man toke a litill horne with watir
and sprengid þe fire þerwith, and anoon it quenchid. And þanne his
kynne cryid and seide: 'Allas, oure sone is made an enchau⟨ntour⟩.'
And as þay wold haue klymyd vp on laddris, sodeynly þay were made
so blynde þat þay sawȝ not þe laddris. And þanne oon of hem seide and 65
cryid: 'Why enforce ȝe ȝou so gretly aȝens hym? See ȝe not how God
fiȝtti⟨th⟩ for hym and ȝe take noon hede? Cesseth anoon leste þe wrathe
of God fall vpon ȝou.' And þanne many of þoo þat sawȝ þis myracle
bileuyd in our⟨e⟩ Lord Ihesu Crist; and þe kynnysmen of hym deide
within .xv. dayis ⟨aftir⟩ at oo tyme and were buryid in oo pitte. 70

In a tyme as þe apostul was in þe cite of Nice, the citezenys come to
hym and seide þat þer were .vij. fendis withoute þe cite nyȝ the heigh
weie, þat sclowȝ all men þat come by hem. And þanne the apostul
comaundid þe fendis to come afore hym. And anoon þay apperid in
liknesse of houndis, and he comaundid hem þat þay schol⟨d⟩ goo þere 75
as þay schold dissese no creature, and anoon þay | vanished away. And
whan the peple sauh this myracle thei bileued anon in oure Lorde
Ihesu Crist. In a tyme as the postil come toward another cite, he met
men beryng a deed body of a ȝong man. And then the apostul asked
howe he deyed, and they seide that .vij. gret houndis had strangled 80
hym. And then the apostil seide with a wepyng voice: 'A, good
[blessid] Lorde, I wote weel that thei weer [the] .vij. fendis that I put
oute of the cite of Nice.' And than he made his prayer to God, and
anone he aroos fro deth vnto lif and foloued the apostul.

In another tyme ther come to him wardis fro fer cuntre .xl. yong 85
men sailyng in the see for to receyve of hym doctryne of crist[en]
feith. The devil, hauyng envi vnto hem, reised suche a tempest in the
see that thei weer al drowned togedres. And [when] her bodies wer
found on the see side, thei weer brought afore the apostul and anone
bi hys preyer thei weer reised fro deth to liff. And therfor it is rad in 90
an ympne that he yildid the liff of .xl. yong men that weer drowned in
the see.

And thus the blessid apostul Seint Andrewe, whilis he was in |
Achaia, he fulfillid all þe cuntre with churchis and conuertid þe pepul G f. 2ʳ
[to] þe feith of oure Lord Ihesu Crist, and tauȝt þe wif of Egie þe 95
feithe and baptisid hire. And whanne Egie hurde þat, he come to þe
cite of Patras and constraynyd þe cristen pepul to doo sacryfise. Seint

H2 f. 3ᵛᵃ

---

61 an heigh] on hight A1   63 kynne] frendes A1   70 .xv.] .v. A1   buryid]
leyde A1   76–8 And . . . Crist] *om.* A1   82 blessid] *om.* H2   the] *om.* H2
86 cristen] Cristis H2   95 to] of G   oure Lord] *om.* H1A1

Andrewe come aȝens hym and seide: 'It is sittyng to þe þat pretendist
to bee a iuge þat þou knowe þy iugge that is in heuen, and whanne þou
100 knowist hym þat he be worschipid of the, and in hym worschipyng
þat þou withdrawe þy corage fro fals goddis.' And þanne Egeas seide:
'Arte þou þat Andrewe þat prechist [a] fals lawe þat þe princis of
Rome haue comaundid to be distroyid?' To þe wiche wordis Andrewe
seide: 'þe princis of Rome knewe neuer how [þe sone of God came and
105 tauȝt how þat þy ydollis ben fendis but þat] he þat techith the
contrarie displesith God, and he þat displesith hym he partith fro
hym and he herith hym nouȝt, and þerfore þay ben as in þe fendis
prison and ben so ferforthe illudid and desseyuyd þat whanne þe soule
is departid fro þe body sche is all nakid and berith noþyng with hire
110 but synne.' Thanne seide Egeas: 'These ben þe vanyteis þat ȝoure
Ihesu Criste prechid þat was hongid on þe iebett of þe cros.' Thanne
answerid Seint Andrewe and seide: 'He resseyuyd of his fre wille þe
gebett of þe cros not for his gilte but for oure redempcion.' 'How may
þat be?' seide Egeas, 'Sithe he was bitrayid of his dissipul and holden
115 of þe Iewis and crucified with knyȝttis, [did] he þus frely of his owne
will?' þanne seide [Seint] Andrewe and bigan to schewe hym by .v.
resonys how þat Criste Ihesu suffrid deth of his owne fre will. The
furste reson was þis, how þat he come by[for] his passion and tolde his
dissiplis þerof whanne he seide: 'Goo we vp to Ierusalem, for þe sone
120 of man schal be bytrayid.' The seconde, whanne Seint Petir wold haue
withdrawe hym fro his passion, how he vndirtoke hym, seying: 'Goo
bihynde me, Sathanas.' The þridde, whanne he tolde hem þat he
hadde power to suffre deth and to arise the þridde day aȝen. The
fourthe is þat he knewe his traytour Iudas byfore whanne he ȝaf hym
125 þe morcel at his maunde. And þe fifthe þat he ches þe place and
knewe well þat his traytour schold come. And also Seint Andrew
affermyd þat he hadde ben at all þese þyngis, and he seide þat þe
mysterie of þe cros was a grete þyng. To whom Egeas seide þat it
E f. 2ʳᵇ   myȝt not be callid mysterie but rathir turmente. | 'And truli but thou
130 graunt to my seiynges y schall make the proue that misterie.'
        And thanne Seint Andrew said: 'Yf y dred the gibet of the cross y
wolde not preche the glorie therof. I wolde that thou woldest here the
misterie of the crosse, and yef thou wilt beleue it and knowe it thou

        102 a] þat G   104–5 þe sone . . . but þat] þese ydollis bene fendis but þat þe sone of
God come and tauȝt it so G   105 he] om. Hɪ   106 hym¹] God HɪAɪ   110 þe]
om. Hɪ   111 prechid] prechith E   115 Iewis] Iuges Hɪ   did] E, deied HɪGAɪ
þus] this EHɪ   frely] om. E   116 Seint] om. E   118 byfor] by G   126 well] add
ynowȝ G   129 callid] add þe G   133–5 and yef . . . crosse] om. G

schalt be saued. .V. resonis y schall saien the of the misterie of this noble crosse. The furst is that right as the furst man deserued dethe bi 135 the tree in breking the comaundement, right so it was sittyng that the secound man putte awaye dethe in suffering dethe vpon a tree. The secounde, he that was made of vncorrupt erthe and a breker of the comaundement, it was sittyng that he that shuld amend this defaute were purely born of a clene virgine. The .iij. that right as Adam hadd 140 streight oute his hond vnordenatly to the forboden mete, the nwe Adam shuld stroght his vndefouled hondes vpon the tree of the crosse. The .iiij. that right as Adam hadd sueteli tasted the forboden appil, right so the nwe Adam schuld putte away that defauute with the contrarie as to taste eisell and galle. The .v. is that right as Ihesu Crist 145 gaue vs [his] immortalite, right so it was couenable thing that he wold take oure mortalite.' And thanne Egias said to Andrew: 'Tell these vanitees to tho that leven the, and obeie the to me and sacri[fi]se to almyghti God.' Thanne said Andrew: 'I sacrifise eueri day to almyghti God a lambe witheoute spotte, and whanne that lambe is eten of the 150 peple, he lyuithe and is all hole.' Thanne said Egeas: 'How may that be?' Andrew ansuered and saide: 'Take the forme of a disciple and thanne thou schalt know it.' And thanne Egeas in gret wrathe comaundid that he schuld be putte in prison til on the morow.

The day | after, he was brought to the iugement and ledde to the f. 2ᵛᵃ place there as he schuld haue do sacrifise to the ydole[s]. Thanne 156 Egeas sayd: 'Yf thou wilt not obeye to me I schall make the hang on the crosse that thou preisest so moche and with other tormentis that thou schalt be weri of thi part.' Thanne sayd Seint Andrew: 'Ymagin what torment that thou canst and thou schalt fynde me redi and gladd 160 to receyue hem, for the more stable that I schall be in tormentz the more agreable schall I be to my Lord and my Kyng.' And than Egeas comaundid that Seint Andrewe schuld be bete with .xxj.ti men, and whanne that he were so beten that he schuld be bounden to the crosse handes and fete. 165

Whanne he was ledde to the crosse ward, gret concours of peple folued hym and sayden: 'Allas, the blode of the innocent is dampned withoute cause.' And thanne the apostell praied hem that thei wold

136 breking] add of E   138 vncorrupt] a corrupte G   139 that²] add all E
140 purely] pouerly Hı   141 his] add ʽdefouledʼ Hı   140–2 hadd . . . Adam] dide
strecche his defowlid hondis vpon þe tree hym forbode riȝt so it was sittyng þat þe seconde
man G   146 his] om. E   148 sacrifise] sacrise E   154–5 on . . . day] on a daye þe
morowe G   156 ydoles] ydole EG   157 Yf . . . not] but if þou wilte G
165 fete] add ʽ&ʼ Hı

not empeche his marterdome. And whanne he sawe the crosse aferre
170 he saluid it with gret reuerence and sayd: 'O worschipfull crosse, O
blesfull crosse, that were halowed with the precious body of oure Lord
Ihesu Cryst, O blessid tree, that were araied with his membres as with
most precious stonis, before that oure Lord stied vp on the thou were
an erthely dred, and now thou art loue of heuene. O blessid crosse,
175 receiue me now, for I come to the be my desire, and I beseche the that
thou receyue me gladly as for the disciple of hym that honged on the,
for I haue alwayes loued and desired to enbrace the. O thou holy
crosse, that receyuedist the bewte and the nobilnesse of the blessid
membre[s] of oure Lord, the which I haue so long desired and
180 curiously loued, take me fro this dedely prison and yelde me to my
maister, so that he receyue me by the lik as he bought me by the.' And
f. 2ᵛᵇ in this sayeng he dispoiled hym|self and gave his clothes to his
⟨to⟩rmentours. And thanne they hyng hym ⟨o⟩n the crosse as thei
were com⟨aun⟩did, and so hangyng on the crosse he lyued two dayes
185 and preched to twenti thousand men that weren there.

[And thanne al the companie] swore the dethe of Egeas, and
sayden: '[This] blessid holy man, pesible and debonayre, schuld not
suffre thus.' An thanne come Egeas for to take hym downe, and
whanne Seint Andrew segh hym he sayd to hym: 'What, art thou
190 come to us now? Yef thou be come for to haue penaunce and
foryeue[ne]⟨s⟩se thou schalt haue it gladly, and yef thou be come
for to haue me downe trust fully that thi comyng is in veyne, for thou
schalt neuer take me downe alyue, for I see now my Lord and my
Kyng that abideth me.' And whanne they wold haue vnbounden hym
195 thei myght not come to hym, for thaire armes were made so stiffe that
they myght not bowe hem. Seint Andrew segh that the world wo⟨ld⟩
haue take hym downe of the crosse.

⟨Th⟩anne he made his orisoun [in] the crosse as Seint Austin
tellithe in his Confes⟨sioun⟩s and said: 'O blessid Lord, late me not be
200 taken downe aliue, for it is tyme that thou comaunde my bodi to the
erthe. I haue long bore thus heuy charge of my body, and I haue truly
laboured in tho thyngges that thou comaunde[de]st me, I am so miche
⟨tr⟩availled that I wold fayne yef it ⟨liked⟩ thi gret goodnesse to be
discharg⟨e⟩d o⟨f t⟩his obedience. For I recorde me how sch⟨e is

171 blesfull] blessid G   oure] my G   172 his] add blessid G   174 art] add þe G
179 membres] membre E   181 lik . . . the] om. G   186 And . . . companie] om. E
187 This] thus O E   191 foryeuenesse] foryeue⟨s⟩se E   196 the world] þay G
198 in] to E   as Seint] twice E   Austin] add berith witnesse and G
202 comaundedest] comaundest E

gre⟩vous in the beryng, proude in ⟨dauntyng⟩, freel in norsching, and ₂₀₅
I haue ⟨labourid⟩ gladly in her refreynyng. Lord, ⟨thou knowi⟩st how
many tymes the world ⟨hath⟩ besied hym to withdrawe me from the
[purite] of contemplacion, and how ⟨many⟩ tymes he besied hym to
awake m⟨e fro⟩ the slombre of thi suete rest. Of⟨te tyme⟩ he hathe
⟨doo⟩ me sorugh, and ⟨as myche⟩ as I ⟨myght⟩ I haue ⟨mekeli ₂₁₀
withstanden this⟩ | greuous bataile an haue ouercome myn enemye f. 3ra
and [hadde] the victorie by the myght of thi grace. And therfor, Lord,
I requere the, that art rightwys and a debonayre guerdonere, that thou
comaunde me no more to laboure in these periles, but y yeue to the
that thou hast take me, and comaunde sum other with that charge, ₂₁₅
that I no lengger be lette from the, but kepe me ioyfull to the
resureccion so that I may receyue merite for my laboure. Comaunde
my body to the erth that he lette me no lengger, but that I may frely
tende to the that art the well of ioie vndefaillynge.' And whanne he
hadd so saide, a gret lyght come from heuene and environde hym by ₂₂₀
the space of half an oure, that no [creature] myght see hym for gret
brightnesse that was about hym, and with the passyng of that lyght he
yeldid up the spirit. And Maxymilla that was wyf to Egeas biried the
body worschipfully, and Egeas was rauisched with the fende er he
come home to his hous, and deied horribl[y] before all the peple.   ₂₂₅

And men seine that oute of the sepulcre of Seint Andrew ther
comithe manna, whiche is lyke to floure and oyle and it hathe a noble
sauoure of swetnesse, and therby the peple of the contreye knowen
whanne thei schull haue plente of godez, for yef it comc litell the erthe
will bere but litell fruyt that yere, and yef it come plenteuously the ₂₃₀
erthe berithe abundauntly. And it myght well be that it was so in olde
tyme, for his body was born from thennys into Constantinenoble.

Ther was a bisshop that ledde religious liff and hadde to Seint
Andrew gret deuocion and reuerence aboue all seintes, so that in all
thyng that he wold do or saye he wold saye: 'In the worschip of God ₂₃₅
and of Seint Andrew.' Wherfor the enemy of all mankynde hadde gret
enuye to hym, and purposid | to deceyue hym with all his malice, and f. 3rb
transfigured hym into the forme of a right faire woman and come to
the palays of this deuoute bisshop and saide that sche most be

208 purite] pitte E, and putte G (*purte* P2)   besied] wakid G   209 thi] my G
212 hadde] *om.* E   the myght of] þy my3t and G   213 rightwys] right wys E
a debonayre guerdonere] debonaire G   214 yeue] 3elde G   220 environde] ouer
houyd G   221 creature] man E   224 rauisched] resseyuyd G   the] a G
225 horribly] horrible E   all] *om.* G   227 and'] of G   229 come] bere G
237 deceyue] haue desseyuyd G   238 forme of a/right] *trs.* G

240 confessid of hym. The bisshop sent her word that sche schuld be
confessid of [his] penitensere that hadd his full pouere. Sche sent to
hym worde ayein that sche wolde not vttre the preuy thyngges of her
conscience to none creature but to hym only, and so the bisshop was
ouercome and bade that sche schuld [be] brought to hym. And
245 whanne sche was with hym allone sche sayd to hym: 'Sir, I beseche
you haue mercy and pitee on me, for y am as ye see yonge and a
mayde, norsched fro my tendre age in gret delites and borne of a riall
kynrede. But now y come allone in a straunge abite for my fader, that
is a myghti kyng, wolde haue weddid me to a gret prince, and I saide
250 that I hadde abhominacion of all erthely mariage, for I hadde yeue my
virginite to Ihesu Crist, wherfor I will neuer consent to haue other
spouse. But atte the last I was constreined to consent to his wille or
ellis I most haue sufferid diuerse tormentis. And thus preueli I fledd
awaye, for I hadde leuer to be pore and in exile thanne for to lese my
255 virginite. So thanne I herde the praisyng of youre holinesse. I am
come to you as for a souerein refute in hope that I may finde be youre
goodnesse a place of rest wherinne I may be preuely in contemplacion
and eschewe the periles of this present lyff and fle the tribulacions of
this world.'
260 This holy bisshop hering all this mervailed gretly of the gret vertu
that appered in her, consydering the nobilnesse of her high kynrede,
the gret beaute of her body, the brennyng loue that sche hadde to
God, and the honest speche of her, so faire it was. He said to her with
f. 3ᵛᵃ a debonaire voyse: 'Doughter, drede you not and be | sure, for he for
265 whos loue ye haue dispised youreselff and all erthely worschippes, he
will graunt you grace in this present tyme and plente of ioye in tyme
to come. And I that am his vnworthi servaunt offre me and my goodes
to the, and chese you an hous wher ye luste and it schall be redy to
you, and this day I praie you to dyne with me.' She ansuered and said:
270 'Fader, I beseche you require me [of] no suche thyng, for perauenture
sum suspecion of evell myght come, that the light of youre noble
renomes myght be enpeyred.' Th[ann]e said the bisshop: 'Nay,
doughter, that may not be, for we will not be allone but among
mony where that no suspecion of euell may be.'

241 his] om. E   243 to none creature] om. G   244 be] om. E   246 mercy,
pitee] trs. G   251 will] wolde G   253 sufferid] add many G   259 this] þe G
262 the²] and G   264 and] but G   be] bea E   for he] om. G   265 erthely]
worldly G   he] For he G   268 ye luste] ȝou liste G   270 beseche, require] trs. G
of] om. E   271 sum] add evell E   272 renomes] name G   Thanne] The E

Thanne thei went to mete and the bisshop made her sitte before 275
hym. And the bisshop entended gretly to her and biheld her
stedfastely in the visage and mervailed gretly of her beauute, and as
he byhelde her stedfastely anone he was hurte in his soule with fals
desire. The fende that hadde hurte hym perceyued right wel and
beganne to encrese her beauute more and more, so that the bisshop 280
was in that point to haue requered her of synne yef he hadde hadd
tyme and place. With that sodenly ther come a pilgrym to the gate and
beganne to knocke fast, and cried and praied that he myght come inne.
Thanne the bisshop asked of the woman yef sche wold that he come
inne, and thanne sche sayd: 'Late axse of hym furst a question, and yef 285
he canne ansuere therto late hym come inne.'
Thanne thei sought among hem who were sufficiaunt to axse that
question, and ther was none that wolde purpoos it. Thanne said the
bisshop: 'Who is so sufficiaunt as ye, lady? For ye passe vs all in faire
speche and in high wisdom, wherfor ye most | purpoos this question.' f. 3vb
And thanne sche said: 'Gothe and askithe of hym whiche is the 291
grettest miracle that euer God wrought in litell space.' And whanne
the pilgrime herde this question he ansuered and said to the
messangere: 'The diuersite [and] excellence of visages of men, for
among all the visages of men there be not tweye verreily like in all 295
thyng.' Whanne he hadde so said, all thei mervailed of his gret
wisdom. Thanne said the woman: 'The secound question schall be
purposed hym more harder thanne this was for to proue beter his
wisdom. Gothe and askithe of hym where the erthe is highest.' The
pilgrime ansuered and said: 'In heuene imperiall wher that the bodi of 300
Ihesu Crist is.' Thanne thei hadde all gret mervaile of his wisdom and
preised hym gretly. The woman thanne said: 'Yet late hym ansuere to
the thridde question that schall be hardest of all. Go and aske hym
how miche a [s]pace it is betwene the highest heuene and the dippest
pitte of helle.' Whanne the pilgrime herde this question he ansuered 305
and said: 'Go to her that sent the hedir to me and bidde her assoile this
question, for sche canne [miche] beter thanne I, for sche mesurid it
onys and so ded I neuer, for sche fel from that heuene to the deppest
place of helle. It is no woman but a fende that hathe transfigured her

279 and] *add* sche G   284 he] *add* schold G   285 thanne] *om.* G
292 grettest] moste G   294 and] of the E   299 erthe] grounde G   301 his] *add*
gret E   303 hardest] most harde G   304 how . . . highest] wiche is þe moste heighist
place of G   space] pace E   305 pitte] place G   306 the] þou G   307 miche]
om. E   308 that] *add* heighist place of G   309 place] pitte G

310 in liknesse of a woman.' Whanne the messanger herde tell this he was
    gretly aferde, and recorded before all what he hadde herde.

    And thanne the bisshop and all were gretly abasshed, [and] the
    auncien enemye vanisshed awaye sodeynli. And thanne the bisshop
    come to hymselff and blamed hymselff greuously, and with gret
315 sobbyng and wepyng asked foryeuenesse of his synnes, and sent a |
f. 4ra messangere for the pilgrime, but he was gone. And thanne the bisshop
    assembeled the peple togederes and tolde hem all the manere, and
    preied hem that they wolde all be in praier and orisonis till oure Lord
    lust of his grace to schewe to som man what was this pilgrime that
320 hadd deliuered hym of so gret a perill. And that same night it was
    schewid to the same bisshop that it was Seint Andrewe that hadd
    putte hymselff in a pilgrime wede for to deliuer hym from that gret
    mischef. And thanne the bisshop beganne more and more to loue
    Seint Andrew and worschip hym with gret deuocion.

       Here endithe the liff of Seint Andrew, and after beginnithe
       the liff of Seint Nicholas, Cap^m. .ij.^m

    Seint Nicholas was borne in the citee of Patras and was come of noble
    and riche kinrede. His fader was named Epiphanus and his moder
    Iohanna. He was begoten in the furst floure of thaire age, and sithe
    after thei liued in chastite and [l]adden an [heuen]ly liff. The furst day
  5 that he was born, whanne he was bathed he dressid hym vpright in the
    basin, and he wold neuer take the briste but onys on the Friday and
    onys in the Wednisday, and in his tendre age he eschewed the vanitees
    of yonge children. He haunted gladli to the chirche, and after that he
    beganne to vnderstond holi scripture he putte it in werke after his
 10 powere.

    And whanne that his fader and his moder weren parted oute of this
    world he bethought hym how he myght [departe] his richesse to the
    preising of God and not to haue mannys preising. Hit happed so that
 14 one of his neighaboures that was a worschipfull man hadde thre
f. 4rb doughtres virgines. This man | fill in suche pouertee that he was

311 recorded] reportid it G   312 gretly] hugely G   and²] om. E   312–13 the
auncien] þilke dedly G   317 assembeled] gederid G   manere] matere G
324 Seint . . . hym] and to worschip seint andrewe G

EGH2T1A1A2K; H1 begins at 161 *that art*; E breaks off after 293 *come*; in A1 some
letters and words are lost or illegible through rubbing at various points   3–4 sithe after]
aftir þat K   4 liued] *add* stedfaster K   ladden] hadden E   heuenly] holy ET1
8 children] men G   12 departe] putte ET1   15 fill] was falle GK

constreined to deliuer one of his doughters to misgouernaunce of her
body for to gete her levyng bi that fals lucree. Whanne this holi man
Seint Nicholas knewe this he hadde gret pitee and abhominacion of
this wikkednesse. He toke a gret somme of gold and knette it in a
clowt and went priuily bi nyght and caste it inne atte this pore mannes 20
wyndowe. And whanne this man aroos by the morw he fonde this
somme of golde. He was fulfilled with gret gladnesse and thanked
God and maried his eldest doughter. And within a while after the
servaunt of God did in the same wise, and whanne this pore man
hadde founde it he gave thankyng to God, and purposed hym to wake 25
for to wete what he was that hadd schewed to hym so gret charitee and
hym brought oute of so gret mischeeff. Withinne a fewe dayes after
Seint Nicholas doubled that somme and caste it inne priuely as he was
wont to done, and with the sowne of the falle the man awoke and in
gret haste aroos and folwed Seint Nicholas that fledde faste away. He 30
cried after hym and said: 'For Goddes loue fle not so faste, but late me
see the.' And as he pursued hym faste he perceyued and knewe well
that it was Nicholas, and thanne he kneled downe and wold haue kyst
his fete, but he de[u]ied hym and praied hym that he wolde neuer
vtter this dede whiles he lyued. 35
   After this the bisshop of the citee of Myre deied, and thanne the
bisshoppes assembelid hem togedre to purveie a bisshop to that
chirche. And ther was one among other a bisshop of gret auctorite
and all the election hangged on hym, and as he taught hem all that thei
schul[d] be in fastyng and in praiere, that same bisshop | herde that f. 4va
same nyght a voys that said to hym atte the houre of Matenys that he 41
schuld take [good] hede to the gates of the chirche, and that persone
that furst schuld entre into the chirche and hight Nicholas, that he
schuld take hym and sacre hym as for bysshop. And thanne this
bisshop schewed this vision to his felawes and counsailed hem all to be 45
in praiers and he wold kepe the chirche dore. Right as it was schewed
vnto hym, so it fell that atte the houre of Matenys bi purveiaunce of
oure Lord Nicholas come furst, and anone the bisshop toke hym and
asked hym what he hight, and he anone mekely ansuered and said:

   20 this] þat tyme into þe G   21 this¹] *add* pore K   24 wise] *add* ayene T1
26 so] *om.* T1   29 sowne] noyse K   31 so] *om.* G   faste] *add* away T1
34 deuied] denied (?) E, denoydid *or* deuoydid G   39 hangged] honyd *or* houyd G
40 schuld] schull E   41 nyght] *om.* G   42 good] *om.* E   42–3 that . . .
Nicholas] þere he schold fynde oon þat hei3t Nicholas and G   44 hym¹] *add* in G
46 kepe] wayte at K   46–7 G *punct. after* hym *instead of* dore, T1 *has both*   47 that]
ri3t G   48 furst] *add* fro hym G

50 'Nicholas, servaunt of youre holynesse.' Thanne with gret ioye he
brought hym to his felawes, and thei all thanked God with gret
worschip and gret ioye, and sette hym in his chayer, notwithstondyng
that he refused it to his powere, but he most nedis obeye the
ordinaunce of oure Lord for his gret profite and of many other.
55 And like as he was meke and vertuous afore, so he was after, and
encresed in vertues and graces. He was humble and honest in all his
governaunce, wakyng in orisons, streit to hymselff in makyng his body
lene, he eschewed the felawschip of women, meke in receyuinge all,
profitable in spekyng, gladd in techyng, sharpe in correccion.
60   It is redde in a cronicle that the blessid Seint Nicholas was atte the
Counsaile of [Nice], and on a day as schipmen were in the see in gret
perile thei cried with wepyng teres and said: 'O Nicholas, servaunt of
God, yef the thyngges be sothe that we haue herde of the, now proue
thi gret goodnesse vpon us and saue us be thi praiere.' And anone
f. 4vb there apered a man in [the] liknesse | of hym and said: 'Loo, here I am.
66 Called ye me not?' And thanne anone he began to helpe hem in
takelyng of her schipp, and anone the tempest sesid. And thanne he
vanisshed away, and whanne thei were come to his chirche thei knewe
hym anone withoute tellyng of any creature, and yet they hadd neuer
70 sene hym before. And thanne they come to hym and gave
thankyng[es] to God and to hym of thaire deliueraunce. He mekely
praied hem that thei wold sette it all to the gret merci of God and
thaire bileue and not to his merites.
     In a tyme it befelle that all the province of Seint Nicholas suffered
75 gret peyne for hunger, for mete failed allmost to all the peple. And
thanne the servaunt of God herde saye that there were schippes
charged with whete and were ariued atte the port. And thanne anone
he went thedir and preied the schipmen that thei wold helpe the peple
that pershid for hunger of eueri schip an .C. buschels of whete. And
80 thanne thei saiden: 'Holy fader, we dur not, for it is deliuered to vs by
mesure, and we most yelde the same mesure into the emperours
garners in Alisaundre.' And thanne the holi man saide to hem: 'Dothe

50 Nicholas] *add* þe G   youre] oure G   51 thanked] þankyng G   52 gret]
om. K   and²] *om.* G   sette] sacryd K   56 humble] meke G   57 governaunce] *add*
he was G   61 Nice] Mire ET₁   the] thee E   63 be sothe] *om.* G   the²] *add* be
trewe G   63 gret] *om.* K   vpon . . . praiere] *om.* G   64 the] *om.* ET₁K   and said]
om. K   69 hym] *add* and E   70 gave] *add* hym E   71 thankynges] thankyng
ET₁K   75 for¹] and G   77 and were] where þay G   81 and . . . mesure] to
delyver K   yelde] dellyuer G   82 garners . . . thanne] hondis and whanne þay seide
þus G

as I haue preied you, and I behete you in [the] vertue of God that it
schall not be lessid whanne ye come to the garners.' And whanne thei
hadd deliuered hym thei come into Alisaundre and deliuered the fulle 85
mesure that thei hadd resseived. And thanne thei told this miracle to
the servauntes of the emperour, and thei all preised gretly God and
his servaunt. And thanne this holi man departed [the] whete to eueri
man after his nede, so that it suffised two yere not onli for to liue by
but [also] for to sowe.   90
    And as that contre serued to ydolis | the peple worschipped the fals f. 5ra
goddes Dyane, so that in[to] the tyme of the comyng of Goddes
seruaunt Seint Nicholas mony of that cursed religion vsed somme
custumes of panymes vnder a tree halwed to Diane. But this holi man
[chased] oute these custumes of all that contre and comaunded that all 95
tho trees schuld be kutte doune. Thanne the fende was gretli meued
ayenst hym, ordeyned an oyle that bren[nyth] ayenst kynde in water,
and also it brenny[th] stones. And thanne he transfigured hym in
forme of a religious woman and sette hym in a litell vessell and mette
with pilgrimes that went by water to the seruaunt of God. And 100
whanne sche neighed hem sche aresoned hem in this wise: 'Al he[i]le
frendes, I wote well ye goo to the seruaunt of God, and fayne wolde I
goo with you, but I may not. Wherfor I praie you that ye wolde bere
this oyle to his chirche and in rememberaunce of me that ye will
anoynt the walles of his halle therwith.' And whanne sche hadde said, 105
anone sche vanisched away. And thanne thei mette with another
schipp and goodly peple therinne, among whiche peple ther was a
reuerent persone lik to Seint Nicholas, and said to hem: 'What hathe
that woman said vnto you that ye mette with and what [hathe] sche
brought you?' Thei tolde hym all [bi] ordre. And thanne saied he to 110
hem: 'Douteth not but that is that fals Diane, and that ye preue that I
saie sothe, castith this oyle into the see.' And whanne thei hadde so do
the see waxse afere in that partie and brent a gret while ayenst kynde.
And thanne the bisshop and that honest mayne vanished away, and
whanne thei were londed thei come to this holi man and said: 'Verily 115

    83 the] om. ET1   84 lessid] lesse T1   85 hym] hem G   88 the] this E
89 suffisid] add fully K   liue by] ete G   90 also] only E, om. K   91 peple] add þat
G   91–2 the fals goddes Dyane] fals goddis G, fals goddys dyane K   92 that] om. G
into] in E   95 chased] chastised ET1K   97 hym] add and GK   brennyth] brent E
98 brennyth] brennyd E   in] add the ET1K   99 sette] hid K   101 sche¹] he K
Al heile] alheule E   105 sche] he K   hadde] þus G   108 Nicholas] add hym silfe K
109 hathe] om. E   110 bi] the ET1   110–11 And . . . hem] om. T1   111 ye] I K
114 bisshop] schip G

thou art he that apered to vs in the see and deliuered us out of the
fendes hondes.' |

f. 5rb   In that tyme ther were men that rebellid ayenst the emperour of
Rome, and the emperour sent ayenst hem thre princes, that is to
120 knowe Neponcion, Vrsyn and Apolyne. Thei ariued atte the port of
Adrian, for the wynde was contrarie to hem, and the blessid Seint
Nicholas praied hem to dyne with hym. And as thei were with hym it
happed that the consult, corrupte by money, hadd comaunded that
.iij. innocent knyghtes schulde be biheded. And whanne the holi man
125 wost it he praied these thre princes to come with hym in haste, and
whanne [thei] come to the place there as thei schuld be bihedid, he
fonde hem on her kneis, thaire eyghen bounde, and the man loftyng
up his swerde redi ouer her [hedis]. And thanne Seint Nicholas sette
afere with the loue of God putte hymselff hardeli bitwene hem and
130 toke the suerde of the mannes honde and caste it fer from hym, and
vnbounde her eyghen and ledde the innocentis sauf with hym. And
anone he went into the iugement to the consult and fonde the gates
schette. He anone openid hem with strength, and thanne the consult
come ayenst hym and wolcomed hym. The holi man hadde dispite of
135 his salutacion and said to hym: 'Thou enemie of God, breker of the
lawe, by what foly or misauenture hast thou be consentaunt to so gret
a felonie and now durst loke us in the visage?' And whanne he hadd
gretli reproued hym and chidde hym he was repentaunt and atte the
preiers of the[se] thre princes he resseived hym to penaunce. And
140 whanne the messengers of the emperour hadd resseiued his blessyng
thei went her waye and ouercome her enemyes withoute schedyng of
blode.

And thanne thei retorned to the emperour and were resseiued with
f. 5va   gret worschip. Thanne fell | it so that somme hadd envie to the wele of
145 the[se] princes and ymagened treson ayenst hem, and what be praier
and be yeftes thei were falsli accused to the emperour of treson ayenst
his mageste. And whan the emperour herde it he was fulfilled withe
gret wrathe and comaunded that thei were putte in prison withoute
mo questionis and that thei were slayn that same night. And whanne

117 fendes] deuelis G   118 In] Also in G   men] *om.* K   119 thre] þe G
121 the blessid] þe bisshop G, hyt plesyd T1K   122 praied] to pray T1K
123 consult] counsel G   money] many G   that²] *add* the EG   126 thei¹] he E
128 hedis] bodi ET1, bodyes K   128–9 sette afere] affreynyd it G   129 putte]
puttyng G   hardeli] hard K   hem] hym G   132 to] of G   133 consult] counsaill G
139 these] the ET1K   141 her waye] awey G   144 wele] welthe G, welfare T1
145 these] the E   148 comaunded] *add* hem G   149 that same] þe first G

these princes knewe this by the portour that priueli hadd told hem, 150
thei rente her clothes and cried, weping bitterly. And thanne
Neponcien remembered hym how blessid Seint Nicholas hadde
deliuered thre innocentes, and preied his felawes that thei wolde
require his helpe. And as thei were in her praiers Seint Nicholas
appered to hem, and also he apered to Constantine the emperour and 155
said [to] hym: 'Whi hast thou take these princes with so gret wrong
and haste iuged hem to the dethe [withoute cause]? Arise hasteli and
comaunde that thei be deliuered, or ellis I schal praie to God that he
schal arayse many batayles ayeinst the in whiche thou schalt be caste
downe and be made mete to bestis.' And thanne the emperour hauyng 160
gret drede and merveil asked: 'What art thou that art by night entered
into my palays and durste saye to me suche wordes?' He ansuered: 'I
am Nicholas, bisshop of Mire,' and with that he vanished away, and
apered to the provost in the same wyse and with a sterne voys said to
hym: 'Thou that hast lost witte and mynde, whi hast thou bene so 165
hardy to consent to the dethe of these innocentis? Goo anone and
ordeyne for her deliueraunce, or ellis thi bodi schall rote and be ete
with wormes and thou and thi meny schal be distroied.' Thanne the
provost with gret drede said: 'What maist thou be that manast me | so f. 5vb
gretli?' He ansuerid and said: 'Wete it well that I am Nicholas, bisshop 170
of the citee of Mire,' and therwith he vanished away.

And thanne eche of hem awoke and tolde to other her dremes, and
anone thei sent for the princes. And whanne thei were come the
emperour said to hem: 'What whichecraft canne ye that ye haue [this
nyght illu]ded vs with dremcs?' And thanne thei said that thei coude 175
neuer that craft ne thei hadde in no wise deseruid dethe. And [thanne]
the emperour said: 'Knowe ye any man that hight Nicholas?' And
whanne thei herde that name thei helde up her hondes to heuene
warde and praied oure Lorde that by the merites of Seint Nicholas
that he wolde delyuer hem of this present perile that thei were inne. 180
And whanne the emperour hadd herde of hem the lyf and the
miracles of Seint Nicholas he said to hem: 'Goo hennys frely, and
thankithe God that hathe deliuered you by the praiere of hym, and

151 and . . . bitterly] *om.* G   153 thre] the GT1   156 to] *om.* E
157 withoute cause] *om.* ET1K   157–8 that he schal] to T1   159 caste] þrawe K
162 palays] place H1T1   164 apered] *ins. above del.* preied H1   165 hym] *add*
What G   lost] *add* þy G   169 manast] manacist GK   172 eche] euery G
173–4 the emperour] to the Emperour he G   174–5 this nyght] *om.* E   illuded]
blynded EH1T1K   176 thanne] *om.* EH1T1K   179–80 by . . . hem] þay my3t be
delyueryd G   182 hennys] þens H1

berithe hym of youre iuelys, and praiethe hym that he manace me no
185 more, but that he praie for me and for my reaume to our Lorde.' And
a litell while after the forsaid princes went to the servaunt of God and
kneled downe to his fete humbly sayeng: 'Verreli thou art the
seruaunt of God and a true worschiper and louer of Ihesu Criste.'
And whanne thei had al tolde hym by ordre, he lifte up his hondes to
190 heuene and gave preysing and thanking to God, and sent these princes
ayen wel taught in vertues into her owne contre.

And whanne oure Lorde lust to take hym oute of this worlde, he
praied oure Lorde that he wolde sende hym his aungeles, and as he
enclined his hede he seigh the aungelis comyng to hym, and thanne he
f. 6ʳᵃ knewe wel that he schulde passe oute of this | worlde [and] he bigan
196 this psalme *In te Domine speraui* vnto [this verce] *In manus tuas Domine
commendo spiritum meum*, and with that worde he yeldid vp the spirit
the yere of oure Lorde .CCC.xl. and thre, withe gret melodie of all
heuenli spirites. And whanne he was beried in the tombe of marbill, a
200 faire welle of oyle sprong oute of the hede and another of water atte
the fete, ant into this daye there comithe oute holy oyle of his bones
that helithe al maner of siknesse. And a man of holi lyff was
successoure of hym [that] was putte oute of his sege be enuious
men. And thanne anone the welle of oyle stynt rennynge, and whanne
205 he was reconsiled ayen sche ranne her cours ayen. Longe tyme after,
the Turkes had distroied the citee of Mire, and thanne ther come thedir
.iiij. knyghtes of Barre, and .iiij. monkes schewed hem the sepulcre of
Seint Nicholas, and thei opened the sepulcre and founden the bonis
fletyng al in oyle. And thanne thei bere it worschipfulli into the citee of
210 Barre in the yere of oure Lorde a thousand foure score and .xv.

In a tyme ther was a man that hadd borued of a Iue a somme of
money and swore vpon the auutere of Seint Nicholas that as sone as
he myght he wolde paie hym ayein, for the Iue wolde none other plege
haue. And thanne he withhelde this money longe tyme til atte the last
215 the Iue asked hym his money, and he said sikerly that he hadd paied
hym. And the Iue made hym come to iugement, and the othe was

185 our Lorde] my lord god K   187 humbly] mekely G   188 of ²] *add* oure
lord G   192–3 he . . . Lorde] *om.* G   193 sende] send *with* d *on erasure* H₁   his
aungeles] an aungel G   195 and] *om.* EH₁T₁K   196 this verce] *om.* EH₁T₁K
196–7 G *leaves space for Latin*   196 *Domine*] *om.* H₁T₁K   198 .CCC.] *add* ȝere G,
.CCCC. K   200 another] *add* welle K   203 of ¹] aftir GK   that] and EGK   sege]
sete G   205 sche] he G   her] his G   209 it] hem T₁   213 hym] *add* his
money G   214 he] þei H₁   this] hym his G   til] *om.* T₁   216 come] go K   to]
add the E

putte vpon the dettour, and he brought with hym an holow staffe
whereinne the money was putte be his wile and malice, and he bere
this staffe in his | honde as for to susteine hym as it semed. And whanne f. 6rb
he schuld swere he toke the staffe to the Iue to kepe, and thanne he 220
swore that he hadd paied hym more thanne he borued of hym. And
whanne he hadd made his othe, he toke his staffe ayein of the Iue. And
thanne he that hadd do this fraude went quite. Hit happed that he felle
in slombre in a karfoke and a cart come with gret strengthe and slowe
hym and breke his staffe ful of golde, and it schadde oute al aboute. And 225
whanne the Iue herde and seigh this he was al meued of this gret
frauude, and mani men counsailed hym to take this money. He refused
it in al wise but yef he that was dede come ayein to lyff by the merites of
Seint Nicholas. He said also yef that he liued ayein he wold resseiue
baptime and schulde be cristenid. And thanne he that was dede rose 230
ayein fro dethe to lyff, and the Iue was cristened.

    Another Iue sawe the miracles of Seint Nicholas. He ordeined hym
an ymage of the seint and sette hym in his hous, and whanne he went
oute he comaunded the ymage to kepe his hous and his goodes and
said: 'Lo, Nicholas, here is al my goodes. I charge the to kepe hem 235
wel, and yef I misse any of hem I schal reuenge me vpon [the].' In a
tyme the Iue went oute, and theues come and toke al the goodes away
and lefte nothing but the ymage. Whanne the Iue come ayein and
fonde al his good gone, he aresonid the ymage by suche wordes: 'Sir
Nicholas, I hadd putte you in myn hous for gret truste that ye schulde 240
haue kept wel my good. Whi haue ye kept it no beter? I telle you truli
that ye schull resseiue cruel torment | and haue the peyne that f. 6va
longithe to the theuis, and I schalle reuenge myn harme in thi
tormentis.' And thanne he toke the image and bette it and tormented
it cruelli, wherof ther fille a grete mervaile, for whanne the theuis 245
departed these thingges this holi seint apperid to hem al forwounded
and saide to hem: 'Whi haue I be so cruelli beten and tormented for

   217 putte] *om.* K   218 wile] will H₁GT₁   221 more . . . hym] *om.* K
222 his] this H₁T₁   223 that¹] *add* thus EH₁T₁K   224 in slombre] into a sclow₃ G
karfoke] *del. with* cartsclade *in margin* H₁, carte sclade GT₁, cartesoke K   225 schadde]
schaterid G   226 herde and] *om.* G   229 yef . . . ayein] þat if he lyuyd G
230 cristenid] cristen G   rose] turned H₁T₁   231 ayein] *om.* K   fro dethe] *om.* H₁T₁
and] *add* thanne EH₁T₁K   231 cristened] *add* and belevid in God K   232 Another]
add time an oþer G   234 kepe] *add* wel G   235 Lo] to H₁T₁   here . . . goodes]
om. G   236 the] *om.* E   237 theues] þe Iewis G   239 suche] þese G
240 putte] *ins.* H₁   242 torment] *add* þerfore G   244 bette it] bite hym G
245 it] hym G   mervaile] miracle H₁T₁   246 thingges] goodes K   247 and¹] '&'
H₁   haue] am H₁T₁   be] *del.* H₁, *om.* T₁

youre gilt? Se ye not how my bodi is al torent and the blode rennyng
downe by gret stremis? Gothe fast and yeldithe ayein those thinges
250 and the goodes, or ellis the wrathe of God schall falle vpon you, that
alle schalle knowe youre defauutes and ye schulle be hangged alle.'
And thanne thei said: 'What art thou that tellist vs these wordes?'
Thanne he saide: 'I am Nicholas, servaunt of Ihesu Crist, the whiche
the Iue hathe so cruelli beten for ye toke awaye his good.' And thanne
255 thei were gretli aferde and come to the Iue and tolde hym how he
hadde done to the ymage and al the miracle, and yalde hym al his
good. And so the theuis come to the waye of rightwisnesse and the Iue
to the faithe of Ihesu Crist.
    In a tyme also a man ther was that halowed eueri yere [solempnely]
260 the feste of Seint Nicholas for loue of a sone that he hadd that went to
scole. And the fende that hadde enuie to this deuocion transfigured
hym in liknesse of a pilgrime and come to his gate and axsed almesse.
The fader comaunded his sone that he schulde bere almesse to the
pilgrime. The childe dede as he was bode and folued after the
265 pilgrime to take hym almesse, and whanne he come to a karfont the
fende toke the childe and strangelid hym. [And] whanne the fader
herde [this] of his sone he made gret wamentacion and pitous sorow,
f. 6ᵛᵇ wepte and | bere the bodi of his sone to his chaumbre and saide: 'A,
my dere sone, that this mishappe is falle to the! A, Seint Nicholas, is
270 this the guerdon that I resseiue for the worschip that I haue done to
you?' And as he said these wordes the childe anone openid his eighen
and awoke as though he hadd slept, and arose al hole and sounde.
    Also ther was a noble man that preied to Seint Nicholas [that] he
wolde be mene to oure Lorde that he myght haue a sone, and he
275 behight hym that he wolde bring his sone to his chirche and offre a
cuppe of golde with hym. He hadde a sone after his desire, and
whanne the childe come to resonable age the fader ordeined the cuppe
of golde. And whanne the cuppe was made, hym liked so wel the
shappe therof that he withhelde that cuppe and [let make] another of
280 the same wight and value. Thanne he toke his viage bi the see towarde

---

249 gret] faste G   249–50 thingges and the] om. K   251 alle¹] add folke G
252 these] suche H₁T₁   257 good] add ayen K   theuis] Iewis G   258 to] was
baptisid and toke K   of] add oure lord G   Crist] om. K   259 solempnely] om.
EH₁T₁K   262–4 and come . . . pilgrime] om. K   265 karfont] Carfouke G
266 the childe] om. K   And] om. EGK   267 this] om. E, 't'his H₁   of his] ins. H₁
wamentacion] lamentacion K   270 guerdon] reward G   271 you] the G
273 that²] om. E   274 be mene] one word E   274–5 and . . . sone] om. G
275 bring] offre K   279 let make] made E

Seint Nicholas, and as he was in the see he comaunded his sone to
bring hym water in the furst cuppe, and as the childe wolde haue take
water he fille ouer the borde [into the see withe the cuppe] and was no
more sene. Yet the fader notwithstondyng al this he fulfilled his avowe
withe gret weping and sorugh for his sone. And whanne he come to 285
the auutere of Seint Nicholas he offered the secounde cuppe, and
anone it was thrawe doune of the auutere with gret violence. And
thanne he toke up the cuppe ayein, and it was throwe doune further
thanne before. And so the thridde tyme, that all the peple hadde gret
meruayle and come to see this thing. And sodeinli the childe come 290
hole and sounde and brought the furst cuppe, and tolde to alle the
peple that whanne he fille into the see anone the b[lessid] Seint
Nicholas come | to hym and kepid hym fro harme. Thanne was the G f. 7ᵛ
fadir full of ioie and offrid vp bothe cuppis to Seint Nicholas.

Ther was anoþir riche man þat hadde a sone by þe meritis of Seint 295
Nicholas, and þis riche man made a chapel of Seint Nicholas in his
manere and halewid euery ȝere solempnely þe feste of Seint Nycholas.
And þis place was biside þe londe of Agareyns. And so it happenyd
þat þis child was take into seruage to þe kyng of þat londe. The ȝere
folowyng whanne þe fadir hilde deuoutly þe feste of Seint Nicholas, 300
the childe stode bifore þe kyng and hilde a riche cuppe in his honde,
and as he þouȝt hym of his takyng and of þe sorowe of his frendis and
of þe ioie þat he was wonte to see in his fadris hous in þat day, he
bigan to sigh wondir sore. And þanne þe kyng askid hym the cause of
his sighyng, and he tolde hym. Thanne seide þe kyng: 'ȝit for ouȝt þat 305
þy Nicholas can doo þou schalte abide here now.' And þanne
sodeynly þer blewe a scharpe wynde that made all þe hous to tremble,
and þanne þe child with þe cuppe in his hond was lifte vp and sette
bifore his fadris ȝatis, so in þat solempnyte all his frendis were fulfillid
with grete ioie. And it is redde elliswhere þat this ȝonge man | was G f. 8ʳ
born in Normandie and wente ouer þe Grete See and was taken of the 311
sowdan. Ofte tymys he was beten bifore þe sowdan, and as he was
beten on a Seint Nicholas Day, what for sorowe of his betyng, what
for the remembraunce of þe ioie þat he was wonte to haue in þat day,

283 into the see/withe the cuppe] *trs.* EHₗTₗK   284 fulfilled] filled HₗTₗ
285 withe] *add* ful G   287 thrawe] drawen G   288 throwe] caste G   doune] *om.*
HₗTₗ   289 thanne] *add* it was G   290 see] *om.* Hₗ, *damaged & illeg.* Tₗ   sodeinli]
secondly *with* od *over* ec Hₗ   292 blessid] bisshop EHₗK, *damaged & illeg.* Tₗ
296 man] *ins.* Hₗ   297 halewid] made K   303 ioie þat] Iewe þat he was wiþ and
how K   305 ȝit] Ye HₗTₗ   306 þanne] þe *del.* Hₗ, *om.* Tₗ   307 sodeynli]
secoundli Hₗ   308 sette] *add* euen G   309 fulfillid] filled HₗTₗ   312 bifore] of Tₗ

315 he made his prayere to Seint Nicholas, and þanne sodeynly he fill on
sclepe, and whanne he awoke he fonde hymself in þe chapel of his
fadris, where alle his frendis were in grete ioie and ȝauen souereyne
worschip and þankyng to oure Lord God and to the meritis of the
holy Seint Nicholas.

[Here endeth the life of Seint Nicholas, and þan biginneþe
þe life of Seint Luce þe virgine, Cap. .iij.].

Seint Lucye the holy virgyne was of þe kynrede of Sirakuse, and
whanne sche hurde þe renoun of Seint Agas that was talkid of in all
Cisile, sche hadde grete devocion to here. Hir modir Euticia had
suffrid þe blody flix the space of .iiij. ȝere and myȝt not be curid þerof.
5 It befelle in a solempnyte as þay were atte messe sche hurde þe gospel
þat makith mencion how þat oure Lord helid a woman of þat sekenes.
And þan Lucie seide to hir modir: 'Modir, if ȝe leue these þyngis þat
ben seide here, leue [verily] þat Agas hath alweyis presentid hym with
hire for the [wiche] sche suffrid passion, and y dare wel seie if þou
10 leue and towche hir sepulcre thou schalt be parfitly hole.'
    Thanne whanne alle were goon, the modir and þe douȝtir abiden in
prayeris bisidis þe sepulcre, and Lucie fille asclepe and sawȝ Seint
Agas in þe myddis of aungellis arayid with precious stonys [and] seide
to hire: 'My sustir Lucye, deuoute virgyne to God, wherfore requerist
15 þou of me þat þou mayste ȝeue anoon to thy modir? For sche is helid
by thy bileue.' And þanne Seint Lucie awoke and seide to hir modir:
'My modir, be ȝe of good comforte for ȝe be parfitly hole, and y
biseche ȝou for þe loue of hire þat hath helid ȝou by hir prayeris þat
fro hensward ȝe speke neuer to me of no mariage, but þat ȝe wolde
20 ȝeue me in [dowry] ȝeue it to pore men.' And þanne þe modir seide:
'A, douȝtir, schette rathir myne eyen and lete me deie or y doo soo as
þou biddist me.' Thanne seide Lucye: 'A, good modir, þat ȝe ȝeue
aftir ȝoure lif ȝe ȝeue for ȝe mowe no lenger haue it ȝoureself, and for
þat ȝifte ȝe deserue litill þanke. And þerfore ȝeue whilis ȝe leue and

317 where] *add* his fader and H1T1, *add* he and K   souereyne] soueraigneli H1T1

GH2H1A1A2; A1 is rubbed and largely difficult to read from 47 to end.   *Rubric
supplied from* H1, *not written into space provided in* G.   2 all] *ins.* H1   3 to here] *om.*
H1   Euticia] *add* speke þe wiche G   5 a] *add* day of G   8 here] *ins.* H1   verily]
alway G   alweyis] *om.* H1   presentid hym with] present'ed' H1   9 wiche] woman
whom G   13 and] þat G   18 þat . . . hir] *om.* H1   19 hensward] hens forward
H1   þat] *add* that H1   20 dowry] mariage G, *so on erasure* H1 (*douaire* P2)   22 þat]
add þat H1   24 ȝeue] *add* the H1

þanne schal 3e haue þanke and guerdon.' And whanne þay were come 25
home a3en, euery day þay bigan to selle of her þyngis and 3af largely
to þe pore. And in þe mene tyme þat þay departid þus her goodis and
heritagis it come to þe knowliche of hym þat schold haue weddid hire,
and he enquerid of hir norice what it mente. And þe norice answerid
sotilly þat his wif had founde betir possession þat sche wold bye in his 30
name and þerfore sche solde so hir þyngis. And þe fole leuyd þat it
hadde be a worldly possession and he bigan to be a sellere of thyngis. |
And whanne all was solde and 3euen to þe pore, he accusid hire to þe   G f. 8ᵛ
consulte Paschasien and seide þat sche was cristen and dide a3ens þe
ordynauncis of [þe] emperouris.   35

And þan Paschasien bade hire doo sacryfise to [þe] ydollis. She
answerid and seide: 'þat sacryfise þat likith to God is for to visite þe
pore and helpe hem in her nedis. And for y haue no more good y offre
myself to God in verrey sacrifise.' And þanne Paschasien seide: 'þou
my3ttist well seie þese wordis to a cristen fole as þou arte, for to me 40
þou seyist hem in veyne þat [kepe the] ordynauncis of princis.' To
whom Lucie seide: 'þou kepist þe ordynancis of thy princis and y
kepe þe ordynaunce of my God. þou dredist thy princis and y drede
my God. Thou wilte plese hem and y coueyte to plese my God. þou
wilte not wrathe thy princis and y will not wrathe my God. And 45
þerfore doo þou þat þou þynkist profitabul to the, and y will doo þat
that y see profitabul to me.' And þanne Paschasien seide: 'þou haste
dispendid thy goodis and thyne heritage in ribaudrie, and þerfore þou
spekist as siche oon as þou arte.' To whom Lucie seide: 'I haue sette
myne heritage in sure place for y wiste neuer what corrupcion of body 50
ne of þou3t was.' Thanne Paschasien seide: 'Who ben tho corruptouris of bodyis and of þou3tis?' And þanne Lucie seide: '3e amongis
3ou þat techen þe soulis to forsake her creatour, and also þay ben
corruptouris of bodyis þat put her delectacion in temporel goodis
bifore spirituel goodis.'   55

Thanne Paschasien seide: 'Whanne betyngis come þanne wordis
schal cese.' To whom Lucie seide: 'The worde of God schal neuer
cesse.' Thanne seide Paschasien: 'Arte þou þan God?' And Lucie

---

28 haue weddid] wede H1   29 and . . . hir] '& he asked her' H1   30 his'] þis H1
þat²] þan H1   34 Paschasien] Faspasien H1 and so throughout Lucy   35 þe] om. G
36 þe] om. G   37 to God] ins. H1   38 nedis] nede H1   41 kepe the] kepith G
ordynauncis] ordinaunce H1   42 kepist] spekest H1   ordynancis] ordinaunce H1
46 þou þinkest] þe thinketh H1   46–7 and . . . me] om. H1   47–8 haste dispendid]
spendest H1   49 sette] om. H1   51–2 corruptouris] corump't'ours H1   52 3e]
þre G   53 þay ben] ye be H1   56 betyngis] beting'es' H1   þanne] om. H1

answerid: 'Y am þe seruant of God þat seithe: "Whanne ȝe be bifore
60 kyngis and princis þenkith neuer what [ȝe] schal seie, for it is not ȝe
þat spekith but it am y þat schal speke in ȝou."' Paschasien seide:
'Then is the holy gost in the?' To whom Lucie seide: 'Tho þat lyuen
chaste ben þe templis of God and of þe holy gost.' And Paschasien
seide: 'Y schal make þe [to be] ladde to þe bordel and þere þou schalt
65 lese þyne holy goste.' Thanne Lucie seide: 'The body may not be
corrupte but if it come by consente of þouȝt, for þouȝ þou make me to
be corrupte with strengthe, my corone of chastite scholde encrese, for
it lithe not in þy cursid power to brynge me to consente ne my wille
therto. See here my body redy to all turmentis þat þou canste deuyse.
70 Why taryist þou, sone of þe fende? Bygynne to doo bitymys th[e]
desire of thy peynys.' And þanne Paschasien made to come forth
cursid ribaudis and lecherous and bade hem goo to hire and deffowle
hire till sche were dede. And whanne þay wolde haue drawen hire to
þe bordel þe holy goste made hire so heuy þat sche myȝt in no wise be
75 mevid. And þanne Paschasien made to come a .M.ˡ men and fifty
oxen, and alle þay myȝt not remewe þe virgyne. And þanne were
callid forth þe enchauntouris for to remeve hire by enchauntementis,
but þay myȝt not in no wise remeve hire. And þanne seide Paschasien:
'What maleficis ben tho þat a mayde may not be remevid with a .M.ˡ
Gf.9ʳ men?' | Wherto Lucie answerid and seide: 'þay ben noon maleficis but
81 þay ben beneficis of Ihesu Crist. For þouȝ þou settist ten þousand
men moo, ȝit scholde y be witheoute remeuyng as y am now.' Thanne
Paschasien was fulfillid with wrathe and comaundid þat a grete fire
schold be made aboute hire and made caste picche and tarre and oyle
85 brennyng hote vpon hire. And þanne Lucie seide: 'Y haue askid a
terme of my martirdom, for y wolde take awey þe drede of suffryng
deth of trewe beleueris, and also for y wolde restreyne þe weyis of ioie
to mysbileuers.'
      And whanne þe frendis of Paschasien sawȝ þat he was ful of
90 anguissh and trowbul, þay toke a spere and putte it þoruȝ hir þrote.
And ȝit sche loste neuer hir speche therfore, but sche seide: 'Y
denounce ȝou þat þis day is ȝouen pees to the Chirche, and
Maxymyan is þis day dede and Dioclician is put oute of his kyngdom.

60 and princis] *om.* H1   ȝeˡ] y G   63 chaste] chastinli H1   of God and] *om.* H1
64 to be] *om.* GH1   bordel] *add* hous G, bordelles H1   66 make] madest H1
67 be] *ins.* H1   68 me to] my H1   69 body] ʽbody' is H1   all] *add* þe H1
70 the] thy GH1   71 Paschasien] *add* seide and G   74 bordel] *add* hous G
77 to] *om.* H1   by] *om.* H1   81 ben] *ins.* H1   82 yˡ] *om.* H1   84 caste] ʽto
puteʼ H1   86 awey] *om.* H1   89 ofˡ] *ins.* H1   90 trowbul] troubeled H1

And as my sustir Agas is ordeynyd to be the defenderesse of
Cathanense, so am y ordeynyd to pray for þe cite of Ciracuse.' And 95
as þe virgyne seide þese wordis, the mynystris of Romaynys come in
and token Paschasien and bounde hym and ladde hym to þe
emperoure, for þe prouost had hurde seie þat he hadde rubbid all
þe provynce. And whanne he was come to Rome þe senatouris accusid
hym, and he was convicte and punyschid and resseyuyd sentence of 100
his hede smytyng of. And þe virgyne Seint Lucie was neuer remevid
oute of þe place where sche was smyten till prestis come and toke to
hire þe precious sacramente, and whanne sche hadde worschipfully
resseyuyd it sche and all þe pepul seide 'Amen'. Sche 3olde vp þe
spirite and hir holy body was buried in the same place. And now hir 105
bonys reste at Venyse. Sche suffrid deth in the tyme of Constantyn
and Maxymyan the 3ere of oure Lord thre hundrid and ten.

[Here endeþe þe life of Seint Luce, and þan beginneth þe
life of Seint Thomas of Inde, Cap. .iiij.].

As Seint Thomas þe apostul was in Cesare, oure Lord apperid to hym
and seide: 'The kyng of Inde, Cundophorus, hath sente his prouost
Abbanes for to seken men þat konnen of þe crafte of masonrie. Come,
and y schal sende þe to hem.' Thanne seide Thomas to oure Lord: 'A,
good Lord, sende me whereeuer þou liste, but sende me not to hem of 5
Inde.' And þanne seide oure Lord: 'Goo sewrely and drede þe nou3t,
for y schal be þy kepere and whanne þou hast conuertid þe pepul of
Inde þou schalt come to me by þe corone of martirdome.' And þanne
Thomas seide: 'þou arte my Lord and y am þy seruant, thy will be
fulfillid.' And as þe prouoste wente þoru3 þe market to seke a crafty 10
man, oure Lord seide to hym: 'What wilt þou beye, 3ong man?' þanne
he seide: 'My lord hath sente me hidir for to gete hym here seruauntis
þat ben tau3t in the crafte of masonrie, for þay moste make hym a
paleis aftir the werke of Rome.' And þanne oure Lord toke hym
Thomas and seide hym þat he hadde grete experience in þat crafte. 15
    And þanne þay come saylyng to a cite where a kyng made þe mariage
of his dou3tir and hadde lete crie þat all schold come | to þe mariage of Gf. 9ᵛ

96 mynystris] ministresse H1   98 seie] seid H1   103 sche] om. H1

GH2H1A1A2; A1 has tear removing parts of the text from 1 to 5 *whereeuer*, 35 *felaschip*
to 41 *and*, 75 *gretly* to 79 *merueylously*, 114 *arisen* to 120 *wisdom*, 154 *as* to 155 *worde*; E
resumes at 167 *And   Rubric supplied from* H1   4 þe] *ins.* H1   hem] him H1   4–5
A good Lord] *om.* H1   5 þou] þe H1   10 crafty] *add and subp.* a H1   11 What]
add þing H1   15 seide] told H1

his dou3tir or ellis þay schold wrathe the kyng. So it befell þat þe
prouost and Thomas wente among oþir, and at þe feste amongis oþer
20 mynstrellis þer was a mayden and hilde a tabur in hir hond and songe
þerwith, and euery man sche seide [somme] preysyng. And whanne
sche saw3 the apostul sche wiste wel þat he was of Ebreu, for he ete not
among hem but hadde vp his eyen to heuen, and as þe mayden songe in
Ebreu afore hym sche seide: 'þe God of Ebrewis is oon allone þat made
25 all þyng, heuen and erthe and þe see.' And þanne þe apostul wold haue
made hire recorde hir wordis a3en, and þe botiller saw3 þat and with his
honde 3af the apostul a grete buffet vndir þe cheke. Thanne þe apostul
seide: 'It is beste for the þat þis be for3euen the in tyme to come and
þou be [punyschid] now and resseyue a transitorie wounde, wherfore y
30 telle þe or y departe oute of þis [place] þat honde þat hath smyten me
schal be boren awey with houndis.' And þanne þis man wente forth to
fette watir at þe welle, and a lyon come and deuourid hym and dranke
his blode, and houndis come aftir and al torente þe body, and a grete
blak dogge toke þe ri3t arme and brou3t it into þe halle among hem alle
35 as þay were at þe dynere. And whanne þay saw3 þis all þe felaschip was
abasshid, and þe mayde recordid þese wordis and caste hir tabre doun
and sche felle doun to the [fete of þe] apostul and resseyuyd cristen
faith.

       And þanne þe apostul at þe requeste of þe kyng blessid þe 3ong
40 mariage and seide: 'Lord, 3eue to þese children the blessyng of thy
ri3t side, and putte in her þou3t sede of lif.' And whanne þe apostul
was goon þer was founde in eche of her handis a palme ful of datis.
And whanne þis 3ong [mariage] had eten of þe frute þay felle asclepe
anoon, and þanne þay [seen] a liche dreme [euerech of hem] for hem
45 semyd that a kyng richely arayid with precious stonys [beklippid] hem
and seide: 'Myne apostul hath blessid 3ou, wherfore 3e moste come to
euerlastyng lif.' And þerwith þay awoke and tolde eche oþir her
dremys, and þanne þe apostul come to [hem] and seide: 'My kyng
hath now apperid to 3ou and hath brou3t me hidir and þe doris ben
50 schette, so þat my blessyng may be fruteful in 3ou and þat 3e haue
purite of 3oure flessh, the wiche is quene of all vertuis and frute of

      19 and at . . . oþer] ins. H1   21 somme] om. G   preysyng] add þerwith to somme G
22 wiste] knew H1   of] an H1   29 punyschid] perischid G   30 place] paleis G
me] om. H1   37 fete of þe] om. G   39 kyng] add he G   3ong] om. H1
43 mariage] man maried G   44 seen] hadde G   euerech of hem] om. G
45 beklippid] he klippid G   hem] ins. H1   46 seide] add hem G   Myne apostul]
Mypostell changed to My'n a'postell H1   48 hem] hym G   seide] s'e'ide H1
49 ben] om. H1

perpetuel saluacioun. For virgynyte is sustir of aungellis, possession
of all [goodes], victorie of klennesse, lordschip of faithe, discomfiture
of fendis and [suerte] of euerlastyng ioie. Luxvrie is engendrid of
corrupcion, and of corrupcion comyth pollicion, and of pollicioun 55
comyth synne, and of synne is confusion engendrid.' And as he seide
þese wordis [two aungellis] apperid to hem and seide: 'We ben þe
aungellis þat ben ordeynyd to kepe ȝou. And ȝe like well all the
techyngis of þe apostul we schul offre to God all ȝoure desiris.' And
þanne þe apostul baptisid hem and tauȝt hem diligently the faith. And 60
longe | tyme aftir þis wif þat heiȝt Pelagian was sacrid with þe holy G f. 10ʳ
veyle of religion and suffrid martirdom, and hir husbond was sacrid
bisshop of þat cite.

After þis þe apostul and Abbanes come to the kynge of Inde and the
kyng deuysid to þe apostul a merveylous paleis and toke hym grete 65
tresouris to make it. And whilis þe kyng wente into anoþer prouynce,
þe apostull ȝaf all þe tresoure to þe pore. And þe apostul was alwey in
predicacion two ȝere hole or þe kyng returnyd aȝen and conuertid to
þe faith pepul withouten nombre. And whanne þe kyng come home
and knewe what Seint Thomas had doon, he putte hym and Abbanes 70
in the deppist prison that he hadde and purposid fully to brenne hem
bothe.

And in þis mene tyme deide [Gad], þe kyngis brothir, and was leide
in a riche sepulcre. The .iiij.ᵉ day he þat had be dede he aroos to lif
and all were gretly afrayid and fledden. Thanne he seide to his brothir: 75
'Brothir, þis man þat þou purposist to brenne and scle is þe special
frende of God almyȝtty and þe aungellis of God seruen hym. And þay
haue ladde me into paradis and schewid me a riche paleis all of gold
and seluer and precious stonys merveylously ordeynyd, and whanne y
merveylid of þe beaute þerof þay seide to me: "þis is þe paleis þat 80
Thomas hath made for þy brothir." And whanne y bisouȝt [hem] þat
y myȝt be portere, þanne þay seide to me: "Thy brothir hath made
hym vnworthy to haue it. If þou [wilt] dwelle here we schul pray to
oure Lord þat he will arere the so þat þou mayste bye it of thy brothir,
ȝeldyng hym þe same money that he wenyd [to haue] loste."' And 85
whanne he hadde þus seide he ran to þe prison where þe apostul was

53 goodes] goddis, klennesse of alle vertuis G   of ²] add all Hı   54 suerte]
sikernesse G   Luxvrie] Lecheri Hı   57 two aungellis] an aungell G   61 þis] add
his G, add þe on erasure Hı   70 he] add merveled gretli and Hı   73 Gad]
Godophorus G   74 he þat] trs. G   77 of¹] ins. Hı   81 hath] so changed to had
Hı   hem] hym G   83 wilt] om. G   85 to haue] he hadde G

and prayid hym to forȝeue his broþir and dide of his cheynys and
prayid hym þat he wold doo on a precious clothe. Thanne þe apostul
seide: 'Wotist not þou wel þat þoo þat hauen myȝt in heuenly þyngis,
90 [how þei setten litul bi erthli þinges?']
  And whanne þe apostul come oute of prison, the kyng come aȝens
hym and fille doun to his [fete] and askid forȝeuenesse. And þanne the
apostul seide: 'God hath grauntid ȝou grete þyngis [whan he hath
grauntid ȝou secrete þingis,] and þerfore leue in Ihesu Crist and be
95 baptisid so þat þou may be a prynce of euerlastyng kyngdom.' And
þanne þe kyngis brothir seide to þe apostul: 'I haue seyn þe paleis þat
þou hast made for my brothir and y am come for to beye it.' And
þanne the apostul seide to hym: 'þat is in thy brotheris wille.' And
þanne seide the kyng: 'Nay, brothir, y wil haue þat paleis myself, and
100 þe apostil schal make the anoþir. And if perauenture he may not, þat
same schal suffise to þe and to me.' Thanne seide þe apostul: 'Many
riche paleysis ben in heuen þat were arayid and ordeynyd fro þe
bygynnyng of þe worlde þat ben bouȝt by price of faithe and of almys.
And þerfore ȝoure richesse may well goo bifore ȝou to þat paleis, but
105 þay mowe not come aftir ȝou.'
  And a monyth aftir, þe apostul made all þe pepul of þat prouynce to
assemble, and whanne þay all were assemblid he comaundid þat all þe
G f. 10ᵛ febul and þe | seke schold be brouȝt forth. And þanne he made his
preyeris ouer hem, and whanne þe pepul þat [were] tauȝt seide 'Amen,'
110 a merveylous liȝt dessendid fro heuen þat smote doun to þe erthe þe
apostul and all þe pepul þe space of half an houre þat þay lay as dede.
And þanne þe apostul aroos and seide to all þe pepul: 'Arisith alle, for
my Lord is come as thondir and liȝtnyng and hath helid vs alle.'
Thanne þay arisen all hole fro all maner of febulnesse and sekenesse þat
115 þay hadde. þanne þay glorifiden oure Lord God and the apostul.
  And þanne þe apostul bigan to teche hem þe degreis of vertuis. The
firste is þat þay bileueden in God þat is oon essence and trebul in
personys, and þanne he schewid hem in þre examplis sensiblis how
þre personys ben in oon essence. The firste ensampul is this: in a man
120 þer is wisdom, and of wisdome þer comyth vndirstondyng, mende
and konnyng. Konnyng is þat that þou hast lernyd, þe mende kepith
it þat þou forȝete it not, þe vndirstondyng þat þou fele it in siche wise

  90 how . . . þinges] om. G erthli] erli H1 92 fete] kneis G 93–4 whanne . . .
þyngis] om. G 95 of] add the H1 100 perauenture] be auenture þat H1
109 were] he G 114–15 þat þay hadde] om. H1 117 oon] add in G
118 schewid] biseched H1 examplis] 'thre examples' H1

þat þou can schewe it and teche it. The seconde ensample is how þat
in [a vyne] there be þre þyngis, the tre, the lef, and þe frute, and ȝit all
is but oo vyne. The þridde ensampul is þat in þe hede of a man ther 125
ben also þre þyngis, that is siȝt, heryng, and smellyng, and ȝit þere is
but oon hede. The seconde degre is þat þay resseyue bapteme. The
þridde that þay kepe hem fro fornycacion. The fourthe þat þay kepe
hem fro couetise. The fifthe þat þay restreyne her glotonye. The sexte
þat þay holde her penaunce. The seuenthe þat þay perseuere in [þese] 130
þyngis. The .viij.ᵉ that þay loue hospitalite. The nynthe, þyngis þat
[ben nedefull] thay asken þe wille of God. The tenthe þat þay
eschewen þyngis that ben not to doone. The enleueneth þat þay
doo cherite to enemyis and to frendis. The .xij.ᵉ þat þay sette her
diligence to kepe þese þyngis. And whanne he hadde þus made his 135
predicacion there resseyuyd bapteme þre skore .M.ˡⁱ men withoute
women and children.

And þanne he wente into þe Grete Inde and þere he was gretly
worschipid by signys and myraclis, for he ȝaf siȝt to Sanctice the dere
frend of Migdonye the wif of Carisien þe kyngis cosyn. Thanne seide 140
Migdonye to Sanctice: 'Y desire gretly to see þis holy man, and y
wiste in what wise.' Thanne sche chaungid hir clothyng by þe counsel
of Sanctice and putte hire among oþir pore women in womannys
clothyng and come thidir as the apostul prechid. And he bigan to
preche of þe wrechidnesse of þis lif, sey120ng þat þis present lif is freel 145
and sogette to many auenturis, and is so fleyng þat whanne a man
wenyth to holde hire sche fleith and vaneschith awey.

And þanne he bigan to teche hem by foure resonys þat þay schold
gladly here þe word of God. He likenyd the worde of God to foure
maner of þyngis: to a col[e]re, for sche enlumynyth the eye of oure 150
vndirstondyng; to a sorep, for it pur[g]ith | oure affeccion fro all Gf.11ʳ
flesshly loue; to an emplastre, for it helith þe woundis of oure synnys;
to mete, for it norischith vs and ȝeuyth vs delite in heuenly loue. And
riȝt as þese þyngis avaylith nouȝt to þe seke but if he take [hem] in
hymself, riȝt so þe worde of God availith nouȝt to þe seke soule but if 155
it be hurde deuoutly.

123 þat þou² . . . teche it] 'can chewit and techit' H1   124 a vyne] þe veyne þat G
all] add þis H1   129 her] hem fro H1   130 þese] siche G   132 ben nedefull]
om. G   asken] add þat þay be leful aftir G   140 wif] wise H1   of²] om. H1
141 Migdonye] Magoude (?) H1   143 women in] om. H1   145 sey120ng . . . lif] om.
H1   147 and vaneschith] om. H1   149 He] Thei changed to he H1   150 colere]
coloure G   151 purgith] purith G   152 loue] loues H1   154 hem] it G
155 so] in þe same wise H1

And as þe apostul prechid he conuertid Migdonee, and þanne sche reffusid hir husbondis bedde in all wise. Ca[r]isien seyng þat ordeynyd [þat þe] apostul was sette in prison. þanne come Migdonye 160 to hym and askid hym forȝeuenesse þat he was sette in prison for hire. Thanne he comfortid hire goodly and seide he wold suffre all paciently. Thanne Carisien prayid þe kyng þat he wold sende þe quene his wifis sustir to hire to assaye if sche myȝt calle hir aȝen fro þis cristen religion. And whanne þe quene was sente thidir sche was 165 convertid by hire þat sche wold haue peruertid, for whanne sche sawȝ þe myraclis þat þe apostul dide, sche seide: 'Truly þay ben cursid of E f. 7ra God that leue not in his werkis.' | And thanne the apostill taught shorteli hem that were there of .iiij. thingges, that thei shulde loue the Chirch and worschip prestes and gadre hem ofte togedre to here the 170 worde of God.

And whanne the kyng seigh the quene he asked her wher sche hadde bene so long, and sche ansuered and saide: 'I wende that Migdeyne hadd bene a fole, and sche is right wise, for sche hathe brought me to the apostill that hathe made me knowe the waye of 175 trouthe, for truli thei bene to gret folis that leuyn not in Ihesu Crist.' Ne neuer after the quene wold not come in the kingis bedd, wherof the kyng was gretli abasshed and said to his cosin: 'Whanne I wolde haue recouerid thi wiff I haue lost myn, for myn is now worse to me than thin is to the.'

180 And thanne the kyng comaunded that the apostill were brought before hym bounden hondes and f[e]te, and whanne the kyng seigh hym he bade hym that he schulde reconsile her wives to her husbondes ayein. Thanne saide the apostill to the kyng and shewed hym bi .iiij. ensamples that thei aught not obeie to hem as long as thei 185 were in errour ayenst the faith, that is to wete be the ensample of the kyng, the toure and of the welle, saieng in this wise: 'Thou that art a kyng will not haue vnclene seruise but pure and clene servauntes, and sithe thou louest this how trouest thou thanne that God louithe chastite and clene seruise? What am I thanne to blame though I labour 190 and preche that God be loued of his servauntis that he louithe? I haue made hym an high toure, and thou biddest me distroie it. I haue

158 Carisien] Catisien G   seyng] seying H1   þat] add þe G   159 þat þe] om. G
167 leue] ben H1   168 were there of] ther were G   169 ofte] om. G   172 that]
add þe H1   176 neuer] om. G   not] om. H1   178 recouerid] reconuertid G
haue²] om. H1   181 and fete] and fote E, om. G   184 hem] him H1   186 toure]
tonne H1   that] om. G   187 will] þou wilte G

digged this toure in gret dipthe and haue brought forthe a quik welle,
and thou | woldest that I schuld stoppe it.'   f. 7rb

Than was the kyng wrothe and comaunded [to] bryng forthe peces
of yren brennynge, and made the apostill goo barfote vpon hem. And   195
anon bi the will of God a welle sprang vp and quenched alle the
brennyng peces. Thanne the kyng bi the counsaile of his cosin made
hym be putte in a brennyng furnais the whiche was so refresshid with
atempre colde that he went oute witheouten any disese. And thanne
saide Carisience to the kyng: 'Make hym offre sacrifice to one of oure   200
goddes that he may renne in the wrathe of his God that deliuer[eth]
hym thus.' And as thei wold haue constreined hym therto he saide to
the kyng: 'Art not thou more noble and more worthi thanne thin
ymage that is peinted after the? Whi dispisest thou thanne the verray
God and worschipest a peinture?' Than saide the kyng: 'What spekist   205
thou to me of comparisons? Do sacrifice to oure god or ellis thou
schalt dye.'

Than the apostill comaunded in Ebrew to the deuell that was
within the ydole that as sone as he schuld knele before hym that he
schulde breke the ydole. Anon the apostill knelid adoune, seieng: 'Lo,   210
what, I worschip here not the ydole, I worschip not the metall, I
worschip not the false ymage, but I worschip oure Lorde Ihesu Crist,
in whos name I comaunde the deuel that hidest the witheinne that
ydole that thou tobreke that fals ymage.' And anone he melt away as
wexse. And whanne the bisshopes of the temple saien this thei with   215
speres rennen thorughoute the apostill and saiden: 'I schall venge the
wronge of my god.' The kyng and Carisien fledden away for thei sein
that the peple wolde reuenge the apostill and brenne the | bisshop al   f. 7va
quik. Thanne the cristen men beren the bodi of the apostill and beried
it worschipfulli.   220

Long tyme after, the yere of oure Lorde .CC. and .xxx.^ti, the bodi
of the apostill was born into Edice, the citee that somtime was said
Rages citee of Mede. The emperour Alisaundre brought hym thedir
atte request of Sirriens. In that citee no man herburith no Iue ne no

192 dipthe] depþ'e' H1   194 to bryng] bryng E, *om.* G   195 of] and H1
brennynge] *om.* H1   goo] *add* forþe H1   198 so] *om.* H1   200 offre] do fre H1
201 deliuereth] deliuerid E   204 the²] þy G   206 god or] goddis and G
209 within] with yow *with* yow *del. and* 'in' *above it* H1   209–10 that he schulde breke
the ydole] *om. and paraph after* anon H1   210 Anon] *add* as G   215 bisshopes]
bisshop H1   216 the apostill] hym G   217 god] goddis G   fledden] ranne G
218 brenne] brent H1   bisshop] bisshopps H1G   222 the citee] *om.* H1
223 emperour] *add* of G   224 herburith] he'r'b'er'eeth H1

225 tiraunt, ne no paynim may not leve there sithe that Abaga[r] kyng of
that citee deserued to haue a pistel of the writyng of oure Lordes
honde, for yef [any] enemyes arisen ayeinst the citee a childe that is
cristenid shall stonde vpon the walle and rede the pistell, and in the
same day, what bi the vertu of the writyng of oure sauioure and bi the
230 merites of the apostill, the enemyes schullen fle or ellis make pees.
   Isodorie in the Boke of Liff and of Dethe of Seintes saiethe in this
wise: 'Thomas the apostill and disciple of Ihesu Crist, semb[l]able to
the saueoure, harde of byleue, preched the gospel in the parties of
Mede of Hi[rquien]s to the Bra[c]hiens, and that same entering into
235 the parties of orient perced the bowelles of the peple by his
predicasion, and so continued til he was persid thorugh his bodi in
resseiving glorious marterdome.' Crisostom saiethe that whanne
Thomas come to the parties of the thre kyngges that come to worschip
oure Lord he baptised hem and thei were made helpers to the cristen
240 faithe.

      Thus endithe the lyff of Seint Thomas of Ynd the apostill,
      and here beginnithe the Natiuite of oure Lorde Ihesu Crist
      and Sauioure, Cap. .v.^m

   The Natiuite of oure Lorde Ihesu Crist was done and fulfilled fro the
f. 7vb   tyme of Adam | .vM.^1 and .xxviij. yere, and after som other ys saieng
.vjM.^1, and after Eusebe of Cesare in his Cronicles .vM.^1 and .ixC. In
the tyme of Octauian emperour, whanne the sone of God come into
5 this worlde, alle peple ioieden that the only emperours of Romayns
lordschipped ouer all. He was called Octauyan, and Cesar also after
Iulius Cesar that was his vncle, also he was called Augustus for the
encresing of the comune of Rome, for the dignite of the emperial
honour that was furst ennobled with the name fro the difference of
10 other kyngges. For as oure Lorde wolde be bore to yeue us euerlasting
pees, right so [he] wolde that the tyme of pees schulde worship his
natiuite.

   225 Abagar] Abagat E, *so with* t *changed to* r H1   226 deserued] desirid G
227 honde] handis G   any] *om.* E   228 cristenid] cristen H1   229 oure] *add* lorde
H1   231 Seintes] seint sith G   232 of Ihesu Crist] *om.* G   semblable] sembable E,
semblid G, sembelabe *changed to* sembeled *and followed by* like *del.* H1   234 Hirquiens]
Hisqs E, Hirqs *bar over* q H1, Turchies G   Brachiens] brathiens EH1, brakyens G
235 perced] perischid G   236 continued] conteined H1G   persid] perischid G
thorugh] *add* oute E

   EH1GH2A1A2; A1 has lost some words around 27   3 .v.] .vj. H1   4–5 whanne
. . . emperours] *om.* G   4 the²] te E   10 be bore] bifore G   11 he] *om.* E

Cesar that was lorde of alle the world wolde wete how many provinces, how many citees, how many castellis and townes, and how myche peple were in the world, and as it is saide in the Stories he comaunded that alle men schuld go to thaire citees where thei hadde be born and that eueri man schulde yeue a peny of siluer to the prouost of the prouince, whiche peny schulde haue the ymage of Cesar and his name wretin aboue. And this was called descripcion or profession, but that was said bi diuerse consideracionis. Sche was said profession, for whanne eueri man schulde yelde that peny he schulde leie it vpon his hede and knowlache to the provost withe his propre mouthe that he was soget to the emperour of Rome, and this profession was opin confession for it shulde be done before alle the peple. Also it is said discripsion, for whanne the nombre of hem that beren the money vpon her hedes a certayn tyme hadde take it to the provost thei were countted by sertayn nombre and putte in writyng.

And the furst discripcion was | made of the prouost of Sirie, Cirin. And for that Iudee is the midel of oure habitacion it was ordeined that it schulde begynne there, and after bi the contrees aboute. And this discripcion was cleped vniuersall for that the other were made bi parties, either for that the furst discripcion was made to the provost in the citee. The secounde was made of the citees in the contre before the massage of Cesar.

And Ioseph, that was of the kynrede of Dauid, went from Nazareth into Bethlem. And the tyme of childyng of the blessid Virgine Marie fel that same tyme, and for he knewe not whanne he shuld come aycin, he ledde her withe hym into Bethelem, for he wolde not leue [her] in straunge governaunce the tresour that was comitted hym of God, but he wolde diligently kepe it hymselff. And as Frere Bartilmew witnessith in his compilacion in the boke of the Childehode of Crist, the Virgine seigh whanne sche neighed to Bethlem the toon parti of the peple wepte and that other partie lough. Thanne the aungell expowned to her the cause and saide: 'The partye of the peple of paynymes that schull resseiue blessyng in the sede of Abraham reioysen hem, and the partie that wepen is the partie of Iuees that bene reproued of God bi thaire desertes.'

And whanne thei come bothe into Bethlem thei myght gete hem no

15 in¹] *add* all G   18 ymage] name G   27 countted] committed H₁G
28 discripcion] writyng G   29 Iudee] ende G   31 cleped] callid G   33 contre]
cuntreis G   38 her²] *om.* E   43 wepte] ʼioyedʼ H₁   partie] *om.* H₁   lough] longeth
or lougeth H₁   45 of¹] *ins.* H₁

hous, for thei were pore and multitude of other hadde all take up.
50 Thanne thei turned hem to [a] comon place that was bitwene .ij.
howses and was hilled aboue and called the diuersorie, wher men of
the citee assembled togederis to speke and to dyne in idell dayes, or
ellis for distemperaunce of the tyme, or ellis as som sayn that the
churles of the contrey, whanne they come to the market, thei wolde
f. 8rb teye | there thaire bestis, and for that cause was there a crache redie
made. And thanne Ioseph teied his oxse and his asse to the crache and
abode stille there with the blessid Virgine, and sche that was ladi of
alle the world was content withe that litell hous.
    So it befell vpon a Sonday that the blessid Virgine Marie broght
60 forthe her blessid sone and laide hym in the crache vpon the haye, and
as the Maister of Stories tellithe that the blessid Eline brought sithe
that same haye to Rome, and as sum sayn that the oxe and the asse
restreyned them of etyng of the heye after that he was leide theron.
    And it is to wete that the natiuite of oure Lord Ihesu Crist was done
65 mervailously for to be schewed multiplyingli and profitably. Sche was
done mervaylously as wel of the moder partie as of the child. Of the
partie of the moder for sche was virgine in childyng and a pure virgine
after, and that sche was virgine in beryng her childe and after it is
schewed us in fyve maners. Furst bi the profit Ysaie in the seuenthe
70 chapitour: 'Lo, a virgine shall conseive and bere a childe.' Secoundly
be the yerde of Aaron that floured and bare fruit and by [the] 3ate of
Ezechiell the whiche was alwaye close. And the thridde by hym that
kept her, for he was trwe witnesse of her virginite. Ferthely bi verray
profe, for as it is redde in the Boke of oure Saueoure of his
75 Childehode, whan the tyme of childyng of the blessid Virgine was
come, Ioseph kepyng the custume of women went oute to call
mydwives, of the whiche that one hight Zebel and that other
Salome. And thanne whanne Zebel myde her and founde her virgine
sche cried and saied that a virgine hathe born a childe, and Salome
f. 8va leued her not but wolde haue | proued it, and anone her honde dried
81 vp. And thanne the aungel apperid to her and comaunded that she
shuld touche the childe and anone sche shulde be hole. The .v. [by]
euidence of miracle, for as Innocence witnessithe how pees was atte

50 a] om. E, the H1   .ij.] om. G   51 hilled] heled H1   was hilled . . . wher] om. G
52 idell] add placis and in ydel G   61 of] add þe H1   62 sum] add men G   63 the]
om. G   65 to] it schold G   67 childyng] bering hir childe H1   67–8 and a
pure . . . childe] ins. with her om. and replaced by of H1   68–9 after it is schewed us] it
was schewid vs aftirward G   69 seuenthe] ins. H1   71 the²] om. E   74 is] ins.
H1   78 whanne] om. H1   myde] ney3id G, so on erasure H1   82 by] om. EH1

Rome .xij. yere, and therfor the Romayns made a faire temple of pees
and putte witheinne the ymage of Rome, and asked counsaile of the 85
god Appoline how long that temple schulde dure, and thei hadde
ansuere: 'Til a virgine shulde bere a childe.' And whanne they herde
that they sayden that yt schuld last thanne for euer, for they
vnderstode that it was vnpossible a mayde to bere a childe euer.
And thanne thei wrote vpon the gates of the temple this title: 'This ys 90
the temple of euerlastyng pees.' But the nyght that the Virgine
brought forthe her sone the temple fell downe, and now ther ys the
chirche of Seint Marie the Nwgh.

Secoundely sche is mervaylous of the partie of the child, the thing
of euerlastyng, ansyen and nwe assembled togedre in one persone 95
mervelously. The thing euerlastyng is the godhede, the aunsien thing
ys the flesche that was take of Adam, the nwe thing ys the saule that
was made of nwe. And Andrewe saithe hereof: 'God hathe made thre
the best werkes merveylously, for he hathe ioyned togedre God and
man, moder and virgine, feithe and mannes hert. This is a mervaile 100
aboue alle mervayles, for to ioyne togedre erthe and God, mageste and
infirmite, so gret filthe and so gret hyghnesse, for ther is nothing
higher thanne God ne nothing so lowe as erthe. And the secounde is
wonder mervaylous and was neuer herde before, that a virgine schulde
[bere a childe and] be a moder and abide a virgine after. | The .iij. is f. 8ᵛᵇ
more lower thanne the furste or the secounde, but sche is not moch 106
lasse wonderfull, that is how a man ys hert canne beleue that God is
man and that the Virgine abode virgine after her childynge.

Thirdely sche was mervailous of the partie of the maner of
childyng, for the childyng was aboue kynde, wherfor it was sittyng 110
and reson sithe that sche conseyued virgine that sche schuld bere
God. She was aboue mannes condicion for sche bere her childe
withoute disese or sorw, she was aboue custume for sche conseiued of
the holi gost, for the Virgine conseyued not by mannes sede but be
devyne enspiring, for the holi goost toke and formed the body of the 115
right chaste and purest blood of the Virgine. In this wise God shewed
the .v. manere of makyng of man, for as Seint Anselme saithe: 'God

90 title] stile G   92 ther] þeˈrˈ H1   the²] there a G   93 Nwgh] add euen faste
by G   94 thing] þyngis G   95 ansyen] are seyn G   96 aunsien thing] ausensing
or ansensing G   98 hereof: God] here of oure lord god that he G   100 and²] in G
103 higher thanne God] so heigh as G   105 bere a childe and] om. EH1   be a moder
and abide] leue stille G   virgine] add vndefoulid G   110 the] om. H1   112 God]
add for G   mannes] add kynde and aboue mannys G   113 or] of H1   114 for the
Virgine conseyued] om. G   sede] fere G

may make man in foure maners, the one is witheoute man and woman
as he dede Adam, of a man witheoute woman as he did Eue, of man
120 and woman as the comune vsage is, of a woman witheoute a man as it
is shewid this day mervailously.'

Secoundely his natiuite was shewed this day bi alle manere of
creatoures. Ther ys one manere of creatoure that hathe only being, as
stones, another that hathe being and lyvynge, as trees, another that
125 hathe beyng and felyng and levyng, as bestis, and the .iij. that hathe
being, lyving, feling and vnderstondyng, as aungels. And be all these
creatoures was shewed this day the natiuite of oure Lord, furst be
stones, as by the distruccion of the temple of Romayns, as it is [said
aboue], by the ymage of Rome that [f]yl that day and many other
f. 9ʳᵃ images that felle in diuerse places. Men | rede in the Maister of Stories
131 that Ieconie the profit, after the dethe of Golye, come into Egipt and
tolde to hem that her ydolis schul[d] falle whanne a mayde schulde
bere a childe, and therfor the prestes of the ydoles made an ymage of
[a] virgine bering a childe in her lappe and sette her in the most
135 secrete place of her temple. Thanne the kyng Tolomee asked hem
what it ment, and thei saiden that it was a misterie that the grettest of
hem helde of the holi profit, wenyng fulli that it schulde befalle.

And so sche was shewed bi the purete of the erthe, for the nyght of
the natiuite of oure Lorde the derkenesse of the eyre was turned al to
140 light of the day. And as Orose and Pope Innocent witnesse, a welle of
water was conuerted into the licoure of oyle and ranne into [Tybre],
and al that day the welle sprong largely, and now is there the chirche
of oure Lady ouer the [Tybre]. And Sibilla hadde profesied before
that whane the welle of oyle schulde springe that the Saueoure shuld
145 be born.

Also [as] Orose saithe, the kyngges of the orient weren vpon an hille
beholdyng vp to heuene wher thei seen appere to hem a woman withe
a faire childe in her arme, a crosse vpon his hede, and that childe
aresoned the kynggez and bade hem go into Iudee and ther thei
150 shul[d] fynde a childe bore. And that same day thre sonnes appered in

119 Adam . . . did] `Adam &' H1        122 his] `h'is H1   123 one] no *changed to* oo
H1   124–6 another . . . aungels] *these two clauses trs. in* G   126 lyving] *om.* G   as]
add men and G   128–9 said aboue] *trs.* E   129 fyl] tyl EH1   day] *add* stode *del.* H1
130 in¹] *add* Rome and in oþir G   of¹] *add* the H1   132 schuld] schull E   134 a¹]
the E   bering] *ins.* H1   136 a] *add* grete G, so *ins.* H1   137–8 wenyng . . . purete]
om. G   138 purete] pouerte H1   erthe] ȝere G   for] or H1   139 oure] hir G
141 into] *twice* E   Tybre] the tymbre E, Tyber *with* ber *on erasure* H1   142 there] *om.* H1
143 the] *om.* G   Tybre] tymbre E, tymbre *with* m *del.* H1   144 schulde] gan G
146 as] *om.* EH1   150 shuld] shull E

the orient to hem and litell and litell thei comen togedre to one sonne, wherby was betokened the knowlache of the Trinite and of God appered to alle the world, or ellis that he was bore in whom thre thingges were assempled, flesche, soule and the godhede. It is redde in the Maister of Stories that the day of the natiuite these thre sunnez | 155 apered not, but it was before the tyme [after the dethe] of Iulius Cesar, f. 9rb and Eusebe saiethe in his Cronicle, and Innocent also, that whanne the emperour Octavian hadd putte alle the world vnder his subieccion that the peple wold haue worschipped hym as a god. And that wyse lorde knewe well that he was dedely, wolde not take on hym the 160 worschip that longed to an vndedly. And yet the emperour atte her enordinat request lete call Sibylle the profetesse, and desired to wete by her prophesie yef any gretter thanne he were to be born in the world. And as he hadd assembeled his counsayle the day of his natiuite vpon this thing and as Sibyll was in her chaumbre to avise 165 her, in the middes of the day a cercle of golde apered about the sunne, and in the middel of the sonne ther was a right fayre virgine bering a childe in her arme. And than Sibill sheued this thing to the emperour, and as the emperour mervailed gretly of this vision he herde a voys that saide: 'This is the auuter of heuene.' Thanne said Sibyll to hym: 170 'This child is gretter thanne thou art, and therfor worschip hym only.' And that same chaumbre is kept in the worship of [the] Virgine Marie and is yet called Virgine Marie Auuter of Heuene.

Thanne the emperour, whanne he vnderstode that thes childe was gretter thanne he, he offered ensence and refused to be called god. 175 And of that saiethe Orosee: 'In the tyme of Octauian as aboute the houre of tierce in the pure and clene shininge eyre apered sodenly a cercle in the forme of the reynbowe and beclipped the sonne in suche wise as he were to come that hadd made the sunne and the world.' In this same tellithe Eu|trope [and] Timothe of stories that is found in f. 9va auncient stories of the Romains that Octauian in the .xxv. yere of his 181 regne he entred into the Capitole and enquered curiously who shuld governe after hym the empire of Rome, and thannne he herde a vois that saide to hym: 'A childe of heuene engendered of lyving God

151 litell and litell] liȝtly G   152 of²] how G, *so on erasure* H1   155 of¹] *add* þe G   156 the¹] *changed to* þat H1   after the dethe] *om.* E, *ins.* H1   157 and¹] as G Cronicle] Cronyklys G   159 wyse] *add* oure E, *om.* G   160 on] vp'on' *with* vp *on erasure* H1   165 this] *om.* G   166 about] *add* rounde G   168 sheued] 'schewid' *above del.* berid G   thing] virgyne G   170 that] and G   172 the²] oure lady and E 176 saiethe] seide H1   177 houre] oueir G   180 same] *add* manere H1   and] *om.* E 181 auncient stories] the auncience G   .xxv.] .xv. H1   182 empire] Emperoure H1

185 witheouten tyme, that schalle be hasteli born of a mayde vncorrupte
and witheoute spotte.' And whanne he herd this he edified an auutere
and sette this title theron: 'This is the auutere of the sonne of God
lyving.'
      Also sche was sheued by the creature that hathe being and lyving,
190 as plantes and trees. For as the seintes seine, the vynes of [Engaddy]
that beren the bawme floured and bare fruit and [gaue] licour.
      Also by the creatoure that hathe being, lyving and feling, as bestis.
For whanne Ioseph went to Bethlem with Marie with childe he ledde
with hym an oxse and an asse, perauenture for to selle for to paie
195 money for hym and for the Virgine and for to live withe the
remenaunt, and the asse for to bere the Virgine. And thanne the
oxe and the asse knewen oure Lorde bi myracle and worschipped hym
vpon her knees. And as Eusebe saiethe in a cronicle, a litell tofore the
natiuite of oure Lorde that as sertain men went to the plowe the oxse
200 said to the men: 'Men schalle defend and oxen shall profit.'
      And it was sheued bi the creature that hathe being, lyving, feling
and discernyng, [so] as [a] man. For atte the oure of the natiuite the
shepardes woken vpon the keping of her beestis, so as thei were
acustumed in the lengest and in the shortest nightes in the yere. In the
205 auncien tyme the paynyme had an vsage that in euery stacion of the
sonne, as about Cristemasse and aboute the Seint Iohn[is tyde], to |
f. 9ᵛᵇ wake the nyghtes for the worship of the sonne, the whiche vsage, for
that the Iues and the paynimes duellid togedre, the Iues toke this in
custume as thei did. Thanne the aungell of oure Lord appered to hem
210 and denounsed hem that the saueoure of the world was borne and
gaue hem tokenis how thei schulde find hym. And with that thei seen
and herd multitude of aungels that songen: 'Ioye be to God and right
high thingges and pes to men of good wille.' Thanne come the
schepardes and founde alle as the [aungel] hadde tolde hem.
215   Also sche was shewed bi Cesar August that made a generall
comaundement that none schuld calle hym his lorde, so as Orose
witnessithe. For perauenture whanne he sawe that vision aboute the
sunne and remembered hym of the fallyng of the Temple and of the

     186 edified] ordeynyd G   189 Also . . . lyving] *om.* G   190 and] of G   vynes]
veynes Hɪ   Engaddy] enigaddy E   191 gaue] thanne EHɪ   192 lyving] om. Hɪ
193 Bethlem] Egipte G   194 selle] add or Hɪ   197 asse] add wiste and G
200 the men] hem G   201 And] Also G   lyving] *om.* G   202 so] ve E   a] *om.* E
203 keping] k'ep'ingges Hɪ   206 the Seint Iohnis tyde] the Seint Iohn E, seint Iohns
Hɪ   207 whiche] *add* was þe Iewis G   209 hem] him *changed to* hem Hɪ
214 aungel] aungels EHɪ   217 he] þay G

welle of oyle and that ther shuld be a gretter born in the world thanne
he, he wold not be called nother lorde ne god. Also it is redde in a   220
cronicle that whanne the day of the natiuite of oure Lorde Ihesu Crist
neyghed, Octauian comaunded that men shulde make grete highwayes
thorugh the world, and he forgave to the Romaynes alle her dettes.
And also she was schewed by the Sodomytes that in that nyght were
all quenched, [wherof Ier[o]mye seith vpon þis cause: 'Liȝt was born   225
to hem, for so grete [it] apperid to hem alle þo þat vsid þat synne þat
þay were alle quenchid], and Ihesu Crist did it for to take hem awaye,
so that in that nature that he hadde take so gret filthe schuld not be
founde no more.' And Seint Austin saieth that whanne God seigh that
synne ayeinst kynde so done of man he lothed to be in the flesche.   230

    Also the natiuite is sheued profitabely, furst to the confusion of the
fende, for he hathe no power ayeinst vs as he hadde before, wher[of] it
is sayde that Seint Hue, abbot of Cliny, sawe in the Vigile of the
Natiuite how oure | Lady Seint Marie helde her sone in her armes and   f. 10ra
saide: 'The day is now that the wordes of the profete bene renewed.   235
Wher is now the fende that bifore this day hadde so moche powere of
man?' And thanne come the fende from benethe for to contrarie the
wordes of oure blessed Ladi, but his wikednesse disseiued hym, for as
he went aboute the offices of the freres to take away her deuocion and
for to make hem leve in his lesson, the symple beddes of the dortre   240
and the pacience of the chapitre drove hym oute.

    It is redde in the boke of Pers de Clyni that in the Vigile of the
Natiuite of Ihesu Crist the blessed Virgine appered to Hugh de Clyni
and helde her sone in her arme, and the childe plaied with his moder
and saide: 'Lo, moder, how the Chirche haluith the day of my natiuite 245
withe gret ioye. Wher is the power now of the fende? What may he do
or saie?' And thanne the fende was sene come oute of a depe pitte, and
saide: 'Though y may not come into the chirche where that thei
preisen the, yet schall I entre into the dortour or into the fraitour or
into the chapitour.' And whanne he wolde haue entered into the   250
chapitour he fonde the dore to streyte and he to gret, and whanne he

wolde haue entered into the dortour he fonde the dore so lowe and he
so high, he fonde the dore of the froytour fulfilled with charite and
fervense, of couetise to here her lessones and sobernesse of mete and
255 drinke, and so he went awaye al confused.

Also this fest was shewed profitabeli for to gete foryeuenesse of
synnes. It is redde in the boke of Ensaumples that a sinfull woman fell
in despeire for her mysgouernaunce, for whanne sche bethought her
of the peynes of helle she felt herselff so gilti that sche hadde |
f. 10ʳᵇ deserued hem alle, and whanne she thought on paradise she felt
261 herselff vnclene, and whanne she thought on the passion she felt
herselff vnworthi to apere tofore his woundes. And atte the last sche
bethought her that litell children be lyght for to please, and thanne she
coniured hym by the goodnesse of his childehode that he wolde haue
265 mercy on her, wherfor she deserued to here a voys that sayde to her:
'Thi synnes be foryeue the.' Also she was shewed to couer oure
infirmite, for as Seint Bernard saieth, mankynde was that tyme
travelled with [thre] sykenesse, in the begynnyng, in the middell,
and in the endyng, and that was to be born, to live, and to dye. The
270 birthe was foule, the lyving pervers, and the dethe perilous. Oure
Lorde Ihesu Crist come ayenst this tr[e]ble maladie, for he brought
thre remedyes, for he was clene and lyued and deyed. His natiuite
purged oure, his lyff taught oure, and his dethe distroied oure dethe.

Also she was for to meke oure pride, wherof Austin sayethe that the
275 humilite of Ihesu Crist the sone of God shewed vs in his incarnacion
thre covenable ensaumples in sacrament and in medisine. In ensaumple for man shulde folw hym, in high sacrement for that the boundes
of oure synne were vnbounde, in souereyne medisyne by the whiche
the stynk of oure pride shulde be heled. For the pride of the furst man
280 was heled by the humylite of oure saueoure, and we shul[d] knowe
how the mekenesse of oure saueoure ansuere[th] conably to the pride
of the traytour. The pride of the furst man was ayeinst God, euen to
God, and aboue God. It was ayeinst God whanne he breke hys

252–3 so¹·²] to H₁G   253 high] add And þanne G   254 here her] her H₁G
lessones] les's'ons H₁   and¹] of G   256 fest] firste G   257 Ensaumples that]
Ensample of G   woman] add þat G   260 whanne] om. H₁   261 on the passion]
om. G   265 she] he H₁   she . . . voys] þer dissended a voice to hire G   to her] om. G
266 couer] cure H₁   268 thre] the gret E, grete G   271 treble] trouble E, troble H₁
273 oure¹] add lorde del. and subp. H₁   oure³] on erasure H₁   276 ensaumples]
Ins's'amples H₁   in¹] In E   277 folw] so lowe H₁   high] þe G   278 of . . .
vnbounde] om. G   280–1 and we . . . saueoure] 'we schuld know God' H₁
280 shuld] shull E   281 ansuereth] ansuered EH₁   282–3 euen . . . ayeinst God]
om. G

comaundement, for he hadde comaunded that he shulde not ete | of f. 10va
the fruit of knowyng of good and euel. It was even to God, for he was 285
euen atte the thought to be God and leued the fende whanne he sayde:
'Ye shulle be even as goddes knowyng good and euell.' Aboue God,
for as Anselme saiethe, in willyng that God wolde not thei putte her
wille vpon the wille of God. But the sone of God humbled hymselff
for mankynde and not ayeinst mankinde, euen withe men in a likely 290
manere of beryng, for he was bore of a woman, aboue man for he was
born of a virgine.

Thus endithe the Natiuite of oure Lorde Ihesu Crist and
Saueoure, and here beginnithe the lyff of Seint Anastace,
Cap^m. .vj.^{m}

Anastace was born of right noble Romayns, doughter of Pretextat, a
noble paynyme, her moder hight Fauste, and Anastace cristenly
taught in the faithe of Ihesu Crist of blessed Grisogone, and she
was yeue to wyff to Papillion. She feyned her to be syk and kepte her
euer from hys felawship. And thanne he herde that she vsed to visite 5
cristen men that were in prison in a vile habite and one chaumbrere
withe her and mynistred to hem her sustinaunce. And thanne he
shette her vp streiteli so that she hadde no sustinaunce, and so he
purposed that she shuld deye for hunger, that he wolde be deliuerid of
her. And whanne she supposed that she shuld deye for hunger [she 10
sent to Grisogone] pitous leteres, and thanne he sent her ayein
comfortable wordes. And in the mene tyme her husbond deied, and
thanne she was deliuered of prison.

And she hadde thre fayre chaumbr[er]es withe her, alle sustres, the
one name was Sapen, the secounde Clyonia, and the .iij. | Citenee. f. 10vb
Thei were cristen and wolde not obeye to the prouost, wherfor he 16
enclosed hem in a chaumbre wher as the vessell of the kechin was
kept. And the prouost that brenned cursidly in her love went to hem
to fulfill his cursed lust, and as sone as he was entered he waxse madde

285 knowyng] cunnyng G   even] wene G   287 Aboue God] *punct. after, not before* G   290 men] *om.* H1

EH1GH2A1A2   1 noble] *add* kynrede a G, *add* 'kynred of' H1   3 was] *ins.* H1
4 euer] *om.* G   5 herde] *add* telle E   6 vile] veile G   one] a G   7 hem] her G
9–10 that . . . hunger] *ins.* H1   10 she^3 . . . Grisogone] *om.* E, she sent H1
11 leteres] *add* to here fader 'Grisogon' H1   14 chaumbreres] chaumbres EH1
15–16 Citenee. Thei] Citees H1   18 love] *add* and EH1   19 cursed] *add* will and G
entered] *add* the hous G

20 and went to haue take the virgines and toke pottis and pannes and
cawdrones and clipped hem and kissed hem, and whanne his fals lust
was fulfilled he come oute blacke and foule and horrible to beholde
and all hys clothes torent. His servauntes that aboden witheoute
whanne they sawe hym in that arraye thei wende he hadde be vexed
25 with a fende and beten hym withe roddes and fledde [all] awaye and
lefte hym ther allone. And thanne he went to the emperour to pleine
hym of this thing, for sum smote hym with roddes, sum spette in his
visage and boffeted hym withe her hondes, wenyng verely that he
hadde be mad. [And] all this tyme he sawe nothing of hymselff, how
30 foule he was, and therfor he mervayled [ouer] mesure what cause it
myght be that thei dede to hym so gret dispite that were wont to do
hym so moche worschip. And hym thought that he was clothed al in
white clothes, and whanne he knewe by other how foule he was he
wende the virgines hadde made hym so by sum wichecraft, and
35 comaunded anon that thei shulde be dispoiled al naked before hym,
that he myght se hem, and anone her clothes cleuyd so faste to her
s[k]innes that thei myght not be take of in no wise. And sodenly the
prouost fell aslepe and slept so harde that he routed, that al his peple
wondered on hym, ne they myght not awake hym for no stering.

f. 11ʳᵃ   And atte | the laste these virgines resseived croune of marterdome,
41 and Anastace was betake to the provost that yef he might make her do
sacrifice he shulde haue her to his wyff. And whanne he hadde
brought her into his chaumbre he wolde haue take her in his armes,
and anone he waxe alle blynde. And thanne he went to his goddes and
45 asked hem whedir he shulde escape that disese. Thei saied to hym in
this wise: 'For that thou hast wrethid and troubelid Seint Anastace
thou art deliuered to vs and shall be tormented with vs in euerlastyng
peyne.' And as he was ledde home he ended his lyff wrechidly in the
hondes of his servauntes.

50   And thanne was Anastace take to another provoste to kepe her in
prison, and whanne he herde that sche hadde gret possession[s] he
saide to her: 'Anastace, yef thou wilt be cristen do as thi God
comaundithe the, for he saiethe: "Whoso will be my disciple forsake
all and folw me." And therfor yeue me all that thou hast and than thou

23 aboden] *add* hym G   25 all] *om.* E   awaye] *add* fro him EH1   27 smote] *ins.*
H1   28 wenyng] venyng H1   29 And] *om. and punct. after* tyme E   30 ouer] of
EH1   37 skinnes] shinnes E   41 yef] *om.* H1   42 shulde] wolde G   haue] *add*
taken G   44 went] *add* anoon G   47 tormented] trowblid G   48 wrechidly] in
wrecchednesse H1, full wrecchidly G   50 Anastace] *add* was *del.* H1   51 herde] *add*
telle E   possessions] possession E

shalt be verray cristen and go where thou wilt.' And she ansuered: 55
'Nay, thou hast misvnderstonde, for my God comaundithe: "Selle al
that thou hast and yeue it to the pore," and not "to the riche." Thou
art riche, and therfor yef I gave it to the I shulde breke the
comaundement of my God.'

And thanne was Anastace putte into a cruel prison for to be slayn 60
withe hungre, but she was fedde withe heuenly mete be Seint
Theodore, that two monthes before hadde resseyved crowne of
marterdome. And atte the laste she was sent into exile into the ile
of Palmers withe .CC. virgines, wherein thei founde many that hadde
be sent thedir before for the name of Ihesu Crist. And a fewe daies 65
after, the | prouost made hem alle come before hym, and he made f. 11rb
Seint Anastace be bounde to a pelere and br[ent] her in a gret fere and
slowe alle the other by diuerse tormentis. And ther was one that hadde
ofte be dispoiled for the loue of Ihesu Crist, and atte the laste she
saide: 'Take as ofte and as moche as ye wille, for I am sure inow ye 70
may not take Ihesu Crist away fro me.' And Seint Apoline made a
chirche in her gardin and beried witheinne worshipfulli the bodi of
Seint Anastace. And she suffered dethe vnder Dioclicien that beganne
about the yere of oure Lorde two hundred thre score and sevene.

Here endithe the liff of Seint Anastace, and nexst beginnithe the lyff of Seint Steuene the furst martir, Cap^m.
.vij.^m

Seint Steven was one of the .vij. dekenis that were in the seruise of the
apostelis. For whanne the noumbre beganne to encrese of the disciples
of genteles that were conuerted, sum beganne to murmure and to
groche ayenst hem that were conuerted of the Iues, for that the olde
women weren refused to serue, or ellis for thei were eueri day more 5
greued thanne the tother in seruise. Whanne the aposteles seen the
murmure and grochinge begonne for the widwes, thei assembeled hem
togedre to see how thei myght staunch this murmure. And thanne thei
saiden: 'It is no[t] right that we leve the worde of God and serue atte
the tables. The Glose saithe that the mete of the sowle is beter thanne 10

55 she ansuered] þan sche seide G   56 comaundithe] *add* to G   60 slayn]
slai`ne´ H1          67 brent] brought E          68–9 hadde ofte] oft`e´ had H1   70 Take]
om. G   72–3 witheinne . . . Anastace] hire þerin worshipfully G

EH1GH2A1A2   *Rubric* Steuene] Stheuene E   1 was] *om.* H1   3 genteles]
gentilnesse G   4 of] to H1   6 in] *add* her G   8 myght] *add* beste G   9 not]
no E   10 thanne] *add* þe H1

bodely mete. And therfor, good bretherin, lat enquere among you
men of good name and thei be wise and full of the holi goste, that we
f. 11ᵛᵃ may ordeine hem | vpon this werke, "that thei mow mynister and
serue aboue hem that haue ministred", and we shull abide in orison
15 and in predicacion.' And [this worde] liked hem alle, and thanne thei
chese oute seuene, of the whiche Steuene was one the furst and the
maister. Thei brought hem to the apostelis and thei leiden her hondes
vpon hym and ordeyned hem in that office. Steuene full of grace and
of strengthe dede gret wondres and signes among the peple. And
20 thanne the Iues manased hym and wolde haue ouercome hym and
assailed hym in thre maners, that was bi witnesse, be disputacion, and
bi torment. But he ouercome hem in disputyng, he ouercome her fals
witnesse, and hadde the victorie of his tormentis, and in eueri bataile
he hadde helpe of heuene, in the furst the holi gost that ministred hym
25 what he shulde saye, the seconde the visage of the aungell that fered
the fals witnesse, the .iij. he sawe Ihesu Crist redi to helpe hym and
conforte hym in his marterdom. In beholdyng shorteli the stori we
mowe wel see alle these thingges.
   For as the blessed Steuene dede many thyngges and preched ofte
30 [to] the peple, the Iues made the furst bataile ayenst hym [for to haue
ouercome hym] bi disputacion, for sum of the sinagoge arose up that
were called libertynes, the whiche were the sones of hem that were
deliuered, that ben tho that hadde bene before in seruage and were
made free, for tho that contrarieden furst ayenst the faithe weren of the
35 kynrede of tho that were in seruage, and also tho of [Hirenensiens],
that bene said of Sirene the citee, and of hem of the citee, and other
that weren of Celicie and Dasee, disputyng withe Steuene. That was
f. 11ᵛᵇ the furste | batell. And thanne he putte the victorie after and seithe
thei myght in no wise withestonde his wisdom, for the holy gost spake
40 in hym.
   And whanne thei seye that they myght not ouercome hym in no
wise, they [be]thought hem malicyously and ordeyned two fals
witnesse to accuse hym of .iiij. blames. Thanne thei brought hym

   12 and thei] and *del.* þei *subp.* þat H1, þat þay G   15 this worde] these wordes EH1
17 hem] hym G   18 hem] hym G   20–1 and wolde . . . assailed hym] *om.* G
22 disputyng] disputacion H1   her] hem in her G   25 fered] *add* in G
26 witnesse] witnessis G   redi] *ins.* G   30 to¹] *om.* E   30–1 for . . . hym] *om.* E
31 sinagoge] Synagogis G   34 contrarieden furst] were made firste contrarious G
35 Hirenensiens] her nensiens E, hire nensiens G, Mensiens H1   36 Sirene the citee]
þe Cite of Cirene G   hem of the citee] þe Cite of Peyme G   38 seithe] so H1
39 no] *add* maner G   42 bethought] thought E   43 to accuse hym] *om.* G

to iugement, and thanne these fals witnesse accused hym of .iiij.
thyngges, that was of the blaspheme of God in Moyses and in the 45
lawe, in the tabernacle and in the Temple. This was the secounde
bataile. And thanne all tho that weren in the iugement sawe the visage
of hym as the visage of an aungell. And that was the victorie of the
secounde batayle. For whanne these fals witnesse hadde alle saide,
thanne the prince of prestes saide to Stevene: 'Now it is thus, what 50
saiest thou now?' And Seint Steuene [exc]used hym by ordre of al that
[the] fals witnesse saide ayeinst hym. Furst of the blame anentes God,
seyng: 'The God that speke to faders and profetis, that was the God of
ioie,' and preised hym in thre thingges. 'This worde "ioie" may be
expowned in trebel wise. The God of glorie is the yever of lawes, so as 55
it is wretin in the Bokes of Kyngges: "Whosoeuer shall see my name I
shalle glorifie hym." The God of glorie may be saide conteyning
glorie, so as it is saide in the Prouerbes: "Richesse and ioie bene withe
me." [Or] the God of ioie is that God that glori only is dieu to.' And
thus he preised God in thre maners, in that he is glorious, glorifiant 60
and glorified.
    And after he excused hym of the blame of Moyses, preisyng hym
gretly in the same wise [of] thre thyngges, that is [of] feruour of loue,
for he slow the Egipcien for he smote the Ebrew, and of the miracle
that | he dede in Egipte, also of the familiarite that he hadde with God f. 12ʳᵃ
in the desert wher he spake with hym ofte tymes frendely. And after, 66
he excused hym of the thridde blame that was in the lawe, [in preisyng
the lawe] in thre maners, furst be reson of the yeuere that was God, of
[the] reson of the minister that was Moyses that was so gret a profit,
and be the reson of the ende for she yeuithe euerlasting lyff. And 70
thanne he purged of the ferthe blame of the tabernacle and of the
Temple. He preised thus the tabernacle in foure maners, for she was
comaunded of God to be made and was shewed by a vision that it was
acomplised of Moyses for that the arche of tesmonage was witheinne.
And he saide that the Temple hadde succeded to the tabernacle. And 75
this blessed Seint Steuene purged hym of that was opposed to hym.

    46 and . . . Temple] *om.* H1   50 prince] prinsis G   51 excused] aclused E,
conclued H1   hym] hem H1   52 the¹] *om.* E   saide] seist H1   blame] blaspheme G
anentes] a3ens G   59 Or] er E, Here G, *or changed to* er (?) H1   glori only] gloriousli
H1   dieu] dyeu (?) H1, 3ouen G   60 glorifiant] glorificant G   62 hym²] it so G
63 of¹] for E   of²] *om.* E   of loue] *om.* G   64 Egipcien] *add* and G   67–8 in² . . .
lawe] *om.* E   69 the¹] *om.* E   70 she yeuithe] siche endith G   71 purged] *add*
hym G   72 preised thus] preysith G   73 a vision] avision EH1   it] *om.* H1
74 witheinne] with Esue (? Esne) G   75 he] *om.* G   76 that] *add* he H1G   to hym]
of G

And thanne the Iues seien that thei myght not ouercome hym in this manere, thanne thei toke the thridde bataile ayeinst hym, so atte the laste thei might ouercome hym be no tormentis. So that whanne
80 the blessed Steuene sawe it he thought to kepe the comaundement of oure Lorde and enforsed hym to refreyn hem in thre maners, [that is] be shame, be drede and be loue. Furst be drede in blamyng the hardenesse of her hertis, and saide: '[Ye] contrarie alwayes to the holi goste with harde hedis, that is to saie withe opstinat spirites and withe
85 vnpitous hertis, right as youre faders that persecuted the prophetis and slewe hem that anounsed the comyng of oure Lorde.' The Glose puttithe hem in foure manere of malice, the furst that thei contraried the holy gost, the secounde that thei slowe the prophetis, the thridde that by cause therof the malice encresed, the ferthe that thei slowe
f. 12rb hym | in her last malice. But for thei were as the wicked woman thei
91 coude haue no shame ne they coude not leue her malice, but whanne thei herde these thyngges thei withesaide hem in her hertis and gnast her tethe ayeinst hym.

And after that he corrected hem withe drede, bi that he tolde hem
95 [t]hat he seye Ihesu Crist in the right side of God the fader redy to helpe hym and to condempne his aduersarie. For Seint Steuene, that was full of the holy gost, loked vp to heuene and seigh the glorie of God and saide: 'See here that I see heuene open and the sone of man stondyng in the right side of the vertu of God.' And thogh it were so
100 that he hadde corrected hem by shame and bi drede, yet thei [lefte] not her malice but weren worse than before, and stopped her eres that thei wolde not here her blames, and crieden withe highe voys and made a sauute ayenst hym withe one wille, and drove hym oute of the citee and stoned hym to dethe, wenyng to do after the lawe of hym
105 blamyng and comaundynge that he shulde be stoned [with]oute the castelles. And these two fals wetenesse that after the lawe shulde caste the furst stone, thei dede of her clothes for to be [the] more freer in castynge of thaire stones, and thei leide hem atte the fete of a yong man that hight Saulis and after was called Paulus, and for he kept her

77–8 And . . . hym] *om.* H1   78 toke] *add* hym G   79 thei] þeˋïˊ H1
80–1 of . . . hem] *om.* G   81 that is] *om.* E   83 Ye] the EG   86 anounsed]
vnavisid G   Lorde] *add* god G   88 slowe] shew *del.* ˋslowˊ H1   92 gnast] gronde G
93 hym] hem H1   95 that] what E   96 to condempne] condempned H1
97 and] *add* seide he G   98 and²] *add* see G   100 lefte] loste E   101 weren
worse] *on erasure* H1   104 and] ˋ&ˊ H1   105 he] *ins.* H1   withoute] to oute of E, wᵗ
on erasure oute *folllowed by* of *subp.* H1   106 castelles] castel H1   lawe] lawes EH1
107 the] *om.* E   freer] fre *on erasure* H1   109 he kept] to kepe H1

clothes that they shuld not be lette to stone hym, he was partinere in 110
the stonynge of hym.

And whanne he seigh that he myght not withedrawe them of thaire
malice ne by shame ne by drede he toke the .iij. manere so that he
myght drawe hem by loue, and the loue that he shewed hem was not
litell whanne he praied for hym and for hem that his passion myght 115
not be putte abak, and that | it shulde not be sette to hem for synne f. 12ᵛᵃ
hym stonyng and tormentyng, he seyeng: 'Lorde Ihesu Crist resseive
my spirit.' And whanne he was on his knees he cryed with an high vois
seyeng: 'Lorde sette not this to hem for synne.' And this was a
mervailous loue, for he preyed for his tormentours on his knees, as tho 120
he made rather orison for hem thanne for hymselff. And as the Glose
saiethe, he kneled for the wikednesse of hem was so moche that hym
nedid gretly to make humble praiere. For in his passion he preied for
hymselff and saide: 'Fader, into thin hondes I recomende my sperit,'
and for his tormentours: 'Fader, foryeue hem.' And whanne Seint 125
Steuene hadde so saide he slepte in oure Lorde and is not dede, for he
offered hymselff a sacrifice of loue and dileccion and slepte in hope of
resurreccion.

And the stonyng of Seint Steuene was done in that yere that oure
Lorde stied vp into heuene, in the monthe of August in enteryng of 130
the .iij. day. Seint [G]amaliell and Nichodemys, that weren aboute the
consultes of [the] Iues for the cristen, beried hym in the felde of
Gamaliel and made gret wepyng upon hym. Thanne was ther made   .
gret persecucion of cristen that were in Ierusalem, for whanne blessid
Seint Stevene that was one of the princes was slain, they beganne to 135
do suche persecucion vpon the tother cristen that alle the cristen that
were lefte fledde oute of the citee alle aboute in alle the provinces of
Iues sauf onli the apostelis, lik as oure Lorde comaunded, seyeng: 'Yef
thei pursue you in one citee fle into another.'

Seint Austin tellithe that [the] blessid Steven was made noble [be] 140
shewyng of many myracles, and that he reysed by hys merites .vj. that
were | dede and heled many one of diuerse siknesse and langoures. f. 12ᵛᵇ
And withe tho he tellithe [other] diuerse miracles worthi to be spoken

111 the stonynge of hym] her stonyng G   112 not] *ins.* H1   them of] *om.* G
114 hem²] him *changed to* hem H1   115 hym] hem G   hem] þenne G
117–18 seyeng . . . was] *om.* G   123 in] *om., no punct. after* praiere *but after* passion G
126 so saide] seide þese wordis G   127 dileccion] delectacion G   131 day] *no punct.*
EG   Gamaliell] Samaliell E   132 the¹] *om.* EH1   133 made²] *om.* H1
134 cristen] *add* pepul G   136 do suche] seche G   136 alle] *om.* G   139 thei] I
erased 'þei' H1   140 the] *om.* E   be] withe E   143 other] many EH1

of. For he saiethe that the floures that were sette vpon the auutere of
145　Seint Steuene, whane men putte hem vpon the seke anone thei were
merveilousli cured, and also the clothes of the auutere sette vpon the
seke heled many one, for as it saide in the .xxij.^{ti} chapitre of the Citee
of God that these floures taken vpon the auutere were leied to the eyen
of a blynde woman and she resseived sight anone. And also he saiethe
150　in that same boke, a man that was maister of a citee whos name was
Marcial and was mysbileued and wolde in no wise be conuerted, and
so it fell that he was gretli seke, and his sone in lawe Gendre was right
a true man come into the chirche of Seint Steven and toke of the
floures and putte hem preuili vnder hys lordes bedde ys hede, and as
155　sone as he hadde slept vpon hem he cried in the morw that they
shulde bryng the bisshop to hym, but the bisshop was not atte home,
and than thei brought hym the prest. [And] whan he sawe the prest he
charged hym that he shulde teche hym to beleve in the faithe of God
and baptise hym anone. And as long as he leuyd after he hadde euer in
160　his mouthe: 'Lorde, resseive my spirit,' and yet he wost not that tho
wordes hadd bene the last wordes of Seint Stevene.

He tellithe also another miracle in the same place that ther was a
ladie that hight Petronie, and she hadde a grevous siknesse of long
tyme and she hadde sought many remedyes and she felt none ease.
f. 13ra　And atte the laste a Iue toke her | a ryng withe a stone and bade that
166　sche shulde hang it by a lace nexst her skyn and she shulde haue
helthe. And whanne she seigh that it availed her not she went to the
chirche of the furst martir and besought humbeli the blessid Seint
Steuene for her helthe, and thanne sodenli witheoute that the lace was
170　vnknette or broke the ryng felle to grounde and thanne sche felt
herselff al hole.

Also he tellithe in the same boke a full merveilous miracle. In
Cesaree of Capadocy ther was a noble ladi whos husbond was dede,
but she had [.x.] children left withe her, sevene sones and thre
175　doughtres. In a tyme thei hadde wrethid her moder and she cursed
hem, and the devine veniaunce folued sodenly the curse of the moder
so that thei were all smite with one likly peyne whiche was ful
horrible, for thei trembeled horribli in alle her membres, for whiche

148 taken] *ins.* H1　　　150 was^1] *add* a E　　　153 of^2] *om.* G　　　154 bedde ys]
bedde H1, *om.* G　　　155 hem] *om.* H1　morw] morne H1G　　　157 And] *om.* E　And
. . . prest] *ins.* H1　　　157–8 he charged] *on erasure* H1　　　158 in the] yn *subp.* 'þe' H1
158–9 that . . . hym] *om.* G　　　166 hang it] hanged H1　lace] case G　　　168 humbeli]
mekely G　　　174 .x.] .xij. EH1　thre] .v. H1　　　176 the^1] þei *with* i *erased* H1　curse]
corps *changed to* cors H1　　　178 for thei . . . horribli] *om.* G

thing thei myght not duelle in thaire contre for shame and sorw that
thei hadde. Thanne thei beganne to go ast[r]ayeng thorugh the world, 180
and what partie euer thei wente thei were wondered on [of] alle tho
that seie hem. And so it fell that [.ij.] of them, a brother and a suster,
come into Iponens. The brother hight Paule [and] the suster Pauladie.
Ther thei founde Seint Austin the bisshop and tolde hym what was
befalle to hem, and thanne Seint Austin counsailed hem that thei 185
shulde go to the chirch of Seint Stevene and praie hym herteli of
helpe. Thanne thei went and haunted the chirche .xv. dayes before
Ester and praied herteli to the seint for to haue her heele, and on Ester
Day whanne alle the peple were present Paule entered sodenli into the
chaunsell and sette hym in praier | withe gret deuocion and gret f. 13ʳᵇ
reuerence before the auutere, and tho that were there abode the ende 191
of this thing. He arose fressheli and gladli witheoute any trembelyng
of eni part of hym, and thanne he was brought to Seint Austin and he
shewed hym to the peple and saide to hem that in the morw he wolde
telle hem alle the case. And as he spake vnto the peple the suster of 195
hym was there trembelyng of alle membres. She arose and entered
into the chaunsell of Seint Stevene and anone she fell aslepe, and
sodenli she rose vp and was hole of alle her membres and was shewed
to the peple also, and thanne worshippes and thankyngges were yeven
to God and to the holi Seint Stevene of the [hele] of bothe. 200
It is to knowe that the blessed Seint Stevene suffered not dethe on
this day but in the day that the Chirche makithe feste of his inuencion,
and yef men aske whi the festes bene chaunged so we shall saie you
whanne we shal speke of his inuencion the cause. But late this suffise
you atte this tyme, for the Chirche wille and hathe ordeyned so the 205
festes that folwen the Natiuite of Ihesu Crist for two causes. The furst
is to Ihesu Crist that is cheeff and spouse that all his felawshippe be
ioyned to hym. For Ihesu [Crist the] spouse of the Chirche born in
this worlde hathe ioyned to hym thre felawes, of whiche felawes it is
saide in the Canticles: 'My white loue and rede chosen among many 210
thousandes,' white as of Seint Iohn the Ewangelist the precious

179 thaire] þat G   180 astrayeng] asteayeng E   181 of] om. E, ins. H1
182 And . . . them] om. G   .ij.] mani E, many del. H1   183 and] om. E
185 Austin] add þe bisshop G   198 her] om. G   199 worshippes . . . yeuen] þay
worschippiden and 3auen her þankyng G   200 of¹ . . . bothe] om. H1   hele] helpe E
201 suffered] offered H1   203 we shall saie] thrice with first two del. H1   204 speke]
add to 3ou G   205 you] om. H1   wille] add so G   207 his] þis H1G   208 Crist
the] cristes EH1   209 thre] þe G   of whiche felawes] 'of þe wiche felawis' H1
211 white] om. G

virgine and confessour, rede as to Seint Stevene the furst martir,
chosen of thousandes as of the virgynel felawship of innocen[tis]. The
f. 13ᵛᵃ secounde reson is that the Chirche hathe gadered | in maners of
215 marteres after [the] degrees of her dignitees, the whiche the natiuite of
oure Lorde was cause. For ther bene thre ma[r]ters, the furst be wille
and be werke, the secounde be wille and not in dede, the .iij. not in
wille but in dede. The furst was of Seint Stevene, the secounde of
Seint Iohn, and .iij. of the Innocentis.

Here endithe the lyff of Seint Stevene, and nexst beginnithe the blessed lyff of Seint Iohn the Ewangelist,
Capitulum .viij.ᵐ

Seint Iohn the Apostill and Ewangelist, byloued of oure Lord and
[chosen] virgine, after the Whitsontide that the aposteles weren
departed he went into Asie, and ther he edified many chirches. And
thanne the emperour herde of his gret name [and] called hym to his
5 presence and made hym be putte in a tonne fulle of oyle boyling before
hym, and he went oute therof as clene and as pureli witheoute harmyng
of hym as he was pure and clene witheoute corrupcion of flesche. And
whanne the emperour seie that he wolde not leue prechyng for all that,
thanne he sent hym into exile into the ile of Pathmos, and ther he
10 duelled allone and made the Apocalips. And in that same yere the
emperour was slain of the senatoures for his gret cruelte, and alle that
he hadde done was repeled ayein. And thanne Seint Iohn that was
brought into Pathmos withe gret wronge he was brought into Ephasim
withe gret worschip, and alle the peple ronne ayenst hym and saide:
15 'Blessed art thou that comest in the name of oure Lord.'
    And whanne he come into the citee, Drusiane his frende that
f. 13ᵛᵇ ha[dd]e gret|li desired his comyng was born dede, and her kynrede
Neuenys and [Or]felius saiden to Seint Iohn: 'A, good lord Seint
Iohn, see here Drusien that we beren, that obeied to alle [thi]

213 Innocentis] innocence EH1   214 reson] resonde H1   gadered] *add* togedris G
maners] man G   215 marteres] *on erasure* H1   the¹] *om.* E   216 thre] the H1
marters] maters EH1, maner of martris G (*martirs* P2)   217 in²] by H1
218 Innocentis] Innocence H1

EH1GH2A1A2; H2 breaks off after 67 *reyne*; A1 breaks off after 97 *nature*; E has been
damaged by liquid at 136–7, 161, 186–9.   1 Ewangelist] *add* þe H1G   2 chosen]
Euuangelist E, *om.* H1   4 and] *om.* EH1   14 ronne] of Rome come G
17 hadde] hathe E   comyng] *add* home G   18 Orfelius] Sifelius E   18–19 A . . .
Iohn] *om.* H1   19 thi] the E

techyngges and norshed vs alle, desired gretly thi comyng and saide: 20
"A, wel were me yef I myght see the apostell of God er that I deide,"
and now thou art comen she may not see the.' And thanne the apostell
comaunded to sette downe the bere and vnbynde the body and saide:
'Oure Lorde Ihesu Crist arere the, Drusian, arise vp and go into thin
hous and make redi my mete.' Anone she arose and went into her hous 25
and fulfilled the comaundement of the apostill, and her semed that she
was not come fro dethe but awaked from slepe.

Another day after, one Craton philosofre gadered togedre the peple
in the market place for that he wolde shewe hem how this worlde were
to dispise. And he hadde made two yonge men bretheren to beye 30
precious stonis, also he made hem selle al her heritages, and bade hem
breke tho stones tofore alle. So it felle that the apostell passed by that
place and cleped the philosofre to hym, and that manere of dispising
that he dispised the world he reproued it in thre maners by thre
resonis: 'The furst reson is this, he that lokithe after the preisyng of 35
man is blamed of God. Secoundly for by that despite synne is not
heled and therfor it is in veyn, right as the medicine ys called veyne
that curithe not the syknesse. The thridde for the dispite of the
worlde is gerdonable to hem that yeven her good to the pore. Yef thou
wil be perfite go and selle alle that thou hast and yeue | to the pore.' f. 14ra
And thanne saide Craton: 'Yef thi maister be verray God make these 41
stones hole ayein so that the prise that thei coste may be yeue to the
pore, and that thou do to the worschip of thi God as I haue do it to the
preysing of man.' And thanne the blessed Iohn toke the partics of the
stones in his honde and made his praiere and anone they were alle holc 45
ayein as euer they w[e]re. Thanne the philo[so]fer and the .ij. yong
men leued in God and solde the stones and gave the price to the pore
men and folued the apostell.

And .ij. other yong men bi the ensaumple of hem solde alle that thei
hadde and gave it to pore men and folued the apostell. And on a day as 50
thei seen her owne servauntes shine in precious clothes and they were
in pore mantellis thei begonne to shewe hevi chere. Seint Iohn that
perceyued this made bryng to hym yerdes and smalle stones of the
riuere and conuerted hem into golde and into precious stones. Bi the
comaundement of the apostell thei went to [the] goldesmithes to wete 55

25 Anone] *no punct.* E, anon *followed by paraph* H1, and anoon *preceded by punct.* G
arose] *add* anon H1   31 selle] self G   32 breke] *add* all G   alle] *om.* G   alle. So]
Also H1   34 the world] *om.* G   35 furst . . . this] resonys ben þese G   36 by] *om.*
H1   37 veyn] *add* For EH1   43 to the¹] to H1, *om.* G   46 were] ware E
philosofer] philofer E   49–50 And . . . apostell] *om.* G   55 the²] *om.* EG

if thei were verray true, the whiche said truly that they hadde neuer
sene beter golde ne finer stones. And thanne the apostell saide to hem:
'Gothe and beyethe youre lond ayein that ye haue solde, for ye haue
lost the guerdon of heuene, and therfor flourithe here that ye mowe
60 fade, and bethe ryche in temporall rychesse that ye may be beggers
witheoute ende.' And thanne the apostell beganne to dispute a gret
while ayeinst richesse, shewyng that there bene .vj. thingges that
shulde withedrawe oure thought fro disatempre richesse. The furst ys
the scripture, as of the storie of the riche man and of the pore lazar.
f. 14rb The secounde is | nature, for a man is bore naked and witheoute
66 richesse. The .iij. is creature, for the sonne and the mone and the
sterres, the reyne and the eyre yeuen comonli to alle thaire benefices.
The ferthe is fortune, for men saien that [the riche] is sirvaunt to the
peny and to the deuell for he pursuithe not the richesse but is pursued
70 of the deuell, for as the gospell saiethe he that louithe money is made
seruaunt therof. The .v. is the besinesse therof, for thei laboure nyght
and day in the getyng and in the kepyng and miche drede in
[the] lesyng. The .vj. is the euell auenture, and shewithe that richesse
is cause of euell auenture, that is in getyng double euell, of the euell
75 present, that is pride, of the euell to come, that is euerlastyng
dampnacion.

And as he disputed ayeinst richesse, men brought a dede man that
hadd bene wedded but .xxx.ti dayes before. Thanne come the moder
of his wiff and other withe gret wepyng and sette hym atte the
80 apostelis fete, besechyng hym that he wolde arere hym in the name of
oure Lorde like as he dede to Drusyan. And thanne the apostell
we[p]t longe and praied, and anone he arose up. Thanne the apostel
charged hym that he shulde telle to these yonge men in what peyne
thei bene ronne and what ioye thei haue loste, and thanne he tolde
85 [many] of the ioyes of paradise and of the peynes of helle, and thanne
he saide to tho two wrechis: 'I seigh youre good aungels that kepen
you wepe and the fende laugh,' and saide hem that thei hadd loste the
euerlasting palais of ioye that bene made of precious stones and of
89 mervailous lyght and full of all delites and of all glorious euerlastyng
f. 14va ioyes. And thanne he tolde hem | .viij. [of the] peynes of helle that

56 true] add golde G, so ins. H1   66 is] add to a G   67 eyre] erthe G   68 the
riche] richesse E   73 the¹] om. E   euell] deuel with d erased H1   75 is¹] add in E
79 other] anoþer H1   hym] hem H1G   82 wept] went EH1   83 to these] too þeies on
erasure H1   these] þis G   men] man G   peyne] poynte H1   84 thanne he] þay G
85 many] om. EH1   the¹] add Iewis del. G   86 he] þay G   87 fende] deuel H1
88 palais] place H1   of²] ins. H1   and] om. H1G   89 of¹] ins. H1   90 of the] om. E

tho sufferen that bene there, that bene wormes, derkenesse,
betyngges, colde, hete, sight of fendes, confusion of synnes,
wepingges. And thanne tho two that were arered and made disciples
of Seint Iohn kneled downe atte the fete of the apostill and besought
hym of foryeuenesse for hem, and thanne the apostell saide to hem: 95
'Dothe penaunce this .xxx.^{ti} dayes and praiethe til these yerdes and
these stones turne into her furst nature.' And whanne this was done
he saide to hem: 'Gothe and berithe hem ayein.' Thei dede so and
receyued the grace and vertues that they hadde before.

And whanne the blessed Iohn hadde preched ouer al Asye, the 100
prestes of the ydoles meued a grete debate in that tyme among the
peple and drowen Seint Iohn to the temple of Dyane and wolde haue
constreyned hym to yeue sacrifise. And Seint Iohn parted the game
betwene hem and saide er thei shulde praie Dyane that sche wolde
distroie the Chirche of Ihesu Crist, er Iohn schulde praie to Ihesu 105
Crist that he distroie the temple of Dyane, and yef thei spedde he
wolde do sacrifice to the ydoles, and yef he distroied thaire temple thei
shulde leue in Ihesu Crist. And as the most parte of the peple
consented to this sentence and alle the peple went oute of the
temple, and thanne the apostell praide and sodenly the temple fell 110
adowne and the ymage of Dyane was al destroied.

And thanne Aristodomus, bisshop of the ydoles, meued gret
discorde to the peple so that it was like to haue hadde bataile betwene
hem. Thanne saide the apostell: 'What wilt thou that I do to apese
the?' And he saide: 'Yf thou wilt that I leue in thi God, drinke | of the f. 14vb
venyme that I schall geue the, and yef it do the none harme thou hast 116
proued that he is a verray god.' And thanne the apostell saide: 'Do as
thou wilt.' [And he saide to hym:] 'But I wille that thou see other deye
byfore the to that ende that thou drede it the more.' And thanne went
Aristodome to the provost and asked of hym two men that were 120
condempned to the dethe and gaue hem the venyme before alle [the
peple], and as sone as thei hadde dronke it thei deyed. And thanne the
apostell toke the cuppe and made the signe of the crosse, and thanne
he drank of al the venyme and he felt neuer harme therof, for the
whiche thyng alle beganne to preise oure Lorde. Thanne saide 125

91 tho] *add* that E   sufferen] suffrid G   93 and] þay G   94 kneled] knele G
98 ayein] *add* and E   99 grace] *add* of god E   they] he G   103 the] his G
104 er] oþer H1   wolde] wil H1, schulde G   106 spedde] spake G   107 do] *om.* G
109 went] *om.* G   114 apostell] apostoles *with final* s *erased* H1   thou] *om.* H1G
118 And . . . hym] *om.* EH1G (*et il luy dist* P2)   121–2 the peple] *om.* E
125–6 Thanne . . . Aristodomus] *om.* H1

Aristodomus: 'Yet I doubte, but yef thou areise these two that bene
dede thanne I shall beleue verili.' And thanne the apostell toke hym
his cote, and he asked whi he toke it hym, and thanne he saide: 'For
thou shalt be confused and parte fro thi mysbeleue. Go,' saide he, 'and
130 putte the cote vpon the dede bodies and saie to hem that "the apostell
of Ihesu Crist hathe sent me to you, chargyng you that ye arise in the
name of Ihesu Crist."' And whanne he hadde so done thei arose
anone. And thanne the apostell baptised the bisshop and the prouost
withe al her kynrede, and thanne thei made a solempne chirche in the
135 worship of Seint Iohn.

The blessid ⟨Clement⟩ tellithe in the .iiij. boke of th⟨e Stori
Ecc⟩lesiast, ⟨and it⟩ is founde bi ⟨other that the blessid⟩ apostell
[conuerted a] goodli yong man and toke hym into the gouernaunce of
a bisshop. And witheinne a litell tyme after the yong man lefte the
140 bisshop and become a prince of theues. Thanne the apostell come to
f. 15ra this | bischop and asked hym to haue ayein the yong man that he toke
hym to kepe, and thanne the bisshop was sore abasshed. Thanne Iohn
perseiued that and asked hym more besili: 'Wher is that yong man
that I toke you and charged you withe hym so gretly?' And thanne he
145 saide: 'Truly, fader, he is dede and duellithe in yonder mountayne
withe theues and he is become her alder prince.' And whanne he
herde that he rent his clothes and saide: 'A, thou art a feble keper,
[thou] hast suffered thi brother to lese his soule.' And anone he toke
an horse and rode fast to the mountayne, and whanne the yong man
150 seigh hym he was sore ashamed and toke his horse and fledde. Thanne
the apostell forgate his age and smote the hors with [the] spores and
cried after hym that fledde: 'Right dere sone, whi fleest thou thi fader?
Drede the not, sone, for I schall yelde acountes for the to Ihesu Crist,
and truli I schalle gladly deie for the lik as Ihesu Crist deied for us.
155 Turne ayein, sone, turne ayein, for Ihesu Crist hathe sent me to the.'
And whanne he herde this he turned ayein and repented hym and
wepte bitterly, and the apostell felle doune to his fete and kessed hem
as thou he hadde be purged bi penaunce. And thanne the apostell
praied for hym and fasted and ga[t]e hym foryeuenesse, and after that
160 [h]e was of suche vertue that Seint Iohn ordeined hym to be a bisshop.

126 two] add men H1   128 and thanne he saide] om. H1   130 saie] seid with d
erased H1   131 chargyng you] om. H1   138 conuerted a] commended E
139 tyme] om. H1   139–41 lefte . . . man] om. G   141 this] his H1   142 Iohn]
Clement G   147 rent] add all G   148 thou] that EH1   hast] add so G
151 the³] his E   152 fledde] add and seide G   157 hem] him H1   159 and
fasted . . . hym] om. G   gate] gaue E   160 he] be E

It is ⟨redde in⟩ the ⟨Stori⟩ aboue said in the Glose ⟨vpon⟩ the Cronicle of Iohn that whane he was in Ephese he bathed hym in a bath, and he seigh in the same bathe a strong heretyk that hight La Chernice. And thanne anone he lept oute of the bathe and saide: 'Fle we hennys lest the bathe falle vpon us, | for Chernice the enemy of f. 15ʳᵇ trouthe bathes hym here.' And as sone as they were oute the bathe 166 felle downe.

Cassiadore saiethe in the boke of Dolacionis that a man hadd yeue to Seint Iohn a parteriche and he plaied hym therwithe adayes whanne hym lust, and a yong man passed by hym with his felawship and seigh 170 hym plaie withe the brydde, and saide to his felawship: 'See how this olde man plaiethe withe a bridde.' And thanne Seint Iohn that knewe in spirit what he saide called the yong man to hym and asked of hym what he helde in his honde, and he saide that it was his bowe. And the apostell saide: 'What do ye therwithe?' And he saide: 'We shete 175 beestes and briddes.' And the apostell asked how, and [he] bent his bowe and drowe it vp witheoute more. And whanne he seigh that the apostell saide no more to hym he vnbent his bowe ayein, and Seint Iohn saide: 'Sone, whi vnbendest thou thi bowe?' And he ansuered: 'For yef it were long bent yt shulde be febeler to shete wel.' And 180 thanne the apostell saide: 'Lo, [so] it farithe bi the freelte of mankynde, but yef it be sumtyme vnbent it may not endure in highe contemplacion. The egle is the bridde that fleithe highest and most clerely beholdithe the sonne, and yet [bi] necessite of kynde hym behouithe that he descende lowe. Right so whanne mankynde with- 185 drawith ⟨hym⟩ a litell fro contemplacion he ⟨puttith hymself heigher bi a renewed streng⟩th and bre⟨nneth more feruently⟩ in heuenly thingges.

⟨As⟩ Seint Ierom witnessithe that whanne the blessed Seint Iohn in his last age dwellid in Ephesim and he was bore for age to the chirche 190 betwene his dissiples | and comonly he hadde these wordes to hem: f. 15ᵛᵃ 'Sones, l[o]uen ye togederes.' And atte the last thei wondered that he saide it so ofte, and thanne thei saide to hym: 'Maister, whi saie ye allwaye these wordes?' And he ansuered: 'For it is the comaundement of oure Lorde, and yef it be only kept it suffisethe.' 195

161 It is] This G   163–4 La Chernice] lachernyte G   165 Chernice] charnyce H1, lachernite G   168 Dolacions] Diolatius H1   169 parteriche] partrich *with* t *on erasure* H1   adayes] and aroos H1, *add* and G   170–1 and seigh . . . felawship] *om.* H1 172 that] *om.* G   173 in spirit] his spirite and G   saide] *add* he G   man] *add* a yene H1 176 briddes] *add* therwith G   he] *om.* EH1   180 wel] with H1   181 so] sone E, sone so H1   184 bi] the E   192 louen] lyuen E, louen *with* n *erased* H1

Helinant tellithe that as Seint Iohn the Euuangelist wolde write the
gospell he ordeyned furst a fastyng so that alle shulde praie that he
myght write wortheli, and men sayen that he wrought this holy werke
in a full secrete place, and as long as he was in the devyne werke ther
200 felle neuer wynde ne reyne to lette hym, and yet men sayen that the
elementes kepen that same reuerence to that place.

And whanne Seint Iohn was of fyue score and .ix. yere, and as
Ysodore saiethe in the thre score and sevenetene yere after the passion
of oure Lorde vnder Trayen the emperour, oure Lorde apered to hym
205 with his disciples and saide: 'Come, my beloued, to me, for it is tyme
that thou dyne withe me atte myn borde with thi bretheren.' And
thanne Seint Iohn arose and beganne to goo, and oure Lorde saide to
hym: 'Thou shalt come on Sonday to me.' And whanne the Sonday
come he assembeled alle the peple to the chirche that had be made in
210 his name and preched to hem a noble sermon, and taught hem that
thei shulde be stable in the faithe and besi in the comaundementis of
God. And after that he lete make a pitte al square besides the auuter
and made the erthe be caste oute of the chirche, and thanne he went
downe into the pitte, his hondes straught vp to God and saide: 'Lorde,
215 I bede myselff to thi dinere and I yelde the thankingges of that I am
f. 15ᵛᵇ suche that I aught to | taste of thi metes, and thou knowest that I
desire hem withe al myn herte.' And whanne he hadde ended his
orison so gret a lyght shined vpon hym that none myght beholde hym.
And whanne the light was parted the pitte was found fulle of manna,
220 and yet she springgith in that place this same day so that sche is sayne
spring vp in the bothom of the pitte as smal grauell lik as springgen in
quyk welles somtyme.

Seint Edward [the] kyng and confessour hadde suche a deuocion to
Seint Iohn that he wolde werne no man that asked hym anything in
225 the worship of Seint Iohn the Euuangelist. [So it befel that a pilgrime
asked hym almis in the name of Seint Iohn the Euuangelist], and his
aumenere was not nye so that the kyng hadde nothing to yeue hym
but the ryng of his fyngger. And long tyme after a knyght of Inglond
that was beyende the see, he resseyued the ryngge of that pilgryme for
230 to bere to the kyng by suche wordes that he shulde saie to the kyng:
'He to whom and for whom thou gauest the ryngge sende it the ayein,
and thi thanke is to come in euerlastyng blisse,' wherby the kyng

196 write] *add* worthily G   198 he] *ins.* H1   204 Trayen] Tracian H1
206 thi] my G   214 straught] *om.* H1   221 smal] *add* as E   223 the] *om.* E
225 the Euuangelist] *om.* G   225–6 So . . . Euuangelist] *om.* E, *ins.* H1

vnderstode well that it was Seint Iohn that come to hym in liknesse of the pilgryme.

Isodorie saiethe also in the boke of the Natiuite of the Lyff and of 235 the Dethe of Seintes, Seint Iohn meued into golde wilde yerdes, and of the stones of the riuere he made precious stones and reformed ayein the broken stones into her furst nature, he reformed the wedu to lyff by hys comaundement and also a yong man, he dronke dedely venyme and escaped of the perile, and tho that were dede therwith he restored 240 hem to lyff. This saide Isodore.

Here endithe the lyff of Seint Iohn the Ewangelist, and
after beginneth the lyff of the Innocentis, Cap^m. .ix.^{m} |

The Innocentes were slayn bi Herode Askalonytees. For holi writte f. 16ra saiethe that there were thre Herodes of gret renoun of her owne fame and of her cruelte, the furst Herode Askalonyte vnder the whiche oure Lorde was born, the secounde was Herode Antipas that slew Seint Iohn the Baptist, and the .iij. was Herode Agrippes that slow Seint 5 Iames and dede putte Seint Peter in prison. But we shull saie of the storie of the furst.

It is redde in the Maister of Stories that Antipater wedded the nece of the kyng of Arabie, by whiche he hadde a sone that he called Herodes that was after Askalo[n]ytees. And this same toke the 10 reaulme of Iudee of Cesar August, and thanne was furst take away the ceptre of Iudee. And th[i]s Herodes hadde thre sones, Antipater, Alexander and Aristobole, and they were of one moder born in Iudee. And thanne they were sent to Rome for to be taught in alle the liberall artes, and after that whanne they come from her studye and duelled 15 withe her fader, this Alexander was ryght sharpe in ansueryng and in chydyng with her fader of the succession of the kyngdome. And the fader was wrothe and wolde haue putte Antipater tofore that other, and the twayne conceyuyng this treted priuely the dethe of her fader, and thanne the fader putte hem awaye from hym, and anone they 20 went to Cesar to pleyne of the wrong that her fader hadde done to hem.

And in this mene tyme the .iij. kyngges come into Ierusalem and

236–7 and . . . precious stones] *om.* G   239 he²] þat G

EH1GA2; A1 resumes at 10 *same*   2 thre] *om.* G   10 Askalonytees] Askalomytees EH1   12 this] thus E, þus *changed to* þis H1, þese .iij. G   19 the¹] *add* oþer H1   treted] tredid G

asked of the natiuitee of the nwe kyng, and whanne Herodes herde
25 that he was gretly troubled and dredde lest any were born of lynage of
f. 16rb verray kyngges that wold | assaile hym and putte hym oute of his
rewme. Thanne he praied these kyngges that whanne they hadde
founde hym that thei wolde late hym wete and he wolde come and
worship hym, but his fals entent was to slee hym. Thanne the kyngges
30 turned annother waye towardes her owne contre, and whanne he sawe
that thei come not he wend that thei hadde bene deseyued by the vision
of [the] sterre and that they durst not for shame come ayein to hym, and
for that cause he made no more enqueryng of the childe. But whanne
he herde what the shepardes hadde saide and what Symeon and Anne
35 hadde prophesied he dred hym gretly and helde hym scorned of the
kyngges. And thanne [he] beganne to ordeyne [for] the dethe of [the]
children that were in Bethelem, for he wold slee with hem hym that he
knewe not.

And thanne by the techyng of the aungell Ioseph fledde into Egipt
40 into the citee of Hermopolyn and was ther .vij. yere vnto the dethe of
Herode. And after the prophesie of Ysaie, whanne oure Lorde entered
into Egipte the ydolis fille doune, and it is saide that ryght in suche
wise that whanne the children of Israel passed oute of Egipte that ther
was none house but that [the] eldest born deied, right so atte oure
45 Lordes comyng into Egipte ther was no temple but that the ydole felle
downe. Cassioder tellithe in the Storie Parted in Thre that in
Hermopolyn of Thebayde ther ys a tree that is called perfides that
availeth gretly to alle manere syknesse, for the leef or the rynde
bounde to the necke of the seke it helithe anone. And as the blessid
50 Virgine Marie fledde into Egipte withe her sone the tree bowed downe
to the erthe and worshipped goodly Ihesu Crist.
f. 16va   And as Herode | ordeyned for the dethe of the chyldren he was
somned bi lettere to come before Cesar to ansuere to the accusacions
of his sones. And as he went thorugh Tharsee he vnderstode that the
55 shippes of Tharsee hadde passed ouer the kyngges, and made to
brenne hem in his madnesse like as Dauid hadde prophesied tofore,
sayeng: 'He shall brenne the shippes of Tharse by despit of
wodenesse.' And as the fader pleded tofore Cesar ayeinst his sones
it was diffined vtterli that the sones shuld obeie to the fader in alle

28 he] om. G   32 the] a E   35 hym^{1,2}] hem G   36 he] om. E   for] om. E
the²] om. EHi   40 Hermopolyn] Crymopolyn G   44 the] om. E   45 ydole]
ydoles EHi   47 Hermopolyn] Erymopolyn G   Thebayde] so with The on erasure Hi
perfides] persidis GHi   50 the tree] þei Hi   55 passed] del. and ins. 'ledde' Hi,
ladde G

thyng and that he shulde yeue to suche as hym luste. And thanne 60
Herode turned home ayein and was more hardi bi confirmacion, and
sent to sle alle the children that were in Bethelem fro the age of two
yere vnto the age of one day. For Herode hadde herde of the thre
kyngges the natiuite of the child fro the day that the sterre appered,
and for that yere was passed and that he hadde be atte Rome annother 65
yere he shewed his wodenesse ayeinst the children that were aboue the
age of Ihesu Crist and binethe the age of .ij. yere, and dradde that this
yere that the sterres serued wolde not haue transformed hym in more
gretter age. And this sentence is most vsed and holden most true.

And after Crisostome sche is expouned otherwise where he saiethe 70
of .ij. yere and witheinne that it be vnderstonde from .ij. yere into
fyve, for he saiethe that the sterre apered a yere bifore the natiuite of
oure Lorde Ihesu Crist. And whanne Herode hadde vnderstonde bi
the kyngges he went to Rome and abode there another yere, and
wende that oure Lorde hadde be born whanne the sterre apered, and 75
bi þat he wende that oure Lorde hadde bene | two yere olde, and fro f. 16ᵛᵇ
two yere to fyve yere he dede moche persecusyon. And of this they
haue euydence, for they saie that the bones of sum of the Innocentes
bene so large that they myght not be but they passed two yere olde,
but men may ansuere ayein that men were more that tyme thanne thei 80
be now.

And this same Herode was punished forthewithe, for as Macrobes
saithe in a Cronicle that a litell sone of Herodes was withe the norse
and he was slayn by auenture amonges other of the cruel bochers. And
thanne was fulfilled that was saide bi the prophete: 'The voise of the 85
weping and of the crieng is her[d]e in Rama, þat of the piteouse
moders in Rama, that is high in heuene.'

It is saide in the Maister of Stories that God the most ryghtwise
iuge suffered not the ryght gret felonye of Herode to be vnponished,
for bi the devyne iugement he that hadde made many wydues of her 90
childeren he was made widue of his owne. For Alexaundre and
Arystoboll were suspecious to hym, for a man that was of thaire
counsaile and of thaire felawship confessid to the kyng that Alexaundre hadde behight hym gret geftes if he wolde enpoisen his fader,
and also his barboure hadde tolde hym that thei behight hym gret 95

62 sent] seint E   64 the²] a G   65 that he] *om.* G   68 that the] þᵗ þis *with* þᵗ
on erasure H₁   sterres] sterre H₁G   69 most²] for H₁   71 of] in G
78 euydence] obedience H₁   85 prophete] prophesie H₁   86 herde] here E, *om.* G
Rama] Roma H₁   87 Rama] Roma H₁   88 of] *add* þe H₁G

giftes yef he wolde kitte his throte whanne he shulde shaue hym, for
thei saide: 'It is no fors of that olde dotarde that kembithe his hede to
seme yong.' And thanne the fader was wrothe and made sle hem
bothe, and ordeyned Antipater to be kyng after hym and that Herodys
100 Agrippe shulde be kyng after Antipater. And aboue alle he norisched
Herodys Agrippe and Herodyene the wiff of Phelip that he hadde bi
f. 17ra Aris|toboll and loued hem as thaire fader. And for double cause
Antipater conceyued double hate ayeinst his fader and wolde haue
enpoisoned hym, and Herodis hadde knowlage therof and did putte
105 hym in prison. And whanne the emperour herde that Herode hadde
slain his sones, he saide hym hadde leuer be Herodes pigges thanne
Herodes sone, for the Iue sparithe hys pigges and he sleith his sones.

   And thanne he fell in a grevous siknesse, for he hadde a strong feuer
and his body roted, his fete suolle, his hede shoke, he was fulle of
110 stynkyng vermyn, horible wormes growed in his fleshe that frette
hym, he kowghed and ofte was tormented with sighyng. And thanne
by hys fesicianes he was putte in oyle and in fyre and take oute as
dede, and thanne he herde saie that the Iues abode his dethe with gret
ioie, wherfor he lete take of the most yonge men that were of the Iues
115 and putte hem in prison, and saide to Salome his suster that 'the Iues
purposen to make gret ioie atte my deying, and yef thou wylt do my
comaundement there shall be inow that shall wepe and sorugh. As
sone as thou seist that my sperit is passed sende to the prison and sle
all tho yonge men, so that Iudee shall sorugh and wepe for me quik or
120 dede.'

   Hys custume was that after his mete he wolde pare an appel and ete
it, and as he helde the knyff in his honde he loked that there were none
aboute hym to lette hym. He lefte his honde to smyte hymselff, but a
cosin of hys was fast by hym and lette hym. And thanne it was
125 thorough the halle that the kyng was dede, wherfor Antipater hadde
f. 17rb gret ioie and behight grete yeftes to the kepers to le|te hym oute. And
whanne Herode wost it he hadde gretter sorugh of [the] ioye of his
sone thanne of his owne deth and sent anone into the prison to sle
hym, and ordeyned Archelaum to be kyng after hym, and deied the .v.
130 day after. He was ryght vnfortunat in other thyngges and ryght cursed
in his owne. And thanne Salome his suster slowe all tho that the kyng

---

   102 hem] him H1   102-3 And . . . fader] *om.* G   107 Iue] Iues EG   sparithe]
sparid G   sleith] sclow3 G   110 growed] growned E   111 kowghed] þoughed H1
118 my] *om.* H1   sende] *add* men G   119 sorugh] *add* for me G   126 to²] and G
127 gretter] grete`r' H1   the] *om.* EH1

hadde comaunded her to sle. Remy in his Original vpon Mathew saiethe that Herodes slow hymselff withe a knyff wherwith he pared his appelis, and that Salome his suste[r] slow the Iues as he hadde ordeyned.   135

Here endithe the lyff of Innocentis, and af⟨ter⟩ beginnithe the lyff of Seint Thomas of Caunterbery, Cap^m. .x.^m

Seint Thomas of Caunterbery whanne he duelled in courte withe the kyng of Englonde he seigh many thyngges done ayeinst his religion, and he went from thennes to the erchebisshop of Caunterbery where he was goodly resseived and made his archedeken. And atte the last by the praiere[s] of the erchebisshop he was made chaunceller of Inglond   5 so that by his grete witte he myght defende the Chirche fro the assauute of wikked men. And the kyng loued hym so tenderly that after the dissese of the erchebisshop he made hym erchebisshop, but he refused it long tyme till atte the last he was ouercome by obedience to take the charge and bere the burden. And anone sodenly he was 10 chaunged into another man and clothed in heer nexst hym called the hayre and made his body lene by fastyng. And he used not only the hayre to his sherte but his nether clothis also of here doune to his | knees, and he coueryd so suttelli hys holinesse with honest clothyng   f. 17va that it was not perceyued, for the apparaill of his clothyng outeward 15 was conformed to the maners of eueriche. And euery day he woshe the fete of .xiij. pore men and fedde hem and [gaue] to euery man .iiij. d.

The kyng enforsed hym to turne hym to his wille ayenst the Chirche and wolde haue vsed the custumes that his predecessoures hadde ayeinst the fraunchise of the Chirche and that they also [weren] 20 confermed by hym, but he wolde in no wyse consent therto, and in suche wise he gete the wrethe of the kyng and of [the] princes. In a tyme it fell that he was constreyned bi the kyng for to go withe other bisshoppes and was manassed by sentence of dethe and was deceyued

132 her] for G   134 suster] suste E

EH1GA2; E has text crossed through and *Vacat* added at the end of the initial and closing rubrics and twice within the Life.   2 seigh] savgh *on erasure* H1   4 atte the last] *om.* G   5 praieres] praiere E   6 witte] my3t G   7 the kyng] þay G 8 dissese] deth G   11–12 called the hayre] *om.* G   16 eueriche] euery archebisshop G   he] *add* visitid and G   17 gaue] thanne EH1   man] *add* he yaf H1   18–20 hym¹ . . . hadde] *om.* G   20 Chirche] *add* weren E, *so add and del.* H1, *add* with his lordis G 20–1 and . . . hym] And þat þei also confermed bi hym *del.* H1   20 weren] *om.* EH1G (*feussent* P2)   21 by hym] *om.* G   22 wrethe] *on erasure* H1   the³] *om.* E, his H1

25 by the counsaile of gret men, so that he acorded by worde to the wille
of the kyng. But whanne he seighe that this thing touched the perile of
the soules, he tormented hymselff gretly bi penaunce and suspended
hymselff of his office till he was restabled ayein bi the pope. And
thanne after he wolde that he shulde conferme in dede bi writyng that
30 he hadde saide bi worde, and he withesaied it myghtili and left up the
crosse and bare hym upryght oute of the court, and thanne the wicked
cried ayeinst hym saieng: 'Take the theef, hang the traitour.'

And thanne two true barons come to hym wepyng and tolde hym
sikerly in counsaile that two gret barones hadde swore his dethe.
35 Thanne the seruaunt of God, dredyng more for the Chirche thanne
for hymself, fledde to the pope Alisaundre that receyued hym goodly
and recomaunded hym to the chirche of Clyny, and sithe he come into
f. 17ᵛᵇ [Fraunse]. And thanne the kyng sent to | Rome to make the legatis
come to defende this thyng, and he was withesaid atte all, and for that
40 he toke gretter hatered ayeinst the erchebisshop and toke alle the
goodes that long[ed] to the [erche]bisshop and to hys meyne and
exiled alle his kynne. But Seint Thomas lefte neuer but contynually
praied for the reawme of Inglond and for the kyng. And thanne it was
re[uel]ed to Seint Thomas that he shulde come ayein to his chirche
45 and that he shulde go to oure Lorde bi payne of marterdome, and
thanne in the .vij. yere of his exile it was graunted to hym to retorne
ayein, and he was receyued of all withe gret worship.

And a fewe dayes before his marterdome a yonge man deyed and
was arerid ayein bi miracle, and he tolde that he hadde be ladde vnto
50 the souerain ordre of seintes, and ther he seigh a sege voide and he
asked for whom it was, and it was saide to hym that oure [Lorde]
keped this sege for the gret prest of Inglond, Thomas.

Ther was a symple preste that song euery day masse of oure Ladi.
He was accused to the erchebisshop and he aresoned hym and fonde
55 hym in symple connyng and heelde hym for an ydiote and suspended
hym of his masse and of his office. On a tyme as Seint Thomas hadde
leide his hayre vnder his beddes hede for to haue seude it whanne he
myght, the blessid Virgine Marie appered to the preest and saide to
hym: 'Go to the erchebissop, and saie hym that she for whos loue

29 bi] *ins.* H1   33 true] *add* bisshopis G   38 Fraunse] flaundres EH1
39 withesaid] *so with* w *on erasure* H1   41 longed] longithe E   erchebisshop] bisshopriche
EH1   44 reueled] releued E, *so changed to* revelede H1   come] *add* home E   45 go] *add*
ayene H1   oure] his G   49 be ladde] belid G   50 he²] y G   51 Lorde] *om.* E
52 keped] kepith G   55 hym in] *trs.* H1, hym G   connyng] *om.* G   58 the²] 't'his H1
59–60 and . . . wont] *om.* G

thou were wont to syng thi masse hathe sowed his heyre that liethe in 60
suche a place, and it is sowed withe rede silke and he shall redely finde
it there as he le[id] it, and that sche sent the to hym bi this token that
he do aweye the entr[edyt] that he hath | made.' And whanne the f. 18ʳᵃ
erchebisshop herde this he was gretly abasshed and fonde al lyk as he
hadde saide, and anone he relesid hym the entredit and charged hym 65
to kepe this in gret counsaile.

After this he defended the right of the Chirche as he dede before, ne
neuer wold turne to the kyng bi strengthe ne by praiere. And thei seigh
that they myght not bowe hym in no wise, the knyghtes of the kyng
withe forse and armes comen into the chirche where the erchebisshop 70
was. He herde [it] and come ayeinst hem and saide: 'See me here.
What will ye?' And thanne thei saide with cruel voys: 'We bene come
to slee the, as thou shalt wete.' Thanne he saide mekely: 'I am here
redy for to suffre dethe for the loue of God and for to defende the
fredom of the Chirche, but y charge you in Goddes behalue and upon 75
the peyne of perpetuell curse that ye do none harme to none of hem
that bene here. Miselff and the Chirche I recomaunde to God, to the
blessid Virgine Marie and to Seint Denys.' And whanne he hadde so
saide his worshipfull hede was smyten withe suerdes of these cruel
men and his holy brayne was shedde in the pament of the chirche, and 80
thus was he sacred martir [to oure Lorde] in the yere fro the
Incarnacion a thousand an hundred seuenti and foure.

And as the prestes wolde do for hym the seruice of the dede and as
thei begonne *Requiem*, the aungels weren redy and breke the voys of
the singgers and beganne *Letabitur iustus in Domino*, the masse of 85
marteres, and thanne the clerkes folued them after. This was a
gracious chaunge of oure Lorde þat the song of wepyng was turned
into the song of preisyng, and that he to whom they hadde begonne
suffrage of dethe was preised withe the prey|syng of marteres. And the f. 18ʳᵇ
nobill holinesse of the glorious martir of oure Lorde was proued bi the 90
aungels that putte hym with so gret worschip in the catheloge of
martires, for he sufferid dethe in the chirche [and for the Chirche], in
holy tyme and in holy place, bitwene the hondes of religious prestis,
so that the holinesse of hym and the cruelte of Goddes enemys weren

61 redely] redi H1   62 leid] lefte E   that'] þan H1   the] *add* prest H1
63 aweye] *add* fro þe G   entredyt] entrodyk E   63–5 that . . . entredit] *om.* G
68 turne] turn'e' *with* t *on erasure* H1   69 bowe hym] make hym to obeye G
70 into] to H1   71 it] *om.* E   72 What] wat *on erasure* H1   voys] wise G   81 to
oure Lorde] *om.* E   85 in Domino] *om.* G   87–8 of wepyng . . . song] *om.* G
89 suffrage] suffrages H1G   92 and for the Chirche] *om.* EH1

95 the more shewed. And oure Lorde lust to do many gret myracles for
hym, for bi his merytes the blynde hadde sight, the deef heryng, the
halte her ryght lymes, and the dede were turned to lyff, and there as
hys vestementis that were [wete] with his blode were waschin and the
water therof was medicine to many syknesses.

100   Ther was a lady of Inglonde and coueited gretly to haue [hadde]
graye eyen for to be the more goodli in the sight of the peple, and for
þat cause she avowed to Seint Thomas for to visite his sepulcre
barefote. And whanne she hadde made her praiere and wolde haue
risen she was verray blinde, and thanne she aperseyued her defauute
105 and repented her and praied Seint Thomas to restore her to her olde
eyghen that she hadd before and she wolde neuer desire graye eyen
more, and oure Lorde by the merites of Seint Thomas herd her and
she was res[tor]ed to her sight.

   A [s]cornere brought to his lorde symple water in stede of the water
110 of Seint Thomas, and his maister saide to hym: 'Yef thou stalyst euer
anything of myn, Seint Thomas graunte that thou bryng me neuer of
his water, and yef thou art no theef bryng forthe the water.' And he
f. 18ᵛᵃ consented, for he wost well that he hadde filled his boxse with | water,
and anone he opened it and he fonde it all voide and drye, and so the
115 servaunt was founde a lier and proued of thefte.

   Ther was a tame bridde that hadde lerned to speke, and as he flewe
oute a sparhauke pursued hym and he beganne to saie as he hadde
lerned: 'Seint Thomas, helpe [me].' And anone the sparhauke felle
downe dede and the bridde askaped.

120   Ther was a man that Seint Thomas hadde moche loued and was
falle in greuous siknesse, wherfor he went to the tombe of Seint
Thomas to praie for his helthe, and he hadde his askyng. And as he
turned ayein al hole he beganne to drede hym that this helthe
perauenture was not best for his soule, and thanne he turned ayein
125 to the sepulcre and praied that yef this helthe were not profitable to
his soule that the siknesse myght come ayein, and anone he turned as
before.

   The devyne veniaunce beganne to werke so wonderfully ayeinst tho
that hadde slayn hym that one al torent hymselff bi peces withe his
130 owne fyngers and nayles, the tother rotted as they went vpon the

95 Lorde] *ins.* G   gret] *om.* H1   98 wete] white E, wet *over del.* wight (?) H1
100 hadde] *om.* E   105 her to] *trs.* G   108 restored] resseiued E   109 scornere]
Cornere E, 's'cornere H1   water¹] *add* of *erased* Seint Thomas *del.* H1   112 and . . .
water] *om.* G   113 filled] felte G   114 and he fonde it] *om.* H1   118 me] *om.*
EH1   126 he] it G, *om.* H1   130 they] he G

erthe, some hadde the pallasie, som were mad and deyed cursidly.
And thus oure Lord punished these cursed tyrauntes for loue of his
holy martir.

Here endithe the lyff of Seint Thomas of Caunterbery, and
nexst begynnithe the lyff of Seint Siluester, Cap^m. .xj.^m

Seint Siluester was the sone of a ryghtwys quene and was taught of
Cy|rin prest, and he loued souereynli hospitalite. Thimothe, a ful   f. 18vb
cristen man, was resseiued of hym in his hous that was escheued of
other for the persecucion, and that Timothe a yere after receyued
crowne of marterdome for the stedfast prechyng of Ihesu Crist. And 5
Tarquyen the provost wende that Timothe hadde gretly abounded in
richesse, and he asked hym of Siluester and manased hym withe
dethe, and [whanne] he wost verili that Timothe hadde no good he
comaunded to Siluester to do sacrifice to ydoles or elles in the morw
he shulde suffre diuerse tormentes. And thanne Seint Siluester saide 10
to the prouost: '[Fole], thou shalt deye tonyght and receyue euerlastyng torment and, wilt thou or no, thou shalt knowe hym for a verray
God that we worship.' And that same nyght as he wolde haue swolued
a mossel of fische it abode in his throte and wolde nother up ne
downe, and so he was strangelid and deied cursidly the same nyght 15
and was ledde into hys tumbe with moche wepyng. And Seint
Siluester was broght oute of prison withe moche ioye and he was
not only loued of cristen men but of panymes me'r'veylously.

His lokyng was like an aungell, clere in wordes, pure in body, holy in
his werkes, wise in counsaile, cristen in the faithe, ryght pacient in 20
hope, ful of charitee. And Melchisedek bysshop of the [cite], whanne he
was dede, Siluester that refused it was chosen bisshop by accorde of alle.
And he putte the names of orphelyns, of wydowes, of the pore, in a
paper and ordeyned for hem. He fasted the Wedenysday and the
Friday and the Saterday [and] ordey|ned to be kepte, and he kept the f. 19ra
Thourseday as he dede the Sonday. And the Iues saide to the cristen 26

EH1GA1A2; A2 changes to Hand B at 104 day; D begins at 239 the sone and breaks off
after 378 of (þe), M begins at 173 not and ends at 343 praiere and   1 ryghtwys] ryght/
wyse E, ryght wyse H1G (iuste S)   2 Cyrin] a G   7 manased] manasseth H1
8 whanne] om. EH1   10 suffre diuerse] trs. with suffre repeated in margin H1
11 Fole] om. E, ins. after deye H1   tonyght] the night H1   12 or no] not G
16 was] om. H1   ledde . . . tumbe] bore with histring G   20 his werkes] werkyng G
cristen . . . ryght] om. H1   21 cite] see EH1   whanne he] om. E, ins. H1   22 was
dede] ins. H1   25 and²] om. E

that the Sabot aught rather to be halowed thanne the fifte day, and he
ansuered: 'Nay, for bi the comaundement of the apostell that day men
shulde haue compassion of the sepulture of [Ihesu Crist].' And they
30 saide that it suffised to faste oo Saterday in the yere for the sepulture.
And thanne Siluester saide: 'Ryght as euery Sonday is worschipped
for the resurreccion, ryght so euery Saterday most be hadde in
reuerence for the sepulture.' And thanne they acorded to the
Saterday, but they strofe gretli for the Thouresday and saiden that
35 she [shulde] not be amonge [the] sollempne dayes [of] the cristen.
And thanne Seint Siluester shewed the dignite of the day in .iij.
thyngges, for that oure Lorde steyed up into heuene in that day, and
ordeyned the sacrement of his precious body and blode, and in that day
the Chirche makithe [the] creme. And thanne alle obeyed to his resones.
40   And whanne Constantine dede persecucion vpon the cristen
Siluester fledde into a mounteyn withe his clerkes. And thanne
[this] Constantyne by desert of that persecucion of tyrauntrie
become mesell. And atte the laste bi the counsaile of the prestes of
idoles .iij. thousand children were brought to be slayn so that he
45 myght be bathed in the hote freshe blode. And thanne whanne he
went oute to the place wher that the bathe shulde be ordeyned and
arrayed, the moderes of the children comen rennyng ayenst hym
wepyng and cryeng piteously, and whanne Constantine seigh and
herde this he wepte for compassion and made his chayere to abide
f. 19rb and | sette hym up and saide to heryng of alle in this wise: 'Now ye my
51 lordes and knyghtes and alle that bene here, takithe hede what I shall
saie to you. The dignite of the empire of Rome is brought forthe of the
welle of pitee, the whiche hathe yeue this ordenaunce, that whosoeuer
sle a childe in bataile [his hede shall be] smete of. And how shulde not
55 this be to gret a cruelte for to do to oure owne children that we
defende to do to others? What shall it availe us to ouercome straungers
yef we be ouercome withe cruelte? For to ouercome straunge naciones
[is] bi strengthe of fyghtyng men, but to ouercome vices and synnes
comithe of vertues of good maners. And in this bataile we haue bene
60 the most myghti, and in this bataile we shalle be strengger thanne

27 fifte day] .vj. dai H1, sonday G   28 comaundement . . . apostell] aposteles
comaundement H1   29 Ihesu Crist] *trs.* E   30 oo] þe G   31 Ryght] *om.* G
35 shulde] wolde E   the^1] tho E   of] after E   39 the^2] *om.* E, his G   42 this] *om.*
EH1   50 heryng] euerech H1   alle] *add* men E   52 empire] Emperoure G
54 his . . . be] shall haue the hede E   55 owne] *om.* G   58 is] if EA2, if *del.* H1, *om.*
G   bi] *add* þe G, *add* 'þe' H1   and] of H1

oureselff. For who shalle be ouercome in this bataile shalle haue the victorie, for after the victorie he shalle be ouercome yef the victorie be ouercome withe felonye. Now late thanne pitee conquere in this batayle, and we mowe lyghtli be a conquerour of alle yef we be conquered withe pitee, for he prouithe hymselff to be lorde of alle that 65 is servaunt of pitee. This is my conclusion. It is beter that y deye sauynge the worship of the lyff of these innocentis thanne I receyue a cruell lyff, and yet the recoueren is vnsertayne, and that is certeyne though she be recouered it is withe cruelte. Wherfor I comaunde that alle these children bene yolden ayein to her moders.' And withe that 70 he gaue hem gret giftes and ordeyned hem chariotes and other caryage ynow to bryng hem home, and the moders that come thedir withe | gret sorugh and wepyng went home ayein withe gret ioye, and thanne f. 19va the emperour turned ayein to his palais.

The nyght foluyng Seint Peter and Seint Paule appered to hym and 75 saide to hym: 'For that thou hast dradde to shede innocentis blode oure Lorde Ihesu Crist hath sent us to the to yeue [the] counsaile how thou shalt haue thin helthe. Sende after the bisshop Syluester that is hidde in the mountayn of Syratym and he shalle shewe the the piscine wherein thou shalt be plunged thries and so thou shalt be cured of thi 80 leper. And thou shalt yelde this goodnesse to God so that thou shalt destroie the temples of [the] ydoles and restable ayein the chirche[s] that thou hast destroied and from hennes forwarde worschip almyghti God.' And whanne Constantyne awoke he sent anone knygtes to Siluestre, and whanne he scighe hem he wende to haue benc ledde to 85 haue receiued marterdome, and thanne [he] recomaunded hymselff to God and comforted his felawship, and whanne he come to the emperour the emperour rose ayeinst hym and saide: 'We haue ioye of thi comyng.' And Siluester salowed hym, and thanne the emperour tolde hym alle [his] dreme by ordre and asked hym what goddes thei 90 were that appered to hym. Siluester ansuered and saide that thei were no goddes but aposteles of Ihesu Crist. And thanne the emperour preide the bisshop that he wolde bringe before hym the ymages of [the] apostoles, and also sone as he seigh hem he saide [that] tho that appered to [hym] were wonder like hem. And thanne Siluester made 95

61 oureselff] oure bileue G   68 recoueren] recouer G, recouering H1   70 yolden] deliuered H1   73 gret^2] om. H1   74 ayein] om. G   76 to hym . . . shede] om. G 77 the^2] om. E   79 Syratym] Syratyim E   the the] þe H1   82 temples] tempull G the^2] om. E   ydoles] idoll G   chirches] chirche E   85 hem] add come H1   86 he] om. E 90 his] the EH1   asked] add of E   94 the] tho E   that^1] om. EH1   95 hym] me EH1 thanne] add seint E

hym faste alle a weke and made hym nwe in the faithe and to deliuer
f. 19vb alle the cristen oute of prison. And whanne the | emperour descended
in the water of baptime a gret lyght shined vpon hym, and he went
oute alle hole and clene and saide that he hadde saien Ihesu Crist.

100   And the furst day of his baptime he ordeined this lawe, that Ihesu
Criste shulde be worschipped in the citee of Rome [as] verray God.
The secounde he ordeined that whoso blamed Ihesu Crist he shulde
be punished. The .iij. [day] whosoeuer dede any wrong to the cristen
he shulde lese half his good. The ferthe day he ordeyned that right as
105 the emperour was hede of the worlde, so the bisshop of Rome shulde
be hede and lorde of al holy Chirche. The .v. day whosoeuer flee to
holi Chirche for to haue refute that he be kepte from alle disese. The
sixte that none edifie no chirche withoute licence of his prelate, and
specialli in Rome. The .vij. daye that the dymes of reall possessiones
110 were take to the edifieng of chirches. The .viij. day the emperour
come to Seint Petres chirche and mekeli accused hymselff weping
[for] his synnes, and after that he toke his picois and digged furste in
the erthe for to make the foundement of the gret chirche, and [he]
bere oute .xij. baskettes vpon his owne shuldres.

115   And whanne Eline moder of Constantine emperour that duelled in
Bethanie herde this thing, she sent hym letteres and preised hym
gretly of that he hadde lefte and renou[ns]ed to worship false ymages
[of] ydoles, but she blamed hym gretly that [he] hadde lefte the god of
Iewes and worshipped a man that was crucified. And thanne the
120 emperour wrote to her ayein that she shulde come to hym and bryng
with her the maistres of [the] Iwes, and he wolde bryng [on] his side
f. 20ra the doctours of the cristen, and thei shul[d]e dispute | togederes and bi
thaire disputacion it shulde apere whiche faithe shuld be most true.
And thanne Seint Eline come to Rome and brought withe her an
125 hundred and fourtie of the most wisest of the Iewes, among the
whiche there were twelue that shuld ansuere before alle other bi gret
wysedom and faire speche. And whanne Siluester and his clerkes and
the Iwes weren assembeled before the emperour for to dispute, they
ordeyned bi comune acorde that two right wise panymes and proued

101 as] and E   103 day] om. E   whosoeuer dede] who so doth G   105 was] is
H1   of^1] add al E   106 and lorde] om. H1   108 sixte] add day G   109 daye]
om.   dymes] demes changed to dymes H1   of] add þe H1   112 for] of E, for on erasure
H1   furste] om. H1   113 he] om. E   117 renounsed] renoued EH1, renouellid G
(renoncie P2)   false] add goddis G   118 of] and EH1   he] om. E   120–1 ayein . . .
her] and to G   121 the^2] om. E   on] in E   122 shulde] shulle E   124 Seint]
seiþe changed to seinte H1   126 gret] om. G

of gret trouth for to be iuges and for to yeue sentence of thingges that 130
shulde be saide, that one was called Craton and that other Zenaphille,
and it was confermed among hem that whiles the parties schulde
speke [the tother] shulde be stille and not speke.

Thanne beganne the furste of the twelue, that hight Abiathar, and
saide: 'In as moche as these cristen sayen for to be thre goddes, the 135
fader, the sone and the holi goste, it is certayne that thei do ayeinst the
lawe, for he saiethe that "I am allone, and ther nis no God but I." And
after that thei sayen Ihesu Crist to be a god for that he dede many
myracles here in erthe. Many one haue there be of oure lawe that
deden gret myracles and yet thei toke neuer vpon hem the name of 140
godhede so as [this] Ihesu Crist dede þat thei worshippen.' And
[to that] ansuered Seint Siluestre and saide: 'We worship one God,
but we saie not that he was sone allone that he ne hadde ioye of the
sone. And therfor wille we shewe in oure bokes the trinite of persones.
For we saie hym the fader of whom the prophete saide: "He called me 145
and saide: 'Thou art my fader.' " We saye of the sone: "Thou art | my f. 20rb
sone." We saie of hym the holi goost of the whiche that same saiethe:
"The spirit of the mouthe of hym is al the vertue of hem." And in that
he saide: "Make we man to oure ymage and to oure liknesse," thus
shewithe clereli the pluralite of persones and vnite of the godhede. 150
For though it be so that there bene .iij. persones [yet] ther is but one
God, right as we mowe shewe here by a visible ensaumple.' And
[thanne he toke] the porpre of the emperoure and made thre plites and
saide: 'Lo, here bene thre plites and but one clothe, right so the thre
persones bene one god. And to that thou saiest that Ihesu Crist shulde 155
not be leued for his myracles and that many seintes dede myracles and
seyden not hemselff God, I telle the pleinly that God wolde neuer late
them passe witheoute sharpe peyne that were lefft vp in pride ayeinst
hym, as it appered to Dathan and Abiron and many other. And howe
myght they thanne lye and saie that they were goddes whanne they 160
were none, and he that saiethe hymselff to be God hadde no payne and
was [in] felawship withe vertue and strengthe?' Thanne the Iues saide:

130 for to be] ins. above del. þat the H1   132 parties] partie G   133 the tother]
to other thei E   135 for to] þat þer G   goddes] personys and oo god G, as E del. with G
reading ins. H1   136 that] ins. H1   137 I²] oon G   138 many] om. G
139 haue] of siche G   be] ins. H1, add þat dide del. G   140 gret] om. H1   141 this]
om. E   142 to that] tho E   147 hym] om. G   148 hem] hym G   150 the²]
'þe' G   151 yet] that E, þat subp. H1   152 thanne] om. EG   he toke] the cote E,
add the cote and H1   154 bene] om. G   155 bene] om. G   156 be leued] beleued
E, be byleuyd G   157 the] om. G   159 appered] appereth H1   162 in] om. EH1

'Abyathar is ouercome withe Siluester, for reson will it yf he were not
God and saide hym to be God he myght not yeue lyff to the dede.'
165 And thanne he was take away.

Thanne come forthe the secounde, that hyght Zonas, and saide that
Abraham in takyng circumcisyon was halowed of God and alle the
chyldren of Abraham were iustified bi circumcision, and thanne he
that hathe not be circumsised shall not be iustefied. And thanne
170 Siluester ansuered and saide: 'It is sertayne that Abraham was
f. 20ᵛᵃ plesaunt to God before the circumci|sion and was called the frende
of God. The circumcision halowed hym not but faithe and rightwisnesse made hym plesaunt to God, for he toke not circumcision in
halowing but in diuision.' And [thanne] he was ouercome.

175   The thridde come foorthe, that hight Godelias, and saide: 'Youre
Ihesu Crist, how myght he be God whanne ye afferme that he was
borne, tempted, traied, dispoiled, bounden and yeuen drinke eisell
and galle, deied and was beried, [sithe] alle these t[h]yngges myght
not be in God?' To that ansuered Siluester: 'We schull proue bi youre
180 owne bokes that alle these thingges [were] saide before of Ihesu Crist.
For of his natiuite saide Isaie: "Lo here the virgine that shall conceyue
and bere a childe." And of his temptacion saide Zakarie: "I seigh
Ihesu Crist a gret prest before the aungell, and Sathanas was in [his]
right side." Of the treson saith the psalme: "He that ete of my brede
185 counsailed the treson to be done vpon me," and of his dispoillyng that
same saithe: "Thei deviden my clothyng and putte lotte vpon hem."
For to be made drinke eysell and galle the same saith: "They gave
galle in my mete." Of that he was bounde saiethe Esdras: "Ye bynde
me not as youre fader that deliuered you from the [l]onde of Egipte,
190 and the tyrauntes before the sege of the iuge, ye haue made me lowe
and haue taken me to hang on a tree." Of the sepulcre saiethe
Ier[e]mye: "In the sepulcre of hym the dede shal quicken."' And
whanne Godelias wost not what to ansuere he was putte oute bi
sentence.

195   And thanne the ferthe come in, that hight Amicias, and saide:
'Siluester affermithe to be saide of Crist that is saide of other, wherfor
f. 20ᵛᵇ it ap|pertenithe that he preue that it hathe be saide before of his Crist.'
And Siluester ansuered: 'Thanne shewe thou me annother that was

174 thanne] that E, in þat H1   176 ye afferme] *changed to* he affermed H1
177 bounden] *om.* G   178 deied] dede G   was] *om.* G   sithe] sight EH1M
thyngges] tyngges E   180 were] was E   181 saide] *om.* G   that] *om.* G
182 temptacion] passion G   183 and] of G   his] the EH1M   189 londe] bonde E
192 Ieremye] Ieromye E, Ierome G

conceiued of a virgine, that dranke eisell and galle, that was crowned
withe thornes, crucified, dede, buried, and arose from dethe to lyve 200
and stied vp to heuene.' Thanne saied the emperour: 'Yef he canne
not shewe that it was another, wete it fulli that he is ouercome.' And
whanne he myght not do it he was take thennes.

And thanne the .v. was brought forthe, that hight Dochet, and
saide: 'Yef Crist were born of the sede of Dauid and halowed as ye 205
saie, hym neded not to be halowed ayein as he was after.' Thanne
saide Siluester: 'Right as circumcision toke his laste ende in the
circumcision of oure Lorde, right so oure baptime toke begynnyng
[in] the baptime of oure Lorde, and thanne he was not baptized for to
be halowed but for to halwe.' And thanne he helde his pees. Thanne 210
saide the emperour: 'Dochet wolde not [holde] his pees yef he coude
saie the contrarie.'

Thanne was brought forthe the .vj., that hight Thussy, and saide he
wolde that Siluester wolde 'expowne to us the cause of this virginal
childyng.' And to that Siluester saide: 'The erthe of whiche Adam was 215
made was virgine and witheoute corrupcion, for she hadde neuer be
open to drinke mannes blode ne hadde neuer hadde the c[ur]se of
thornes ne sepulture of dede ne she hadde neuer be ete of serpentis.
Wherfor it behou[ed] that a nwe Adam were made that right as the
serpent hadde ouercome hym that was born of the erthe virgine were 220
ouercome of hym that was born of the Virgine Marie, and that he
hadde ouercome in para|dise were made temptour of oure Lorde in f. 21ra
the deserte, and for that he hadde ouercome Adam in etyn[g] were
ouercome of oure Lorde in fastyng.'

And whanne he was thus ouercome another, that hight Beniamyn, 225
come forthe and saide: 'How myght youre Cryst be the sone of God
that was tempted withe the fende so [that] atte the ende he was
constreyned to make brede of stones, and anone he was leffte up vpon
the hyght of the Temple for to worship that same fende?' Thanne
saide Seint Siluester: 'Yef the fende ouercome Adam in that he leued 230
hym and ete of the appill, right so it is trewe that the fende was

202 it²] add well and G   206 neded] nedeþe H1M   halowed] add as del. H1   after]
on erasure H1   208 toke] add in þe with in del. H1   209 in] that E   210 but . . .
halwe] ins. H1   211 holde] om. E   213 the .vj.] om. G   215 was] ins. H1
216 was] om. G   217 curse] crosse EH1MG (maudicon P2)   219 behoued] M,
behouithe EH1G (conuint P2)   221 he] add 'þat' H1   222 ouercome] add 'Adam' H1
temptour] temptouris G   223 hadde] wolde G   etyng] etyn E   225 he was] ins. H1
226 forthe] om. G   youre] om. H1   227 the¹] a G   that²] om. E   228 leffte up]
sette G   229 Thanne] And changed to þan H1   230 Seint] om. H1   Yef] Of H1

ouercome and dispised of Ihesu Crist in fastyng, and it is trewe that he
was not tempted as God but as man. He was tempted in thre maners
for that he wolde take awaye alle these temptaciones from us and
235 [yeue] us [a forme] and [a] rule for to ouercome temptacions.'

And thanne was Beniamyn ouercome, and ther come another, þat
hight Archell, and saide: 'It is trewe that God is souereynli parfit and
hathe nede of nothyng. Wherfor hadde he thanne nede that he shulde
be born in Crist, and wherfor callest thou Crist the sone of God? For
240 it is trewe that before that he hadde a sone he myght not be called
fader, and thanne yef he after be called fader of Crist he is meueable as
in that.' Siluester ansuered and saide: 'The sone was engendered of
the fader before all tyme for to make that that was not, and he was
born in tyme for to reforme that was loste. And though he myght do it
245 bi his onli worde, yet bi his owne rightwisnesse he myght not beye
ayein man but yef he hadde bene a man and but he suffered dethe. |
f. 21rb And that was not of inperfeccion but of perfeccion. And bi that
appere[th] it that worde to be saide of the sone that the prophete
saiethe: "Myn hert hathe putte oute a good worde." For God was
250 alway fader, and his sone is the worde of hym, and the wisdom after
Dauid: "Myn herte putte oute a worde etc." He was alwayes wisdom
after that: "I went oute of the mowthe of the right hye and was furst
engendered before alle creatoures." He was alwayes vertue after this
sentence: "Before alle [hillys I was engendered and before alle] wellys
255 [of] waters weren." And whanne the fader was neuer witheoute worde
that is wisdom and vertue, how wenest thou that this [name] be come
to hym in tyme?' And thanne he was putte awaye.

And the .ix., that hight Iubal, come forthe and saide: 'It is true that
God ne condempneth ne vncondempnithe not mariage ne blamithe it
260 not. [Whi] thanne denye ye that he was not born in mariage but yef [ye]
thought to hyndre the dignite of maryage? And yet ouer [that], how
was he tempted that is myghti, how suffered he dethe that is vertue,
and he that is lyff was dede? Atte the ende thou shalt be constreyned to

235 yeue] thanne EH1M, *add* `to ȝefe´ H1   a forme] enforme EH1M   a²] *om.* EH1M
236 come] was H1   237 souereynli] so uereynli E, so verreli H1, so/uereynli M
243 all] olde G   244 though] þouȝt G   247 that¹] *om.* G   248 appereth]
appered E   250 alway] halewis G   253 this] his G   254 hillys . . . alle] *om.*
EH1M   255 of] and EH1M   weren] *om.* G   256 name] may EM, mai *del. and ins.*
name be H1   be come] become E, come H1   257 in] *add* of EH1MG (*en temps* P2)
258 And] *add* þanne G   Iubal come forthe] Iubas Camborth G   It is] *trs.* G
260 Whi] whanne E, Whan *changed to* Whey H1   ye] he *changed to* ȝe E, he H1   thought]
taught H1   261 [that] *om.* E   263 he] *om.* G   EH1MG *begin sentence at* Thou,
but a paraph before´Thou *has been erased in* H1

saye that ther were two sones, one that the fader engendered, another
that the Virgine bare. And how myght it be done that man that is 265
receyued suffered dethe witheoute hertyng of hym he is receyued?'
Siluester ansuered: 'We saie noght that Ihesu Crist was born of a
virgine to condempne mariage, but resonabli the causes of the
virgynial chylding worshipen rather mariages in as moche as the
Virgine that bare Ihesu Crist was bore in maryage. Ihesu Crist was 270
tempted for he wolde surmounte alle temptaciones of the fende. He
suffered dethe for he wolde surmounte alle passi|ones. He deied for he f. 21ᵛᵃ
wolde destroie the empire of dethe. The sone of God is one only in
Ihesu Crist, and ryght as he is verray the sone of God so is he one in
Crist, and right as he is one only God in Crist invisible [right so Ihesu 275
Crist is visible. He is invisible] in as moche as longithe to God, and
visible in as moche as he is man. For mankynde taken may suffre
dethe witheoute lesion of hym that takithe it. And it may be shewed bi
ensaumple of the pourpre of the kyngges that was wolle, and whanne
the dye[r] toke this wolle he gaue it coloure of purpure. And whanne 280
she was deyed and sponne into threde, I aske the this question, whedir
the coloure of purpure of the riall dignite was sponne, either the wolle
whiche was his manhede. And yet was the purpure coloure whiche
was his godhede withe the wolle his manhede whanne he suffered
dethe in the crosse, but the passion was al hole in the manhede.' And 285
thanne was he ouercome.

  The .x., that hight Thara, come forthe and saide: 'This ensaumple
likithe me not, for it most nedes be that the coloure is turned withc the
wolle.' And whanne alle ayeinsaide it Seint Siluester saide: 'I shalle
shewe the annother ensaumple. A tre that the sonne shineth on, 290
whanne a man hewith it the tree receyuithe the stroke and the
bryghtnesse of the sonne felithe no disese. Right so whanne þe man
suffered, the Godhede suffered not.'

  And thanne the .xj., that hyght Siloo, saide: 'Yef the profites haue
devined these thingges of thi Crist that bene of so gret folies and iapes, 295
yet we wolde fayne wete the causes of his passion and dethe.' Thanne

264 another] *add* þanne G   265 that²] *add* a G   266 receuyed¹] resonyd G
witheoute] 'with'oute H1   267 that] *add* þat H1   270 bore . . . was] *ins.* H1
273 one] *om.* G   274 and right . . . in Crist] *om.* G   275–6 right . . . invisible] *om.* E
277 taken may] *trs.* H1   279 pourpre] propretre H1, power G   280 the] *add*
'pouer' H1   dyer] dye EM   281 she] it G   282 of¹] *add* the E   sponne] *add* 'þe
whiche was his godhede' H1   283–4 manhede . . . his¹] *om.* G   287 Thara come]
Tharacaon co G   288 that . . . is] *add* 'þat þe colour is be' *del.* H1   coloure is]
colouris G   292 þe] *changed from* a E   296 causes] cause G

Siluester saide: 'Ihesu Crist hadde hunger for to fulfelle us, and thruste for to refresche us with euerlastyng drinke, he was tempted for to deliuer us from temptacion, he was holden and bounden for to f. 21vb deliuer | us from the boundes of the fende, he was dispised for to
301 bryng us oute of despite of fendes, he was bounden for to vnlowse the knotte of [curs], he was made lowe for to enhaunse us, he was dispoiled for to hide oure nakednesse of the furst disobeisaunce, he receiued a croune of thornes for he wolde yelde us the floures of
305 paradise that were loste, he was hangged in the crosse for he wolde condampne the couetise that was come of the tree, he tasted eysell and galle for that he wolde bryng man in the londe that rennithe oyle and hony, he receyued deth for to yeue us vndedlynesse, he was beried for to blesse the sepulcres of the dede, he stied into heuene for to open us
310 the gate, he sitte in the right side of [his] fader for to enhaunce the praiers of [true] peple.' And as Siluester saide these thyngges, the emperour [and] alle that other peple beganne gretly to preise Siluester.

And thanne the .xij., that hight Zambry, saide bi gret despite: 'I
315 mervaille gretli that ye that bene so wise iuges leuen the wordes of so gret trufulles and that ye discriven the myght of God to be enclosed vnder mannes reson. But late us cese of wordes and go we to the dede. For I schalle preue hem foles that worshipen the crucified, for I wote well that rocches ne no livyng creature may endure to here the name
320 of almyghti God. And for that I wolle proue that I saie trouthe, bryng hedir to me a cruell and a fyers boole, and as sone as that name I shall soune in his ere he shall deie.' Thanne saide Siluester: 'Hou [lernydest] thou that name whan thou myghtest not here it?' And Zambri saide: 'It apertenethe not the to knowe that art enemye of
325 Iues.'

Thanne was ther brought a boole that vnnethes an hundred men f. 22ra myght not holde, and as sone as Zambry hadde saide the worde | in his ere he turned up the eyen and deide anone. And thanne alle the Iues assailden gretli Siluester withe huge crie, to whom Siluester saide:
330 'Wetithe well that he hathe named no name of God but the name of a

299–300 temptacion . . . from] *om.* G   300 boundes] handis G   301 vnlowse]
lose G   302 curs] cours E, ours H1M   303 of] Of *beginning new sentence* EM
304 us] vp G   308 hony] *add* and E   310 his] the EM   311 true] pore EM
peple] *add* and true EM   312 and] of EM   314 .xij.] *add* cam G   Zambry] Yambri
H1, *add* and G   319–20 name of] *om.* G   320 of] *add* þe M   that^2 . . . trouthe] and
seide þoru3 G   321 as sone] *om.* H1   that name] *add* is seid H1, *om.* G   shall] *om.* G
322 ere] *add* `&' H1   323 lernydist] berest EH1M   324 that] *add* þat H1M

wicked fende, for oure Lorde Ihesu Crist makithe not onli dede tho
that lyuen but he yeuithe lyf to the dede. For to sle and not to make
lyue ayein longithe to lyones and to serpentes and to wilde bestis. If he
wille that I leue that he se[i]de not the name of a fende, late hym saie it
ayein and make to lyue that he hathe slayn. For it is writen of God, "I   335
shalle sle and make to lyue ayein," and yef he may not do it, trustithe
fulli that he named the name of a fende that may slee and not make to
lyue ayein.' And whanne he was constreyned bi the iuges to arere the
bole he saide: 'Late Siluester arere hym [in] the name of Ihesu of
Galilee, and thanne we shull leue on hym. For though he cowde fle   340
withe wynges he coude not bryng it aboute.' And thanne alle the
Iewes behighten to beleue yef Siluester cowde arere hym. And thanne
Siluester made his praiere and went to the bole and sayde in his ere:
'O thou cursed name of dethe, go oute in the name of oure Lord Ihesu
Crist in whos name I lefte the up. Bole, goo forthe debonayrli withe   345
thi bestaile.' Thanne the bole arose mekeli and went forthe, and
thanne alle the Iwes and the iuges weren conuerted to the faithe.

And withein a while after, the bisshoppes of idoles comen to the
emperour and saide: 'Right holi emperour, sithe ye receyued the
feithe of Ihesu Crist, the dragon that was in the pitte hathe slayn a   350
thousand men euery day bi his brething.' And thanne the emperour
counsayled withe Siluester in this matere, | and Siluester ansuered: 'Bi   f. 22ʳᵇ
the vertue of Ihesu Crist I shalle make hym cese of his malice.' And
thanne alle the bisshoppes behight hym to beleue yef he dede that.
And thanne appered Seint Peter to Siluester that was in his praiers   355
and saide: 'Goo downe suerly to the dragon thiselff and two prestes
that thou haue withe the, and whanne thou comest into the place saie
in this wise: "Sathanas, abide in this place vnto the comyng of oure
Lorde Ihesu Crist, borun of a virgine, crucifyed, beried, and risen
ayein from dethe to lyff, and sitte in the ryght honde of his fader, that   360
shalle come to iuge [the] quik and [the] dede," and thanne bynde his
mowthe with a threde two tymes and sele it with a ryng that hathe a
crosse, and ye shul come after me hole and sounde and shul ete of the
brede that I haue made for you.'

And thanne Siluester went doune withe two prestes and bere with   365
h[y]m many lanternes, and thanne saide the wordes that Peter

331 dede] deþ `to' Hı, deth to G   334 seide] sende E   a] þe Hı   337 a] þe Hı
338–9 the bole . . . arere] om. G   339 in] om. EM   342 beleue] add in God G, so ins.
Hı   thanne] add seint HıG   346 bestaile] bestes alle Hı   347 and the iuges] om. G
349 Right] om. G   351 bi his] bi hire Hı, his G   brething] bretheren G   356 and
saide] ins. Hı   361 the¹˒²] om. EHı   366 hym] hem E

bade hym saye, bounde and seled his mouthe, [and] whan he come up
ayein he fonde two enchauntours that hadde folued hym for to see the
ende and were as dede with the stynke of the dragon. And Seint
370 Siluester brought hem forthe hole and sounde withe hym, and anone
they were conuerted and a gret multitude of peple witheoute nombre
withe hem. And thus bi [the] merites of Seint Siluester weren the
peple of Rome deliuered from double dethe, þat is to knowe for the
worshipping of ydoles and [fro] the venyme of the dragon.
375 And in the ende whanne the blessid Seint Siluester neighed his
dethe, he taught the clergy that they shuld haue charite among hem
and that they shulde diligentely governe her chirches and kepen her
f. 22ᵛᵃ shepe fro the | bytyng of wolues. And thus he taught and saide, [and]
he slepte [blessidli] in oure Lorde Ihesu Crist.

Here endithe the lyff of Seint Siluester, and nexst
beginnethe the Circumcision of oure Lorde Ihesu Crist,
Capᵐ. .xij.ᵐ

Fowre thyngges maken the day of [the] Circumcision of oure Lorde
worshipfull and solempne. The furste is the vtas of his natiuite, the
secounde the imposicion of his nwe name, the .iij. the effusion of his
blode, the ferthe the token of the circumcision.
5 The furst thing is the vtas of the natiuite, wherein we beseche that
þat we haue lacked to fulfille in his feste, that is to saie the Office of his
birthe where men were wont to syng som tyme in the worship of the
blessed Virgine Marie *Vultum tuum et c.*
The secounde thing is the imposicion of the nwe name bryngynge
10 helthe, for this day was yeue hym the [nwe] name that the mowthe of
God named, the name witheoute whiche ther nys none other vnder
the heuene that may make us sauf, the name of whiche Seint Bernard
saieth that it ys hony in the mouthe, suete melodie in the ere, ioie in
the herte, the name that rennythe as oyle, and that precheth, fedithe
15 and kepithe in mynde, it assuageth and callithe on that same and it
anointeth.

367 bade hym saye] had seide G   and²] *om.* E   369 and] *add* `þei´ H₁, *add* þay G
370 forthe] *om.* G   372 the¹] *om.* E   Seint] *om.* H₁   373 for] from H₁
374 fro] for E   375 blessid] bisshop G   377 her¹] þe G   378 and²] *om.* E, `&´
H₁   379 blessidli] besili EH₁   Ihesu Crist] *om.* H₁

EH₁GA₁A₂   1 the²] *om.* EH₁   7 wont] *ins.* H₁   7–8 in . . . *et c*] *space left
only for the Latin* G   10 nwe] true EH₁   12 sauf] *add* saue G   14 precheth]
precheð H₁G   16 anointeth] anoieþ H₁

And as the gospell saiethe, he hadde thre names, sone of God, Ihesus and Cristus. He was called sone of God in as moche as he was of God, Ihesus in as moche as he was assembeled to the manhede, Cristus in as moche as he is man, and persone devine in as moche as to 20 the humanite. And of these trebel names saieth Seint Bernard: 'Ye that bene in pou|der wake and preisen God. Lo, here how he comithe f. 22vb withe hele, he comythe with oynement, he comithe with ioie, for Ihesus comithe not witheoute hele, ne Crist witheoute oynement, ne the sone witheoute ioie, for he is helthe, unccion and ioie. But before 25 his passion he was not perfitely knowe that he hadde the trebel names. He was knowe of somme thou it were but of fewe.

And after the resureccion these trebell names were glorified, the furst as to the certeynte, the secounde as to the cominitee, and the thridde as to [the] reson of the name. The furst name is the sone of 30 God, and that name aperteynith most to hym, as Seint Hillarie saith in the boke of the Trinite: 'He is knowe in diuerse maners for to be verely þe sone of God. O only sone of God is oure Lorde Ihesu Crist, for the fader witnessithe it, the aposteles preche it, religio[u]s leuen it, the fendes confessen it, the paynimes knewen it, and the Iues denyden 35 it. We kn[o]wen oure Lorde Ihesu Crist by name, by natiuite, by nature, bi myght, and bi procession.' The secounde name is Crist, that is as moche to saie as anoynte, for he was anoynted with the oynter of gladnesse before his participans. And bi that he sei[t]h 'oynt' he shew[ith] that he was prophete, champion, preste and kyng. These 40 foure persones weren somtyme anoynt. He was prophete in techyng doctrine, champion in ouercomyng the fende, preste in reconsilyng of pees, [kyng in gerdonyng] of gerdons. And for that [he was] named Crist. Seint Austin therfor saiethe: 'Cristen is a name of verrey rightwisnesse, of bounte, of purete, of pacience, of clennesse, of 45 humanite, of innocence, and of pitee. | How defendest thou that name f. 23ra appropred to the in whiche ther bene so many notable thingges? He is cristen that is not only by name but be werke.' The .iij. name is Ihesus. 'This name,' saiethe Seint Bernard, 'is of suche vertue that as

19 assembeled] asymplid G   20 to] *om.* G   21 trebel] trembel *with* m *del.* E
22 pouder] *add* & EHı   23 hele . . . with³] *om.* Hı   26 trebel] þre G
27 somme] þe sone G   29 cominitee] communyte G   30 the¹] *om.* E   33 O]
ins. Hı, *om.* G   only] *add* þe Hı   God is] *om.* Hı   34 religious] religiones EG
35 knewen] knowen Hı   denyden] denyen Hı   36 knowen] knewen E
38 anoynte] anoynted Hı, oyntid G   39 seith] seigh E   40 shewith] shewed EHı,
swetith G (*demonstre* P2)   43 kyng in gerdonyng] *om.* E   he was] *trs.* E   44 therfor]
þerof Hı   45 purete] pouerte Hı

50 many tyme as thou recordest it so many tymes thou shalt be
comforted. He defendethe from ydell thougthes and comfortithe
tho that bene assailed withe the fende, he yeuithe wisdom and
vertue, he drawithe to hym good and honest condiciones and
norische[th] chaste willes.'

55   Secoundely he is sayed the welle seled that springethe oute in foure
stremes, wherof Seint Bernarde saiethe: 'Ihesus is the welle seled of
whom springgen oute foure stremes, for he is to us oure wysdom, oure
rightwisnesse, oure halowyng, and oure redempcion; wisdom in
predicacion, rightwys in absolucion of synnes, holy in conuersacion,

60 redemptor bi his passion.' And in other places saith Seint Bernard:
'There rennen oute of the name [of] Ihesu quik spryngges, that is to
saie worde of sorughe in whiche is betokened confession, also water of
clensyng wherinne ys betokened compunccion.'

        Also this is the medicine [wher]of Seint Bernard saiethe: 'This

65 name Ihesus ys medicyne, and re[f]reineth the strengthe of wratthe, yt
appesith the bolnyng of pride, he helithe the woundes of enuye, he
restreyneth the fere of lecherie, and it quenchith the flame of
coueitise, it attemperithe the thruste of auarice, and chasith oute all
filthe and wrechidnesse.'

70   Also this name Ihesus is lyght, [as] Seint Bernard saiethe: 'Wenest
thou that so gret and so sodeyn a lyght of feithe myght come into this
worlde but only bi the vertue of this name Ihesus? This is the name
f. 23rb that Seint | Paule bere afore the gentiles, and the voys therof was
[l]yght brennyng fulle of suetnesse.' Wherof Seint Richarde of Seint

75 Victorie: 'Ihesus is a comfortable and delectable name of good spede
and of good hope,' where he saithe: 'Swete Ihesu, be to me Ihesus.'

        Also this is a name of gret vertue, wherof Pers of Rauenys saith:
'Ihesus is the name that yeuithe lyght to the blynde, hering to the
deef, goyng to the lame, speking to the domme, liff to the de[d]e, and

80 the vertue of this name chasithe oute alle the pouer of fendes.'

        Also this is a name of gret excellence and of hynesse, wher Seint
Bernarde saiethe: 'The name of my saueoure, of my brother, of my

50 tyme . . . many] *om.* G   54 norischeth] norisched E   55 seled] sealed *with* a
subp. H1   56–7 wherof . . . stremes] *om.* H1   61 of²] *om.* E   63 compunccion]
compassion G   64 wherof] of EH1   Bernard] *add* þat H1   65 refreineth]
restreineth E   66 he¹] *om.* H1   68 all] þe H1   69 filthe] *add* as seint bernard
seith G   70 as] and E   70–1 Wenest thou that] we wiste not how G   72 Ihesu
. . . name] *om.* G   73 bere] bere`þ´ H1   gentiles] gentilues E   74 lyght] hyght E
Wherof] *add* seiþe H1   75 and delectable] *om.* G   good] god H1   75–6 spede . . .
good] *om.* G   79 dede] dethe E   80 chasithe] chased H1   of] *add* þe H1
81 hynesse] heuynesse G   82 The name] *changed to* þis name `is´ H1, this name is G

flesche, the name hid fro worldes but he is sheued in the ende of
worldes, a name merveylable, a name incomperable, a name inestim-
able.' 85

And this name Ihesus was yeuen of euerlastingnesse, of the aungell,
and of hym that men wende hadde bene his fader, that was Ioseph.
Ioseph is as moche to saie as saueoure.

The .iij. thing is the effusion of the blode of Ihesu Crist, [for on this
day he began furst to shede his blode for us,] the whiche he wolde 90
after shede in many maners. He shadde his precious blode for us in .v.
maners and .v. tymes: furst in his circumcision; the seconde tyme in
orison tofore his passion, whanne he suette blode and water; the .iij.
tyme in scourgyng; the ferthe in his crucifieng; and the .v. in [the]
openyng of his side, and that was the sacrement of oure redempcion. 95
And ther went oute blode and water, and that signified that we shulde
be clensid bi water of baptime and that hit most haue his strengthe of
the precious blode of Ihesu Crist.

The ferthe and the laste thing is | the signe of his circumcision, the f. 23ᵛᵃ
whiche he toke on this day. Ihesu Crist wold be circumcised for many 100
causes. The furst cause was for that he wolde shewe that he hadde take
verray mankinde, for he wost well that many wolde saie that he hadde
not take a verray bodi but a fantastik bodi, wherfor he wolde be
circumcised for to destroie that errour and shedde oute his blode in
that place that thei myght see that he was verray man and that a 105
fantastik body hathe no blode.

Men sayn þat of the flesche of the circumcision of Ihesu Crist the
aungel brought to Charles the Gret and he putte it worshipfulli in
Aays in the chirche of Oure Ladi. And after that it was translated to
Chartres. And now thei sayn that it is atte Rome withein the chirche 110
that is called *Sancta Sanctorum*, and ther they sain also is the precious
nauill of oure Lorde Ihesu Crist. And this same day is made stacion in
that chirche of *Sancta Sanctorum*.

84 merveylable] mervaill H1   86 And] *add* as G   yeuen of] euen for H1
euerlastingnesse] euerlastyng G   91 shede] schewe G   94 the³] *om*. E
96 signified] signifieþe H1   97 hit] vs G   his] the G   100 circumcised]
circumcidid G   100–1 for many causes] *ins*. H1   102 well] *om*. H1   106 hathe]
had H1   blode] *on erasure* H1   112 day] *om*. G

Here endithe the Circumcision of oure Lorde, and nexst
beginnithe the fest of the .xij.^{te} day whiche is called
Epiphanye, Cap^m. .xiij.^m

The Epiphanie of oure Lorde is worshipped by foure myracles, and
therfor sche is named by foure names. For on this day the .iij. kyngges
comen whanne thei hadde sain the sterre fro orient to worship oure
Lorde in Bethelem, Seint Iohn baptised oure Lorde in the flode of
5 Iordane, and [the] water was turned into wyne, and he fedde .vM.¹
men with .v. loues.

Whanne oure Lorde was but thre dayes olde the .iij. kyngges come
to hym by the sterre that ledde hem, and for that is this day called
[the] Epiphanye as it is saide aboue, for the sterre appered thanne an
f. 23vb high and shewed | well to these .iij. kyngges that Ihesu Crist was
11 verray God. And in that same [day] .xx.^{ti}.ix. wynter after, as he
neyghed the .xxx.^{ti} yere, after Beede he was .xxx.^{ti} yere full and the
Chirche [of Rome] affermithe it to holde, thanne he was baptized in
the flode of Iordan. And therfor it is called Epiphanye, of Theos, that
15 is as moche to saye as God, and of Phanus, that ys to saie apparicion,
for thanne the Trinite appered, the fader appered in vois, the sone in
fleshe, the holy goste in lyknesse of a douve. In that same daye the
yere after, whanne he was .xxx.^{ti}.j. yere, he turned water into wyne,
and therfor it is saide Beth[f]anye, of Beth, that is to saye hous, and
20 Phanos, aparacion, for by the miracle done in the hous he appered to
be verray God. And in that same day the yere after, whanne he was
.xxx.^{ti}.ij. yere, he fedde .v. thousand men with .v. loues, so as Bede
saiethe in an ympne that is songe in many chirches, that beginnithe in
this wise, *Illuminas altissimus*. And for that is she saide Phagyphanie,
25 of Phage, that is as moche to saye as mete. But of this myracle
wh[ether] it was done in this day it is doute, for it is not expressely
redde in the Original of Bede. And also for that that Iohn saieth wher
he spekithe of this thing that it was nigh Ester. And the apparicion is
thanne made thries on this day. The furst was made by the sterre in

EH1GA1A2; H2 resumes at 41 *Herode whanne*; D resumes at 168 *in*. The more
substantial omissions from G in this chapter are also omitted from H2, and from D
when running.   2 sche] it G   5 the] *om*. E   7 thre] .xij. H1   9 the¹] *om*. E
11 day] *om*. E   12 .xxx.^{ti ¹}] *add* wyntir aftir as he ney3id to þritty G   Beede] dede G
13 of Rome] *om*. E   18 yere²] *add* olde G   19 Bethfanye G] Bethanye E, Bethenai
H1   22 yere] *add* there EH1   24 *Illuminas altissimus*] *space left blank* G
Phagyphanie] Plaginaphye G   25 Phage] Plage G   26 whether] whanne E   it²]
þer G   27 that that] þat G   29 made¹ . . . was] *ins*. H1

the crache, the secounde by the vois of the fader in the flode of Iordan, 30
the .iij. in turnyng water into wyne, the .iiij. by the multeplyeng of the
brede in the desert. The furst apperyng was made this day of the .iij.
kyngges, and for that we will folue the storie therof.

Whanne oure Lorde was born, the .iij. kyngez come into Ierusalem,
of whiche the | names bene in Ebrewe *Arcellus, Damerius, Damascus,* f. 24ra
and in Greke *Gorgalath, Malgalach, Sarachi,* and in Latyn *Iasper,* 36
Melchior, Balthasar. And ther bene thre causez whi these kyngges
bene called Magi, for this name Magus is as moche to saie as an
enchauntour, a scornere, or wise. For some [sayne] that these kyngges
were called after ther gouernaunce, that is to saie scorners, for that 40
thei scorned Herode whanne they turned not ayein to hym. And
whanne Herode seigh that thei turned not ayein to hym, he was
troubled. And therfor saiethe Seint Cr[i]sostome þat these kyngges
were called Magos for that thei hadde bene wicked doers but thei were
conuerted after, for whanne oure Lorde wolde shewe to hem his 45
natiuite and bryng hem to hym so [that] be that signe he shewed that
he wolde yeue pardon to synners. And Magos is as moche to saie as
wise, for Magus in Ebrewe is to saie scribe, in Greke philosophie, in
Latin wise, and therfor thei bene saide Magi as grete in wisdom.

And these thre kyngges come with gret companye into Ierusalem, 50
but the cause that they come thedir sethe oure Lorde was not born
ther Seint [Remy assigneth] foure resones. The furst for they knewe
well the tyme of the natiuite of oure Lord but thei knewe not the
place, and for that Ierusalem was a citee riall and that souerein
presthode was there, thei hadde suspecion that so noble a child shulde 55
not be born but yef it were in so noble a citee. The secounde for that
thei myght the sonner wete the place of his natiuite for the wise men
and [the] maistres of [the] lawe duelled there. The .iij. that the Iwes
myght not sain: 'We knewe not the place of his natiuite and we knewe
not the tyme, | and therfor we leued not,' for the kyngges shewden the f. 24rb
tyme [to the Iues] and the Iues sheued the place to the kyngges. [The 61
.iiij. that be the curiosite of the kyngges] the slouthe of the Iues shuld
be condempned, for the kyngges leuedyn [oo] only prophete and the

37 these] *add* .iij. H1   39 or] of H1   sayne] some E   42 seigh] *ins.* H1   hym]
add and G   43 Seint] *add* Iohn G, *so ins.* H1   Crisostome] Crosostome E
44 hadde bene] were G   45–6 his . . . hem] *ins.* H1   46 that¹] *om.* EH1   47 is]
add also G   49 Magi] *om.* G   51 sethe] seieþ H1   52 Remy assigneth] Remya
singeth EH1   53 not] wel G   58 the¹] *om.* EH1   the²] *om.* E   59 knewe¹]
know H1G   knewe²] know H1G   60 leued] leue G   shewden] shewen H1   61 to
the Iues] *om.* E   61–2 The . . . kyngges] *om.* E   63 oo] *om.* EH1   onely] *add* the E

Iues wolde not leue many prophetes; the kyngges soughten a straunge
65 kynge and the Iues wolde not seke thaire owne; the kyngges come
from ferre contre and the Iues weren nye. The kyngges weren
successours of Balaam and come to the vision of the sterre bi the
prophecie of her fader that saide: 'A sterre shalle arise of Iacob and a
man shal be born of Israel.' Crisostom putte another cause wherfor
70 that they come in his Original vpon Mathew in affermyng that some
saide that there were a certayne that toke [kepe to] the secretes of
heuene, and thei chosen .xij.ᵉ of hemselff for to take continuelli hede,
and yef any of hem deied hys sone or som other of his kynne shulde be
in his stede.

75   And these .xij.ᵉ went vpon an high hille and wa[s]hed hem and
praied oure Lorde that he wolde shewe hem that sterre that Balaam
hadde saide hem before. And so it felle that on the day of the natiuite
of oure Lord, so as thei were there a sterre apered to hem aboue the
hille that hadde the fourme of a fayre litell childe and another sterre
80 that shined bright vpon his hede, the whiche aresoned the kyngges,
seyeng in this wise: 'Gothe in gret haste into the londe of Iudee and
ther ye shulle fynde the kyngge that ye seke.' And Austin putte
another cause whi that they remeued for the sight of the sterre, for it
myght be that an aungell appered to hem and saide: 'The sterre þat ye
85 see is of Ihesu Crist. Gothe and worship hym.' And Leon putte an
f. 24ᵛᵃ nother | cause and saithe that bi the sterre that apered so clere to hem
the doctrine of God was taught in her hertis.

And thanne thei begonne anone to goo. But how thei come in so
shorte tyme as in .xiij. dayes the space of so many myles fro orient into
90 Ierusalem that is in the middes of the worlde, it may be saide after
Seint Remy that so blessed a childe as thei hasted to seke myght
lightly bring hem in as shorte tyme as hym luste. And it may be saide
after Ierome that thei come vpon dromedaries that bene swifte bestes
and rennen more in a day thanne an horse in thre dayes.

95   And whanne thei come into Ierusalem thei asked and saide: 'Where
is he that is born the kyng of Iwes?' Thei asked not yef he were born,
for thei beleued verrily, and asked: 'Wher is he born?' And as som
myght aske hem: 'How knowe ye that he is born?' thei ansuered: 'We
haue sain his sterre in orient and bene come to worship hym, that is to

64 leue] *ins.* H1   65 seke] *om.* G   owne] *add* propre kynge G   71 kepe to] *om.*
E, `kepe´ to H1   73 kynne] kende G   75 washed hem] wached hem E, *so with* cc *on*
erasure H1, watchid G (*lauoient* P2)   77 day] *add* of þe dai *del.* H1   82 that] and G
83 for¹] fro G   85 putte] puttith G   86 saithe] seid H1   89 so] *om.* H1
92 as¹] a H1G   93 Ierome] Ieremie H1   99 sain his] the G

saie we that were in orient sene his sterre shewing his natiuite, whiche 100
was sette vpon Iudee.' And as Remy saieth in his Original: 'Thei
confessid hym verray man, verray kyng and verray God be these
wordes: a verrei man whanne thei said: "Where is he that is born?";
verrey kyng whanne thei saide: "Kyng of Iues"; verrai God whanne
thei said: "We bene come to worship hym," for it was comaunded 105
that ther shulde none be worshypped but God allone.' And after
Crisostome thei confessed that same to be verrai God be worde, by
dede and bi yeftes.

And whanne Herode [herde this he] was troubled, and al Ierusalem
withe hym. This kyng Herode was gretly troubled [by] thre causes: 110
the furst he dredde [lest] that the Iues wolde refuse hym as a straunger
and take this nwe born kyng for her lorde, wherof Crisos|tome saieth f. 24ᵛᵇ
that ryght [as] a light wynde takithe awaye the bowe of a tree that
stondithe an high, right so a light renomes troubelithe hem that bene
enhaunsed and sette in the hille of dignite; secoundely lest he were 115
blamed of the Iues if eny were called kyng the which the emperour
hadde not ordeyned; thirdeli, that as Gregori saiethe, whan the kyng
of heuene was bore the kyng of [the] erthe was wrothe. What
meruaile, for erdely [high]nesse was confounded whanne the highnesse of heuene apered. 120

Alle tho of Ierusalem were wroth and troubled withe hym for thre
causes. The furst was for that [that] the comyng of that rightwise
kynge shulde lette them that thei myght not reioyse the empire; the
secounde for to flater the kyng that was wrothe for to shewe hem
wrothe withe hym; the thridd that right as wyndes troublen the waters 125
and make hem to turne and meve, right so whanne kyngges contrarien
togeders the rewmes bene troubled, where thei dradde that the
present kyng and the kynge to come shulde falle in contencion
wher thorugh thei shulde be lapped in tribulacion. And this is [the]
reson of Crisostome. 130

And thanne Herode assembeled alle the prestes and the wise men of
the lawe and enquered of hem where Crist shulde be born. And
whanne he hadde lerned of hem that he shulde be born in Bethlem of

105 was] is G   106 be] ins. H₁   worshypped] add and del. H₁   but] add he G
109 Herode] he H₁   herde this he] thus E   110 by] withe E   111 lest] om. E
wolde refuse] refusid G   112 take] toke G   113 as] om. E   takithe] so with tak on
erasure H₁   115 he] add we del. H₁   116 eny] add kyng G   118 the²] om. EH₁
119 erdely] erthly H₁G   highnesse] heuinesse EH₁   121 tho] add þat were G
122 that²] om. E   rightwise] two words E   123 them] him changed to hem H₁
124-5 for² . . . hym] om. G   125-45 that . . . thridde] om. G   129 the] om. E

Iudee, he called to hym these kyngges priueli and enquered of hem
135 bisily the tyme of the sterre for to knowe what he wolde do and the
kyngges come not ayein to hym, and saide [hem] that whanne they
hadde founde the childe thei shulde sende hym worde and he wolde
come and worschip hym as thei dede, but his fals cursed entent was to
slee hym.

f. 25ᵃ   And wetithe well that as | sone as thei were entered into Ierusalem
141 thei loste the condit of the sterre for thre resones. The furst was for
that thei shulde be constreyned for to enquere the apperyng of the
sterre as bi the certeficacion of the prophesie, and so it was done; the
secounde cause was that as sone as thei [asked] mannes helpe thei loste
145 the devine helpe; the thridde was for [that] the tokenes of his natiuite
were yeven to true peple, and therfor this token of withedrawyng of
the sterre was yeuen to hem that were as yet misbileuers, and for that
she appered not to hem whiles they were among the Iues.

But as sone as thei come oute of Ierusalem the sterre apered and
150 went before hem til [he] come ouer the place wher þe childe was. Of
this sterre and of what maner she was Remy putte .iij. opiniones in his
Original. And som sain that it was the holi gost, as he that after
descended vpon oure Lorde whanne he was baptized in lyknesse of a
white douue, that same shulde apere to the .iij. kyngges in liknesse of a
155 sterre. The other, as Crisostome, saiethe that it was the aungell that
apered to the shepardes and that same apered to the kyngges. But he
apered to the shepardes that were Iues right as to hem that used reson
in resonable fourme, and to the panymes he apered in an vnresonable
fourme as to hem that were vnresonable. Some other sayn that it is
160 more credible that it was a sterre nwe made the whiche, his seruice
done, turned ayein to her propre mater.

And after [that] þat Fulgens saiethe thus, that sterre was difference
to other in thre thingges: in sittyng, for she was not sette in place
certayn in the firmament, but hanged in the middell of the eyre nye to
f. 25ʳᵇ the erthe; also in shinyng, for she | was more bryghter thanne other,
166 and þat shewith well in as moche as the light of the sonne myght not

134 kyngges] þinges *changed to* kinges *subp. with* kynges *in margin* H1   135–6 and . . .
hym] *del.* H1   136 hem] hym E   139 hym] hem H1   144 asked] loste E
145 that] *om.* E   147 sterre] *add* þat G   147–8 that . . . hem] *twice once marked for
deletion* H1   150 he] thei EH1   152 that²] *ins.* H1   154 shulde] childe *changed
to* shulde H1   155 The other as] The oþer was *changed to* oþer waise (?) H1   155–9
The other . . . were vnresonable] *om.* G   161 done] sone G   mater] *changed to* nature
H1, nature G   162 that¹] *om.* E   163 thre thingges] the þre kyngis G   sette] *om.*
H1

shadwe the clere lyght of her shynyng, but atte mydday sche apered
ryght bryght; and went before the kyngges in manere as it hadde bene
a gyde. The thre other difference bene touched in the Glose of
Mathew: the furst difference is in makyng of the sterre, for alle the 170
other were made fro the begynnyng of the worlde in one manere; the
secounde deference is in offys, for the other bene made in signes and
in tyme like as Genesis saiethe, and this sterre was made to shewe the
waye to the kyngges; the thridde difference is enduryng, for the other
bene made to last eucr, and this whanne his office was done turned 175
ayein to his furst mater.

  And whanne thei sene the sterre ayein thei were fulfelled with gret
ioie and entered into the hous and seen Mari and the childe, and thei
withe gret reuerence and drede kneled doune and worshipped the
childe and offered gold, encence and myrre. Hereof spekith Seint 180
Austin and saithe: 'O childehode to whom the sterris bene sogettis, of
whom this gretnesse of soueraigne preisyng is, the aungels preisen,
the sterris seruen, kyngges dreden. O thou blessed litell hous that art
made the sege of God.' Seint Ierome saiethe: 'O heuenli palais wherin
duellith a kyng not crowned but God corporat, to whom was 185
ordeyned an harde crache in stede of a softe and precious bedde,
thou hast the hynes of a smokyng hous, but she is worshipped bi the
seruice of sterres. I am abaished whanne I see thi pore cloutes in the
tone side and heuene in that other side, I wonder whanne I see a
begger in a crache þat is clere aboue alle the sterres.' And yet | saiethe f. 25ᵛᵃ
Seint Bernarde: 'What do ye kyngges that worshipen a litell childe 191
hidyng hym in a litell hous wrapped in vile clowtes? Is this the same
God? What do ye that offre to hym golde? Is he a kyng? Wher is his
riall halle? Wher is the felawship of his courte? Is not his halle a stable
and his trone a crache and the felawship Marie and Ioseph?' These 195
kyngges semed foles for they shulde be made wise. And of that saith
Seint Hillary in the secounde boke of the Trinite: 'The Virgine hadde
a childe but the childe is of God. The childe wepithe but the aungels
bene herde praising hym. The dignite of the myght is not loste thou
the mekenesse of the flesche be pershed.' Of this saiethe Seint Ierome 200

---

167 atte] as H1   169 thre] þirde H1   169–76 The . . . mater] *om.* G
176 mater] *changed to* nature H1   178 seen] sawe *on erasure* H1   181 childehode]
childe holde EG, childe be holde H1 (*enfance* P2)   184 wherin] where H1
184–90 Seint . . . yet] *om.* G   186 softe] lofte H1 and] *add* a H1   188 cloutes]
cloþes H1   190 saiethe/Seint Bernarde] *trs.* G   192 clowtes] clothis G
193 that] *add* ye H1, *om.* G   194 the] his H1   194–5 of his . . . felawship] *om.* H1
195–200 These . . . pershed] *om.* G   198 wepithe] wept H1

vppon the Pistell to the Ebrewes: 'Beholdithe the cradell of Ihesu
Crist and sethe the heuene togeders, beholde the childe weping in the
crache and herkenithe therwithe the aungels preysing hym. Herode
pursuithe hym but the kyngges worship hym, the philosofers
205 vnknewe hym but the sterre sheued hym, he is baptized of his
servaunt but the uoys of God is herde ouer hym, he is plunged in
the water but the holi goste descended vpon hym in likenesse of a
douve.'

Ther bene diuerse resones whi these kyngges offered to hym yeftes.
210 The furste reson is for that the custume of anciens was that none
shulde entre with voide honde to God ne to a kyng, and tho of Caldee
weren custumed to offre suche yeftes. The secounde is, as saieth Seint
Bernard, thei offered golde to þe blessed Virgine for to comfort her
pouertee, the ensence ayeinst the stinke of the stable, the mirre for to
215 comfort the membres of the childe and to take awaye al wicked
f. 25ᵛᵇ vermyn. The thridde cause for that golde longithe | to [the] truage,
ensence to sacrifice, mirre into the sepulture of dede, and bi these thre
thyngges [bene] signified in God Ihesu Crist pouste roial, devine
mageste and humane dethe. The ferthe is for that golde signifiethe
220 dileccion, ensence orison and myrre mortifieng of the flesche, and
these thre thingges we aught to offre to Ihesu Crist, that is to wete a
right precious dignite, a right deuoute soule, and a right chaste and
pure bodi.

These thre thyngges bene signified bi the thre thyngges þat weren
225 in the arke. For the yerde that floured signified the pure flesche of
Ihesu Crist that arose from dethe to lyff, wherof Dauid sai[eth]: 'My
flesche shall floure ayein.' The tables wherin the comaundementes
weren wreten signified the saule, where al the tresours of connyng
bene and al the wisdom of God. The name signified the dignite of
230 Ihesu Crist, that hathe al sauoure [and] al suetnesse. And bi the golde
that is most precious of alle metalles is vnderstonde the right precious
devinite; by the ensence the soule ryght devoute, for the ensence
signifieth deuocion and orison, wherof Dauid saiethe: 'Myn orison
shall be dressed before the as worthi ensence;' bi the mirre that
235 kepithe fro corrupcion is signified the corrupte fleshe.

202 the¹] ȝe G   203 and herkenithe] om. G   203–212 Herode . . . yeftes] om. G
210 that . . . that] om. H₁   212 Seint] om. G   216 the] om. EH₁   218 bene] om.
E, he G   219 humane] humanyte G   221 offre] affre changed to offre H₁
224–37 These . . . region] om. G   226 wherof] wherefore H₁   saieth] saide E
230 and²] om. E   232 the soule] om. H₁   232–3 for . . . orison] om. H₁

And thanne these kyngges that were taught in her slepe that thei shulde not repaire to Herode be turned ayein into her owne region. Se now how these kyngges wenten and comen, for thei come bi the condit of the sterre and were taught of the prophete and went home ayein by the condit of the aungell, and after þat thei rested in Ihesu 240 Crist, and the bodies atte Melane in the chirche that is now of oure bretherin, and now thei lyen atte reste in Coloyne.

Here endithe the fest of the Epiphanie, and thanne beginnithe the lyff of Seint Paule the | Hermite, Capitulum f. 26ʳᵃ .xiiij.ᵐ

Poule the furst hermite, as Seint Ierom saiethe that wrote the lyff of hym, witnessithe that whanne the feruent persecucion of Decy regned he went into a gret deserte and duelled there in a pitte fourti yere witheoute knowlage of man. And it is saide that this Decyen was of Galilee and hadde double name. He beganne the yere of oure Lorde 5 two hundred fifti and sixe. And whanne Seint Paule seigh so mani diuerse tormentes done to [the] cristen he fledde into the desert. And in that tyme two yongge men were taken that were cristen. T[h]e tone of hem was anointed alle the bodi withe hony and was sette in the brennyng of the sonne for to be perced and stonge withe the speres of 10 harnettes and waspes and alle other flies. The tother was leide in right a softe bedde in a delitable place wher ther was atemperaunce of eyre, the sowne of stremes, songe of briddes, suetnesse of floures couered withe fruit and floures of diuerse coloures, but he was so bounde that he myght not helpe hymselff withe fote nother withe honde. And 15 thanne [was] ther brought to hym [right] a faire yonge woman but ful vnchast [and] ful vnchasteli and wrechidly demenid this cristen man, and he, fu[l]felled withe the loue of God, whan he felt in his flesche steryng[es] contrarie to reson and he hadde none armure wherwith he myght defende hym from that cursed enemye, he bote his owne tonge 20 of withe his tethe and spete it in the visage of that vnshamefull woman, and the [anguyssh] therof chased awaye the temptacion, and

---

236 kyngges] þinges *changed to* kinges H1

EH1GDH2A1A2   1 hermite] tyme G   5 Galilee] Galee H1   7 the¹] *om.* E
8 The] te E   9 of hem] *om.* G   was¹] *om.* H1   10 perced] perischid G
16 was] *om.* E   right] *om.* EH1   17 vnchast . . . ful] *om.* G   and¹] *om.* E   and¹ . . .
vnchasteli] *om.* H1   18 fulfelled] fufelled E   19 sterynges] steryng EH1
21 of¹] *om.* G   it] *om.* G   22 anguyssh] anger EH1

thus he deserued victori of preysing. And thanne Seint Paule fered bi
f. 26rb thaire pey|nes and bi other and went into the desert.

25   [In] that tyme Antony duelled among the monkes and thought that
he wolde be furste in hermytage, and it was shewed hym in a vision
that ther was another hermyte [in deserte moche beter than he]. And
as he sought hym bi the forest[es] and wildernesse he mette a man that
was halff man and halff horse that shewed hym the waie in the right
30   honde. After [that] he mette a beeste that bere the fruit of palmers that
was [abouen] man and dounwarde in the fourme of a goete, and he
charged hym that bi vertue of oure Lorde that he shulde telle hym
what he was. He ansuered: 'I am a satirell, lorde of the wodis after the
erroure of panymes.' And atte the laste he mette a wolffe that brought
35   hym to the celle of Seint Poule. And Poule felt that Antonye come,
and shet faste his dores. And Antonye praied hym to open, for he
wold neuer parte thennes but rather deie euen there. Thanne Paule
was ouercome and opened the dore, and anone thei clipped eche
other. And whanne dyner tyme come a rauene brought double that he
40   was wont to do of brede, and Seint Antony wondered of this. Thanne
Poule saide that eueri daye oure Lorde mynistred to hym in suche
wise, 'and this day oure Lorde hathe doubeled my lyueray for my
geste sake.' And thanne ther beganne betwene hem a meke stryff who
was most worthi to parte the brede. Poule saide that his geste,
45   Antonye saide that his oste, and atte the laste thei sette on hondes
bothe atte onys and made euene partie.

And as Antony retorned ayein and neighed his celle he seigh the
aungels bering the saule of Poule an highe towarde heuene, and
f. 26va thanne in alle haste he turned ayein and fonde the body of | Poule
50   dressid on his knees in maner as he hadde praied, so that it semed
verrili that he lyued. And whanne he sawe hym dede he said: 'A, holi
soule, thou hast shewed atte thi dethe what thou vsed in thi lyff.' And
as he [ne hadde wherwith] to make the pitte ther come anone two
lyones that made it, and whanne he was beried thei turned ayein to the
55   wode. And Antony toke the cote of Poule that was woue of palmes and
werid it in highe daies. He passed aboute the yere of oure Lorde two
hundred foure score and seuene.

    25 In] And E   27 in deserte/beter than he] trs. E   moche] om. EH1
28 forestes] forest E   wildernesse] wildernessis G   30 that'] om. E   palmers] so with
rs subp. H1   31 abouen] a boond E, abouen on erasure H1   33 what] w'h'at H1   a]
om. H1   satirell] Satirell EH1   36 open] add 'it' H1, add it G   40 to do] om. H1G
50 hadde] om. G   51 that] as H1   53 ne hadde wherwith] was aboute EH1
55 toke] add ayene H1

Here endithe the lyff of Poule the Hermyte, and after
begynnithe the lyff of Seint Remygie the holi confessour
and doctour, Capitulum .xv.^m

Remigye a noble doctour and glorious confessour of oure Lorde was
before his natiuite seen to be born in suche a wise as an heremyte seigh
it. For as the persecucion of Vandalyens hadde wasted nygh al
Fraunce an holi man, a recluse that was blynde, praied ofte to oure
Lorde for the pees of the Chirche of Fraunce, and the aungell of oure 5
Lorde appered to hym in a vision and saide to hym: 'Knowe it well
that the same woman that hight Alyne shall haue a childe that [shall]
hight Remygie, and he shal deliuer the peple fro the assauutes of
wicked men.' And whanne he awoke he went to the hous of Alyne and
tolde her that he hadde herde, and for that she wolde not leue hym for 10
she was olde he saied to her: 'Wete wel that whanne thou shalt yeue
that childe sowke thou shalt anointe myn eighen with thi melke and
restore myn eighen to the sight.'
   And whanne alle these thyngges were falle Remegye fledd | the f. 26vb
worlde and entred into reclusage. And as his renome encresed, 15
whanne he was .xxij.^{ti} wynter olde he was chosen to be erchebisshop
of alle the peple. And he was of so gret a debonairte that the wilde
sparowes come to his boorde and toke mete of his honde. In a tyme
[as] he was herborued withe a ladi and she had but litelle wyne,
Remigy wente into the sellere and made a crosse ouer the tonne, and 20
as sone as he hadde praied the wyne sprong up aboue the vessell and
ranne in al the sellere.
   And as Cloouys kyng of Fraunce was in that [tyme] paynym and
wolde in no wise be conuerted by his wyff that was a full cristen ladye,
and he seigh that gret peple witheoute nombre come vpon hym, 25
thanne he made his avowe to that god that his wiff worshipped [that]
yef he wolde geve hym the victorie of [these straunge] peple he wolde
receyue the faithe of Ihesu Crist. And whanne he was come to his
desire that he hadde the victorie, he went to Seint Remygie and
requyred of hym baptime. And whanne he come to the funtstone ther 30
myght no creme be founde, and therwithe ther come a dowue and

   EH1GDH2A1A2; D breaks off after 36 *hadde*   1 was] *twice once del.* H1   5–6 for
. . . Lorde] and he G   7 shall^2] *om.* E   10 tolde] told *with* ld *on erasure* H1   12 that]
þy G   eighen] þanne G   13 myn . . . the] hym þanne to my G   14 whanne] *om.* G
these] *twice* E   19 as] *om.* E   he] 's'he H1   21 up] *om.* G   22 tyme] *om.* E
24 vpon] to G   26 that^3] *om.* E, *add* tyme G   27 these straunge] this strong EH1
30 come] *add* 'in' H1

brought a viole in her beke fulle of creyme, [and] the bisshop toke that
of the sonde of oure Lorde and anointed the kyng therwithe. And this
violl is yet kept in the chirche of Reynes, wherwith al the kyngges of
35 Fraunce that haue bene sithen haue bene anointed into this day.

And thanne longe tyme after, so as Genebaude hadde wedded the
moder of Seint Remygie and that one hadde lefte that other bi cause of
religion, the blessed Remygie ordeyned Genebaude to be bisshop of
f. 27ʳᵃ Laon. And as Genebaude | made diuerse tymes his wyf come to hym
40 bicause of visitacion and for to teche her to encrese in vertues, but atte
the laste bi custume of this visitacion he was enflavmed [with] the
coueitise of lecherie and come to the synne so that sche conceiued and
bere a sone. And thanne she sent to the bisshop and lete hym knowe
therof. Thanne he was foule confused [and] sent to her that sithe it
45 was gote in theft that it shuld be called Theef. And for there shulde be
no suspecion he lete his wyff come to hym as she dede before, and so
after the furste synne they fille in the secounde. And whanne she
hadde a doughter she sent [it] to the bisshop, and he sent her to saie
that it shulde hight Foxe. And atte the ende he repented hym and
50 went to the blessid Seint Remygie and fille downe atte his fete and
wolde haue take awaie the stole of his necke. And whanne he hadde
shewed to Seint Remygie how it was befalle hym, he conforted hym
goodly and closed hym vp in a celle where he abode .vij. yere, and all
that tyme Seint Remygie gouerned his chirche. The seuent yere after
55 on a Sher Thoursday as he was in his praiers, an aungell come to hym
and saide that his synnes were foryeuen hym and comaunded hym to
go oute. He ansuered and saide: 'I may not, for my lorde Remygie
hathe shette the dore and seled it withe his seall.' Thanne the aungell
saide to hym: 'For thou shalt knowe þat heuene is open to the, this
60 dore shal open to the witheoute brekyng of the seall.' And anone the
dore was open as he hadde saide. And thanne Genebaude laide hym
downe in the dore and saide: 'Though my lorde Ihesu Crist come to
f. 27ʳᵇ me I maye not go oute but yef my lorde Remigy that shette me | up
here come to me.' And thanne Remigy bi the tellyng of the aungell
65 come to Laon and restabled Genebaude [in] his place, and he
perseuered in holi werkes vnto his dethe. And Theef his sone
succeded after hym to the bisshopriche and was an holi man. And

32 viole] *so with* e *erased* H1   and] *om.* EH1   38–9 to . . . Genebaude] and G
40 to²] the H1   41 with] bi E   44 and] *om.* E   48 it] *om.* E, *add* to seie H1
50 blessid] bisshopp H1   53 all] at G   59–60 this . . . open] *ins. with* þe *for* this H1
60 to the] *om.* H1   65 Laon] allone G   in] to E   66 perseuered] resseyuyd G
And] *add* the G

in the ende blessed Remigie rest in pees noble bi many vertues about
the yere of oure Lorde fiftee.

Here endithe the lyff of Seint Remigy, and after foluith the
lyff of Seint Hillari the bisshoppe, Capitulum .xvj.ᵐ

Hyllarie the bisshop of Poyters was born of the region of Aquitayne,
and he proceded as the sterre of Lucifer among other sterres. This
same before hadde a wiff and children and in seculer abite he liued lik
a monke, and atte the ende he profited so in lyff and in cunnyng that
he was chosen to be bisshop. And thanne as blessid Seint Hillarie 5
defended not onli his citee but alle the reawme of Fraunce ayeinst the
heresies, he was sent atte the request of two bisshoppes heretikes in
exile with blessid Eusebe of Versillis by the emperour that was maister
of heresyes. And thanne as the heresie of Aryene encresed in euery
place and the emperour hadde yeue leue that alle shulde assemble to 10
dispute of the trouthe, Seint Hillarie come atte the request of .x.
bisshopes that myght not suffre his faire speche and than he was
constreined to go into Peitowe.

And as he come to the ile of Galiarre that was fulle of serpentes, he
entered in and chased oute the serpentis bi his lokyng and sette a staffe 15
in the middes of the ile and gaue hem no fredom to take more place
mo thanne he assigned hem | and marked hem, the whiche party of the f. 27ᵛᵃ
ile is no londe but see. And as he come to Poiters a dede childe
witheoute bapteme was releued bi his orison and restabled to lyff
ayein. For he laye so long in orison that thei arose togedre, Hillari 20
from orison and the childe from dethe.

And as Apra his doughter wolde haue take an husbond he preched
her so deuoutely and he confermed her in the purpos of holi virginite.
And whanne he considered that she was stabeled, he praied oure
Lorde that he wolde resseiue her and suffre her no lenger to lyue, and 25
a litell after that she passed to oure Lord and he beried her. And
whanne the moder of this blessid Apra hadde considered this thyng
she required hym that he wolde gete her that same grace that he dede
to his doughter. He dede so and sent her before to the kyngdom of
heuene bi his praiers. 30

EH1GH2A1A2   14–15 he² . . . serpentis] *ins.* H1   16 no] mo *changed to* no H1
18 no] noon of þe G   Poiters] Pʻoʻiters H1   19 restabled] restablischid G   22 as]
om. G   23 and] þat G   of] *add* the E   24 stabeled] stabul G   27 blessid]
bisshop *del.* H1   28 that¹] and G

In that tyme Leon the pope was corrupte bi the wikkednesse of
heresies. He assembeled a Counsaile of alle bisshoppes sauf only Seint
Hillari was not sent for, but he come vnsent for. And whan the pope
herde he comaunded that none shulde ryse ayeinst hym ne yeue hym
35 no place. And whanne he was among hem the pope saide to hym:
'Thou art Hillary the Galle,' and he saide: 'I am not Galle, but I am a
bisshop of Fraunce.' Thanne saide the pope: 'And I am Leon, iuge of
the sege of the apostoyle of Rome.' And Hillarie saide: 'If thou be
Leon, that is not of the linage of Iuda, and thou iuge that is not in the
40 sege of thi mageste.' And thanne the pope arose up [bi] despite and
saide: 'Abide till I come ayein, and I shall yelde the that thou haste
f. 27ᵛᵇ deserued.' [And] Hillarie saide: 'Yef thou come not ayein, who | shalle
ansuere me for the?' And he saide: 'I shalle come anone and reffreyne
thi pride.' And as the pope went to ese hymselff he pershed by a
45 sodein flixe in puttyng oute alle his bowelles and so he ended his lyff
cursedly. And in the mene tyme Seint Hillari seigh that none wolde
make hym place. He suffered all pesibly and sette hym mekely downe
in the erthe and saide: 'The erthe is oure Lordes.' And anone the
erthe wher as he satte arose up till [it] come to the highthe of other
50 bisshoppes. And whanne tydyngges come that the pope hadde ended
his lyff so wrechidly, Hillari arose hym vp and confermed the
bisshoppes in the faithe of holi Chirche and sent hem alle confermed
to her propre places.

But this myracle of the dethe of the pope Leon is douted, for the
55 Maister of Stories ne that Parted in Thre spekithe no worde therof,
and that the cronicle witnessith it not that in that tyme ther was no
pope of suche a name, and Ierome saiethe that the Chirche of Rome
was allewayez witheoute defoulyng of heresye and shal be alwaye. But
it may be saide that ther was that same tyme a pope that hight so, that
60 was vnduely chosen [but] hadde goten the [sege] withe tyranny, or
ellis perauenture it was Lyberien that obeyed to Constaunt the
heretik, that was by another name callid Leon.

And at the laste many miracles done bi Hillarie, he fille grevously
seke, and whan he knewe that his ende neyghed he called to hym
65 Leonce, a preste that he loued moche, and bade hym go oute and yef
he herde anythyng that he shulde come telle hym anone. He dede as
he was boden and come ayein and tolde hym that ther was grete |

32 assembeled] *on erasure* Hɪ   33 for²] *om.* G   40 bi] in EHɪ   despite]
despute G   42 And] *om.* E   49 up] *ins.* G   it] he EHɪ   52 of holi Chirche]
om. G   60 but] and EHɪ   sege] *see* EHɪ

tumulte in the citee. And as he woke tofore hym and abode his ende f. 28ra
and bede hym go oute ayein atte midnyght and report hym what he
herde. And whanne he tolde hym that he herde nothyng, sodenly a 70
grete lyght entered into the hous, the whiche lyght the prest myght
not endure ne suffre, and the light parted litell and litell, and thanne
he passed to oure Lorde, and floured aboute the yere of oure Lorde
four hundred and fourti vnder Constant the emperour.

And as two marchauntes hadden a loef of comune, the tone of the 75
marchauntes offered the loef maugre that other to the auuter of Seint
Hillarie, and anone the loef was parted a two and that one parte abode
withe hym that hadde refused to offre the loef.

Here endithe the liff of Seint Hillarie, and nexst beginnithe
the lyff of Seint Makarie, Cap^{m}. .xvij.^{m}

Makarie went oute of a place of desert and entred [in] the sepulture of
a dede man and leyed his hede downe vpon the dede bodi in stede of a
pilow. And the fende thought to make hym afraied and called the bodi
as he had bene a woman and saide: 'Arise up, go we to the bathe.' And
the other fende þat laye vnder Makaries hede saide as thowe he hadde 5
be dede: 'I haue a straunge man vpon me that I may not arise.' And
Makarie dred hym nothyng [for no fere] but bete the body and saide:
'Aryse vp yef thou maist.' And whanne the fendes herde hym thei
fledde crieng with highe vois: 'Allas, thou haste ouercome us.'

In a tyme as Makary went toward his celle the fende come rennyng 10
ayeinst hym withe a sithe and wold haue smiten hym, but he myght
not. | And thanne he saide hym: 'A, thou Makarie, thou makest me to f. 28rb
suffre gret violence, for I may do nothyng ayeinst the. And I doo as
thou doest, thou fastest and I ete not, thou wakest and I slepe not, but
one thing is wherin thou ouercomest vs most.' Thanne the abbot 15
saide: 'Wherin is that?' And the fende saide: 'Humilite, wherfor I may
do nothyng ayeinst the.'

Whanne the temptaciones troubled hym he wolde arise and caste a
grete sacke full of grauel vpon his shuldres and went so many dayes
thorugh the desert. And Theosebe mette with hym in a daye and 20

69 midnyght] 'mydde' night H1   73 and . . . Lorde] om. G   76 maugre] in
angre H1   that other] the subp. oþer del. and subp. H1   77 that] add oþer del. H1
78 to offre] om. G

EH1GH2A1A2   1 in] to EH1   4 he] it G   5 saide] om. G   6 be] add
'þe' H1   straunge] strong G   7 for no fere] om. EH1   9 fledde] add hym G
13 And] add 'þat' H1   as] om. H1   14 wakest] walkest E

sayde to hym: 'Fader, whi bere ye so grete a burdon vpon you?' And
Makarie saide: 'I slee hym that sleith me.'

   In a tyme the abbot Makarie seigh the fende in mannes liknesse and
hadde on a lynen clothe al torent, and by euery hole of the rentyng
25 ther hyng a viole. Thanne saide Makarie to hym: 'Whedir goest thou?'
And he said: 'To thine hous to yeue drinke to thi bretheren.' Makari
saide: 'Whi berest thou so many violes?' 'I bere hem to the taste of thi
bretherin, that yef thei lyke not one they shull assaie of another, and so
the thridde till sumwhat shall plese hem.' And whanne he come ayein
30 Makarie asked hym how he hadde spedde. He saide: 'Not, for thei
bene al halowed sauf one that hight Theotist, and he hathe receyued
of my drinke.' Thanne Makarie arose up and went thedir and fonde
[the] brother gretly tempted. He conuerted hym by his holy exhorta-
cion. And after that Makarie met ayein with the feende and asked hym
35 whedir he went. He saide: 'To thi bretheren.' And whanne he turned
ayein the holy fader saide: 'What do my bretheren?' And he saide:
'Ful euel thei do.' 'Whi so?' saide Makarye. 'For they bene al holy,
f. 28va and | this is my most sorugh, for one that I hadde wonne is now loste
and made the most holy of hem alle.' And whan Makarye herde that
40 he thanked oure Lorde.

   In a day Seint Makarie fonde the hede of a dede man, and whanne he
hadde made his praiers he asked of the hede of whom he was, and he
saide: 'Of a panyme.' Thanne saide Makarie: 'Wher is thi soule?' And
he saide: 'In helle.' He asked hym yef he were depe, and he saide that he
45 was as depe as the erthe is ferre fro heuene. Thanne Makarie saide: 'Is
there any mo depper thanne thou?' He saide: 'Ye, the Iues.' Thanne
Makerie saide: 'Is ther any more depper thanne Iues?' Thanne saide
the hede: 'The deppest of alle bene fals cristen men that were bought
[of] the blode of Ihesu Crist and despisen the price therof.'

50   As Seint Makerie went in a ferre desert he stiked a roser by euery
halff myle for to come the same [way] ayein. And whanne he hadde
laboured .ix. dayes he rest hym in a place, and the fende gadered vp
alle these rosers and layde hem atte his hede, wherfor Makarie
laboured sore in his turnyng ayein.

55   There was a brother gret[li] travailed in his thoughtes, and as hym
thought therfor he profited nothing in his sell he purposed to go oute

22 sleith] fleith *del.* `wold sle´ H1, wolde scle G   33 the] his EH1   36 saide¹]
add Makarie G   40 oure Lorde] god/oure lorde *marked for trsp.* H1   41 Makarie]
Ma`ka´ri H1   man] body G   44 yef] where H1   he] she G   49 of] with EH1
50 desert] *add* place G   51 way] day E, waie *with* w *on erasure* H1   53 hem] him H1
55 gretli] gret bi E

and duell amonge the peple, supposing to profit more. And whanne he
hadde tolde Makary his thoughtes, he saide: 'Sone, thou shalt ansuere
in such wise to thi temptaciones: "That I do, I do it for Ihesu Crist,
and for hys loue I wille kepe the wallis of this selle."'   60

So as Makarie hadde slayn a flee that bote hym and he seigh moche
blode come oute of hym, he repreued hymselff that he | reuenged hys   f.28ᵛᵇ
propre wrong and went into deserte and duelled there .vj. monthes al
naked til he was al forbetin with flies. And after that he rested in pees
in oure Lorde shinynge bryght bi many gret myracles.   65

Here endith the liff of Seint Makary, and after foluithe the
liff of Seint Felixe, Capᵐ. .xviij.ᵐ

Felixe, otherwise called Enpinces, is saide of the place where he
rest[ith] either of the greves bi whiche he suffered dethe, for pinche [is
to saie] greef. And som sayn that whanne he was a maister of children
that he was full rigerouse to hem, and thanne he was takyn of the
panymes, and for he confessed freli Ihesu Crist he was taken into the   5
hondes of the children that he hadde taught, the whiche slowe hym
withe her pointles and her brocches and greffys. And yet [it] is not
seyn that the Chirche holdithe hym a martir but a confessour. And
thei bade hym that he shulde sacrifice to euery ydole.

And whanne Mychine the bisshop and Valerien fledden the   10
persecucion of paynemes, that bisshop was tormented withe hunger
and threst so that he felle to the erthe as halff dede. Thanne bi the
aungell of oure Lorde Felix was sent to hym, but he bere nothing
withe hym to comforte hym, and as he went he seigh bisides hym an
honycombe hangynge [on] an hege and the hony springed aboute his   15
mowthe, and thanne he toke the honycombe and leide it on his
shuldres and bare it forthe with hym. And after that whanne the
bisshop was dede Felix was chosen into bisshop.

And as he preched the pursuers of the faithe sought hym. He dede
hym in a litell hole among broken walles, | and anone bi the wille of   f.29ʳᵃ
[God] the crevise of the walles were fulfilled withe [copwebbis], and   21
tho that pursued hym seigh that [and] thei wende that ther hadd bene

59 I do it] ins. H1   63 duelled] 'd'welled H1   64 forbetin] forbiten G
EH1GH2A1A2   2 restith] rested E   greves] grif G   is] ins. H1   2–3 is/to
saie] trs. E   4 rigerouse] so with ri on erasure H1   7 it] om. E   9 ydole] Idolle
with ll on erasure H1   15 on] of E   springed] springynge H1G   20 hole] holde E, so
with d subp. H1   21 God] om. E, ins. H1   copwebbis G] Cobles E, cobles (?) changed to
cobwebes H1   22 and] om. E, '&' H1

nobodi and parted from thennis. And Felix went thanne into another
place and toke his sustinaunce thre monthes of a wydowe, and alle that
25 tyme he seigh neuer the visage of her. And atte the ende whanne the
pees was he turned ayein to his chirche and rest in oure Lorde.

And this same hadde a brother that hight Felix als. And [whanne]
this Felix was constreined to worship the ydoles he saide: 'Ye bene
youre goddes enemyes, for [yef] ye bryngge me to hem I shall blowe
30 ayeinst hem as my brother dede and they shull al tobreste.'

This Felix tilled a gardine, and there were som that stale his wortes,
but they myght not oute of his gardine but dalue there alle the nyght
diligentely, and in the morw Felix salued hem and they knowlaged her
defauutes and went home ayein to her howses.

35 The panymes wolde haue hadde Seint Felix, and sodeinli so gret
passion toke hem that thei beganne to crie and rore like madde bestis.
And thanne Felix saide to hem: 'Saiethe that Ihesu Crist is verray
God and youre sorugh shal sece.' And thanne they saiden soo, and
anone thei were hole.

40 The bisshop of the ydoles come to hym and saide: 'Sir, as [sone as]
my god seigh the he beganne to flee, and I asked hym whi he fledde
and he saide me: "For I may not suffre the vertue of this Felix." And
sethe my god dredithe the so moche I aught moche more drede the.'
And thanne Felix confermed hym in the faithe and baptized hym.

45 Felix saide to tho that worshipped Apoline: 'If Apoline ys verray
f. 29rb god late hym telle me | what I [holde] in myn honde.' He helde in his
honde a scrowe that the orison of oure Lorde was wretin in. And
Apolyne coude not ansuere, wherfor þe panymes conuerted hem to
oure Lorde.

50 And atte the laste, whanne he hadde saide his masse and yeuen the
pees to the peple, he leyde hym doune in orison vpon the pauement
and passed to oure Lorde.

24 wydowe] wyndowe E, *so with* n *del.* H1   26 he] *om.* G   27 whanne] as E, *om.*
H1   28 Ye] þay G, Ye (?) *changed to* þei H1   29 yef ye] ye E, ye`f' H1   31 were]
om. G   35 hadde] *om.* G   36 hem] him H1   37 Saiethe] *on erasure* H1, *om.* G
40 sone as] *om.* EH1   41 seigh] sei3h *with* i3h *on erasure* H1   46 holde] haue EH1

Here endith the lyff of Seint Felix, and after foluithe the
liff of Seint Marcell, Capitulum .xix.^m

As Marcell souerayne preste was atte Rome and blamed Maximyen of
his gret cruelte that he dede to the cristen, and as he saide his masse in
a ladies hous that he hadde sacred and made a chirche, þat emperour
was wrothe therwith and made of the chirche a stable of mules, and
made Seint Marcell to serue there the bestes vnder good kepyng. And 5
he deyed in that seruyse many yere after and went to oure Lorde
aboute the yere of oure Lorde [two] hundred foure score and seuene.

Here endithe the lyff of Seint Marcell, and nexst foluithe
the liff of Seint Antonie, Capitulum .xx.^m

Whanne Seint Antonye was of the age of .xx. yere he herde redde in
the gospell: 'If thou wilt be perfit goo and selle al that thou haste and
yeue it to the pore.' And thanne he solde [alle] and dede so and lyued
an heremytes lyff. And he susteyned temptaciones of the fende
witheoute nombre. In a tyme as Antony hadde ouercomen the 5
sperit of fornicacion bi vertue of faithe, the fende come to hym in
forme of a | blacke childe and knowlaged that he was ouercome [bi]   f. 29va
hym. And thanne he besought God that he myght se the spirit of
fornicacion aspiynge the yong peple, and whanne he seigh hym in the
forsaide forme he saide: 'Thou hast appered to me in an horrible 10
forme, wherfor I shalle drede the no more.'

Another tyme, as Seint Antonye hidde hym [withe]in a tombe, gret
multitude of fendes comen aboute hym and tormented hym so that his
seruaunt bere hym vpon his shuldres, and as alle tho þat were there
wept hym as dede, alle thei felle aslepe, and Antony revigured 15
sodeinly and made his man bere hym ayein faste to the tombe. And
as he laye vpon the erthe for anguishe of his woundes, thei come ayein
to the assaute and apered in diuerse formes of bestes and withe her
hornes and nayles alle torent hym ayein more cruelly thanne he was
before. And thanne sodenly apered a mervailous light that chased 20
away alle the fendes, and thanne [anone] Antony was heled, and he

EH1GH2A1A2   3 hadde] om. G   þat] þa`t´ þe H1   7 two] an EH1   foure
score] .viij. G

EH1T1GH2A1A2, D resumes at 7 knowlaged   3 pore] add man G   alle] om. E
7 bi] withe E   12 withein] in E   13 aboute] a followed by erasure of (?) ll followed by
bought H1   14 as] ins. H1   15 revigured] refigurid G   18 assaute] assowde with
owde on erasure H1   21 anone] om. E, ins. H1

vnderstode that God was there and saide: 'O where were thou, go[o]d
Ihesu Crist, whi commest thou not atte the begynnyng to helpe me
and for to hele my woundes?' Thanne oure Lorde saide: 'Antony, I
25 was here, but I abode to see [thi] stryf, and for thou hast wel foughten
I shall make the preised thorughoute the worlde.' The blessed Antony
was of so gret brennyng of loue that whanne Maximyen the emperour
slowe the cristen he folued the martires for to haue bene martered
withe hem, and he was fulle of sorugh for no man wolde yeue hym
30 marterdome.

As he went in a tyme into another desert, he founde a disshe of
seluer [bi the waye and saide to hymselff: 'From whennes cometh this
disshe of seluer] wher no man walke[th]? If it hadde falle from a
f. 29ᵛᵇ travayleng man he | shulde haue herde the sowne in the falle. O thou
35 fende, this is thi werke, thi will shall neuer chaunge myn.' And as he
saide that the dische vanished away as a smoke. And after that he
fonde a gret gobet of verray golde, but it was as it hadde bene
brennyng fere.

And thus he fledde to the mountaynes and was there twenti wynter
40 shynyng by many miracles. In a tyme as Antonye was rauished in
spirit he seigh al the worlde besette with snares, and thanne he cried
and saide: 'Allas, who shall ascape these snares?' And he herde a voys
that saide: 'Humilite.' Som tyme whanne he was lefte vp in the eyre
withe aungels the fendes wolde haue de[u]yed that he shuld not haue
45 passed, purposyng ayeinst hym the syn[n]es of his natiuite, to whom
the aungelles saiden: 'Acountith not that that is effaced bi the pitee of
Crist. And yef ye canne tell any sethe he was monke, saieth on faste.'
And whanne thei hadde failed of her purpose Antony was bore an hye
[all] deliuered from her malice.

50 Antony wolde saie som tyme of hymselff: 'I seygh in a tyme the
fende high of body that durst saie that he was vertue and purveiaunce
of God, and saide to me: "Antonye, what wilt thou that I yeue the?"
And I spette hym in the visage and was al armed with the name of
Ihesu Crist, and he vanisshed awaye. And after that the fende apered

22 good] god EH₁G   23 begynnyng] add 'for' H₁   25 to see] add 'how þay and
þou diden and y am come to helpe þe but y abode to se' H₁, so G   thi] the E   26 the¹]
add well H₁   thorughoute] þoruȝ G   29 wolde] on erasure H₁   31 a¹] an oþer G
another] add place G   32–3 bi . . . seluer] om. EG   33 walketh] walked EG
35 myn] 'my' mynde H₁   41 besette] set H₁   43 whanne] ins. H₁   44 deuyed]
denyed (?) E   45 synnes] sygnes E   46 that²] om. G   effaced] deffacid G
47 ye] he G   sethe] such 'sithe' H₁   49 all] and EH₁   malice] purpos G   50 in a]
sum G

to me so high that his hede touched [the] heuene, and whanne I hadde 55
asked hym what he was he saide me that he was Sathanas. And thanne
he saide: "Whi assailen me in suche wise thi monkes and these cursed
cristen?"' And Antony saide: 'Withe good right thei done it, for thei
bene ofte tormented bi thi malice.' Thanne saide the fend: | 'I disese f. 30ʳᵃ
hem not, thei wrathe me al togederes, I am now brought to not, for 60
Crist regnithe ouer all.'

An archer [in] a tyme seigh Antony plaie hym withe felawship and
lowgh hym to scorne. And thanne Antony saide to hym: 'Putte thin
arowe in thin bowe and shete.' And whan he hadde done so the
secound tyme and the thridde the archer saide: 'I may so longe shete 65
that I drede me to breke my bowe.' Thanne saide Antony: 'Right so it
farithe bi gosteli werkes, for if [we] wil streche us ouer mesure we
shull be the sonner broken, wher[for] it behouithe atte some tyme for
to restresse rigoure.' And whanne he hadde herde it he parted al
confused. 70

In a tyme a man asked Seint Antony: 'What shall I do to plese
God?' He ansuered and saide: 'What place that euer thou go in, haue
euermore God before thi sight, and in al thingges that thou shalt do
take the witnesse of holi writte, and wher that thou art sette, parte the
not lightly. Kepe these thre thingges and thou shalt be sauf.' 75

An abbot asked of Antony and saide: 'What shall I do, Antony?'
And he saide: 'Truste not in thin owne rightwisnesse, kepe continence
of thi bely and of thi tongge, and repent the not of thing that is
passed.' And Antony saide hym ouer: 'Right as fishes that tarien from
the water deyen, right so a monke tarying [oute] of his celle, duellyng 80
withe seculers, deyen from thaire holy purpos.' And yet saide Seint
Antony: 'Whoso sitte in his selle allone he restithe and is oute of thre
batellis, of spekyng, of sight, and of hering, and fighting but withe
one, that is with the hert.'

Certeyne bretheren went in a tyme withe a good auncien fader to 85
visite Seint Antonye. Thanne Antonye saide: 'Bretheren, ye haue
founde goode | felawship in this olde fader,' and thei saide: 'Ye.' f. 30ʳᵇ

55 the] *om.* EH1   56 me] *om.* G   57 assailen] *add* `ȝe' H1, *add* ȝe G   suche]
this G   58 saide] *add* that EH1   59 thi] þe H1   60 hem] him H1   62 in] on E
63 thanne] *om.* H1   65 thridde] *add* tyme G   67 we'] *om.* E, *ins.* H1   streche]
strengthe H1   68 wherfor] wher E, where`for' H1   69 restresse] refresshe G
71 In a tyme/a man] *trs.* G   73 thi] þe H1   77 And he saide] *ins.* H1   78 bely]
body *on erasure* H1, body G   tongge] *add* and of þy bely G   80 oute of] of E, fro H1
85 Certeyne] *preceded by* `A' H1   bretheren] brother H1   86 Bretheren] Broþer H1,
add he seide G

Thanne saide Antony to the olde fader: 'Fader, thou hast founde good
bretheren withe the.' He ansuered and saide: 'I haue founde hem
90 good, but ther is no gate to thaire habitacion. Whoso will may entre
into the stable and vnbinde the asse.' And he saide it for þat cause,
that whanne ther was anything in thaire herte it was anone atte her
mouthe in to moche talkyng. Thanne the abbot Antonye saide: 'It
behouithe to knowe that there be .iij. bodely mevyngges: that one is of
95 nature, that other is of plente of metes, and the .iij. of the fende.'

Ther was a brother that hadde forsake the worlde but not pleinly,
for he hadde witholde sum thyng. And Antonye saide to hym: 'Goo
and beye som flesche.' He went, and as he come ayein houndes al
torent hym. And thanne saide Antonye: 'Tho that renounsen the
100 worlde and withe[holde] money withe hem in suche wise be totoren
with fendes.'

And as Antony was tormented by enoye in desert he saide: 'Lorde
God, I wolde be saued, and I may not for my thoughtez.' And thanne
he seigh a man that satte and wrought, and after he arose and praide,
105 and this was an aungell of oure Lorde that saide to hym: 'Do this and
thou shalt be sauf.'

[As] the bretheren in a tyme asked Antonye of the estate of soules,
the nyght foluyng a vois called hym and saide: 'Arise and see.' And he
arose and seigh a long dredfull man that his hede streched to the
110 heuene and defended to some that hadde wynges that thei myght not
flee to heuene. And other there were that hadde wynges þat fleghen
freli to heuene that he myght not lette, and therwithe he herde gret |
f. 30ᵛᵃ ioie medeled withe sorugh. And than he vnderstode that [it] was the
acorde of soules and the fende that defended hem to go an highe, and
115 he sorued that the soules of seintes fleen so freli that he myght noght
witholde hem.

It fell on a tyme that Seint Antonye praied withe his bretheren and
he behelde to the heuene and seigh a sorifull vision, and thanne he
kneled hym downe before God and praied hym that he wolde
120 distourbe that felonye that it felle not. And thanne he saide to his
bretherin that asked hym of this thing with gret wepyngges and gret
sobbyngges that suche a felony hadde neuer fall in the worlde afore.

92 it] þer G   anone] `a´noon G     93 in to] into EHıG     94 to] add `be´ Hı   of]
add oo del. Hı   99 renounsen] recouysyn G   100 witheholde] withe E   money] mony
with o on erasure Hı   wise] add shull E   102 enoye] `noye´ with preceding letter erased Hı
103 thanne] `þan´ following erasure Hı   104 wrought] þoght changed to wroght Hı
107 As] And E, An Hı   the bretheren] þe broþer on erasure Hı   112 not] ins. Hı
113 it] is E, þis Hı   114 acorde] corde Hı   120 distourbe] distroble Hı

'I seigh,' he saide, 'an auuter of Ihesu Crist biclypped with multitude
of men that al torent the auutere with thaire spores, whiche
signifie[th] that the catholik faithe shal be gretly tormented and 125
men shull be made lyk to bestis [and] shullen tobreke the sacrementis.
And thanne a vois was herde that saide: "Men shullen haue
abho[min]acion of myn auutere."' And two yere after the Ariens
come and al tobreste the vnite of the Chirche and defouled baptime,
and the cristen sacrified on the auuter as beestis.   130

And as a duke of Egipte, Malachin by name, tormented the virgines
and the monkes al naked amonge the comune, Antony wrote to hym
in this wise: 'I see the wrathe of God aboue the, and therfor leue for to
pursue the cristen lest that wrathe fall on the, for she manassheth the
withe dethe.' And this cursed fole redde this lettre, and he lough and 135
spette theron and caste it to the grounde and tormented the bringgers
withe betyngges and sent to Antony suche wordes: 'For thou hast so
gret cure of mon|kes oure disciplyn of riguore shalle come to [the].' f. 30ᵛᵇ
And .v. daies after, he light vpon his hors that was right debonayre
and he was [throwe] doune to the erthe and al torent withe the same 140
hors and was dede withein thre daies.

[As] some bretherin required to here of Antonye wordes of
edificacion he saide to hem: 'Haue ye not herde oure Lorde saieng:
"If any smyte you on that one cheke turne hym that other."?' And
thei saide: 'We mowe not fulfell that.' Thanne saide he: 'Atte the leest 145
suffre pacientli with that one cheke.' And thei said: 'We mowe not.'
And Antonye saide: 'Atte the hardest wil not to smite more thanne
thou woldest be smiten.' Thei saide: 'That mow we not do neither.'
Thanne saide Antonye to his disciple: 'Goo make redy a bitter iuys to
these bretherin, for thei bene to delicious. Oonli orison is necessarie to 150
you.' And these thingges be redde in the Lyff of the Olde Faders.

Whanne [the] blessed Antony was of the age of an .C. and .v. yere
he kissed his bretheren and rested in oure Lorde vnder Constant that
regned the yere of oure Lorde thre hundered and fourt[ye].

124 whiche] with G   125 signifieth] signified E   that] with G   126 and] om. E,
'&' H1   128 abhominacion] abhortacion EH1   134 wrathe] wreche (?) G
138 the] you EH1   139 after] ins. H1   140 throwe] drawe E   142 As some]
And some E, Assone G   144 hym] add to E   145 leest] laste H1G   147 hardest]
add we H1   148 That mow we] we mowe G   152 the¹] om. EH1   153 Lorde]
add 'the xvj kalendes of Februar' H1   154 fourtye] fourtene E

Here endithe the blessed lyff of Seint Antonye, and nexst
foluithe the lyff of Seint Fabian, Capitulum .xxj.

Fabiane was a citezein of Rome, and as the peple was assembeled
whanne the pope was dede for to [chese] another, he come to the
register for to knowe who shulde be it. And a white douue descended
vpon hym and alle mervailed therof. He was chose pope.
5   This same, as Damassien saithe, sent thorugh al the cuntreies seuen
f. 31ra dekenes and toke | hem seuene subdekenes that gadered togedre al the
dedis of [the martirs] and brought hem to hym. This same, as
Haymon saiethe, ayeinstode the emperour Philipe that wolde haue
be atte the Vigile of Ester communed, but he suffered hym not to be
10 atte the seruice til he hadde confessed his synnes and was repentaunt.
[And] atte the laste whanne he hadde be .xiij. yere pope he was
crowned bi marterdome by the comaundement of Dessen and hadde
his hede smetin of, and suffered dethe aboute the yere of oure Lorde
two hundered.

Here endithe the lyff of Pope Fabian and Seint, and after
foluithe the lyff of Seint Sebastian, Capitulum .xxij.^m

Sebastian was a ful cristen man and was of the kynrede of Nerbone
and citezein of Melane, and was so beloued withe Dioclicien and
Maxymien emperours that they toke hym the lordeship of the furst
felawship of knyghtes and comaunded hym alwayes to be bifore hem.
5 And this bere alwaye the mantell of knyghthode to that ende that he
myght comfort the soules of cristen that he seigh defaille in tormentes.
And as the blessed and right noble men Marcellyn and Marke
bretherin were iuged to the deth for the loue of Ihesu Crist, and ther
come her kynrede to hem for to take hem from her good purpos, and
10 ther come his moder al dissheue[l]e rendyng her clothes and shewed
hem her brestes seyeng: 'O right dere children, was ther neuer moder
suffered the sorugh that I endure and [suffre] for you. Allas, wreche, I
lese my sones withe her owne wille, the whiche yef enemyes hadde

EH1T1GDH2A1A2; in E, *Pope* is deleted and *buschop* substituted throughout
2 chese] teche E, chese *on erasure* H1   3 white douue] white dovue *with* te dovue
on erasure and 'saule' *above* H1   7 the martirs] maistres EH1   11 And] *om.* E

EH1T1GDH2A1A2   *Rubric deleted but still legible* E   4–5 to be . . . alwaye] *om.* G
4 hem] him H1   5 this] he *on erasure* H1   6 defaille] defaylid G   7 blessed]
bisshopp H1   10 dissheuele] dissheuede E   rendyng] rentynge H1G   11 hem]
hym G   12 I] 'y' H1   suffre] suffered E   Allas] *add* y G

take away fro me I wolde haue folued to the dethe. But this | is a nwe f. 31rb
maner of dethe to me bi whiche the yougthe of my sones is loste of 15
thaire owne will, and the bochers bene praied to smite, thei desire to
be loste, and the dethe is taught to come. This is a nwe wepyng and a
sorifull waillyng bi whiche the violence [of kynrede] is constreyned to
lyue.' And as the moder talked, come the fader ledde betwene his
servauntes, his hede strawed withe pouder, saide suche wordes to 20
[the] heuene: 'I am come to my sones going to the dethe withe thayre
good willes for to seye many thyngges, for that I hadde ordeyned to
my sepulture I most wreche must dispende vpon the sepulture of my
sones. O my derrest sones, the staffe and sustinaunce of myn age and
the double lyght of myn herte, whi loue ye so well the dethe? O ye 25
yonge men, comithe and wepithe vpon these yonge thynges that of
her owne fre will perishe hemselff. Ye olde men, comithe and wepithe
with me vpon my sones, comithe hedir, ye faders, and defende hem
that ye suffre no suche thyng. Myn eyen, go ye oute in wepyng so that
I see not my sones slayn before my sight.' 30

And as the fader saide these thingges the wyves of these yonge men
come bryngyng her yonge sones before hem wepyng and crieng and
sayden: 'Allas, Syres, to whom will ye leue us and oure children?
Allas, youre hertis bene harder thanne iren that despisen youre fader
and moder and kyn and refusen youre frendes and caste oute youre 35
wives and renye youre children and take youreself to the bochers of
youre propre wille.' And among these thynges the hertes of the
yonge men bygonnen to tendre. Thanne Seint Sebastiane per|ccyued f. 31va
this and come to hem and said: 'O ye right stronge knyghtes of Ihesu
Crist, willethe not to lese the euerlastyng crowne of ioie for these 40
cursed wordes.' And thanne he saide to thaire kynne: 'Drede ye not,
for thei shull not be parted fro you, but thei gone tofore you for to
araye the howses of he[uen] for you. For fro the begynnyng of the
worlde this lyff hathe deceyued all tho that ioyen in hym, [and
defoulen hem] þat abiden withe hym, and despisen tho that ioien in 45
hym, and she is so [un]sure and vncertayn that she lith to alle. This

15 bi] *add* `þe' H1   yougthe] ioye H1   sones] synnes G   of²] fore H1   16 thei]
þy G   18 of kynrede] *om.* E, *ins.* H1   21 the¹] *om.* E   23 vpon] aboute G
24 and¹] *add* þe H1   27 Ye olde men] þe olde man G   28 hedir] *om.* H1   ye] þe G
defende] þe fend G   31 these¹] *ins.* H1   34 youre¹] oure G   36 renye] *changed
to* rente H1, rente G   41 kynne] kinrede H1G   Drede] *om.* G   42 you²] *om.* H1G
43 heuen] hem EH1   For] *om.* G   44 hym] hem *changed to* him H1   44–5 and
defoulen hem] *om.* E   45 abiden] abideth H1   46 unsure] mesure EH1G (*elle nest sy
seure* P2)   lith to] light with H1

[lyff] techithe to be a theef whoso obeyethe to hym, to be yreux so that he wexe madde, a lyer that he deceyue. She comaundithe to do wikednesse and felonye, she techith all vnresonable thyngges. But this
50 passion and this persecucion that thei suffre here hetithe today and col[d]ithe tomorw, she comithe in an houre and gothe in another oure. But the euerlastyng sorugh renewethe more feruentely and multepliethe more brennyngly, she is enflaumed for to punische the sor[ier]. Wherfor late us enforce oure corages in the loue of
55 marterdome, for therin the fende wenithe well to ouercome and wynne gret thingges. But whanne he wenith to take he is take, whanne he holdith he is ouercome, whanne he tormentithe he is tormented, whanne he strangelithe he ys slayn, whanne he chasithe he is despised.'
60 And as the blessid Sebastiane pr[ech]ed these thingges and like other, Zoe the wiff of Nichostrate, the whiche kepte these seintes, hadde lost her speche. She kneled downe to the fete of Seint Sebastiane and asked foryeuenesse bi signes. And than Sebastiane
f. 31vb saide: 'If I be the seruaunt of Ihesu Crist, and if [the] thingges be | true
65 that this woman hathe herde of my mouthe of Zakarie the profyte of Ihesu Crist.' And with that worde the woman cried and saide: 'The worde of thi mouth is blessed, and tho bene blessed that beleuen that thou hast saide. For I seigh an aungell before the holdyng a boke wherin was wrete al that thou hast saide.' And whanne her husbonde
70 herde that, he fell downe to the fete of Seint Sebastian and praied hym of foryeuenesse and vnbounde anone the marteres, besechyng hem that thei wolde go her waye, the whiche saide that in no wise thei wolde not leue the victori that they hadde vndertake. And than oure Lorde gave so gret grace and so gret vertue in the wordes of Seint
75 Sebastian that he ne confermed not only Marcell and Marke in stable wille of marterdome, but also Terqynlyn her fader and her moder [and] many other women that he conuerted to the faith, and Polikarpe the prest baptised hem alle.
And Tequilyne that was sore vexed with a grevous siknesse was
80 heled as sone as he was baptized. And than the prouost of Rome praied Tarquilyn that he wolde bryng hym sumbody that coude hele hym, for he was vexed with a greuous siknesse. And whan Polikarpe

47 lyff] loue EH1   51 coldithe] colithe E   52 oure] om. G   54 sorier] sorren EH1   55 ouercome] add me E   56 wynne] add withe E   56–7 to take . . . he is^1] ins. with he is del. H1   57 he tormentithe/he is tormented] trs. G   58 chasithe] on erasure H1   60 preched] praied EH1   60–1 and like other] om. G   64 the^2] these E   66 and saide] ins. H1   77 and^1] withe EH1

and Sebastiane were [come] to hym he praied hem that he myght haue
helthe. Sebastiane saide hym that he shulde furst renye his ydoles and
yeue hym power for to breke hem, and so he shulde resseiue helthe. 85
Than Cromasien prouost saide that his servauntes shuld do it and
not he. Sebastiane saide: 'Thei bene dredfull and [doute] [to] breke
hem, and yef the fende hurte any of hem bi any occasyen þe
misbeleuers wolde saie that they were hurte for they breke her
goddes.' And so Policarpe and Seint Sebastiane | distroied mo f. 32ra
thanne .CC. ydoles. 91

Thanne after that thei saide to Cromasien: 'Whi hast not thou
receiued helthe the whiles we breke the ydoles? It is certayne that thou
hast not take away thi misbeleue, or elles thou kepest priuely sum
ydoles.' And thanne he shewed hem a chaumbre wher al the light of 95
sterres was innc, wherfor his fader hadde dispended more thanne
.CC. pais of golde, by whiche he knewe before al thyng þat was to
come. Thanne saide Sebestian: 'As longe as thou kepest that hole thou
shalt neuer be hole thiselff.' And as he was acorded that it shulde be
broke, Tyburcien his sone, that was a noble yong man, saide that he 100
wolde neuer suffre that so noble a werke shulde be destroied, 'but for I
will not be sain contrarie to my fader helthe, late ther bene ordeyned
two furneis brennyng, and whanne the werke shall be destroied yef
my fader resseive not his helthe ye two shull be brent in the furneis al
quik.' And Sebastian [saide]: 'Be it as thou hast saide.' And as thei 105
[to]breke that chaumbre, the aungell of oure Lord appered to the
provost and tolde hym that his helthe was yolde hym, and anone he
was hole and ronne after hym for to haue kessed his fete, but he
deuyed hym for he hadde not yet resseiued baptime. And so Tyberien
his sone withe a thousand foure hundered of her meyni were baptized. 110

And Zoee was take and tormented so longe with the vntrue beleuers
that she gaue vp the spirit. And whanne Tarquilin [herde] that he
come forthe and saide: 'Allas, whi leue we so longe? Women gone
afore vs to the croune of marterdome.' And a fewe dayes after he was
stoned to the dethe. And Tyburcien was comaunded that he shulde go 115
barfote vpon brennyng coles or elles do sacrifice to the ydoles, | and f. 32rb

83 come] brought EH1T1   87 he] by *changed to* y H1, by G   doute] dare not EH1,
add not G (*doubteroit* P2)   to] *om.* E   88 hurte] hurde *corrected in different hand* G
94 thi] þe H1   98 saide] *add* seint EH1   99 be²] *add* dispisid or G   101 a] *om.*
H1   102 will] wold H1   fader helthe] Fadris he G   ther] here H1   105 saide]
ansuered EH1   106 tobreke] breke E, two breke H1   of oure Lord/appered] *trs.* G
108 kessed] *add* hym and G   111 Zoee] *add* that E, she H1, 3oure G   112 herde]
om. E, 'saw' H1   113 so] þus H1   115 the] *om.* G

thanne he made the signe of the crosse vpon the coles and went vpon
hem barfote seyeng: 'Me thinkithe that I go vpon floures [of] roses in
the name of oure Lorde Ihesu Crist.' To whom Fabien prouost saide:
120 'We knowe well that youre Ihesu Crist is a techer of sorcerie.' To
whom Tiburcien saide: 'Holde thi pees, thou cursed wreche, for thou
art not worthi to nemene so holi a name ne so suete a name.' And than
the prouost was wrothe and comaunded that he shulde be byheded.
And thanne Marcell and Marke were sore tormented and bounden to
125 a piler, and as thei were sore bounden thei saide in synginge: 'Loo,
how good and ioifull it is bretheren for to duelle togederes.' To whom
the provost saide: 'Ye wreches, dothe awaye youre madnesse and
deliuer youreselff.' And thei saide: 'We were neuer so wel fedde. We
wolde that thou woldest late vs stonde here till the spirites went oute
130 of the bodies.' And than the prouost comaunded that they shulde be
persed thorugh with speres, and so they fullfelled her marterdome.
    And after that the prouost accused Sebastian to the emperour, and
he made hym come before hym and saide: 'Sebastiane, I mervaile of
the, for I haue always sette the with the furst of my palays, and thou
135 haste now abaied and cried ayeinst myn hele and into the wronge of my
goddes.' Thanne Sebastian saide: 'I haue alway worshipped Ihesu
Crist for thine helthe, for the astate of the empire of Rome I haue
alwaye worshipped God that is in heuene.' And thanne saide
Dyoclicien and comaunded that he were bounde in the middes of a
f. 32va feelde and that he were thorughe shote withe arowes. And than | they
141 shotte atte hym so that thei filled alle the bodi withe arowes that he was
like an irchon, so thikke the arowes stode oute of hym in eueri side, and
thei wende he hadde be dede and went her waye. And within two dayes
after he was deliuered and stode vpon the degrees in the palais. So as
145 the emperour come from his wycked doyng to the cristen, he reproued
hym greuously. Thanne the emperour saide: 'Is not this he Sebastian
that I comaunded for to be slain withe arowes?' To whom Sebastian
saide: 'Oure Lorde hathe refused me for that I shulde assemble you
togederes and reproue you of the wickednesse that ye do to the
150 servauntes of Ihesu Crist.' And thanne the emperour comaunded
that he were so longe beten withe st[au]es til he yelde up the sperit, and

118 of] and EH1   120 youre] add lorde EH1   122 nemene] name G   name¹] man
H1   123 byheded] hilde G   124 Marcell] Ma`r'cellH1    126 good] go`o'd H1
127 Ye wreches] þe bochers H1   133 made] bade H1   before] to G   135 now] om. H1
abaied] disobeyid G   137 empire] emperoure G   138 saide] om. G   139 and] om. G
140–41 And . . . arowes] so G   142 stode oute of] steden on G   143 he] þay del. `he' G
144 after . . . deliuered] twice E   146 not . . . he] it not þis G   151 staues] stones E

sithe made caste the body into a preuey that he shulde not be worshipped of the cristen as a marter. And the nyght foluyng he apered to Seint Luce and re[uel]ed her where he was and comaunded her to bery hym atte the fete of the apostelis. She dede as she was 155 comaunded, and suffered dethe vnder Dyoclisien and Maximyen that begonnen to regne the yere of oure Lorde .CC.iiij.^{xx}.vij.

Seint Gregori tellithe in the furst boke of his Dialoge that a woman of Toskane whiche was nwe wedded was preied of other women for to go withe hem to the dedicacion of the chirch of Seint Sebastiane, and 160 the nyght that she shulde go in the morwe she was stered in her flesche that she myght not absteyne her from her husbonde. And in the morw she hadde gretter shame of men than | of God and went f. 32vb thedir, and anone as she was entered in the oratorie where the reliques of Seint Sebastian were, the fende toke her and began to torment her 165 before alle the peple. And thanne the preste toke the couerture of the auuter and couered her, and anone that preest assailled [the fende]. And thanne her frendes saide that thei shulde speke to the enchauntours that they shuld enchaunte the fende. But as sone as thei were enchaunted, bi the right wisdom of God a legion of fendes 170 .vjM^l.vjC.lxvj. entered into her and tormented more sharpeli thanne before. A noble and an holi man þat hight Fortunat heled her bi his praiers.

Hit is redde in the Dedes of Lumbard[es] that in the tyme of Kyng Gilbert al Ytaile was smeten with so gret pestilence that vnnethes the 175 quik myght bery the dede, and that pestilence was principalli at Ro[m]as and atte Pauy. And thanne the good aungell appered visibli and comaunded to the wicked aungell that bare a staffe that he shulde smite and make hem departe. And as many tymes as he smote an hous, so many deied oute therof. And thanne it was shewed to a man that 180 this pestilence shulde neuer cese til they hadde halowed an auuter atte Pauye in the name of Seint Sebastian. And it was do in the chirche of Seint Petre, and thanne this pestilence cesed. And the reliqes of Seint Sebastian were from thennes born to Rome.

Seint Ambrose saiethe in his Preface: 'The bloode of the blessed 185 martir Sebastien shedde, Lorde, for the confession of thi name, hathe

152 into a] in þe G   154 reueled] releued EG, *so changed to* reueled H1
159 preied] 'bede' G   167 the fende] that preste E, þe fende *on erasure* H1
168 shuld] *add* doo G   170 God] *add* anoon G   171 .vjC.] v^C. H1G
tormented] *add* 'hire' H1   sharpeli] *add* hire G   172 thanne] *add* þay dide G, *so ins.* H1
174 Lumbardes] Lumbardie E   of^2] *add* the H1G   177 Romas] Ronas E, Ronas *with*
minim ins. H1   186 Sebastien] *add* was G

knowlaged thi mervailes that thou fulfelle[st] in [the] stabilnesse of thi
f. 33ra vertues and | yeuithe profit to oure stodies and doth helpe towardes
the to thine enemyes.'

> Here endithe the liff of Seint Sebastien, and thanne
> beginnithe the liff of the blessed virgine Seint Annes,
> Cap^m. .xxiij.^m

Seint Anneis the right wise virgine, so as Seint Ambrose tellithe that
wrote her liff and her passion, loste the dethe in the .xiiij. yere of her
age and fonde lyff. The childehode was counted bi hys yeres, but she
was aunsien of her age and of gret wisdom, yong of bodi but olde of
5   corage, faire of visage but more faire of faithe.
In a day as she come fro scolys, the sone of the prouost loued her
and behight her precious stones and richesse withoute nombre so that
she wolde acorde to be his wyff. To whom Anneis saide: 'Goo hennes
fro me, sheparde of dethe, begynnyng of synnes, norshing of felones,
10 for I haue another loue.' And than she beganne to preise her loue and
her spouse of .v. thingges that bene couenable betwene the spouse and
the spouse, furst of the nobilnesse of kynrede, of the manere of bewte,
of the habundaunce of richesse, of the [vigour] of strengthe and
myght, and of the excellence of loue, and saide in this wise: 'He that is
15 full fer more noble thanne thou bi kynrede and bi dignite, of whom his
moder is a virgine and the fader knewe neuer woman, to whom the
aungelis seruen, of whos beauute sonne and mone meruailen, of whom
richesse neuer faillen ne disencresen, bi whos sauoure the dede
quikken, the sike bene comforted, of whom the loue is chastite, the
20 touching is continence and the assembelyng virginite.' And these .v.
f. 33rb thingges she putte in one auctorite, of whom the nobilnesse is | most
high, the myght is most stronge, the beholdyng most fayre, the loue
most suete and the grace grettest of alle other.
And after she putte .v. benefices that her spouce yeuithe her and to
25 all other spouces, for he makithe hem noble withe the ring of faithe,

187 knowlaged] knowlech'ed' H1   fulfellest] fulfelled E   the] thi E   thi²] om. G
188 helpe] helthe changed to helpe H1

EH1T1GDH2A1A2; L begins at 22 myght; T1 breaks off after 15 bi¹   3 counted bi]
countted to H1   4 aunsien] come sithen G   of²] add riȝt G   7 behight her] by
liȝt G   8 to be] om. G   11 of . . . spouse¹] om. G   12 spouse] spowser G
12 of²] add the H1G (de P2)   13 vigour] dignite EH1   17 mone] add þay G
17–18 of² . . . faillen] om. H1   20 .v.] foure G   21 one] om. G   22 high] faire in
hire G, faire on erasure 'in hire' H1

he clothes and arrayethe hem with many diuerse vertues and byndeth
hem bi the passion of his blode, he [ioyneth] hem to hym bi the bonde
of loue and makithe hem riche withe heuenli tresours of ioye, and she
saide ouer: 'This is he that hathe betrouthed me withe his ryng in my
right side, he hathe beclipped my necke withe precious stones, he 30
hathe clothed me with a mantell of tissu of golde and he hathe araied
me withe right noble broches, and he hathe sette his signe in my
visage so that I take none other loue thanne hym, and hathe arayed my
chekes withe his blode. He hath now streyned me withe his chaste
clippynges and his bodi is now ioyned to myn, and hathe shewed me 35
his tresours that mowen not be nombered, the whiche he hathe
behight me yef I perseuer and kepe me to hym.'
   And whanne this yong mad man herde this he leide hym downe sik
in his bedde, and the phisicianes saide that he was sik for loue, so that
the fader of hym tolde it to the virgine all the cause of his siknesse. 40
And she saide hym that she myght in no wise breke the alliaunce of
her furst husbonde, and the pr[o]uost enquered what he was that
Anneis vaunted her so gretly of, and sum tolde hym that she saide that
Ihesu Crist was her spouse. The prouost thanne exhorted her withe
faire blandishe wordes, and sethe manased her withe dredfull wordes. 45
To whom Anneis saide: 'What | wilt thou do? For thou maist neuer f. 33ᵛᵃ
haue that thou requerest. I praise neuer thi faire wordes ne thi
manasing.' Than the prouost saide: 'Chese one of two thyngges,
eyther thou shalt sacrifice to oure goddes in the clothyng of goddes, or
ellis thou shalt be brought to the bordell as other comune women 50
bene.' For he myght not do her no wrong for cause she was of noble
kynrede, but onli bi cause that he putte vpon her that she was cristen.
To whom she ansuerid: 'I tell the pleinli I shal neuer sacrifice to thi
goddis ne I shall neuer be defoilled withe straunge filthes, for I haue
with me the keper of my body that is the aungell of oure Lorde.' 55
   Thanne the prouost comaunded that she shulde be dispoilled and
brought naked to the bordell. And anone oure Lorde made her here so
longe and so thicke þat she was beter clothed withe her here thanne
she was before withe her owne clothyng. And whanne she was entered
into that place of filth, she fonde the aungell of oure Lord redy that 60
illumined all the place withe gret lyght and brought her a right white

27 ioyneth] L, yeuithe EHɪG   28 hem] om. Hɪ   29 betrouthed] bitrow`þ´ed
Hɪ   his] þis Hɪ   35 me] add nowe Hɪ   42 prouost] pruost E   43 of] to on
erasure Hɪ   44 exhorted] hurted G   47 neuer²] neþer Hɪ   50 to] into E
51 cause she] marked for reversal Hɪ   of] om. Hɪ   54 defoilled] defouled Hɪ
straunge] strong G   58–9 withe . . . before] þan G   59 clothyng] clothis G

clothe to do on her. And so that place of a bordell was turned into a
place of orison, and for grete lyght men come thennes more cle[n]er
thanne thei went inne.

65   And thanne the sone of the prouost come to the bordell withe other
yong men and taught hem to go before to her. And whanne thei were
entered anone thei were repentaunt, and for that miracle he called
hem cursed wreches and went in hymselff in gret wodenesse. And
whanne he wolde haue touched her the bryghtnesse of the light come
f. 33ᵛᵇ ayeinst hym, and he yelded no worshippes ne | thankyngges to God,
71   wherfor he was anone strangeled of the fende. And whanne the
prouost herde it he come to her withe gret weping and axed her
diligentely the cause of his dethe. To whom Anneis saide: 'He of
whom he wolde fulfell the wille toke pouer vpon hym and slough
75   hym, and whanne his felawes sayn the miracle of God thei turned
ayein all dredfulli withouten any harme.' Thanne saide the prouost:
'In that it shall apere that thou hast not do it bi art magyke yef thou
maist axe grace for hym that he myght be releued ayein to lyff.' And
thanne Anneis went to orison and praied hertely oure Lorde, and
80   anone the yonge man arose from dethe to lyff and preched oure Lorde
Ihesu Crist openly. And thanne the bisshopes of the ydoles meued
gret contencion to the peple and cried seying: 'Take awaye this wiche
from us that chaungithe the hertes and meuithe the corages of the
peple.' And whanne the prouost hadde sayn so gret a myracle he
85   wolde fayn haue deliuered her, but he durst not for the striff of the
peple, wherfor he ordeyned another vicarie that hight Aspasien and
went his waye all sorifully for he myght not deliuer her.

And thanne the nwe vicarie comaunded that she shulde be caste in a
gret fyre, and whanne that she was in the middell of the fyre the fyre
90   departed in two partyes and brent the peple of misbeleuers. And
thanne Aspasien charged that thei shulde putte a spere thorugh her
throte, and so her spouse white and rede hathe sacred her to hym
virgine and marter. She suffered dethe as men leuen in the tyme of
Constant the Gret in the yere of oure Lorde .CCC.ix. And as the |
f. 34ʳᵃ cristen and her kynrede [entered] her with gret ioie vnnethe thei
96   myght ascape for the panymes that casten stones ayeinst hem.

A ryght holy virgine Emerenciane, whiche was felow to her though
it were so that she was nwe in the faithe, as she satte besides the

63 lyght] *om.* G   clener] clerer EH1G (*plus net* P2)   66 to²] *om.* H1   69 he] *ins.*
H1   78 went] *add* ayene H1   80 preched] preysid G   86 sorifully] sorowful G
95 entered] bere E, *om.* H1   96 hem] him H1   97 virgine] *add* that hight E

sepulcre of her and reproued the paynimes of her wyckednesse thei
stoned her to dethe. And thanne anone the erthe trembeled and 100
thunder and lytenyng was so grete that it slowe many of the paynimes,
so neuer sithe they durste hurt none that come to the sepulcre of that
virgyne. And the body of Seint Emeranciane was leide besydes the
sepulcre of Seint Anneis. And as her kyn woke the .viij. day atte her
tombe thei seigh a companye of virgines clothed withe clothes of 105
golde, among the whiche thei seigh blessed Seint Anneis clothed
withe like clothyng and a lambe whitter thanne any snowe in her right
side. Thanne she saide: 'Beholdethe me and bywepithe me not as
dede, but ioye ye withe me, for I haue receyued the right shynyng
seges with alle other virgines.' And for this vision is halowed 110
secoundely the fest of Seint Anneis.

Constaunce the doughter of Constant was sik of a strong siknesse,
and whanne she herde this vision sche come to the tombe of Seint
Anneis, and as she was in orison she fell aslepe and seigh in vision
Seint Anneis that saide to her: 'Constaunce, yef thou wilt werke stably 115
and leue in oure Lorde thou shalt anone be deliuered.' And withe this
worde she awoke and felt herselff perfitely heled, and thanne she
receyued bapteme and founded a chirche vpon the body of the
virgine, and there she abode in her virginite and assembeled there
many virgines by her | ensaumple.   f. 34rb

Ther was a man that hight Paulyn and vsed the office of preste in 121
the chirche of Seint Anneis and beganne to be tormented bi
temptacion of the fleshe. This symple man, that wold not in no
wise wrathe God, askcd leue of the pope to marie hym. Thanne the
pope, consideryng the bounte [and] the sympelnesse of hym, toke 125
hym hys rynge withe an emeraude and comaunded hym to go to his
chirche where an ymage of Seint Anne[is] was peinted and praie her
that he myght take her to his wyff. This symple man dede so, and
anone the ymage putte forthe her fyngre and he sette the rynge
theron, and she drewe her fyngre to her and kepte the rynge faste, and 130
ther anone al the temptacion was take awaye of the preste. And yet as
men saye the ryng apperithe vpon the fynger of the ymage. And also it
is redde that whan [the pope behelde the chirche of Seint Anneis] he
saide to a preste that he wolde yeue hym a spouse to norishe and to
kepe, and that he ment bi the chirche of Seint Anneis that he wolde 135

101 thunder] þondred H1G   104 woke] a woke E   108 bywepithe me] wepith G
109 dede] ȝe dide G   ye] *ins*. H1   110 seges] þyngis G   125 and] of E, and *on
erasure* H1   127 Anneis] Anne E   133 the Pope . . . Anneis] *om*. E, *ins*. H1

committe to hym. And thanne he toke hym a rynge and comaunded hym to wedde the ymage, and the ymage putte forthe her fyngre and withdrewe it with the rynge, and so he wedded her.

Of this virgine saiethe Seint Ambrose in the Boke of Virgines: 'This
140 virgine here praisen yong and olde and children. Ther nys no more to praise thanne tho that mowe be praised of men, wherfor witheoute nombre prechen this marter. Abaashin you alle whanne they speken, that ye be witnesse of so gret diuinite, for yet mysht she not bi age be arbitrere of herselff. She made atte the ende that it was leued of God
f. 34ᵛᵃ that that was | not leued of man, for what thyng that is ouer kynde
146 longithe to the maker of kynde. This is a newe maner of martir, that she that was not couenable yet to haue pain and that nature hadde a strong stryff of the victorie, was couenable to be crowned and to haue the maistrie of vertues, the whiche bere the iugement of her age. And
150 right as the nwe maried haste[th] to go to the chaumbre, this virgyne went gladde and ioyfull a gret pase to the place of torment.'

Seint Ambrose saiethe also in his Preface that the blessed Anneys despised the delites of nobilnesse, she deserued the heuenly dignite, in levyng the desires of mannes felawship [she hath fonde the felawship]
155 of the euerlastyng kyng, and she receyving a precious dethe for the confession of Ihesu Crist is made therwithe like to hym and endelesly to ioie with hym.

Here endithe the liff of Seint Anneis, and after begynnethe the lyff of Seint Vincent martir, Capitulum .xxiiij.ᵐ

Seint Vincent was of the noble kinrede, but he was more noble bi faithe and bi religion, and he was a deken of Seint Valerie bisshop, to whom, for that he hadde a lettyng in his tongge, he commytted his charge so that he ne ten[d]ed to nothyng but to orison and to contemplacion.
5 And bi the comaundement of Dasien, Vincent and Valerien were drawen and caste into a cruel prison. And whanne the prouoste wende that they were perished bi hunger and peyne, he comaunded that thei shulde come byfore hym, and whanne he seigh hem hole and gladde he

140 praisen] preisith *with* ith *on erasure* H1   and²] *om.* G   141 men] me G
143 so] *om.* H1   diuinite] dignyte G   144 it] *changed to* þis H1   leued] loued H1
144–5 God . . . of] *om.* G   145 leued] loued H1   146 maker] marter H1
147 that²] *add* marter *del.* H1   150 hasteth] hasted EG   153 despised] displesed
H1   deserued] desoxenyd G   154 she . . . felawship] *om.* EG   157 to] with H1

EH1GDH2A1A2L   1 was¹] *om.* H1   4 tended] tented E, entendid G   to¹] *add*
do E   8 hem] him H1

was wrothe and | saide: 'What saiest thou, Valerye, that vnder the f. 34ᵛᵇ
name of thi relygion thou doest ayeinst the decreez of princes?' And 10
as Valeri ansuered softely, Vincent saide to hym: 'Worshipfull fader,
murmur not so dredfull thought but crye withe a deliuer vois, and
fader, yef thou comaundest me, I shal go ansuere to the iuge.' To
whom he saide: 'Right dere, it is longe agoo that I comitted to the the
cure of spekyng, and now I ordeyne the to ansuere for the faithe 15
wherfor we be come hedir.' And thanne Vincent turned hym to
Dacyen the iuge and saide: 'Thou haste holde into now wordes for to
reneye the faithe, but wete it wel that this is gret felonye towardes the
wisdom of cristen peple for to blame in renyinges the worship of oure
Godhede.'   20
    And thanne Dasyene comaunded that the bisshop were sent into
exile and that Vincent [as] a presumptuous yonge man were streight
oute in the torment that is called eculee, and it is made as a crosse in
trauers wherof the twey endes bene fasted into the erthe, and alle hys
membres weren tobroste for to afere the tother cristen. And whanne 25
he was al torent Dacien saide to hym: 'Nou, thou Vincent, how saiest
thow now thi wreched body is al torent?' Thanne Vincent smyling
saide to hym: 'This is al that I haue euer desired.' And thanne the
prouost more wrothe thanne before beganne to manase hym of alle
manere of tormentis. Thanne Vincent saide [to hym]: 'O thou cursed 30
creature, wenest thou to anger me? So moche more greuously that
thou shalt bygynne in me turmentyng, so moche more mercy will oure
Lorde God haue on me. Arise up, thou cursed, and bi al thi wicked
spirit | thou shalt be ouercome, for thou shalt see me by the vertue of f. 35ʳᵃ
God more mow suffre thanne thou hast myght to turment me.'   35
    And thanne the prouost beganne to crie and [to smyte the bochers]
withe scourges and withe roddes. And thanne Vincent saide to hym:
'What saiest thou, Dacien? Thou thiself vengest me of my
tormentoures.' And thanne the prouost was al madde for angger
and saide to the bochers: 'Right cursed that ye be, ye do not. Whi 40
faillen youre hondes? Ye haue ouercome mordereres and vouutereres
that thei myght nothyng holde vnder youre hondes and among youre

---

12 murmur] mornyth G   dredfull thought] dredfully G   but] to H1
13 comaundest] mayste comaunde G, 'mayste' comaundest H1   14 the the] þe G
18 is] *om.* H1   19 renyinges] reny G   22 as] and EH1   24 fasted] fitget H1,
fichid G   27 now] *add* by G, *so ins.* H1   is al torent] *om.* G   28 euer] *om.* G
29 prouost] *add* was E   30 to hym] *om.* E   36 to smyte the bochers] bade the
bochers smyte EH1   38 Thou] though H1G   my] *om.* G   41 mordereres] merthes
H1   voutereres] a voritus (?) G   42 nothyng] not G

tormentes, and this [onli] Vincent ouercomithe you all.' And thanne
the bochers [to]drewe his body withe combes of iren that the blode
45 ranne al aboute his body so that his boweles apered thorugh hys
ribbes.

Thanne Dacien said to hym: 'Vincent, haue pitee of thiselff so that
thou myghtest recouer thi faire yougthe and spare the tormentes that
bene to come.' Thanne Vincent saide: 'O thou venemouse tonge of the
50 fende, truste it well that I drede not thi tormentes that bene to come,
but I drede more only that ther thou feynest the to haue pitee of me,
for the more wrothe that I see the the gladder am I. I will not in no
wise that thou les[s]e thi tormentes, so that thou mayst knowe that
thou art ouercome in all thingges.' Than was he take from that
55 torment and was brought into a torment of fire, and Vincent blamed
the bochers for they abode so longe to do hym payne. And thanne he
went vpon the gredill withe his owne wille, and ther was he rosted,
brent and b[r]oyled thorugh all his membres, and he was takked to the
f. 35rb gredill withe sharpe | naylles of iren brennyng, and whan the blode
60 ranne in the fire the lemes of fire ronnen vp thorugh all his woundes
and toke his bowellys and boyled oute of hem all manere moyster till
he was made vnmevable, but alwayes withe his honde[s] leffte vp to
heuene he praied to oure Lorde.

And whanne the mynistres hadde tolde to Dacien he saide: 'Allas,
65 we be ouercome, liuithe he yet. Yet to that ende that he may lenger
lyue in payne, closith hym up in a derke prison and bringeth thedir
right sharpe broken shellis, and bindithe his fete to a poste, and late
hym lye there witheoute eny maner comfort vpon the broken shellis,
and whanne he is dede late me wete it.' And the cruell mynistres
70 obeyed to hym as to a ryght cruell lorde, but the kyng for whom he
suffered that payne turned it into ioye, for the derkenesse was chased
awaye oute of the prison with right gret lyght, and the peces of the
sharpe shellis were torned into softenesse and suetnesse of all manere
of floures, his fete were vnbounde and he vsed of the comfort and
75 worship of aungelis. And as he went vpon the floures syngyng withe
the aungels, the suete sowne of the songe and the suete sauoure of
floures that was merveylous streched up oute of the prison. And

43 onli] *on erasure* H1, holi E   44 todrewe] withdrewe E   50 that bene to come]
om. G   51 ther] *om.* G   of] on G   52 more wrothe that] wroth more G   the the]
þe G   I. I] y G   53 lesse] L, lese EG, leue H1   58 broyled] boyled EH1
60 in] into H1   the lemes of fire] and G   vp] oute G   62 hondes] honde E
65 that ende] *om.* H1   68 maner] more G   69 dede] turmentid to deth G
76 sowne . . . suete] *om.* G

whanne the kepers hadde perceiued this thorughoute the creueys of
the prison what ioye was there, they conuerted hem to the faithe.

And whanne Dacyen herde this thyng he was al madde and saide: 80
'What shal we now do? We bene ouercome. Now late hym be brought
into a softe bedde | withe softe clothes lest he be made more glorious, f. 35va
and whanne he is sumwhat comforted and strengthed we shull
ordeyne nwe tormentis for to punishe hym.' And whanne Vincent
was brought into a right softe bedd and hadde rest a litell while therin, 85
he yelde vp the spirit to God aboute the yere of oure Lorde
.CCC.iiij^{xx}.viij. vnder Diocli[si]en and Maximien.

And whanne Dacien herde it he made gret sorugh and saide that
now he was ouercome, 'but sithe I myght not ouercome hym levyng I
shall punishe hym dede, for though I myght not haue the victorie yet 90
shall I fede me of his payne.' And thanne his body was caste into a
felde for to be deuoured withe bestes and briddes bi the comaundement of Dacien, but it was kepte anone withe the keping of aungels,
and bestis also kept it witheoute touchyng, and after that ther come a
ravon al enf[amyn]ed that chased away [other briddes withe her 95
wynges, and also she chased away] a wolff withe bityng of her bille and
withe cryeng, and thanne she turned her hede towarde the holi body
to biholde hym as he that mervailled of the keping of aungels.

And whanne Dacien herde this he saide: 'I trowe I shall not
ouercome hym dede.' And th[anne] he comaunded that thei shulde 100
fasten a mylnstone about his necke and caste hym into the see so that
he that myght not be wasted in the erthe withe bestis be deuoured in
the see with fishes. And the shipmen that beren his body into the see
cast hym therin, but the body was sonner aryved thanne the shipmen
and was founde of a lady and of other bi [the] reuelacion of Ihesu Crist 105
and was worshipfully beried of hem. |

Austin saiethe of this martir: 'The blessed Vincent ouercome in f. 35vb
wordes, ouercome in peynes, he ouercome in confession, he ouercome
in tribulacion, [he ouercome bruled], he ouercome drowned, he
ouercome quik, he ouercome dede. This Vincent was tormented for 110
the loue of God, he was scourged [for] to be taught, he was beten for

78 creueys] greues H1   85 into] forth in H1   hadde] *om.* G   87 Dioclisien]
Dioclien E   89 not] *add* with victorie G   90 yet] þere G   93 keping] wepyng G
94 also] *om.* H1   95 enfamynyd] enflaumed EH1   95–6 other . . . away] *om.* E
97 thanne] *om.* G   100 thanne] ther E, þan *on erasure* H1   101 that] *om.* H1G
102 be] but G, be *changed to* bot H1   104 thanne] and *changed to* þan H1   105 the]
om. E   108 he ouercome²] *om.* G   109 he ouercome bruled] *om.* E   bruled]
broylyng G   drowned] drownyng G   110 This] Thus G   111 for¹] *om.* E

to be made stronge, he was brent for to be purged.' Ambrose saide of
this marter in this manere: 'Vincent was tormented, beten, scourged
and brent for the holi name of God, and his corage was neuer
115 chaunged, for he brent more withe [the] fire of heuene thanne
withe the fire of the gredyrne, he was more bound withe the drede
of God thanne of the worlde, he desired more to please God thanne
the market, he hadde leuer dye to the world thanne to God.' And
Austin saiethe elliswhere: 'A mervailous syght is sette before oure
120 eyen, a felenous iuge, a blodi turmentour, a martir vnouercome, a
striff of cruelte [and] of pitee.'

Prudencien that was noble in the tyme of Theodesien the olde that
beganne the yere of oure Lorde .viijC.iiij^{xx}.vij., he saide how that
Vincent ansuered to Dasien in this wise: 'The tormentis of the prison,
125 the hokes drawyng, the fire brennyng and the dethe that foluithe is
but game to cristen men.' And Dasien saide: 'Byndethe hym and
ouerdrawe hys armes from hye to lowe, strechyng oute the iointes of
his membres so myche that his bones departen that his brethe come
oute bi the trewens of his membres.' And Goddes knyght lough of all
130 this and blamed the blodi hondes for they putte no dipper the yrne
hokes in his membres. And whanne he was in the prison the aungell of
f. 36ra God saide to hym: 'Arise, | thou noble martir al sure, for thou shalt be
oure felawe among the holi felawship. O thou knyght vnouercome,
more mighti thanne any other, these sharpe and strong tormentes
135 dreden [the] as a conquerour.' And Prudencien criethe: 'O thou art
only noble of the worlde, thou berest only the victorie of double batell,
and therfor thou haste goten the two crownes.'

Here endithe the lyff of Seint Vincent, and nexst beginnethe the liff of Seint Basile bisshop, Cap^m. .xxv.^{m}

Basile was a worshipfull bisshop and a noble doctour, and Philesiene
bisshopp of Dyaconye wrote his lyff, and it was shewed to an holi
hermyte that hight Effraim of what holynesse he was, for as the saide

---

112 saide] seith G   114 God] crist G   corage] *so on erasure* H1   115 the] *om.* E
119–20 oure eyen] vs þanne G   120 felenous] felawis G   vnouercome] oon ouercome G
121 and] *om.* E   122 that¹] *on erasure* H1   123 of oure Lorde] *om.* G   124 the]
þy G   127 strechyng] strechith G   129 trewens] krenys G   130 hondes]
houndez H1   133 vnouercome] oon ouercome G   134 any] meny H1G
135 the] *om.* E   criethe] cride *with* de *on erasure* H1, cride G   137 crownes] *add* of
heuen G, *so ins.* H1

EH1GDH2A1A2L   1 and Philesiene] of Philosofie *changed to* & of Philosien G

Effraym was rauished in spirit he seigh a pilere of fere of whiche the
ende touched the heuene, and herde a vois seyeng: 'Suche is Basile the 5
grete as this pilere that thou seest here.' And thanne the hermite come
into the citee on a tuelfe day only for to see this man, and whanne he
seigh hym clodid in a fayre vestement goyng worshipfulli a procession
with his clerkes, he saide to hymselff: 'I haue trauayled in vayn as y
see, for he that is in suche worship may not be as I seigh, for we that 10
haue born the charge of colde and of hunger bene not suche, and this
that is in suche highnesse and suche worshipes for to be a pilere of
fere, I mervayle gretly of this thing.' And thanne Basile seigh these
thingges in spirit and made the hermyte for to come to hym, and
whanne he was come thedyr he seigh a tonge of fire spekyng thorugh 15
his mowthe. And thanne saide the hermite: 'Verily this is the grete
Basile a pilere of fere, verily spekith | the holy goste thorugh his f. 36rb
mouthe.' Than Effraym saide to hym: 'Syr, I praie the that thou axse
grace for me that I may speke Greke.' And thanne Basile saide: 'Thou
hast asked a grete thinge.' But yet he praied for hym, and anone he 20
speke Greke.

Another hermyte seigh another tyme Seint Basile go well besain in
abyte of a bisshop and despised hym in his thought, seyeng: 'Lo what
delyte he hathe to go in suche bobaunce.' And a vois ansuered hym
and saide: 'Thou delitest the more in strokyng of thi catte thanne 25
Basile in al hys araye.'

The emperour, that was a chersere of the Arryens, toke from the
cristen a chirche and gaue it to the Arrienes. Thanne Basile went to
hym and saide: 'Emperour, it is writen that the worship of a kyng
yeuithe rightwisly. Whi hast thou thanne comaunded that the trewe 30
catholike be putte fro thaire chirche and that she be yeue to the
Arienes?' And than the emperour saide: 'Basile, thou turnest ayein to
thi chidyngges. What hast thou to do therwith?' And he said: 'It sit me
forsothe to deye for the trouth.' And thanne Demoscenys, prouost of
the metis and a norisher of the Ariens, spake for hem flateryng 35
wordes, to whom Basile saide: 'It sittithe the to medle of the kyngges
potage and not of the devyne techyngges.' And anone he held hys pees
al confused. And thanne the emperour saide to Basile: 'Goo and iuge

---

8 a²] *on erasure* H1   12 highnesse] heuynesse G   be] *ins.* H1   13 these] *om.* G
15 of] *add* the E   16 this] *om.* G   19 grace for] *so with* ace for *on erasure* H1
22 besain] besy H1   24 to . . . bobaunce] in apparail G   25 catte] *on erasure* H1,
cote G   28 cristen] *on erasure* H1   a chirche] *ins.* H1   31 thaire] þe G
32 ayein] ayeinst E, ayenst *with* st *erased* H1   33 chidyngges] tidyngis G

betwene hem, but not after the inordinat loue of the peple.' And he
40 went thedir and saide before alle the catholiques and the Arryenes that
they shulde shette the dore of the chirche and sele it withe her
signettes of euery partie, and that the chirche shulde be to hem bi the
f. 36ᵛᵃ orison of whom she were opened. And whanne it liked | [to] the
Arryens thei preiden thre dayes and thre nyghtes, and whanne they
45 come to the dores of the chirche it wolde not be opened. And thanne
Basile withe procession come to the chirche and made his orison and
putte lyghtly withe the ende of his crosse and saide: 'Princes, open
youre gates.' And anone thei opened and thei went in and yolde
thankyngges to God, and thanne the chirche was yolde ayein to the
50 catholiques.

Thanne the emperour made behight gret thyngges to Basile, as it is
redde in the Story Parted in Thre, if he wolde consent to his purpose.
And Basile ansuered: 'These thingges longen to children, for tho that
bene made fatte withe the devyne scripture ne will not suffre in no
55 wyse þat oo silable be corrumped of the devyne techingges.' And
thanne the emperour havyng despite saide that he wolde yeue
sentence of the exile of hym, and as he wolde haue wretyn it hymselff,
the furste penne breke, the secounde and the thridde, and thanne he
was so aferde that he myght not write but breke the scrowe in gret
60 anger.

A worshipfull man, Herarde by name, hadde a doughter only that
he wolde sacre to oure Lorde, but the enemye of mankynde that
perceyued this thing set afire [one of] the seruauntez of this Herard in
the loue of this same mayde. And whanne he seigh that it was
65 impossible for hym that was a servaunt to come to the clippyng[ges]
of so noble a mayde, he went to an enchauntour and behyght hym gret
quantite of money yef he wolde helpe hym in that nede. To whom the
f. 36ᵛᵇ en|chauntoure saide: 'I may not do it, but yef thou wilt y shall sende
the to the fende my lorde, and yef thou do that he will bidde the thou
70 shalt haue thi desire.' And thanne the yonge man saide: 'I shall do
whateuer he biddithe me.' And thanne this enchauntoure made a

39 inordinat] ordynate G   40 alle] om. G   42 hem] hym G   43 it] on erasure
H1   to] om. E   44 thei] om. G   44–5 thei preiden . . . chirche] repeated with
prayeden for preiden E   45 opened] thei opened not E, so with þei and not del. H1
46 Basile] add wente G, so ins. H1   procession] add and G   47 crosse] add vp the
dore G   51 made] om. G   is] add seide and G   54–5 scripture . . . devyne] om. G
55 silable] Basile H1   62 enemye] heremite changed to enmie H1   63 one of] L, on
EG, on 'of' H1   65 clippyngges] clippyng EH1   66 behyght] he heiȝt G
67 money] mone'y' H1   71 made] seide he wold make G

lettre and sent it to the fende bi the yonge man in these wordes: 'My
lorde, for that it behouithe me hastely and curiously withedrawe sum
from cristen religyon and bryng hem to [do] thi wille so that thi party
be eueri day multeplied, I sende you here a yonge man that brenn[ith] 75
in the loue of suche a mayde and praieth you that he may haue his
desire, so that ye glorifie in hym, and fro hennys forward I may
assemble other to the,' and toke hym the lettre and sayde to hym:
'Goo and be atte suche an houre atte midnyght vpon the sepulcre of a
panyme, and caste vp this lettre into the eyre and anone the fendes 80
will come to the.' He went thedir and dede so, and the prince of
derkenesse come enviround withe multitude of fendes, and whan he
hadde redde the lettre he saide to the yong man: 'Wilt thou leue in me
yef I fulfill thi will?' And he saide: 'Lord, y leue in the.' And the fende
saide: 'Renye thi Ihesu Crist.' 'Y renye hym,' he saide. Thanne saide 85
the fende: 'Ye cristen men bene full of trecherye, for whan ye haue
nede to me ye come to me, but also sone as ye haue hadde youre will
ye renye me anone and gone to youre Ihesu Crist, and he receyue[th]
you, for he is full debonayre. And therfor yef thou wilt that I fulfill thi
will, make me a lettre wretin with thine owne honde wherinne thou 90
shalt confesse to haue renyed thi Crist and thi baptime and al cristen
profession, and that thou art my | seruaunt to be condempned withe f. 37ra
me atte the iugement.' And [anone] he wrote this lettre with his
propre honde, how he renyed Ihesu Crist and putte hym in the seruise
of the fende. And thanne anone the fende called the spirites of 95
fornicacion and comaunded hem to go to the forsaide mayde and sette
her al afire in the loue of this yonge man in suche wise that she may
not endure witheoute hym, the whiche spirites went anone and sette
her al afire so that this maide fell doune to the erthe and wepte and
cried and said to her fader: 'Haue pitee on me, fader, for I am 100
greuously tormented for the loue of this yong man that is withe þe.
Haue pitee of myn inwarde sorugh and shewe me the loue of a fader,
and ioyne me to hym that I loue and for whom I am thus peinfully
tormented. And yef thou do not thou shalt see me in shorte tyme
deye, and thou shalt yelde for me acountes atte the day of iugement.' 105
Thanne saide the fader wepyng to his doughter: 'A, wreched
doughter, what is befalle on the now? Allas, whi is my tresoure

72 sent] sende G   74 do] *om.* EG   75 brennith] brenned E   76 you] þe G
77 ye] þou G   79 an houre atte] a G   of] *add* suche E   84 And²] *add* þanne G
86 Ye] þe G   88 receyueth] receyued E   89–90 that . . . will] *om.* G   92 art]
add renyed G   seruaunt] *twice* E   93 anone] *om.* E   with] *add* my seruant and with G
95 thanne . . . fende] *om.* G   102 of¹] on me and G

stole awaye from me? Allas, whi is the light of myn eyen quenched? A,
doughter, al my ioie hadde bene to haue ioyned the to an heuenly
110 spouse in hope to haue be [the] rather saued bi the, and now thou art
woxe madde in wrechidnesse. Yet, doughter, late me ioyne the to God
so that thou not lede myn age with sorugh into helle.' And she cried
continuelly, sayeng: 'Fader, eyther thou most fulfille my desire or ellis
thou shalt see me deye anone.' And she wepte bitterly as though she
115 wolde haue go oute of herselff. Thanne the fader that was sette in gret
f. 37rb discomfort was deceyued bi the counsayle | of f[r]endes and fullfilled
her wille and gaue her to this yonge man to wiff withe moche of his
substaunce and said: 'Go, my wrechid doughter, with alle.' And as
they were wedded togedre this yong man entred not into the chirche
120 ne made not the signe of the crosse ne dede nothyng like a cristen
man, the whiche was perceyued of many that saide [it] to his wyff in
this wise: 'Wete it well that he that thou hast chosen to thin husbonde
is not cristen ne entre[th] not into the chirche.' And whanne she herde
it she dradde gretly and felle to the erthe and beganne to scrache with
125 her fyngers and to bete her breste and sayd: 'Allas, whi was I born that
I ne hadde bene dede anone as I was receyued into this worlde?' And
whan she hadde tolde her husbonde that she hadde herde, he saide it
was not soo but al was fals that she hadde herde. And thanne she
saide: 'Yef thou wilt that I leue the, late us entre into the chirche
130 tomorw togedre.' And whanne he seigh that he myght hyde it no
lenger he tolde her al by ordre of al hys governaunce, and whanne she
herde it she wepte withoute mesure and hasted her to goo to the
blessed Basile and tolde hym al that was fall to her husbond. And
thanne Basile called the yong man to hym and herde all these
135 thyngges of hym, and he saide to hym: 'Sone, wilt thou turne to
oure Lorde?' 'Ye, Sire,' he saide, 'full fayn, but I may not, for I haue
renyed Ihesu Crist and haue confessed the fende, and I haue wretyn
the renyeng with myn owne honde and haue yeue it to the fende.' And
139 thanne Basile saide to hym: 'Dere frende, drede the not, for he is
f. 37va debonayre | and will receyue the repentaunt.' And anone he toke this

---

108 the] þis G   109 haue ioyned] ioyne G   110 haue] *om.* G   the^1] *om.* E
112 not . . . age] 'be' *with* not ledde *on erasure* H1, be not ledde G   113 eyther thou]
ye H1   115–16 sette . . . was] *om.* G   116 frendes] fendes E, f'r'endez H1
118–19 as they were] whanne þay schold be G   119 togedre] *om.* G   not] *om.* G
120 ne^1] and G   not the] no H1   121 it] *om.* E   123 entreth] entred E   chirche]
add as cristen G   124 scrache] scratte H1, kracche G   125 fyngers] hondis G
127 hadde^2] *om.* G   129 leue] loue H1   130 that he myght hyde] it he hidde H1
132 her] it G   137 confessed] L, *add* to EH1G

yonge man and crossed hym in the forhede and shette hym faste up
thre dayes, and sith he visyted hym and asked hym how it was withe
hym. And he saide: 'Sir, I am in gret torment and may not suffre her
clamours ne the fere[s] of hem, and they shaken the lettre vpon me
and sayen: "Thou comest to us and not we to the." ' And thanne ayein   145
he signed hym withe the crosse and closed hym vp ayein and praied
for hym. And certayne dayes after, he come ayein to hym and sayde:
'How doest thou, sone, yet?' And he saide: 'Fader, I herde aferre the
manases and the feres of hem, but I seigh hem not.' And thanne he
gave hym ayein mete and blessid hym and closed the dore and went   150
and praied for hym. And atte the fourty dayes ende he come ayein and
asked hym: 'How doest thou yet, sone?' And he saide: 'Wel, holy seint
of God, for I seigh the in a vision fight for me and ouercome the
fende.' And after that he ledde hym withe hym and sembeled al the
clergy and the peple and taught hem to praie for hym, and holdyng   155
the honde of the yong man ledde hym to the chirche. And the fende
come with multitude of wicked spirites and visiblie toke the yong man
and enforsed hym to take hym oute of the seintez honde, and he
beganne to crie and saide: 'Helpe me, holy seint of God.' And the
cursed fende assailled hym withe so gret strengthe that he drowe the   160
holy man with hym a gret waye. Thanne saide the holy man to hym:
'O thou right wicked aboue al other, ne suffisith not thi dampnacion
to the but thou most tempte the creatures of myn.' | And thanne the   f. 37ᵛᵇ
fende saide, heryng all the peple: 'Basile, thou doest me gret
preiudice, for we went not to hym but he come to us and renyed   165
his Crist and knowlaged me his lorde. Lo here his lettre wretin
withe his owne honde þe whiche I holde in myn honde.' Thanne
Basile saide: 'We shull neuer cese of praiere till thou haue yolde
ayein the lettre.' And as Basile praide and [lefte] his hondes to the
heuene the lettre was brought to hym thorugh the eyre and taken in   170
his honde so that all the peple seigh it. And thanne he saide to the
yong man: 'Knowest thou this lettre?' And he saide: 'Ye, Sir, it is
wretyn with myn owne honde.' Thanne Basile al torent the lettre
and ledde þe yong man forthe to the chirche and made hym able to

143 her] þe G   144 feres] fere EH1   145 sayen] seyden G   ayein] anon H1
147 sayde] add to hym G   149 manases] man`a´cez H1   150 ayein] om. G   the
dore] hym aȝen G   152 thou] om. G   holy] add fadir and G   157 visiblie] bisili H1
158 he] ins. H1   159 to crie] om. G   165 renyed] so on erasure H1   166 his³] is a
H1   168 thou] we H1   168–9 yolde ayein] trs. followed by the del. H1   169 and
lefte] and E, and 'left' H1, liftyng G   170 brought . . . thorugh] to hym þrowe in G
171–2 to . . . saide] om. G   172 it is] þay ben G   173 owne] om. G

175 [h]ere the holy seruise and enfourmed hym wel and toke hym ayein
to his wyff.

A woman ther was also that hadde done many gret synnes, the
whiche she wrote in a lettre of parchemyn, and the most greuous she
sette all binethe and toke this lettre to Seint Basile that he shulde praie
180 for her that tho synnes myght be effased bi his praiers. And whan he
hadde praied and opened the lettre she founde all her synnes effaced
saue the most grevous. Th[a]nne she said to Basile: 'Seruaunt of God,
haue pitee on me and gete me foryeuenesse of this, lyke as thou hast
done for [the] other.' And he saide to her: 'Goo hennys fro me,
185 woman, for I am a synfull man and haue nede of foryeuenesse as
thou.' And as she was importune to hym he saide: 'Goo to the holy
man Effraym, for he may gete the that thou desirest.' And she went to
the holy man and tolde hym how Seint Basile hadde sent her to hym.

f. 38ʳᵃ And | thanne he saide: 'Doughter, goo thi way, for I am a synner, and
190 turne ayein to Basile, for he that gate the foryeuenesse [of] the furst
may wel gete the the same grace for the remenaunt. And hast the fast
that thou maist fynde hym alyue.' And whanne she come into þe cite
she seigh men bere Seint Basile to beryeng, and thanne she beganne to
crie after hym and seye: 'God se and iuge by[t]uene me and the, for
195 thou were myghti inow to praie for me and sendest me to another.'
And than she leyde the scrowe vpon the bere, and withinne a while
after she toke it ayein and opened it and fonde her synnes al effaced.
And thanne she and al that were there preised hym and thanked God.

Bifore that this holy man passed oute of this world, he fell in a gret
200 siknesse of whiche he deyed. Thanne he called to hym a Iwe that hight
Ioseph bi name that was right wys in the art of medicine, the whiche
he loued miche for that he seigh before that he shulde conuerte hym
to the faithe. He praied hym taste his pounce, and so he dede and
founde therby that he shulde deye in haste, and anone he saide to his
205 meyne: 'Makith redy that is nedefull to his sepulture, for he shall deye
anone.' And whanne Basile herde it he saide: 'Ioseph, thou woste not
what thou saiest.' And thanne Ioseph saide: 'Sir, wete it well that
whanne the sonne goth doune this day [the sonne goth doune], that is
to saie thou shalt deye this day whanne the sonne gothe downe.' And

175 here] bere E   176 wyff] *add* and to god G   181 she] he G
182 Thanne] Thnne E   183 this] þese G   184 the] that E   190 he] *ins.* H1
of] atte E   194 seye] seide G, sey`d′ H1          God] good G, go`o′d H1   se] *changed to* ser
H1G   bytuene] bymene EH1   me and] thou *on erasure* H1   the] me H1   197 it²] *om.*
H1   200 Iwe] man G, iewe *on erasure* H1   203 pounce] spounce E   206 it] þis G
208 the sonne goth doune²] *om.* EH1

Basile saide: 'Yef I leue till tomoru none what wilt thou saye?' Thanne 210
Ioseph saide: 'Yef thou lyue to that houre I will deye.' And thanne
Basile saide: 'Thou shalt deye verily in synne but thou shalt | leue in f. 38rb
Ihesu Crist.' 'I wote well,' quod Ioseph, 'what ye mene, and yef ye liue
atte that houre I will do as ye sayn.' And thanne the blessed Basile,
though it were so that after nature he shuld haue deyed anone, he gete 215
dilacion of oure Lorde vnto the morw the houre of none and lyued.
And whanne Ioseph see it he was abaisshed and leued in oure Lorde,
and thanne Basile ouercomyng the febilnesse of the bodi by the vertu
of corage he rose hym vp fro his bedde and entred into the chirche and
baptised hym with his owne hondes, and after that he turned to his 220
bedde and yelde goodly the spirit to God, and floured aboute the yere
of oure Lorde .CCC.lxx.

Here endithe the liff of Seint Basile the bysshop, and next
beginneth the liff of Seint Iohn the Awmonere, Cap^m.
.xxvj.^m

Seint Iohn the Awmenere, that was a patriarke of Alisaundre, was in a
tyme in his praiers allone and seigh a right faire mayde stondyng
before hym and bere a crowne of olyues on her hede. And whan he
seigh her he was gretly abaisshed and asked what she was, and she
sayde: 'I am Misericorde, that brought forthe the sone of God. Take 5
me to thi wyff and thou shalt fare well.' And thanne he vnderstondyng
that the olyue signified merci and byganne from that day forward to
be so mercyfull that he was called Awmonere. And he called alway
pore men his lordes, and therof it came that Hospitalers callen pore
men her lordes. And thanne he called to hym al his servauntes and 10
saide to hem: 'Gothe thorugh the citee and writeth alle the names of
my lordes.' And he | seigh that thei vnderstode hym not. He saide: 'I f. 38va
mene tho that ye call pore men and beggers and I calle hem my lordes
and saie that they bene myn helpers, for truste it well thei mowe helpe
us and gete us the kyngdom of heuene.' And for he wolde stere folke 15
to do almes, he vsed to tell a merye tale.

  There were sum tyme, as he saide, beggers the whiche seten and

211 thou] add do & G   211–12 And . . . deye] om. G   212 leue] bileue verrili E,
bileue H1G (viuras P2)   213 ye^1,2] þou G   214 ye sayn] the same G   blessed]
bisshop H1   215 he^1] she with s erased H1   219 chirche] chambre G

EH1GDH2A1A2L   1 a patriarke] om. G   3 on her hede] in hir hond G
5 sone] summe G   God] gold G   7 forward] om. G   8 so] om. G   11 thorugh]
add alle H1

warmed hem ayeinst the sonne and hadde there mery talis of almes
folke and blamed the wicked and preised the good. Thanne was there
20 in the citee a riche man [and a mighty] that hight Theolonair, but he
was right cruel to pore men for he wold chace hem oute bi gret despite
tho that come to his house. And as ther was neuer one of these pore
men that hadde any almesse of hym, than one of hem saide to that
other: 'What will ye geue me yef y gete of hym almes this day?' And
25 they leide a wageoure that he shulde not, and than he went his waye
and turned right to the hous of this riche man and stode atte the gate
askyng almesse. And whanne this riche man come and seigh this pore
man atte [his] gate he hadde gret despite and wolde haue [throwe]
sumwhat atte his hede, but he coude fynde nothyng, til atte the last
30 ther come a seruaunt of his brynging a basket full of brede, and he
toke a loef of the basket and threwe it atte the pore manys hede. And
he toke the lofe and ranne faste to his felawes and saide truly that he
hadde receiued þat loef of Pers ys owne honde.

And thanne two dayes after, the riche man was sik and atte the
f. 38ᵛᵇ dethe, and as he was rauished in sperit and | seigh that he was sette in
36 iugement and som putte his wicked dedes in a balaunce, and in that
other parti of the balaunce there were sum clothed in white that weren
all sorifull and mournyng for they hadde nothing to putte in that other
balaunce. And one of hem saide: 'Truly we haue nothing but one rie
40 loef that he gaue to God ayeinst his will but two dayes agoo.' And
thanne thei putte that lofe in the balaunce, and hem semed that the
balaunce were euen. Thanne thei sayde to the riche man: 'Multiplie
this rie loef, or ellis [thou] most be deliuered to these blacke fendes.'
And thanne he awoke and saide: 'Allas, yef a rye loef haue so moche
45 availed me that I gaue in despite, how moche shulde it haue done yef I
hadde geue all my good to pore men?' As this riche man went on a day
clothed with riall vestimentis, a pore man al naked come to hym and
asked hym sum clothing for the loue of God to hille hym with, and
anone he dispoiled hym and gaue hym his riche clothe, and anone this
50 pore man solde it. And whanne this riche man wost it that he hadde
solde the clothe and dispended it, he was so sori that he wolde ete no
mete but [saide]: 'Allas, I am not worthi that the pore man haue

20 and a mighty] *om.* EH1   25 his waye] þidre H1   28 his] the E   throwe]
drawe E   29 til] but G   30 brynging] bering H1   32 faste] *om.* G   33 Pers
ys] his G   36 and¹] *add* þat G   36–7 and² . . . balaunce] *om.* G   38 sorifull and]
sori ful of H1   in that other] into her G   41 hem] hym H1   43 thou] the E, ʒe G
45 it] I H1   48 hille] hele H1G   49 clothe] clothyng G   51 dispended it]
dispendidded H1   52 saide] *om.* E, *ins.* H1

[mynde] vpon me.' And the nyght folueng whanne he slepte he seigh one that was brighter thanne the sonne and bere a crosse vpon hys hede, the whiche was clothed withe the same clothe that he hadde 55 yeue to the pore man, and saide to hym: 'Whi wepist thou, Tholonayre?' And whanne he hadde tolde hym the cause of his sorugh he saide to hym: 'Knowest thou this clothe?' And he saide: 'Ye, Sir.' And thanne | oure Lorde saide: 'I haue be clothed therwith f. 39ra sethe thou gauest it me, and I thanke the of thi good will that thou 60 haddest pitee of my nakidnesse and clodist me.'

And whanne he awoke he beganne to blesse the pore and to saye: 'Oure Lorde leuithe, and he late me neuer deie till I be one of his pore men.' And whanne he hadde al yeue to pore men his good, he called one of his nye servauntes that he truste most on and saide to hym: 'I 65 will telle the a counsell, and butte thou kepe it truly and do as I will bidde the I shall selle the to straunge men.' And thanne he toke hym .x. li. of golde and saide to hym: 'Go into the citee and beye sum mercerye, and whanne thou hast do so, go and selle me to sum cristen man and take the price of me and yeue it for the loue of God to pore 70 men.' And the servaunt refused it. And thanne he saide: 'Truly but yef thou do it I shal sell the.' And thanne he ledde hym as he hadde saide and solde hym to a marchaunt, and he was clothed in vile clothing as a servaunt, and he receyued the price for hym and gaue it to the pore. 75

Thanne this Pers Theloneye was made an vnder servaunt in the kichin and dede all the foule offices of the hous, and was often tyme beten and despised and called madde fole. But oure Lorde appered to hym often tymes and shewed hym his clothyng and comforted hym, and verily the emperour [and] all other weren sori of the losse of Pers 80 Theloneire. And so as worthi men come fro Constantinople to the place there as he was, the maister of Pers praied hem to dyner, and as thei satte atte her mete on of hem seigh hym passe before hem and behelde hym and saide: 'Truly yender yonge man resembelith | gretly f. 39rb to Sir Pers Theolonaire.' And as thei loked beter they sai[d]e: 'Verrily 85 it is he. Late us rise and take hym.' And whan Pers vnderstode that he

53 mynde] pite E   56 the] *add* same E   57 Tholonayre] 'Theolonayre' *above del.* Thonoleyre H1   62-3 to saye . . . he] seide to oure lord G   63 be] *add* made G his] þy G   64 al . . . good] ʒouen all his good to pore men G   66 will²] *om.* G 67 selle the] sey it G   72 the] myself G   ledde hym] dide G   73 to] *ins.* H1 76 vnder] vnde'r' H1   80 verily] *om.* G   and²] of E, & *on erasure* H1   84 behelde] biheded *changed to* bihe'l'de H1   85 they] *om.* G   saide] saie EH1   Verrily] *add* þat G, so *ins.* H1   86 is] was G, 'w'as H1   whan] *ins.* H1

was aspied he fledde priuely. And the porter was bothe defe and
dvmme and opened the gate bi signes, but Pers made no signes but
comaunded hym bi worde, and [he] herde anone and receyued his
90 speche and ansuered hym, and he went his waye. And the porter
turned into the hous, and alle hadde mervaile whanne thei herde hym
speke. Than he saide: 'He that was in the kychen is gone oute and
fledde awaye, but wetithe wel that he is the seruaunt of God, for as
sone as he bade me open the gate ther come oute of his mowthe a
95 flawme of fire that touched my tongge and myn eres and anone I
receyued heryng and spekyng.' And thanne all in gret haste ronnen
after hym, but thei myght not fynde hym. And thanne alle tho of the
hous deden penaunce for thei hadde so wrechidly tretid hym that was
so worthi and so blessed.
100 A monke ther was that hight Vitall that purposed to assaie yef he
myght stirre Seint Iohn to arere any disclaundre ayeinst hym, and
come into a citee and went thorugh alle the bordelles of wreched
women and saide to euery bi ordre: 'Yeue me this nyght and do no
fornicacion.' And thanne he entered into an hous of hers and praied al
105 the nyght in a cornere vpon his kneis for hem, and in the morutide he
went his waye and charged hem that they shulde not discouer hym to
none. But one of the women whanne he was gone tolde his lyff and his
f. 39ᵛᵃ governaunce, and as the olde man praied she was anone | vexed with
the fende. And thanne all that other cursed women saiden her: 'God
110 hathe yeldid the as thou hast deserued, for thou hast lyed vpon hym.
He come in for to do fornicacion.'
Thanne whanne it was nyght the forsaid Vitall saide in heryng of
all: 'I will go yender for suche a lady abidithe me.' And whanne some
blamed hym he ansuered as though he hadde be wrothe: 'Haue I no
115 body as other men haue? Is God only wrothe withe monkes? Thei
bene verryli men as other.' Thanne sum saide to hym: 'Take a wyff
and chaunge thin habite so that thou sclaunder not other.' And he
made hym wrothe and saide: 'Goo youre waye. I will not here you.
Who leste to defame, late hym, and sm[y]te his hede ayeinst the wall.
120 Ye be not ordeined of God aboue me as my iuges. Gothe and takithe
hede of yourselff, for ye shull not yelde acountes for me.' And this he
saide an hygh with a crieng vois. And thanne men pleyned to Seint

89 hym] *ins.* H1   he] *om.* E   94 sone as] *om.* H1   96 haste] *add* þay G   98 tretid]
tredid G   100 assaie] 'a'sai H1   101 to] *om.* G   ayeinst] and ȝens G   and] a'nd' H1
102 a] þe G   109 her] here H1G   113 all] oon G, *so ins.* H1   some] *ins.* H1
117 And] but G   119 smyte] smote E   122 men] 'some' H1, *om.* G

Iohn of his gouernaunce. Oure Lorde harded so the herte of hym that
he gaue no credence to her wordes, but praied God that he wolde
shewe to sum creature his werkes after his dethe and that it were not   125
turned hem to synne that defamed hym. And in this mene tyme he
hadde conuerted many of the forsaid women and made hem religious.

In a morwtyde as he went from one of this comune women he mette
a man that entred for to do fornicacion and gaue hym a bofette and
saide: 'Thou wicked man, whi amendest thou not thi wicked lyving?'   130
And he saide hym: 'Leue me ryght well that thou shalt haue suche a
bofette | that alle Alisaundre shall assemble to wonder on the.' And   f. 39ᵛᵇ
after that the fende come in lyknesse of a man and gaue hym a bofette
and saide: 'This is the bofette that [the] behight Vitall the abbot.' And
anone he was rauished withe the fende and tormented so that alle the   135
peple drowe to hym and wondered vpon hym, but atte the laste he was
repentaunt and heled bi the praiers of Seint Iohn. And thanne whanne
the servaunt of God neighed his ende he lefte his writyng to his
disciples: 'Ne iugethe neuer before the tyme.' And whanne the
women confessed what he dede, all glorified God.   140

A pore man in the abite of a pilgrime come to Iohn and asked
almesse, and he called his dispenser and bade hym geve the pilgrime
.vj. d. And whanne he hadde yt he chaunged his clothing and come
ayein to the patriarke and asked almesse ayein. And he called his
dispenser and bade hym geve hym .vj. d. of golde. And whanne he   145
hadde yeue hym and was gone, the dispenser saide to his lorde:
'Fader, atte youre request this man hathe twies resseiued almesse this
day and hathe chaunged his clothing.' And Seint Iohn feyned as
though he hadde not wost it. And he chaunged his clothing ayein and
come the thridde tyme to Seint Iohn and asked hym almesse. And   150
thanne the dispenser putte to his lorde priuily shewyng hym that it
was the same beggere. Thanne Seint Iohn saide to his dispenser:
'Yeue hym .xij. d. lest perauenture it be my Lorde Ihesu Crist that
assaiethe where he myght [more take] thanne I may yeue.'

In a tyme it fell that the patricyen that was lorde of the | contre   f. 40ʳᵃ
wolde putte sum money of the contrey into marchaundise, and the   156

123 harded so] herd it so þat *with* it *del.* H1, herde so *with* so *del.* G   128 went] come
H1   from] *add* thens *del.* H1, *add* hem G   comune] *om.* G   130 wicked] *om.* G
131 hym] *om.* H1   134 the²] thou E, y G   140 women] *add* weren G, *so ins.* H1   what
. . . dede] he deide G   glorified] *add* 'in' H1   God] *om.* G   141 to] *add* seint G
142 dispenser] dispenser H1, disposer G   145 dispenser] disposer G   146 dispenser]
disposer G   149 though] *om.* H1   151 dispenser] disposer G   it] he H1G   152 to
his dispenser] *om.* G   155 patricyen] Patriarke G   156 and] *add* than E

patriarke wolde in no wise consent therto but that it shulde be yeue to
the pore, so that ther was gret contencion betwene hem two and
departed al wrothe. And whanne euesong tyme come the patriark sent
160 bi an ershebisshop to the patricien and saide: 'Sir, the sonne is nygh
go to rest.' And whanne the patrice herde that he wepte and come to
hym and asked hym foryeuenesse.

As a neuewe of the patriarke hadde resseiued a gret wronge of a
taverner, he compleined hym to the patriarke weping and myght in no
165 wise be comforted. And the patriarke ansuered and saide: 'What is he,
sone, that durst wrathe the? Leue it wel, sone, that I shalle this day do
suche a thyng ayeinst hym that Alisaundre shal mervaile theron.' And
whanne he herde that, he was well comforted and wende that he
shulde haue be greuously beten. And Seint Iohn seigh that he was
170 comforted, he beganne to kesse hym and saie: 'Sone, thou art verrey
neuewe of myn humilite, wherfor make the euer redi to receyue
betyngges, chydingges and wrongges of all, for verrey affinite is not
only of flesshe and of blode, but of the strength of vertues.' And
thanne he sent for hym that hadde done hym this wronge and made
175 hym fre of all pencion and of all truage. And all tho þat herden it
mervayled gretly, and than thei vnderstode that he hadde saide before.

The patriarke herde that anone as the emperour is [crowned] the
maner is suche that the werkemen that maken the sepulcres shullen
f. 40rb take foure or five litell peses of marbell of diuerse coloures and co|me
180 to hym and aske hym of what marber or of what metaill his lordship
lest comaunde that his tombe be made of, so that for this cause Iohn
was ordeyned to lete make his sepulcre. But alway he lete it be
vnperfite til his laste ende, and whiles he was withe the clergie he
ordeined some to go to hym and seyne: 'Sir, youre monyment is not
185 perfitely made. Comaundith that it be fullfelled, for that ye knowe not
whanne the theef comithe.'

A riche man that for he seigh Seint Iohn hadde foule clothes vpon
hym and vpon his bedd, for that he hadde yeuen to pore men al his
good clothes, he bought to hym right a precious couerture and gaue it
190 to blessed Seint Iohn. And in a nyght as it laie vpon hym he myght not
of al that night slepe for he thought that .CCC. of his lordes myght

160 patricien] Patriarke G   161 go] *om.* G   patrice] Patriarke G
165 ansuered] hurde G   he] the E   169 greuously beten] *trs.* E   170 saie]
seid HıG   172 affinite is] affynitees Hı, affynyte G   177 crowned] L, comunyd E,
commined Hı, comen G   180 what²] *om.* HıG   metaill] metallez HıG
183 vnperfite] *om.* G   189 bought] brouȝt G   191 that²] þanne G, þan than *with*
final n *changed to* t Hı

well haue be couered therwithe. And al that nyght he made his wamentacion, seyinge: 'A, how many ther be of my lordes all bemyred, [how many wet withe the reyne], how many streyne the tethe togedre for colde that lyen and slepen in the market place, and 195 thou wreche deuourest the grete fisches and restes[t] in thi chaumbre withe al thi wickednesse and vpon a couertoure of .xxvj. pounde for to warme thi wrechidnesse.' And thanne the meke Iohn wolde neuer be couered therwith after, but anone in the morwtyde he made sell it and gaue the price therof to the pore. And whanne this riche man seigh it 200 he bought it ayein and toke it to the blessed Iohn and praied hym that he ne wolde no more sell it but kepe it | to hymselff. And as sone as he f. 40ᵛᵃ hadde it he solde it ayein and yaue the price to his lordes. And whanne the riche man herde it he bought it ayein and toke it to Seint Iohn and saide to hym full goodly: 'We shull see who shall faill, other thou in 205 the selling or I in the beyeng.' [And thus] thei pleied ofte in beyeng and in sellyng, the riche man se[y]ing þat men might well dispoile the riche in this manere witheoute synne for the entent to yeue it to the pore, and bothe shulde wynne in this manere, that one in savyng of soules, the tother in getyng gerdon.   210

And [whanne] Seint Iohn wolde draue men to do almesse, he hadde in use to tell of Seint Scrapion, whan he hadde yeue his mantell to a pore man he mette another that was fullfelled with colde and yaue hym his cote and satte al naked. And as a man asked hym: 'Fader, who hathe dispoiled the?' And he shewed hym the gospell that he helde in 215 his honde and saide: 'This dispoiled me.'

And after that he seigh another pore man, and thanne he solde the gospell and yaue the price to the pore man. And whanne men asked hym where his gospell was he ansuerid and saide: 'The gospell comaundithe and saithe: "Goo and sell alle that thou hast and yeue 220 to the pore." I hadde this same gospell and I haue solde hym like as he comanded.' So as he hadde comaunded for to yeue almesse to any that asked hym, the pore man hadde despite for he gaue hym but fiue penyes and biganne to chide hym and to despise hym in his visage. 224 And whanne Seint Iohnis men seigh | and herde hym thei wolde haue f. 40ᵛᵇ

---

192 well/haue be] trs. H1   couered] rekeuered H1G   194 how¹ . . . reyne] om. E wet] wente G, went with n erased H1   196 restest] restes E   199 after] on erasure H1 201–4 the blessed . . . it to] om. G   206 And thus] L, Of this EG, of þis followed by punct. H1   pleied] playnyd G   207 seying] L, seing EH1G, add well H1G 211 whanne] L, om. EH1G   215 hathe despoiled] is þat despoileth H1, is he þat dispoylid G   And] om. G   222–3 So . . . hym¹] EG capitalise as if this belongs to preceding sentence

betin hym, and thanne the blessed Iohn defended hem, seyeng:
'Sufferith, bretherin, sufferithe, that he curse me not. I am now
fourti yere and haue blamed Ihesu Crist bi my werkes and may not
suffre o chidyng of this man.' And thanne he comaunded þat the sacke
230 of money shulde be opened to hym that he myght take as moch as
hym luste.

In a tyme after þat the gospell was redde thei went oute of the
chirche and ta[l]ked there of idell materes, and the patriarke
perceyued hem and folued after hem and satte doune amonges
235 hem, and alle thei hadde meruayle therof. And thanne he saide to
hem: 'Sones, ther as the shepe be, the sheparde most be also, and
therfor either ye most entre withe me into the chirche or elles I most
abide withe you here.' And this he dede ones or twies, and therbi he
taught the peple to abide in the chirche.

240 As a yonge man hadde rauished a nonne and the clerkes blamed this
yonge man before Seint Iohn and saiden that he was acursed as he that
hadde loste two soules, his owne and the nonnes, than Seint Iohn
refreined hem in saieng: 'Sone, it is not so, but I shewe you that ye do
two synnes. Furst ye do ayeinst the comaundement of oure Lorde that
245 saiethe: "Ne iugithe not and ye shull not be iuged." Secoundely that
ye wete not of certain wher thei haue synned vnto this day and haue
repented hem.'

[Many] tymes it fell that he was rauished in his orison and he was
herde despute withe oure Lorde bi þe wordes: 'So, good Lorde Ihesu
250 Crist, soo, I in parting and thou in mi[ni]string, lat us see the whiche
f. 41ʳᵃ shall ouercome.' And as he was seke of the feueres | he seigh that he
neighed his ende and saide: 'I yelde the thankingges, Lorde God, for
that thou haste enhaunsed my wrechidnesse, requering thi bon[t]e
that oo thinge I drede be not shewed to me atte my deyeng, that is that
255 I haue comaunded to yeue to the pore the goodes of other.'

And whan he was dede his worshipfull bodi was leide in a sepulcre
wher the bodies of two bisshoppes hadde bene beried, and these two
bodies yaue mervailous place to the body of Seint Iohn and lefte hym
the place al voide.

260 A litell tyme before that he deied ther was a woman hadde done an

227 Sufferith] suffre suffre H1   sufferithe] om. H1G   not] del. H1   229 thanne]
þere G   233 talked] taked E   238 this] þus G   240 a nonne] Anoone G
244 Furst] add for H1G   247–8 G punct. only after tymes   248 Many] Often E,
ony G, on a on erasure H1   tymes] so with s erased H1   249 þe] these H1   250 thou]
om. G   ministring] mistring E   253 enhaunsed] enchaungid G   bonte] bonde EH1G
(bonte P2)   254 atte] al H1G   257 of] on erasure H1   259 the] om. G

horrible synne and durste not be shriuen to none man, and thanne
Seint Iohn saide: 'Atte the leste write it and ensele it and bringe it to
me, and I shall praie for the.' She graunted hym and wrote her synne
and seled it diligentely and brought it to Seint Iohn. And a litel tyme
after he fell seke and deied, and whanne she herde that he was dede 265
she wende for to haue be shamed and confused for euer, wenyng that
he hadde lefte the scrowe in sum other mannes hondes, and she went
to the tombe and ther she cried, hidously weping and saieng: 'Alas,
alas, I wende to haue eschewed my confusion, and now I am made
confusion to all other.' And as she wepte bitterly and praied Seint 270
Iohn that he wolde shewe her wher he hadde done her writyng, and
than [sodeinly] the blessed Seint Iohn come oute of [his] tombe in the
abite of a bissop and in eueri side of hym a bisshop, and saide to the
woman: 'Whi hastest thou us so faste? Whi ne sufferiste thou us to
take sum rest, neither me ne these seintes that bene with | me? Loo, f. 41rb
here oure stoles al bewette withe thi teres.' And thanne he toke hir her 276
scrowe ayein al enseled as it was before and saide to her: 'See here the
sele and open the scrowe and rede it.' And whanne she hadde opened
it she founde al effased and founde wretin in this manere: 'Thi sinne is
foryeuen bi the praier of Iohn my servaunt.' And thanne she yelde 280
thankyng to God, and Seint Iohn turned into his tombe with the two
bisshops. And he was ennobled aboute the yere of oure Lorde .vjC.v.
in the time of Focas the emperour.

Here endithe the liff of Seint Iohn the Awmenere, and
nexst foluithe of the Conuersion of Seint Paule, Cap^{m}.
.xxvij.^{m}

The conuersion of Seint Paule the Apostell is made in the same yere
that oure Lorde suffered dethe on and Steuen [was] stoned, and not in
the naturell yere but aperyng, for Ihesu Crist suffered dethe in the
.viij. kalend of Auerell, and Steuen suffered dethe in that same yere
.iij. dayes in August.   5
    Thre resones bene assigned whi the conuersion of hym is more

262 EG *have no punct.*, H1 *has* Atte   leste] laste EH1G (*moins* P2)   263 shall] *ins.*
H1   264 tyme] *ins.* H1   267 the] his H1   269 made] madde *with second* d *subp.*
H1   270 and] sche G   272 sodeinly] *om.* E   his] the E   276 al] alwey H1
bewette] be wette E, `be´ wete H1   278 it] *om.* G   282 ennobled] envoiued H1

EH1GDH2A1A2L   1 Seint] *om.* H1G   2 was] *om.* EH1G (*fut* P2)   4 .viij.]
om. H1G   5 .iij.] .iij.^{e} E   6 Thre] The *changed to* Tre H1

[h]alowed thanne of other seintes: furst for the ensaumple that no
synner, whateuer he be, falle in dispeir of foryeuenesse whanne he
seithe hym that was in so grete a gilte be now in so gret worship and
10 ioye; secoundeli for ioie, for as the Chirche hadde gret sorugh in his
persecusion, right so hadde she gret ioie in his conuersion; thriddely
for the gret myracle that oure Lorde shewed [in] hym, whanne of a
right cruel persecutour he made a true prechour.

f. 41ᵛᵃ   The conuersion of hym was merueilous | because of hym that dede
15 it, of hym that ordeyned it, and of the pacient. Bi the reson of hym
that did it, that was Ihesu Crist that shewed there mervelous myght in
that he saide: 'It is harde to the to hurte ayeinst [the] pricke.' And in
that he meued hym so sodenly, for anone as he was chaunged he
ansuered and saide: 'Lorde, what wilt thou that I do?' And vpon this
20 word saiethe Seint Austin: 'The lombe slayn of the wolfes made of the
wolfe a lambe, for he made hym redy now to obeye that before
enforced hymselff to pursue.' Secoundely he shewed mervaylous
wisdom. It was a mervaylous wisdom whanne he toke from hym
the bolwyng of pride in offering the lowe thingges of humilite and not
25 the highnesse of mageste. For he saide to hym: 'I am Ihesus of
Nazareth,' and called not hymselff God ne the sone of God, but he
saide: 'Take the lownesse of humilite and putte awaie the thisteles of
pride.' Thriddeli he shewed his pitous debonairte that signified in þat
that he that was in dede and will of persecucion he conuerted. Though
30 it were soo that he hadde a wicked will, as he that sighed al of manaces
and hadde euel enforsinge, as he that went to the prince of prestes, as
in avauntyng hymselff bi wicked dede that he wolde lede the cristen
bounden into Ierusalem, and therfor he went and for that cause the
viage was right wicked. And notwithstondyng al this the gret merci of
35 oure Lorde conuerted hym.

    Secoundeli she was mervailous by reson of the ordyner, that is of
light þat he ordeyned atte his conuersion. And men sayn þat that light
f. 41ᵛᵇ was dispositiff, sodeyn, gret and heuenly, and | that lyght of heuene
biclipped [hym] sodenly. Poule hadde in hym thre vices: the furst was
40 hardinesse, in that he saide: 'I will go to the prince of prest[es],' and as
the Glose saiethe, not called but of his propre will and by enuye that

7 halowed] alowed E   8 he be falle] bifalle G   9 seithe] segh H₁G   a gilte]
agilite G   12 in] L, to EH₁G   13 true] cruel G   16 there] þe G   17 the²]
a E   22 Secoundely] sikerly G   24 bolwyng] bollyng H₁   29 that²] om. G
31 prince] princes H₁G   34 viage] visage H₁G   37 light¹] add 'of heuen' H₁
that he . . . lyght] om. G   39 hym¹] hem EG   40 hardinesse] hardenesse H₁
prestes] prest E   41 his] add owne E

meued hym; the secound was pride, the whiche is signified in þat he
saide sighyng [al] full of ma⟨n⟩asez; the .iij. was the carnell entent that
he hadde in the laue, and of that saiethe the Glose vpon this worde: 'I
am Ihesus, I, God of heuene, that speke to the, the whiche thou 45
wenest dede bi [thy] witte of a Iwe.' And that diuine lyght was sodein
for to fere hym hardy, she was grete for to bete hym downe that was
high and proude into lownesse of humilite, sche was heuenly for sche
shuld chaunge [his] carnall entent into the heuenly. Or it may be saide
that this ordenaunce was in thre thingges, in the vois crieng, in the 50
light shinyng, and in the vertue of the myght.

Therdeli she was mervailous by reson of the pacient, the whiche
was Poule in whom this conuersion was done. That is to wete, he was
[th]rowe downe to the erthe, he was blynde and fast .iij. dayes. He was
[th]rowe doune for he shulde be areysed. And Austin saiethe: 'Poule 55
was beten doune for to be blynde, and he was blynde for to be
chaunged, he was chaunged for to be sent, he was sente for that he
shuld suffre dethe for trouthe.' And yet [saieth Austin]: 'The
tormentour was hurte and was made a trewe leuer, the pursuer was
hurt and was made a prechoure, the sone of perdicion was hurt and 60
was made a vessell of eleccion.' He was blynde for to be enlumyned,
and that was as to his derke entendement, and thanne in tho thre
dayes that he was blynde men sayen | that he was taught in the gospell, f. 42ra
for he lered it neuer of man ne bi man as he hymselff witnessithe but
bi the reuelacion of Ihesu Crist. And Austin saieth: 'I seie that he was 65
a verrey champion of Ihesu Crist, taught of hym and dressed of hym,
crucified with hym and glorified in hym, and made [lene] in the
flesche so that [that] flesche was ordeined to the effecte of blessed-
nesse, and euer after þat the bodi of hym was stabled and ordeined to
all goodnesse. He coude well suffre hunger and habundaunce, and was 70
taught in all thyngges and in alle places, and suffered gladli alle
aduersitees, tormentours, tirauntes and peple full of wodenesse, and
ouercome hem as flies. Dethe [and] torment or any peynes he
acounted not but as the plaie of children and he embraced hem

43 al] as E   45 I²] om. G   46 thy] a E, the H1   of a Iwe] om. G   diuine]
diuyinte H1, dymme G   47 to²] add be subp. H1   48 high] hi with e on erasure H1
49 his] her E   the] add the E, om. G   54 throwe] drowe E, þorowe H1
55 throwe] drowe E   57 chaunged] add And E   58 saieth Austin] seint Austin
saieth E   59 was hurte and] om. H1   leuer] louer G   62 as] om. H1   to] add the
del. H1   tho] þe del. H1, om. G   64 lered] lereded H1   it] om. H1G   65–6 And . . .
Crist] om. H1G   67 with] of G   lene] L, loue EH1G   68 that²] om. E   73 and]
or E   or any] her with H1   he] she H1G

75 gladly, and hym thought hymselff more worshipped to be bounde
with a cheyne thanne to be crowned as a kyng, and he receyued
gladlier woundes thanne other men [wolde] yeftes.

It is redde of hym that thre thingges weren in hym that were ayeinst
the thre thingges that weren in oure furst fader: for ther was in hym a
80 lefftyng vp ayenst God, and Paule was in the contrarie for he was
streched doune to the erthe; there was in oure fader openyng of
eyghen, and in Paule the contrarie, he was blynde; there was in oure
fader etyng of the fruit deuyed, and in Paule the contrarie for he dede
abstinence of couenable metes.

Here endith of the Conuersion of Seint Paule, and nexst
foluith the lyff of Seint Pa[u]line, Cap^m. .xxviij.^m

Paul[a] was a noble lady of Romaynes, of the whiche Seint Ierome
f. 42rb wrote the lyff by this wordes. | 'If all the membres of my body were
torned into tonges and that all my membres myght speke mannes
voyse, I myght not saye nothing worthi to the vertues and holynesse of
5 the noble and worshipfull Paul[a], that was noble of kynde but moche
more noble of faithe and bi holynesse and sumtyme myghti in
richesse, but she is now more ennobled withe the pouerte of Ihesu
Crist. I witnesse in Ihesu Crist and in his aungeles and in the same
aungell that was felawe and keper of that merveilous woman that I
10 may nothing saie suffisaunt to the grace of her ne in the mowthe of the
preisers of hir, but that I haue to saie I putte it for witnesse of the leste
of her merites. And yef the reder [wille] wete the vertues of her, she
lefte her pore the most pore of all, and right as among many stones the
precious stone shinithe and the bryghtnesse of the sonne derkith and
15 shaduithe the litell light of sterres, right so surmount[ed] she the
vertues and þe myghtes of all bi her humilite. She was the lest in alle
for to be the grettest in all, for of as moche as she dispised herselff
most she was the more enhaunsed of God, for in the fleyng of ioye

77 wolde] done E   78 thingges] kyngis G   79 thingges] kyngis G
83 deuyed] denyed (?) E

EH1GDH2A1A2L   *Rubric* Pauline] Paline E   1 Paula] L, Pauline EH1G
2 this] 't'his H1   3 tonges] *changed to* touchez H1, teuchis G   5 Paula] L, Paulyne
EH1G   kynde] kyn H1   6 of] by H1   mighti] *add and erase* I H1   7 ennobled]
enuolued H1   8 I . . . Crist] *om.* G   9 aungell] aungellis G   10 grace] *add* 'of
God and' H1, *so* G   mowthe] L, mowthes E, mone þere H1G   12 wille] *om.* EG
wete] *ins.* H1   13 the most pore] *om.* H1   15 of] *add* þe G   surmounted]
surmountithe E   16 her] his G   the] *om.* G   in] of H1G   17 in] of H1G   of]
om. G   18 more] *corrected from* moste G

she deserued ioie, the whiche foluithe vertue as a shadue and leuithe
hem that coueyten hym and s[u]ithe hem that dispisen hym.   20

'This same here hadde .v. children, that was B[l]esile, vpon the
dethe of whiche I conforted Paule atte Rome, the whiche seint [lefte]
Pa[m]achien her heyr and prouost of her thingges, to whom we made
a litell boke vpon the dethe of her, and to Eustoche that is now a
precious iuell in holy places in the Chirche of virginite, and Eufyne 25
that | wrethed the corage of her moder for that she deyed witheoute f. 42va
ripenesse of age, and [Thoroch, after] the whiche she lefte beryng as
she that wolde no more seruc to [do] the office of mariage, but she
hadde obeied to the will of her husbond that desired to haue an eyre
male. And whanne her husbond was dede she bewepte hym so that 30
there failled litell that she ne hadde deide for sorugh, and than sche
conuerted hir so to the seruise of God that she desired to haue the
same dethe that he hadde. And what shall I more [saie]? The grete and
the noble houses and the right gret richesse of bifore she gave to the
pore.   35

'She was so enflaumed bi the vertues of Paulyne the bisshopp of
Antioche and of Epiphanes that were come to Rome that she purposed
her fully to leue her owne contrey. And what more, wherfor abide I?
Here brother, her cosynes, hir frendes, and yet most of all her owne
children folued her. But the sayle was drawen vp and the ship driuen 40
forthe withe the condyt of ores, and the litell Thoroche helde up her
hondes beseching vpon the riuage, and Rufine [redy to be maried]
praied her to abide his weddyng and halff deied in wepyng, and
she alwaies helde her eyen towardes the heuene and [trowyd]
fe[l]onye in her sones and pitee in God. And she vnknowe herself 45
[a moder for that sche arayed herselfe] to be [the] servaunt of God,
and she was tormented in her bowels right as men hadde drawe oute of
her membres, and she faught withe sorugh and sofered plenier
creaunce hem ayeinst the right of nature, and [though] that reioysing 49
[her] corage coueited the loue of children to be grettest after | kynde, f. 42vb

19 she deserued ioie] *twice* E   20 that^1] and G   coueyten] coueyted H1   suithe] L,
seithe E, sey H1G   21 Blesile] besile E, bisily G   22 lefte] L, lost EH1G
23 Pamachien] Pannachien EG   25 in^1] *add* þe H1   Eufyne] Easyne G   26 that^1]
þe G   wrethed] wrecched H1G   27 Thoroche after] L, thorugh EH1G   lefte]
loste G   beryng] lernyng G   28 do] *om.* E   29 obeied] abeyid G   33 saie] saide
E, seie *with second* e *on erasure* H1   34 the^1] *om.* G   39 Here] *so with final* e *subp.* G
41 ores] Corys G   litell] *om.* H1   42 Rufine] refyne H1   redy/to be maried] L, *trs.*
EH1G   44-5 trowyd felonye] L, towardes fekonye EH1, toward Foconye G   46 a
moder . . . herselfe] L, *om.* EH1G   the] *om.* E   47 oute of] *om.* G   49 though] L,
thow EH1G   50 her] of E

yet she lefte hem alle for the loue of God. She comforted her only in
Eustace, that was felawe in her viage. And in the mene tyme that the
ship sailed foorthe in the see alle tho that were withe her withinne
[behylde] the riuage, and she helde her eygen to heuene and turned
55 hem fro that she myght not beholde witheoute sorugh and torment.

'As she come to the place of the Holi Londe, the prouost of
Palestyn that knewe right well the worthinesse of her, the peple of her,
sent before his meyni to araie a gret palace for her, but she chase a
litell selle and visited euery day the holy places withe so gret stody and
60 [withe] so gret feruoure that but the cause of hasting to other hadde
bene she myght not be drawe from the furst. And whanne she kneled
before the crosse she worshiped in beholdyng oure Lorde as though
he hangged on the crosse, and whanne she was entered into the
sepulcre wher he arose, she kessed the stone that the aungell hadde
65 take away from the monument and beclipp[ed] the places wher the
holi body hadde layn and drowe into her mouthe the desired waters of
beleue that she coueited. And alle Ierusalem is witnesse of the teres
and wepingges shedde of her eyen and oure Lorde hymselff that she
praied to.

70 'And fro thennys she went into Bethelem and entered into the pitte
of oure saueoure and seighe the holi place and swore, heryng myselff,
that she seigh withe the eyen of her beleue the childe wrapped in
clothes and weping in the creche, and the kyngges worshippyng oure
Lorde, and the sterre shyning vpon the Virgine and moder, and the
f. 43ra sheparde[s] norisching the bestis that come to se the sone | of God that
76 was made for to deie, thanne the begynnyng of Iohn the Euangelist
the whiche is: *In principio erat uerbum et uerbum caro factum est*, and
she seigh Herodes in his wodenesse sleyng children, Mari and Ioseph
fleing into Egipte, and speke with ioie medeled withe teres and saide:
80 "God saue the, Bethelem, hous of pes, in the whiche is born the brede
that descended from heuene, God saue the, Eff[r]ata, contrey
plentevous, [of] the whiche plente Dauid speke in this wise: 'Verrely
we shull entre withinne the tabernacles of hym and worship the place
where the fete of hym stode;' and I, right wreched synner, am iuged

52 viage] visage G, *so with* s *erased* H1   54 behylde] L, besiled EH1G   55 H1G
punct. after that   58 palace] place G   H1 *punct. after* her   59 so] *om.* G
60 withe] *om.* E   61 whanne] *om.* G   63 he] *add* hadde G   65 beclipped] L,
beclipping EH1G   68 that] *om.* H1G   73 creche] cros G   75 shepardes]
sheparde E   76 the²] *om.* H1G   77 *In . . . est] space left blank* G   80 Bethelem]
L, Bethelemes EH1G   81 Effrata] Effata E   82 of] *om.* E   83 worship] L,
worshiped EH1G

worthi to kesse the [cre]che in whiche oure Lorde cried full litell, and 85
in the pitte in the whiche the Virgine bare God. Here is my reste, here
shall I duelle, therfor I haue chosen it and my saueoure chase it
before me."

'She demened herselff by so gret humilite that who that see her and
hadde saine her before in her gret worship he wolde not haue leued 90
þat it hadde bene she but the leste of her chamberers, and whanne she
was ofte tymes enviround withe the felawship of virgines she was the
lowest of all in speche, in habite and in goyng. And sithe that her
husbond was dede she ete neuer withe man, knewe she hym neuer so
holy or in highnesse of a bisshopp, ne she entered neuer sithe into no 95
batthe but yef she were sike, ne hadde neuer sithe softe bedde though
she were in right a greuous feuer, but laye vpon the harde grounde in
strayles of heire, and þat she acounted her reste, but her reste myght
be called nyght and day in orison for the most parte continued. And
she wepte for her lyght synnes | that men wolde haue wende that she f. 43rb
hadde be gilty in right greuous synnes, and as she was ofte taught of vs 101
that she shulde spare her eyen and kepe hem to the lesson of the
gospell, she saide that "the face shulde be troubled that I haue so ofte
peinted withe coloures ayeinst the comaundement of God, and the
body shulde be tormented that hathe tended to so many delites, for 105
the long lawghyng most be recompensed withe weping, and the
softe and precious clothes of selke most be chaunged into sharpenesse
of heire, and I that haue plesed man and the world desire now to plese
Ihesu Crist."

'And yef I wolde preche in that same chastite among so many 110
vertues it shulde be outrage, the whiche whanne she was atte Rome
was ensaumple to alle ladies of the citee, for she demened her so that
neuer renome of none euell word ther durste [no]ne feyne ayenst her.
And I confesse myn erroure, that whanne she was to moche
abandoned in yevynge I vndertoke her and purposed her th[i]s 115
saieng of the apostell: "It apertenithe you not to refreshinge as to
other but tribulacion, but it most be of qualite in tyme, so that youre
habundaunce be to the nede of hem, and so it behouithe to purvei that

85 creche] L, chirche EG, *so changed to* crarche (?) H₁   87 haue] shall *del.* `haue' H₁
89 demened] demed H₁G   herselff] her life H₁   91 she'] `sche' H₁, so G   leste] *so on
erasure* H₁   92 was'] *om.* G   96 hadde neuer] *trs.* G   97 right a] *trs.* G
99 continued] conteynyd H₁G   104 comaundemente] comaundementez H₁G
106 recompensed] recompessed H₁, recompellid G   withe] bi H₁   107 softe and]
softenes of G   into] *add* þe GH₁   108 world] worldis G   110 that] þe G
113 neuer] euer G   none²] ne E, not G   feyne] seyne G   115 this] thus E

thing that men wolde fayne do thei mowe not alwaies do." And I saide
120 to her many other thingges, the whiche she with gret shame and fewe
wordes receiued, and I calle oure Lorde to witnesse that she dede all
for Ihesu Crist and that she desired to deie so pore that she wolde not
leue one peny to her doughter and to her owne [body] atte [her] laste
ende were lapped in a straunge suayre. And she saide me whanne I
f. 43va asked her: "I shalle finde men ynow that will yeue me one, | and yef a
126 pore man haue not of me that I may yeue of other, if he is dede of
whom shall his soule be asked?"

'She wolde not dispende her money in stones that be transitori here
withe erthe, but [she dispended hem in quycke stones] that be founde
130 aboue erthe, of the whiche Seint Iohn saiethe in the Apocalipse that
the citee of the grete kyng is made of. She toke vnnethes oyle in her
mete the high festes so that one thing myght be supposed of her, that
is that she dede faste fro wyne, fro licoures, fro fysshes, fro melke, fro
hony, from eyren, of this and of other thingges that bene soffte in the
135 taste, in the whiche thingges takyng sum wenen to be right abstinent,
and yef thei haue fulfilled thaire belies thei wene he be a di[s]pitous
man that blamithe hem. She was so debonaire that for the grete
brennyng of vertues it semed to sum that it was halff madnesse, and
whanne men saide her that the brayne most be sostened and norished
140 she ansuered: "We bene made tresoure beholding to the worlde, to
aungels, and to men, and so we be foles to Ihesu Crist, and one
Goddes foole more wise is thanne many men."

'After oure chirch that she hadde take to the gouernaunce [of men],
she ordeined thre chirches and putte witheinne hem thre felawshippes
145 of virgines that she hadde assembeled of diuerse prouinces, as many
noble as of mene and lowe kinrede, in suche manere that thei were
departed at thaire werke and atte thaire mete, but in psalmes and in
orison[es] thei were ioined togedre only. And whanne they chidden
togedre amonge hemselff she wolde reherce hem withe softe wordes,
150 and breke the flesche of the yong virgines by double and ofte
f. 43vb fasting|ges, and loued beter that the stomake shulde ake thanne the

119 wolde] *add* ful H1   123 leue] lyue *with* y *del.* `e´ G   to her²] to *over del.* doo G
body] doughter E   her³] the E   124 straunge] stronge H1   125 shalle] *add* ʒe G
one] eyen G   and] A G   126 of other] *del.* H1   127 his] þis H1G   128 wolde]
wol H1   129 she . . . stones] L, *om.* EH1G   134 of¹,²] fro G   this] `t´his H1
136 dispitous] dipitous E, de`s´pitous H1   137 hem] him *changed to* hem H1, hym G
138 brennyng] benygnyte G   139 brayne] veynys G   143 of] *om.* H1   of men] L,
thanne E, men H1G   145 as] of H1G   146 mene] men H1G   148 orisones]
orison E   togedre] *om.* H1   whanne] what G   149 she] `c´he H1   150 ofte] of
H1G

thought be dissolut, sayeng that the clennesse of body and of clothing
is filthe to the soule and that thing that is not or light among men of
the worlde is full hevi and greuous among religious. And þof she gaue
al thingges large[ly] to the sike of fleshe and of metes, in her owne 155
persone she wolde nothing take whanne she was seke, and in that she
was not egal, for tho thingges that she dede to other in pitee she
torned to herselff in hardinesse.

'I shalle tell that I haue hadde experience of. It fell in the right
brennyng hete of Iulit that she was in a brennyng feuer and after that 160
men wende she wolde haue deied, but she turned to lyff bi the merci
of God, so that phisicianes saiden that she most drinke and vse smal
wyn and drinke no water lest she fill into a dropsi. And I praied to the
blessed Epiphanes the bysshop that he wolde bidde her and enioyne
her to drinke wyne. For she was of wise and of subtile engine she felt 165
anone and smyled vpon hym, and who stered hym therto she tolde
hym. And what ouer? Whanne the blessed bisshop come to her and
after many exortaciones went oute from her ayein, I asked her how she
hadde done, and she ansuered: "I haue so moche profited that withe
moche payne I haue stered this olde man that I shall drinke no wyne." 170

'She was debonaire to her husbonde and in weping milde, and she
breke myghtly her sensualite, and moste ayeinst her children, for in
[the] dethe of her husbonde and children she was euer in perell of
dethe. And whanne she signed her withe the crosse in the forhede and
in the breste, the impression of the crosse enforsed her ayeinst | the f.44ʳᵃ
moderli sorugh and asuaged and ouercome the corage; the faithefull 176
mynde and the bowels of the moder were troubled, so sche ouercome
the freelte of the body and was ouercome.

'She helde in gret rememberaunce holi scripture, and as she loued
the stori and saide that it was the foundement of trouthe, yet she 180
folued more the spirituel vnderstondyng, and be that hyghnesse she
defended the edificacion of the soule. And she speke another tonge,
the whiche thing is not lyght to the envious. She lerned the tonge of
Ebrewe, the whiche I lerned of my yougthe withe grete paine and
many an harde swete for pite, and witheoute [ce]sing euer thenkyng 185
theron leste she lefte me er I her, she lered hem in suche wise that she

152 that] ins. H1   155 largely] large E   of] add þe G   in] om. H1G
156 nothing] þinge H1G   158 hardinesse] changed from hardenesse H1   164 he]
she with s erased H1   165 of²] om. G   167 what] whan H1   ouer] euer H1G
Whanne the] þat H1   to] ins. H1   168 many] money H1   172–3 for . . . children]
om. H1G   173 the] om. E   180 and] sche G   185 an] and G, and del. H1   for]
of H1   cessing] L, lessing E, lesing H1G

song all her psalmes in Ebrew and sowned that worde withoute any
other properte of Latyne tonge, the whiche thing we see into this day
in Eustache her doughter.

190   'We haue into this tyme driven oure shippe by good wyndes and
oure shippe hathe coruen the right passing waters of the see in
rennyng, and now oure talkyng rennithe in estaffys that bene litell
shippes. What is he that myght tell Paula ys deyeng witheoute weping?
She fell in right gret febilnesse and [founde that she] desired for to
195   leue us and for to be [more] pleinly withe oure Lorde. Wherfor abide I
so long and make my sorw more long in abidyng in other thingges?
[The] right wis among women felt the dethe be [in] her, and a party of
the body and of the membres wexen colde and she felt but only the
brethe a litell mevyng [in] here holy brest for to passe forthe, and
200   thanne she saide softely this vers: "[Lorde], I haue loued the beauute
of thine hous and the habitacion of thi glorie." And thanne she saide:

f. 44ʳᵇ   "Lorde of vertues, | how miche haue y coueited thi biloued taber-
nacles. Mi soule faillethe in the beyng of oure Lorde. I haue rather
chosen to be despised in the hous of my God thanne to duelle in the
205   tabernacles of synners." And whanne I asked of her whi she helde her
still and whi she ansuered not to me crieng and soruyng, she ansuered
me in Greke that she hadde no sorugh, for she felt that all thingges
were pesible and in quiete. And thanne she recorded this vers withe
eyen closed into she yeldid vp the soule withe so lowe a voys that
210   vnnethis I myght vnderstonde her.

'And ther was no monke hidde in his celle in the desert ne no
virgine that most bisiliest kepte the secrete places of her chaumbre but
that they hadde wende that it hadde be sacrilege if thei hadde not be
atte the office that she were worshipfully leide in the pitte beside the
215   chirche. And Eustoche the worshipfull virgine doughter of her myght
not be drawe from her moder, kissing her and euer hauing her eyen to
her visage, and enbraced the body and wolde haue bene beried withe
the moder, and God [is] witnesse that she lefte neuer a peny to her
doughter but money of straungers, and that more wonder is she lefte

188 thing] iuge *del.* 'thinge' H₁   190 shippe] L, shippes EG, shepes *changed to*
shippes H₁   194 founde . . . she] L, *om.* EH₁G   195 more] *om.* E   oure] oute
changed to oure H₁   197 The] L, is EH₁G   in] L, to EH₁G   199 in] L, it E, at
H₁G   200 Lorde] *om.* E   203 in the] *twice* G   oure] my H₁   206 me¹] my
changed to me H₁   208 pesible] passibull G   209 so lowe a] a lowe G
211 the] *om.* H₁   212 the] *add* moste G   214 the¹] *om.* H₁   216 not] *om.*
G, *add* to *subp.* H₁   eyen] þen G   218 is] L, to EH₁G   219 wonder is]
wondrez H₁, wondir G

her gret multitude of bretheren and susteren that was an harde thinge 220
to sustene and wicked in the puttyng awaye. Oure Lorde saue the,
Paula. Helpe, I praie the, the laste age of hym thi worshipper.'

Here endithe the lyff of Seint Pauline, and nexst beginnithe
the lyff of Seint Iulian, Capitulum .xxix.

Iulian was bisshopp of Emans, and men sayne that he was Simon the
lepere that | oure Lorde heled of that siknesse and he that bede oure f. 44ᵛᵃ
Lorde to dinere, the whiche the apostelys ordeined hym to be bisshop
of Eman[s] after the ascencion of oure Lorde. And this same bisshop
was ennobled withe many vertues, for he areised thre men from dethe 5
to lyff be his merites, and after that he slepte in oure Lorde. This is
that Iulien the which [as] men sayn that traueling men praien vnto for
good herburgh bicause that oure Lorde was herborued atte his hous.
[But] it is more verrily sain to be another Iulien the whiche
vnwetingly slowe his fader and his moder, of whom the stori shall 10
be sette here witheinne.

Ther was also another Iuliane of a noble kynrede of Dauuergne, but
miche more noble be faithe, for bi hys owne will he offered hymselff to
the persecutours be desire of marterdome. And atte the laste the
prouost Crispine sent his servaunt and comaunded that he shuld be 15
slaine, and whanne this Iulian herde that he rose hym vp and offered
hymselff witheoute any drede to hym that asked aftcr hym. And
thanne he smote hym a stroke and slowe hym, and thanne the hede
was lefte vp from the erthe and born to Seint Frayoll his felaw for to
manasse hym withe the same dethe yef he wolde not sacrifie anone to 20
the ydoles. And whanne he wolde not in no wise consent thei putte
hym to dethe and slowe hym and putte oute the hede of Seint Iulian
withe hym in a toumbe. And many yere after Seint Mamertyn the
bisshop of Viene fonde the hede of Seint Iuliane betwene the hondes
of Seint Freyoll as hole and | as sounde as though he hadde be beried f. 44ᵛᵇ
in the same day. 26

Among other thingges the myracles of this Iulian most be tolde, for
as [a dragon] hadd stole the shepe of Seint [Iulian] and þe schepardes
forbede hym in the name of of Seint [Iulian], he ansu[e]red: 'Iulian

EH1GDH2A1A2L; D somewhat damaged 188–98, 217–end   3 to be] *twice once del.*
H1   4 Emans] Eman E   bisshop] blessid H1G   5 ennobled] enuolued H1
7 as] that E   8 herburgh] *add* and H1   9 But] L, for EH1G   23 Seint] sente
to G   28 a dragon] drakyn E, Adragoun G   Iulian] Iohn EG, Iulian *on erasure* H1
29 Iulian] Iohn EG, Iohn *subp.* 'Iulian' H1   ansuered] ansured E

30 etithe no moton.' And a litell after he was striken withe a strong feuer,
and whanne the feuer laboured hym he knowlaged that he was al sette
afere withe that martir and bede men to caste water on hym to
refresshe hym, and anone ther come oute so gret a smoke and so foule
a stinke of his body that alle fledden that were aboute hym, and anone
35 after he deied. So as Seint Gregor tellithe, ther was a plowman þat
wolde eere a felde in a Sonday, and anone he was contracte in his
hondes and the instrement that he clensed the share of his sool withe
fille oute of his hondes. And he was heled two yere after in the chirche
of Seint Iulian.
40   Ther was also another Iulian that was brother to of Seint Iulien,
and these two bretherin come to the cristine emperour Theodesien
and required hym that he wolde geve hem powere that in what place
thei founde any temples of ydoles that thei myght destroie hem and
edefie chirches of Ihesu Crist, and the emperour graunted hem gladly
45 and wrote oute lettrez that alle [peple] shuld obeye hem [and helpe
hem] in paine of lesyng of her hedes. And thanne as the blessed Iulien
and Iulyn made a chirche in a place that is called Gant, and by þe
comaundement of the emperour all tho that passed bi that way shulde
helpe hem to thaire werke.
50   And so it fell that there come men with a carte, and that one saide to
f. 45ra that | other: 'What excusacion mowe we make that we mowe passe
frely and not be ocupied withe this werke?' And thanne thei saide:
'One of vs shall lye doune in the carte as dede and we shull couer hym
with a clothe and we shull saie that we carie a dede man, and so we
55 shull passe frely.' And thanne thei toke a man and caste hym in the
carte and saide to hym: 'Lye stille and close thin eyen and lye as thou
were dede til we be passed.' And whanne thei hadde couered hym as
dede, thanne thei come to the se[r]vauntes of God, Iulian and Iulyn
saide to hem: 'Good sones, abide a whiles and helpithe us to oure
60 werke a lytell.' And thei ansuered and saide: 'We mowe in no wise
abide for we carie a dede man witheinne oure cart.' Thanne saide
Seint Iulian: 'Whi lye ye so, my sones?' And thei saide: 'We lye not,
Syr, but it is as we sain.' And thanne saide Seint Iulian: 'So falle it you
after the trouthe of youre sayeng.' And thanne thei drove forth the

carte and went her waye, and whanne thei were gone a good waye 65
thennes thei went to the carte and called thayre felawe and bade hym:
'Arise and driue the carte that we mowe go the faster.' And he remeued
not. Thanne they beganne to crie and to calle on hym and saide: 'Whi
tariest thou so longe? Arise and stere the oxen.' And whanne he
ansuered not thei went to hym and vncouered hym and founde hym 70
dede, and thanne so grete drede fell to hem and to alle other that none
durst make a lesing [after that tyme] to the servaunt[es] of God.

Ther was another Iulien as I saide before that slow his fader an his
moder bi ignoraunce. For as this Iulien yong and noble | went on a day f. 45rb
to hunt he founde an herte and folued hym, and sodenli the hert 75
turned ayein and saide to hym: 'Thou foluest me, wete well that thou
shalt slee thi fader and thi moder.' And whanne he herde þat, he
dredde leste it shulde falle to hym as the herte saide and fledde away
priuely and lefte all that euer ther was, and come into a fer contrey and
fell in seruice of a noble prince and gouerned hym so nobly and so 80
worthely bothe in bataile and in paleis that alle men hadd ioye of hym.
And thanne the prince made hym knyght and weddid hym to a
chastelyn that was wedowe, and gaue hym a faire ca[s]tell withe her
with gret lordshippes that longithe therto.

In this mene tyme the fader and the moder of Iuliene weren in gret 85
sorugh for her sone and wenten al aboute the straunge contreyes to
seke hym and asked in alle places after her sone. And atte the laste thei
hapened that thei come to the same castell ther Iulien was lorde. And
Iulien was thanne go oute, and whanne the wiff of Iulien seigh hem
and hadde enquered what thei were and thei hadde tolde her alle that 90
was befalle hem of her sone, and she vnderstode þat thei were her
husbondes fader and moder, as she perauenture had ofte tyme herde
of her husbonde like case, and receiued hem goodly and lefte hem her
owne chaumbre and her bedde for loue of her husbonde and toke
herselff another for the tyme. In the morw erly the chastelyn arose and 95
went to the chirche, and as fortune wold, Iulien come home the same
morw|tide erly and purposed to awake his wyff, and come into the f. 45va
chaumbre and founde two slepe togederes, and anone supposed that it
hadde bene his wyff and sum other man, and in verrey wodenesse of
ielosie he drowe his suerde and slowe hem bothe. 100

67 driue] d`r'yue H1   71 drede] derkenes G   72 after that tyme] L, *om*. EH1G
servauntes] L, servaunt EG, seru`a'nt H1   83 castell] catell E   92 ofte tyme] *om*. G
herde] *add* before G   93 like case] *om*. G   hem¹] *twice once del*. H1   94 for . . . husbonde]
om. G   96 wold] *add* she H1   98 slepe] asclepe G   100 drowe] *add* oute G

And whanne he went oute of the chaumbre he mette his wiff
comyng fro the chirche, and whanne he seigh her he hadde mervaile
and asked her who thei were that slepte in her bedde. Thanne she
saide with gret gladnesse: 'A, Sir, it is youre fader and youre moder
105 that hauen sought you so longe withe gret sorugh and laboure, and I
haue leide hem in youre chaumbre.' And whanne he herde that he fell
downe as dede, and whanne he awoke he beganne to wepe right
bitterly and to saie: 'Alas, I most wreche, what shall I do? For I haue
slayn my right dere fader and moder. Now is the worde fulfelled of
110 the herte, and whanne I wende to eschewe this sorifull dede I most
cursed haue fulfelled it. Now fare well, my dere[st] wiff, for I shall
neuer rest from hennes forward till þat I knowe that oure Lorde hathe
receiued my penaunce.' And she with gret sorugh saide: 'Oure Lorde
defende that euer I leue you, for the while that ther is lyff in my body
115 ye shull neuer go witheoute me, for sethe I haue parted with you in
ioye I shall be partener of your sorw.'

And thanne thei went togedre besides a grete flode where many
men perisched, and there besides in that desert thei made a litell
hospitall for to do there penaunce and for to bere ouer all tho that
f. 45vb wolde passe, and for to receiue hem | into the hospitall and mynster to
121 hem after her power. And longe after that tyme, whanne Seint Iulian
reste hym aboute midnyght al forweried and the wedyr [was] colde
and a gret froste, he herde a vois that wepte piteously and cried:
'Iulian, helpe me ouer for Goddes loue or ellis I perische for greuous
125 colde.' And whanne he herde that voys he arose al sodenly and passed
the colde water and founde that pore creature that deied nigh for
colde, [he] toke hym up and bere hym to his hous and light the fere
and dede al his diligence to warme hym. And as he myght in no wise
make hym take warmthe he toke hym in his armes and bare hym to his
130 bedde and hilled hym diligently. And a litell after he that apered to be
so sike and as a foule lepre stied vp shinyng into heuene, saieng to his
oste: 'Iulian, oure Lorde hathe sent me to the, sendyng the to saie that
he hathe receiued thi [penaunce] and ye bothe shull reste in oure
Lorde witheinne a litell tyme.' And anone he vanished awaye, and
135 thanne a litell after, Seint Iulian and his wyff, fulfellid with good
werkes and grete almes, slepten in oure Lorde Ihesu Crist.

101 the] his G   102 hadde] *add* gret E   108 to saie] saide G   111 derest]
dere E   113 And] A`nd' H1   114 the] ther E   115 parted] departid G
119 there] her H1G   122 was] *om.* E   125 al] *om.* G   127 he] *om.* EH1
130 hilled] helid G, heled `him' H1   diligently] *add* him *del.* H1   132 the²] *add* me G
133 penaunce] L, pacience EH1G   135 good] Goddes H1G

Another Iulian ther was that was nothing holi but right cursed, that
is to wete Iulian the apostata. This Iulian was furste a monke and
feyned hym to be of gret religion and, as Maister Iohn Bylett tellithe
in the Somme of the Office of the Chirche, how ther was a woman that 140
hadde .iij. pottis full of golde, and she couerid the pottis aboue withe
asshen that the golde shuld not apere, and thanne she toke the pottis
to Iulien to kepe, wenyng þat he hadde bene right an holy man | bifore f. 46ra
many of thother monkes. And whanne Iulian hadde these pottis in
keping, in a day he desired to wete what was withinne hem, and 145
whanne he hadde loked and founde al that golde he toke oute al that
golde and filled the pottes with asshes. And a litell while after the
woman come for her pottes, and he deliuered hem to her full of
aschen, and whanne she asked her golde she myght not proue it that
she toke hym any for she hadde no witnesse, for the monkes before 150
whom she deliuered the pottis sawe nothing but aschen withinne. And
so Iulian hadde that gold, [and withe alle that golde] he went to Rome,
and bi that golde he dede so moche that witheinne a litell tyme after he
was made consult of Rome, and after that he was so haunsed into the
empire.   155
And fro his yougthe he was taught in art magike and it plesed hym
gretly, and hadde withe hym many maistres therof. In a day, as the
Stori tellithe that is Parted in Thre, that his maister, the whiche hadde
taught hym in his yougthe, was parted from hym, and as he was allone
he beganne to rede the coniu+rementes, and anone [a grete] multitude 160
of fendes in manere of blake Ethiopens appered before hym, and
whanne Iulian seigh hem he dredde hem and made the signe of the
crosse, and anone thei vanished away, and whanne his maister was
come ayein he tolde hym how it was befall hym. Thanne his maister
saide that the fendes dreden gretly and haten the signe of the crosse. 165
And [thanne] whanne Iulian was so [haunsed] into the empire, he
remembered [hym] vpon that thing and become in alle apostata, and
for he wolde werke bi that art magike he destroied the | signe of the f. 46rb
crosse in eueri place wher he come and was a persecutour of cristen as
moche as laye in his pouere, wenyng that other [wayes] the fende[s] 170

141 full . . . pottis] ins. H1   143 bene] add a EG   an] om. G   146–7 he toke . . .
golde] om. H1G   147 and] he G   148 her¹] he'r' E   149 not] ins. H1
150 any] none H1   152 and . . . golde] om. E   alle] om. H1   153 he¹] sche G
moche] add þerwith H1G   that²] om. H1   witheinne] In H1G   160 coniuremementes]
coniurentez H1, coniowratis G   a grete] L, om. EH1G   162 hem²] hym G
166 thanne] om. E   haunsed] hated E   167 hym] om. E   170 wayes] wise E
fendes] L, fende EH1G

wolde not obeye hym. And as it is redde in the Liff of Faders that whanne Iulian was come downe into Percie he sent a fende into the occidente for to bringe hym an ansuere from thennes, and whanne this fende come into a place ferre thennes aboute [a] .x. iorneis, he
175 abode still there withoute meving, for ther was an holy monke that preied nyght and day, and thanne he turned ayein witheoute any effecte, and whanne Iulian seie hym he saide: 'Whi haste thou taried so longe?' And than the fende saide: 'I haue abidde alwayes a monke that preied, to wete yef he wolde cese perauenture of his praieng that I
180 myght passe, and he sesed neuer, wherfor I may not passe but am come ayein witheoute any effecte.' And thanne Iulian saide bi grete disdeyne that he wolde take veniaunce on that monke. And as the fendes behight hym victori of hem of Perse, his maister saide to a cristen man: 'What trowest thou now what the carpenter sone doth atte this tyme?' And he
185 ansuered: 'He makithe redi a sepulture for Iulian.'

As men reden in the stori of Seint Basile, and Philibert bisshop of Chartres witnessith it also, whanne Iuliane come in Cesarie of Capadoce Seint Basile come ayeinst hym and sent hym thre louis of barly, [and] Iulian hadde despite therof and sent hym ayein heye and
190 luste not take the loues, but saide: 'Thou hast sent us mete that longithe to dvm bestes. Take ayein that thou haste sent us.' And
f. 46ᵛᵃ Basile saide: 'We haue sent vnto the suche mete as I leue | withe, and thou hast sent me suche mete as thou norishest thi bestes with.' And thanne he, wrothe, ansuered: 'Whan I haue submitted the Persans I
195 shall distroie this citee, and I shall pare hym so nygh that he shall mowe [better] be called "beryng whete" [than] "susteynyng men".' And the nyght foluyng Basile seigh in a vision in the chirche of Oure Ladi grete multitude of aungels and in the middes of hem a woman sitting in a trone that saide to tho þat were there: 'Calle anone to me
200 Mercurie that he may sle anone Iulian the apostata that blamithe so proudeli my sone and me.' And that Mercuri was a knyght that hadde bene slayn of Iulian before for the faith of Ihesu Crist. And anone Seint Mercurie come withe his armes that were kepte ther witheinne, and she comaunded hym to go to the bataile and he dede [so]. And

173 occidente] add And H1   174 aboute] om. G   a²] om. E   .x.] add 'dayes' H1
iorneis] dayis iourney G   175 that] and H1   177 hym] 'þe fende' H1, om. G
180 sesed] ceseth H1G   184 trowest] add trouest E   186 Philibert] add also H1
187 it] om. H1   189 and¹] L, om. EH1G   heye] on erasure H   190 not] add 'to'
H1, add to G   194 Persans] personys G, Perses on erasure also in margin H1
196 better] om. E   than] the EG   201 that²] om. H1   203–6 that . . . armes] om. G
204 she] he changed to she H1   so] also E

whanne Seint Basile awoke he went to the place wher this holy 205
Mercurye was beried withe his armes and opened his sepulcre and
fonde nother hym ne his armes. And thanne he enquered of hem that
kepte hym who hadde take hym awaye, and he suore to hym that same
nyght he was there as men kepte hym alwayes. And thanne Basile
went his waye and come ayein in the morwe and fonde the body of 210
hym and his armes and the spere al blody. And anone one that come
from the oste saide: 'So as Iulian the emperour was in his hoste, an
vnknowen knyght come in his armes and smote his horse with his
spores and withe hardi corage ronne to Iulian and smote hym thorugh
withe his spere, and thanne sodenly he vanished away.' And this 215
Iulian, so as [the] Storie Part[ed] in Thre saiethe, as he sighed deyeng
he filled | his honde withe his blode and saide: 'Thou hast ouercome, f. 46ᵛᵇ
Galelien, thou hast the victorie.' And so crieng he deied cursidly.

Here endithe the liff of Seint Iulian, and nexst beginnithe
Septuagesme, Capᵐ. .xxx.ᵐ

The Septuagesme signifiethe the tyme of deuiacion, that is as moche
to saie as the tyme of goyng oute of the right waye; the Sexagesme
signifiethe the tyme of renouacion; the Quinquagesme signifiethe the
tyme of remission; þe Quadragesme signifiethe the tyme of spirituall
penaunce. 5

The Septuagesme beginnithe the Sonday that men synggen
Circumdederunt me, and endithe the Sonday after Ester. And the
Septuagesme is ordeyned for th[r]e resones, as it is contened in Sum
of the Office of the Chirche that Maister Iohn Belet made, that is to
saie for the redempcion, the whiche the holy faders ordeined hit, and 10
also for þe worship of the ascension in whiche oure kinde ascended
into heuene and was enhaunsed aboue all the felawship of aungels,
this fifte day was holde solempne and worshipfull, and for that men
shulde not faste, for in the furste begynnyng of the Chirche this day
was as solempne as the Sonday, and than ther was made a procession 15
solempne for to represent the procession of the disciples and of the
aungels. And therfor it is knowen for a comune prouerbe that the day

208 hymʳ] L, *add* and EH1G   211 his] *om.* G   212 in] to H1G   216 the] L,
om. EG, *ins.* H1   Parted] partithe E   sighed deyeng] sanke down G

EH1GDH2A1A2L; D damaged till 2 *goyng* and from 40–44, 61–71   2 waye] day
H1G   8 thre] the E   11 kinde] king H1G   13 fifte] first H1G   15 than]
om. G

of Thoursday is called cosin to Sonday for that it was in olde tyme
solempne as Sonday, but for as moche as festis of seintes bene comen
20 nwe and halowed so ferforthe that the multeplieng beganne to be
grevous to the Chirche, this feste of Thoursday cessed. And thanne
f. 47ʳᵃ for to make a recompense for tho dayes, the holy faders | haue
ordeyned a woke and ioyned [it] in abstinence lik to Lenten and called
it Septuagesme.

25 [The] other reson is [signifyeng, for by that tyme is] signified
deuiacion, exile and tribulacion of al mankinde from Adam into the
ende of the worlde, the whiche exile is ledde bi the turnyng ayen of
.vij. dayes and of .vijMˡ. yere, for bi the Septuagesme we vnderstonde
.lxx. yere. Fro the begynnyng of the worlde vnto þe ascencion we
30 acounte .vjMˡ., and as moche as foluithe after into the ende of the
worlde is comprehended in the .vijMˡ., of whiche only God wote the
terme. And in the .vj. age of the worlde Ihesu Crist toke us oute of this
exile and yelde us [by] bapteme the stole of innocence in hope of
euerlastyng guerdon, but whanne the tyme of oure exile shall be
35 fulfelled he shall araie vs perfitly with bothe stoles. And therfor in this
tyme of deuyacion and of exile we take awaye the songe of gladnesse,
and the Saterday tofore Ester we sing one Alleluya, reioising vs in
hope to [haue the] euerlastyng pees, and as recouering the stole of
innocence bi Ihesu Crist in the .vj.ᵗᵉ age of the worlde, and after this
40 Alleluya men synggen the Tracte bi the whiche is signified the trauaile
that we shulde haue in fullfellyng the comaundementes of God. And
the Saterday after Ester in the whiche as it is saide Septuagesme
cesithe, we synge two Allel[u]yas, for whanne the terme of this worlde
shal be fulfelled we shull receiue double stole of glorie.

45 Another reson is for the representacion, that the Septuagesme
representithe .lxx. yere that the children of Israel weren vnder
chetivison of Babiloyne, and as they dede awaye her songges,
seying: 'Howe shul[de] we syng songges of oure Lorde in a straunge
f. 47ʳᵇ londe?', right so we do a|waye oure songges of preisyng. And after that
50 thei hadde licence to turne ayen into Ciro in the .lx. yere thei beganne
ayein to reioyse hem, and we were the Saterday of Ester, as in the .lx.
yere, Alleluya in representing her gladnesse. But for al that thei

20 ferforthe] foresothe H₁G   22 tho] þe G   23 it] L, *om.* EH₁G   in, lik to]
trs. G   25 The] L, That EH₁G   other] ouer H₁G   signifyeng . . . is] *om.* E   for . . .
signified] *om.* H₁G   29 *after* yere *no MS has punct.*   31 of²] *add* `þe´ H₁   33 by]
the E, þe *del.* `by´ H₁   37 reioising] refresshyng G   38 haue the] *om.* E
41 shulde] shul H₁   43 synge] syngyng G   Alleluyas] Allelyas E   48 shulde]
shull E

travailed sore in makyng hem redy to turne ayein and to gadre her
thingges togedre, and for that cause we syng anone after the Tracte
that signifiethe her trauaile, and in the Saterday that the Septuagesme 55
fallethe we syng tw[o] Alleluyas in figure of her pleine ioye by whiche
thei come ageyn into [her] contre.

And in this tyme of chetevite of the children of Israel representithe
the tyme of oure pilgrimage, for right as thei were deliuered in the .lx.
yere, right so [were] we in the .vj.^te age of the worlde, and right as they 60
trauayled in gaderyng togedere her thingges and to bere her fardeles,
right so we being deliuered labouren and trauailen to fulfell the
comaundementes of God. But whanne we shal be come home to oure
contrey oure trauaile shal be ended and perfit ioye shal be hadde, and
thanne we shul sing double Alleluia in bodi and in soule. 65

In this tyme of exile the Chirche hathe be gretly depressed bi many
tribulacionis and putte almost in [the] anguishe of despaire, sighyng
hili, and crieth in the Office and saieth: 'The wepingez and the
wayllingges of dethe haue beclipped me.' And the Chirche shewith
her multeplyeng tribulaciones that she hathe, nameli for the wiked- 70
nesse done, for the double peyne putte in her and for the gilte done to
other. But for she shulde not falle in despeire ther is putte to her .iij.
remedies of hele in the pistel and in the gospel and [.iij. medes]. The
remedie is that yef | she will be perfitely deliuered that she laboure in f. 47va
the vine of the soule in drowing oute vices and synnes, and sithe that 75
she renne in the estate of this liff by werkes of penaunce, and after that
she fyght strongely ayeinst the temptaciones of the fende. And yef she
do this she shall haue trebel her mede, for the peny shall be yeue to hem
that laboure, and to the renner in fleing, and to the fighter corone.

And for that the Septuagesme signifiethe the tyme of oure 80
chetevison, it is yeue us remedie bi the whiche we mow be deliuered
of oure cheteuyte by rennyng in fleyng, bi bataile in fityng, bi the peny
in vs ayeinbeying.

56 fallethe] L, faillethe EH1, fallid G   two] tw E   57 her] L, the EH1G
60 were] om. E   61 togedere] add in E   62 and] to G   63 be] om. G
66 hathe] haue changed to ha`th' H1   67 the¹] om. E   68 hili] gretly G   73 .iij.
medes] L, in mede EH1G   78 trebel] travaile changed to trebaile G

Here endithe Septuagesme, and nexst foluithe Sexagesme,
Cap^m. .xxxj.^m

The Sexagesme begynnethe the Sonday that men synggen *Exurge
Domine* and ys termined in the .iiij.^te fery after Ester, and was
ordeined for redempcion, for the significasion and for representacion.
[For redempcion], the whiche Melchisedek and Siluester the pope
5 ordeyned it, for it was ordeyned in the lawe that eueri Saterday men
shulde ete twies, for þe abstinence that men hadde susteyned in the
Friday, in the whiche men aughten faste at alle tymes, but yef kynde
were ouer febled. And thanne for the redempcion of the Saterdayes in
that tyme thei [added] a woke of Lente and called it Sexagesme.
10 Another^e reson is for significacion, for that .lx.^e signifieth the tyme of
widowehode of the Chirche and the weping for her for the absence of
f. 47vb her spouse, for the fruit of .lx.^ti is done to the widowes. And | in
conforting her for the absence of her spouse that is rauished into
heue[n] ther is yeuen to the Chirche two wingges, that is to saye .vij.
15 werkes of mercy and the fulfelling of the .x. comaundementes of the
lawe. Sexti is as moche to saye as .vj. tymes ten, so that by .vj. is
vnderstonde the .x. comaundementis of the lawe. The thridde reson is
for the Sexagesme signifiethe not only the tyme of widowhode but
representithe þe mistery of oure redempcion, for bi ten is vnderstonde
20 man, that is the .x. dragma, for he was made to restore the fallyng
downe of the .ix. orderes. Er man ys vnderstonde bi .x., for that he is
of foure humoures as to the body and he hathe .iij. vertues as to the
soule, that is mynde, vnderstondyng and will, that bene made for to
serue the blessed Trinite, so that alle leuen truly that same and hym to
25 loue feruentely and euer to holde hym in oure mynde. By the .vj. bene
vnderstonde .vj. misteries by the whiche man the .x. dragme is bought
ayein, that is to saye the incarnacion, the natiuite, the passion and the
goyng downe into helle, the resureccion and the ascension. And for
þat it is saide the Sexagesme vnto the .iiij.^te fery after Ester that men
30 synggen *Uenite benedicti patris mei et cetera*, for tho that vsen the
werkes of mersi shullen here that songe: 'Comith [ye] blessed children
of my fader', so as that same Ihesu Crist witnessithe, ther as the gate is

EH1GDH2A1A2L   1 Sexagesme] septuagesme G, *so with* þ *changed to* x H1
Sonday] Second day H1G   that] þanne G   4 For redempcion] L, *om.* EH1G   5 it^1
. . . ordeyned] *om.* H1   7 men] *ins.* H1   8 febled] feble H1G   9 added] L,
hadden EH1G   11 for^1] of H1G   14 heuen] the heued E, heuen *with* uen *on erasure*
H1   16 .vj.] se`xe´ H1   21 of] as G   26 .x.] *om.* G   28 goyng] doyng G
30 patris] patres G   *et cetera*] *om.* G   31 ye] the EG

now open to her spouse and shall vse the clipping of her spouse. And
he techithe her in a pistell that she shall suffre pacientely as Paule
dede the absence of his spouse in his tribulacion, and the gospell 35
techithe here that she | be alwaies in good werkes, and that sche that f. 48ra
ha[dd]e cried as in dispaire: 'The wailyngges of dethe haue beclipped
me,' that now she was comyng to herselff requerith in the Office to be
holpen of her tribulaciones and for to be deliuered from hem, saieng:
'Arise, Lorde, whi slepest thou?' And she saieth thre tymes: 'Arise.' 40
For there bene sum in the Chirche that bene greued by aduersite but
thei be not caste oute, and other that bene greued and caste oute, and
other that bene nother greued ne caste oute. Notwithstonding tho that
ne suffre none aduersite, it is to drede leste that prosperite breke hem.
Wherfor the Chirche criethe that he arise, as to the furst in 45
comfortyng hem, for it semithe hem as though he slepte; and she
crieth that he arise as to the secounde in [conue]rtyng hem, for it
semithe hem as though he hadde turned awaye his visage fro hem and
in a maner caste hem fro hym; and he crie[the] that he arise as to the
thridde in helping hem in her prosperite and to deliuer hem.   50

Here endithe Sexagesme, and nexst foluith Quinquagesme,
Cap^m. .xxxij.^m

The Quinquagesme durithe fro the Sonday that men synggen *Esto*
michi Domine and endith on Ester Day. And she is ordeyned for
fullfellyng, for signifieng and for representing. [For] fulfelling, in as
moche as we aught to faste .xl. daies like as Ihesu Crist dede, and
ther bene but .xxxvj.^ti daies to be faste, for as moche as men fast not 5
the Sondaies for the ioie and the reuerence of the resureccion of oure
Lorde and for the ensaumple of oure Lorde Ihesu Crist that ete two
tymes in that daye, whanne he | entred into his disciples the gates f. 48rb
being closed and thei brought hym of a rosted fische and of an
honycombe, and he ete ayein withe the disciples whanne they went to 10
Emaus. And for to fullfelle the Sondaies the .iiij. dayes bene sette to.
And also the clergi consider[ed] how they went before the laye peple
bi ordre and thought that they most go before hem bi holinesse and

37 hadde] hathe E   40 tymes] thingez *del.* timez H1   47 the] *om.* G
conuertyng] comfortyng E   49 criethe] cried E

EH1GDH2A1A2L   3 For] L, *om.* EH1G   5 faste] *add* not þe sondaies H1
6 the Sondaies] *om.* H1   10 they] he G   12 considered] considerith E   the²] þei
changed to þe H1, þer G

begannen to faste two dayes before the comon peple, so that an hole
15 woke is put to, the whiche is called Quinquagesme.

And as Seint Ambrose saiethe, the thother reson is for significacion,
for Quinquagesme betokenithe tyme of remission, that is penaunce,
wherinne all thingges be foryeue. [The] fifti yere was of ioie, that was
the yere of remission, for thanne dettis weren foryeue, servauntes
20 were deliuered of thraldome and alle turned ayen to her possessiones.
By whiche yere is signified that by [penau]nce dettes of synne[s] be
foryeue and al were take oute of the seruage of the fende and retorned
to the possessiones of heuenly houses.

The .iij.ᵉ reson is for the representacion, for the Quinquagesme
25 signifieth not only tyme of remission but representith the tyme and
astate of blessidnesse. For in the fyfti yere servauntes were made fre,
and in the fifty day from the day of the lambe sacrified the lawe was
yeuen, in the fyfti day fro Ester the holy goste was yeuen, and therfor
representithe this nombre blessidnesse, for therinne is receiued
30 fredom and liberte and knowlache of trouthe and perfeccion of
charite. Thre thingges be necessarie to us the whiche bene [purposed]
f. 48ᵛᵃ to us in the pistell and in the gospell | to that ende that [the] werkes of
penaunce bene perfit, that is to saie charite, that is purposed to vs in
the apistell, mynde of oure Lordes passion, and faithe, that is [to]
35 vnderstonde by ellumyninge of the blinde. And that is purposed in
the gospell for that stedfast beleue made his werkes acceptable, for it is
inpossible to plese God witheoute faithe, the mynde of the passion,
wherof Seint Gregor saiethe: 'If the mynde of the passivn be truly
brought to mynde, ther is nothing but that it makithe it to be suffered
40 euenli with go[o]d wille.' She continuethe charite, for as þe same
clerke saiethe, the loue of God may not be idell, for wher she is she
dothe gret thingges, but yef she leue to werke that is not loue.

And right as [at] the begynnyng the Chirch in despeire of herselff
hadde cried: 'The waylinges of dethe *et c.*,' and after that in comyng
45 ayen to herselff she asked helpe, right so she, whanne she hadde
conceiued trust of hope of foryeuenesse, she praied and saide: 'Lorde,
be to me my protectour in God.' And in that Office she requirithe .iiij.
thingges, that is defence, stabilnesse, refute and condut. For all the

18 The] for E   20 of] from H1G   21 yere] þer G   penaunce] L, pacience
EH1G   synnes] L, synne EH1G   28 in . . . yeuen] *om.* H1   30 perfeccion]
persecucion H1G   31 purposed] L, *om.* EH1G   32 the³] L, *om.* EH1G   34 to]
om. E   39 mynde] *add and del.* H1   40 good] godd E   continuethe] conteynyth G
43 at] *om.* E   46 trust] crist G   47 God] good E   requirithe] required H1G

children of the Chirche, either thei bene in grace either in gilte, either
in aduersite or [in] prosperite. And she aske[th] for hem that bene in 50
grace stabelnesse that thei bene confermed, to hem that bene in gilte
she requirithe refute of God, for hem that bene in aduersite defence,
and to hem that bene in prosperite she askethe condut þat they mow
be brought to God by innocence.

And the Quinquagesme endithe as it is saide on Ester Day, and she 55
makithe penaunce a nwe | lyff to spring vp. For in this tyme is often f. 48ᵛᵇ
tyme songe the psalme *Miserere mei Deus secundum magnam miseri-*
cordiam tuam, that is the psalme of penaunce and of remission.

Here endithe Quinquagesme, and than foluithe Lente,
Capitulum .xxxiij.ᵐ

The Lente beginnithe the Sonday that men synggen *Inuocauit me*
Dominus, and the Chirche that was so broken before [withe] tribulaciones and hadde cried: 'The wailingges of dethe,' and after she was a
litell respeired in callyng helpe she saide: 'Arise up *et c.*,' now [she
sheweth] that she is herde and saithe: 'He callithe me and I haue herde 5
hym *et c.*' And it is to knowe that the Lente contenithe .xlij. dayes
withe the Sondaies acounted, and whanne the .vj. Sondaies be take
awaye ther remayneth but .xxxvj. dayes of abstinence, that is the
dyme of alle the yere, but the .iiij. dayes before be sette therto so that
the noumbre of .xl. dayes bene fulfelled, for that oure saueoure 10
halowed hem before with fasting.

And thre resones mowe be assigned whi we kepe the faste in that
noumbre of fourty. The furst saiethe Austin [that] Mathew putte
fourti generaciones, and for that oure Lorde descended to us in the
noumbre of fourty for that we shulde stie up and come to hym in oure 15
fourti[th] nombre. And that same assignethe another reson and saieth:
'To that we haue the nombre of fourti to ioine to the nombre of fourti
we aught ioyne to the p[eny], for yef we will come to the blessed reste
it behouithe us to laboure alle the tyme of this present lyff. And oure

50 in²] *om.* E   asketh] asked E   51 grace] grete G   E *ends sentence after* gilte, H1G
ambiguous   In H1 *a corrector has inserted a rough paraph after* confermed   52 requirithe]
required H1G   God] good E   defence] *add* and to hem þat ben in prosperite defence *del.*
H1   55 as] þat G   57 psalme] *add* of remission E

EH1GDH2A1A2L   2 withe] by E   3 after] *add* þat G   4–5 she sheweth] L,
ye shewe EH1G   5 He] and G   13 that] L, *om.* EH1G   16 fourtith] L, fourti
EH1G   18 peny] payre EH1GL (*denier* P2)

f. 49ʳᵃ Lorde duelled .xl. dayes withe his | disciples, and the .x. day after he
21　sent hem the holi goste.'

　　　The .iij. cause assigneth the Maister in the Somme of the Office of
the Chirche and saiethe: 'The worlde is devided in foure parties and
the yere in foure tymes, and man ys made of foure elementes and of
25　.iiij. complecciones, and the nwe lawe is ordeyned by foure euuange-
listes and the olde lawe that we haue passed was in the ten
comaundementes. And therfor it behouithe that the peny be multeplied bi foure and foure, that is that we make in suche wise the
noumbre of fourti, that is that we fulfell the comaundementez of the
30　olde lawe and [of] the nwe lawe al the tyme of this lyff. And as [we]
haue said, oure bodies be of .iiij. elementes and thei haue in vs as it
were .iiij. seges, for the fire is in the eyen, [the eyre] in the tonge and
in the eres, lightnesse for to do synne is in the membres engenderyng,
the erthe is in the hondes and in other membres. And thanne is
35　curiosite in the eyghen, in the tonge and in the eres, lightnesse of
synnyng is in the membres engendering delit, and in the hondes and
other membres is crueltee. And these foure confessed the publican
that stode aferre. He confessed lecheri þat is stinkyng as though he
saide: "Lord, I dare not neygh the [leste] I stinke in thi nose." In that
40　he durst not left vp his eyghen he confessed curiosite. In that he bete
his breste with his hondes he confessed cruelte. And [in] that he saide:
"Lorde, be mercifull to me sinfull," he confessed lecherie and
lightnesse that is promte to synne.'

　　　And Gregori in his Omelyes putte .iij. resones and saiethe: 'Whi
45　the nombre of fourti dayes is kepte in abstinence it is for that the
f. 49ʳᵇ vertue of | the ten comaundementes of the lawe be fulfelled bi the .iiij.
bokes of the gospell. For in this dedly tyme we bene of the .iiij.
elementes and be [the] delite of the same bodies we contrarie to the .x.
comaundementes of oure Lorde, and for as moche as we haue
50　despised the ten comaundementez of the lawe bi the desire of the
fleshe, it is worthi that we torment that fleshe bi the nombre of .iiij.
tymes .x. And [fro] the furst daye of the Quadragesme into Ester ben
sixe wekes that bene .xlij. daies, and whanne sixe Sondayes bene take
away ther leuithe .xxxvj. dayes in abstinence, and whanne the yere is
55　brought aboute by .CCC.lxvj. dayes so we yeue to God as the dyme of
oure yere.'

　　　22 The] These G　　cause] causis G　　　30 of¹] L, *om.* EH1G　　we] L, I EH1G
32 the eyre] L, *om.* EH1G　　36 synnyng] synne H1G　　　39 leste] L, lorde EH1G
41 in] L, to EH1G　　48 the¹] L, *om.* EH1G　　52 fro] L, for EH1G　　ben] by G

And .iiij. resones bene assigned whi we kepe not this faste in that
tyme that Ihesu Crist faste[d], for he beganne to faste sone after his
baptime, and these .iiij. resones assignith Maister Iohn Belett in his
Somme. The furst is that yef we will arise with Ihesu Crist that 60
sofered so moche for vs it is sittinge that we suffre payne withe hym.
The secounde is that bi that we foluen the children of Israel that [in]
that tyme went furst oute of Egipte, and after that they went oute of
Babiloyne, and it is proued bi that þat anone as thei were oute they
halowed the Paske, and so we folwing hem fast in this tyme so that we, 65
be going oute of Egipte and [oute] of Babiloyne, that is of this worlde,
deserue to entre into the londe of euerlasting ioie. The .iij. reson is
that for the tyme of Veer, the whiche chaufith the blode, causith most
the brennyng of vnclennesse, wherfor to restreyne the vnordinat
mevyngges of | the body we faste in that same tyme for a souerayn f. 49ᵛᵃ
gosteli remedie. The ferthe cause is for that anone after oure faste we 71
shulde receiue oure Lordes body in the blessed sacrement. For right
as the children of Israel tormented hemselff [in] etyng wilde letuse
and bitter before thei ete the lambe, right so we shulde furst be
tormented [by] penaunce so that we myght worthely resseiue the right 75
pure lambe of liff.

Here endithe the storie of Lente, and nexst foluithe of the
Quatertens, Capᵐ. .xxxiiij.ᵐ

The fasting of .iiij. tymes, whiche ys called Ymber, were ordeyned of
thc pope Calixte, and these fastes be done .iiij. tymes in the yere after
the tymes of the yere, and therof ther bene assigned many resones.

[The] furst is for that Veer is hote and moyst, Somer is hote and
drie, Autumpne colde and drye and Winter colde and moist. We faste 5
in Veer for that we shulde attempre [in vs] the noying humoure of
vnclennesse, in Somer for that we shulde chastise in vs the wreched
hete of couetise, in Autompne for that we shulde chastise in vs the

57 faste] feste HıG   HıG start new para. at in   58 fasted] faste it EHı   60 yef
we will] he wold G, so with he changed to we Hı   62 in] L, into EHıG   63 tyme]
add he G   66 oute²] om. E   of³] in HıG   67 the] þis Hı   68 Veer] birthe G
the whiche] om. G   chaufith] causeth Hı   blode] add `&' Hı   72 shulde] shull HıG
73 in] en E   letuse] leuys G   74 ete] add of E   shulde] shal HıG   75 by] withe E
76 pure] faire G

EHıGDH2AıA2L   3 assigned] signyd G   4 The] L, And EG, And `þe' Hı
6 in vs] L, om. EHıG   humoure] humouris G   8 chastise] chast Hı

drinesse of pride, in Winter for þat we shulde chastise the coldnesse of
10 vntrouth and of malice.

The secound reson is, whi we faste .iiij. times in the yere, for the
furste fastyng is made in Marche in the furst woke of Lenten, for the
vices shulde wexen drie in vs if they myght not in all be quenched and
that the herbes of vertues be brought forthe in vs freshe and grene and
15 suete smellyng. The secounde fast is atte Whitsonday, for thanne
f. 49vb come the holy goste and we aught to be feruent in the holi goste. | The
.iij. bene in Septembre before Mychelmasse, for in that tyme fruites
bene gadered, wherfor we aught yelde to God the fruites of good
werkes. The .iiij. is made in Decembre, for thanne the herbes deyen
20 and we shulde be mortefied to the worlde.

The .iij. reson is for þat we folowe the Iues. The Iues fasten .iiij.
tymes in the yere, byfore Paske, byfore Whitsontide, in Septembre
byfore that thei sette her tabernacles, and in Decembre byfore the
Dedicacion.

25 The [.iiij.] reson is for that man is of .iiij. elementes as to the body
and of .iij. myghtes, that is resonable, coueitous and irouse as to the
soule. And [therfor] that these thingges bene attemp[r]ed in us we
fasten .iiij. tymes in the yere bi thre dayes, so that the noumbre of .iiij.
bene reported to the body and the noumbre of thre to the soule. These
30 be the resones of Maister Iohn Belett.

And as Iohn Damaciane saiethe that the .v.^{te} reson is for that in
Veer the blode multepliethe and in Somer col[e]r and in Autumpne
malecoly and in Winter flewme. And thanne we faste in Veer for to
enfeble the blode of flessheli coueitise and of inordinat gladnesse, for
35 the sanguyn is luxurious and gladde; in Somer for that the col[e]r of
wratthe and of fallace be made feble, for the colerik is naturelly angrie
[and hatefull]; in Autumpne for that malecoly of coueitise and of
tristesse bene made feble, for the malicolyous is naturelly [colde],
coueitous and hevi; in Winter for that the fleume of moistour and of
40 slouthe bene made feble, for the fleumatik is naturelly moist and
slowe.

The .vj. reson is for that Veer is likened to the eyre, Somer to fere,
Autumpne to the erthe, Wynter to the water. And we faste in Veer for

---

14 vertues] add `be' del. H1   18 wherfor . . . the] om. H1   20 mortefied]
mortized H1 G   21 .iij.] L, .iiij. EH1 G   25 .iiij.^{1}] L, .vj.^{te} EH1 G   27 therfor]
L, om. EH1 G   attempred] L, attempted E, accepted H1, accepte G   in] to G   30 the]
add .iij. E   31 that^{2}] add þat G   32 coler] colour E, kelith G   35 coler] L,
colour E, coles H1 G   37 and hatefull] om. E   38 tristesse] trostez H1, yeousteis
second letter unclear G   colde] om. E   39 hevi] evy G

to daunte in vs the eyre of elacion and of pride, in | Somer for to daunt f. 50ra
in vs the fere of coueitise and of avarise, in Autumpne for to daunt the 45
erthe for the coldenesse and the derkenesse of ignoraunce, in Wynter
for to daunt the water of lyghtnesse and disatemperaunce.

The .vij. reson is for that Veer is lykened to childehode, Somer to
wexen in age, Autumpne to sadnesse or strengthe of age, Winter to
gret age. We fasten in Veer for that we mowe be children [by] 50
innocence, in Somer that we mowe be stable bi good wexing and
encresing, in Autumpne that we mowe be sadde by good attemper-
aunce, in Winter that we mowe be olde bi wisdom and bi honeste of
lyving or ellis that we make satisfaccion of that we haue misdone in
these .iiij. ages. 55

The .viij. reson putt[ith]e Maister William Dauuser and saiethe
that we faste the .iiij. tymes of the yere for to make satisfaccion of that
we haue mysdone in al the tymes of the yere. And the faste is ordeined
in thre dayes so that we do satisfaccion in oo daye that we haue
misdone in an hole yere, [or] thei be done in a Wednisday for that 60
oure Lorde was betrayed that day of Iudas, in the Friday for he was
crucified in that day, and in the Saterday for in that day he was beried
and laye in the sepulcre, and the disciples weren sorifull of the dethe
of oure Lord.

Here endithe the Quatertemps, and nexst foluith the liff of
Seint Ignacien, Capitulum .xxxv.^m

Ignacien was the disciple of [blessed] Seint Iohn the Euuangelist and
was bisshop of Antioche. And we reden that he sent a letter to the
blessed Virgine Marie with suche wordes: 'To Marie bering Ihesu
Crist, I her humble Ignacien, newe frende to Seint Iohn [thi] disciple,
the whiche desirithe thi comfort to haue more perfit knowlage of 5
Ihesu Crist thi sone, of | whom I haue herde and perceiued so many f. 50rb
mervayles that I am abasshed in the heryng, and I desire in my corage
to be made more certayne of thingges herde, bi the that were most
familyer withe hym and nyest ioined to hym and most knowyng of alle
his counsels. God kepe the, and the nwe frendes that be withe me 10

---

46 coldenesse] colenys G   47 and] *add* the E   50 by] L, to EH1G
52 encresing] *add* In Autumpne þat we mowe be stable bi goode wexinge and encresinge
del. H1   56 puttithe] L, putte EH1G   William] Silam H1, Gillam G   60 or] *om.* E

EH1GDH2A1A2L; A1 largely illegible from 21 *gret* to 95 *the emperoure*   1 blessed]
L, *om.* EH1G   3 blessed] Blessed *on erasure* H1   4 thi] L, the EH1G

confessin this of the [and in the] and for the.' And thanne the blessed moder of God ansuerid hym in these wordes: 'To Ignacien, the frend of the humble disciple, of the servaunt of Ihesu Crist. Tho thingges that thou hast herde and lerned of Iohn of Ihesu Crist bene trwe. Leue
15 hem verily, and holde and kepe truly the avowe that thou hast made to cristen faithe, and late thi liff and thi maners acorde to thine avowe. I shall come with Iohn to certefie þe and hem that bene with the. Stonde and werke myghtely in the faithe, and be not meued with no persecucion of cruelte, but fare well and thi sperit ioye in God thi
20 saueoure.'

Ignacien was of so gret autorite that Denys the disciple of Poule that was souerain in philosephie and so perfit in connynge of diuinite brought to conferme his sayengges the wordes of blessed Ignacien for auctorite. [So] as he witnessithe in the Boke of Devine Names, some
25 repreued the name of loue in devine thingges sayeng that a devine name is as miche name of 'loue' as of 'dileccion'. He will shewe that the name of loue apertenithe to vse in devine thyngges and wrote in this wise: 'The devine Ignacien saieth: "The crucified is my loue."'

Men rede the Stori Parted in Thre that the blessed Ignacien [herde]
30 the aungels synggen antemes vpon an hill, and of that he ordeyned the
f. 50ᵛᵃ antemes to be songgen in the chirche and | to entune the psalmes after the antemes.

As the blessid Ignacien hadd longe tyme praied oure Lorde for the pes of the Chirche, dredyng the perile not of hymselff but of other
35 that were not stable in the faithe, he went ayenst Troien the emperour, that was the yere of oure Lorde an hundred, and as he come fro the bataile havyng the victorie and thretyng the cristen withe manace of dethe, he confessed hymselff frely that he was cristen. And thanne Troien bonde hym faste withe cheynes of yren and toke hym
40 to .x. knygthes and comaunded hem to lede hym to Rome, manassing hym that he shuld there be deuoured withe wilde bestes. And as he was ledde to Rome he sent letteres to alle the chirches and confermed hem in the faithe of Ihesu Crist, amonge the whiche he wrote [to] the chirche of Rome, as it is redde in the Stori Ecclesiast, praieng that thei

11 and in the] om. E   12 these] þis H1G   wordes] wise G, so on erasure H1
14 thou] þˋoˊu H1   of Iohn] om. H1G   Ihesu Crist] Iˋoˊhu Crist H1   16 late] L, add
hem that bene with the EH1G   17 Iohn] Ihesu H1   18 faithe] fire H1G
21 autorite] auaunte G   24 So] om. E   of] L, add the EH1G   25 in] om. G
sayeng] ins. H1   26 shewe] add þat þe name of loue is of dileccion he will shew H1, so
with as for is G   27 vse] vse with e erased H1, vs G   29 herde] L, saide EH1G
39 thanne] þat H1G   41 there] add haue G   43 hem] om. G   to] om. E

wolde not lette his marterdome, in whiche he saide in this wise: 'I am   45
brought fro Syrri vnto Rome [and] I will fight with bestes in londe and
[in] water nyght and day enlased and bounden withe cheynes, withe
ten wolues knyghtes ordeined to kepe me, the whiche for oure good
dedes bene þe more cruel, and we be the beter enformed be thaire
felonye. O ye helthefull bestis that bene arraied to me, whanne shull   50
ye come forthe, whanne shul thei like to use my flesche? I shall
beseche hem to deuoure me leste perauenture thei drede to touche my
fleshe, as thei haue done to other, I shall [enforce] hem [and falle in
the middes of hem] seyeng: "Foryeue me I praie you," for I wote what
is expedient to me, fyre, the crosse, beestes, departyng of bones,   55
rentyn[g] of alle the mem|bres and of al the body, and al these   f. 50vb
tormentes bene ordeined ayeinst me by the arte of the fende and shall
be fulfelled in me for that I deserue to se Ihesu Crist.'
    And whanne he was comen to Rome Troien saide to hym:
'Ignacien, whi hast thou made Antioche to rebell and conuerted my   60
peple to [thi] cristiante?' To whom Ignacien saide: 'Mi will were that I
might conuerte the and that thou myght alwaies hold the strengthe of
princehode.' And than Troien saide: 'Sacre[fie] to oure goddes and
thou shalt be prince of all the prestes.' And thanne Ignacien saide:
'Neither I will sacrifie to thi goddes ne I coueite not thi dignite. Thou   65
maist do withe me as the luste, for thou shalt neuer chaunge my
purpos in no manere.' Thanne Troien saide: 'Gothe bete his shuldres
withe lede and rent oute his sides withe hokes and rubbe his backe
with sharpe stones.' And whanne thei hadde done al this to hym he
was euer in one plight. Thanne Troyen saide: 'Bring forthe hote   70
brennyng coles and make hym goo barefote vpon hem.' To whom
Ignacien saide: 'Neither brennyng fire ne boyling water may not
quenche the charite that I haue in Ihesu Crist.' And Troyen saide:
'Thei bene e[n]chauntementes, for we defende in oure lawe that thei
bene not, but do thow that make hym suffre so mych.' [To whom   75
Ignacien saide]: 'We cristen vse not enchauntementes, for we defende
in oure lawe that thei be not, but do thou awaye thi wickednesse that
worshippest [the] ydoles.' Than Troien saide: 'Al torent his backe

---

46 and¹] L, om. EH₁G   47 in] om. E   48 ten] xij H₁   50 ye] þe H₁G
53 enforce] L, comforte EH₁G   53–4 and . . . hem] om. E   54 me] om. H₁G
56 rentyng] rentyn E   60 to] add be E, 'to' H₁   61 thi] om. E   63 Troien]
Troicien H₁G   Sacrefie] L, sacre the EH₁G   64 the] oure G, 'ovre' H₁
65 goddes] god G   coueite] conuerte G, so changed to coueyte H₁   thi] in H₁G
66 the luste] þu list H₁G   74 enchauntementes] echauntementes E   75 do thow]
trs. G   75–6 To . . . saide] om. E   78 the] om. E

with hokes and sethe frotithe his backe withe salt.' To whom Ignacien
80 saide: 'The passiones atte this tyme be not worthi the ioye that is to
f. 51ra come that shal be shewed to vs.' And thanne | Troyen saide: 'Take
hym hennys anone and bynde hym withe cheynes and putte hym in
the lowest place of the prison, and late hym be there witheoute mete
or drinke and thre dayes after deliuer hym to be deuoured of bestes.'
85   The .iij. day after, the emperour and the senatoures and all the
peple assembeled [for] to see the bisshop of Antioche fight with wilde
bestes. Troyen thanne saide: 'For that Ignacien is so proude and full
of despit, lete [bynde] hym faste and ma[k]e two lyones come to hym
for to deuoure hym so that ther be leffte no remenaunt of hym.' And
90 thanne Seint Ignacien saide to the peple that weren there: 'Ye men of
Rome that beholden this [strife], thenkith well that I trauayle not in
veyne, for I suffre not this for my wickednesse but for purete of my
soule.' And as it is redde in the Stori of Ecclesiast he beganne to saie:
'I whete of Ihesu Crist shal be ground withe the [tethe] of bestes, for I
95 shall be clene brede.' And whanne the emperour herde that, he saide:
'Grete is the pacience of cristen men. What Greke wolde suffre so
moche for his god as he dothe?' To whom Ignacien ansuered: 'It is not
bi my vertue that I suffre but bi [the helpe] of Ihesu Crist.' And
thanne Ignacien called the lyones to hym for thei shulde devoure hym,
100 and thanne two cruel liones ronnen to hym and strangeled hym only,
but they touched not his flesche in no wise. Whanne the emperour
seigh this he went his way with gret mervayle and comaunded þat yef
any luste to berie hym that thei were not deuyed, for whiche thing the
cristen toke the body and beried it worschipfully.
f. 51rb   And as Troyen hadde receiued the letteres | in whiche the secounde
106 prouost hadd gretly preised the cristen that Troyen hadde comaunded
to slee, he sorughed for that he hadde done to Ignacien and
comaunded that fro thennes forward that they were no more
sought, but yef any felle that he were punished.
110   Men rede that among alle these cruel tormentes he cesed neuer to
calle in the name of Ihesu Crist, and whanne the turmentours asked
hym whi he named so ofte that name he ansuered: 'That blessed name
is wretin in my herte, [and therfor I may not but that I calle hym].'

79 frotithe] fretith G   84 dayes] ins. H1   86 for] om. E   87 and] add so E
88 lete] lede G bynde] L, om. EH1G make] made E   91 strife] om. E   94 tethe]
thete E   95 that] what H1G saide] add 'he seyde' H1   98 the] L, om. EH1G
helpe] vertue E   102 mervayle] anger H1G   103 deuyed] denyed (?) E
109 felle] lif G   113 and . . . hym] om. E

And tho that [hadde] herde this wolde proue after his dethe of this
thing and toke his herte oute of his body and kitte it a tweyne and 115
fonde witheinne al wreten withe lettres of golde this name 'Ihesu
Crist', and many leued in God for this miracle.

Of this seint [saiethe Seint] Bernard vpon the psalme of *Qui habitat*:
'This Ignacien was a gret auditour of the disciple that Ihesu loued, of
the reliques of whiche marter oure pouerte is made riche, and in many 120
apisteles that he wrote he salued Marie beryng Crist.'

Here endithe the liff of Seint Ignacien, and nexst foluithe
of the Purificacion of oure Lady, Cap^m. .xxxvj.^m

The Purificacion of oure Lady the blessed Virgine Marie is made the
.xl.^ti daye after the natiuite of oure Lorde, and this feste is called bi
thre names, Ca[n]delmas, Ypo[p]ant, and the Purificacion. She is
called Purificacion for that atte the .xl.^ti daye fro the natiuite of oure
Lorde the blessed Virgine come to the Temple for to be purified after 5
the lawe, [though she were not bounde vnder suche lawe], for the lawe
comaund[ed] in Leui|tique that a woman that hadde conceyued and f. 51va
brought forthe an eyre male was not clene and that she shulde abstene
her .vj. wokes fro the felawship of man and fro entering into the
Temple. And .vij. dayes passed she was made clene as to the felawship 10
of man, but not to entre into the Temple before the .xxx[iiij].^ti day.
And whanne these .xl.^ti dayes weren fullfelled she went to the Temple
and the childe withe her and offered hym vp with yeftes. And yef it
were a doughter the dayes weren doubeled as wel for the felawship of
man as f[or] the entering into the Temple. 15

And thre resones mowe be whi the lawe comaunded that the childe
shulde be offered into the Temple in the .xl.^ti day. [That one reson is
that by that is vnderstonde that right as the childe is brought in the
.xl.^ti daye] in the material Temple, right so the fourty day after his
concepcion the soule is often tymes putte into the bodye as into his 20

114 hadde] *om.* EG   wolde] wold *changed to* word *and add* 'wold' H1, word G
118 saiethe Seint] L, *om.* EH1G   habitat] *add* 'seyth' H1   121 apisteles] *so with a subp.*
H1, apostlis G

EH1GDH2A1A2LT2; A1 breaks off after 200 *yeft*   2 feste] *om.* T2
3 Candelmas] Caldelmas E   Ypopant] L, Ypotant EH1G   3–4 She . . . Purificacion]
om. T2   6 though . . . lawe²] *om.* E   7 comaunded] comaundithe E   Leuitique]
leuique H1G   11 .xxxiij.^ti] .xxxiiij.^ti E, .xxxij. H1   12 Temple] peple H1
13 with] *om.* G   15 for] T2, fro EH1G (*quant a* P2)   16 comaunded] comaundith G
17 That] There is H1   reson] *add and subp.* is H1   17–19 That . . . daye] *om.* E
18 in¹] into H1   19 day] *om.* T2

temple, as it is saide in Historia Scolastica, notwithestondyng the
philosophers sayn that in the .xlvj.^{ti} day the bodi is made perfit. The
secound reson is that right as the soule in the fourty day is putte into
the body and defouled with the body, that body and soule togeders
25 entering in the fourty daye into the Temple be clensed of that
defoulyng by sacrifise. The .iij. that by that entre it is to vnderstonde
that tho deseruen to entre into the heuenly temple that kepen the
comaundement[es] of the lawe withe the faithe of the .iiij. euuange-
listes.

30   To her that bringethe forthe a woman the dayes [be] doubled as to
the entre of the Temple, as they bene doubled in the [formacion] of
the body, for right as in fourty dayes the body of a male is fourmed
and made perfit with the soule putte withinne, in lyk wise the body of
f. 51vb the | woman is perfit in .iiij^{xx}. dayes and the soule putte withinne.
35 And whi for the body of a woman is latter perfit withein the wombe
thanne the body of a man and the soule latter putte inne may be
shewed by .iij. resones and the naturell reson[es] left. The furst is for
that oure Lorde wolde take flesche in the fourme of a man so that bi
þat cause he wolde worship the sexe of man and do hym gretter grace,
40 he wold that the [male] were sonner fourmed [and] the moder sonner
purified. The secound reson is for that woman synned more thanne
man, so [that] right [as] the corse was doubeled outeward to the
worlde, right so they shull be doubeled inward in the wombe. The .iij.
is by that it is vnderstond that the woman trauelled more God in a
45 maner thanne man in that she offended furst and more, for God is in a
maner trauailed in oure wicked dedes, wherof saith Ysaie in the .xliij.^e
chapitre: 'Thou makest me to serue to thine iniquitees', and 'I
travailed in susteynynge.'

      The blessed Virgine was not bounde to this purificacion, for she
50 bere no childe by man but by devine e[n]spering. And therfor seiethe
Moyses: 'Tho that haue conceiued by man,' and it was none nede for

21 Historia] historiall G   the] þat H1GT2   23 in] into   24 the¹] *add* body
subp. G   28 comaundementes] comaundement E   30 To her] *no MS has punct.*
suggesting new sentence   that] and G   be] L, *om.* EH1G   31 entre] encres T2
formacion] fornicacion E   33–4 in . . . withinne] *om.* T2   34 the¹] a H1, *add* wo (*at*
end of column) E   37 the] be H1   resones] reson E   left] *om.* H1GT2   39 sexe]
seythe T2   40 male] maler *with* l *almost turned into* k E   and] L, *as* EGT2, & *on erasure*
H1   41 synned] synnes H1, is synne is G   42 man] mannys G   so that] *on erasure*
H1   that] as E   as] that E   corse] crosse H1   43 in] to H1   44 it] *om.* H1GT2
trauelled] travaylith G   47 iniquitees] inquietis G   48 EG *no punct. after*
susteyninge, H1 *punct. ins.*   49 Virgine] *twice once del.* H1   she] *om.* T2
50 enspering] espering E   51 by] *om.* G

to saie it to other women, for alle hadde brought forthe bi felawship of
man but onli she, and therfor he saide it for he wolde not arere no
blame to the moder of God, so as Seint Bernard saiethe.

But she herselff wolde submitte her to the lawe for .iiij. resones. 55
The furst reson is for she wolde yeue ensaumple of humilite, wherof
Seint Bernard saieth: 'Verrily, blessed Virgine, thou haddest no cause
ne nede of purificacion, ne thi sone nother hadde no nede of
circumcision. Be thou among women as one of hem', that is as
moche to saye as by similitude, | 'for thi sone is in like wise in the f. 52ra
middes of children.' And this humilite is not only by the moder, but 61
she was also bi the sone that wolde in that submitte hym to the lawe,
for in his natiuite he hadde hymselff as a pore man, but in his
circumcision as a sinfull man, as a pore man and as a servaunt. As a
pore man for he chase the offering of [pore men], as a sinfull for he 65
wold be purified with his moder, as a servaunt in that he was bought
ayein. And in [the] same wise after he wolde be baptized, not for to
purge his gilte but for to shewe his gret humilite, for he wolde take in
hym all the remedies that were ordeined ayeinst the original sinne, not
for no nede that he hadde but for to shewe his gret humilite, and that 70
tho remedies were nedefull to us in that tyme.

.V. maneres of remedies were ordeyned ayeinst the synne originall
bi processe of tyme, and after [that] Hugh de Victore saieth that .iij. of
hem be ordeined in the lawe of kinde, the whiche bene oblaciones,
dymes and sacrifices, and bi these thre expressed the werke of oure 75
redempcion. For the manere of beyeng ayein was signified bi the
oblacion, and the price was signified by the sacrifice in whiche was
sheding of blode, and the thing bought was signified bi the dyme, for
man is signified by the .x. dragme. And thanne the furst remedie was
oblacion, Caym offered yeftes to God of his cornes and Abell of his 80
beestes. The secound was the dyme that Abraham offered the prest
Melchisadech, for after Seint Austin they gaue dymes for tho thingges
that thei hadde cure of. The .iij., after Seint Gregore saiethe, that
sacrifices weren remedye ayeinste the original synne. | For it f. 52rb

52 it] *add* is GT2   to²] to her *on erasure* 'but it was seyd to al' H1   other] 'o'þer H1
55 .iiij.] *add* enchesons *subp.* T2   56 wherof] wherfore H1GT2   60 for] off T2
thi] the H1   is in] in *changed to* is T2   62 she] hit G   also] only T2
63 hadde] was GT2   man] *om.* H1   65 for he chase] *twice once del.* H1   pore
men] L, a pore man EH1G   67 the] *om.* ET2   69 hym] *om.* T2   73 after]
on erasure H1, afore T2   that] L, *om.* EH1GT2   Hugh] Hwe *with* w *on erasure* H1
Victore] victorie H1G   77 oblacion . . . by the] *om.* T2   81 offered] *add* 'to' H1
84 For] *on erasure* H1

85 behou[ed] that one of the kinrede atte the leste were true, and for as
myche as perauenture that neither were true, therfor come the ferthe
remedie whiche was circumcision, the whiche auailled were the true
or vntrue. But for that remedie myght not availe but only to malis, ne
the gates of heuene myght not be opened therby, therfor come after
90 the sacrement of bapteme that is comune to all and opened the gatis of
paradis.

And oure Lorde toke the furste remedie whanne he was presented
in the Temple of his kynne. And the tother remedie he toke in a
maner whanne he fasted fourti dayes and fourti nyghtes, in as moche
95 as he hadde no wordely goodes to paie his dyme to God, [he offered to
God] the dyme of dayes. He toke [the] thre whanne his moder offered
a paire of turtelys or of dovues for hym to do sacrifice, or ellis whanne
he offered hymselff sacrifice in the crosse, the ferthe whanne he was
circumcised, the .v. [whanne] he receiued bapteme of Iohn.
100   The secound reson is in that he fulfelled the lawe, for as he hymselff
saiethe he come not to breke the lawe but to fulfell it. For yef he hadde
passed the lawe in this thing the Iues myght haue excused hem and
saide: 'We will not receiue thi worde ne thi doctrine for thou art vnlike
to oure faders and kepest not the comaundementz of the lawe.' In this
105 day Ihesu Crist and his moder virgine submitte hemselff to trebel
lawe: furst to the lawe of purificacion in signifiaunce of vertue, so that
whanne we haue al do as moche as we canne or may we mow saye that
f. 52ᵛᵃ we be vnprofitable servauntes; secoundely to the lawe | of redempcion
in ensaumple of humilite; therdely in ensaumple of humilite and of
110 pouerte.

The .iij. reson is that he made to cese the lawe of purificacion, for
right as whanne lyght comithe derkenesse cesithe, and whanne the
sonne apperithe the shadw voideth, right so whanne oure verrey
purificacion come, the whiche was Ihesu Crist, the figured purifica-
115 cion cessed, for he purified vs in suche wise that the faders be not
bounde to solucion ne the moders to purificacion ne to the entering
into the Temple, nether the sones to that redempcion.

The ferthe reson is that he taught us to be purified, for purificacion
is made in .v. maners of cace, that is to saie of diffame for whiche we
120 aught to purge vs, that is to wete: bi othe, that signifiethe renounsing

85 behoued] behouithe E   leste] laste G   87 true] tu (?) *changed to* tr`u′ H1
88 malis] malice H1GT2   95 wordely] worldes T2   95–6 he offered to God] *om.* E
96 the²] *om.* E   98 he] *add* hadde E   99 whanne] *om.* E   104 kepest] kepte T2
109 therdely . . . humilite] *om.* G   117 nether the] nere T2   120 othe] oþer T2

of sinne; bi water, [that] signifiethe washing of bapteme; bi fire, that
signifiethe the infusion of the holi goste; by witnesse, that signifiethe
plente of good werkes; bi bataile, that signifieth refusing of temptacion.

Whanne the blessed Virgine come to the Temple she offered her
sone and bought hym ayen withe .v. sicles, whiche is a maner of   125
money of sertayn wight. But it is to knowe that sum of the furst born
were bought ayein, that is to saie the furst engendered of the .xj.
linages that were bought ayein withe .v. sicles; some were not bought
ayein, as the furst of the Leuytes, but whanne thei come into her last
age thei shulde always serue in the Temple of oure Lorde, right as   130
the furst fawnes of beestes that were clene were not bought ayein but
offered to oure Lorde. And som were | chaunged so as the furste coltes   f. 52ᵛᵇ
of asses that were chaunged into shepe, and sum were slayn as the
furst whelpes of dogges. And thanne Ihesu Crist that was of the
kinrede of Iuda, that was one of the .xj., it apperithe that he shulde be   135
bought ayein, wherfor thei offered to oure Lorde for hym a payre of
turteles or two pigones of doves, for that was the offering of pore
folkes and a lambe was the offering of rich men. [And he] seith not the
pigeons of turtelis but of dowues, for tho of dovues mowe alwaies be
founde but not of turteles. And also he saiethe not a paire of dovues as   140
he dothe a paire of turteles, for the dovue is a luxurious bridde and the
turtel a chaste bridde. But a litell afore the blessed Virgine Marie
hadde receiued a gret somme of golde, wherbi it semithe that she
myght haue well a lambe, for it is to suppose withoute doute after
Seint Bernard that the kingges offered gret charge of golde, for it is   145
not likly that suche kyngges as they were wolde offre litell yeftes to
suche a childe, but always the blessed Virgine witehelde it not to
herselff but gaue it anone to the pore, or ellis perauenture she kepte it
for to make her puruiaunce in the [seuene] yere that she was in Egipte,
or elles perauenture thei offered not in gret quantite for cause that   150
thaire offering was in significacion. And the expositour putte thre
oblaciones to haue be made of oure Lorde: the furste was made of hym
bi his kynrede, the secound was made for hym of the briddes, and the
.iij. he made in the crosse for all. The furste shewithe his humilite, for
the lord of the lawe submitted hym to the lawe; the secounde [h]is   155

    121 that¹] L, and EHıGT2   126 money] mone G   127 bought] brou3t G
engendered] engendereth T2   128 linages] lynage HıG   130 of] om. HıG
136 bought] bo3t with bo on erasure Hı, brou3t GT2   138 And he] L, A E, And ʼheʼ
Hı, and GT2   139 of¹] om. T2   143 wherbi] where T2   144 haue] add right
T2   suppose] L, add that EHıGT2   145 kingges] kynge HıGT2   149 seuene]
seson of the E, cecond Hı, seuone G, seson T2   155 his] is EHıGT2 (sa P2)

f. 53ra pouerte, for | he chase the offering of the pore; and the thridde that he
shewed his gret charitee, for he suffered for the sinfull.

The propertees of the turtull bene these: she fleithe high, she
waylithe in syngyng, the comyng of Ver she vouchithe, she liuithe
160 chastely and hathe but one make, she norishithe her chikenes bi
nyght, she fleithe al dede thing. And the propertees of the dove bene
these: he gaderithe the greynes, he fleithe in felawship, he hathe no
galle, he wailethe, and cherisithe and touchithe his felawe with his
beke, he makithe his neste in stones, he fleithe the sparhauuke as his
165 enemy, he hurtithe not with the beke, he norishith his pigones two
and two.

Secoundly this feste is saide *Ipo[p]ante*, that is to saie Presentacion,
for that Ihesu Crist was presented into the Temple, or ellis *Ipo[p]ant*
may be saide Metyng Togederes, for that Symeon and Anne went
170 ayeinst oure Lorde whanne he come to the Temple, and it is saide
Ipo[p]ant of *ypo*, that is as moche to saye as Goo, and also it is as moche
to saye as Ayeinst. And thanne Symeon toke hym in his armes. And it
is to wete that thre beryngges or .iij. mevyngges were this day made of
oure Lorde. The furste of verite, for he that is verite, [that] ledithe al
175 men hymselff, that is [waye], in hymselff, suffred this day to be ledde
and born of other, and the gospell saiethe so as they ledde the childe
or bere hym to the Temple. The secounde is of bounte, for he that is
only goodly and holy wolde be purified withe his moder as though he
hadde be foule. The .iij. is of mageste, for he that berithe al thingges
180 bi the vertue of his word suffred hymselff to be born in the armes of an
f. 53rb olde man, notwithe|stondyng that he susteined hym that bere hym, so
as he saiethe: 'The olde man bere the child, and the childe governed
the olde man.' Thanne Symeon blessed hym and saide: 'Lorde, lete
thi servaunt in pees after thi worde.' And Simeon called hym bi thre
185 names, Sauacion, Light and Glorie. And the reson of these thre names
mow be take in foure maners. Furst after oure iustefieng, so that it be
saide saving [in] levyng and in foryeuyng oure synnes, for Ihesus is as
moche to saie as Saueoure, for that he makithe his peple sauf fro her
synnes, that he is called Light in yevyng grace, and Glorie to the
190 peple. Secoundely for oure regeneracion, for furst the childe is blessed
and baptized and he is clensed fro synne as to the furst, and the candel

157 his] is H1   162 in] *add* his H1   164 beke] bill T2   167 Ipopante] L,
Ipotante EH1G   168, 171 Ipopant] L, Ipotant EH1G   174 he] *om.* H1   that^2] L,
om. EH1GT2   175 waye] to wete E   181 bere] for T2   182–3 bere . . . man]
ins. H1   184 servaunt] servauntes EH1   187 in^1] and E, and in H1GL, and iij T2
(*en* P2)   188 fro] for GT2   190 regeneracion] generacion H1

light is take hym as to the secound, and for the .iij. he is offered vp to the Temple. Thirdely for the procession of this day, for furst the candeles bene blessed, secoundly thei bene lyght, thirdely they be take into the hondes of true cristen puple, ferthely they entre into the 195 chirche synginge. For the trebel name of this feste, for she is saide Purificacion as to the purgyng of synne, by that she is saide Saueoure; she is saide Candelmasse as to lyghtenyng of grace, and for that he is saide Lyght; and it is sayde also *Ipo[p]ant*, that is Presentacion as to the yeft of glorie, and for that he is saide the Glorie of the peple of 200 Israel. Or it may be said for oure Lorde is preised in this canticle right as pees, lyght and glorie, [as] pees for he is mediator, as hele for he is redemptor, as light for he is conditor, as glorie for he is gerdoner.

And this feste is saide | thirdely Candelmasse, for that men bere f. 53ᵛᵃ candelis brennyng in thaire hondes. And whi the Chirche hathe 205 ordeyned to bere candeles light in thaire hondes mow be assigned .iiij. resones. The furst for to take awaye the custume of errour, for som tyme in the kalendes of Feuerere al the citee of Rome vsed from .v. yere to .v. yere to goo aboute al the nyght withe torches and brondes of fire in the worship of Februs moder of Marce, god of bataile, for 210 that he shulde yeue to theire sones the victorie of thaire enemyes, and that space of tyme was saide Lustre, that is to saye shynyng of lyght. The Romaynes in the same wise sacrifiden to Pluto the god of hell in that tyme and to other goddes of hell, and they deden it for they wolde haue merci [of] hem, and thei offered to hem sacrifices solempne and 215 weren al nyght in the preising of hem withe torches and brondes of fire brennynge. And the wyves of the Romaynes, so as the pope Innocent saiethe, made in that day feste of lyghtes and toke th[ere] begynnyng of the fables of some poetis. For thei saide that Preserpyne was so fayre that Pluto the god of helle co[uei]ted her and rauisshed 220 her and made her goddesse. And her kynrede sought her long tyme by wodes and forestes withe torches and brondes, so that [the] ladies of Rome represented this thing going aboute Rome withe torches and lyghtes. [And] for it is full harde to breke an olde custume, the cristen

198 he] `sc´he H1, sche G    199 Ipopant] L, Ipotant EH1G    200 yeft] yefts E he] it T2    202 lyght] right G    as²] L, and EH1GT2    203 gerdoner] g`w´erdener H1, governure T2   206 mow] nowe T2   208 kalendes] calenders T2 208–9 from .v. yere to .v.] euery *on erasure* H1   209 to .v. yere] *om.* G   210 Marce] Mars *on erasure* H1   211 yeue] if T2   212 of¹] and T2   213 wise] twise *with* t *erased* H1   215 of] on EG   sacrifices] sacrafice H1GT2   218 there] thaire E 220 coueited] conuerted E   222 so] *changed to* for H1, for G   the] L, *om.* EH1GT2 223 represented] `re´presented H1   224 And] *om.* E

225 that weren conuerted myght vnnethes leue this custume, and bi cause
therof Serge the pope meued this custume into beter, that is to wete
f. 53vb that the cristen that day shulde go aboute | the chirche withe candeles
blessed and lyght in the worship of the blessed Virgine Marie, so that
the solempnite shulde holde but that she shulde be done for other
230 intencion.

Secoundely, for to shewe the purete of the Virgine, for som that
herde that the Virgine hadde be purified wenden that she nedid of
purificacion; and for to shewe that she was right pure and right clene,
for that the Chirche ordeyned that we shulde bere torches and lyghtes
235 brennyng, right as the Chirche saide that bi that token this blessed
Virgine hadde no nede of purificacion but shined al in puretee. And
she was conceyued of a sede that was al clene and al purified in the
wombe of her moder, and in the comyng of the holy goste she was
purified, clensed and halowed so that no spotte ne none inclinacion of
240 synne abode in her, but the vertue and the holinesse of her streched
oute to other and was shedde so largely that she quenched in other the
inordinat mevyngges of fleshely coueitise. And the Iwes sayden
though Mari were right faire yet myght she neuer be coueited of
man, and the cause is for the vertue of [her] chastite peersed al tho þat
245 behelde her and putte oute from hem al wicked coueitise. And therfor
she is lykened to the cedre, for the ceder sleithe al serpentes bi his
sauoure, and the holynesse of her shine[d] in other that she slow in
hem all fleshely mevyngges. Also she is likened to myrre, for right as
myrre sleithe wormes, so the holinesse of her quenchi[d] all fleschely
250 coueitise, for she hathe this prerogatyff before all tho that euer were
halowed and is purest virgine aboue all virgines, for the holinesse of
f. 54ra other was not pored out to other, ne her | chastite quenched not the
inordinat mevyngges of other, but the vertue of chastite of the blessed
Virgine Marie persed thorugh hem that were vnchaste and yelde hem
255 anone chaste as to her.

Thirdeli, for the representacion [of the procession] of this day, for
Marie [and] Ioseph and Simeon and Anne made this day a worshipfull
procession and presented the childe Ihesus in the Temple. So that in

226 therof] *so with* of *erased and add* of H1, *om.* T2   wete] with H1   230 intencion]
`in'tencion T2   235 right] *om.* G   this] his T2   236 puretee] poverte T2
244 her] L, the EH1GT2   peersed] preesed T2   247 shined] L, shinethe EH1GT2
249 sleithe] fleith G   quenchid] L, quenchithe EH1GT2   251 holinesse] holiest H1G
252–3 ne . . . other] *om.* H1GT2   256 of the procession] L, *om.* EH1GT2
257 and¹] L, *om.* EH1GT2   258 procession] L, *add* and beren candeles of wexe
brennyng EH1GT2

this day we make procession and berin candeles of wexe brennyng in
oure hondes, so bi that light that eueri man berithe is signified Ihesu 260
Crist borne into the Temple. It is to knowe that in a wexse candell
bene thre thingges, that is to saie wexe, mache and fire. Bi these thre
bene signified thre thingges that weren in Ihesu Crist: wexe, that
signifiethe the fleshe of Ihesu Crist that was born of a virgine
vncorupt, right as the bees maken the hony withoute coniunccion 265
of that one er that other; the mache hidde in the wexe signifiethe the
right white soule of hym hidde in the fleshe; the fire or the light
signifiethe the devinite, [for] oure Lorde is a fire wasting. Wherof a
vercifiour made this vers:

> Hanc in honore pie candelam porto Marie.   270
> Accipe per ceram carnem de uirgine ueram.
> Per lumen numen magestatisque cacumen.
> Dum lichinusque latet spiritus inde patet.

The whiche vers is as moche to saie in Englishe: 'In the worship of the
meke Virgine Marie I bere this candell; vnderstonde bi the waxe is the 275
verrey flesshe of the Virgine, the mageste bi the lyght, the highnesse
of the godhede, by the mache hidde in the wexe shewith the spirit.'
    The ferthe is for oure techyng, for we aught to be taught in that yef
we will be purified before God and clensed we shulde haue | in us thre f. 54ʳᵇ
thingges, verrey faithe, good werkes and good entencion. For the 280
candell brennyng in the honde is faithe withe good werkes, for right as
the candell withoute light is saide dede and the lyght witheoute
candell lightethe not but bene bothe dede togeders, right so faithe
witheoute good werkes and good werkes witheoute faithe is dede. And
the mache wit[h]inne the wexe hidde is the right entencion, wherof 285
Seint Gregor saieth: 'Thou the werke be in open the entencion may be
hidde witheinne.'
    Ther was a lady of noble kinrede that hadde gret deuocion to the
blessed Virgine Marie. And she hadde made a chapell besides her

261 into] 'in'to H1   a wexse candell] wexe candellis G   262–3 that is . . .
thingges] om. G   263–4 wexe . . . Crist] om. T2   264 signifiethe] signified H1G
born] om. H1   266 signifiethe] signified H1GT2   267 white] whiche changed to
whight with ght del. and 't' ins. H1   268 for] of E   wasting] wastineng H1
269 this vers] þese vercis G   270–3 space left for verses T2   270 porto] porta G
274 lichinusque] linchinus que E   275 candell] candellis G   278 taught] tought
del. 'taȝt' H1   280 faithe] add and H1   282 witheoute²] add þe H1GT2
283 lightethe] om. G   bene] both del. H1   bothe] om. G   284 witheoute²] with
with oute second with del. H1   and good werkes] ins. H1   285 withinne] wit Inne E
286 in open the] ins. H1

290 hous and hadde a preste of her owne, and eueri day she wolde here a
masse of oure Ladye. And so as the feste of the Purificacion neighed
the chapileyne went oute ferre thennes for gret besinesse that he
hadde to done, and that lady myght not that day haue no masse. And
as it is redde ellyswher that she hadde yeue for [the] loue of the
295 Virgyne as myche as she hadde or myght gete and her owne clothes, so
that whanne she hadde yeue her mantell she myght not go to the
chirche but was withouten masse that day, wherfor she was full sori.
And thanne she entered into her chapell and was sodenly rauished in
spirit byfore the auuter of oure Lady, and her semed that she was in
300 right a fayre chirche and a noble, and she behelde and seigh a gret
companye of virgines that come, and right a faire virgine aboue all
other crouned withe a riche crowne and went before, and whanne all
were sette ther come another companye of yonge men that were sette
f. 54ᵛᵃ downe | also bi order. An thanne come one that bere a gret assemble of
305 torches and toke the furst to the virgine that went before other, and
after to eueri of the other virgynes and yonge men, and after that thei
come to this ladie and toke her a light, whiche she receiued gladly.
And she loked into the quere and seigh two queresters that helde two
torches, and the deken and the subdeken and þe prest revished goo to
310 the auuter as tho that wolde syng her masse. And it semed her that
Laurence and Vincent weren accolites and that two aungels weren
[deken and subdeken] and Ihesu Crist was the prest. And whanne the
Confiteor was done two right faire yonge men went into the quere and
bygonne the office of þe masse with high voys right devoutely, and
315 these other that weren in the quere folued. And whanne it come to the
offering, the quene of virgines withe the other that weren in the quere
offered her torches to the preestis on her knees so as it is accustumed.
And as the preste abode that lady that she shulde come and offre her
torche, and she wolde in no wise come, than the quene of virgines sent
320 a massenger to her and sent her worde that she dede vngoodly to make
the preste abide so long. And she ansuered that the preste shulde
procede in his masse, for she wolde not offre her torche. And thanne
the quene sent another messangere, and she saide pleinly that the
torche that was geve her she wolde not forgoo in no wise. And thanne
325 the quene comaunded to the massenger and saide: 'Go to her ayein
and praie her to offre her torche, and yef she will not, take it from her.'

294 the¹] *om.* E   298 thanne] þere G   her] þat H₁GT₂   303 yonge] *om.* G
306 after¹] *add* that E   307 a] *om.* G   gladly] *add* And after that thei come to this
ladye E   312 deken] dekenes EG   and subdeken] *om.* E   326 yef] *om.* H₁G   will]
wold *with* d *erased* H₁

And whanne he hadde done his message and she wolde in no wise
offre | her torche, he wolde haue take it from her, but she helde faste, f. 54vb
and he drewe, and she defended myghtely, so that whanne they hadde
long stryuen the torche breke sodeinly and halff lefte in her honde. 330
And with this hasti brekyng she come ayein to herselff and fonde
herselff before the auuter ther as she was sette, and the halff broken
torche in her honde, wherof she was gretly mervailed and yelded gret
thankyngges to the blessed Virgine Marie that hadde not lefte her that
day withoute masse, but hadde suffered her to be atte suche a seruise. 335
And she putte in sauf keping the torche and helde it for a gret relyque,
and it is saide whosoeuer be touched with that torche is made hole of
al maner siknesse.

A lady seigh in a nyght in her slepe so as she was with childe that
she bere a baner died al in redc coloure. And as sone as she awoke she 340
loste her witte, and the fende tormented her so that her semed that þe
cristen faithe that she hadde holde into that tyme was redy to go fro
her bytwene her brestes. And she myght in no wise be cured, til in a
nyght of the Purificacion she woke in the chirche of Oure Lady, and
by her moste holi merites she receyued perfite helthe. 345

Here endithe the feste of the Purificacion of oure Lady,
and nexst foluithe the lyff of Seint Blase, Cap^m. .xxxvij.^m

As Seint Blase schined in alle vertues and holinesse, the cristen [men]
chase hym to be bisshop [in] the citee of Sabast in Capadoce, and
whanne he hadde receiued the bysshopriche he [fledde] into a pitte for
drede of the persecucion of Dioclician, and ther he lyued the lyff | of f. 55ra
an heremyte, and briddes brought hym his mete, and they wolde come 5
togederes to hym and wolde in no wise go fro hym til he hadde paued
hem with his honde and blessed hem. And as sone as any bridde was
syk thei wolde [come] to hym and were heled anone.

The prouost that was than of [that] region sent oute his knyghtes

327 he] she *with* s *erased* H1, sche GT2 and] *om.* T2   330 breke] brest H1 sodeinly]
denli T2   331 hasti] hastly GT2 she] he T2 and] *add* she T2   332 ther] *om.* T2
333 wherof] wherefore H1GT2   333-4 gret thankyngges] yn grete þonkes H1
335 hadde] *on erasure* H1   336 helde] *so with* de *on erasure and* i *changed to* e H1
337 and] *add* as GT2   339 childe] *add* and T2   340 bere a] *om.* T2

EH1GDH2A2L; A1 resumes at 4 -*cucion*   1 men] man EG, *so changed to* men H1
2 in^1] L, of EH1G   3 fledde] L, fell EG, went *on erasure* H1   5 briddes] bestis *on*
erasure H1   7 bridde] *subp.* 'beste' H1   8 come] L, turne EH1G   9 that^2] L,
the EH1G

10 for to hunte for hym and they myght no game fynde, and so by
auenture thei come to the pitte where Seint Blase was and founde gret
multitude of bestes that weren before hym. And thei assailed hem, but
they myght in no wise take none, wherfor thei went thennys al
abasshed and tolde to [her] lorde, and thanne anone he sent many
15 knyghtes and comaunded hem þat they shulde bring to hym Blase
with alle other cristen that myght be founde. And that same nyght
oure Lorde appered to hym sayeng: 'Arise up and offre sacrifice to
me.' And anone the knyghtes come to hym and saide: 'Arise vp, the
prouost sent for the.' And Blase ansuered: 'Sones, ye be right
20 welcome, for I see well that my Lorde God hathe not foryete me.'
And thanne he went forthe with hem and cesed neuer to preche and
dede many myracles before hem.

And thanne there was a woman that hadde a sone whiche was
strangeled with a bone of a fysche that was turned thuart ouer his
25 throte and deied, and she brought hym to the fete of this seint and
praied hym with piteous teres that he myght be heled. And thanne
Seint Blase sette his honde vpon hym and praied to God that the
childe myght be hole and alle tho that requered helpe in the name of
hym for that disese that thei myght be holpe, and anone the childe was
f. 55rb heled and ly|ued. Ther was a woman [that] hadd but [o] pigge, and
31 come a wolff and toke hym away with strengthe, and thanne she
praied Seint Blase that he wolde ordeyne that she myght haue her
pigge ayein. And he saide her in smylyng: 'Be not wrothe, woman, for
thou shalt haue thi pigge ayein.' And anone the wolff come and
35 brought the pigge ayein to the woman.

And whanne he come into the citee he was putte in prison by the
comaundement of the prince, and the nexst day he was comaunded to
come before hym, and whanne the prouost seigh hym he salued hym
and saide to hym with smothe wordes: 'Ioie haue thou, Blase, frende
40 of oure goddes.' To whom Blase saide: 'Ioie to the, go[o]d prouost,
but saye not that they bene goddes but calle hem fendes, for thei shull
be deliuered to euerlasting fire with hem that worship hem.' And
thanne was the prouost wrothe and made hym to be beten withe
staues and shette up ayein into the prison. To whom Blase saide:
45 'Thou mad man, wenest thou to take fro me the loue of my God with
thi paynes? Thenke wel that he is in me to my strength and comfort.'

14 her] L, the EH1G   30 that] and EH1   o] L, a EH1G   34–5 And . . .
woman] om. H1   38 whanne] ins. H1   39 hym] add 'frende' H1   44 shette]
se'n't H1, sette G

And the pore wydoue that hadde recouered her pigge bi Seint
Blase, she went and slowe hym and bare to Seint Blase the hede and
the fete with brede and a candell, and he mekely thanked her and said
to her: 'Offre euery yere a candel in my name, and whosoeuer do it 50
shal fare wel.' She dede so alwayes and hadde gret prosperitee.

After þat whanne the prouost hadde made hym to be take oute of
prison and myght in no wise encline hym to hys goddes, he made hym
hangged | vpon a tre and all his body to be rent withe combes of yren, f. 55ᵛᵃ
and after that he was ledde ayein to prison. And thanne .vij. women 55
folued the traces of his blood and gadered it up, and as sone as it was
aspied they were taken and constreyned to do sacrifice to the fals
goddes. To whom thei saide: 'Yef thou wilt [that] we worship youre
goddes, lat hem be born to yender ponde and washen clene so that we
mow worship hem the more clenly.' Thanne was the provost gladde, 60
and as sone as it myght be done he fulfelled that they hadd saide. And
thanne the women toke thaire goddes and threw hem in the middes of
the ponde and saide: 'Now shull we see yef thei be goddes.' And
whanne the prouost herde it he was wode for anger and smote hymself
and saide to the ministres: 'Whi ne hadde not ye kepte oure goddes 65
þat thei hadde not be caste in the water?' And thei ansuered: 'These
women speken to the in trecheri and threw hem in the water.' The
women ansuered and saiden: 'The verrey God sufferithe no trechery,
but yef thei weren goddes thei shulde haue know before what we
wolde haue do to hem.' 70

And thanne the prouost full of wrethe comaunded that men shuld
bryng hym in that one syde moltin lede and combes of iren and .vij.
habirgones al brennyng, and in that other parte .vij. smockes of lynen
clothe, and saide that thei shulde chese whiche of the tweyne thei
wolde. And one of hem that hadde two children ranne hardely before 75
and toke the smockes and th[r]ewe hem into [the] chemeney
brennyng, and the children saide to the moder: 'Right suete moder,
leue us not after the, but as | thou hast fedde us withe the suetnesse of f. 55ᵛᵇ
thi melke fulfell us now withe the suetnesse of the heuenly kyngdom.'
And thanne the prouost comaunded that thei were hangged vp and al 80
todrawen withe tho combes of iren, and þe fleshe of hem was as white
as melke, and melke ranne from hem in stede of blode. And as thei

57 do sacrifice] sacrifie G   fals] holy *del.*'fals' H1   58 that] *om.* E   youre] þy G
64 for] *ins.* H1   67 speken] *om.* G   68 sufferithe] suffrid G   69 thei²] þay *with*
y *on erasure* H1   we] he *changed to* we H1   76 threwe] thewe E   the²] a E
78–9 the suetnesse of thi] þy swete G

were in this torment and suffered it paciently the aungell of oure
Lorde come to hem and comforted hem and saide: 'Drede you not, for
85 the good werker that well begynnith and well endith he deseruithe to
be preisid of hym [that hirithe hym], and whanne his werke ys
fulfelled he receyuith hys hyre for his labour and possedithe ioie for
his hire.'

And thanne the prouost comaund[ed] that they were take thennes
90 and putte in a brennyng fire, and anone by the devine grace it
quenched and they went oute witheouten any harme. Thanne the
prouost not wetyng what he myght do saide to hem: 'Leue youre
enchauntementes and worship oure goddes.' And they ansuered:
'Performe that thou hast vndertake, for we be now called to the
95 kyngdom of heuene.' And thanne he gaue the sentence and
comaunded that they shulde be byheded, and whanne thei shulde
receyue marterdome they worshipped Ihesu Crist on her knees,
sayeng: 'Lorde God, that hast take us oute fro derkenesse and hast
brought vs to this suete lyght and made us thi sacrifice, receyue oure
100 soules and make hem come to euerlasting lyff.' And so thei hadde her
hedes smete of and passed forthe to oure Lorde.

And after that the prouost comaunded to bring forthe Blase before
hym and saide: 'Or thou shalt worship oure goddes now or neuer.'
f. 56ra Thanne Blase saide: 'O | thou wrechid felon, do what thou wilt, for I
105 drede the not. I take the here my body vtterly.' And thanne he
comaunded that he shulde be [throwe] in a ponde, and Blase blessed
the water and anone it was drie. And thanne he said to hem: 'Yef
youre goddes be verrey, shewe us the vertu of hem and enterith inne
hedir.' And thanne .lxv. men entered into the ponde and were
110 drowned anone. And thanne the aungell of oure Lorde descended
fro heuene and saide: 'Go oute, Blase, and receyue the crowne that is
arayed to the of oure Lorde.' And whanne he went oute the prouost
saide to hym: 'Thou hast al ordeyned that thou wilt not worshippe
oure goddes.' And thanne Blase saide: 'Knowe it well, thou wreche,
115 that I am the servaunt of God and will worship no fendes.' And
thanne anone he comaunded that he were beheded. And thanne he
praied to oure Lorde that whosoeuer hadde siknesse in þe throte or for

83 it] *om.* H1   84 hem¹] him H1   85 werker] werkis *with* is *subp. and* 'er' *in
different hand* G   86 that hirithe hym] L, *om.* EH1G   89 comaunded]
comaundithe E   91 quenched] L, *add* anone EH1G   93 oure] ȝoure G, youre *with* y
erased H1   96 thei] *ins.* H1   99 thi] þis H1G   105 vtterly] witterly H1G
106 throwe] drawe E   108 verrey] *add* goddis G   109 .lxv.] .xv. *on erasure* H1,
.xv. G   117 for] in H1

any other siknesse that þei requered his helpe inne that they myght anone be herde, and a voys fro heuene saide that it shulde be do as he hadde praied. And so he was beheded withe [the] two litell children 120 aboute the yere of oure Lorde .CC.iiij^{xx}. and seuene.

Here endith the life of Seint Blase, and nexst beginnith the life of Seint Agas, Capitulum .xxxviij.

Agace the noble virgine was right faire of body and of thought and worshipped alwayes God in al holinesse in the citee of Cathenense. Qynsyn that was consult of Cecyle was not noble but vnchaste man and a coueitouse and worshiped the ydoles, and enforced hym to take Agace. And for he was vnnoble in takyng one that was | noble it was to f. 56rb drede, for he that was vnchaste wolde use her b[ew]te amysse, he that 6 was coueitouse wolde take her richesse, and he that was an ydolater wolde make her sacrifice to ydoles.

And thanne he made her be brought before hym, and whanne she was brought he knewe that her purpos was vnmeuable and toke her to 10 a comune woman that hight Affrodisse by name and to .ix. doughteres that she hadde that weren alle right wicked and vnclene, so that bi thaire filthe and foly and wyckednesse they shulde chaunge her corage, behightyng her now gladnesse now sorugh, so þat be byhestes and manasses thei myght take her from her good purpos. To whom 15 Agace saide: 'My thought and myn entencion is sadder thanne any stone, for it is founded in Ihesu Crist. Your wordes bene wynde, youre behestes bene reyne, and youre dredfull manasses bene but iapes, for whateuer thei do thei mowe not make the foundement of myn hous to falle.' And withe that sayeng she wepte and praied euery 20 day, trustyng to come to the ioie of marterdome. And whanne she hadde bene there .xxx. dayes Affrodisse seigh that she was vnmeuable. She saide to Quy[n]ciane: 'A stone myght rather be made softe and iren turned to softenesse of lede thanne the thought of this mayde myght be turned fro the entencion of cristen faithe.' 25

And thanne Quyncien made her be brought before hym and saide to her: 'Of what condicion art thou?' And she saide: 'I am not only a

---

118 that'] *add* `jif' H1   119 shulde] *ins.* H1   120 the] tho EH1G

EH1GDH2A1A2L; E breaks off after 78 *with*   1 thought] youthe H1G   3 Qynsyn] Quyncian`e' *with* cia *on erasure* H1   6 vnchaste] *preceded by erased letter* H1   bewte] L, bounte EH1G   12 .ix.] þe G   16 thought] trouthe G   22 vnmeuable] vnable G   23 Quynciane] Quyciane EG, *so with misplaced macron over* u H1

noble woman but I am also of noble kynrede, as alle my kynrede beren
witnesse.' To whom Quyncien saide: 'Yef thou be noble, whi sheuest
f. 56ᵛᵃ thou bi thi werkes to be a persone | seruyng?' And she ansuered: 'I
31 shewe me a seruyng persone for I am the seruaunt and handmayden of
Ihesu Crist whom I serue.' Thanne Quyncien saide: 'Thou saiest and
affermest thiselff noble. Hou art thou thanne a servaunt?' She
ansuered and saide: 'It is souerein noblesse for to be seruaunt of
35 Ihesu Crist.' Thanne Quincien saide: 'Chese whiche thou wilt, either
do sacrifice to oure goddes or ellis receiue diuerse tormentis.' And she
ansuered and saide: 'Suche be thi wiff as Venys thi goddesse, and
suche be thou as Iubiter thi god.' And thanne Quincien comaunded
that she shulde be bete withe boffetis aboute her hede, sayeng to her:
40 'Ne iangle not so withe thi presumptuous mouthe to iniurie of the
iuge.' And thanne Agas saide to hym: 'I meruaile that thou, a man
wise, art wrapped in so moch folye that thou saiest hem thi goddes
that thou and thi wiff wolde not resemble and thou saiest it iniurie to
lyue after her ensaumple, for yef thei bene goddes [I] haue wisshed
45 the a good thing, and yef thou blame her felawship thou felest as y
doo.' Thanne Quincyen saide: 'What haue I to do withe thine veyne
wordes? Either thou shalt sacrifice to the goddes or I shall make the
deye bi diuerse tormentes.' And Agas ansuered: 'If thou behight me
wilde bestes and whan thei here the name of God her cruelte will
50 asuage; and yef thou deliuer me to fere the aungeles of heuene will
ministre a suete dewe; yef thou make me receyue woundes or
tormentis I haue the holy goste witheinne me bi whom I despise all
these thingges.' And thanne he comaunded that she were drawen into
f. 56ᵛᵇ the prison for she confounded hym withe her wor|des tofore the
55 comune, and she went gladly and gloriously as thou she hadd be
boden to a good dyner, and recomaunded her [strif] to oure Lorde.
    The day foluyng Quincyen saide: 'Renye thi Crist and worship
oure goddes.' And whan she hadde refused it he comaunded that she
were hangged on the crosse turned upsodoune and the two endes
60 fastened in the erthe and ther to be tormented. And thanne Agas
saide: 'I delite me in these peynes as he that herithe good tidyngges or
seithe that he hathe long desired, or as he that hadde founde gret

28 as . . . kynrede] *ins.* Hɪ   beren] *so with* be *on erasure* Hɪ, weren G   34 souerein]
sone seien *with last* e *on erasure* Hɪ, sone seyn G   37 goddesse] goddes Hɪ   39 to]
ins. Hɪ   40 to] *add* the G, *so ins.* Hɪ   43 it] þat þe G   44 I] *om.* EG, *ins.* Hɪ
47 or] *add* ellez HɪG   51 dewe] dew *with* w *on erasure* Hɪ   53 thingges] goddis G,
so on erasure Hɪ   56 strif] furst E, self G, *so on erasure* Hɪ   57 oure] *add* lordis and G
60 to] *ins.* Hɪ   61 peynes] peyntis G

tresoures. For the pure whete may not be putte in the gerner but yef
the chaffe and the straw be gretly beten and defouled and take away.
Right so my soule may not entre into paradys with crowne of 65
marterdome but yef I suffre my body to be tormented with bouchers.'
And than Quincyen comaunded that her brestes shulde be drawe of,
and whanne thei hadde be longe drawen thei were cutte of. Thanne
Agas saide to hym: 'O thou cruel and wicked tyraunt, art thou not
ashamed and confused that thou hast made cutte of a woman that 70
[thou] thiselff soukedest in thi moder? I haue withinne my soule hole
brestes wherwith I norishe al my wittes, the whiche I haue fro my
yougthe sacred to oure Lorde.'

And thanne he comaunded that she were putte ayen in the prison
and defended that no leche shulde entre to her ne no man shulde 75
mynister her neither brede ne water. And aboute mydnyght an
auncien man come to her hauynge a litell childe before hym bering
light and diuerse medicines and saide to her: 'Though it be so þat the
madde and wicked provost hathe tormented the with his tormentis,
thou hast more tormented hym with | þy answeris, for þou3 he haue Gf. 69ʳ
drawen of þy brestis, þe grete plente of his turmentis turnyd hym to 81
bitternesse, and for y was þere whanne þou suffredist y seigh well þat
þy brestis my3t resseyue cure of hele.' To whom Agas seide: 'I putte
neuer [bode]ly medicyne to my flessh, and it were a foule þyng to lese
þat y haue so long kepte.' And þanne þe auncien man seide to hire: 85
'Dou3tir, drede þe nou3t, ne be not abasshid, for y am a cristen man.'
And Agas seide: 'Wherfore schold y be a[sham]id sithe þou arte of
grete age and y al torente with turment þat no man may take delite in
me? But y þanke þe, holy fadir, of þat þou woldist putte þy cure to
me.' And þanne he seide: 'Why wilte þou not suffre þat y hele the?' 90
Sche answerid and seide: 'For y haue my Lord Ihesu Crist þat by his
oonly word and comaundement curith and helith all þyngis.' And
þanne þe olde man smylid and seide: 'I am þe appostul of Ihesu Crist,
and wite welle þat in the name of hym þou arte helid, for he sente me
to the.' And with that Seint Petir vaneschid awey. And þanne þe 95
blessid virgyne Agas fill doun prostrate and þankid God of þat sche
fonde hirself helid and hir pappis restorid to hir breste. Hir keperis
weren abasshid for the grete light þat þay seyen and purposidden to

63 gerner] garner *with final* ɼ *on erasure* H₁   yef] *om.* H₁   70 woman] *add* `brestes´ H₁
71 thou²] *om.* E   soukedest] sukedest *with* ke *on erasure* H₁   74 the] to G   77 auncien
man] aungel G   78 the] þu *changed to* þei (?) H₁   79 madde and] made a H₁
83 hele] L, helpe GH₁   84 bodely] redily G, bodely *with* bo *on erasure* H₁
87 ashamid] abasshid G   88 turment] turmentis G   98 þat] þanne *changed to* `þat´ H₁

fle awey and leue þe prison open, praying hir to goo awey. And þanne
100 sche seide: 'God deffende þat y schold fle and lese þe corone þat is
ordeynyd for me or that y putte my keperis in tribulacion for me.'
    So þanne .iiij. dayis aftir, Quyncien seide to hire þat sche schold
worschip þe goddis oþir resseyue greuous turment[is]. Thanne seide
G f. 69ᵛ Agas to hym: 'þy wordis ben veyne | and full of folie and deffoulen þe
105 eyre. þou cursid wiȝt withouten witte or vndirstondyng, how woldist
þou þat y schold worschip þy goddis and leue God of heuen þat hath
helid me?' And Quyncien seide: 'Who hath helid the?' Agas seide:
'Ihesu Crist, the sone of God.' 'How derste þou,' he seide, 'name
Crist bifore me aȝen sithe y will not here of hym?' Thanne Agas seide:
110 'As long as y schal lyue y schal calle Crist with herte and mouthe.'
And Quyncien seide: 'Now y schal see whethir Crist schal hele þe or
noo.' Thanne comaundid he þat men schold brynge broken scherdis
[of shellis] and strewe hem þikke in the flore and þrowe brennyng
colis vpon hem, and make hir nakid and turne hir vpon hem. And as
115 þay were aboute to ordeyne þerfore, a right grete tremblyng of þe
erthe bigan and turmentid so þe cite þat þat oo partie fill doun and
sclewe two of Quyncienys counsellouris. Thanne alle þe pepul come
and cryid vpon hym seying: 'We suffre þis vengaunce for þe turmente
that þou doist to Agas withoute reson.' And þanne Qyuncien drede in
120 that oo parte the tremblyng of þe erthe and in þat oþer þe meuyng of
the pepul and comaundid þat sche were putte aȝen in prison, where
sche prayid and seide: 'Lord Ihesu Crist, þat formedist me and hast
kepte me fro my ȝouthe and kepte my body fro all filthe, and hast take
fro me the loue of þe world, and hast made me to ouercome the
125 tormentis and hast ȝeue me aȝens hem þe vertu of pacience, now good
Lord resseyue my spirite and comaunde me to come to þy mercy.'
And whanne sche hadde seide þat with a grete voice, sche ȝaf vp þe
spirite the ȝere of oure Lord .CC.liij. vnder Dacien þe emperoure.
    And as good cristen pepul anoyntid þe body for to putte it into þe
130 sepulcre, ther come a faire ȝong man clothid in selke with moo þanne
a .C. men with hym riȝt faire and wel biseyne, clothid all in white,
wiche meyne had neuer be seyn bifore of hem, and sette a t[a]bul at
hir hede of marbul, and anoon [dis]apperid fro þe sight of alle. And in
þe tabul were writen þese wordis: 'Holy mynde of good wille,

103 turmentis] turment G   111 whethir] add in del. H₁   þe] ins. H₁   113 of
shelles] L, of sherdes del. H₁, om. G   115 grete] ins. H₁   122 and] ins. H₁
124 to] ins. H₁   129 into] in῾to´ H₁   132 sette] fet del. sette H₁   tabul] tubul G
133 disapperid] þeron apperid G, þey on apered with y on erasure H₁ (desaparut P2)
134 good] go῾e´de H₁

worschip to God and to þe cuntre dellyueraunce.' The wiche writyng 135
is in this wise vndirstond: sche was holy in þou3t; sche offrid frely
worschip to God; and sche was dellyueraunce of þe cuntre. And
whanne this | myracle was hurde and puplisshid paynemys and Iewis G f. 70ʳ
bygonne to worschip hir sepulcre.

And þanne whanne Quy[n]cien wente for to enquere hir richessis, 140
two horsis bygunne to fight togedris as he passid by hem, and þat oon
smote hym with his fote and þat oþer bote hym, and so bitwene hem
þay þrewe hym in a flode þat he myght neuer be founde aftir.

And whanne þe 3ere was turnyd a3eyne aboute þe feste of hire, a
grete hille [nye] þe cite brake vp and put oute fire þat dessendid fro þe 145
mountayn as a streme and brente rochis and erthe and come toward
the cite. And þanne grete multitude of paynemys dessendid fro þe
hille and fledde to þe sepulcre of Seint Agas and toke þe kouerynge
wherwith þe sepulcre was helid and sette it a3ens þe fire, and anoon þe
fire abode and passid not ouer. 150

Of þis holy virgyne seith Seint Ambrose: 'A, blessid virgyne and
nobul, þat deseruyd þat oure Lord schold worschip þy blode by þe
praysyng of martirdom. A, þou nobul and glorious, worschipid [with
double beaute, that] among þe scharpe turmentis were sette bifore by
schynyng myraclis, þat deseru[ed]yst to be curid of þe apostull by his 155
visitacion and so maried to God the eyre ressesyuyd the, and at þe
glorious entryng of þy membris schynyng where the felaschip of
aungell[is] schewyng þy holynesse and þe dellyuerance of þe contre.

[Here endeth þe life of Seint Agas, and next beginneth þe
life of Seint Vedast, Cap. .xxxix.]

[V]edaste was ordeynyd of Seint Remye bisshop of Aras, and whanne
he come to þe 3ate of the cite he fonde þere two pore men [þat] askid
of hym almys. þat oon was lame and þat oþir was blynde, and he seide
to h[e]m: 'Y haue with me neythir gold ne seluer. Y 3eue 3ou þat y
haue.' And þanne he made his prayer and helid hem bothe two. And 5

135 þe] *ins.* H1   The] Tʰh'e H1   140 Quyncien] Quycien G   142 fote] fete H1
145 nye] *so changed to* by H1, *by* G   fro] frome *with* me *del.* H1   152 deseruyd]
deseruest H1   153 A] L, And GH1   153–4 with . . . that] *om.* G   154 beaute]
bent H1   155 deseruedest] L, deseruyst G, dissereuest H1   156 the²] the / the *with*
first del. H1

GDH2H1A1A2L   *Rubric* Vedast] L, Sedast H1, *space left for Rubric* G
1 Vedaste] L, Sedast GH1   2 þat] L, and GH1   3 hym] him *changed to*
hem H1   4 hem] hym GH1 (*leur* P2)

as a wolf dwellid in a waste chirche that was all forloste and koueryd
all with breris, he comaundid þat he schold goo þens and come no
more there. The wolf [dide] as he was comaundid.

  And whanne he hadde conuertid myche pepul by worde and by
10 werke, in the .xl. ȝere of his bisshopriche he seigh a beme of fire þat
come fro heuen into his hous, and þanne he considerid that his ende
G f. 70ᵛ neyȝid, so þat a while aftir þat he reste in pees about the | ȝere of oure
Lord .vC.

  And as his body was born to ben enteerid, Audomere, a blynde
15 man, was ful sory þat he myȝt not see þe body of hym, and þanne
anoon he resseyuyd his sight, and aftir þat he loste his sight aȝen at his
owne request and of his owne fre wille.

      [Here endith the life of Seint [V]edast, and next biginneth
      the life of Seint Amande, Cap. .xl.]

Amandis was born of nobul kynrede, and as he entrid into a chirche
and walkid aboute þe monasterie he fonde a grete serpente, and anoon
he constreynyd hym by his orison and by þe vertu of þe cros to goo
aȝen to his pitte with[oute eny] comyng oute, euer þere to abide. And
5 Amandis wente to þe sepulcre of Seint Martyne and dwellid þere .xv.
ȝere and werid þe heire and was sustenyd with barly brede and water.

  And aftir þat as he was come to Rome and woke in þe nyght in the
chirche of Seint Petir, oon of þe keperis of þe chirche putte hym oute
vnhonestly. And þanne Seint Petir apperid to hym in his sclepe bifore
10 þe ȝatis of [the] chirche and tauȝt hym þat he schold goo into Fraunce
and blame þe kyng Dago[b]ert for his wikkid dedis, and he dide so,
wherfore þe kyng was wrothe and putte hym oute of his rewme. And
as þe kyng hadde no issewe he made his prayer to God and hadde a
sone, and þanne he byþouȝt hym who schold cristen his sone, and
15 sodeynly it fill in his mende þat Amande schold doo it. And þanne was
Amande souȝt and brouȝt to þe kyng, and the kyng knelid doun to
hym and askid forȝeuenesse and prayid hym þat he wold baptise his
sone þat oure Lord hadde ȝeue hym. He grauntid hym goodly þe
firste requeste, but þe second he [denyed] hym and wente his wey, for

  8 dide] and G   14 enteerid] entred H1   16 and aftir . . . sight] om. H1

  GDH2H1A1A2L   *Rubric* Vedast] Sedast *changed to* Vedast H1, *space left for rubric* G
  4 withoute eny] with GH1 (*sans jamais* P2)   euer] ouer H1   8 of þe chirche/putte
  hym oute] *trs.* G   9 vnhonestly] vn onesly H1   10 the] L, his GH1
  11 Dagobert] Dagovert G   19 denyed] neyghid G

he dradde hym to be ocupied in seculer ocupacionys. But atte laste he 20
was ouercome by prayers and grauntid to þe kyng to be rulid aftir
hym, and as he baptisid þe childe and alle hilden her pees, the ʒong
child answerid: 'Amen.'

And þanne the kyng made hym bisshop of Troies, and as he seiʒ þat
þe pepull dispised þe worde of God he wente into Gascoyne, and as a 25
iogelor skornyd hym of his wordis he was anoon raueschid with þe
fende | and al torente hymself with his owne tethe and confessid G f. 71ʳ
hymself þat he hadde doon iniurie to þe seruaunt of God and di[ed]
anoon cursidly. A[s] þis holy man wissh his hondis in a tyme anoþer
bisshop made kepe þe water of his hondis, and aftir þat a blynde man 30
was helid therwith.

A[s] he wold make a chirche in a place by þe kyngis wi[lle], a
bisshop of þe nexte cite was [wroth] þerwith and comaundid to his
seruauntis þat þay schold put oute Amandes or ellis scle hym. Thay
come to hym and told hym in gile þat he schold goo with hem and þay 35
wold schewe hym a couenabul place to make a chirche on. He knewe
bifore þe malice of hem and wente with hem in haste vnto a grete
mountayne where he wende to haue ben sclayne, for he desirid gretly
martirdome. But anoon þat hille was koueryd with so grete a reyne
and tempeste þat þay myght not see hym and þay wende verrely to 40
haue deide. And þanne þay knelid doun bifore hym and askid hym
forʒeuenesse [that] þay myght goo þens [a lyfe], and þanne he made
his prayere and sodeynly þer was faire and cle[r]e wedir, and þanne
þay wente aʒen to her propur placis and Seint Amande eskapid by þe
goodnesse of oure Lord and dide meny oþer grete myraclis. And sithe 45
he restid in pees, and flowrid aboute þe ʒere of oure Lord .vjC. and
twenty in the tyme of Rakle.

[Here endeth the life of Seynt Amande, and next foloweth
the life of Seynt Valentyne, Cap. .xlj.]

Valentyne was a worschipful preste wiche Claudien þe emperour
made come bifore hym and [asked him and] seide: 'Arte þou
Valentyne? Why arte not þou of oure frendschip to worschip oure

27 owne] *ins.* H1   28 died] L, dide G, dud *erased* died H1   29 As] L, And GH1
32 As] L, And GH1   wille] with G   33 wroth] L, brouʒt G, brought *changed to*
wrought H1   42 that] L, for GH1   a lyfe] and lyue GH1   43 clere] clene G
45 oþer] *add* many *del.* H1

GDH2H1A1A2L   *Space left for rubric* G   2 hym] him *on erased paraph* H1
asked hym and] L, *om.* GH1

goddis and renounce th[i] wikkid lawe ful of vanyte?' To whom
5 Valentyne seide: 'If thou knowist þe grace of oure Lord þou woldist
not seye as þou doste but withdrawe þy corage fro ydollis and
worschip God þat is in heuen.' And þanne oon þat was bifore
Claudien seide: 'Valentyne, what seiste þou of þe holynesse of oure
goddis?' And Valentyne seide: 'Y sey noþyng of hem but þat þay were
10 cursid men ful of all filthe and wrechidnesse.' þanne seide Claudien:
'If þy Criste be verrey God, why seiste þou not þat he is so?' And
þanne Valentyne seide: 'Verrely Crist is oonly God, and if þou wilte
leue on hym thi soule schal be sauyd, thy comune goodis schal |
G f. 71ᵛ encrese, and victorie schal be ȝeue the of þyne enemyis.' þanne seide
15 Claudien to all þe pepul of Rome þat stode aboute hym: 'Loo, how þis
man spekith wisely and riȝtwisely.' And þanne seide þe prouost: 'See
ȝe not how þe emperour is disseyuyd? How myȝt we leue þat we haue
holde fro oure ȝouthe?'

And þanne þe wille of Claudien was chaungid and Valentyne was
20 taken to a prince in kepyng, and whanne he had ladde hym to his hous
he seide: 'Lord Ihesu Crist [þat] arte verrey light, enlumyne this hous
so þat þay knowe the as verrey God.' And þanne þe prince seide to
hym: 'Y merueile þou seiste þat Criste is verrey light. If he wold ȝeue
sight to my douȝtir þat hath be long blynde I schal doo as þou seyste.'
25 Thanne Valentyne prayid and gete sight to his blynde douȝtir and
conuertid hym and alle his housold. And þanne þe prouost comaundid þat Valentynys hede schold be smeten of þe ȝere of oure Lord
.ijC.iiijˣˣ.

[Here endeth the lif of Seint Valentine, and next biginneth
þe life of Seint Iulian, Cap. .xlij.]

Seint Iulian þe virgyne was weddid to Eulogiene prouost of Nicho-
medie, but sche wold in no wise consente to hym but if he wold
resseyue þe faith of Ihesu Crist. And þanne hir fadir comaundid þat
sche schold be greuously beten and dellyueryd to þe prouost. And
5 þanne the prouost seide to hire: 'A, þou my right swete Iulian, why
dispisiste þou me and forsakist me in siche wise?' Sche answerid and
seide to hym: 'If þou worschepe my God y wold obeye the, or ellis
þou schalt neuer be my husbond.' Thanne seide þe prouost to hire:

4 thi] the GH1 (ta P2)   6 not] ins. H1   16 and riȝtwisely] om. H1   21 þat]
L, þou GH1   enlumyne] L, enlumyned GH1

GDH2H1A1A2L   Space left for rubric G

'Madame, þat may y not doo, for þe emperoure wold sone make my
hede to be smyte of if y dide þat.' Thanne seide Iulian: 'If þou 10
d[re]dest here a dedly emperoure, how trowist þou þat y drede not þe
vndedly emperoure? Wherfore doo as þou wilte, for þou mayste not
disseyue me.'

And þanne þe prouost made hir greuously to be beten with roddis
and made hir honge all a day by hir here and powrid on hir hede hote 15
multen lede. And whanne he saw3 þat it greuyd hire in no wise he
vnbounde hir of hir cheynys and closid hir a3en in the prison. And
þanne þe fende apperid to hire in liknesse of an aungel and seide:
'Iulian, y am þe aungel of oure Lord þat sente me to the for to telle the
þat þou scholdist doo sacrifise to þe goddis so þat þou be no more 20
turmentid ne suffre þyself to deie so wikkidly.' | And þanne Iulian Gf. 72ʳ
prayid to oure Lorde with wepyng teris and seide: 'Lord God, suffre
me not to perissh, but schew me what he is þat sterith me to þis þyng.'
And þanne a voice seide to hire þat sche schold take hym and aske
hym what he was and constrayne hym to telle hire. And whanne sche 25
[hadde] askid hym what he was he seide þat he was a fende and þat his
fadir hadde sente hym to hire for to desseyue hire. Thanne Iulian
seide: 'Who is þy fadir?' He answerid: 'Belzabub, that sendith vs [to]
all yuellis, and if we be ouercome with cristen men he makith vs
greuously beten, and y knowe well þat y am come hidir for my harme 30
for y may not ouercome the.' Among oþer þyngis he knowlechid hire
and seide þat his ocupacion was gretly to temp[t]e hem þat were
aboute the mysterie of þe sacrament and hem þat tendi[d] to orisonys
and predicacionys. And þanne Iulian bonde his hondis bihynde his
back and keste hym doun to hir fete and bete hym scharply with þe 35
cheyne wherwith sche was bounde The fende cryid and seide:
'Madame Iulian, haue mercy on me.'

And aftir þat þe prouost comaundid þat Iulian were brou3t oute of
prison, and whanne sche wente oute sche drowe the fende aftir hire
faste bounden crying and seying: 'Madame Iuliane, doo not me þis 40
spite, for y schall neuer greue the more. Men seyen þat cristen pepul
be piteuous, but þou hast no pite of me.' And sche made as sche toke
no [hede] of his crie but drewe hym þoru3 þe market and aftir þrewe
hym in a grete diche and a foule.

11 dredest] deidest G   not] subp. H1   17 the] om. H1   26 hadde] om. G
28 to] ta G   30 am] ins. G   hidir] thidir G   32 tempte] tempre G
33 mysterie] mynsterie G   tendid] L, tendith GH1   42 þou] ins. H1   43 hede]
kepe G

45   And whanne sche was comen to þe prouost sche was sette in a
whele so þat all hir bonys were tobrosten þat men myȝt see þe marie of
hi[r] bonys. And þanne þe aungel of oure Lord brake þe whele and
helid hire in a moment, and whanne þoo þat were þere seiȝ þis þay
leuyd in God and were anoon bihedid by nombre .vC.xj^{xx}. and ten
50 women. Aftir þat sche was putte in a vessel full of hote multen lede,
and anoon þe lede wax as tempre as a bathe. And þanne þe prouoste
cursid his goddis that myght not punyssh a maide þat dide hem siche
wrong and dispite. And þanne he comaundid þat sche schold be
hedid, and as men ladde hir to be hedid þe fende þat sche hadde beten
55 apperid in þe forme of a ȝong man and cryid seying: 'Spare hir nouȝt,
for sche blamyth oure goddis and hath bete me þis nyght full
greuously. Ȝelde hire þat sche hath deseruyd.' And whanne Iulian
G f. 72^v openyd a litill þe eyen for to | see who it was þat seide siche wordis, þe
fende fledde crying: 'Allas, allas, y trowe þat sche will take me aȝen
60 and bynde me.' And whanne þe blessid Iulian was bihedid, the
prouost saylid in þe see with .xxiiij.^{ti} men, and a tempeste come
and drownyd hem, and whanne þe see hadde caste vp þe bodyis þay
were deuourid with bestis and briddis.

[Here endeth the life of Seint Iulian the virgine, and next
foloueth the feste called *Cathedra Sancti Petri*, Cap. .xliij.]

The chare of Seint Petir is solempnely worschepid of þe Chirche, for
þe blessid apostull Seint Petir was so haunsid in þe chaire of bisshop
in Antioche. And þe ordynaunce of þis solempnyte hath .iiij. causis.

    The firste is, whanne þe blessid Petir prechid in Antioche
5 Theophile the prince of þe cite seide to hym þus: 'By what reson
turnyst þou my pepul fro my lawe?' And þanne Petir prechid hym þe
faith of Ihesu Crist, and þanne anoon he made hym to be putte in
prison and bounde faste with cheynys and lete hym be withoute mete
and drynke. And as Seint Petir faylid almoste for hungre he toke

47 hir] his G   48 hire] *ins.* H1   49 .xj.^{xx}] .xj. H1   55 þe] *ins.* H1
57 hire] *ins.* H1   61 .xxiiij.^{ti}] .xxiij. H1

GDH2H1A1A2L; A1 breaks off after 153 *of*; H1 misplaces 98 *oure* to 183 *sympul* from
f. 73ra to middle of 44 Matthias, ff. 74ra-75rb, beginning by repeating *that is ayenst God.* At
foot of f. 74rb in a 15th-century hand: *At þe marke aboue shuld begyn that begyneth to `a' lyke*
marke in þe lefe next her folowing. And þat þat begyneth at þis marke shuld be at such an opur
marke in þe lefe next befor this; and in margin of f.75rb *tha foloweth her shuld be in first side of*
the lefe next befor this at þe sign in þe midel margyn.   Space left for rubric G   1 The
chare] Thare H1   2 apostull] apostoles *with final* s *erased* H1

to hym strengthe and lifte vp his eyen to heuen and seide: 'O þou 10
Lord Ihesu Crist, helper of all þoo þat ben in sorowe, helpe now me
þat am ouercome ney3 with þis tribulacions.' To whom oure Lord
answerid and seide: 'Petir, wenyst thou to be lefte of me? Oþir
dispisi[st] þou my bounte, if þou dredist not to seie siche þyngis? Y
am redy and schal helpe þe in þy sorowful bataile.'   15

And Seint Poule hurde þanne speke of þe pr[ison]yng of Seint Petir
and come to Theophile and seide hym þat he was a souereyne werker
in dyuerse craftis and þat he kouthe kerue in tre and in stone and
peynte tentis and make meny oþir nobul werkis. And þanne he was
gretly prayid of Theophile to dwelle with hym in his courte. Within a 20
fewe dayis aftir, Poule come priuyly to Petir in[to the] prison, and
whanne he saw3 hym as dede and wastid he bigan bittirly to wepe, and
almoste he was failid in wepyng and klippid hym and bigan to seie in
this wise: 'A, brothir Petir, my glorie and my ioie and half my lif, take
a3en thy vertuous for my comyng to the.' And þanne Petir openyd the 25
eyen and knewe hym and bigan to wepe, but he myght not speke to
hym, and þanne Poule in haste openyd his mouthe and putte in mete
and he resseyuyd it. And whanne Petir was comfortid with mete he
ranne to Poule and [kiss]id hym and wepte togedris [bothe] a grete
while. And þanne | Poule turnyd a3en pryuyly f[ro] hym and seide to Gf.73ʳ
Theophile: 'A, þou good Theophile, thy glorie is grete and þy 31
curyosite is frende to honeste, but a litill fawte defamyth the.
Remembre 3e not what 3e haue doon to hym that worschipi[th]
almyghty God þat is callid Petir, as þou3 he were an enchaunter. He is
now so disfigurid and so fowle and so wastid in all þyngis þat he is 35
brou3t to nou3t and in hym is noþyng lefte but a litill of the tvnge.
Allas, why putte 3e siche a man in prison? Trewly and he were owte at
3oure wille as he was wonte he myght be full profitabul to the in many
þyngis, for as summe seyn of hym he helith of all maner sikenesse and
he arreysith fro deth to lif.' Thanne Theophile seide to Poule: 'These 40
ben but fabullis þat þou seiste, for if he couth arrere the dede he
couthe dellyuer hymself oute of prison.' And thanne seide Seint
Poule: 'He doth as Ihesu Crist dide þat arrerid þe dede as men seide,
and 3it he wold not come doun of þe cros. And by that ensampul Petir
woll not dellyuer hymself ne he dredith not to deye for Ihesu Crist.' 45

10 to hym strengthe] `to´ del. strenght vnto hym H1   12 þis] so with s subþ.G
14 dispisist] dispisid G   if] If as for new sentence GH1   16 prisonynge] presentyng G
21 into the] L, in G, into H1   29 kissid] L, askid GH1   bothe] om. G   30 fro] for G
32 fawte] defaute H1   33 3e¹] þe H1   worschipith] worschipid G   40 arreysith] ariseth
H1   42 couthe] wold H1   Seint] om. H1   44 not] ins. H1   45 woll] wold H1

To whom Theophile seide: 'Make hym þanne arrere fro deth to liff
my sone þat hath be dede this .xiiij. ȝere and þat he ȝelde hym to me
bothe hole and sounde.' Thanne Poule bihiȝt hym and entrid to Petir
in the prison where he was and tolde hym how he hadde height þe
50 resussytynge of þe sone of þe prince. And þanne Petir seide to hym:
'Poule, þou hast byhight a grete þyng, but if God wile it schal be to þe
ful light.' And þanne Petir wente oute of þe prison, and whanne he
hadde prayid vpon þe sepulcre of þe dede, anoon he aroos fro deth to
lif. But it is [not] all likly to be trewe þat Poule schold feyne hym by
55 mannys wilis to konne siche craftis, or þat [the] sentence of þat [30]ng
man schold haue be suspendid .xiiij. ȝere. And thanne Theophile and
all the pepul of Antioche bileuyd in oure Lord Ihesu Crist and many
oþer, and maden a glorious chirche and sette in þe myddis [þereof] a
cheyre of grete heighthe and sette Seint Petir þerynne þat he myght
60 be seyne and hurde of all þe pepul.

And of þat firste worschip the Chirche makith feste, for þe prelatis
of þe Chirche bigan þanne furste to be so haunsid by place, by myght
and by name. And þanne was fulfillid þat was seide of Dauyd: 'Thay
enhaunsid hym [in] the Chirche of þe pepul.'

65   And it is to wite þat þer be .iij. maner of chirchis in wiche Seint
Petir was enhaunsid, that is to seye in the Chirche militacion,
G f. 73ᵛ malignancion and trivmphancion. And | in th[is] trebul chirche was
he enhaunsid like as þe Chirche halowith this trebul feste of hym. He
is enhaunsid in the Chirche militacion hauyng lordschip on hire and
70 gouernyng here in the feithe and in good werkis preysably, and þat
appertenyth to þe solempnyte of that day þat is seide the Chaire of
Seint Petir, for he toke þanne þe cheire of a bisshop vpon Antioche
and gouernyd hire .vij. ȝere preysably. Secondly he was enhaunsid in
the chirche of wikkid men in brekyng hire and wastyng hire [and] in
75 conuertyng hire to the faith, and þat appertenyth to þe seconde feste
þat is seide of Cheynes, for þanne he wastid the chirche of wikkid men
and conuertid myche pepul to the faith. Thridly he was enhaunsid in
the Chirche of victoriaunce entr[yng] blessidly in hire, and that is to
the .iij.ᵉ solempnyte the wiche was his passion, for þanne he entrid
80 into þe Chirche of victoriaunce.

And it is to wite þat þe Chirche makith .iij. tymys in the ȝere feste

46 arrere] arere *on erasure* H1   50 to] *ins.* H1   54 not] L, *om.* GH1   55 the]
L, *om.* GH1   30ng] þyng G   58 þereof] *om.* G   59 of] *add* golde *del.* G   64 in]
L, to GH1   67 this trebul chirche] L, these trebul (trembell H1) chirchis GH1
68 enhaunsid] haunsed H1   74 in¹] in/in *with first del.* H1   and wastyng hire] *om.* H1
and²] L, *om.* GH1   78 entryng] entretyng G   79 .iij.ᵉ] .iiij.ᵉ G   81 .iij.] .iiij. G

of hym by mony resonys, that is to seie for his priuylage, for þe office,
for þe benefice, for [the] duete and for ensampul. For þe [priuylage,
for þe blessid Petir was] priuylegid more þanne othir in .iij. þyngis,
for wiche .iij. priuylegis þe Chirche worschipi[th] hym .iij. tymys 85
in the ȝere. He was bifore othir more worthy of auctorite for he was
prince of the appostullis and toke þe keyis of þe kyngdom of heuen, he
was more brennyng in the loue of God for he louyd Ihesu Crist more
feruently þanne othir so as it is witnessid in many placis of the gospel,
and he was more profitabul in vertu, for as it is radde in the Dedis of 90
þe Appostlis the seke were helid by þe schadowe of Seint Petir.

Secondly for þe office, for he hadde office of prelate aboue all the
Chirche, and riȝt as Seint Petir was prince and prelate of þe Chirche
þat is strechid oute in .iij. partyis of þe world, in Assie, in Aufrike and
in Europe, so the Chirche halowith .iij. tymys in the ȝere the feste of 95
hym. Thridly for þe benefice, for he hadde resseyuyd power to bynde
and vnbynde, wherby he dellyuerith vs fro .iij. maner of synnys, that
is of þouȝt, of word, of dede, þat is aȝens God, oure neighbore and
aȝens oureself. Or þis trebul beneficis may be vndirstond þe vertu þat
the synful man resseyuyth by þis heuenly keyis of the Chirche. The 100
firste is the absolucion of synnys schewid, the second is the chaungyng
of the peynys of purgatorie into temperel peynys, the þridde is þe
relessyng of temperel peynys. And for þis trebell | beneficis is Petir G f. 74ʳ
worschipid in the Chirche .iij. tymys. Fourthly for dewte, for [Seint]
Petir hath ordeynyd vs trebul refeccion, by word and by ensampul 105
and by temperal comforte or by helpe of orison, and for þat we be
bounde to worschip hym .iij. tymys. The .v.ᵉ is for ensample, þat no
synful ne falle in dispeire þough he hadde þries renyid Crist as Petir
hadde, but doo as he dide, confesse hym with herte, with mouth and
with werke. 110

The seconde cause of þe ordynance was this, wiche was taken in the
boke of Clement. For whanne Petir prechid þe word of God and he
neyghid to Antioche, all tho of the cite come aȝens hym barefote and
in her schertis þrowyng asshis vpon her hedis, doyng penaunce of þat
þay were accordid aȝens hym with Symeon Magus the enchauntour. 115
And whanne Seint Petir sawȝ þeyre penaunce he ȝeldid þankyngis to
God. And þanne þay brouȝt bifore hym all þoo þat were seke or vexid

83 the] L, *om.* GHᵢ   83–4 priuylage . . . was] *om.* G   85 worschipith]
worschipid G   86 in the ȝere *begins sentence in* Hᵢ, *ambiguous in* G   88 Crist] *add*
with Hᵢ   89 feruently] feruent Hᵢ   is witnessid] witnesse Hᵢ   93 prelate] L, *add*
aboue GHᵢ   98 God] *add in margin versus* G   neighbore] neighbours Hᵢ
104 Seint] *om.* G   116 he] ye *changed to* he Hᵢ

with fendis. And whanne he saw3 hem he callid þe name of oure Lord
vpon hem, and anoon ri3t grete light apperid there, and þanne all were
120 helid and ronnen aftir hym and kissid þe [pase] of his fete where he
hadde passid. And þanne within ten dayis aftir, moo þanne [.x]M¹.
men resseyuyd bapteme, and Theophile prince of the cite made his
hous to be ordeynyd and blessid [in to] a chirche and made sette
þer for Seint Petir an heigh cheire for to be hurde and sene of [all] þe
125 pepul. Ne these thyngis ben not contrarie to þoo þat ben seide aboue,
for it may well be that by the doynge of Poule that Seint Petir was
resseyuyd of Theophile ioyously and of all the pepull, but whanne
Petir was partid Symon the [en]chauntour peruertid and meuyd the
pepul greuously a3ens Petir, and aftir þat þe pepul dide penaunce and
130 resseyuyd hym a3en worschipfully.

And also þis feste of þe Cheire of Seint Petir was wonte to be callid
the feste of Metis of Seint Petir, and þerof may be take the .iij. reson
of the ordynaunce therof. It was an auncien custume of paynemys, as
Iohn Billet seith, þat euery 3ere in the monethe of Feuerere on the
135 .iij.ᵉ day to offre metis vpon þe tumbis of her kyn[ne], and þanne þe
fendis wold waste it by nyght and þe paynemys trowidden þat þe
mete[s] hadde ben vsid of þe soulis gooyng aboute the tombis as
schadowis. And as þe same clerk seith þat the auncien pepul were
Gf.74ᵛ wont to seie þat whanne þe soulis weren in | the bodyis þay were seide
140 soulis, and whanne þay ben in helle þay ben callid wikkid, and whanne
þay were lifte vp into heuen þay callid hem spiritis, and whanne þay
were newly leide in þe sepulcre or þat þay wente aboute þe tvmbe þay
callid hem schadewis. This wrecchid errour and custume myght
vnnethe be take awey of cristen men, the wiche thyng the holy
145 fadris seighen and vndirstoden and wold distroye þis falce errour and
custume, and ordeynyd þe f[e]ste of þe [Chaire] of Seint Petir as well
as of that of Rome as of that of Antioche in þat same day þat þe oþer
was wont to be doon, wherfore sume callid þe feste 'of the mete of
Seint Petir'.

150 Ferthely þis feste was ordeynyd for reuerence of the corone of
clerkis, and it is to knowe aftir þat sume seyn þat þe corone of clerkis
bigan þere firste. For whanne Seint Petir prechid in Antioche þay

120 pase] L, place GH1   121 within] add an G   .x.] L, a GH1   123 in to] L,
om. GH1   124 þer for] þerfore G   Petir] add on G   all] L, om. GH1
128 enchauntour] Chauntour G   129 a3ens] L, add seint GH1   132 reson]
resonys G   135 kynne] L, kyng GH1   136 waste] cast H1   trowidden] trowen H1
137 metes] mete G   146 feste] faste G   Chaire] L, Chirche GH1   147 of¹] at H1
150 of²] the G

schouen his hede in þe heighist parte þerof in dispite of cristen name,
the wiche was aftir ȝeuen in worschip [to] all þe clergie þat was doon
in dispite to þe appostul of Ihesu Crist. Thre þyngis ben vndirstonde 155
in the corone of a clerk, the furste is þe shauyng of the hede, the
kuttyng of the here, and the forme of the cercle. The schauyng of þe
heighist parte of þe hede is doon for .iij. resonys, þe wiche Seint
Denys assignyth two of hem in the Ierarchie of the Chirche and seyeth
þat þe schauyng or kuttyng of the here signyfyith clennesse and [not] 160
a curious lyf, for in kuttyng awey of the here ther folowen .iij. þyngis,
kepyng of klennesse, a defformy[te] and a nakidnes. Klennesse for as
myche as filthe is ofte tymys gederid in the here; a difformyte for here
is a maner of an ornament, and þerfore schauyng signyfieth clene lif
and not a curious lif, þat is to seie þat clerkis scholden haue clennesse 165
of þought withynne and not queynte and curiouse cloþyng outward;
the nakidnesse of the hede signyfyith þat þe clerk schold be ioynyyd
to God withoute eny mene and beholde gladly the glorie of oure Lord.
The kuttyng of þe here is doon for þat it is to vndirstond þat all
outragious and foule thoughtis schold be kutte oute of the mynde of a 170
clerk, and þay schold alwey haue the [eere] to here the word of God
and take awey fro hymself all temperalteis but oonly to his necescite.
   And þe figure of the [cercle] is made for many resonys. Furste þis
figure hath nothir bygynnyng ne endyng. Secondly þat þis figure hath
no cornere, the wiche bitokenyth þat þe clerk schold haue no filthe in 175
his lif, for þere as heris | ben there is gladly filthe. Seint Bernard seith Gf.75ʳ
þat þay schul[de] haue trouthe in her doctryne, for trouthe louyth no
corneris. And Ierome seith þridly for þat þis figure is þe moste faire of
all figuris, for God made in þis figure all heuenly creaturis, wherfor it
bitokenyth þat clerkis schold haue beaute within her þouȝt and 180
withoute in her conuersacion. Ferthely for þis figure is þe moste
sympul of all figuris, for as Seint Austyn seith þer is no figure so
sympul for sche is but of oo lyne, the figure of the [cercle] is enclosid
all oonly in line, by the wiche is vndirstond that the clerk[is] schold
haue sympulnesse of a dowue, aftir þe autorite of Poule þat þay schold 185
be sympul as dowuys.

   154 to] L, of G, to *erased* `of´ H1   155 appostul] appostullis G   159 Ierarchie] *so*
changed to Iearchie H1, Iearchie G   160 þe schauyng] `t´he `s´hauyng H1   not] L,
no`o´n H1, in G   161 a] *subp.* H1   162 defformyte] defformyd G   171 eere]
here G, eere *changed to* here H1   to] *add* the G   here] `h´ere H1   172 hymself] hem
selfe H1   173 cercle] L, clerk GH1   177 schulde] L, schul GH1   trouthe¹]
drou`t´he G   183 of¹] *ins.* H1   lyne] life H1   cercle] L, clerk GH1   184 clerkis]
clerk G

Here endith the chayryng of Seint Petir, and nexte folwith
the lyf of Seint Math[ie] the Apostle, [Cap. .xliiij.]

Math[ie] þe appostul was sette in the place of Iudas, but we will furste
deuyse the natyuyte of þe traytour Iudas. It is radde in a storie, þough
it so be þat i[t] be apocrify, þat þer was a man in Ierusalem þat height
Ruben, and by anoþer name he was callid Symeon. He was of þe
5 kynrede of Iuda, and as by Ierome of the kynrede of Isakar, and þat
man hadde a wif þat hight Tiborea. And in a nyght as þay had leyne
togedris Tiberea fille asclepe and hadde a merveylous dreme wherof
sche was gretly affrayid and told it to hir husbond with grete sorowe in
this wise: 'Me dremyd that y brought forth a wikkid sone þat was
10 distruccion of alle oure pepul.' Thanne Ruben seide to hire: 'It is a
wikkid þyng and vnworthy to be spoke of, for y trowe þat þou were
raueschid with sume wikkid spirite.' And þanne seide sche: 'If so be
that y fele þat y haue conseyuyd and þat y bryng forth a sone,
withoute faile it is no wikkid spirite but a trewe reuelacion.'
15   And þanne þe tyme passyng forth sche brou3t forth a sone, wherof
the fadir and the modir were gretly trowblid and bygan to þenke what
þay mary might beste doo, and as þay dred to scle her child and also thay
w[old] not norissh þe distruccion of her owne kynrede, thay putte
hym in a litill bote and lete hym flete forth in the see, and þe wawis of
20 the watir ladde hym to the yle of Skariot, and of þat was he callid
Iudas Skariot. And þe quene of þat yle wiche hadde no child wente to
disporte h[ir] vpon þe ryuage of þe see and saw3 þis bote þat the
wawis of þe see drof vp and doun. Sche comaundid to loke what was
withynne, and þanne þay fonde within a litill child, and whanne sche
25 saw3 it sche seide sighyng sore: 'A, y schold be glad and y hadde a
child of so faire a forme as this is, I schold not þanne be priuyd oute
Gf.75ᵛ of | my rewme, but he schold succede aftir me.' And þanne sche made
to norissh the child priuyly and feynyd hirself to be with child, and
atte laste sche lyed and seide þat sche hadde brou3t forth the sone and
30 the renome hereof was puplischid þorugh þe rewme. And þe prince
hadde grete ioie for that ly[ngnye] þat he hadde and all his pepul were
gretly gladid, and þanne he was noreschid aftir þe noblesse roial. And

GDH2H1A2L; E resumes at 51 [*the*] *sone* (*his sone*), A1 at 113 *of;* D breaks off after 128
it; at 76 *moder* H1 inserts a passage from 43 Chair of Peter, 14 lines up f. 74ʳᵃ, to f. 75ʳᵃ l. 6.
Rubric Mathie] L, Matheu GH1   1 Mathie] L, Mathew GH1   3 it] L, I G, I't' H1
8 gretly] L, *add* merveylid and GH1   told] toke *changed to* told H1   9 dremyd] L, *add*
sche seide GH1   18 wold] will G   þe] *add* distroyid *del.* G   22 hir] hym G
31 lyngnye] L, lyuynge G, lying (?) nye H1

within a litill while aftir þe quene conseyuyd by þe kyng and brouȝt
forth a sone. And whanne the children weren growen in age thay were
euer chydyng and brawlyng togedre, and Iudas dide often tymys 35
wrongis to þe kyngis sone and made hym to wepe. And þanne þe
quene [that] knewe well þat Iudas perteynyd not to hire and [was]
wroth herwith and bete hym often tymys, but he lefte not þerfore to
doo harme to the child. And so atte laste it was knowen þat he was not
verrey sone to the quene, and whanne Iudas knewe it he was gretly 40
aschamyd and sclewe priuyly þe kyngis sone. And whanne he hadde
doon so he dradde gretly to be iugid to the deth and stale awey and
fledde into Ierusalem with þo men þat bere the trewe and putte
hymself into þe c[ourt]e of Pilate þat was þanne prouost. And for þat
þyngis likly ben sone mette and accordid, Pilate fonde Iudas 45
couenabul to his condicyonis, wherfor he hadde hym in grete cher
and Iudas was maister of all the c[ourt]e and all was rewlid aftir his
wille. It fille on a day þat Pilate bihilde oute of his paleis and sawȝ an
appul tre and hadde grete desire to ete of the frute þerof that he wiste
not what to doo. And þat same gardyn longid to Ruben the fadir of 50
Iudas, [but] þe fadir knewe not | [the] sone ne the sone the fader, for E f. 57ʳᵃ
Ruben wende that his sone hadde be drowned in the see, and Iudas
knewe [neither] his fader ne his contreye. And than Pilate called Iudas
and saide to him: 'I haue so gret desire to haue of [the] fruite of that
gardyne that I wote not what to do.' And thanne Iudas was meued and 55
anone went and lepte into the gardin and toke hastely of the appelis.
And in the mene tyme come Ruben and founde Iudas taking his
appeles, and they begonne gretly to striue togederes and to chide, and
after chiding thei begonne to fight and harmed eche other, and the
ende was [such] that Iudas smote Ruben withe a stone in the partie 60
wher the necke ioyned to þe [hede] and slowe hym. And thanne
he bare the appeles forthe withe hym and tolde to Pilate as it was
falle hym.

And whanne the day was gone ande night come Ruben was founde
dede in his gardyn, and it was none otherwise knowen but that he 65
hadde deied sodeinly. And thanne Pilate gaue al the good of Ruben to
Iudas and Tibore his moder to his wiff. In a daye as Tiborea sighed
sore Iudas asked her diligentely the cause of her sighing. She ansuered

37 that] L, *om.* GHɪ   was] L, and G, and was Hɪ   38 bete] bite G   43 trewe]
trewage G   44 courte] cuntre G   46 cher] cherste G, cherʻteʼ Hɪ (*cher* P2)
47 courte] L, cuntre G, court *changed to* contre *with* ʻtreʼ *repeated above* Hɪ   50 longid]
longeth Hɪ   51 but] L, for GHɪ   theʼ] his E   53 neither] L, neuer EHɪG
54 the] that E   60 such] L, this EHɪG   61 hede] L, ende EHɪG

and saide: 'Allas, I am [the] most vnhappi woman of all women, for I
70 haue drowned myn owne [childe] in the waues of the see, and nowe I
haue founde myn husbonde dede, and Pilate hathe added sor[ugh]
vpon sorugh of me most cursed and most wreched that hathe ayeinst
my wille coupeled me to the by mariage.' And whan sche hadde tolde
alle her auenture and Iudas hadde tolde her [ayein] of his findyng, it
75 was founde that Iudas hadde slayne his fader and hadde wedded his
moder. And thanne he was stered to penaunce by the teching of his
f. 57rb moder | and went to oure Lorde Ihesu Crist and asked hym
foryeuenesse of his synnes. And vnto this it is redde [in] the forsaide
stori of apocrifum, but wheder it be to rede or none that leue I in the
80 will of the reder.

And thanne oure Lorde made hym his disciple, and fro his disciple
he chase hym to apostle and was so well beloued and familier with
hym that he made hym his proctour and bare the purs with money
and stale that was [yeuen] to God. And in the tyme of the passion of
85 oure Lorde he was sori that the oynement that was worthe thre
hundred pens hadde not be solde þat he myght haue stole of the pens,
and thanne he went and solde oure Lord for .xxx.^{ti} pens, of the whiche
eueri peni was worthe .x. pens of rennynge moneye, and so he
recouered the harme of the oynement that was worthe thre hundred
90 pens. Or ellis as sum sayne he stale awaye the tenthe parte of that þat
longed to Ihesu Crist, and for the tenthe parte of the oynement that he
hadde lost he sold oure Lorde for .xxx. pens, the whiche notwithestonding he, brought to hymselff bi penaunce, brought the pens ayen,
and thanne he went and hangged hymselff, and whanne he was
95 hangged he braste atwo and his boweles ranne oute. And the
mouthe was defended that there shulde nothing passe ther, for it
was not sitting that the mouthe shulde be so horribly defouled that
hadde so late touched so blessed and so holy a mouthe as the mouthe
of Crist. And also it was worthi that the entrayles that hadde
100 conceiued so foule a treson were brosten and shedden oute, and the
throte that the vois of treson went oute of were bounden withe a
f. 57va corde. And so | he deied in the eyre, for he that hadde wrethed the
aungels in heuene and the men in erthe were take awaie fro the region

69 the] *om.* E   70 childe] sone E   71 added] hadd'e' *with* h *erased* H1, hadde G
sorugh] so you E   74 alle] of H1G   ayein] *om.* E   78 in] to E, in *on erasure* H1
84 yeuen] L, ther Inne EH1G   85 thre] þ'r'e H1   89 recouered] keuered H1,
rekenyd G   90 sum] *add* men E   parte] peny G   96 ther for] therfor E
101 of¹] the E   of²] *om.* H1   102 that] *om.* H1

and the contre of angeles and of men, and he was sette in the eire withe fendes. 105

Whanne the aposteles weren togederes *in cenaculo* betwene the ascension and [the] Whitsonday, Seint Peter seighe that the noumbre of the .xij. aposteles was lassed of the whiche that oure Lorde hadde chosen in that nombre for to preche the faithe of the Trinite in the foure parties of the worlde. He rose up in the myddes of his bretheren 110 and saide: 'We most ordeine another in stede of Iudas that may witnesse withe vs the resurreccion of Ihesu Crist, for oure Lorde saide to us: "Ye shull be witnesse of me in Ierusalem and in al [Iu]de and Samary and into the ende of the world." And for as moche as none may bere witnesse but tho that haue seine it, one of these men that 115 haue bene with us alwayes and hau[e] seen the myracles of oure Lorde and herde his doctrine most be chosen.' And thanne thei ordeyned tweyne of [the] .lxxij. disciples, of the whiche that one was Ioseph that was surnamed Iustice for his holinesse, he was brother to Iames Alphees, and Mathi of whos preysing I stinte as nowe, for it suffisithe 120 hym for a preysing to be chosen apostel. And thanne they went to her prayers and saide: 'Lord that knowest the hertes of men, schewe vs whiche thou hast chosen of these two men that shal take þe place of this misterye of apostell the whiche Iudas loste.' And thanne they yaue hem lottes and the lotte fille vpon Mathie, and thanne he was 125 sette withe the [.xj.] aposteles. | And as Seint Ierom saiethe, it sittithe f. 57ᵛᵇ not us by this ensaumple to vse lottes or sortes, for the priuilage of fewe men makithe no comon lawe. Bede saieth also that it was sitting to kepe the figure into tyme that the trouthe come, for the verrey sacrifice was sacrificed in the passion, but it was fulfelled atte 130 Whitsontyde, and therfor vsed thei sorte in the eleccion of Mathye that they vncorded not in the lawe in the whiche the souerein preste was chosen by sorte. [But] after Whitsontyde that the trouthe was fulfelled thei made .vij. dekenes not by sorte but be eleccion of the disciples by praier, and by leying of the aposteles hondes vpon hem 135 they were ordeyned. Of these sortes that they maden saiethe Seint Ierom and Bede that they were suche as they vsed in the olde lawe of whiche men vsed ofte. And Seint Denys saiethe, [the] disciple of Seint Paule, that it was an inordinat thing to thenke or wene that was

104 contre] courte H1   106 the¹] *om.* E   112 vs] 'vs' H1   113 Iude] ynde E 116 haue²] hau E   118 the¹] L, *om.* EH1G   120 stinte] studie H1   123 hast chosen] shalt shesen H1   124 of] *add* the G   apostell] aposteles H1   126 .xj.] L, .xij. EH1G   127 us] *om.* H1   132 vncorded] encordid G   133 But] L, And EH1G   138 the] L, that E, that the H1G   139 that²] þat that G

140 sorte, and he saiethe that it semythe hym that the sorte was nothing
elles but a beme and a devyne shyning fro heuene that was sent vpon
Mathie by the whiche it was shewed that he shulde be take vnto
apostell, and this saiethe he in the boke of the Ierarchie Ecclesiastice.
And of the sorte that fell dyuynely vpon Mathye some other sayne in
145 other manere and not relygiously, as I deme I shall saye her intencion
and myn, for it semith me that for to name this worde sorte
thearticum, whiche is shewyng of a maner yefte.

Mathye receyuyng [this] yefte of God was receyued in the felawship of the aposteles, and this Mathye toke in sorte the contre of
150 [Iude] and ther was in predicacion as apostell and dede many
f. 58ʳᵃ myracles | and rest in pees. And it is redde in many places that he
suffered the gebette of the crosse and that he, crowned by suche
marterdome, stied up to heuene. And men sayn that his body is atte
Rome in a stone of marbre in the chirche of Seint Mari the More and
155 that his hede is shewed there to the peple. And in another legende it is
founde atte Treues.

And it is redde amonge other thingges that Mathie was born in
Bethelem of the noble lynage of Iuda. He was sette to scole and in
shorte tyme he toke al that connyng [of the] lawe and of the prophetes
160 and dredde vanitee and ouercome by good condiciones his childisshe
yeres. And his corage was taught to vertues, and þat he myght be the
more couenable to vnderstondyng he was lyghtly meued to misericorde, he was not lyffte up by prosperite but constant in aduersitee,
and witheoute drede. He enforced hym to fulfell by werke that he
165 conceyued by witte, and he shewed the doctrine of the mouthe bi the
werkes of the honde. And as he preched thorugh [Iu]de he enlumyned
the blynde, he clensed lepres, he chased oute fendes, he heled the halt
and the deef and gaue lyff to the dede. And whanne he was accused
before the bisshop he ansuered to many [o]biecciones that ye calle
170 crymes and saide: 'It apertenithe not to [saye] many thingges, for the
name to be cristen is no name of crime but a name of glorie.' To whom
the bisshop saide: 'Yef space of tyme be yeuen to the wilt thou repent
the?' And thanne he saide: 'God defende that I parte by apostasie fro
the trouthe that I haue [o]nes found.'

141 and] or G   142 by] *ins.* H1   143 the¹] this H1   148 this] the E
150 Iude] ynde E   apostell] apostlis G   153 marterdome] *add* he H1   159 of the¹]
L, *om.* EH1G   lawe] *om.* H1   164 EH1G *punctuate or capitalise to indicate new sentence
at* and   165 shewed] chosed H1   166 Iude] ynde E   169 obiecciones]
abiecciones E   170 saye] so E   172 to . . . thou] til þu wilt H1   173 defende]
'de'fende H1   174 ones] nes E

And Mathie was thanne right wise in the lawe, clene of body, wise 175
of | corage and sharpe in assoyling questiones of holy scripture, f. 58ʳᵇ
purueide of counsaile and not [lettyng] in his talkyng. And as he
preched in [Iu]de he conuerted moche peple bi sygnes and by
mervayles. And the Iues hadden enuye of hym and putte hym vp in
iugement, and two fals witnesse accused hym and dede caste many 180
stones ayeinst hym, and whanne they hadde stoned hym he was smete
withe an axe in the manere of Rome. And thanne, his hondes streched
up to heuene, he yelded up the sperit and required that the stones
were leyde withe hym in his sepulture in witnessing of [his]
marterdome. The body of hym was bore out of [Iu]de to Rome and 185
fro Rome it was translated to Treues.

It is redde in another legende that Mathie come into Masedoyn and
there he preched the faithe of Ihesu Crist. And thei gaue hym a drinke
medeled withe poison that shulde make blynde alle tho that dronke
therof, and he dranke in the name of Ihesu Crist and hadde none 190
harme therof, and ther hadde bene made blynde withe that drinke mo
thanne .CC.l., the whiche he touched withe his hondes and made hem
alle to see. Thanne the fende appered to hem in lyknesse of a childe
and bade hem to sle Mathie or elles he wolde destroye her lawe. And
as Mathie was among hem alle they sought hym thre dayes and coude 195
not find hym. The .iij.ᵉ day he appered to hem and sayde: 'I am he
that ye tormented the hondes behynde the backe and the rope aboute
the necke.' And thanne they putte hym in prison, and there the fendes
appered to hym and mowed vpon hym aferre | but they durst not f. 58ᵛᵃ
neigh hym, and thanne oure Lorde come to hym with gret lyght and 200
lefte hym vp from the erthe and vnbounde hym and comforted hym
suetely and opened the dore and lete hym oute of prison. And whanne
he was oute he preched the worde of oure Lorde, and whanne he
seighe that sum were harded in her malice he saide to hem: 'I
denounce you that ye shuld descende into helle quicke.' And anone 205
the erthe opened and swalowed hem, and the other were conuerted to
oure Lorde.

177 lettyng] lette E   178 Iude] ynde EG   184 his²] high E, his *changed to* hie Hɪ
185 Iude] ynde E   191 that] *om.* Hɪ   197 ye] *om.* Hɪ, þe G

Here endithe the liff of Seint Mathie the Apostell, and
nexst beginnith the lyff of Seint Gregori, Cap^m. .xlv.^m

Gregorie was of the kinrede of [the] senatoures of Rome. His fader
was called Gordien and his moder Siluia. And in his yougthe he
atteyned to the souerein hyghnesse of philosephie and gretly abundant
in richesse, but alwayes he thought to leue al that and putte hym to
5 religion, thenking that the ferther that he withedrawe hym fro his
owne contre so moche he shulde the more suerly serue God. And
thanne he serued the worlde .vij. yere in abite of a iuge, and thanne
beganne to falle to hym moche besinesse of the worlde so that he was
witheholde withe herte and mynde.
10   And in the ende whanne his fader was dede he made .vij. chirches
in Cecile and .vij. witheinne the walles of Rome in his propre heritage
in the worship of Seint Andrew the apostell, and one in whiche he
leffte the ornamentes shyninge of golde and of siluer and of selke and
clothed hymselff withe a vile habite of [a] monke. And ther come he
f. 58vb with|inne shorte tyme to so gret perfeccion of vertue that in the
16 beginnyng of his conuersion he myght be acounted in the nombre of
perfite men, the perfeccion of whom myght well be perceiued bi his
wordes that he putte upon the Dyaloge, wher he saiethe in this wise:
'O thou wreched soule putte fro thine ocupacion, rememberithe hym
20 by his wounde that he was somtyme in the monasterie, whanne alle
worldely thingges were putte vnder fote, how he shulde appere noble
in alle thingges that bene yeuen yef he hadde not acustumed to thenke
but in heuenly thyngges, for though that he were witheholde witheinne the body, yet he passed the cloyster of the fleshe [by]
25 contemplacion so ferforthe that the deth that wel ney is peyne
[to all] he loued as þe entre of lyff and guerdon of his trauaile.' And
atte the laste he tormented his body by suche distresse that he was so
seke in the stomake that vnnethe he myght defye any mete, [and] he
suffered diuerse tymes so gret anguishe that he was ofte nye dede.
30   In a tyme whanne he duelled in a chirche where that he was abbott
and wrote devine thingges, the aungell of oure Lorde come to hym in
gyse of a pore man and requered hym in weping that he wolde haue

EH1GH2A1A2L; D resumes at 40 *in*, breaks off again after 284 *thought*, and resumes at
411 *diuynely*; H1 breaks off after 168 *hast* and resumes at 327 *blode*; E breaks off after 527
chirches   Where [*pope*] is printed, it has been over-written in E by *bushop*.   1 the²] *om.* E
4 that] *om.* G   14 a²] *om.* E   21 noble] *om.* H1   24 by] L, in EH1G
25 wel ney is] wolney his H1   26 to all] L, *om.* EH1G   28 and] L, *om.* EH1G
29 suffered] *add* 'of' H1   tymes] metes H1

pitee of hym. He made yeue hym .vj. pens of siluer, and thanne he
went his way, and come ayein the same day and saide that he hadde
moche loste and litell receyued. And thanne he made yeue hym as 35
moche as he dede before, and yet he come ayen the thridde tyme and
beganne to crie sorer thanne he dede before that he wolde haue pitee
of hym. But whanne Gregori herde of the procutour of the chirche
that he hadde no more to yeue but one dische | of siluer that his moder f. 59ra
hadde lefte hym in whiche she was wont to sende hym potage, he 40
comaunded anone she were yeue to the pore man, and he toke it gladly
and went hys waye. And as he re[uel]ed it after it was an aungel of
oure Lordes

In a day Seint Gregorie went by the market of the citee of Rome,
and as he went he seighe children of ryght a fayre forme, of faire 45
visages and shyning here, fulfelled withe passing beauute. And thanne
he asked of the marchauntes of what contrey they were that were
brought to sell. They saide that they were of the Grete Bretayne,
'wherof all tho that bene there duellyng bene of like beauutee.' And
thanne he asked hem yef thei were cristen, and thanne the march- 50
auntes saide: 'Nay, but they be holden and bounden in the errour of
paynymes.' And thanne Gregori cried and wailled sorifully and saide:
'Allas, what sorugh that the prince of derkenesse shuld haue
possession of so faire a peple.' And thanne Gregori asked how that
peple were named, and the marchauntes said in Latin: '*Anglici* thei 55
bene called,' that is as moche to saye as Englysche men. And thanne
Gregori saide: 'They mowe well be called *Anglici* right as aungeles, for
they hauc visages lyk aungeles.' And thanne he asked hem of what
province, and they saide: 'Of Irlonde.' And thanne Gregorie saide:
'They may well be of Irische, for it is sittyng that the ire of God be 60
take awaye from hem.' And he asked of the name of her king, and the
marchauntes saide that he hight Alle. And thanne Gregorie saide: 'He
is well called Alle, for it behouithe to synge in his contrey "Alleluya".'
Than anone Gregorie went to the [pope] and asked of hym withe gret
instaunce that he myght be sent for to conuerte | hem of Inglond. And f. 59rb
as he hadde take the waye the Romaynes were gretly displesed of his 66
goyng, and went to the [pope] and saide to hym in this wise: 'Holy

33 .vj.] .vij. H1   35 thanne] *om.* G   yeue] 'ʒeue þat' *with* þat *del.* H1   41 she]
subp. 'it' H1   42 he reueled it] it was reuelid G   reueled] releued E   44 of¹] in G,
of *changed to* in H1   47–8 that were . . . they were] 'they seid' H1   51 be holden]
beholden E   53 that] *ins.* H1   57 They] the *changed to* thi H1   58 haue] hadde G
60 Irische] Irissh *on erasure* H1   ire] tre *changed to* Ire H1, tre G   61 name] *on erasure*
H1   65 conuerte] ouere come H1

fader, thou haste wrethed Seint Peter, for thou haste destroied Rome
that haste suffered Gregorie goo from hennes.' And thanne the [pope]
70 hadde drede and sent anone for to repele Gregorie by messengers.
And Gregorie hadde tho gone thre iorneyes, and whiles other rested
he turned hym into a privi place for to rede, and thanne ther come
vpon hym *locusta*, that is a maner grassope, and lette hym to rede. And
thanne by the exposicion of his name that is saide '*Locusta*', that is to
75 saye 'stonde in one place', she taught hym that he shulde cese
ther witheoute passyng forthe. And thanne as by sperit [of] prophecie
he stered his felawes to go anone, but or they myght remwe the
messangers of the [pope] come vpon hem, and though it were so
that he were full hevy therof he was constreyned to turne ayen. And
80 thanne the [pope] toke hym from his chirche and ordeyned hym his
diaken cardinall.

In that tyme the riue[r] of Tymbre went oute of his cours and
encresed so moch that he ranne aboue the walles of the citee of Rome
and dede caste downe many houses. And in the myddes of that flode
85 there descended into the see a gret dragon withe gret multitude of
serpentes, but whanne thei were drowned the see caste hem vp so that
the corrupte eyre beganne to stinke of hem, wherfor ther come a gret
pestilence so that men sawen openly arues come fro heuene and men
seen how thei smote many and whom the[i] luste. And the furste of
f. 59ᵛᵃ alle was the [pope] Pelagien and slowe | hym witheoute any tarienge,
91 and after that it descended so into [the] other comune peple and there
were gret multitude dede of tho that duelled in the citee.

But for as moche as the Chirch of God myght not stonde witheoute
a gouernour alle the peple chase Gregorie to [pope], though it were so
95 that he refused it withe al his herte and powere. And whanne he
shulde be blessed and that corrupcion destroied, he made a sermon to
the peple and ordeyned processiones and letanyes and taught hem alle
that they shuld praie to God more ent[ent]iffly. And as alle the peple
were assembeled and praied to oure Lorde, that corrupcion waxe so
100 madde that in one houre she slow .iiijˣˣ. men, but for al that he lefte
not to exorte the puple for to praie into tyme that the devyne party
shulde chase awaye that pestilence.

71 gone thre] goten ther *with* t *in* goten *del.* Hɪ   75 she] she *with* s *erased* Hɪ
76 ther] therewith Hɪ   ther witheoute] therwithe oute E   of] L, in EHɪG   78 hem]
him Hɪ   79 that he were] *om.* Hɪ   82 tyme] *ins.* Hɪ   riuer] L, Riues EG, Reyne`r´s
or Reyue`r´s Hɪ   Tymbre] *so with* m *subp.* Hɪ, Tybre G   83 he] it G   aboue] abought
Hɪ, ouer G   85 there] that *on erasure* Hɪ   88 arues] *so with* w *over* u Hɪ
89 thei] the E   91 the] *om.* E   98 ententiffly] entiffly E, `r´entifly Hɪ

And whan the procession was done he wolde haue fledde awaye,
but he myght not, for men kepte nyght and day the gates of the citee
and woke for the same cause. And atte the laste he chaunged his habite 105
and praied som marchauntes that he myght be caried priuely in a
tonne and leyde in a carte and so priuely caried oute of the citee. He
fledde into forestes and sought priue places and caves, and there he
was thre dayes and thre nyghtes. And as the peple sought hym
curiously, a leme of fire descended from heuene vpon the place where 110
he hidde hym, and a religious persone seighe the aungell descendyng
and styeng vp by that leme, and thanne he was take of alle that peple
and was brought ayein and made souerain bisshop.

And alway he styed up to that hynesse of worship ayeinst his wylle,
and tho that reden his wordes mowe | perceyue it clerely, for he f. 59ᵛᵇ
saiethe [thus] in his apistell Anarace [patricien]: 'Whanne ye writte to 116
me,' he saiethe, 'of my contemplacion, ye renue to me my ruyne, for I
haue herde that I haue loste withinne me whanne I stied vp outewarde
to the cure of this gouernement witheoute my desert. And wetithe
well that I am so dewed with teres of sorugh that I may vnnethe speke. 120
And therfor calle me no more faire but bitter, for I am [alle] full of
bitternesse.' And also he saiethe in other places: 'Ye knowen and
writen that I am comen to the order of apostel. Yef ye loue me
wepithe, for I wepe witheoute cessing, and I praie you that ye praie to
God for me.' And he saiethe in a prologe vpon his Dyologe: 'By the 125
occasion of pasturell cure my corage sufferithe the nedes of seculer
men and is defouled withe the pouder of erthely dedes or werkes after
the faire forme of her reste. Whan I beholde what I haue loste, that I
bere is more greuous to me, and I am now thrawen in the gret flodes of
the see and the shippe of my thought is blowen withe the wyndes of 130
stronge tempest. And whanne I remembre me of the furst lyff and
retorne myn eyghen bacwarde and whanne I see the riuage, I sighe.'

But for that the pestelence was atte Rome yet as she was before, he
made processiones thorugh the citee in the manere as he hadde
custumed and aboute the towne withe teres and wepingges and in a 135
tyme of Ester. And as sum sayen an ymage of the blessed Virgine
Marie was atte Rome, the whiche they sayen that Seint Luke the
apostell that was a peintour and [a] noble phisician hadde made, the

107 He] She *with* s *erased* H1   108 priue] priuely EH1   114 of] and H1
115 reden] dreden *with initial* d *erased* H1   116 thus] L, this EH1G   patricien] L,
Patrien EH1G   ye] he H1   writte] write H1G   117 ye] *changed to* he H1
121 alle] *om.* EG   128 faire] fire H1   132 sighe] seigh G   136 sum] *add* men E
137-8 the apostell] the euangeliste *on erasure* H1   138 a²] *om.* E

whiche ymage they sayen was right lyke to the blessed Virgyne Marie
f. 60ʳᵃ in alle thyngges, and | Seint Gregorie made to bere that image
141 worshipfully before the procession. And thanne al the derkenesse
[and al] the trouble of the eyre went awaye and gaue place to the image
right as it fledde, and myght not endure the presence of the image,
and after the image [all clere]nesse and purete often tyme was. And
145 thanne as that [pope] saiethe, voises of aungeles weren herde singyng
and sayeng: 'Quene of heuene, be gladde, alleluya, for he that thou
des[erued]est to bere, alleluya, is arisen like as he saide, alleluya.' And
thanne Seint Gregori putte therto: 'Praie to God for us, we beseche
the, alleluya.' And anone Seint Gregorie seigh vpon the castell of
150 Cressent the aungell of oure Lorde that helde a blody suerde and
wiped it and putte it in his she[th]e, and therby he vnderstode that the
pestilence cesed. And thanne afterward alwayes that castell was called
the Castell of the Aungel. And thanne Gregorie after that, so as he
hadde alwayes in will and desire, sent Austin, Mellitum and Iohn and
155 some other into Englonde and conuerted hem by her praieres and by
her merites to the cristen faithe.

The blessed Gregorie was of so gret humilite that he wolde be
preised of none. For he wrote in this manere to Stephene the bisshop
that hadde preised hym in his lettres: 'Ye haue shewed to me
160 [vnworthi] moche more fauour thanne I am worthi to here by youre
letteres, for it is wreten: "Praise no man the whiles he leuithe." And
alwaies though I haue be vnworthi to here suche thingges, I beseche
you that I may be made worthi by youre praiers, so that yef ye haue
saide any goodnesse to be in me, that I may be by youre praiers that I
165 am not, thoughe ye haue saide soo.' And he saieth in a pistell to
f. 60ʳᵇ Narracien patricien | in this wise: '[Ye] fourme preisingges by the
clauses of youre scriptures in makyng similitude of my cause and of
my name. Siker, dere brother, thou hast called the ape lyon that in the
same manere we beholde us to haue done, for ofte tymes we haue
170 called the scabbes whelpe leopart or tygre.' And in a pistell to
Anastasium, patriarche of Antioche, he saiethe: 'Wherfor calle ye
me the mouthe of God, and ye saie that I am lyght that in speking may
profit and shyne to moche peple, I confesse to you that ye haue

140 to] two H1   142 and¹] L, of EH1G   al] *om.* E   143–4 and² . . . image]
om. G   144 all] L, and EH1G   clerenesse] L, clennesse EH1G   often] of H1
146 Quene] *so with* q *on erasure* H1   147 deseruedest] desirest E, deseruest H1
149 vpon] *om.* G   151 shethe] shede E   154 sent] seint *changed to* sent H1
159 Ye] Ґe′ H1   160 vnworthi] L, *om.* EH1G   166 Ye] L, the EH1G
167 clauses] causis G, chaunses H1

brought in gret drede my folisshe demynge. I considre what I am and
I finde in me nothing of these good signes, I considre what ye be and I 175
deme not that ye mowe lye. And whan I wolde leue that ye sayn, myn
infirmite withesaiethe it, and whan I wolde dispute that ye haue saide
in my preising, youre holinesse withsaiethe me.'
And verrily wordes that souned vantinge or vanyte he refused hem
in al wise. He wrote also to Eulogien, patriarke of Alisaundre, saieng: 180
'In the writinge of youre apistell ye haue olde peinted wordes of
proude cleping in callyng me pope vniuersall, wherfor I requere youre
holinesse that ye do so no more, for it is withedrawe us that is yeuen to
other. I wil no more thanne reson requerithe of wordes to be
enhaunsed but of maners, ne I [acounte] no worship in that I 185
knowe bretheren to lese her worship. Lat hem go than, suche
wordes that blowen by vanite and hurten charitee.' And for that
Iohn, bisshopp of Constantynople, wolde take to hym this name of
vanytee and hadde graunte of the senatoures to be called pope |
vniuersell, he wrote in this wise of that Iohn: 'What is he that ayeinst f. 60ᵛᵃ
the statutes of the gospell and ayeinst the decrees of the canons wille 191
take a nwe name? Wolde God he were verrely one true membre of the
Chirche that coueitithe to be called vniuersall.' Also he wolde not þat
his bretheren bisshopes shulde write to hym sayeng: 'Ye comaunded
me,' wherof he writethe in a pistell to Eulogiom bisshop of Alisaundre 195
in this wise, seyeng: 'Youre charitee hathe wrete to me seyinge: "As
[ye] comaunded", [whiche] wordes of comandement I praie you that
ye putte awaye fro me, for I knowe wel what I am and what ye be. In
open places ye be my brother[s] but in vertues ye be my fader[s].'
Also for souerein humilite that was in hym he wolde not that the 200
ladyes of Rome shulde calle hemselff in writing to hym his chamberers
or handemaydenes, wherfor he wrote to Rusticane the wiff of Patrice:
'I haue receiued in youre letteres one thing that displesith me, for that
thing the whiche myght haue be saide one tyme is rehersed to ofte,
that is "Youre seruaunt". I bi that charge that I haue receiued am 205
made seruaunt to alle. By what reson canne ye saye that ye be my
servaunt, and namely [ye] to whom I was properly sogette before that
y receiued this estate of bisshoppe? And therfor I requere you in the
name of almyghty God that ye sende no [more suche wordes] in youre
writynge.' He was the furste that named hymselff in his letteres 210

185 but] *om.* G   acounte] L, coueite EG   197 ye] L, he EG   whiche] L, withe EG
199 brothers] brother E   faders] fader E   207 ye] L, *om.* EG   209 more suche
wordes] L, wordes and namely suche EG

'Seruaunt of the servauntes of God' and ordeyned to calle all other in
the same wise.

f. 60vb　　And also whiles he lyued he wold | not publishe his bokes for verrey
mekenesse that was in hym, but saide that thei were nothinge worthe
215　in comparison of other. Wherfor he wrote to Innocent prouost of
Aufrike in suche wise: 'For that ye haue luste to sende to us for the
exposicion of Seint Iob we reioyse us in youre desire, but yef ye
coueyte to be made fatte in good pasture redithe the werkes of the
blessed Austine youre contreyeman and in comparison of his bulted
220　floure requerithe not oure brenne, for truly I wille not while I lyue in
this dedely prison yef I haue saide anything that it be lyghtly
publisched to the peple.'

It is redde sertainly in a boke translated oute of Greke into Latin
that an holy fader whiche hight Abbot Iohn went to Rome for to visite
225　the holy reliques and the corseintes of Seint Peter and Paule aposteles,
and whanne he was come thedyr the blessed Gregorie the pope went
thorugh the citee, and whanne this holy fader seigh hym he wolde
haue gone ayeinst hym to haue done hym reuerence as hym aught.
And whan the blessed Gregorie seigh that he wolde knele to hym he
230　kneled adoune furst and wolde neuer arise till the holy fader arose
furst, and in that it was gretly preised the humilyte of hym.

And he was so large in yeuyng almes that he minystred not only the
necessitees of hem that were present, but also to hem that were in the
mounte of Synay of monkes. He hadde wreten al the names of pore
235　folkes and susteyned hem frely. And he ordeyned a chirche in
f. 61ra　Ierusalem and founde the necessitees to the | servauntes of God
that were there, and he paied eueri yere .lxxx. li. of golde for the
dispens of euery day to thre thousand servauntes of God, and euery
day he wolde calle pilgrimes to his borde. And among whiche there
240　come in a tyme one that he wolde for humilite haue geue water to, and
as Gregori turned hym to [take] the euer, anone sodeinly he was gone
that he wolde haue yeue water to. And as he mervayled of this dede,
the same [nyght] folwyng oure Lorde saide to hym in a vision: 'Thou
hast other dayes receiued me in my membres, but this day yesterday
245　thou haste receiued me in myn owne selff.'

Another tyme he comaunded his chaunceller that he shuld bidde .xij.
pilgrimes to dyner. He dede his comaundement, and whanne thei were
sette to dynere the pope beheld and seigh .xiij., and thanne he called to
hym his chaunceller and asked hym whi he hadde sette .xiij. there ouer

241 take] L, goo to E, haue go to G　　243 nyght] *om.* E　　244 day] *add* and G

his comaundement. The chaunceller tolde hem and founde but .xij. 250
[and saide to hym: 'Fader, leue me welle, ther bene but .xij.'] And
thanne Gregori avised hym and seigh a propre man atte the dynere þat
chaunged his visage ofte, that now he semed a worshipfull auncien man
withe faire hore here, and anone ayein he semed yonge. And whanne the
dynere was done he ledde hym into his chaumbre and asked hym 255
diligentely what he was and what was his name, and he saide to hym:
'Whi askest thou my name that is mervailous? I am that pore shipman
that thou gauest the dische of siluer to the whiche that thi moder was
wont to sende the withe potage, and wete well that fro the day that þou
gauest me that dische oure Lorde ordeyned the to be bisshop of his 260
Chirche and successour of Peter the apos|tel.' Thanne Gregorie saide to f. 61rb
hym: 'How knowest thou that oure Lorde [hadde] ordeined me to be of
his Chirche?' And he saide: 'For I am an aungel of his and am sent hedir
to kepe the alwayes, and al thing that thou praiest of hym that thou
myghtest gete it by me.' And thanne he vanished awaye. 265
   In that tyme ther was an hermyte that was a man of gret vertue and
hadde forsake alle thing for the loue of God sauf a catte that he loued,
and somtyme amonge he wold holde hym in his lappe and playe with
hym. And this hermyte praied to God that he wolde vouchesauf to
shewe hym withe whom he shuld be heuenly guerdoned in the blisse 270
of heuene as he that nothinge posseded for the loue of hym, and than
it was shewed hym in a nyght that he shulde be guerdoned withe
Gregori the pope of Rome. And whan he herde this he sorughed
gretly, wenyng that his wilfull pouerte had lytell availed hym sethe he
shulde haue his guerdon withe hym that habounded so gretly in 275
wordely richesse. And as this hermyte made nyght and day collacion
by grete sighyng betwene Gregori is richesse and his pouertee, he
herde another nyght oure Lorde that saide to hym: 'The possession of
richesse makithe not a man only riche but only his coueitise. How
durst thou make comparison betwene the richesse of Gregori and thi 280
pouertee, sethe thou louest more thi catte that thou handelest and
strokest eueri day thanne he dothe alle the richesse that he hathe, for
he dispisethe hem and yeuith hem frely to eueri man.' And thanne
this hermyte yaue thankyngges to God and thought that his merite
hadd | bene wel ordeyned for yef he myght haue bene guerdoned f. 61va
withe Gregori, and beganne euery day to praie to God that he myght 286
deserue to haue his duellyng withe Gregori.

251 and . . . hym] *om.* G   and . . . xij.] *om.* E   260 his] þis G   262 hadde]
hathe E   270–2 in . . . guerdoned] *om.* G

As Gregori was falsly accused to the emperour Moris and to his
sones vpon the dethe of a bisshop, he saide in this wise in a lettre þat
290 he sent witheoute his name: 'O thyng is that thou shalt saie shortely to
oure lordes, that yef we the seruaunt of hem wolde haue entermeted of
the dethe and of the harme of Lombardes, the men of Lombardye
hadd not atte this day neither kyng ne duke ne erle and that hadde
bene to his confucion, but for I drede God I drede to medle of the
295 dethe of any creature.' Loo, how he was full of gret humilite, for ther
as he was souerain bisshop he called hymselff servaunt of the
emperour and called hym his lorde. And loke what innocens he was
of, for he wolde not consent to the dethe of his enemyes. So as Moris
persecuted Gregorie and the Chirche, he wrote in this wise among
300 other thingges: 'For that I Gregori am synfull, I beleue that in so
moche ye plese the more God that ye torment me gretly.'
    In a tyme a man clothed in the abite of a monke and helde a naked
suerde in his right honde and stode withe hardy chere ayeinst the
emperour and brandisshed his suerde on hym and tolde hym that he
305 shuld be dede. And thanne Moris was sore aferde and cesed to do
persecucion fro that tyme forwarde, and praied Seint Gregori that he
wolde praie for hym to oure Lorde that he wolde ponische hym in this
worlde of the misdedes that he hadde done and that he were not
f. 61ᵛᵇ ponished in the laste iuge|ment. In a tyme Moris seighe hymselff
310 brought into iugement before the iuge and that the iuge cried: 'Bryng
forth Moris.' And anone the ministres toke hym and brought hym
before the iuge, to whom the iuge saide: 'Wher wilt thou, Moris, that I
yelde the þe wicked dedes that thou hast done?' He ansuered: 'My
Lorde, here, and I beseche the spare me in the worlde to come.' And
315 anone the devyne vois comaunded that Moris and his wiff and his
children were deliuered to Foce, a knyght, for to be slayne. And so it
was done, and so Foce slowe hym and alle his meyni withe suerde, and
thanne he succeded after hym in the empire.
    As Seint Gregorie song [the] masse on Ester Day in þe chirche of
320 Oure Lady the Maior and he hadde saide: '*Pax Domini*,' the aungell of
oure Lorde withe high vois [ansuered]: '*Et cum spiritu tuo.*' And
therfor makithe the pope stacion on Ester Day to that chirche, and
whanne he saiethe '*Pax Domini*,' none ansuerithe hym in token of that
miracle.   Ther was in a tyme that Troyan the emperour hasted hym

291 we] *add* were G   seruaunt] seruauntis G   292 G *begins new sentence at* the men
299 wrote] wrou3t G   312 Wher] whether G   319 the] L, his EG
321 ansuered] L, saide EG

gretly to goo to [a] batayle, and a woman that was widow come 325
ayein[s]t hym weping and saide: 'My lorde, I beseche the that thou
vouchesauf to venge the blode of my sone that is slayn.' And Troyan
saide to her yef he torned ayein from the batayle hole and sound he
wolde revenge hym. Thanne saide the wedow: 'Who shall revenge
hym yef thou abide in the batayle?' And Troyan saide: 'He that shall 330
be emperour after me.' And thanne the wedue saide to hym: 'What
shall it profite þe yef another do me right?' And Troyen saide: 'Siker
nothing.' Thanne saide the wedue: 'Now were it not beter for you to
do me ryght and receyue merite for youre good dede thanne another |
dede it?' And thanne Troyan meued by pitee light downe of his horse f. 62ra
and venged the innocentes blode.   336

And men saien that so as the sone of Troyan rode thorugh the citee
of Rome to lustely and lete his horse renne to rechelesly, he slowe the
sone of a wedue, and whanne the wedue had tolde it to Troyan in gret
wepinge, he toke that sone that hadde done the dede to the wedue in 340
stede of her sone and gaue her gret lyuelode.

And in a tyme that Gregori went thorugh the market of Troyan he
bethought hym of the gret rightwisnesse and debonairte of that iuge,
[he] come to the chirche of Seint Peter and beganne to wepe for the
errour of hym right bitterly. And thanne he herde a devyne vois 345
saieng to hym: 'Lo, I haue saued Troyan fro euerlastinge payne, but
kepe the dilygentely fro hennes forward that thou praie for none that
is dampned.' Damacien tellithe in a sermon that Gregori praieng for
Troian herde a vois that saide to hym: 'I haue herde thi praier and
foryeuen Troian.'   350

And as he said that thinge alle the orient and occident beren
witnesse. And vpon this same some sayn that Troian was repeled
ayein to lyff and hadde grace for to deserue foryeuenesse, and so he
hadde euerlasting ioye and he was not fynably ordeined to be
dampned in helle by sentence diffinitif. And some other sayen that 355
the soule of Troian was not symply assoiled from euerlasting payne,
but his payne was suspended vnto the day of dome. And sum othe[r]
sayen that the peyne of his torment as to the place and to the maner
sumwhat taxed vnder a condicion, that was as longe as Gregori praied 359
for hym, so that bi the mercy | of God the place and the manere was f. 62rb

---

325 a¹] om. E   326 ayeinst] ayeint E   329–30 Thanne . . . hym] 'What' H1
330 yef] if changed to 'wher'of H1   saide] add to hir G   338 rechelesly] rechesly H1G
344 he] om. EH1G (il P2)   347 praie] p'ra'y on erasure H1   357 other] othe E
358 peyne] peynes E

sumwhat chaunged. And [o]ther, as Iohn Diaken that compiled this legende, saiethe that men fynden not that he praied but wepte, and God assoileth and hathe pitee ofte and foryeuithe that man [that] mekely desirithe and dar not aske. And he saiethe that the soule of
365 hym is not all deliuered oute of hell ne sette in paradys but symply deliuered fro the torment of hell, that is to wete that the saule that is in helle by the pitee of God felith not the torment that is in helle. Other sayen that euerlasting peyne is in two thingges, that is in sensible payne and in payne of harme, the whiche is for to be witheoute [the]
370 sight of Ihesu Crist. As to the furst the euerlasting peyne is withedrawe, as to the secounde she abideth and is withholde.

It is saide that the aungel of oure Lorde saide to Gregori thus: 'For thou hast praied for a dampned saule chese one of two thingges, either thou shalt be two dayes in purgatori, or elles all the dayes of thi lyff
375 thou shalt be laboured with continuel languoure[s] and siknesse.' The whiche chase rather to be al his lyff vexed withe sorugh and siknesse thanne for to be two dayes [tormented] in purgatorie. Wherfor it fell that he always sithe was either sike in the feuer, either tormented withe potagre, either that he was gretly greued withe other gret
380 sorughes and diseses, or tormented in the stomake mervelously, wherof he saiethe in a pistell: 'I am greued withe so gret potagre and withe so many gret and diuerse sorughes and diseses that my liff is to me right a greuous bataile, and almost I am ouercome euery day in
f. 62ᵛᵃ sorughe, and I | sighe in abyding the remedie of dethe.' And in
385 another place he saiethe: 'My sorughe is sum tyme to litell and som tyme to gret that she sleithe me. But she is made suche to me that I that am eueri day nye [dede am] putte oute fro dethe, and I am so infecte withe the drinke of this noyfull humour that the lyff is peinfull to me and I abide the dethe withe gret desire, the whiche I wene to be
390 remedie to my gret waylingges.

There was a woman that offered eueri [Son]day brede to the blessed Gregorie, and whanne he hadde songe his masse he offered to her the body of oure Lorde and saide: 'The bodi of oure Lorde Ihesu Crist kepe the to euerlastyng lyff.' And she by her gret folye smyled, and
395 Gregorie seing that withedroue his honde fro her mouthe and putte that partie of the oost vpon the auuter, and than he asked that lady

361 other] there EH1G (*les autres* P2)   362 not] *so with* t *on erasure* H1
363 that²] *om.* E   365 paradys] *add* ne H1   369 the²] *om.* E   370 peyne is]
peynes E   375 languoures] languoure E   376 chase] cause G   rather] *om.* H1
377 tormented] *om.* E   387 dede am] L, *om.* EH1G   391 Sonday] L, day EG, dai
'synghyng' H1   392-3 the . . . Lorde¹] '& seid' H1

before alle the peple how or by what cause she dorst laugh, and she
saide: 'For that thou callest the brede that I haue made with myn
owne honde the body of oure Lorde.' And thanne Gregori turned
hym to preier for the mysbeleue of this woman, and whanne he arose 400
he founde vpon the auuter that partye of the brede that he hadde leyde
as moche as a fynger conuerted into fleshe, and so this lady was
conuerted to the faithe. And thanne he praied ayein and founde that
partie of fleshe conuerted into brede, and thanne he toke [it] to [this]
lady to vse. 405

There were also sum princes that asked sum precious relyques of
hym, and he gaue hem a litell of the domatyk of Seint Iohn the
Euuangelist, the whiche they toke, and sithe they yelde hem ayein by |
gret despite. And the blessed Gregori asked a knyff and made his f. 62ᵛᵇ
praier and beganne to prik the clothe, and anone the blode come [of 410
the pointerie], and so it was diuynely shewed hou the reliques weren
precious.

In a tyme a riche man of Rome hadde lefte his wyff, and for that he
was depriued fro the communyalte of Rome bi the [pope], and he was
right sorie, but he myght in no wise eschewe the auctorite of the 415
[pope]. He requered helpe of the maistres of sorsery, and thei behyght
hym that they wolde by her charmes sende a fende to the horse that
the [pope] rode on that shulde torment hym so longe that the horse
and the maister shuld perische bothe. And as Gregorie was on a tyme
lyght on his horse þe enchauntours and the fende made the horse so 420
wode that no man myght hold hym. And thanne Gregorie by devine
reuelacion knewe that the fende had be sent and made the signe of the
crosse and deliuered the horse from this present wodenesse, and the
maistres of this malefice weren perpetually blynde. And thanne thei
knowlaged her synne and come to the grace of holy bapteme, and he 425
wolde not yelde hem her sight ayen lest they wolde haue turned ayein
to her cursed artes, but comaunded that they shulde be founde of the
chirche goodes.

It is redde in a boke that is called Lymo that the abbot that was of
that chirche denounsed to the [pope] Gregorie that there was a monke 430
in that place that hadde tresoure by hymselff, and the [pope] cursed
hym for to afraye the other monkes, and a litell while after that monke
deyed or Gregorie woste it. He was sori of that he was dede witheoute

397 she¹] he G   404 it] this E   this] the E   406 precious] add þyngis and G
407 hem] corrected from hym H₁   410 prik] on erasure H₁   410–11 of the pointerie]
L, on the point EH₁G   421 no man] none H₁G   424 malefice] malice H₁

f. 63ʳᵃ absolucion, | and thanne anone he wrote an orison in parchemyn in the
435 whiche he assoyled hym of the bonde of cursinge, and toke it one of
his dekenes and comanded hym that he shulde rede it vpon his graue.
He dede his comaundement, and the nyght foluyng he that was dede
appered to the abbot and shewed hym til that tyme he hadde be hold
in [stronge] prison, but yesterday he saide he was vnbounde.
440   Gregorie ordeyned the Office and s[o]nge of the Chirche and the
scole of singers, and for that he made two habitacles, one besides the
chirche of Seint Peter and another faste bi the chirche of Latran, and
ther yet atte this day is the bedde wher he laye whanne he ordeyned þe
songes and the preisyngges of God, the yerdes that he ma[na]ssed
445 withe the children, and the Antiphoner of songe, and there they be
holde [in] gret reuerence.
Whanne the blessed Gregorie hadd sitte in the sege of [pope] .xiij.
yere .vj. monthes and .x. dayes, he passid to oure Lorde full of high
vertues. And [these] vers [bene] wreten in his tombe: 'Suscipe terra tuo
450 corpus de corpore sumptum.' And this was in the yere of oure Lorde
.vjC. and .vj. yere vnde[r] Foce the emperour.
And after the dethe of Seint Gregorie a gret [famine] assailed alle
the contre, so that the pore peple that Gregorie was wont to fede frely
come to his successour and saide to hym: 'Goode lorde, thi
455 holy[n]esse graunte us that we perische not amonge us that were
wont to be fedde be oure holy fader Gregorie.' And the [pope]
ansuered hem in despite in suche wise: 'Thoughe Gregorie wolde
receyue all the peple for to haue souerayn preysing, we mowe not fede
f. 63ʳᵇ you.' And so he sent hem ayein alle voyde. And | thanne Seint Gregori
460 appered to hym thre tymes and blamed hym of that he was to
holdynge and to euel spekynge, and he wolde neuer amende hym
the rather. And thanne he apered to hym the ferthe tyme and
vndertoke hym and gaue hym a dedely stroke on the hede so that
he was contynuelly laboured with sorugh in the hede that he ended in
465 shorte tyme his lyff.
And as this [famine] lasted yet, sum envious byganne to talke euell
of Gregorie and saide that he hadde wasted the tresoure of the
Chirche as a wastour, and therfor thei stered other to brenne his

438 be hold] behold E   439 stronge] om. E   440 songe] sange E   443 day]
ins. above tyme subp. H1   444 manassed] massed E   446 in] withe E   449 these]
this EG   bene] is EG   450 yere] yeres E   451 vnder] vnde E   Foce the
emperour] trsp. and marked for correction H1   452 famine] L, hyngre EH1G
455 holynesse] holymesse E   463-4 so . . . hede] om. H1   466 famine] L, hungre
EH1G   468 stered] add eythir H1

bokes. And as they hadde brent some and wolde haue brent mo other,
Pers deken his famylier, withe whiche he hadde disputed of the foure 470
bokes of the Dialogis, saide right hastely that it myght not avayle for
to putte awaye the mynde of hym, for the ensaumples of hym were in
many diuerse parties of the worlde, and he saide that it was sacrilege
for to brenne suche and so many bokes of so noble a fader, vpon whos
[hede] he hadde sene full ofte the holy goste in lyknesse of a douue. 475
And in the ende he ledde hem to this sentence, that he wolde afferme
by his othe that he hadde saide of the douue, and as sone as he shuld
haue affermed it he shulde deye and they shulde stint for to brenne
the bokes, and but yef it be so yef he abode alyue after he graunted to
haue his hondes brent withe the bokes. And it is saide verrayly that 480
Seint Gregorie hadde saide hym before that as sone as he shulde
shewe the miracle of the douue he myght not lyue after. And thanne
the worshipfull deken | Pers come and brought the boke of the f. 63ᵛᵃ
gospelles withe hym and suore, and as sone as he hadde touched the
boke for to suere and had born witnesse of the holinesse of the blessed 485
Gregorie he was str[ange] and oute of sorugh of dethe and gaue vp the
sperit amonge the wordes of verray confession.

A monke of the chirche of Seint Gregorie assembled nyghe hym a
company of ribauudes, and the blessed Gregorie appered to another
monke and saide to hym: 'Tell that monke that he parte fro that foule 490
companye and do penaunce, for he shall deye witheinne foure dayes.'
And whanne þat other monke herde this thing he dradde hym gretly
and ded penaunce and putte oute that foule felawship, and anone he
was taken withe a feuer that from the morutyde on the .iij. day vnto
Tierce he putte oute the tonge by so grete hete so that it semed to all 495
other that seighe it that it hadde bene his laste sigh. And whanne the
monkes in the laste ende said before hym her psalmes they beganne to
saie euell of hym, and he that was dede quykened anone and opened
the eyghen and smyled and saide: 'Oure Lorde foryeue you, my
bretheren. Whi saie ye euel of me? Ye haue lette me gretly, for I haue 500
be as gretly accused of you as of the fende, and I wost not to whos
malice I myght ansuer furst. But, goode bretheren, whanne ye see in
any tyme any that shall passe oute of [the] worlde, saiethe none euel
but haue compassion and praiethe [for hym] as for hym that gothe

475 hede] L, *om.* EG, 'schulder' H1   476 this] his H1   477 douue] do'u've H1
477–8 by . . . affermed] *twice* H1   479 and . . . so] *twice* E   486 strange] strong E
487 of] and H1   493 felawship] felashipp *with* s *on erasure* H1   496 sigh] sight
H1G   503 the] this E   504 for hym¹] *om.* E, for *del.* H1   as for hym] *om.* G

f. 63vb withe | his accusour to so streite a iugement. For I haue bene in
iugement withe the fende, but by the helpe of Seint Gregorie I haue al
wel ansuered to his abiecciones, and I am but only ouercome withe
one abieccion, for whiche I wexe rede and am thus trauailed as ye see
and yet I may not be deliuered.' And whanne the bretheren asked hym
510 wherfor it was, he saide: 'I dar not saye, for whanne Seint Gregorie
comaunded me for to come to you, the fende compleyned hym gretly
and wende that I shulde turne ayein to do penaunce that God myght
foryeue me, for whiche thinge I haue yeue plege the blessed Gregorie
that I shall not shewe that thinge to none.' And anone therwithe in
515 crienge he saide: 'O Andrewe, Andrewe, thou shalt perishe in this
yere that by thi wicked counsaile haste putte me in perile.' And anone
he turned horribly the eyghen and deyed. Ther was a man in that citee
that hight Andrewe, that in the same moment that the monke praied
þat he shulde perische whanne he deyed he fell in so gret languoure of
520 greuous siknes that his flesshe fell from hym al roted, and yet he
myght not deye for no peyne that he susteyned. And thanne he made
assemble the monkes of Seint Gregorie ys chirche, and thanne he
confessed to hem that he withe the forsaide monke hadde stole sum of
her charteres and solde hem to other strangers for hyre, and this saide
525 anone he deyed in the wordes of [his] confession.

In that same tyme, so as it is redde in the lyff of Seint [Eugene] that
G f. 84^v in that tyme men helde more in chirches | þe Office of Seint Ambrose
þanne þe Office of Seint Gregory, so þat þe pope of Rome assemblid
the Counsel in wiche he ordeynyd þat þe Office of Gregory schold be
530 vnyuersely kepte, of wiche thyng Charlys þe kyng was executour, so
þat whanne he wente by sume prouyncis he constreynyd all þe clerkis
by manacis and by turmentis and brente all þe bokis of the Office of
Seint Ambrose and put in prison meny rebel clerkis. And þanne þe
blessid Ewgeny bisshop wente to þe Counsel and fonde þat þay were
535 departid .iij. dayis tofore, and alwey he [gouerned] þe pope so by his
wisdome þat all þe prelatis þat hadde be at þe Counsel þat were partid
.iij. dayis bifore he repelid hem aȝen. And whanne þis Counsel was
assemblid togedre, oo sentence was ordeynyd of all þe bisshopis, þat
þe messale of Gregory and þe messale of Ambrose were sette vpon þe
540 awter of Seint Petir þe appostul, and all þe ȝatis of þe chirche were
wel closid and schette and enseallid with þe seallis of meny bisshopis

507 wel] *om.* H1   524 saide] *add* he deied H1   525 his] this E, *om.* H1
526 Eugene] L, Gregorie EH1G   527–8 Ambrose . . . Seint] *om.* H1   528 Gregory]
del. with Ambrose *ins.* H1   535 gouerned] L, grauntid GH1   540 all] at H1

diligently, and þat þay pray all ny3t so þat oure Lord by sume token schewe hem wiche [he] wille be more [holde] of auctorite in the Chirche. And so it was doon as he hadde ordeynyd, and in the morowe þay openyd the 3atis of the chirche and fonde bothe messe 545 bokis [open] vpon the awter. And as sume seyn, þe messe boke of Seint Gregori was all [vnbounde] and disparkelid abrode on þe awter and þe messe boke of Seint Ambrose was oonly open in þe same place where it was leide, by wiche tokenys þay were dyuynely tau3t þat þe Office of Gregory schold be schadde þoru3 all þe world and þat of 550 Ambrose schold oonly be kepte in his owne chirche, and þe holy fadris ordeynyd it as þay were tau3t by God.

Iohn the deken tellith, he þat compilid þe lif of Seint Gregory, þat whanne he wrote the lif of hym a man in habite of [a] prest come to hym sclepyng, and as hym thought he was bifore hym writyng at a 555 lanterne and was clothid aboue with [a ri3t] white and so smalle and fyne cloth that þoru3 þe þin[n]es of þe ouer cloth men my3t see the colour of the nether cloth. He wente alwey nerre and nerre and my3t not kepe hym fro lawghyng, and whanne Iohn askid hym why þat he þat was a man of so nobul an office schold lawgh, and he seide: 'For 560 þou writist of the dede þe wich þou sey neuer alyue.' And Iohn seide hym: 'þou3 y saw3 hym neuer in þe | visage, 3it y write of hym þat y G f. 85ʳ haue knowe by redyng.' And þanne he seide to hym: 'þou doste as þou wilte, and y wille doo that y may.' And anoon he quenchid his lanterne and come so faste to hym ward þat he cryid so faste þat he 565 wente he schold haue smyte hym þoru3 with a swerd. And anoon Seint Gregory come thidir, and Seint Nicholas bere hym felaschip in the ri3t side and Piers deken in the lifte side, and seide to hym: 'O þou man of litill faith, why dredist þou?' And þat enemy hidde hym vndir þe curteyn of þe bedde. Thanne Gregory toke of þe hond of Piers a 570 grete brond of fire þat he hadde and bygan to broyle the visage and þe mouth of þat aduersarie and made hym as black as an Ethiope, a man of Ynde. And þanne a sparkle of þe brond fill vpon þe white cloth and brente it all, and þanne he apperid all black, and Piers seide to blessid Gregory: 'We haue made hym blac ynow3.' And Gregory answerid: 575

543 he] L, *om.* GHı   holde] L, *om.* GHı   546 open] *om.* G   547 vnbounde] L, oon hand G, on hande Hı   disparkelid] displed Hı   550 schadde] shewed Hı 554 a²] *om.* G   555 thought] semed Hı   556 a ri3t] *trs.* G   557 thinnes] L, þyngis GHı   ouer] *add* the Hı   561 þou] thow *with* ow *on erasure* Hı   sey] segh Hı seide] *add* 'to' Hı   564 anoon] *om.* Hı   565–6 so² . . . haue] *om.* Hı 566 þoru3] *add* oute G   569 litill] lyght Hı   570 Thanne . . . hond] *om.* Hı 572 hym] *om.* Hı   573 sparkle] spark Hı

'We haue not made hym blak, but we haue schewid þat he is blak.'
And þanne þay lefte her grete liȝt and wente her wey.

Here endith þe liff of Seint Gregory, and nexte folwith þe
liff of [Seint] Longius, [Cap. .xlvj.]

Longius was oon of þe knyghtis þat was with oþer at þe crucyfying of
oure Lord, and by þe comaundement of Pilate he perschid the side of
oure Lord with his spere, and whanne he sawȝ the signys and tokenys
þat were in the deying of hym, as þe derkyng of the sune, the
5 tr[em]blyng of þe erthe, he leuyd in oure Lord. And for þat, namely
þat as sume seyen þat his eyen were trowblid by siknesse eythir by
age, he toke by cas of auenture of þe blode of Ihesu Crist that ranne
doun by his spere and towchid his eyen, and anoon he sawȝ clerly.
And [þanne] he renounsid þe knyȝthode, and by the ordynaunce of
10 the appostlis he was in Cesar in Capadoce .xxviij. ȝere and leuyd the
lif of a monke, and myche pepul he turnyd to Ihesu Crist as wel by
word as by ensample. And whanne he was taken of þe prouost of þat
cuntre and he wold not sacrifie, þanne þe prouost comaundid þat all
his tethe schold be rasid oute of his hede and his tvnge kutte of, but he
15 loste neuer his speche for all þat, but toke an axe and braste doun all
þe ydollis and seide: 'If þay be goddis we schul see.' And þe fendis þat
wente oute of þe ydollis entrid into the prouost and within his felawis,
and þay al torente hemself as madde men and knelid doun to Longius.
And þanne he seide to the fendis: 'Why dwelle ȝe so in the ydollis?'
G f. 85ᵛ And þay answerid: 'For þere | as Ihesu Crist is not namyd ne his signe
21 is not, there is oure habitacion.'
And whanne þe prouost was made and hadde lost his siȝt Longius
seide to hym: 'Wite it wel þat þou mayste not be hole into þe tyme þat
þou haue sclayn me, and as sone as y am dede y schal pray for the and
25 gete the hele of body and soule.' And anoon he comaundid þat
Longius were bihedid, and þanne þe prouost wente to þe body of hym
and knelid doun wepyng and dide penaunce, and anoon he resseyuyd
his siȝt and endid his lif in good werkis.

576 he] *ins. H1*   577 wente] yede H1

GDH2H1A1A2L   *Rubric* Seint²] L, *om.* GH1   5 tremblyng] trowblyng G
erthe] eyre *del.* erthe G   6 þat¹] *om.* H1   9 þanne] L, anoon GH1   18 torente]
rent H1   hemself] him *changed to* hem H1   20 namyd] naylid *del.* namyd G
23 þou . . . þat] ʿwhanʾ H1   25 hele] L, helpe GH1

Here endith þe liff of [Seint] Longius, and nexte bygynnyth
the lif of Seint Benet, [Cap. .xlvij.]

Benet was born of the prouynce of [Nur]sie, and whanne he was sette
by his frendis to þe studye of liberal science at Rome, he lefte fro his
childhode his lernyng and wente to deserte, and his norice þat louyd
hym tendirly folowyd hym vnto a place þat is callid Alphide. And
þere sche borwid a syve for to klense whete in, but sche putte it 5
rechelesly vpon a borde and it fill doun and braste. And þanne the
norice wepte and whanne he saw3 hir wepe he wente and prayid, and
whanne he aroos fro prayer sche fonde it all hole.

Aftir þat he fledde | priuely fro his norise and come into a place E f. 64ra
wher he was thre yere withoute knowing of any man but of one 10
Romayn that was a monke, whiche mynistred to hym ententifly. And
for that the waye was longe fro Romaynes chirche vnto the pitte wer
Benet was, he knette a lofe in a longe corde and so he vsed to putte it
doune to hym. And also he [hadde] teied to the corde a litell belle that
the servaunt of God myght here whanne the Romaine brought hym 15
his brede. But the olde enemye the fende hadde enuye of þe charitee
of that one and of the refeccion of that other; he caste a stone and
braste the belle, but notwithestonding Romayn lefte neuer for þat to
ministre to hym. After that oure Lorde apered to a preste in vision þat
ordeined his mete in an Ester Day and saide to hym: 'Thou ordeynest 20
delites for the, and my servaunt is tormented withe hungre in suche a
place.' And thanne he rose anone and fonde the place withe gret payne
and labourc, and thanne he saide to Benet: 'Arise and lete us ete
togedre, for it is Ester Day.' To whom Benet saide: 'I wote well that it
is the Pasch of oure Lorde in that I haue deserued to see you that am 25
putte so fer from men.' But yet he wost not that it was the solempnite
of Ester Day. To whom the preste saide: 'Verrily this is the fest of the
resurreccion of oure Lorde, wherfor I am sent to the for thou shuldest
take the refeccion.' And thanne they blesse[d] oure Lorde and toke
her mete. 30

As Seint Benet tellithe that on a daye ther come a black bridde that
is called in Latin *merula*, and this bridde flewe so bisily aboute his

GDH2H1A1A2L; E resumes at 9 *priuely*; D breaks off after 49 *streitely*, resumes at 168 *he*,
and breaks off again after 287 *her*   *Rubric* Seint¹] *om.* GH1   1 Nursie] Musie G, Mircie
H1   5 syve] *on erasure* H1   6 doun] *om.* H1   8 sche] he *changed to* sche H1
9 Aftir] *on erasure* H1   14 hadde] L, *om.* EH1G   15 whanne] L, *add* the EH1G
17 other] *add* 'and' H1   18 notwithestonding] L, *add* the EH1G   19 in] *add* 'a' H1, *add*
a G   22 anone] *om.* G   29 blessed] blesse E   32 flewe] fleeth H1

f. 64rb visage that he myght haue take | hym, but anone he made the signe of
the crosse upon hym and the bridde fledde awaye. And thanne anone

35 the fende brought before hym a woman that he hadde sene sum tyme
before and enflaumed [so] his corage in her beauute that almost he
hadde purposed to haue lefte the desert. But anone by the grace and
goodnesse of almyghti God he come to hymselff, and whanne he
perceiued his errour he wailed and sorued and dispoiled hymself and

40 threw his body among the breres and thornes, and ther he turned his
naked bodi to and fro til he was al towounded, and thus the woundes
of þe fleshe dede awaye the woundes of the mynde. And after this
tyme ther growed neuer temptacion in his body.

The renome of this holi man encresed so gretly that whan the abbot

45 of the monasteri was dede alle the colage of bretheren come to hym
and requered hym to be thaire fader and thaire gouernour. He longe
werned hem and denyed hem, saieng that he coude not acorde withe
thaire maners, but atte the laste he was ouercome and consented to
hem. And as he constreined hem to kepe more streitely her rule, thei

50 repented and reproued hemselff that they hadde chosen hym to her
gouernour by the strengthe of whom her crokednesse most be brought
to the rule of rightwisnesse. And whanne thei seighe and felte that
vncustumed thingges n[oy]ed hem and that he made hem leue her
olde custumes, they maliciously medled venom withe his wyne and

55 offered hym to drinke. But Seint Benet made the signe of the crosse |
f. 64va ouer it and anone the verre that the venom was inne braste in peces as
it hadde bene caste withe a stone. And thanne he vnderstode wel that
it was a drinke of dethe that the signe of lif hadde destroied, wherfor
he rose anone and saide pesibly: 'Bretheren, God foryeue [it] you, for

60 I tolde you wel before that myn condiciones were not couenable to
youres.'

And thanne he parted from hem and went into a place wher he
duelled allone, and there he encresed me[r]vaylously in graces and
vertues, and that was shewed by mervailous signes so that moche

65 peple come to hym, and thanne he ordeyned .xij. monasteries. And in
one of these chirches ther was a monke that myght not abide longe in
praier, but the whiles other were in praier he wolde anone go oute and
do sum wordely ocupacion. And whanne the abbot of that place hadde

34 fledde] flyȝ G　　　36 so] to EHı　　　41 to] two Hı　　　42 þe] his G　　þe . . . of]
so ins. with his for þe Hı　　the²] his on erasure Hı, his G　　　53 noyed] L, newed EG,
meued Hı　　　55 But] and Hı　　　56 verre that] ve`r´re `þat´ Hı　　verre . . . peces]
venym braste the verre to pecis þat it was ynne G　　　59 foryeue] forbede G　　it] om. EG
63 there] om. G　　mervaylously] mevaylously E　　　64 was] om. Hı

tolde it to Seint Benet, he went thedir on a day and thanne he seigh
how that right a blacke childe drewe oute [this] monke by the hemme 70
of his coule. And thanne he saide to the abbot of that chirch and to
Maure the monke: 'See ye not,' quod he, 'who it is that drawithe
hym?' Thei ansuered and saide: 'Nay.' Thanne saide Seint Benet: 'Go
we to orison that ye mowe see hym.' And whanne thei hadde praied
Maure the monke seigh hym, but not the abbot. And that same day 75
whan her praier was fulfelled Seint Benet founde th[is] monke oute,
and thanne he toke a sharpe rodde and smote hym for his blyndenesse,
and fro that day forward he abode stille and parted not fro orison. And
so the auncien enemy durst no more | take lordship of hym, but fledde f. 64ᵛᵇ
away from hym as though he hadde bene sore beten.   80
    As it is wretin, thre of these monasteries weren sette vpon roches on
a high hell where they drowe thaire water withe a gret laboure and
peyne, and as the bretheren hadde praied the seruaunt of God that he
wolde come and visite these chirches, and whanne he hadde graunted
hem, in a nyght he with a childe withe hym went vp into that 85
mountayn and ther he praied longe in a place, and whan he hadde
done he leyde there thre stones for a token. And whanne he was
turned ayein to his owne duelling place the bretheren come to hym for
that same cause, and thanne he said to hem: 'Gothe into the roche
wher ye shull finde thre stones leide and diggethe ther a litell, for oure 90
Lorde may wel yeue water from thennes.' Thei went thedir and
founde the roche al moyst and sueting, and anone thei made a place
caued withinne, and sodeinly thei sene it full of water, þe whiche
water aboundithe into this day so sufficiently [that she descendeth] fro
the hight of that helle vnto the fote of the hille.   95
    In a tyme it felle that as a man mowed doune the breres aboute the
place wher this holi man duelled, it fell so that the irne of his syth fille
away from the tree and fill doune into a right depe place, and as the
man made moche sorughe therfor Seint Benet toke the handell and
helde it ouer the place, and anone the sithe come to the handelle.   100
    A yonge [monke] that hight Placidas went oute for to fette water
and fell into the water and was born | forthe withe the water nye a f. 65ʳᵃ
bowe shotte thennes. And the servaunt of God that was in his selle

70 this] L, the EH1G   74 we] ye H1   76 this] the's' E   77 toke] fande
changed to toke G   sharpe] smarte G   89 hem] him *changed to* hem H1
90 diggethe] digged H1   94 aboundithe] hab'o'undeth H1   that . . . descendeth] L,
om. EH1G   96 aboute] and fonde G   98 right depe] *trs. and marked for reversal* H1
98–9 the man] thei H1   99 handell] handefulle H1   100 handelle] hondefull H1
101 monke] L, man EH1G   102 fell] *add* downe H1

knewe it anone in sperit and called to hym Maure and tolde hym what
105 was falle of the childe and bade hym goo and take hym vp. And
whanne he hadde take his blessing Maure went hastely, and as he
wende he hadde gone vpon the londe he went vpon the water vnto he
come to the child, and thanne he toke hym by the here and droue hym
oute of the water. And thanne he come to this holy man and tolde hym
110 how it was befalle, and he acounted this miracle nothing thorugh his
merites but to the obedience of Maure.

Ther was a prest that hight Florentine and hadde gret enuye to this
holy man wherfor he bithought hym in a gret malice. He toke a loef
and enpoisoned it and sent it to hym as it hadde be in waie of charitee.
115 He goodly receiued it and dede caste it [to] a crowe that was wont to
take brede of his honde and bade hym take the loef and bere it into
suche a place that no creatoure myght take it. And thanne the crowe
beganne to renne aboute the loef withe the beke open and spredde his
wyngges and cried as though he saide that he wolde obeie but he
120 myght not fulfell þe comaundement. And thanne the seint
comaunded hym twies thries and saide: 'Arise in the name of Ihesu
Crist suerly and caste it as I haue saide the.' And thanne he toke it atte
þe laste and bere it forthe, and thre dayes after he turned ayen and
toke his porcion of this holy man as he was custumed before. Whanne
f. 65ʳᵇ this Florentyne seigh that he myght | not sle the body of the maister,
126 he thought he wolde assaie to sle the soules of his disciples. He made
.vij. maydenes al naked to daunce, synge and playe in the gardyne of
the monasterie that the monkes myght be stered to synne and to
vnclennesse, the whiche thing the seruaunt of God seigh in his selle
130 and dredde the synne of his disciples. He gaue place to his enemye
and toke som of his bretheren with hym ande chaunged his duellinge.
And Florentine that was in his soler seigh how he went, wherof he
hadde gret ioye, and sodeinly forthewith he fell from his soler doune
and was slayne. And thanne Maure knowing this ranne after the
135 servaunt of God and saide: 'Turne ayen, Benet, for he that pursued
the is dede.' And whanne he herde that he wepte sore, as wel for that
his enemye was dede in hate as for þat his disciple ioyed of the deth,
wherfor he enioyned hem penaunce for they reioysed the dethe of her
enemye.
140   And thanne the servaunt of God Benet went into another place and

107 vnto] vntill G   108 to] `vn'to Hı   hym¹] add vp G   110 this miracle] ins.
Hı   111 obedience] obeciens Hı   112 hadde] add a E   113 He] and G
115 to] in E, to on erasure Hı   127 daunce] add `&' Hı   136 for that] as for Hı

chaunged not his purpose, for he went to the mounte Cassion wher he
founde a temple of Apolayne, the whiche he sacred into a chirche of
Seint Iohn Baptist and conuerted al the peple aboute and toke hem
from her ydolatrie. But the auncien enemye whiche was full of wrathe
apered to hym right horribly and enforced hym ayeinst hym and caste 145
visibly flawmes of his eyghen and fro his mouthe and saide: 'Benet,
Benet.' And whanne he seigh that he ansuered not he saide to hym:
'Thou cursed and not blessed, whi | pursuest thou me in suche wise?' f. 65ᵛᵃ
   In a day [as] the bretheren wold lefte vp a stone to putte it to werke,
it was so hevy that thei myght not, and thanne there come grete 150
multitude of men, but thei myght not remeue it. And whanne Seint
Benet herde this he come theder and gaue them hys blessinge, and
thanne anone they leffte it vp lightely ynow, and thanne they
perceiued that the fende hadde made it so hevy. And whanne they
had made that werke a litell high the fende appered to Seint Benet and 155
saide to hym that he shulde goo to his bretheren that laboured, and
thanne the holy man sent hym by a massage to saie: 'Bretheren,
werkithe wisely, for the wicked sperit is come to you.' And the
messenger hadde vnnethe fulfelled his worde but the fende [th]rewe
downe the walle, and withe the falle it slowe a yonge monke. But Seint 160
Benet made hym be brought to hym in a sacke the dede childe al
tobrosten and arered hym to lyff and made hym goo ayein to his
werke.
   A seculer man of honest lyf hadde in custume eueri yere to visite
Seint Benet fastinge, and in a day as he went thedir an other man fell 165
in felawship with hym, and as hym thought he bare mete in his bosum
for the viage, and whanne the day was up wel he saide: 'Brother, late
us take sum mete that we be not ouerweried in the waye.' And he
saide that he wolde in no wise taste any mete in the waye. And thanne
he helde his pes atte that ty|me, but atte the laste withein a while after f. 65ᵛᵇ
he stered hym ayein, but he wolde not consent in no wise. And atte 171
the laste whanne that the houre was passed and they had made a gret
vyage they founde a faire medue and a welle and alle thinge that is
delitable to take refeccion. And thanne he that went withe this man
shewed hym those thingges and saide that it were best to take 175
sumwhat and reste hem there a litell while, and whanne the wordes

   142 a²] add child subp. G   147 he saide to hym] om. G   148 me] men G
149 as] om. E   to²] add the E   150 grete] om. G   150–51 and . . . not] om. H1
159 threwe] drewe E   167 and whanne] twice once del. H1   168 in] changed to by
H1   170 pes] add as E   172 that] atte H1   173 is] is changed to was H1, was G

liked to the eeres and the place to the sight he consented to hym. And
whanne he come to the servaunt of God Seint Benet he saide hym:
'Brother, the wicked sperit stered the ones and he myght not preuayle,
180 ne the secounde tyme nother, but the .iij. tyme he hathe ouercome
the.' And thanne he kneled downe to his fete and wepte sore for his
trespace.

Cotila kyng of Goches wold proue yf this holy man had the sperit of
prophecie, toke to a squier of his his real vestement and sent hym to
185 his chirche withe rich aparayle, and whanne Seint Benet seigh hym he
saide: 'Do of, sone, do of, for that thou werest is not thine.' And
thanne he felle downe to the erthe and was aferde for that he hadde
scorned so the holy man.

There was a clerke that was demoniacle the whiche was brought to
190 the servaunt of God for to be heled, and whanne he hadde putte oute
the fende of hym he saide to hym: 'Now loke well that fro hennys
forward thou ete no fleshe ne that thou goo not to receiue holy
f. 66ʳᵃ orderes, for as sone as thou doest thou geuest the to the fende.' | And
as he was kepe in a tyme and seigh that he dede well inow in litell
195 orders, he made as thow he hadde foryete the wordes of the holy man
and putte hem fully abacke and went to holy orders. And anone the
fende that hadde lefte hym toke hym ayein and lefte neuer to torment
hym [til the soule was oute of the body].

A good man sente to Seint Benet by a childe two flasko[ns] of wyne,
200 but the childe hidde that one by the waye and brought hym that other,
and he receiued it goodly. And whan the childe shulde goo he taught
hym and sayde: 'Sone, loke wel that thou drinke not of that fla[skon]
of wyne that thou hast hidde, but turne hym upsedoune and thou
shalt see what is therinne.' The childe was al confused and went his
205 waye, and he thought to preue that he hadde herde; he turned ouer
the flaken and anone ther lepte oute a gret serpent.

In a tyme as this holy man sate atte [his] soper ther stode a monke
before hym that helde the light to hym, and as this monke stode he
beganne to thenke in hymselff by the spirit of pride for that he was
210 sone of a noble man: 'What is this he þat I stonde before to whom I

177 and the] *on erasure* H1   and] of G   184 prophecie] *add* `and´ H1, *add* and G
his²] *del.* H1, *om.* G   193 orderes] horders *with* h *erased* H1   194 he²] *ins.* H1
195 foryete] fore`yete´ H1   198 til . . . body] L, *om.* EH1G   199 flaskons] L,
flaskowse EH1, flaskettis G   201 taught] thought H1   202 that¹] what *changed to*
that H1   flaskon] L, flaken E, Flaskone H1, flaket G   203 hym] it G   206 flaken]
Flascon H1, flaket G   207 his] *om.* E   210 I¹] *ins.* H1   before] *add* the *del.* H1

holde this lyght in his etynge, and what am I that do suche lowly seruise
to hym?' And anone the holy man saide to hym: 'Brother, leue that hert,
what saiest thou now [to thyselff]?' And thanne he called his bretheren
and bede hem to take the light oute of his honde and comaunded that he
shulde be putte oute of the chirche and sette atte reste.   215

One of Goche that hight Zalla that was of the wicked se[c]te of
Arriens in the tyme of Cotile her | kynge, the whiche was so sette afere   f. 66rb
by gret cruelte ayeinst the faithe of holy Chirche in suche wise that
whateuer monke or clerke come before [hym] he skaped not alyue in
no wayes. On a day as this Zalla was sette afere withe the brennynge of   220
his coueytise that wolde rauishe and haue many thingges, and as he
tormented cruelly a [cherle] of the courte and almost slowe hym by
diuerse paynes, so he nye ouercome comaunded hymselff and his
goodes to the servaunt of God Benet. This tormentour herde that and
his cruelte was suspended, so that he wende that the goodes weren   225
take awaye of Benet. And thanne Zalla cesed to torment this [cherle],
but he bonde his hondes behynde hym withe a stronge corde of ledyr
streitely and droue hym forthe before hym and saide that he shulde
shewe hym þat Benet that hadde take away tho thingges. And so the
[cherle] went before til he brought hym to the chirche of the holy   230
man, and there they founde hym sitting alone before the dore of his
celle. And than this velayn saide to Zalla that folued hym: 'Lo here is
that Benet that I tolde you of.' And whan he hadde beholde hym withe
a brennyng sperit and madnesse of thought, wenynge by suche ferfull
chere to do as he was wonte, he beganne to crie and saide withe highe   235
vois: 'Arise up thou faste and take me tho thingges that thou haste
take from this [cherle].' And thanne the servaunt of God lefte vp his
eyen withe the vois of hym and lefte his redyng and behelde hym and
perceyued anone the armes [that] weren bounde of the cherle, | and   f. 66va
atte his lokinge sodeynli in a mervaylous maner the bondes losed more   240
hastely thanne any man myght haue [lo]sed hem. And whan he that
was bounden was so wonderly vnbounde, Zalla was made so dredfull
that he felle downe to the erthe, and the hede of his cruelte he bowed
to the fete of this holy man and recomaunded hym to his praiers. And

211 what] *add* man H1   213 to thyselff] L, *om.* EH1G   216 secte] sette E
218 by . . . faithe] *om.* H1   219 hym] L, *om.* EH1G   222 cherle] L, clerke EH1G
and almost slowe] hadde almost slayne H1   223 he nye] *trs.* H1, he was ney3 G
224 Benet] *preceded by del. paraph* H1   226 cherle] L, clerke EH1G   230 cherle] L,
clerke EH1G   231 alone] And oon H1   232 is] *om.* H1   237 cherle] L, clerke
EH1G   239 that] L, and EG, *om.* H1   cherle] cherle *changed to* clerke H1, clerk G
241 losed] vsed E, vnlosed H1   244 the] his G

245 thanne this holy man arose a litell fro his lesson a[n]d called his
bretheren and made hem take hym vp and bare hym witheinne the
chirche for to resseyue his blessinge. And whanne he was comyn ayen
to hymselff he taught hym that he shulde withedrawe hym from so
gret crueltee. And thanne he toke refeccion and went his waye and
250 asked no more sithe of the ch[erl]e the whiche the servaunt of God
had vnbounde withe his lokyng withoute touchinge.

In a tyme ther fill a gret dirthe in the contreye of C[a]mpannye that
alle peple hadde gret nede of lyuing, and corne was vtterly failed in
the chirche of Seint Benet, and all her brede was so nye eten that whan
255 the bretheren shulde go to her mete they hadde but .v. loues. And
whan the worshipfull fader Benet seigh hem wrothe and troubeled he
beganne to correcte hem withe softe attempre wordes and to comforte
hem alle, sayeng: 'Whi bene ye thus lyghtly troubled for lacke of
brede? This is but one day, tomorw we shull haue habundaunce.' The
260 day foluynge ther was founde before the dore of her celle .CC.
busshels of mele, but it was neuer wist who brought it ne by what
f. 66ᵛᵇ messenger oure Lorde sent it. And | whanne the bretheren seighe that,
they gaue thankingges to God and lerned therby that man shulde not
gretly ne sodeinly be trouble[d] ne drede for habundaunce ne for
265 pouerte.

Men reden that ther was a man that hadde a seke sone of a siknesse
that is called *elephantino*, whoos her fill al [a]way and his chine suall
and his flesshe roted away that it was a piteous thinge to beholde. And
thanne the fader of this childe that was a man of good faithe sent this
270 childe to Seint Benet, and he was anone restored to his furst helthe,
and so they yelded gret thankyngges to oure Lorde Ihesu Crist, and
after [that] the childe perseuered in goode werkes and slepte in oure
Lorde God.

In a tyme as Seint Benet [sente] som of his bretheren into a place to
275 edefie a chirche and ordeyned a daye whanne he wolde come to hem
and shewed hem how they shulde do. And the same nyght before the
day that he hadde sette to goo theder, he apered to a monke in his slepe
whiche he hadde ordeyned aboue other as prouost and shewed hem
eueri place by hymselff where they shulde goodly and sotelly edifien.

245 and] ad E   248 taught] thought H1   withedrawe] *with* o *changed to* a H1
250 cherle] chirche EG, clerke *on erasure* H1 (clerke L, *vilein* P2)   252 Campannye]
Compannye E   253 failed] falled H1   254 so nye] sone G   261 neuer] not G
262 whanne] *ins.* H1   264 troubled] trouble E   267 away] way E   272 that] L,
om. EH1G   274 sente] L, hadde EH1G   277 he¹] thei H1   278 hem] hym G
279 hymselff] hem self H1

And as they toke none hede to this vision but abode alwayes his 280
comynge and they seigh he come not, they turned ayein to hym and
saide: 'Fader, thou behightest us to come, and we haue longe abidde
and thou art not yet comen.' He ansuered and sayde: 'Bretheren, whi
saye ye soo? Ne appered I not to you and sheued you eueri place by
hymselff? Gothe and ordeynithe lyk as ye saye in a vision.' 285

Ther were two nonnes nigh his chirche that were women of nob|le f. 67ra
kynrede that coude not kepe her tongges, but they stered ofte hym þat
was her gouernour to laugh with her many wordes. And whanne he
hadde tolde it to Seint Benet he sent to hem and bade them [to] rule
beter her tongges or elles he wolde curse hem, the whiche sentence of 290
cursinge he putte not forthe in pronounsynge but in assaienge. But for
al that they chaunged not but de[ie]den witheinne a litell while after
and weren beryed in the chirche. And as they songgen the masses the
deken saide as custume was: 'Whoso comithe not withe us go oute.'
And the norise of these nonnes that offered allwayes oblaciones for 295
hem seigh how withe the wordes that the deken saide they went oute
of her sepulcres and passed oute of þe chirche, and thanne she [saide]
it to Seint Benet. He anone toke her the oblacion of his owne honde
and bade her: 'Goo offre for hem, for thei shull no more be acursed.'
And whan that was done the deken cried as he was wont. They laye in 300
pees and were no more sene arise and go oute of the chirche.

Ther was a monke that went oute to visite his kynne withoute
resseyvinge blessinge, and the same daye he deyed, and whanne they
wolde haue beried hym the erthe caste hym vp ayein two tymes. And
thanne thc kynne of this monke come to this holy man and praied hym 305
to yeue this dede monke his blessing, and thanne he toke the sacrement
of oure Lordes bodie and saide to hem: 'Gothe and laieth this vpon his
breste and putte hym in the erthe.' And whanne þat was done the erthe
receyued hym | and caste hym no more up. f. 67rb

A monke ther was in his chirch that myght not abide [there]in but 310
stroue so longe withe the servaunt of God that he lete hym goo, and as
sone as he was oute he mette with a gret dragon withe open mouthe
for to haue devoured hym, and he gretly aferde cried: 'Come hedir
and helpe me, come hedir, for this dragon will devoure me.' And
whan his bretheren come thedir they seye nothing of this dragon but 315

285 saye] segh *with* gh *on erasure* H1   a] *om.* H1   286 nigh] ny`gh´ H1
289 and bade them] *om.* G   to³] *om.* E   292 deieden] deden E, diden H1G   while]
om. H1   293 masses] messe G   297 saide] L, sent EH1, tolde G   298 oblacion]
oblacionys G   299 shull] schold G   300 the deken] *om.* H1   wont] *add* and G
310 therein] in E

brought home this monke to his chirche al trembelynge and pantynge, and thanne he behight that he wold neuer parte from his chirche.

In a tyme whanne al that prouince was full of famyne and the servaunt of God hadde yeue as moche as he myght finde to the peple, so
320 that ther was not lefte in his monasterie [but] a litell oyle whiche was in a vessell of glasse, and ther he comaunded to the sellerere that it shulde be yeue to a pore man. He herde it well, but hym luste not do it, for thanne ther shuld none oyle be leffte to the bretheren. And whanne Seint Benet woste it he comaunded that the vessell with the oyle shulde
325 be caste oute atte the wyndowe, that nothinge of inobedience shulde byde witheinne that place. And thanne the vessell that was caste oute felle vpon a grete roche, but nether the vessel was broke ne the oyle shedde, and thanne he comaunded that the vessell of oyle shulde be yeue hym þat he [b]adde furste. [Thanne he] blamed and vndertoke the
330 monke of euel faithe and of inobedience. And thanne he went to his
f. 67ᵛᵃ praier, and anone a gret tonne that was there was fulle | of oyle and encresed so gretly that it ranne ouer in the pauement.

In a tyme Seint Benet went for to visite his suster, and as they saten togedre atte the borde his suster praied hym that he wolde abide withe
335 her al that nyght. He wolde in no wise graunte her, and thanne she enclined her hede downe and helde vp her hondes and made her priue praier to oure Lorde, and whanne she hadde done and lyfte vp her hede ayein so gret a thonder, so gret a lyghtnynge and so gret a reyne come þat ther was no creatoure that myght stere oute of his hous, and
340 before þat she hadde praied the wedir was full softe and faire, but for she shedde a flode of teres she drowe to reyne the fairenesse of weder. And thanne was Seint Benet wrothe and saide: 'Suster, almyghti God foryeue the that thou hast done.' To whom she saide: 'I praied [the] and thou woldest not here me, and than I praied to oure Lorde and he
345 hath herde me. Now goo hennes and þou mayst.' And so al that nyght they were fedde withe holy talkynge of the loue and suetnesse of oure Lorde. And as he turned ayein to his chirche .iij. dayes after and had his eyghen lefte up to heuene, he seighe the soule of his suster in lykenesse of a dovue peerce heuene, and thanne he comaunded anone
350 that her body were brought to his chirche and putte in a sepulture that he hadde ordeyned for hymselff.

320 but] om. E, ins. H1   323 oyle] om. G   329 badde] L, hadde EH1G
Thanne he] L, om. EH1G   blamed] commaunded on erasure H1   341 weder] wederes
with s subp. H1   343–4 the and] L, and EG, and on erasure H1   347 he] ins. H1
350 putte] add it E

In a nyght as he loked oute of a wyndowe and praied to oure Lorde,
sodeinly he seigh a light come downe vpon hym and was so grete that
hit chased awaye al derkenesse of the nyght, and ther|withe al the f. 67vb
worlde was brought before his eyen, and there he seigh vpon a beme 355
of the sonne the soule of Germayne of a companye born into heuene.
And afterwarde he founde openly that atte that same houre that he
seigh this sight the soule parted fro the body.

In the yere that he shulde deye and passe oute of this worlde he
denounsed to his bretheren the [tyme] and the day. And the .viij. daye 360
after his dethe he comaunded that his sepulture shulde be opened. And
than anone he was smyten withe a feuer, and eueri day the siknesse
engregged, and the .vj. day he made hymselff to be born into the
oratorie, and there atte his passing he armed hymselff withe the body of
oure Lorde and susteyned his pore membres betwene the hondes of his 365
disciples and yelded up the sperit bitwene the wordes of orisones.

And that same day his dethe was shewed to two bretheren, to one
that duelled in a celle and to another that duelled further, for they
seen a way al encortined with manteles and shinyng of lampes
witheoute nombre, and that way streched from the celle of Seint 370
Benet towardes the orient vnto heuene, and a man of worshipfull
habite satte aboue, and whanne they enquered of eueriche what waye
that was and they were ansuered that men wost not, a vois was herde
that saide: 'This is the waye by whiche the servaunt and the frende of
oure Lorde stie[th] into heuene.' 375

He was beried in the oratori of Seint Iohn Baptist in whiche he
destroied the auuter of Apolyne and made there a chirche. He
florished aboute the yere of oure Lorde .vC. and .xviij. vnder the
tyme of Iustine | the olde. f. 68ra

Here endithe the liff of Seint Benet, and nexst beginnithe
the lyf of Seint Patrik, Capitulum .xlviij.^{m}

Seint Patrike beganne to preche aboute þe yere of oure Lorde .CCCC.
.iiij^{xx}., and as he preched the passion of Iesu Crist to the kynge of
Scotlonde he stode before hym and lened vpon his bordone that he

353 and] add it G   360 bretheren] childerenne H1   tyme] oure E   361 he] ins.
H1   363 engregged] encresid G   368 celle] Castelle H1   369 encortined]
entortyned H1   manteles] mancelles H1   373 that^{2}] and H1   375 stieth] stied E

EH1GH2A1A2L   Rubric Patrik] Patriarke with ar erased H1   1 Patrike]
Patriarke with ar erased H1   3 Scotlonde] Irelond on erasure H1

helde in his honde, and [it] was perauenture vpon the fote of the kynge
5 and the point of the bordon persed the kynges fote. And thanne the
kynge wende that the holy bisshop hadde done it wetyngly and other
weyes he myght not receiue the faithe but yef he suffered so for Ihesu
Crist, and therfor he suffered it paciently. And thanne at the laste the
holy man conceiued this thinge that was al abasshed, and thanne anone
10 he heled the kynge by his praiers. And he gate to that prouince that no
venemous beste myght live therinne, and yet he gate more, that the
trees and the lether of that contre bene holsom ayeinst venyme.

Ther was a man that hadde stole a shepe from a neyghebour of his
and eten it, and the holy man hadde often tymes spoken amonge the
15 peple in the chirch that whoso hadde done that dede shulde make
satisfaccion, but none was done ne none wolde knoulage priuely ne
openly, and whanne all the peple was assembeled in a tyme in the
chirche this holy man comanded in the name of Ihesu Crist that þe
shepe shulde blede witheinne the bely of hym that hadde ete hym, and
20 so he dede and he that was gilty dede penaunce.

f. 68rb   He hadde in custume to worship alle the crosses deuou|tely that he
seigh, but in a tyme he passed by a faire crosse that he toke none hede
of but passed ouer. His men asked hym whi he hadde not beholde that
crosse, and whanne he praied he herde a vois vnder the erthe that
25 saide: 'Thou hast not beholde me for I am an hethen man that am
beried here and am not worthi of the signe of the crosse.' And thanne
he made that crosse to be take awaye.

[As] this blessed Seint Patrike preched in Irlond and dede lytell
fruyt among hem, he praied oure Lorde that he wolde shewe sum
30 token by the whiche they myght be adradde and repent hem. And
thanne by the comaundement of oure Lorde he made in a place a gret
sercle withe his staffe, and than the erthe opened witheinne the cercle
and there apered a gret pitte and a depe. And thanne it was shewed to
the blessed Patrik that there was a place of purgatorie, and whosoeuer
35 wolde go downe there he shuld haue none other penaunce [ne fele]
none other harme for her synnes, and many come not ayen that went
thedyr, and tho that come ayein most abide there fro one morw to
another.

And thanne longe tyme after whanne Seint Patrik was dede ther

4 it] his E, *so changed to* it H1   6 holy] *om.* G   12 trees] teeres H1   lether] lepre
H1   ayeinst] of G   14 man] *ins.* H1   15 done] *ins.* H1   16 knoulage] *add* it H1
19 bely] body H1   24 that] and H1   28 As] L, And EH1G   34 blessed]
bisshop G   Patrik] Patriark H1   35 haue] *om.* G   ne fele] *trs.* EH1   36 harme]
add haue EH1   38 Patrik] Patriark H1

was a man that hight Nicholas the whiche hadde done many synnes, 40
but he repented hym and wolde suffre to be purged in the purgatorie
of Seint Patrike. And so as the custume was that other dede, he fasted
.xv. dayes before that he made the dores to be vndo of þat purgatorie
the whiche is kepte in an abbaye vnder kaye. And thanne he
descended into the pitte, and in the side of that pitte he founde a 45
dore and entered witheinne and | there he founde an oratori and f. 68ᵛᵃ
monkes [that] were reuest in aubys entred into that oratorie and dede
her seruise. And thanne they saide to Nicholas that he shulde be sadde
and stedfast in the faithe, for hym behou[ed] to passe by many harde
assaies of fendes. And thanne he asked hem what remedye and helpe 50
he myght haue ayeinst hem. Thei saide: 'As sone as thou felest the
tormented withe peynes saie anone: "*Ihesu Christe fili Dei uiui miserere
michi peccatori.*"' And anone as these men were gone the fendes come
and bade hym to obeye hem and made hym gret promys yef he wolde
[do] it that they wolde kepe hym and bringe hym ayein to his owne 55
place. But whanne he wolde not obeye [to hem] in no wise, than he
herde the voys of diuerse wild bestes, and the criengges of hem
togederes semed as thou all the elementes hadde fallen downe, and as
he trembeled al for the horrible drede he saide: '*Ihesu Christe fili Dei
uiui miserere michi peccatori.*' And as sone as he hadde saide those 60
wordes al that multitude of the horrible bestes were apesed.

And than he went ouer to another place and there he founde a gret
multitude of enemyes [that saide to hym]: 'Wenest thou that thou be
askaped from us? Nay, thenke it not, but now we shull begynne to
torment the.' And thanne there apered a gret and an horrible fere before 65
hym, [and thanne the fendes saide to hym]: 'Yf thou wilt not consent to
vs we shull thrawe the in this fere brennynge.' And whan he refused it
they toke hym and caste hym in that dredfull fyre, and whanne he felt
hymselff tormented he cried anone: '*Ihesu Christe | fili Dei uiui miserere* f. 68ᵛᵇ
michi peccatori.*' And thanne [anone] the fere quenched.   70

And fro thennes he went into another place and [seigh] sum men
brenne in the fere al quik and tobeten withe peces of iren brennynge
and the bodies torent withe tonges of fere þat the bowelles appered

---

47 that¹] *om.* E   aubys] abeys H₁   49 behoued] behouithe E   by] þoru₃ G
51 hem] him H₁   53 *michi peccatori*] *mei* G   55 do] *om.* E   56 to hem] *om.* E
57 wild] wikkid G   60 *michi peccatori*] *mei* G   61 apesed] *add and del.* And þan he
went ouer to anoþer place and þere he founde a grete multitude of þe horrible bestes were
apesed H₁   63 that¹ . . . hym] *om.* EG, 'þat sayde' H₁   66 and thanne . . . hym] L,
om. EG, 'and þay sayde' H₁   70 *michi peccatori*] *mei* G   anone] *om.* E   71 seigh]
saide E, seid *with* d *subp.* H₁   72 tobeten] to beten E, to be beten H₁, beten G

and hadden her belyes toward the erthe and gnew the erthe for sorugh
75 and woo and cried pitously: 'Spare us, spare us,' and thanne the
fendes bete hem more greuously. And he seigh other of whom the
serpentes deuoured her membres and bufones drue her bowelles
aboute withe her brennyng prickes, and whanne Nicholas wolde not
assent to hem he was caste in the same fere and in the same torment,
80 but he was anone deliuered of that peyne. And after that he was ledde
into a place where men were fried in a panne by lemes of fere, and
there was a gret whele full of fere and theron were these men hangged
by diuerse membres, and whanne she was hastely turned she threwe
oute lemes of fyre.

85   And after that he seigh a gret hous that was full of boyling metalles
by pittes, in whiche pittes sum hadde one fote and sum hadde tweyne,
other were witheinne vnto the knees, other vnto the bely, sum to the
breste, sum to the necke, and sum to the eyghen, and in rennynge
thorugh alle these tormentes he called the name of oure Lorde and
90 passed ouer, and behelde withinne a depe pitte, of whiche there went
oute a foule smoke and a stinke that [none] myght suffre the odour
therof, and oute of that place come men brenninge as hote iren in
f. 69ra maner | of sparkes of [brenn]yng fere, but the fendes anone threwe
hem in ayein. And the fendes saide to hym: 'This place that thou
95 beholdest is helle wher Belsabub oure maister duellithe. In this pitte
we shulle now caste the yef thou wilt not consent to us, and be thou
ones there thou mayst neuer askape for ther nys no remedye.' And
than he despised hem and wolde not obeye hem. They toke hym and
threwe hym into the pitte, wher he felt so gret torment and sorugh
100 that he hadde nye foryete the name of oure Lorde, but as sone as it
come to his mynde he saide it in his herte, for he myght not speke for
payne, and anone he went oute al hole and al that multitude of fendes
fledde awaye as ouercome.

   And thanne he was ledde into a place vpon a brigge that he most
105 nedes passe ouer, and that brigge was right streite and polisched as
glas and as sleper as yse yfrosen, vnder the whiche brigge ther ranne a
flode [of] fyre and bremstone. And than he was in despeyre how euer
he myght passe ouer, and atte the laste he bethought hym of that
worde that hadde deliuered hym fro so many periles and went with

   76 fendes] fende H1   hem] him H1   79 was] om. G, ins. H1   83 threwe] add
'hem' H1, add hem G   87 knees] kne/es with first e subp. H1   91 none] no man E
93 sparkes] sparklis G   brennyng] blemyng E   94 hem] hym EH1   in] ther Inne E
100 foryete] so changed from for hete H1   107 of] L, om. E, ins. H1, full of G

good truste forthe and sette [a] fote vpon the brigge and saide his 110
praier. And thanne an horrible and a dredfull crie made hym aferde
þat vnnethes he myght susteyne hym, but alwaye he saide his praier
and was al sure, and so he went forthe, and atte eueri pase he made his
praier and passed surely.

And whanne he was passed ouer he come into a faire mede wher 115
ther was mervelous odour of diuerse | floures, and thanne he seigh two f. 69rb
right faire yonge men that appered to hym and ladde hym into a noble
citee merveilously shyning withe golde and precious stones. Oute of
the gate of that citee ther come a merveilous suete odour that
comforted hym so that it semed hym that he hadde neuer felt 120
sorugh ne smerte ne stinke ne none disese, and thanne they tolde
hym that þat citee was paradys. And as Nicholas wolde haue entered
witheinne the yonge men saide to hym that he most turne ayein to his
mayne and by alle the places that he come by, but the fendes shul[d]
in no wise mysdo hym but fle from hym dredefully wh[anne] they see 125
hym, and .xxx.^ti dayes after he shulde reste in oure Lorde, and thanne
shal he entre into that citee as a perpetuel citezein.

And thanne Nicholas went by the same waye that he was come and
founde hymselff vpon the pitte and tolde to alle the peple as it was
byfalle hym, and .xxx.^ti dayes after he rested goodly in oure Lorde. 130

Here endithe the lyff of Seint Patrike, and nexst beginnithe
the Annunciacion of oure Lord, Cap^m. .xlix.^m

This is called the Annunciacion of oure Lorde, for on this day the
comynge of oure Lorde in flesche was furste [an]nounsed of the
aungell, for it was full couenable [that] the annunciacion of the aungell
shulde come before the incarnacion of the sone of God by .iij. resones:
furst for the ordre of assembeling, so that the ordre of the reperacion 5
ansuere to the ordre of preuaricacion, | that is the vnbeysaunce of oure f. 69va
furste fader, for right as the fende tempted the woman for to drede
and by that drede drawe her to consent and by the consent to synne,
right so the aungell denounsed to the Virgine þat by his anounsynge
she were drawe to bileue, and by her beleue to consent, and by her 10

110 a] L, his EH1G   115 was] hadde H1   121 ne²] in H1   124 shuld]
shull E   125 whanne] L, where EH1G

EH1GH2A1A2LT2; A1 breaks off after 6 *of preuaricacion* (as catchword); D resumes at
275 *man*; G has omitted 117 *leued* to 199 *God*   2 announsed] L, pronounsed EH1GT2
3 that] of E   annunciacion] auncien H1   5 assembeling . . . ordre of] *ins.* H1, *om.* T2
the³] *om.* H1   9 to] *om.* T2

consent to conceyue the sone of God. The secounde reson is the
misterie of the aungell, for the aungell is minister and servaunt of God
and the blessed Virgine was chosen to be moder of God, wherfor it
was sittynge that the servaunt shulde serue to his lady and right
15 resonable that thilke message were done to that blessed Virgine by the
aungell. The .iij. reson is for the recoueringe of the falle of aungels, for
the annunciacion was not only done for the reperacion of mankinde
but also for the reperacion of the falle of aungels, and therfor the
aungels ne owen not to be forclosed fro the knoulage of this misterie
20 no more thanne was the sexe of woman excluded from the misterie of
the incarnacion and of the resurreccion.

And thanne so as the blessed Virgine fro the thridde yere of her
birthe was duellynge withe other virgines in the Temple vnto she was
.xiiij. yere of age and hadde made her avowe to kepe her chastite, God
25 ordeyned for her that she shulde be wedded to Ioseph by his
reuelacion and by the flouringe of the yerde of Ioseph, as it is more
pleinly shewed in the Natiuite of the Blessed Virgine. And thanne
went Ioseph into Bethelem wher he was born for to purueie for the
weddyng, and she torned into Nazareth into the house of her fader,
f. 69vb and Nazareth | is as moche to saie as 'floure'. Of that saiethe Seint
31 Bernard that the floure wolde be born in the floure and of the floure,
in tyme of the floure wher the aungell appered to her and gret her,
sayeng: '*Aue gracia plena, Dominus tecum, benedicta tu in mulieribus.*'
Bernarde sterithe us to foure thingges, the salutacion of Marie [to] the
35 ensaumple of Gabriel, to the reioysinge of Iohn, and to the profit of
the salutacion.

But furst [it] is sittinge to wete whi oure Lorde wolde that his
moder were marie[d]. Vpon that Bernard assigneth foure resones and
saiethe that she was wedded of necessitee to Ioseph, for therby the
40 misterie was hidde fro the fende, and her virginite was proued of the
husbonde, and ther was made puruiaunce as wel for her shamefast-
nesse as for her good name. The ferthe reson is that by that
reprofe shulde be take awaye of [alle] estates of women, that is to wete
of virgines, of wyues and of wedues, for this same Virgine was in that
45 trebel estate; the .v. that she shulde use of the seruise of Ioseph; the

16 recoueringe] rekenynge T2   17 not] *ins.* H1, *om.* T2   19 this] þi`s´ H1, thi
T2   20 woman] women H1T2   23 vnto] till þat G   25 that] *twice* T2
28 into] in T2   30 floure] *add* wold be bore in the floure H1   31 and of the floure]
om. H1   33 *benedicta . . . mulieribus*] & *c* T2   34 to^2] *om.* E   37 it] *om.* E
38 maried] marie E   foure] iiij *repeated in margin* H1   39 of] in T2   43 alle] L, *om.*
EH1GT2   44 and] *ins.* H1, *om.* T2   45 trebel] crewell T2   of] off of T2

.vj. that mariage therby shulde be proued as good; the .vij. that the
genelogye of the man were enhaunsed ordinatly.

And thanne saide the aungell: '*Aue gracia plena, Dominus tecum, et c.*'
And Bernarde saiethe vpon this: 'She had grace in her wombe of the
godhede and in her herte grace of charite and in her mouthe grace of 50
feire speche and in her handes grace of mercy and of largesse.' And he
hymselff saiethe verrily that 'she was full of grace, for of the plentee of
her all taken tho that bene in chetiuyte redempcion, þe sorifull
comfort, the synne[r]s pardon, the rightwisse grace, the aungell[es]
gladnesse, and also al the Trinite ioy|eth, the sone of God toke f. 70ᵃ
substaunce of mankinde.' And thanne he saide after: 'Oure Lorde is 56
withe the, [oure Lorde the father is withe the], that engender[ed] the,
whiche thou conceyuedest; oure Lorde the holy goste is withe the, by
whom thou conceyuedest; oure Lord the sone, whom thou clothedest
with thi flesshe.' [And] as Seint Bernarde saiethe: '*Benedicta tu in* 60
mulieribus, et c.', that is to saie: 'Blessed be thou aboue alle women, for
thou shalt be virgine and moder of God.'

For before that tyme women were sogettis to thre corses, that is to
saye the curs of reproef, the curs of synne and the curs of peyne: the
cours of reproef to hem that conceiued not, wherfor Rachel saide: 65
'God hathe [take away] my reproeff;' the cours of hem that conceiue,
wher Dauid saieth: 'Loo, I am conceyued in synne;' of the cours of
hem that beren children, wher he saieth in Genesis: 'Thou shalt
bringe forthe thi fruit in woo and sorugh.' Wher þe blessed Virgine
Marie is soverreynli blessed aboue al women and to the virginite of 70
her he added plenteuosnesse, and to her plenteuosnesse he added
holinesse in conceyuinge, and in her holy conceyuinge he added ioye
in beringe.

And as Bernarde saiethe, she was saide 'Full of grace' for foure
thingges that shined in her mynde, the whiche were deuocion, 75
humilite, reuerence, puretee, gretnesse of faithe, and sadnesse of

48 *space left for Latin* T2   *et c.*] *om.* H1   50 herte] gerte H1   53 chetiuyte]
captyuite *with* ap *on erasure* H1, captyuyte G   54 comfort] *add* 'is' H1, *add* is G
synners] synnes E   aungelles] aungell EH1G   55 al] *om.* T2   57 the²] oure T2
oure Lorde the father is withe the] L, *om.* EH1G   engendered] engenderithe EH1T2
the⁴] *add* 'the' H1, *add* the G   58 the¹ . . . is] *ins.* H1   holy . . . the] *om.* T2   by] *ins.*
H1   59 conceyuedest] *so with* conceyue *on erasure* H1   oure . . . clothedest] *ins.* H1
60 And] *om.* E   61 *c.*] *benedictus* T2   64 of¹] *add* the E   reproef] 're'proef H1,
proef T2   66 take away] L, *trs.* EH1GT2   69 forthe] 'forth' H1   forthe thi fruit]
om. T2   71 and . . . plenteuosnesse] *om.* T2   72 in¹ . . . her] and T2   and . . .
conceyuinge] *om.* H1   73 in] and T2   75 whiche] *om.* T2   76 sadnesse]
stedfastnesse G

herte. It is saide: 'Oure Lorde is withe the' for foure thingges that
shine[d] to her fro heuene, as the same saieth, which ben the
halwingges of Marie, the salutacion of the aungell, the comynge of
80 the holy goste, the incarnacion of the sone of God. And he saide
'Blessed be thou aboue all women' for .iiij. thingges, as the same
f. 70ʳᵇ saiethe, that shi|nen in her fleshe: she was floure of virginite,
conceyuinge witheoute corrupcion, gret withe childe witheoute
greuaunce, bering her fruit witheoute sorugh.
85   And whanne she herde that, she was troubeled in the worde of the
aungell and thought what this salutacion myght be. And in þat
appere[the] the praisinge of the Virgine in heringe her sobernesse
and temperaunce, for she herde and helde her stille. In affeccion was
preised her shamfastnesse, for she was troubeled, in her thought was
90 preised her wisdom. She was troubeled in her thought of the wordes
of the aungell and not of the sight of hym, for the blessed Virgine
hadde ofte the sight of aungels, but not sayenge suche wordes. Pers of
Rauen saiethe that the aungell was come faire in fourme and dredfull
in worde, wherfor though the sight were plesaunte to her the wordes
95 weren dredfull to her hering. And Bernard saiethe: 'in that she was
troubeled it was of [a] virginal shame, for the vertue of strengthe in
her was not troubeled, in that she was still and speke not but thought
was [by] prudence and discrecion.'
   And [thanne] the aungell comfortinge her saide: 'Drede the not,
100 Marie, for thou haste founde grace before oure Lorde.' And Bernarde
saiethe: 'That grace was of God, pees to man, destruccion of dethe,
reperacion of liff. "Lo here," he saiethe, "thou shalt conceiue and bere
a sone, and his name shal be called Ihesus, that is to saye 'saueour', for
he shal make [his] peple sauf fro her synnes. And this same shal be
105 grete and shal be called the sone of the right high Lorde."' And
Bernarde saiethe that it is he that is the gret God to come, that is to
f. 70ᵛᵃ saye the gret | man, gret doctour and gret prophete.
   And thanne saide Marie to the aungell: 'How may this be done
sithe I knewe neuer man, that is to saye ne I purpose neuer to knowe
110 none?' And so was [she] virgine in thought, in flesshe and in purpos.
But see here how that Marie asked of that she dradde. Whi thanne

78 shined] shinethe EH₁T2   to] on erasure H₁, in T2   79 the¹] EH₁G start new
sentence   86 and] what G   what] that changed to what H₁, þat GT2   87 apperethe]
appered E   Virgine] virginite H₁T2   92 Pers of] Pees of T2, Pees with of changed to
wherof H₁   96 a] om. ET2   98 by] high EH₁T2   99 thanne] L, there
EH₁GT2   101 of¹] om. T2   104 his] us E   106 that is¹] om. G   110 so . . .
virgine] was virginite T2   she] om. E, ins. H₁

receiued Zakarie the wo[un]de for to be deef for his askinge? And therfor saiethe Pers vpon that and assignethe .iiij. causes: 'He that knowithe the priuetees of þe herte seghe not only the wordes but toke hede of her hertes, and she sheued not that thei saide but that thei felt. 115 And the cause of the demaundes were vnlike and of diuerse hope, for she l[e]ued ayeinst kynde, and he dred that was kindely. She asked the ordinaunce holy, and he dradde that thinge that God wolde haue done myght not be vndone. He come not to the beleue by ensaumples sheued, and she withoute ensaumple come to the faithe. She 120 mervailed how she shulde bere a childe and be a virgine, and he disputed of the conceivinge in mariage.' [And] she dradde not of the dede but she asked the ordre and þe maner, for ther bene thre maner of conceyuingges, that one is naturell, espirituel and mervailous, and therfor she asked in whiche of these maners she shulde conceyue. 125

And the aungell ansuered and saide: 'The holy goste shal come in the that shal be made thi conceyvinge.' Wherof it is saide that he was conceiued of the holy goste, and that was sheued by .iiij. resones: furst for the shewyng of his noble charitee, in that it was shewed that by right gret charite of God the worde was made | flesshe, on the thridde f. 70vb chapitour of Iohn, 'So as God loued the worlde,' and this is the reson 131 of the Maister of Sentence; secoundely for the shewinge of grace witheoute desert, so by that he is saide 'conceiued of the holy goste', it is shewed that of only grace, withoute goinge before the merites of any man; this is the reson of Seint Austine; thirdely the vertue of the 135 werke, for bi the werke and the vertue of the holy gooste he is conceiued, and this is the reson of Ambrose; ferthely for the cause mouyng to concepcion. The cause stering to naturell concepcion is the loue betwene man and woman. Right so, he saiethe, is of the blessed Virgine, for the loue of the holi goost brent singulery in [her] hert, and 140 therfor the loue of the holy goost dede mervailles in her flesshe.

And thanne the aungel saiethe after: 'The vertue of the right high shal shadowe in the.' And after the Glose it is thus expowned: the shadowe is wonte to be formed of [the] lyght and of the body [*obiecto*],

112 wounde] L, worde EH1GT2   113 assignethe] askith G   114 seghe] seithe T2   115 she] he G   117 she] he G   leued] L, loued EH1T2   117–199 leued . . . God] *om.* G   119 ensaumples] ensample H1H2   122 And] but E   123 for . . . maner] *om.* H1H2   124 naturell] *add* 'þat oþer' H1   espirituel] spirituell *followed by* is *on erased* e H1   133 is] *om.* T2   134 only] one by H2   136 vertue of the] *om.* H2   139 man and woman] men and wommen H2   140 singulery] surgerli H2   her] *om.* E   140–1 brent . . . goost] *om.* H1   141 dede] and T2   142 The vertue] *om.* T2   143 shadowe] shewe H2   144 wonte] with out T2   the^1] *om.* E   obiecto] L, *om.* EH1T2   144–5 obiecto . . . body] *om.* H2

145 that is to saye of a body sette before the light, and the Virgine myght
    not take the fulnesse of the Godhede as pure man, and therfor
    the vertue of the right high [hathe] shadowe[d] her whanne the
    [vn]bodely lyght of the Godhede toke in her body of mankinde, so
    that she myght in suche wise suffre the lyght of God. This exposicion
150 is seen to be touched of Bernard, that saiethe in suche wise: 'God is a
    sperit and we bene shadowes of his body, and he attempere[th]
    hymselff in suche wise so that by þe *obiectum* of the flesche quikened
    we see the worde made flesche, the sonne in a clowde, the light in a
    shell, the brightnesse in a lanterne.' Right as thou Bernarde saide:
f. 71ʳᵃ 'That maner | wherby thou shalt conceiue of the holy goost is of the
156 vertue of God, and Crist in his most secrete counsaile in shadowinge
    hathe hidde hym in the so that he haue al his desire. As though he
    saide: "Whi askest thou of me that thou shalt now finde in the by
    experience? Thou knowest it blessedly by that doctour whiche is
160 auutour. I am sent to the for to denounce the virgynel conceyuinge,
    and not to make it." [But he] shall shadowe in the, that is to saye that
    he shall refresshe the fro alle he[t]e of vices. "And see here Elizabeth
    thi cosin that hathe conceyued a childe in her age."' And he saide:
    'Loo here,' for to shewe that it was a gret nouelte. And the conseivinge
165 of Elizabeth was shewed Mari for .iiij. causes: the furste was plentee of
    gladnesse, the secounde perfeccion of science, the thridde perfeccion
    of doctrine, and the ferthe seruice of mercie. And therfor saiethe he
    that the conceyuinge of the [bareyne] was shewed to Mari her cosin,
    for that whan miracle is ioyned to miracle ioie is multeplied with ioie.
170 Ether for sothe it is sittinge that the worde whiche shulde be
    published in everi place w[h]ere knowinge is to the Virgine of the
    aungell er she herde it of man, ne that the moder of God were not
    putte oute of the councell of her sone if that whiche was so nighe her
    doune in erthe were vnknowinge to her. Either for this cause, that
175 whan the comynge of the messangere and of the saueoure were taught
    to her, that she holding the order and the tyme of thingges myght
    after beter open the trouthe to wr[i]ters and to prechoures. Either that

146 therfor] *om.* H2   147 hathe shadowed] L, shall shadowe E, had shewed H1T2,
shewed H2   148 vnbodely] one bodely E   149–50 suffre . . . wise] *twice* H1
151 attempereth] attempered E   152 *obiectum*] obieccion H1H2T2   153–4 a shell]
space H2   158 askest] asked T2   160 to²] I H1   the²] thi H1T2   161 But he]
bothe EH1H2T2   shall] all H1   162 hete] hede EH2T2, hete *with* te *on erasure* H1
168 bareyne] L, barstmes E, barynes *with* y *on erasure* H1, Barslnesse H2, Barstynes T2
171 where] were E   knowinge] knowingges H1H2   171–2 Virgine, aungell] *trs.* H2
174 her²] eyre H2   176 holding] holde T2   177 after] *add* be H1T2, be H2
writers] wrters E

she herde that her olde cosin was withe childe, þe same yonge virgine
thought to do her | seruise, so that to that litell profite were yeue place f. 71rb
to serue oure Lorde, and that were made more merueilous by miracle. 180

'A,' seithe Seint Bernarde, 'O thou blessed Lady, yeue an ansuere
hastely, ansuere worde and receyue worde, putte forthe thi worde and
receyue the devine worde, putte forthe a transetorie worde and
receiue the euerlastinge worde. Arise up, renne, and open, arise by
faithe, renne by deuocion, and open by confession.' And thanne Mari 185
withe her blessed hondes streched vp to heuene and saide: 'Lo me
here, the servaunt and handemayde of oure Lorde, be it done to me
after thine worde.' And Bernarde recordithe that before tyme the
worde of God was done to somme in the eeres, to somme in the herte,
to other in þe mouthe, to other in the honde. But to Marie she was 190
done in [the] eere bi the salutacion of the aungell, in the herte by
beleue, in the mouthe by confession, in the honde be touchinge, by the
wombe bi incarnacion, in þe lappe by sustenynge, in the armes by
oblacion.

   Ecce ancilla Domini. Fiat michi secundum uerbum tuum. And thanne 195
saiethe Bernarde: 'I will [not] that this thinge be done to me as by
proclamacion of prechinge or as shewed by figure or as by dremes or
imaginaciones, but I will [it] be enspired priuely, [incarnat] personly,
and put corpora[l]ly in the wombe.' And anone the sone of God was
conceiued in her wombe as perfit God and perfit man, and in that 200
same day of his concepcion he hadde as moche wisdom and myght as
he hadde atte .xxx. wynter.

   Thanne oure Lady went to Elizabeth, and as [she] gret her Iohn
reioysed in his moders wombe. *Glosa*: for he myght not ioye with his |
tonge he ioyed withe his soule and beganne his office to be his f. 71va
messager. And Marie was there to serue her cosin thre monthes into 206
tyme that Iohanne was born, and she was the furste that lefte hym
withe her owne hondes. As it is wreten in the Boke of Rightwise Men
that [on] this daye as the cours hathe ronne aboute, God hathe wrought
many faire and gret thingges whiche bene declared by þese verses: 210

180 serue] seruyse of H2   more] *om.* H2   182 ansuere] ansuered ET2, *so with* d
erased H1, she aunswered a H2   receyue] receyued H1T2, receyued a H2
185 confession] *space* H2   Mari] *om.* H1   186 and] *om.* H1T2   191 the¹]
om. E   192–3 by the . . . sustenynge] *om.* H2   195 *Ecce . . . tuum] space left for Latin*
T2   196 not] L, *om.* EH2T2, 'not' H1   198 it] *om.* E   incarnat] L, in garnet
EH2T2, *so with* Garnet *on erasure* H1   199 corporally] corporatly E   203 she] he
EG   gret] g'r'ete H1   204 *Glosa*] Austyn G, *space* T2   209 on] L, as EH1GT2
209 God . . . wrought] *om.* H1T2   210 verses] *add* here after folowinge T2

Salue festa dies que uulnera nostra coheres.
Angelus est missus, est passus et in cruce Christus,
Est Adam factus et eodem tempore lapsus,
Ob meritum decime cadit Abel fratris ob ense,
215   *Offert Melchisedech, Ysaac supponitur aris,*
Est decollatus Christi baptista beatus,
Petrus ere[p]tus, Jacobus sub Herode peremptus,
Corpora sanctorum cum Christo multa resurg[u]nt,
Latro dulce tamen cum Christo suscipit. Amen.

220 This is the Englishe of these vers: 'Haille right holy day in whom oure
woundes were restreined. The aungell was sent to Marie and oure
Lorde was crucified in the crosse, and Adam was made and in the
same tyme felle, and for the dyme Abel was slayne of his brother,
Melchisedech offered, Isaac was leyde on the auuter, the Baptist of
225 Crist [was] byheueded, and Peter take oute of prison, and Iames vnder
Herodes slayn, and many holy bodies arose withe Crist, the theef with
Crist hathe receiued euerlastinge ioie.'

Here beginnethe a myracle of oure Lady. Ther was sumtyme a
noble knyght that hadde forsaken the worlde and was entered into þe
230 order of Citeaus, and for he was not lettered the monkes ordeyned
f. 71vb hym a maister yef be auenture he myght | anythinge lerne, so that he
duelled longe amonge the monkes. But for none laboure that coude be
done to hym he myght neuer passe these two wordes: '*Aue Maria*,' but
withelde hem so stedfastely in his mynde that what thing euer he dede
235 or what place that euer he was inne he saide hem euer with herte or
with mouthe. And atte the laste he deyed and was beried in the
chircheyerde with other bretheren, and thanne vpon his tombe ther
sprong a precious lelye, and in eueri leef was wreten with lettres of
golde '*Aue Maria*.' And thanne they ronne alle to see this noble
240 mervaile and digged vp the erth of the tombe and founde that the rote
of the lelye come from the mouthe of hym that was passed. And
thanne they vnderstode withe what worship and deuocion he saide
these wordes that God hadde shewed by tokenes so grete meruaile of.

Ther was a knyght that hadde a castell by a comune hye waye, and
245 he vsed to despoile alle tho that passed therby witheoute anye mercye,

214 *ob ense*] L, *obense* EG, *obence* H1   215 *Ysaac*] *Isaie* H1, *Ysaiah with iah on
erasure* G   217 *ereptus*] L, *erectus* EH1G   218 *resurgunt*] *resurgent* EH1
219 *tamen*] *tum* H1   225 was] is E, is *del.* `was' H1   byheueded] *so with* ue *subp.*
H1   228 *space for initial* H *in* G   234 withelde] with holde H1   235 that] *om.* T2
euer²] *om.* H1T2, *oþir* G   239 alle] *om.* H1   242 they] *om.* H1T2

but alwayes he hadde in custume [that] for any besinesse or for any
lettynge that myght falle hym he wolde euery day worship oure Lady
withe the salutacion of the aungell. And so it fell that an holy man and
a religious passed therby, and anone this knyght comaunded that he
were dispoilled. And thanne the holy man praied the robbers that they 250
wolde bringe hym to her lorde, for he hadde a certayne counsaille to
telle hym, and whanne he come to hym he praied the knyght that alle
his meyni and all tho of the castell myght be assembeled and that he
myght preche the worde of God to hem. And whanne the knyght
hadde made hem alle come forthe, the holy man saide: 'þey | bene not   f. 72ʳᵃ
alle here.' And thei saide: 'We bene alle here.' He ansuered and said: 256
'Sekithe diligentely and ye shull fynde some faille.' And thanne one of
hem saide: 'Ther failithe none but the chamberleyn.' Thanne saide
the holy man: 'Verreli it is he that failethe.' And thanne he was anone
sought and brought forth, and as sone as he seigh the holy man he 260
beganne to turne the eyen dredfully and shoke his hede as a madde
man and durst not go no nerre. And thanne saide the holy man to
hym: 'I coniure the by the name of oure Lorde Ihesu Crist that thou
telle us what thou art and telle us al openly the cause of thi comynge
hedir.' He ansuered and saide: 'Allas, I am coniured and constreined 265
by strengthe to speke. Siker I am no man but a fende, but I haue the
forme of man and haue duelled with this knyght this .xliij. yere, for
oure prince sent me hedir to take hede [of] the day that this knyght
grette not oure Lady, and thanne I shulde haue power of hym for to
strangle hym, and so shulde ende his lyff in wicked werkes and be one 270
of oures. But in that day that he saluithe her I may not haue no power
of hym, and I haue loked diligentely fro day to day but he failled neuer
day but that he grette her.'
    And whanne the knyght herde this he was sore abaisshed and
kneled dovne to the fete of this holy man and asked foryeuenesse, and 275
fro thennes forward he chaunged his lyff into beter and lyued and
ended blessidly in the holy seruice of oure Lady. And thanne [this]
holy man saide to the fende: 'I comaunde the that thou go anone from
hennes in the name of Ihesu Crist and duelle in suche a place fro this

246 that] *om.* ET2   248 the aungell] oure lady G   252 he²] *on erasure* H1
254 hem] hym T2   257 fynde] se T2   258 none] *om.* T2   chamberleyn] *so with*
am *on erasure* H1   261 the eyen] ayene T2   263 oure] *om.* T2   264 us¹] *add* all
openly H1T2   al openly] *om.* H1T2   267 .xliij.] .lxiij. H1T2   268 of] L, *on*
EH1GT2   the] *add* to subp. H1   269–70 for . . . hym] *om.* T2   270 strangle]
stranghel *with* el *on erasure* H1   shulde] *add* he G   271 But . . . day] *twice* T2   her] our
lady T2   273 but] *twice once del.* H1   277 this] the E

280 tyme forwarde that thou neuer be so hardy to noye ne disese to none
f. 72rb that seruithe | ne requirithe the helpe of that glorious moder of
Ihesu Crist.' And as he comaunded so the fende went and vanished
awaye.

> Here endithe the Annunciacion, and thanne foluithe the
> Passion of oure Lorde, Capitulum .l.^m

The Passion of oure Lord was bitter by sorughe, by dispitfull, by
illusion, and fruitful by profit, and the sorugh was caused of .v.
thingges. The furst was that the passion was shamefull for the
shamefull place, for that place of Caluary was there wher wicked
5 doers were punished; and after for the dispitouse torment, for he was
dampned to right a foule dethe. And the crosse that tyme was torment
to theues, and there the crosse that tyme was in gret despite she is now
in gret worship. Wherof Austin saiethe: 'The crosse that was torment
of theues is now born in the forhede of emperoures.' Yef God graunte
10 so moche worship to his torment, hou miche yeuith he to his
servaunt? For his shamefull felawship, for he was deputed withe
cursed men, that is to saye withe theues that weren wicked; but after,
one was conuerted that hight Dismas, whiche hynge on his right syde
as it is in the Gospel of Nichodemus, and the other that hynge on the
15 lefte side was dampned, that is to saye Gesmas. To that one he gaue
his kingdom and to that other payne. Ambrose: 'The Lorde and
auctor of pitee hanginge vpon the crosse departed his offices of pitee
to seculer nedes, that is [to witte] persecucion to the aposteles, pees to
his disciples, the body to the Iues, þe spirit to the fader, the messanger
20 to the Virgine, paradis to the theef, helle to the sinfull, the crosse to
f. 72va cristen men | that will do penaunce. Loo here is the testament [that]
Ihesu Crist made atte his deyenge hanginge on the crosse.'
The secounde was for that she was not rightwise, for trecherie ne
gile was neuer founde in his mouthe, and therfor the peyne that
25 comithe wrongfully comithe withe gret sorugh. And they principaly
accused hym withe wronge of thre thingges, that is to saye that he

EH1GDH2A2L; D breaks off after 110 *deliueraunce* and resumes at 492 *that*, and has a
hole affecting from 511 *amonge* to the following rubric *Seint*   1 dispitfull] dispitynge
H1   by³] *om.* G   12 after] *add* 'þat' H1, *add* that G   15 was] is *del.* ` was' H1
16 Ambrose] *add* 'seid' H1   17 hanginge] hang/ginge *with second* g *on erasure* H1
18 to witte] with E   20 the theef] *ins. replacing cancelled* theftes *del.* 'þe theff' H1
21 that] L, of EH1G   26 thre] th`r'e H1

forbade the tribute to be yeuen, and that he saide hymselff kynge, and
that he made hymselff the sone of God. And ayeinst these [.iij.]
accusaciones we saye on Good Friday thre excusaciones, that is to
saye: 'My peple, what haue I do to the?' and that Ihesu Crist 30
reprouithe hem of thre benefetes that he dede thanne, that is to
saye that he deliuered hem oute of Egipte, the gouernaunce of hem in
deserte, the pla`n´tinge of the vine in right good place, as though Crist
sayde: 'Thou haste accused me of the truage, but thou shuldest rather
thanke me for I deliuered the from truage; thou accusest me of that I 35
saye to be a kynge, and thou shuldest rather thanke me of that I fedde
the in desert rially; thou accusest me als of that I make me [the] sone
of God, and thou shuldest rather thanke me of that I haue chosen the
to be in my vine and haue planted the in right good place.'

The .iij. for that it was done of his frendes by despite, for a sorugh 40
shulde be more sufferable if sche were suffered of hem that by any
cause shulde be his enemyes, and of hem that bene straunge, or to
suche as men had do any harme to, but for to suffre of hem that shuld
bene his frendes and nexst to hym, that was of hem of whos kinrede he
was born. Of that saiethe Dauid: 'My frendes and tho that shulde be 45
nexst | to me heelde hem fer fro me.' And Iob saiethe in the .xxx.^ti f. 72vb
chapitle: 'Tho that knewen me parted fro me.' And after it was of thoo
he hadde do moche good to and many gret benefetis, and therof
saiethe Seint Iohn in the .viij. chapitle: 'Many good dedes haue I done
to hem and c.' *Bernardus*: 'O thou good Ihesu Criste, how thi 50
conuersacion was suete among the peple, how thou gauest hem gret
thingges abundantly, how harde and sharpe thou hast suffered by hem
sharpe and hevi wordes, more sharpe and harder strokes, and the most
hideouse torment of the crosse.'

The ferthe was for the gret tendernesse of the body, wherof 55
Dauid saiethe in figure of hym: 'He is as [a] tendre tree worme
eten.' Seint Bernard saiethe: 'O ye Iues, ye bene stones, but ye
smyte right a softe stone of whom comithe a persing soune of pitee
and boillethe oute the oyle of charitee.' Seint Ierom saiethe: 'Ihesu
Crist is taken to [be] beten of knyghtes, and her betingges haue 60

27 hymselff] *add* to be H1   27–8 kynge . . . hymselff] *ins.* H1   28 .iij.] *om.* E
29 excusaciones] accusacions H1   31 thanne] hem G   34–5 but . . . truage] *om.* H1
37 the²] *om.* E   39 my] *ins.* H1   43 any] *add* schame or G   46 fer] *om.* H1
47 knewen] knowen H1G   48 therof] therefore H1   50 *Bernardus*] om. H1,
Bernard *ins. in different hand* G   55 the¹] hir G   56 as] *om.* H1   a] *om.* E
57 ye²] þat G, *del.* `þat´ H1   but] *add* if G   ye³] *ins. above erasure* H1   58 a¹] as E, as
a G   a²] *add* `riȝt´ H1, *add* riȝt G   59 boillethe] boiled H1   60 be] *om.* E

cruelly wounded that holy sacred body in whos breste was hidde
the godhede.'

The .v.^{te} was for that she was vniuersall, for she was in alle parties
and in alle his wittes. This furst sorugh was in the eighen, for he
65 wepte. As the apostell saiethe: 'He stied up that he myght be herde
ferre, he cried strongly that none shulde excuse hem, he added this
clamure withe teres for men shulde haue pitee.' And other tymes
hadde he wepte twies, o tyme in the resureccion of Lazar and that
other vpon Ierusalem. The furst teres weren of loue, wherof sum saide
70 that sene hym wepe: 'Lo, how he loued hym.' The secounde were of
pitee, but tho her⟨e⟩ weren of sorugh. The secounde sorugh w[as] in
f. 73ra his eeres, whanne men saide hym reproues and blames. Ihesu | Crist
hadde specially in hym .iiij. thingges in whiche he herde reproues and
blames: he hadde in hym most excellent noblesse, for as to his devine
75 nature he was the sone of [the] euerlastinge kinge and as to his
manhede he was of the riall kinrede, so that in as moche as he was man
he was kynge of kyngges and lorde of lordes; he hadde in hym perfite
verite, for he is waye of verite and lyff, wher he saiethe of hymselff
'Thi worde is trouthe', for the sone is the worde of the fader. He
80 hadde in hym an vnspekable myght, for alle thingges bene made by
hym and witheoute hym nothinge is made; he is bounte singuler, for
nothing is perfitely good but only God. In these thingges Crist herde
reproues and blasphemes. Furst of his nobilnesse, *Mathi .xiij.^o*:
'Wheder this is not the smithes sone? Is not his moder called Mari,
85 and c.' The secounde as to his myght, *Mathi .xij.^o*: 'This þrouithe
oute no fendes but in the name of the prince of fendes.' Item *Mathi
.xxvij.^o*: 'He makithe other sauf but hymselff he may not saue.' And
thus thei saie that he is vnmyghti, notwithestonding that he is so
myghty that by his only voys he [threwe] downe his pursuers. For he
90 asked hem whom they sought; thei saide: 'Ihesus of Nazareth,' and
anone they fell to the erthe. And therfor saiethe Seint Austine: 'O vois
witheouten any dart smote a cruel companye full of hate, dredfull by
armes, she putte hem abacke and made hem falle to the erthe by the
vertue of the hidde diuinite. What shal he do whan he iugethe, sithe
95 he ferithe so hem þat iugen hym? What shall he mowe do whanne he
regnithe that may do suche thingges whanne he gothe to dye?' The

63 .v.^{te}] firste G   vniversall . . . was] *om.* H1   64 his] *om.* G   66 ferre] fore H1
70 loued] louyth G   71 was] were E, were *changed to* was H1   75 the²] *om.* E
78 hymselff] *add* this H1   82 nothing] noo thing/thyng *with* thing *add. and del.* H1
83 nobilnesse] noblesse G   85 þrouithe] poteth *on erasure* H1   89 threwe] L, may
throwe EH1G   90 hem] *om.* G

.iij. as to trouthe, wherof Iohan saieth in the .viij. chapitle: 'Thou |
berest witnesse of thiselff, thi witnesse is not true. For they saide that f. 73ʳᵇ
he was a lyer notwithestondynge that he is waye of lyff and of trouthe.'
This trouthe Pilate deserued not to knowe, for he iuged not [after] the 100
trouthe. He bygganne his iugement by trouthe [but he abode not in
trouthe], and therfor he deserued to begynne his question of trouthe,
but he deserued not that the ansuere were assoilled hym of trouthe.
Another reson after Austine is wherfor he herd not the assoillinge of
the question of the trouthe, for as sone as he hadd asked it sodeinly it 105
fell in his mynde the custume of the Iues that weren wont to late one
goo in the tyme of Pasch, and therfor he went oute anone and abode
none as[o]ylinge. And after Crisostome the .iij. reson is for he knewe
well that for to assoyle so straunge a demaunde it behoui[d] a gret
space and a gret dilacion of tyme and he hast of deliueraunce of Ihesu 110
Crist, and therfor he went oute anone. And yet it is redde in the
Gospell of Nicodeme that whanne Pilate asked of Ihesu Crist what
was trouthe, he ansuered and sayde: 'Trouthe is in heuene.' Than
Pilate saide: 'Is ther none in erthe?' Ihesu Crist ansuered: 'How may
trouth be in erthe whanne she iuged tho thingges that haue pouer of 115
the erthe?' The fourthe as to his goodnesse, for they saiden that he
was a synner in herte, *Iohn .ix.⁰*: We know well [that] this man is a
synnere and a deceiuer of the peple in his wordes;' *Luc .ix.⁰*: 'This
same meuithe and sterithe the peple thorugh al Iudee bygynnynge fro
Galile into this place, and passithe the lawe in his werkes.' And Iohn 120
saiethe in the .ix. chapitlee: 'This man | is not of God that kepith not f. 73ᵛᵃ
the Sabot.'

The .iiij. sorugh was in hys smellinge, for he myght fele gret
stinke in the Mount of Caluarie wher many dede bodies were roted.
And it is saide in Stories that Caluerie is properly the nakednesse of 125
mannes hede, and for that wicked doers were behedid there and
many bones of hedes were departed there for that cause it was called
Caluarie.

The ferthe was in tastinge, for whanne he cried: 'I am athruste,'

100 after] *om.* E   101–2 but . . . trouthe] *om.* E   102 he deserued] 'he' deserued
he *with second* he *del.*H1   103 the] they E, 't'he G   ansuere] ansuered *with* d *erased* E, *so
with* d *subp.* G   105–6 hadde asked it] asked hadde H1   105 sodeinly] *om.* G   it
fell] *om.* H1   108 asoylinge] aseylinge E   109 straunge] stronge G   behouid]
behouithe E   110 dilacion] deliberacioun G   he hast] þe haste G   115 iuged]
iugith G   116 saiden] seyn H1   117 that] *om.* E   121 kepith] kepte G
127 for] 'þat' H1   126–8 and for . . . tastinge] *a later hand has inked over some words
damaged by liquid* E   128 there for] therefor E

130 thei yauen hym vinegre medeled with gall and eisell and mirre, so that
by [the] vinegre he myght deye the sonner and that his kepers were
deliuered of hym, for thei sayen that tho that bene crucified shullen
deye the sonner yef thei drinke aysell, and therfor thei gaven hym
mirre that his felinge shulde suffre, and the galle to his taste. And
135 Austin saieth: 'His purete was fulfelled withe aysell in stede of wyne,
his suetnesse with galle in stede of hony, the innocent was take for
gilty, he that is lyff deied for the dede.

The .v. so[r]ugh was in touching, for in eueri part of his body fro
the crowne of his hede vnto the sole of his fote was no helthe ne ease
140 but al torment and sorugh in al his wittes, as [Seint] Bernarde
[saiethe]: 'That hede that made aungels to tremble, the right faire
visage before al the sones of man was defouled withe the spettinge of
Iues, the eyen that weren clere[r] thanne [the sonne] were made derke
by the dethe, the eeres that herden the songe of aungels herden the
145 clamour of sinfull men, the mouthe that teche[th] the aungels was
fedde with eisell and galle, þe fete of whom the steppes bene holy were
nayled to the crosse, the body beten, the side opened withe a spere.
f. 73vb And what ouer will ye? Ther was nothing | that abode with hym but
only the tonge to praie for the sinfull and for to recomaunde his moder
150 to his disciple.'

Secoundely his passion was dispitous by illusiones, for he was
dispised and scorned in .iiij. maners. [First] in the hous of Anne wher
he was and receiued spittyngges, bofetes and was blindefeld. Wherof
Bernard saieth: 'O thou go[o]d Ihesu Crist, thi desired visage whiche
155 aungels desiren to beholde was defouled with her orible spettingges
and smiten withe her cruel hondes, they couered his eyen withe a
clothe in despite and spared hym not of cruel betyngges.' And after he
was scorned in the hous of Herode that iuged hym as a fole and as a
madde man of thought, for he myght haue no worde of hym, and
160 thanne was he clothed by despite in white clothinge. Wherof Bernard
seiethe: 'Thou art man and werest a chapelette of floures and I am
God crowned withe sharpe thornes, thou haste gloues on thine hondes
and myn hondes bene pershed with sharpe nayles, thou daunsest and

130 vinegre, eisell] *trs.* G   131 the] that E   132 that¹] *ins.* H1   133 gaven hym]
yif hem H1   136 in] *ins.* H1   137 he] he *on erasure* H1, so G   is] his EG
138 sorugh] sough E   140 torment] torente H1   al²] *add* haste *del.* H1   140–1 Seint . . .
saiethe] saiethe Bernarde E   142 the²] *ins.* H1   143 clerer . . . sonne] L, clere, thanne
EH1G   145 techeth] teched E   151 by] by / by E   152 First] L, *om.* EH1G
154 good] god E   155 her] *ins.* H1   156 smiten] smytyng G   157 clothe] *add* 'and'
H1, *add* and G   160 white] wiche G   161 art] *add* a E

lepest in white clothingges and I am despised of Herode, thou trippest
with thi fete and I trauaile withe my fete, thou strecheste oute thine 165
armes in karolles in crosse wise and I haue straught oute myn armes
on the crosse by reprofe, I haue sorughed in the crosse and thou
reioysest in the crosse, thou haste thi side and thi breste open in token
of veyne glorie and I haue my side persed with a spere for the. But
notwithestonding al this, turne ayen to me and I shall receiue the.' 170

But the cause whi he held hym stille in all the tyme of his passion
before Herode and Pilate: the furst reson is for thei were not worthi to
here his ansuer, the secounde cause is for Eue hadde offended by |
iangelinge and [he] wolde make satisfaccion by holdinge his pees, the f.74ra
.iiij. for whateuer he ansuered it was turned to euel and to despite. 175

The [.iij.] in the hous of Pilate [where] the knyghtes clothed hym in
rede clothe and putte on his hede a crowne of thornes and in his honde
a rede and kneled tofore hym in scorne and saide: 'Heille, kinge of
Iues.' And that crowne of thornes men sayen was of risshes of the see
wherof the pointes be as sharpe as of thornes and as prikkinge, and þat 180
sharpe [crow]ne drewe blode [of] his blessed hede in gret plente.
Wherof Bernard saieth: 'That holy hede was persed with multitude of
thornes into the brayne.' Thre opiniones be putte of the soule, that is
to saie wher she hathe her principal sege, either in the herte, 'for that
wicked thoughtes comen oute of the herte,' either in blood, for that 185
Leuiticus saieth: 'The soule of al flesche is in the blood,' either in the
hede, bycause Iohn saiethe: 'And he putte oute the sperit the hede
enclined.' And anone as that was done the Iues enforced hem to wite
this trebel reson, and for thei wolde take his soule awaye they sought it
furst in his hede in persinge it with thornes vnto the brayne, and thei 190
sought [it] in his blode whanne thei opened his veynes of hondes and
of fete, and thei sought it in his herte whanne thei opened his side.
And ayeinst these thre despites on Good Friday er we vncou[er] þe
crosse we putte .iij. worshippingges in sayeng 'Agios', as in worshippinge hym thre tymes that was despised for us .iij. tymes. 195

Ferthely he was despised in the crosse, Mathi .xxvij.º: 'The princes

165 trauaile] trauailed E   166 karolles] add and G   174 he] I with 'he' in
different hand E, he on erasure H1   by holdinge] byholdinge EH1   176 .iiij.] .iij. changed
to .iiij. E, fourthe G   where] L, ins. H1, whanne EG   179 sayen] add it H1, add þat it G
risshes] richesses H1   180 wherof] weherof E   of] add þe H1   180–1 þat . . .
crowne] þoo sharpe thornys G   181 crowne] L, thorne EH1   of] on E   183 soule]
add Of the soule be .iij. opiniones EH1   187 bycause] for G, bi followed by for on erasure
H1   188 enclined] enclynyth G   191 it] om. E   193 vncouer] L, vncouyre with
r over erased s E, vnconyse H1, vncony se G   195 that] For þat he on erasure H1
196 Ferthely . . . despised] ins. H1

of prestes and the aunsiens withe the scribes saiden in hym
f. 74rb des|pisinge: "If he be kynge of Iues, late hym come downe of the
crosse that we mowe leue in hym".' Bernarde saiethe vpon this place:
200 'He shewed amonge these thingges gret pacience, he preised humilite,
he fulfelled obedience, he made charite parfit, and in token of these
.iiij. uertues the .iiij. corners of the crosse bene araied with precious
stones, and the moste apperinge is charite al aboue, in the right side is
obedience, and in the lefte syde is pacience, and al benethe in the
205 lowest place is humilite whiche is rote of al vertues.'

Alle these thingges that Ihesu Crist suffered Bernard gadered hem
shortely togeders and saide: 'I shall remembre as longe as I shal leue
the laboure that he hadde in prechinge, in werinesse in goinge here
and there, in wakinge in praienge, of his temptacion in fastinge, in
210 wepinge, in awaytes that he hadd in spekinge, and atte the laste of
chidingges, of spittingges, of betyngges, of tresones, of reproues, and
of the nailles that he suffered.

Thirdely his passion is full fruytefull by multeplyenge of profite,
[whiche profite] may be in treble wyse, that is to wete in remission of
215 synnes, in getinge of grace, and in yefte of glorie. And these thre
thinges bene signified in the titell of the crosse, that is to wete 'Ihesus'
as to the furst, 'of Nazarethe' as to the secound, 'kynge of Iues' as to
the thridde, for ther we shull al be kyngges. Of this profit saiethe
Austin: 'Criste hathe take awaye oure giltes that is present, that is
220 passed, and that is to come, tho that bene passed in foryeuinge, the
present in withdrawinge, tho that bene to come in yeuinge grace to
eschewe hem.' And of this profit saiethe he yet: 'Mervaile we vs, |
f. 74va reioyse we vs, praise we hym, loue we hym and worship we hym, for
by the dethe of oure ayeinbyer we be come fro derkenesse to lyght and
225 fro dethe to lyff, fro corrupcion to incorrupcion, fro exile to a good
contre and fro wepinge to ioye.'

It is shewed by .v. resones how profitable oure redempcion was,
that is to wete for she was right couenable to apese God, right agreable
to cure oure siknesse, most effectuel to draw mankinde, most wise to
230 chase the enemy fro mankinde and for to reconsile vs to God.

Furst it was most acceptinge and most plesinge and to reconsile

197 of] *add* þe G   200 preised] *on erasure* H1   204 al benethe] all bigineth H1
207 as¹] *on erasure* H1   209 wakinge] walkinge E   214 whiche profite] L, *om.*
EH1G   215 yefte] yifť H1   216 wete] *add* of E   217 kynge] kinges H1
218 saiethe] *add* seint G   225 incorrupcion] vncorrupcion G, `vn´corrupcion H1
226 contre] courte H1   231 it was] is H1   plesinge] plesaunt G   and] *om.* G
reconsile] *add* `vs to´ H1, *add* vs to G

God, for as Anselme saiethe in the boke *Cur Deus homo*: 'A man may
suffre no harder ne no sharper thinge of his owne will and not of duete
to the worship of God thanne de[the], and in no wise man may yeue
more to God thanne to delyuer hymselff to de[the] for the loue of 235
God.' And that saiethe Paule to the Ephisens: 'He toke hymselff in
oblacion and in sacrifice to God in sauoure of suetnesse.'

And Austine saiethe in the Boke of the Trinite in what maner he
was sacred, apaieng and reconsilinge vs to God: 'What thinge so gretly
agreable myght be receiued as the body of oure prest made flesshe for 240
oure sacrifice? For .iiij. thingges bene considered in oure sacrifice, that
is, to whom men offren and what thinge men offren, an [who] offerithe
and wherfor it is offered, that same mediator betwene that one and
that other in reconsilynge us to God by sacrifice of pees abode one
with hymselff to whom he offered, was hymselff alone the whiche 245
offered and was offered.' And of that we be reconsi|led by Ihesu Crist, f. 74vb
saiethe Austin, that Ihesu Crist is preest and sacrifice, [God and
temple, preest by whom we be reconsiled, sacrifice] wherby we be
reconsiled, [temple in whom we be reconsiled]. And some that preise
litell this reconsiliacion reprouithe Austin in the person of God, 250
sayeng: 'Whanne thou were enemy of my fader I reconsiled the to
hym by me, and thou were ferre fro hym yet I come to the [to] by the,
and whan thou erredest amonge the wodes and hilles I sought the and
founde the amonge stones and stikkes, and [that] rauisshinge wolfes
and wilde bestes shuld not deuoure the I gadered the and vpon my 255
shuldres I bare the and yalde the to my fader. I haue suette and
trauailed, I putte my hede ayeinst the thornes, I offered myn hondez
to the nayles, the spere opened my side. I shall not saye al my iniuries,
but withe al sharpenesse and cruelnesse I was torent, I shedde al my
blode and I haue putte oute my soule. Al this haue I suffered for to 260
ioyne the to me, and yet thou partest fro me.'

Secoundely oure redempcion was most couenable to hele oure
maladye. Conablete is vnderstonde of the partie of the tyme, of the
partye of the place, and of the partie of the maner. Of the partie of the
tyme, for Adam was made and synnid in þe monthe of Marche the 265

232 *Cur Deus homo*] *De Doctrina Cristiana* G   234 of] *om.* Hɪ   dethe] deye E
235 dethe] deye E   239 apaieng] paying G   242 offren] *so with* ren *on erasure* Hɪ
who] L, he EHɪG   246 offered . . . offered] was offrid and offrid bothe G   and was
offered] *om.* Hɪ   Crist¹] *add and* G   247–8 God . . . sacrifice] *om.* E   249 temple . . .
reconsiled] *om.* E   250 in . . . God] *twice with second time del. closing folio and followed by*
of God *on next folio* Hɪ   252 to²] *om.* E   253 erredest] herdest Hɪ   254 that] L,
om. EHɪG

.vj.^{te} ferye and the .vj.^{te} houre, and therfor God wolde suffre dethe in Marche, and in that same that he was anounsed he suffered dethe the same day and the same houre. Secoundely [of] the partie of the place, [for the place] of his passion was considered in treble wyse, as comune
270 or especial or single. The place comune was the londe of promission, the special was the place of Caluarie, the singuler was the crosse. The
f.75ra furst man was formed in plase comune | in th[ese] parties besydes Damaske and was beried in speciall place, for in the same place that Ihesu Crist was beried men sayen that Adam was beried, though it be
275 not [aute]ntik, for after Ierom Adam was beried in Ebron as it is expressed openly by Iosue. And he was deceiued in a singuler place, not by that same tree that Ihesu Crist suffered dethe on, but it is sayde for as moche as Adam was deceyued of the tree that Ihesu Criste suffered dethe on the tree, notwithestondinge that in a storie of the
280 Grekes it is saide that it shulde be the same tree. The .iij. maner of [the] partie of curinge, the whiche maner by likly wise and by contrary wise. By likly wise, so as Austin saiethe in his boke *De doctrina cristiana*: 'Man was deceiued by woman and man was born of a woman, man deliuered man, he dedly deliuered dedly, and the childe
285 bi his dethe.' Ambrose saiethe: 'Adam was born of þe erthe virgine and Crist of the Virgine, he after the ymage of God and this is the image of God, bi the follissnesse of a woman and by the wisdom of a woman, Adam naked and Crist naked, the dethe come by the tree, the lyff by the crosse, Adam in desert, Crist in desert.' By contrarie wise,
290 for the furste man hadde synned by pride, by inobedience and by glotenye, he wolde haue be like to God in hynesse of connynge by passinge of þe comaundement [of God] and by tastinge of the swetnesse of the appill. And for that cures shulde be done by contrarie thingges, therfor was this maner right couenable to do satisfaccion, for
295 she was by humylinge of the diuine will, by fulfellynge and by torment. Of these thre, saiethe the apostell: 'To the furst he meked
f.75rb hymselff, to þe | secound he was obedient, to the thridde vnto the dethe.'

Thirdely she was right profitable to drawe mankinde, [for] the fre
300 will saued nothinge ne myght drawe mankinde so moche to the loue

267 anounsed] anunciate G   268 of] L, by EH1G   269 for the place] L, *om.* EH1G   271 was¹] *add* of H1   272 these] this E   274 sayen] seide G 275 autentik] in antik EH1   276 deceiued] receiued *del.* 'desseyuyd' H1   279 the tree] *om.* G   280 .iij.] *add* in G   281 the¹] *om.* E   282 By likly wise] *om.* G 286 after] *add* of G   292 of God] L, *om.* EH1G   296 saiethe] s'e'ith H1   meked] makith G   299 for] fro E   300 saued] *changed to* saw H1

and to the truste of hym. Bernard saiethe how he drowe vs to his loue
bi this thinge: 'Aboue al thingges, good Ihesu Crist, yeldithe the most
amyable to me the chalise þat thou dr[o]nkest, whiche was the werke
of oure redempcion, for that drawith moste myghtely all oure loues
to þe, for that it is that norischithe oure deuocion most suetely and 305
drawith vs most rightwisly and enbrasethe vs most hastely. And there
as thou [anentisshed thiselff and there as thou] dispuled thiselff of
naturell bemes, ther shined most [thi] pitee, [ther] lyghtnithe most thi
charitee and there stremithe most thi grace.' As the apostill saiethe to
the Romaynes in what maner he drowe us to the truste, 'for he spared 310
not his propre sone but deliuered [hym] to the dethe for vs all.' And
Bernard saiethe how that he yaue us all withe hymselff: 'What is he
þat shulde not be rauisshed with hope for to gete truste, that
vnderstondeth the ordinaunce of his body? He hath his hede enclined
for to kisse vs, his armes streight oute for to clippe us, the hondes 315
persed for to yeue largely, the side open for to shewe vs his loue, and
al his body streched out on the crosse for to yeue hym all to vs.'

Ferthely he was ryght wise to chase awaye the enemy fro mankinde,
wherof Iob saiethe the .xxvj.ti chapitel: 'The wisdom of hym smote
the proude.' Whedir Crist may not take the proude with his hoke, for 320
Ihesu Crist hidde the hoke of his diuinyte vnder the mete of his
humanyte, and whan he wolde take the fende he toke hym | withe the f. 75va
hoke of his godhede vnder the flesshe of his manhede. Of this wise
takynge saiethe Austine: 'The beyer come and the deceiuour was
ouercome. And what dede the beyer to the deceiuour? He laide his 325
snares that was the crosse and putte witheinne the mete of his
precious bloode.' He wolde shede his blode not of his dettour, for
the whiche thinge he parted from his dettours. The apostell callithe
this dette syrograf, the whiche Ihesu Crist bare and f[i]ched it in the
crosse. Of whiche sirograf Austin saiethe: 'Eue borued synne of the 330
fende, she wrote the sirograf and yaue plege and the vsure encresed
vpon her kynrede. She borued synne of the fende whanne she
consented to his wicked techinge ayeinst þe comaundement of God,
she wrote the sirograf whanne she putte her honde to the forboden

303 dronkest] drinkest E 305 to þe] þe del. H1 it] om. G 307 anentisshed
. . . thou] om. E there as thou²] om. G 308 shined] shineþe H1 thi¹] the E
ther²] thei E, þe'r' H1 309 stremithe] streneþ H1, schewith G 310 drowe]
drawith G the truste] 'trust' replacing erasure H1 311 hym] om. E, ins. H1
312 withe] om. H1 316 yeue] add vs E 317 on] of G 318 ryght wise] one
word G 328 the] ins. H1 from his] from changed to fro his H1 329 fiched]
feched E 334 the¹] so G

335 fruit, she yaue plege whanne she made Adam consent to her synne,
and so the vsure of synne encresed in her kynrede.'

B[e]rnarde in reprouynge saiethe ayeinst hem that despisen his
redempcion, by whiche we were bought ayein by the person of Ihesu
Crist, that God hymselff saide: 'My peple, what myght I more haue
340 do for you that I haue not done? What cause hast thou that it [liketh]
the to serue rather myn aduersarie than me? He made you not ne he
fedde you not, but this semithe litell thinge to somme vnthankfull, ne
he bought you not but I bought you, neither withe price of golde ne of
siluer ne withe the sonne ne with the mone ne with none aungell, but I
345 bought you with myn propre bloode. Whi will ye than withoute cause
eschewe to do to me the due seruise of right, ye shulde al thingges
leffte [conuenite] withe me at the leste of the peny of euery day.' And |
f. 75ᵛᵇ for as moche as they deliuered Ihesu Crist to dethe, Iudas thorough
coueitise, the Iues for enuye, Pilate bi drede, it is sittinge to [se] what
350 payne God sent hem for the desert of that synne. As of the peyne of
brynginge forthe of Iudas ye shull finde in the legende of Seint
Mathie, of the payne and of the destruccion of the Iues ye shull finde
in the legende of Seint Iames the Lesse, of the payne and of the
begynnynge of Pilate it is wreten in a story that is apocriff.

355 Ther was sumtyme a kynge þat hight Tyrus that knewe flesshe[l]y
þe doughter of a myller that hight Atus, and the doughter hight
Pilam. By her he hadde a sone, and thanne the moder toke her fader
name and hers togedre and called the childe Pilatus. And whan Pylate
was thre yere olde she sent hym to the kynge, and the kynge hadde a
360 sone by the quene his wyff that was nygh of the same age of Pilate, and
[whanne] these children comen to yeeres of discrecion they wolden
plaie togedre in wrastelinge and withe the [slinge and] atte the balle
and many other games. But right as the sone mulerye was most noble
by kinrede, right so he was founde more [no]ble in al places and more
365 conable in al manere of playes. Thanne was Pilate meued by envye
and with bitter sorugh and slowe priuely his brother, and whanne the
kinge wost it he was wonder sori and assembled counsaile togedre and
asked hem what he shulde do with that cursed sone homycide. Alle

336 so] *on erasure* H₁   the] þere G   of] *add* `þe´ *changed to* `þer´ H₁
337 Bernarde] Barnarde E   340 that¹] þat *changed to* þan H₁   not] *om.* H₁
liketh] liked E, like H₁   341 you] ȝow *with* ȝ *on erasure* H₁   347 conuenite] coueyte
E   leste] lefte H₁G   348 to] *add* the E   thorugh] for G   349 se] L, saye EH₁G
350 of²] *add* þe H₁   355 Tyrus] Titus G   flesshely] flesshe by E   361 whanne] L,
om. EH₁G   362 slinge and] playenge E   363 mulerye] moreli H₁, mulier G
364 noble] able E   367 and¹] an`d´ H₁

they sayden that he was gylti and worthi dethe, and thanne þe kyngge
moued by grace come ayein to hymselff and wolde not [double]   370
wikkednesse vpon wickednesse, but sent hym in ostage for the true
that was due euery yere to the Romaynes, and | bothe he wolde be f. 76ʳᵃ
founde innocent of his sones dethe, and also he wolde fayne be
deliuered of the truage of Romaynes.

In that tyme ther was in Rome the sone of the kynge of Fraunce   375
that the kynge hadde sent thedir for truage, and so Pilate fell in
felawship with hym, but whanne he seigh that he surmounted hym in
wisdom and in al good condiciones he was prikked with enuye and
wrathe and slewe hym. And whanne the Romaynes enquered amonge
hem what men shulde do with hym, some saide that he whiche hadde 380
slayn his brother and hym that was ostage, 'yef he may leve shall be
yet [full] profitable for þe wele of Romaynes'. Thanne saiden the
Romaynes: 'He is worthy to deye, wherfor late us sende hym into the
ile of Pounte, to these men that will suffre no iuge, and late hym be
made iuge ouer hem, yef be any fortune or auenture he myght daunt 385
her cruelte, and yef he may not, [l]ete hym than suffre as he hathe
deserued.' And so Pilate was sent to be iuge ouer þat cruel peple that
slewe thaire iuges. Pilate wiste wel whedir he was sent and that his lyff
stode in auenture by dieue sentence, he thought to kepe hys lyff, what
by promysses and by yeftes, by manaces and by tormentes he   390
submitted that peple to hym. And for he hadde bene [the] veynquor
of so harde a peple he was called of þat ile [of] Pount 'Ponce Pilate'.

Herodes thanne beyng kynge, hering the wisdom of that man,
reioysed hym of [his] wikkednesse as he was hymselff wikked, sent to
hym and stered hym by massages and by yeftes for to come to hym, 395
and whanne he was come to hym he gaue hym his power vnder hym
vpon Ierusalem. And whan | Pilate hadde gadered togedre a gret f. 76ʳᵇ
somme of moneye he went to Rome vnknowynge of Herode and
profered right grete good to Tyberien the emperour and gate of hym
by yeftes that he helde before of Herode, and for this cause they were 400
enemyes, Herode and Pilate. And Pilate in a tyme of the passion of
oure Lorde reconsiled Herode to hym for that he sent oure Lorde to
hym. Another cause of her enemyte is assygned in the Storie of

370 double] done the E   371 true] 'trewage' *replacing erasure* H1, trewage G
376 the kynge] the *with* t *erased* H1   377 but] and H1   382 full] right E
384–5 and . . . iuge] *om.* G   386 lete] bete EG   387 sent] dethe G   389 dieue]
dew *on erasure* H1, dyuyne G   he] He *with* H *on erasure* H1   391 the] in EH1G
392 of²] L, the EH1, *add* þe G   394 his] that E   396 his] *om.* G   400 helde]
hadde G   403 of²] *om.* H1

Scolasties. For one that made hymselff Goddes sone hadde deceyued
405 moche of the peple of Galilee, and whanne he hadde ledde hem into
Galile ther as he said that he wold stie vp to heuene, Pilate come and
slow hym and all his. And for that cause were they made enemyes, for
Herode hadde the lordshipp of Galile, so that euery of these causes
may be true.

410   And after that, whanne Pilate hadde take oure Lorde to the Iues for
to be crucified, he dredde lest the emperour Tyberien wolde be
wrothe with hym for he hadde iuged the innocentez blode, wherfor he
sent a frende of his to Tyberien for to excuse hym. And in this mene
tyme Tyberien fell seke of a greuous siknesse, and it was tolde hym
415 that ther was a leche in Ierusalem that heled men of al maner syknesse
by his word only. He wist not that Pilate and þe Iues hadde slayn
hym. Wherfor he called to hym one of his priue men aboute hym that
hight Volusien and saide to hym: 'Goo anone ouer the see and bidde
Pilate that he sende to me in al haste the leche by whom I may be
420 restored to my furst helthe.' He come to Pilate and hadde saide to
hym the comaundement of the emperour. Pilat was thanne al meued
f. 76ᵛᵃ and aferd | and asked respit [of] .viij. dayes.

And in that space of tyme Volusien met withe a woman that hadde
ben famulier with Crist, whiche hight Veronica, and asked her how he
425 myght finde Crist. And thanne she saide anone to hym withe gret
lamentacion: 'Allas, he was my Lorde and my God. He was [take] for
envye to Pilate, and he hathe dampned hym and comaunded that he
shulde be crucified.' And thanne was Volucien right sori and saide:
'Allas, I am right sori of this, þat I may not fulfell that my lorde hathe
430 comaunded me.' Thanne Veronica saide to hym: 'Whanne my Lorde
went here and preched I was always present, and for that cause I
wolde do make me an ymage, so that whan I shal not be in his
presence the ymage myght yeue me comfort that was made to his
figure. And as I bere a clothe to the peintoure oure Lorde [mette]
435 withe me and asked me whedir I went, and whanne I hadde tolde hym
my cause he asked of me the clothe, and whanne I hadde take it hym
he wyped his visage therwith, [and] anone the blessed figure of hym
abode therinne euene lyk to his owne blessed visage, and I dare well
saye yef thi lorde behelde deuoutely the figure of this image he shall

404 Scolasties] *changed to* Scolastica H1   419 the] þat H1G   422 of] for E
425 finde] haue G   426 he] L, *add* that EH1G   take] *om.* E, 'broȝt' H1
434 mette] L, went EH1G   436 take] ȝeue G   437 wyped] wept H1   and] *om.*
EH1

anone be hole.' He asked her yef this image were to sell for any golde 440
or syluer. She sayde: 'Nay, but it is for to be sene only by good
deuocion and good will. I shall go withe the and bere the emperour
the image that he may see it, and thanne I will come home ayein.' And
thanne come Volucyen withe Veronica to Rome and said to Tyberien:
'Ihesu Crist that thou hast longe desired to see, Pilate and the Iues 445
haue deliuered hym to dethe with|oute cause and hanged hym by f. 76vb
envye vpon the gebet of the crosse. And a lady is come hedir withe me
that hathe brought an ymage of that Ihesu Crist, and yef ye beholde it
deuoutely ye shulle receyue anone the benefete of youre helthe.' And
thanne the emperour anone made streche forth in the waye clothes of 450
silke and made that image be presented to hym, and as sone as he
hadde beholde it he was perfitly hole.

And thanne Pounce Pilate was take by the comaundement of the
emperour [and brought to Rome], and whanne the emperour herde
that Pilate was come he was fulfelled ayeinst hym withe gret wratthe 455
and made hym be brought before hym. And Pilate hadde brought
with hym the cote of oure Lorde that was witheoute zeme and were it
vpon hym before the emperour, and anone as the emperour seigh hym
al his anger was done and arose vp ayeinst hym and coude in no wyse
saye but wel to hym, and he that was in the absence of Pilat so cruel 460
and dredfull was in the presence of hym debonayre and goodly. And
anone as he hadd yeue hym leue to goo, he was hette ayeinste hym
horribly and called hymselff cursed for that he hadde not shewed hym
the wrathe of his corage, and made hym anone to be called ayein, and
suore and saide that he was the sone of dethe and that it satte hym not 465
to lyve vpon the erthe. And whanne he was brought ayein the
emperour salued hym and thanne al his cruelte was gone. And
thanne alle mervayled of the emperour, hymselfe most of all, of
that he felt hymselff so gretly meued ayeinst hym whan he seigh hym
not, and whanne he was present he myght saie none angri worde to 470
hym. And so atte the laste | by the will of God, or perauenture by the f. 77ra
techinge of som good cristen man, they made hym dispoyle hym of
that cote, and thanne anone he toke ayeinst hym his cruelte of corage,
and as the emperour mervailed gretly of that cote it was saide hym
that [she] hadde bene [of] oure Lorde Ihesu Crist. And thanne the 475

---

440 yef] of H1   441 sene] sende H1   453 by] *ins.* H1   454 and[1] . . . Rome]
L, *om.* EH1G   456 and] *om.* H1   459 vp] *om.* G   462 hette] hotte H1
467 his] *om.* H1   469 hymselff] him H1   472 good] *om.* H1   473 hym] *om.* G
475 she] L, it EH1G   of] L, on EH1G

emperour comaunded that he were putte into preson into the tyme he
hadde ordeyned [by] counsayll of wyse men what shulde be done with
hym. And thanne was sentence geuen ayeinst Pilat that he shulde be
dampned to a foule dethe, and whanne Pilate herde this he slowe
480 hymselff withe his owne knyff, and by suche dethe he ended his
wreched lyff. And whanne the emperour herde how he was dede he
saide: 'Now truly he is dede of right a foule dethe whanne his owne
hande hathe not spared hym.'

And thanne was he bounden to a gret melstone and caste into the
485 flode of Tybre, and anone the wicked spirites ioyned hem to this
wiked creature and drowe hym now in the water, now they bere hym
in the eyre, and they meued so mervaylously the wawes with
[thunder] and lytenynge and tempest[es] in the eyre so horrible that
alle the peple were so brought in horrible drede that none wende to
490 haue askaped, [for the whiche thinge] the Romaynes toke hym vp of
the flode of Tybre and bere hym to Vene and dede caste hym in the
flode of Rome. And Vene is expouned as waye of Iehenne, that is to
saye of helle, for it was thanne a place of cursinge. But anone the
wicked spirites were there and diden as they dede before, and thanne
495 the peple myght not endure so greuous tormentes and [toke] vp from
thennes that vessell of malice and sent [it] to be beried in the depe |
f. 77ʳᵇ pitte of Losenge. And whanne they sawe that they were contynuelly
greued withe the forsaid tempestes, they toke hym away and bere hym
ferre and threwe hym and plonged hym in a depe pitte that was all
500 environd withe grete hilles, and in that same places, as diuerse
reporten, ben [sene] to well vp many maculaciones of fendes into
this tyme. Here is contened in the Stori aboue said, and wheder that
she be to recorde or no I leue it in the will of the reder.

But wete ye well that it is redde in the Maister of Stories that Pilate
505 was accused of the Iues towardes the emperour of the violence and of
the slaughter of innocentes, and for that the Iues pleyned that he sette
in the Temple þe images of paynymes, and [that] the money putte in
the Corbonan he toke [to] his propre vsage, and he hadde made in his
hous a condit for to make the water come to hym. For all these causes

476 tyme] *add* that E   477 by] hym E   488 thunder] *om.* E   tempestes]
tempest EH1   490 for . . . thinge] L, and for whiche EH1, wherfor G
492 Iehenne] Iohenne H1   495 toke] *om.* EH1   496 it] *om.* EH1
497 they] þe H1   499 ferre] ferther G   500 places] place G   diuerse] *add* 'folke'
H1, *add* folk G   501 ben sene to well] L, ben to well EH1, wellen G   503 she] it G
504 Stories] *add* It is redde EH1   507 images] image G   that] at EH1   508 to] *om.*
EH1   vsage] vse G

he was deliuered to Lyons in exile [where] he hadde be born, so that 510
he shulde duell there in reproef amonge his owne nacion. And this
myght be, yf that Stori contenithe trouthe, for furst the emperour
ordeyned hym to be deliuered to Lyons in exile, and that he was born
theder before Volucyen retorned ayein to þe emperour. But whanne
the emperour herde that he hadde slayne Ihesu Crist, he repeled hym 515
fro exile and made hym be brought to Rome. Eusebee and Bede sayen
not in her Cronicles that he was sent into exile, but they tellen verrely
that he fell into many mischiefs, and atte the laste he slowe hymselff
with his owne propre honde.

Here endithe the Passion of oure Lorde Ihesu Crist and of
the dethe of Pilate, and nexst foluithe | the lyff of Seint   f. 77va
Secound martir, Capitulum .lj.

Seint Secounde was a noble knyght, [and sith he was a noble knyght]
and a glorious marter of oure Lorde he was crowned by marterdom in
the citee of Astens, and that saide citee is ennoblisshed by his glorious
presence and reioysithe of hym as of her right patron. And this
Secounde was taught in the faithe of blessed Calotero that was holden 5
in prison by the prouost Sapricio in the saide citee of Astens. And
whanne the blessed Marcianus was holden in prison in the citee of
Terdonensi, Saprece þe prouost wolde goo to hym for to make hym
sacrifie, and thanne Secounde went thedir as by cause of disport and
desired to see the blessed Marciane.   10
    And anone [as] he was oute of þe citee of Astens ther come a dowue
and satte vpon his hede, and then Sapres saide to hym: 'Secounde,
seest thou not how oure goddes louen the? They louen the so moche
that they sende briddes fro heuene for to visite the.' And whanne they
come to the flode of Tanage, Secounde herde an aungell of oure Lorde 15
that went vpon the flode and saide to hym: 'Secounde, loke thou haue
stedfast faith in the, and thanne thou shalt folw the fals worshipers of
ydoles.' And thanne Sapres saide to hym: 'Secounde, brother, me
thinkithe I here the goddes speke to the.' Secounde ansuered and
sayde: 'Go we faste there as oure hertes desire.' And whanne thei 20

510 where] L, whanne EH1G   501 nacion] nacions EH1   517 sent] seint H1
518 he] *om.* G

EH1GDH2A2L; D has a hole resulting from an excised initial affecting from 56 *al* to 65
folow and from 89 *Lorde* to end   1 and . . . knyght] L, *om.* EH1G   11 as] *om.* EH1
17 shalt] *add* `not' H1   20 there] þidir G

come to another flode that hight Burin that same aungelle aforesaid
apered to hym and saide: 'Secounde, leuest thou in almyghty God or
f. 77ᵛᵇ ellys perauenture dredest þou | yet?' Secounde sayde to hym: 'I leue
verrily on his passion.' To whom Saprece sayde: 'What is that that I
25 here of the?' And anone he helde his pees. And whanne thei come to
the citee Tridoyne and that they were entered therinne, Marciane
went oute of þe prison by the comaundement of the aungell and come
before hem and saide: 'Secounde, entre into the waye of trouthe and
receyue the victorie of feithe.' And thanne Saprece sayde: 'Who is that
30 spekithe to us as it were a dreme?' Secounde saide to hym: 'This is a
dreme to the, but to me it is a techinge of oure Lorde and [a] comfort.'
    And after that Secounde went to Melane, and the aungell of oure
Lorde brought Faustine and Iouytan, the whiche were holden in
prison, to hym withoute the toun. He receyued bapteme of hem, and a
35 clowde of heuene mynistred water to his bapteme. And anone ther
lyght a dovue fro heuene vpon hym and brought the blessed
sacrement withe hym and toke it to Faustine and to Iouytan, and
Faustine gaue it to Secound. And as he turned ayein fro thennes it was
thanne nyght, and thanne he come to the riuer of Pade, whiche is a
40 reuer that rennyth thorugh þat contre, wher that the aungell of oure
Lorde toke the brydell of his hors and ledde hym ouer the reuer and
condit hym to Trydoyne and putte hym into the prison withe
Marcyen. And [thanne] Secounde gave to Marcyen the yefte that
Faustine hadde yeue hym and sayde: 'The precious body of oure
45 Lorde be withe me in the euerlastinge lyff.' And thanne after that
Secounde went oute of prison by the comaundement of the aungell
and went to his hous.
f. 78ʳᵃ   After that Marcyen receiued sentence to haue | his hede smyten of,
and so it was done, and Secounde toke his body and beried it. And
50 whanne Saprece herd that, he called Secounde before hym and saide:
'By this moche as thou haste done I see well that thou knowlegest to
be a cristen man.' Secound saide: 'Verreliche, I knowlage to be a
verrey cristen man.' Thanne saide Saprece: 'Loo, how thou desirest to
deye of euel dethe.' Secounde ansuered hym: 'That dethe is due to the
55 moche more sharpely than to me.' And whanne Secounde wolde not
sacrifie, Sapres comaunded that he were dispoiled al naked, and than
the aungell of oure Lorde was there redy and ordeyned hym ayein
clothinge beter thanne he hadde before. And than Saprece

25 And¹] om. H₁   31 a²] om. E   35 mynistred] minister'ed' H₁   43 thanne]
L, om. EH₁G   45 me in the] changed to in þe in to H₁   52 be²] on erasure H₁

comaunded that he were hangged vpon a torment that is called eculee.
It is made in maner of a crosse wherof the two endes bene vpwarde 60
and the other two be dunwarde and fastened in the erthe. Theron he
was so longe tormented that his armes went oute of her iointes, but
oure Lorde restored hym anone to helthe. And than he was
comaunded to prison, and whan he was there the aungell of oure
Lord come to hym and saide: 'Secounde, arise vp and folow me and I 65
shall lede þe to thi saueoure.' And thanne he ladde hym into the citee
of Astens and did putte hym into the prison where Caloseren was, and
ther he founde the saueoure of the worlde withe hym. And whanne
Secounde seigh hym he felle doune to his fete, and thanne oure
saueoure saide to hym: 'Secounde, drede the not, for I am thi Lorde 70
and thi God, and I shall take the from al wickednesse.' And so he
blessed hym and stied vp to heuene.

   And in the morw Saprece sent to the prison, and tho that he sent
founde it faste shette, but they | founde not Secounde. And thanne f. 78rb
Saprece went fro Tredoyne to the citee of Astens for to sle Caloceren 75
and sent for hym anone. And thanne his messangers reported to hym
that Secounde was withe Caloceren, and whanne he herde that he
made bothe to be brought before hym and saide to hem in this wyse:
'For that oure goddes knowe well that ye despise hem they will þat ye
deye bothe togedre, and therfor dothe sacrifice or elles receyueth 80
sentence.' And whanne they refused it he made to melte piche and
rosen, and boylinge hote he made it to be pored vpon her hedes and
witheinne her mouthes, and they dranke it as sauourly as though it
hadde be a suete water or clere wyne, and saide withe high and clere
voys: 'A, Lorde, how thi wordes be suete in oure mowthes.' And 85
thanne Saprece gaue sentence ayeinst hem so that Secounde was
beheded in the citee of Astens and Caloceren was sent into Albergame
for to be punished there. And whanne Secounde was beheded aungels
of oure Lorde come and toke his body and bere it withe hem and dede
berie it with gret worship and preysinge. And he suffered dethe in the 90
thridde kalende of Auerell.

   63–4 And . . . prison] om. H1   67 was] ins. H1   77 withe] 'þere with' H1
78 hem] hym G   86 hem] him H1   89 and¹] subp. H1   toke] to kepe H1

Here endithe the liff of Seint Secounde, and nexst
beginnith the lyff of Mari Gipcien, Cap^m. .lij.^m

Mari Egipcien that is called a synfull woman lyued a full harde and
streite lyff .xlvij. yere in desert. And as she was doynge her penaunce
in that desert an holy fader that hight Zozimas passed the flume
Iordane, and as he went thorugh that desert seking yef he myght
f. 78va fynde by auenture any holy fader, and as he went he | seighe going
   6 before hym in [the] deserte a creature that was al naked and þe body al
      blacke [and] bruled thorugh þe hete of the sonne, and that was Mari
      Egipciane. And as sone as she seigh hym she beganne to flee awaye,
      and Zozimas to renne after as moche as he myght. And thanne saide
  10 she: 'Zozimas, fader, whi pursuest thou me? Foryeue me [for] I dare
      not turne my visage to the, for I am a woman al naked, but I praie the
      caste to me thi mantell that I may couer me, and thanne I shall see
      [the] witheoute shame.' And whanne he herde hymselff named he was
      abaisshed and toke her his mantell and kneled downe to her and
  15 praide her to blesse hym. And thanne she saide: 'Fader, it longethe
      beter to the that thou blesse me þat art araied withe the dignitee of
      presthode.' And whanne he herde that she knewe bothe his name and
      his dignitee he mervailed moche more and praied her more hertely to
      blesse hym. And thanne she saide: 'Now blessed be God, the
  20 aȝeinbyer of oure soules.' And as she helde her hondes vp to
      heuene and preyd, the olde man seighe how that she was lefte vp
      from the erthe an arme lengthe fro the grounde and [houered] in the
      eyre. And thanne this holy man beganne to drede lest it hadde ben a
      sperit and feyned to make his orison. And thanne she saide to hym:
  25 'Oure Lorde foryeue the that hast went that I, a vile sinner, were a
      wicked sperit.'

      And thanne he coniured her by the vertue of oure Lorde that she
      shulde tell hym al [her] condiciones. And thanne she saide to hym
      pitously: 'Fader, foryeue me, for yef I shulde tell the myn estate and
f. 78vb gouernaunce thou wolde | fle fro me withe grete drede as fro a
  31 venemous serpent, and thine eeres shulde be defouled with my
      wordes, and the eyre shulde be vnclene of my felthes.' [Thanne] he
      charged her in any wyse to tell hym, and thanne she saide to hym: 'I

EH1GH2A2L; D resumes at 7 *blacke*   3 hight] *add* ȝiȝt H1   5 and] *om.* G
6 the] *om.* E   7 and¹] as E, *as del.* and H1   9 to] *del.* H1   he] she E, *with* s *erased*
H1   10 thou] *add* so H1   for] *om.* E   13 the] *om.* E   22 houered] honoured
EG   25 that¹] *add* 'þou' H1, *add* thou G   27 her] L, *om.* EH1G   32 Thanne]
L, *om.* EH1G

was born in Egipte and in the .xij. yere of myn age I come into
Alisaundre, and ther I putte myselff .xvij. yere to lyue as a comune 35
woman. I de[u]yed neuer to none. And as men of that region toke her
waye towardes Ierusalem for to worship the holy crosse, I praied the
shipmen that ledde hem that they wolde late me come into þe shippe
withe hem, and whanne þei asked hire of me to lede me ouer I saide to
hem: "Bretheren, I haue nothinge to yeue you, but takithe my body 40
for youre hire."

And so they toke me and dede her willes. And so whanne we were
come to Ierusalem and I come withe other to the gates of the chirche
for to worship the crosse, sodeinly and witheoute anythinge [seing] I
was refused and not suffered to entre. And thus I went many tymes to 45
the entre of the gate and sodeinly I was euer putte abacke, and alle
other hadde free entre and founde no lette. And thanne I beganne to
beholde witheinne myselff and thought verrely that all this was befalle
me for my wicked synnes and beganne to bete my breste and to shede
bitter teres and to sigh ryght hevily. And as I stode waylinge full of 50
sorugh I behelde into the porche of the chirch and there I seigh [an
ymage] of the blessed Virgine Marie, and thanne I beganne to praie to
her right pitously that she wolde aske for me foryeuenesse of my
synnes and late me entre to worship the holy crosse, and I behight her
for to forsake the worlde and | for to lyue chaste fro thennes forward. f. 79ra
And as sone as I hadde made my praiere I toke truste in the name of 56
the blessed Virgine and went agayne to the gates of the chirche and
entred withinne withoute any lettynge.

And whanne I hadde right devoutely worshipped the holy crosse a
man gaue me thre penyes wherwith I bought me thre loues, and 60
thanne I herde a voys that saide to me: "If thou passe the flode of
Iordan thou shalt be saued." And thanne I passed it and come into
this desert wher I haue bene .xlvij. yere withoute seing of any man,
and these thre loues that I bere with me endured long and suffised me
.xvij. yere togedre. I haue bene grevously payned a gret while gone, 65
and .xvij. yere togedre I hadd gret tormentyng withe temptaciones of
the fleshe, but by the grace and goodnesse of God I haue al ouercome
hem now, and my clothes that I bere with me bene roten and wasted
many yeres agone. Now [haue I] tolde the al my werkes, wherfor I

36 deuyed] denyed E   region] religion *with* li *subp.* H1   38 shipmen] schipman G
39 to lede me] *om.* H1   40 yeue] ette *del.* `ʒeue´ H1   44 anythinge] oni H1   seing]
saieng E, sening *with first* n *changed to* y (?) thing H1, *om.* G   46 euer] *om.* H1
49 and¹] *add* `y´ H1   51-2 an ymage] L, a virgine EH1, a figure G   64 bere] bare
changed to bere H1   65 togedre] *om.* G   69 haue I] *trs.* E

70 beseche the that thou praie and do praye for me.' And the olde fader
fell downe to the erthe and blessed oure Lorde in his chambr[er]e.
And thanne she saide: 'I praie the, fader, that on Sheresthorsday thou
come ayein to the flom Iordan and bring oure Lordes body [withe
the], and I shall come ayeinst the and receyue the holy sacrement of
75 thine hande, for sethe the tyme that I come to this desert I was not
houseled.'
   And thanne the holy fader turned ayein to his monasterye, and
whanne the yere was passed and Sherthorsday come he toke the
blessed sacrement of oure Lordes body and went to the riuage of flom
80 Iordan, and whanne he come thedir he seigh that woman that was by
f. 79ʳᵇ that other syde of the ryuer, and as sone as she percey|ued hym she
made the signe of the crosse upon the water and come forth vpon the
water to this holy man. And whanne he seigh her he kneled hym
doune mekely to her fete al abaisshed. And thanne she saide to hym:
85 'Loke, fader, that thou do neuer so more, for þat thou hast the
sacrement of oure Lordes body withe the, and also thou shinest by the
dignite of presthode. But I beseche the, fader, that the nexst yere
foluynge thou come to me ayein.' And whanne she hadde receiued the
sacrement she made the signe of the crosse and went ayein vpon the
90 water to desert.
   And the holy man turned ayein to his chirche, and the .iij. yere he
come ayein to the place wher he hadde spoke withe her and founde
her dede. And thanne he beganne to wepe [and] durst not touche her
but sayde to hymselff: 'I wolde fayne bery this holy body so it were not
95 displesaunce to God ne to her.' And as he thought in this wyse he
seigh besydes her hede letteres wretin in the erthe that contened these
wordes: 'Zozimas, berye the body of Mari and yelde to the erthe her
sepulture and praie for me to oure Lorde, by the comaundement of
whom I lefft the world in the secounde kalende of Auerell.' And
100 thanne wost this holy man certainly that as sone as she hadde receyued
her sacrement and turned ayein to desert she ended her lyff to oure
Lorde.
   And [as] this holy man digged the erthe he myght not well laboure.
He seigh a lyon come debonairly to hym, and thanne he saide to the
105 lyon: 'This holy woman comaunded that her body shulde be beried,

71 chambrere] chambre EH1   72 that] add thou E   73–4 withe the] L, om.
EH1G   78 Sherthorsday] sh`e´reforsedi with f changed to þ H1   82–3 and ... man]
to þis holi man and come forþe H1   85 thou²] ins. H1   93 and] L, he EH1G
95 displesaunce] displesing H1   he¹] ins. H1   97 to the] on erasure H1   101 her¹]
the G   to] add þe H1   103 as] L, om. EH1G   105 comaunded] commaundeth H1

and I haue nothinge couenable for to make her pitte, wherfor I
comaunde the that thou digge the erthe withe thi clees till | thou haue   f. 79ᵛᵃ
made a couenable pitte wherinne that I maye bery her holy body.' And
anone the lyon beganne to digge and to arraye a couenable pitte, and
whanne he hadde performed it and she was leide witheinne he went   110
ayein as a debonaire lambe, and the holy man went ayein to his chirche
glorifieng God, and wrote the lyff and þe penaunce of her and
publyshed it ouer all.

Here endithe the liff of Mari Egipcian, and nexst foluithe
the liff of Seint Ambrose, Capitulum .liij.ᵐ

This Ambrose was the sone of Ambrose the prouoste of Rome, and as
he laye in his cradell in a place wher men helde the iugementes, a
swarme of bene come sodenly and al beclipped his visage, mouthe and
al, and entred into his mouthe and comen oute ayein right as they
hadde bene in her owne propre habitacion, and whanne they hadde so   5
done they fleyen up so high into the eyre that they myght not be
perceyued by the sight of no creature. And whanne this was fallen the
fader mervayled gretly and saide: 'Yef this childe may lyue he shal be
a gret and a mervaylous man.' And whanne the childe was more
growen he seigh his moder and his holy suster kisse the prestes   10
honde, he wold in his play putte forthe his right honde and offre it
to his suster to kisse and tolde her that therafter her [behoued] to do
the same [to hym]. She vnderstode not what the childe ment and
refused it.

And [thanne] after that he was taught atte Rome in lecture so   15
ferforthely that he purposed full clerely the causes in iugement,
wherfor he was sent by the emperour Valentyne for to gouerne the
prouince of | Lygurie and of Emurie. And whanne he come to Melan   f. 79ᵛᵇ
it fell so that they failled a bisshop, and the peple were gadered
togeders to purueye for a bisshop of thaire citee. But it fell so that ther   20
was a gret debate betwene the Ariens eretikes and betwene the verray
cristen peple, and the debate was that eueryche wolde haue hadde a
bisshopp of his partye, and for cause that Ambrose come thedir for to

106 pitte] *add* with G   110 and] *twice once del.* H1   113 it] *om.* H1

EH1GDH2A2L; A1 resumes at 214 -*ne* of *anone*²; D breaks off after 301 *truage*
2 iugements] *add* and EH1   4 and¹] *om.* H1   12 therafter] here aftir G
behoued] bhouithe E   13 to hym] *om.* E   15 thanne] that E, *om.* H1   lecture]
lettrure G   16 ferforthely] forthli H1, ferreforth G   18 Emurie] Enjurie H1
20 thaire] þat H1

apese that debate, sodenly a lytell childe that hadde neuer spoken
25 before beganne to speke and saide: 'Ambrose shall be bysshop.' And
thanne anone alle weren acorded to the voys of the childe and saiden
that Ambrose shulde be bisshopp alle togedre withe one voys.

And whanne he wost that, he went vp to the sege and sette hym as a
iuge to putte hem in drede that he were it not, and thanne he went
30 oute of the chirche and ayeinst that he was [custumed] to done
he comaunded in his iugementes to torment persones. And notwithe-
stondyngge that, all the peple cried: 'Thi synne be vpon vs.' And
whan he herde this he was full of sorugh and went to his hous and
wolde not knowlage that he cowde anythinge in philysophie. And yet
35 for he wolde not be bisshopp he made comune women come into his
hous to that ende that he myght turne the peple fro his eleccion, but it
profited hym not, for alway the peple cried: 'Thi [synne] be vpon vs.'
And whanne he seigh that he coude in no wyse turne her hertes fro
hym he fledde awaye aboute mydnyght. And as he went al nyght
40 wenynge to hym that he went into the citee of Cyenyn, in the morw
tyde he founde hymselff before the gate of Melane that is called the
Gate Romayn.

f. 80ʳᵃ　And whanne he was founde he | was kepte of the peple, and whiles
he was in keping the peple sent to the right debonayre emperour
45 Valentyne the relacion of this thinge, the whiche hadde souerayn ioye
that his iuge was of so vertuous gouvernaunce þat he was required to
the noble office of presthode. And thanne the good prouost was gladde
that his worde was fulfelled of hym, for whanne he gaue hym
comaundement to go theder, he saide to hym: 'Go, and do not as a
50 iuge, but foryeue as God dede hanginge on the crosse.' And yet ayein
he was hidde, and whanne he was founde ayein he was but nwe in the
faithe, and thanne he was baptized, and the .viij. day after he was sette
in the chayer of a bisshop. And thanne foure yere after that he went to
Rome, and as his suster that was an holy virgine come and kessed
55 his honde, and thanne he smyled on her and sayde: 'Lo, now it is falle
þat I tolde you, that ye shulde kisse a prestes honde.'

In a tyme as he was gone into a citee for to ordeyne a bisshopp, the
emperour Iustine and other heretykes ayeinsaiden the eleccion of that
bisshopp and wolde that none of his secte were ordeyned. A virgine of

28 a] `a´ H1   30 he was] om. H1   custumed] instumed or iustumed EH1
31 he comaunded] add to EH1, his comaundement G   37 synne] sone E
40 Cyenyn] Cievin G   51 he³] ins. H1   52 and²] add thanne E
54 and as] om. G, del. H1   55 his] ins. H1   57 as] whan H1

the secte of Arienes that was more [bo]lder thanne other went vp and 60
toke Ambrose by the vestementes and wolde haue drawe hym
towardes the partye of the women to that ende that they wolde
haue beten hym and putte hym oute of the chirche. To whom
Ambrose saide: 'Woman, though I be not worthi to do the office of
a preste, [yet] thou oughtest not to be so hardy to sette honde in any 65
preest, lest by the iugement of God other thinge falle the thanne
[well].' And so it felle atte the issue of that thinge confermed his
sayenge, for the nexst day after he | conueyed dede touardes her f. 80ʳᵇ
sepulcre and did yelde her worshipp for the iniurie þat she hadde do
to hym. And this dede fered gretly al the remenaunt. 70

And after he retorned to Melane and suffered there moche sorugh
and awayte of Iustine the emperour, for he stered the peple ayeinst
hym by yeftes and by worshippes, that many enforsed hem for to
sende hym into exile. And one of the heretykes that was more cursed
than another was moued withe so grete despite that he hered an hous 75
faste by the chirche and sette therin a carte made redy in whiche he
shulde be stolen by the procuracion of Iustine and ledde more lightly
into exile, but by rightwyse iugement of God the same day that he
wende to haue rauisshed the bisshopp, the same day fro that same
hous he was ledde into exile in that same carte. 80

This same Ambrose ordeyned the songe and the Office of the
chirche of Melane.

And in that tyme many of tho of Melane weren vexed withe the
fende that crieden withe high voys that they weren tormented by
Ambrose. Iustyne and many of the Aricnes whanne they weren 85
togederes saide that Ambrose yaue money to suche men for to
make hem saye that they were tormented by hym of wicked spirites.
But they fayled full vtterly vpon hym, and anone one of [the] Arienes
that stode there was rauisshed withe a wicked sperit and ranne
amonge hem and cried withe an ydeous voys and saide: 'Wolde 90
God þat alle tho that leuen not the merites of Ambrose weren
tormented as I am.' And thanne alle the other were confused and
toke this demonyakle and drowned hym in a depe pitte full of water. |

Another heretyk that was right a sharpe disputour ayeinst the faithe f. 80ᵛᵃ
and was full euel to be conuerted herde in a tyme the sermone of 95

60 bolder] L, elder EH1G   63 and putte hym] om. H1   64 Woman] wymmen
H1   65 yet] that EH1   in] on G   66 God] Crist G   67 well] wele E
69 do] om. H1G   77 ledde] lete H1G   86 yaue] 3aue with 3 on erasure H1
88 the] om. E   94 disputour] dispitour G

Ambrose, and he seighe an aungell stondinge by Ambrose that saide
in his eere al that he preched to the peple. And thanne he was
conuerted to the faithe of whiche he hadde be a gret pursuer, and
beganne to defende it.

100   In a tyme an enchauntoure coniured the fendes and sent hem to
haue distroied Ambrose, and whanne they hadde assayed and myght
not preuayle they turned ayein and saide: 'We mowe not only neghe
hym, but we maye in no wise neighe the gates of his hous, for alle his
place is environde withe intollerable fire that we bene yet in gret drede
105 of the syght therof.' And as the same enchauntoure was tormented of
the iuge for his wychecrafte, he cryed and saide that he was more
tormented of Ambrose.

So as it fell in a tyme that a demoniacle entered into the chirche of
Melan, the fende lefte hym anone, and as sone as the man went oute of
110 the chirche he toke hym ayen. And whanne the man asked the fende
whi [he dede] so, he ansuered for he dradde Ambrose.

Another heretyk went in a tyme into a chambre wher Ambrose laye
for to slee hym with a spere, for he wa[s] sent by Iustyne [by] yeftes
and by praiers, but as he lefte up his honde for to smyte Ambrose,
115 anone his honde dried vp.

Another heretik was rauisshed withe the fende and beganne to crie
that he was tormented by Ambrose. And thanne Ambrose sayde to
hym: 'Holde thi pees, thou enemye, for Ambrose [tormenteth] the |
f. 80ᵛᵇ not, but thi fals envye is thi torment bycause thou seest men stie vp
120 into goodnesse fro whennes thou fell in a foule manere, for Ambrose
coude not bollen the withe pride.' And than anone he helde his pees.

In a tyme as the blessed Seint Ambrose went in the citee, a man fill
doune to the erthe by caas of fortune and lay al streight, and ther was
one [that] seigh hym falle and lough. Thanne saide Ambrose to hym
125 that lough: 'Now thou laughest beware lest thou fall in the same
wyse.' And anone he fell, and than he was ashamed of hymselff that
[he] hadde laughed of that other.

In a tyme Ambrose went to the paleys of Macedonyen þat was
maister of offices for to praie for a man, but he founde the gates shette
130 and myght not entre witheinne. And thanne he saide: 'Thou shalt
come to the chirche and the gates shull be open, and yet thou shalt not

108 So] add `þat' Hɪ, add þat G      a²] `a' Hɪ   111 he dede] hede E   113 was]
wa E   by¹] from G   by²] for E, for subp. Hɪ   118 tormenteth] tormented E
123 caas] cause HɪG   124 that] and E   to hym] twice E   125 lest thou] on erasure
Hɪ   127 he] om. EHɪ   128 Macedonyen] marterdome changed to marcedonie Hɪ
131 open] opened Hɪ

entre.' And witheinne a litell while after, this same Macydonyen for drede of his enemyes fledde to the chirche, and the gates weren open and yet he coude fynde no waye inne.

This holy Ambrose was of so gret abstinence that he fasted euery 135 day sauf holy festes and Saterdayes. He was also so full of gret largesse that alle that he hadde or myght gete he yaue to þe pore and to [the] chirche and withhelde nothinge to hymselff. He was also of so gret pitee and mercy that whan any creature shulde confesse to hym hys synnes he shulde wepe so bitterly that he shulde constreyne that other 140 partye to wepe by his teeres. He was also of so gret humylitee and of so gret laboure that the same bokes that he endited he wrote | hem f. 81ʳᵃ withe his owne honde but yef he were greued withe any bodely siknesse. He was also of so gret pitee and mercye that whanne he herde of any bisshop or preest that weren passed oute of this world he 145 wolde wepe so bitterly that ther myght none [comforte] hym. And whanne he was asked whi he wolde wepe so for the partynge hennes of holy men that wenten to ioye, he ansuered and saide: 'Wetithe well that I wepe not for hem that bene gone but I wepe that they go before me, and also [for we] shul vnnethes fynde any worthy to putte in her 150 office.' He was also of so gret sadnesse and stabelnesse that he wolde not holde his pees to emperoures and to princes of her vices, but wolde reproue hem right sadly with high voys.

Ther was a man that hadde done right a grevous synne whiche was brought before Ambrose, and whanne Ambrose seigh hym he sayde: 155 'This man most be deliuered to the enemye [to destroie] his flesche that he be neuer hardy to do suche synnes more.' In the same moment as he saide these wordes the wicked sperit beganne to torment hym and al todrewe hym.

Som sayn as the blessed Ambrose went to Rome he was loged in a 160 towne of Toskane with ryght a riche man, and as they talked togedre Ambrose asked hym of his estate. He ansuered and sayde: 'My astate is happi and glorious, for I habounde in richesse, I haue seruauntes and chaumbreres many, I haue abundant lynage of children, and alle thingges comen to me atte myn awne wyll ne ther [fallethe] nothinge 165 contrarie to me [ne] that displesithe me.' And whanne Ambrose her|de f. 81ʳᵇ this he was gretly abasshed and saide to hem that were in his

136 so] om. H1G   137 yaue] add it G   the] om. E   138 chirche] riche H1
146 comforte] L, constreyne EH1G   149 wepe²] add for H1   150 for we] sorugh E
152 but] add 'he' H1   156 to destroie] that destroieth E   162 hym] om. G
165 fallethe] faylethe E   166 ne] om. E

felawshipp: 'Arisethe anone and go we hennys in haste, for oure
Lorde is not in this place. Haste you, Syres, haste you faste, and abide
170 no lenger here lest the devyne vengeaunce take vs here and wrappe vs
togedre withe the synnes of this meyne.' And as thei fledde in al haste
and weren a lytell waye thennes, the erthe opened sodeinly and
receyued that man with al hys godes that longed to hym, so that ther
lefft not [one of] hem. And whanne Seint Ambrose seigh this he saide
175 to hys meyne: 'Loo, bretheren, how God sparithe vs whanne he
yeuith us aduersitees in this worlde, and how he is displesed withe
hem þat he yeuithe alwaye wordely prosperite.' And in [that] same
[place wher] this was done ther abidethe into this day a depe pitte in
token therof.

180   And as Seint Ambrose seigh that auarice, the whiche is vice of alle
euels, encresed more and more in men and specially in hem that
weren sette in noble lordshippes, and that they solden all her werkes
for mede, as well tho that were ordeyned to holy Chirche as other, he
beganne gretly to sorugh and to wepe and praied to God that he
185 myght be take oute of the wrechidnesse of this sorifull lyff. And
thanne he reioysed hym for that he was herde of his praier and tolde
his bretheren that he shulde lyue to the resureccion of oure Lorde.
And a fewe dayes before he fell seke in his bedde, so as he [endited] to
his notary the .xviij. psalme the notarie seighe sodenly a fyre in maner
f. 81ᵛᵃ shapen as a | [shilde] the whiche keuered al his hede, and a litell it
191 entered into his mouthe as to his propre hous wher he shulde duell
and abide, and anone the visage of hym was whitter thanne any snawe,
and anone after she come ayein to her propre coloure. And thanne
that day he made an ende of writynge and of enditinge and myght not
195 make an ende of that psalme, and witheinne a while after he began to
be sik. And thanne the erle of Italy that was atte Melane assembled al
the nobles of the contre and saide to hem that it was lyk gret perile to
falle in Italye yef so noble and so worthi a man shulde parte fro hem
oute of this worlde, wherfor he praied hem to go to the servaunt of
200 God and beseche hym that he wolde aske of oure Lorde space to lyue
yet lenger. And whanne Ambrose vnderstode that by hem he ansuered

169 Syres] series H1   haste you] yow del. H1   171 meyne] add here EH1   fledde]
fley3 G   174 one of] on E   177 prosperite] add 'to' H1, add to G   that] this E
178 place wher] whei E   179 token] tokenyng H1   180 seigh] seith G
181 encresed] encressith G   185 this] his H1   188 endited] L, entitled EH1G
189 psalme] psalmes E   a fyre] after H1   190 shilde] childe EH1   191 he] she E
193 she] he H1   her] add owne E   200 aske] om. G

and saide: 'B[r]etheren, I haue not so lyued amonge you that I haue
shame for to lyue, ne I drede not [to deye] sithe we haue so good a
Lorde.'

In that tyme his foure dekenes stoden togedre and treted who 205
shulde be in his place after his dethe. And they were atte that tyme a
gret waye fro Ambrose wher as he laye, and one of hem named
Symplicien so lowe that vnnethes his felaw myght here hym, and
Ambrose þat was fer fro hem cryed thre tymes and sayde: 'But, Bon,
Bon.' And whan they herde hym they fledde for fere, and whanne he 210
was dede they chase the same Bon that he hadde named.

Honure bisshopp of Versailles that abode the ende of Ambrose was
leide to slepe, and thanne he herde a voys that saide thries: | 'Arise f. 81vb
anone, for he shall departe anone.' He arose and come to Melan in
hast and gaue hym the sacrement of oure Lordes bodye, and as sone as 215
he hadde streched his hondes in crosse wise he yelded vp the spirit
bytwene wordes of prayer, and floured in oure Lorde aboute the yere
of grace .iiijC. .iiijxx.x. And as his body was born to the chirche on
Ester Day, many children that were cristened seen hym right as
though he satte in his chayere as a iuge, and sum shewed hym with her 220
fingre to her fader and moder as they sayen hym stye vp and seyne
that they seen a bryght sterre ouer the body of hym.

A prest as he satte atte his mete beganne to saye euell of Ambrose
before moche peple, and thanne anone he fell so seke þat he was born
to his bedde and ended his lyff there. So as thre bisshopes dyned in 225
Cartage the citee all togederes, one of hem beganne to missaye of
Ambrose, and the other that were there tolde hym how it was falle to
the preste that hadde myssayde of hym, but he toke none hede but
hadde despite therof, and sodeinly he was smyte withe a dedly
wounde and deyed right there. 230

Wherfor it is [to] knowe that this blessid Ambrose is to be
commended in many wyse. Furst in fredom, for alle that he hadde
hit was holy to the pore, wherof he tellithe [of] hymselff how he
ansuered to the emperour whanne he praied of hym a chirche: 'If [ye]
desired anythynge of myn I wold in no wyse werne you, but rent, 235
golde, siluer, heritage and as moche as I haue is [of] the pore.'

Secoundely he is to be commended in purete and clennesse, for he

202 Bretheren] Betheren E, Broþer H1   203 to deye] L, om. EG, ins. H1
216 in] a G   221 moder as] om. G   226 the citee] þay sate G   togederes] L, add
and EH1G   231 to¹] L, om. EH1G   233 hit] hi3t H1   wherof] wherfore H1   of]
L, om. EH1G   234 ye] he E   236 of] L, om. EH1G   237 purete] sprit H1

was a virgine, of whom Seint Ierom saieth that he hadde saide: 'We
f. 82ʳᵃ be|re not only virginite but we kepe it.'
240　　Thirdely in stabelnesse of feith, for he saide to the emperour whan
he asked hym a chirche, and this is contened in the .viij. capitlee of the
decre in the .xxiij. question: 'It is moche beter that ye take my lyff fro
me than my feythe.'
　　Ferthely in couetyse of marterdome, wher it is redde in his pistell
245 whanne Ambrose wolde not deliuer the chirche how that the prouost
Valentinyen sent to hym these wordes: 'Thou despisest Valentinyan,
wherfor I shall haue thine hede.' To whom Ambrose saide: 'God
suffre the to do that thinge that thou manasest, and God take awaye
the enemyes of the Chirche and conuerte al her folyes ayeinst me so
250 that they myght staunche her thruste withe my blode.'
　　Fiftely in stabelnesse of orison, wher it is sayde in the .xj. boke of
the Maister of Stories: 'Ambrose defended hym not ayeinst the
madnesse of the quene with his hondes ne with suerdes but by
continuel praier and fastinge, and arayed by his praier ou[re] Lorde
255 vpon the auutere to be his defendour and the Chirche.'
　　Sextely in abundaunce of teeres, for he hadde .iij. maner of teeres,
the whiche were: teers of deuocion and compassion for the synnes of
other, wherof Paulyne saide in his legende that whanne any man was
shriuen to hym he wolde wepe so bitterly that he most constreyne that
260 other to wepe; also he hadde teeres of deuocion for the desire of
euerlasting lyff as it is saide before, [that] whanne men asked hym whi
he wepte the seintes that passed out of this worlde he saide that he
wepte not for her goinge to blisse but for they were go so ferre before
f. 82ʳᵇ hym; he hadde also teeres of pitee for wrong|ges done to other, wher
265 he saiethe in þe decree in the furste chapitle: 'Ayeinste the Gotheyen
knyghtes my teeres be myn armures, for suche armure longethe to a
prest, ne I aught not neither I may not otherwyse withestonde.'
　　Seuently in stronge perseuerance, of the whiche perseueraunce it
aperith in .iij. thingges. Furst in defendinge the trouthe of the faithe
270 of holy Chirch, wher it is saide in the .xj. boke of the Story Ecclesiast
that Lucyne the moder of the emperoure Valentyne that was moder of
the eresye Aryene beganne to trouble the Chirche and his astate and to
manace the prestes for to dryve hem oute into exile but yef they

238 Seint] *om.* G　　241 capitlee] Chapitre G　　242 the] *om.* Hɪ　　248 suffre]
suffred *with* d *del.* Hɪ, suffrid G　　253 with²] *add* his E　　254 oure] ou E
257 compassion] of passion G　　259 to] of G　　261 that] L, and EHɪG
265 saiethe] seide G　　Gotheyen] goth eyen G　　272 eresye] eretik G

fordede the decrees that hadde be made in Generall Counsell ayeinst
the Arienes, in the whiche batayle Ambrose faught as a stronge walle 275
and a myghty toure ayeinst her. And certainly this is the songe of hym
in his Preface: 'Thou hast confermed Ambrose with so gret vertue of
stabilnesse and made hym noble withe so gret an heuenly yefte that by
hym bene tormented and chased awaye the fendes, and the wykked-
nesse of Arienes putte oute and made feble, and the neckes of 280
[princes] ben yolden humble vnder the yocke of thi seruice.'

Eghtely in the defence of the Chirche, that is to saye that whanne
the emperour wolde haue withdrawe a chirche and made it of his
owne lordshipp Ambrose stode ayeinst hym, as he hymselff witnessithe in the decre .xxiij. in the [.viij.] question: 'I was aresond by an 285
erle that in al haste I shulde yeue a chirche to the emperour, for so the
emperour hadd comaunded, and I ansuered: "If he desire the heritage
of his moder I will withstonde it with al my myght, for | though he f. 82ᵛᵃ
putte my body to dethe or to prison it shall not be ayeinst my wille, for
I will not haue multitude of peple to defende me, ne I shalle not holde 290
me by the auuter, but I shal hate my liff if he were not frely sacrified
for the auuter. I am now comaunded that I shall deliuer a chirche. I
wote well that we be anoynted by the comaundement of the reaws, but
we be confermed by the wordes of scriptures, the whiche scripture
ansuerith that 'thou hast spoken as one of the folisshe women'. 295
Emperour, be not displesed nor greued in that thou wenest to haue
eny imperiall right in the devyne thingges, for the paleis longen to the
emperour and the chirches apertenen to prestes. Seint Nabott
defended the chirches right withe his propre blode, and sithe he
wolde not take his lingne we will not deliuer the Chirche of God. The 300
truage longithe to Cesar, we will not denye it the, but the Chirche
longith to God, and therfor she shall not be yeuen to Cesar. Yef
anythinge were asked me, eyther londe or hous, golde or syluer, that
longithe to me of right, I wolde yeue it gladly, but I may nothing take
awaye ne withedrawe from the temple of God, for I haue receyued it 305
in kepinge and not for to yeue it to none other."'

[Ninthely] in repreuyng al vices and all wyckednesse, whanne it is
redde in the Story Parted in Thre in [a] cronicle that whanne he was
in Thessalonique a gret discorde beganne for that som of the iuges

278 an] and Hı   281 princes] prestes E   282 the²] holy G   285 .xxiij.] L, add C
EHıG .viij.] L, .xviij. EHıG   292 chirche] add þat Hı   295 ansuerith] answerid G
297 longen] longith G   298 chirches apertenen] chirche apperteynyth G   301–2 denye
. . . not] om. Hı   307 Ninthely] L, Neuertheles EHıG   308 a] L, EHıG
309 Thessalonique] Thessalombe followed by illeg. deletion Hı

310 hadde be stened of the peple. Theodore was gretly wrothe therwith
and comaunded that alle shulde be slayn, as well the innocentes that
f. 82vb were not gylty therof | as the thother, so that there were slayn aboute
.vM^l. men. And whanne the emperoure come to Melane and wolde
haue entered into the chirche, Ambrose [ranne] ayeinste hym to the
315 gate and denyed hym the [entre], saieng: 'Emperour, whi knowlegest
thou [not] the grete cruelte of thi pride after the cause of so gret
madnesse? But perauenture þe pouer of thine empire denyeth the
knowlage of thi synne. Thou art a prince, an emperour, but that is a
conseruatour. Withe what [eighen] wilt thou beholde the communyon
320 of the temple of oure Lorde, and withe what fete wilt thou steppe on
the holy temple, how wilt thou streche oute thine hondes to God of
the whiche oure rightwysse blode [f]lowithe yet, with what presumpcion wilt thou receiue into thi mouthe the holy flesshe and blood of
hym, sith by the wodenesse of thi wordes so moche blode is shedde
325 withoute reson and with wronge? Go hennes anone, lest thou encrese
thi furst wickednesse by [thi] secounde synne, knowlache the bondes
wherwith that oure Lorde hathe now bounde the, for that is a full gret
medicine for thine helth.' And thanne the emperour, obeyeng to his
wordes, retorned to his palais with wepinge and sighinge, and whanne
330 he hadde longe wepte ther come to hym Ruffyne that was maister of
his knyghtes and asked hym the cause of that gret sorugh. The
emperour saide to hym: 'Thou felest not my disese, for the chirches
bene open to seruauntes and to the pore, and I may not entre
witheinne hem.' And in that [sayeng] he breke oute in gret sobbynge,
335 to whom Ruffyn saide: 'Yef [ye] wyll I shall go to Ambrose and praie
hym to lese you of the bonde that he hathe bounde you with.' And |
f. 83ra thanne the emperour saide: 'Thou maist not do that touardes
Ambrose, for he dredithe nothinge the imperyal myght, but he
dredithe more for to trespace in þe devine lawe.' But whanne Ruffyne
340 hadde behight hym that he shulde not drede but he shulde be wel
reconsiled, the emperour bade hym goo and hymselff folued a litell
after. And as sone as Ambrose seigh Ruffyn he saide to hym: 'O thou
Ruffyn, thou art turned into the filthe of houndes that hast be doer of

310 Theodore] *changed to* The emperour H1   314 ranne] rode E   315 entre] L,
entering EH1G   knowlegest] knowest H1   316 not] L, *om.* EH1G   318 an] and
H1   is] *om.* H1   319 eighen] thanne EH1G   320 temple] pepul G   321 the] þi
H1   322 flowithe] blowithe EH1G (folowyth L, *decourt* S)   326 thi^i] þe H1   H1G
punct. after wickednesse   thi^2] L, the EH1G   bondes] *changed to* boundes (?) H1
334 sayeng] L, syghinge EH1G   gret] *om.* G   335 ye] y E   praie] prayid G
343 houndes] hondis G

so gret a mortalite, and now in puttinge away the shame of thi forhede
thou art not ashamed to obeye ayeinst the devyne mageste.' And 345
whanne Ruffyne hadde praied for the emperour and tolde how he
come after hym, Ambrose fulfelled with the souerayne loue of heuene
saide: 'I tell the well before that I haue defended hym and shall
defende hym to entre in holy chirche, and yef he will turne hys myght
in the strengthe of a tyraunt I shal receyue gladly the dethe.' 350
    And whanne Ruffyn hadde tolde this to the emperour he saide:
'I shall go to hym that I may entende to his rightfull rebukes.' And
whanne he was come he besought hym that he wold vnbynde hym of
his bondes, and Ambrose ranne ayeinst hym de[u]yeng hym the entre
and sayde: 'What penaunce hast thou done after so gret wrongges?' 355
And thanne the emperour sayde: 'Fader, it longithe to the to ordeyne
and me to obeye.' And [as] the emperour aleged for hym how Dauid
hadde done avouutrye an homycide, Ambrose saide to hym: 'Thou
hast done this felonye.' And [than he was agreable] that he refused not
to do open penaunce, and whan he was reconsiled he entred witheinne 360
the chirche and abode in the chaunsell. Ambrose asked hym what he |
taried there, and he sayde that he abode there to here the devine f. 83rb
seruise. Than Ambrose saide hym: 'Emperour, the place of the quere
longithe to prestes only. Thou shuldest abide this seruise with the
comune peple in the chirche withoute, for the purpure makith the 365
emperoure and not prestes.' And thanne the emperour obeyed hym
anone. And whanne the emperoure come into Constantinenople he
helde hym in the chirche beneth and wolde not come into the
chaunsell, and the bisshopp sent to hym that he shulde entre
withinne. He saide: 'Vnnethe I may [discerne] what defference is 370
betwene an emperour and a preste, ne vnnethe I haue founde eny
maister of trouthe, ne I knowe none [that] is worthi to be called a
bysshop but Ambrose allone.'
    Tenthely he was profitable in holy doctrine, for his doctrine hadd
an high dipnesse of wisdom. Wherfor Ierom saieth in the Boke of .xij. 375
Doctoures: 'Ambrose rauisshed [vpon] the science of depe thingges,
right as a bridde of the eyre the whiles he fleithe into profounde
thingges he is s[ayne] to take fro aboue stabelnesse, for al his sentence
of the Chirche of the faythe bene sadde pelers of alle vertue fulfelled

344 mortalite] mortaill G   thi] þe H1   347 loue] floure H1   354 deuyeng]
denyeng (?) E   357 as] L, *om.* EH1G   358 hadde] *ins.* H1   359 than he was] L,
ther EH1G   agreable] agreably E   361 what] why G   367 into] 'in'to H1
370 discerne] L, deserue EH1G   372 that] *om.* EH1   376 vpon] vp E   science]
sciences E   378 sayne] L, fayne EH1G

380 with high noblesse.' Austine in the Boke of Mariages and Ayeinst:
'Pelagien, maister of heretykes, praisithe in this wise Ambrose and
saiethe: "The blessed Ambrose, of whos bokes al the faithe of Rome
shinithe, the whiche amonge the escriuans of Latine shinethe as a
floure full of suetnesse."' And he saiethe more: 'Of whom the faithe
385 and the right pure witte is abidden in the scriptures, so that the fende
f. 83ᵛᵃ dar not reproue so gret and noble auctoritees.' | For the auncyen
doctoures so as Austine hadde his wordes for gret auctorite, wher
Austin tellithe to Ianiuere that whanne his moder mervailed her why
he faste in the Saterday whanne he was atte Melan, and Austine asked
390 of Ambrose whi it was, and Ambrose saide hym: 'Whanne I goo to
Rome I faste the Saterday. To what chirche that thou shalt come for
enythinge kepe þe custume therof yef thou wylt not be sclaundred.'
And Austine saiethe: 'And I, thenkinge in this sentence, kepe it as
though it hadde come fro heuene.'

Here endithe the lyff of Seint Ambrose, and nexst foluithe
the lyff of Seint Iorge, Capitulum .liiij.

Seint George was a iuge of the kynrede of Capadocie, and come in a
tyme into the prouince of Lybye vnto the citee of Silena. And besides
that citee ther was a stange, a ponde, in the whiche ther was a dragon
that hidde hym therinne, and this dragon hadde many tymes chased
5 the peple that comen armed ayeinst hym, and he slowe by hys
brethinge all tho that he founde. And he wolde come even to the
walles of the citee, for the whiche cause [the] men of the citee were
constreyned eueri day to yeue hym two shepe for to apese his
woodnesse, for whanne he hadd hem not he wolde so assaill the
10 walles of the citee that by the corrupcion of his foule brethe many one
deyed. And thanne they gaue hym so many that bestes fayled
nerehond, and all pasture for her bestes failed and was al dried
thorugh the foule and corrupte eyre that come from hym. And thanne
f. 83ᵛᵇ they toke counsell amonge hem that they wolde yeue hym a man | and
15 a beste so ferforthely that they hadde yeue [hym] all her children,
bothe sones and doughters, for the sorte spared none, and so alle the

385 witte] whiȝt H1   391 that] om. H1   393 kepe it] kepte it EG, kepte changed
to kepe it H1

EH1T1GH2A1A2L   3 a stange] om. G   7 the³] L, om. EH1G   8 apese]
apece with a on end of erasure H1   12 nerehond] neyȝ G   15 ferforthely] ferforth G
hym] hem E   16 bothe sones] ins. H1

children of that peple were wasted awaye. So atte the laste it fell by
sorte that the kyngges doughter shulde be yeue to the dragon, and
thanne the kynge was gretly troubled and saide: 'Take my golde and
my siluer and the halff of my reaume and leue me my doughter that 20
she deye not in suche wise.' To whom the peple sayde by gret
wodenesse: 'Kynge, thou hast made this ordenaunce, and now al oure
children bene dede thou woldest saue thine. Wherfor but yef thou
kepe the ordinaunce that thou haste made and deliuer thi doughter we
shull brenne the and thine hous.' And whanne the kinge herde this he 25
beganne to wepe for his doughter and saide: 'Allas, my right dere
doughter, what shall I do for the, or what shall I saye? For I shall
neuer se thi weddyng.' And thanne he turned hym to the peple and
sayde to hem: 'I praie you that ye yeue me space of .viij. dayes to
bewepe my doughter.' And whanne the peple hadde graunted hym, in 30
the ende of the .viij. dayes the peple turned ayein to hym withe gret
crye, sayenge: 'Why lesest thou thi peple for thy doughter and seest
that we deye continuelly by the brethe of this dragon?' And thanne the
kynge seigh that he myght not deliuer his doughter. He lete clothe her
withe riall clothinge and enbrased her and saide withe wepinge: 'Allas, 35
my dere doughter, I wende to haue hadde and to haue þe norisshed of
thi riall kynrede, and now thou goest to be devowred of a dragon.
Allas, my doughter, I hadde hoped to haue sommed my richesse to thi
mariage, but now thou partest fro me in | piteous manere.' And thanne f. 84ra
he kissed her and lete her goo, saienge: 'By my will, doughter, I hadd 40
leuer haue deyed than thou [haddest] be loste in this wyse.' And than
she kneled downe on her knees and asked his blessinge, and whanne
he hadde blessed her she went forthe to the lake. And as by auenture it
fell that Seint George passed therby and founde that faire yonge lady
pitously wepinge, he come to her and asked her what her ayled 45
and what she was and whi she was so in that place allone. And than
she saide: 'I praie you, Syr, passithe in youre waye and hye you faste
hennes, leste ye perische withe me.' Thanne George saide to her: 'Ne
drede you not, yonge lady, but tellithe me what ye abide here and whi
it is that yender peple stonden so to wonder.' And thanne she saide to 50
hym: 'A, good yonge knyght, I se well that ye haue a noble and a
worthi herte, but whi [desyre ye] to deye withe me? Wherfor high you

17 of] *twice* E   26–7 right dere/doughter] *trs.* H1   30–1 in . . . of the] þe space
of G   31 ayein to hym] hem aȝen G   37 thi] þe G   devowred] wirowed *with* wir *on*
erased sol H1, wirowid G   38 sommed] somond H1   41 haddest] hast E   43 he]
she *with* s *erased* E   46 and what she was] *om.* H1   47 I praie you/Syr] *trs.* H1   in]
on H1   48 saide] *ins.* H1   52 desyre ye] *trs.* E

hennes in all haste.' And George saide to her: 'I shall not parte from
hennes till ye haue tolde me what you aylethe.' And whanne she
55 hadde tolde hym George saide to her: 'Drede you not, lady, in the
name of Ihesu Crist, for I truste to helpe you.' And thanne she saide to
hym: 'Now, good knyght, goo youre waye and perish you not withe
me, for it suffisethe to me that I perische allone.' And as they spake
togedre the dragon beganne to lefte vp his hede of the water, and
60 thanne this yonge mayde beganne to tremble and to quake and saide:
'Flee, good Syr, flee hastely.' And thanne George lepe vpon his hors
and armed hym withe the signe of the crosse and assayled hardely the
dragon that come ayenst hym. And he brandisshed his shelde
myghtely and his spere, and he recomended hym to God and
f. 84rb woun|ded the dragon and threwe hym to the erthe. And thanne
66 George saide to her: 'Throwe thi gerdell aboute his necke and drede
the not, fayre lady, in no wyse.' And whanne she hadde do so the
dragon folued her as a debonayre hounde. And whanne they hadde
brought hym into the citee, the peple that seigh hym ronnen and
70 beganne to flee as they hadde be wode thorugh the wodes and hilles,
and saide: 'Allas, now shull we perishe alle.' And thanne the blessed
Seint George shewed hym to hem and saide: 'Dredithe you not, for
oure Lord hathe sent me hedyr to you for to deliuer you of the paynes
of this dragon. Beleuithe only in God, and be ye baptized euerychone,
75 and than [I shall] slee to you this dragon.' And thanne the kynge and
alle the peple were baptized, and whanne they had receiued holy
bapteme Seint George drewe oute his suerde and slowe þe dragon and
comaunded that he shuld be born oute of the citee. And than most
they haue foure couple of oxen to drawe hym oute into a gret feelde.
80 And in that same day ther were baptized .xx.^{ti} thousand men withoute
women and children. And than the kynge in worship of oure Lady
and of Seint George lete make a chirche of mervaylous gretnesse, and
fro the auuter of the chirche ther [springithe] a quicke well that
[helithe] of all maner siknesse whoso [drinkithe] therof. And thanne
85 the kynge offered to Seint George golde withoute nombre, the whiche
he refused and comaunded that it shulde be geue to the pore. And
thanne Seint George taught the kynge of foure thingges, that was that
f. 84va he shulde take gret cure of the chirches of God, and þat | he shulde
worship prestes, and here goodly the devine seruise, and þat he shuld

57 you] om. H1, 3e G   69 ronnen] comen G   70 the] om. G   75 I shall]
trs. E   79 into] in'to' H1   83 springithe] L, sprange EH1G   84 helithe] L,
heled EH1G   drinkithe] L, dranke EH1G   89 here] he`e´re H1

be almesfull to the pore. And thanne he toke his leue of the kynge and 90
went his waye.

In this tyme Dyoclician and Maximyan were emperours, and ther
was [so] gret persecucion do vnder Dacyen that was prouost that in a
monthe there were crowned by marterdome .xx.^{ti} thousand. And
amonge these tormentis many of the cristen failled and dede sacrifice 95
to the idoles. And whanne Seint George seigh this he was gretly sori
in his herte and went and parted to the pore al that he hadde, and dede
of his clothinge of knyghthode and clodid hym withe the habite of
cristen and lepte into the [middes] of the tyrauntes and saide: 'Alle the
goddes of gentiles bene deuels and oure Lorde God made heuene and 100
erthe.' To whom the prouost, full of wrethe, sayde: 'By what
presumpcion darst thou calle oure goddes fendes? Telle me what
thou art and what is thi name.' To whom he saide: 'I am called George
and am of the noble kinrede of Capadocye, and I am come into
Palestine by the will of God, and I haue lefte alle erthely thing frely 105
for that I myght the more suerly serue to almyghti God of heuene.'
And as the prouost myght in no wyse enclyne hym to his entent he
comaunded that he shulde be putte into a torment the whiche is called
amonge hem eculee, the whiche is a crosse and the two endes fastened
in the erthe, and vpon that torment his body shulde be al torent withe 110
hokes of iren membre fro membre. And whanne | he was all f. 84vb
dismembred, yet he putte in his sides brondes of fyre al brennyng,
the whiche brent hym so greuously that all hys bowels were sene, and
thanne he comaunded that his [woundes] shulde be felled withe salt
and harde froted therwith. And the same nyght Seint Pcter appered to 115
George withe gret lyght and comforted hym full suetely by that
vision, wherof he toke suche comfort that he sette nothinge by his
tormentis. And whanne Dacyen seigh that he myght not ouercome
hym withe peynes, he called to hym an enchauntoure and saide to
hym that [the] cristen men despised his tormentes by her art magyke, 120
'an [they] despise the sacrifice of oure goddes.' And thanne the
enchauntoure sayde: 'If I ouercome not his art I will lese myn
hede.' And thanne he dede his cursed crafte and called his goddes

90 be] *ins.* H1   93 so] L, a EH1G   95 amonge] *add* all G   96 he] *om.* H1
sori] sorwid G   99 the¹] *om.* G   middes] middell E   the²] *om.* H1   100 goddes]
goodes *changed to* goddes H1   deuels] deu'e'ls H1   102 goddes] goddes *with* od *on*
erasure and 'gods' *in margin* H1   105 Palestine] Palestinet *with second* t *del.* H1
107 myght] most G   108 into] in H1G   the whiche] þat G   112 al] *om.* H1
114 woundes] L, bowels EH1G   119 to²] *om.* H1G   120 the] tho EH1
121 they] tho EG, the'i' H1

to helpe hym. And whanne he hadde do he toke wyne and medled
125 withe venyme and toke it to George, and þe seruaunt of God toke it
and made the signe of the crosse therouer and dranke it of witheoute
felynge of any disese. And whanne the enchauntour seigh this he
medeled ayein the wyne with strengger venyme thanne he dede before
and toke it to George, and he made the signe of the crosse therouer
130 and dranke it witheoute any harmynge of hym. And whanne the
enchauntoure seigh al this he fell anone to the fete of Seint George
and asked hym foryeuenesse with sore wepinge, byseching hym that
he myght receyue the sacrement of bapteme. And whanne the iuge
seigh this he made anone the enchauntour to be byheded. And the day
f. 85ʳᵃ foluynge he comaunded þat | George were sette on a whele arayed
136 witheinne and witheoute with sharpe swerdes, but anone the whele
tobraste and George was found al hole. And thanne was the prouost
wode for wrothe and comaunded hym to be thrawe in a caudron full of
hote molten lede. And thanne he made the signe of the crosse therouer
140 and by the vertue therof he satte [therein] as in a goodly batthe.

And whan Dacyen seigh this, that he myght not surmounte hym
withe tormentis, he wolde assaye to ouercome hym withe softe
wordes, and thanne he saide to hym: 'George, my good sone, seest
thou not how debonayre oure goddes bene that so sufferably susteyne
145 the? And yet thou blameste hem, and they be euer redy to foryeue the
yef thou wilt conuerte the to hem. Right suete sone, do now as I teche
the, forsake thi fals lawe and do sacrifice to oure goddes, and thou
shalt haue gret worshippes of hem and of vs.' To whom George saide
with a smylinge chere: 'Whi hadde ye not begonne with fayre wordes
150 rather thanne with tormentes at the begynnynge? I am redy to do
thine askinge.' And thanne Dacien, scorned by this beheste, was
wonder gladde and comaunded to make a crye that alle the peple
shulde assemble to see George parte fro his lawe that hadde so long
stryuen withe the contrary. And thanne al the citee was full of ioye,
155 and whanne George entered into the temple of ydoles to do sacrifice
and alle the peple were there to beholde hym, he kneled downe and
praied to oure Lorde that he wolde vtterly destroie al the temple and
f. 85ʳᵇ the ydoles, so þat atte the preisinge of hym and the | conuersion of the
peple ther shuld nothinge abyde therof. And anone ther descended

124 medled] *add* it G   134 byheded] bihedd *with* hedd *del.* ʼhedidʼ H1   135 on]
in H1   138 in] *add* to G   139 molten] melting H1   140 therein] L, *om.* EH1G
goodly] goode H1   143 thanne] *om.* H1   144 so] *om.* H1   152 the] *om.* H1G
157 wolde] *ins.* H1

fyre from heuene and brent the temple and the goddes and the 160
prestes, and sodenly the erthe opened and swaloued alle so that ther
lefte nothinge therof.

This tellithe Ambrose in his Preface, and saiethe: 'George the right
true knyght of Ihesu Crist, whanne he gouerned the profession of
cristente priuely, he only confessed withoute drede the sone of God 165
among the idolatres, to whom the devyne grace graunted suche
stabelnesse of faithe that he despised the comandementes of the
myght of the tyraunt and dradde not the tormentis of peynes
witheoute nombre. O thou noble knyght and champion of oure
Lorde, that were not deceyued withe the smothe behestes of temporall 170
reynynge, but thi persecutours weren deceyued, and the shewing of
her fals images were thrawe downe into hell.'

And whanne Dacyen hadde sayne these thingges he made George
to be called before hym and saide to hym: 'Whiche bene thi malefices,
thou worst of all men, that haste done suche a felonye?' And thanne 175
George saide to hym: 'What, wenest not thow [that] it be so? Come
ayen with me and thou shalt see me [ayen] do sacrifice.' And he saide:
'Nay, for now I vnderstonde well thi frauude, for thou woldest make
me to be swalued [into] the erthe lyke as thou hast do my temple and
my goddes.' [And thanne saide George to hym]: 'O thou cursed 180
wreche, how mowen thi goddes helpen the that bene not of power to
helpe hemselff?' And thanne the kynge was gretly wrothe and tolde it
to Alyandrine | his wyff and said: 'Allas, I deye and faill for sorugh, for f. 85ᵛᵃ
I see well that I am ouercome of this man.' Sche ansuered and saide:
'Thou cruel tyraunt and wicked bocher, [haue I not] ofte saide to the 185
that thou shuldest not be so cruel to cristen men, for her god fyghteth
for hem? And truste it well that I will be cristen.' And thanne was the
kynge sore abaysshed and saide: 'Allas, with what sorugh art thou now
deceyued?' And thanne he made her to be hangged by the heer right
[c]ruelly and to bete her body with roddes. And whiles men bete her 190
she cried to George: 'O thou light of trouthe, whider trowest thou that
I goo that am not wasshen with the water of bapteme?' And thanne
George saide to her: 'Drede the not, doughter, for the shedinge of thi
blode shall be sette to the for bapteme, and thou shalt haue a crowne.'
And thanne in sayeng her orisons she yelded vp [the] sperit. And this 195

160 and²] *om.* G   173 these] þis *del.* ʾþeseʾ H1   176 that] *om.* EG   it] *ins.* H1
177 with] to H1   ayen] *om.* E   179 to] *om.* H1G   into] in E   180 And . . . hym]
om. E   183 faill] faʿiʾlle H1   185 bocher] broþer H1, brothel G   haue I not] I
haue E   186 god fyghteth] god fiʾȝʾteþe H1   190 cruelly] ruelly E   beteʾ] bete *with*
second e *on erasure* H1   195 yelded] ȝaf G   the] her EH1

witnessith Ambrose in his Preface, sayeng: 'For that the quene of the
peple of Perce comdampned her husbond by cruell sentence witheoute hauynge grace of bapteme deserued victorie of glorious passion,
of the which we mowe not drede but that the rednesse of her blood
200 she had deserued to vnshette the yates of he[uen] and she to entre and
take in possessyon the kyngdom of heuene.'

The day foluyng George receyued such sentence that he shulde be
drawen thorugh all the citee and thanne his hede to be smiten of. And
than he praied to oure Lorde that whosoeuer requered his helpe that
205 he myght haue his requeste. A vois come to hym fro heuene and said |
f. 85vb to hym that it was graunted as he hadde desired. And whanne he
hadde endyd his orison he fulfelled his marterdom and hadde his hede
smyten of. And he was vnder Dyoclician and Maximian that
bygannen aboute the yere of oure Lorde .CC.iiij^{xx}. and seuen. And
210 whanne Dacyen retorned fro the place wher he hadde bene byheded
to his paleys warde, the fyre of vengeaunce descended fro heuene þat
brent hym with al his mynistres.

[Gregory] of Toures tellith that as som folke beren diuerse reliques
of Seint George and they were herborued in a litell oratorie, and
215 whanne the morwtyde come they myght in no wyse remeve the shrine
from thennes till they hadde sum of the relyques there.

It is redde also in the Stori of Antioche that as the cristen went to
besege Ierusalem a semely yonge man appered to a preste and saide
[to] hym that he was Se[i]nt George, the duke of cristen men, and
220 taught hym how that they shulde bere withe hem reliques and he
wolde be withe hem. And whanne they hadde beseged Ierusalem the
Sarizenes defended hem so strongly that the cristine men durste not
go vp vpon the laders to scale the towne. Anone Seint George, clothed
al in white armes and with a crosse of rede in the middes, taught hem
225 how they shulde stie vp after hym suerly and they shulde take þe
citee. And with his blessed comforte they toke hardinesse and toke the
cite and slow all the Sarizenes.

199 rednesse] redinesse H1   200 heuen] L, hem EG, hem *changed to* heuen H1
203 drawen] þrowe G   213 Gregory] L, George EH1G   215 morwtyde]
mornyng G   216 they] he G   hadde] *add* 'left' H1   219 to] *om.* EH1   Seint]
sent E   220 hem] *add* 'his' H1   223 vp] *om.* G   clothed] L, *add* hym EH1G
224 armes] 'h'armes *with* m *changed to* ny H1, armure G   227 Sarizenes] Sazezines
changed to Sarezines H1

Here endithe the lyff of Seint George, and nexst bygynnithe
the lyff of Seint Marke the Euuangeliste, Capitulum .lv.

Seint Marke the Euuangeliste was of the ordre | of dekens and prest, Gf. 113ᵛ
and he was in his bapteme the sone of Seint Petir the appostul and his
dissipul also in the word of God. | He wente to Rome with Seint Petir, Gf. 114ʳ
and as Seint Petir prechid þere the gospel, the good cristen pepul
there prayid Seint Petir þat þe blessid Seint Mark myght write hem 5
þe gospel þat þay myȝt alwey haue it in mende. He wrote it ful trewly
as he hadde hurde it of Seint Petir his mayster, and Petir examynyd it
ful diligently, and whanne he sawȝ þat sche was ful of all trouthe he
aprovid it to be resseyuyd of all trewe cristen pepul. And whanne
Petir sawȝ þat Marke was parfite in the feith he sente hym into 10
Aquyle, and þere he prechid þe word of God and conuertid to þe faith
of Ihesu Crist grete multitude of pepul. And þere he wrote þe gospel
like as he dide at Rome, the wiche into this day is schewid in þe
chirche of Aquyle and is þere kepte by grete deuocion. And atte laste he
brouȝt to Rome to Seint Petir Ermagorin, a man of the cite of Aquyle 15
þat he hadde conuertid to þe faith of Ihesu Crist for to ordeyne hym
bisshop of Aquyle. And whanne Ermagoryn hadde resseyuyd þe
bisshoprich and the office and gouernyd long the chirche of Aquyle,
he was take of þe mysbyleuers and crownyd withe martirdom.

And Marke was sente by Seint Petir into Alisaundre, and þere he 20
prechid furste the word of God. And in [his] furste entre into
Alisaundre, so as Philo þat was þe moste sotill man of Iewis seith,
þat he assemblid þere grete multitude of pepul and ordeynyd hem in
faith and deuocion and for to kepe continence, and Papie bisshop of
Ieropolis deuysith and clerith in nobul wise the riȝt preysyngis of 25
hym. And Piers Damacien seith also of hym: 'Oure Lord hath
ennoblid [hym] with so gret gracis in Alisaundre þat all þoo þat
come þan by hym to the knowleche of þe feithe fleyȝen to þe heignesse
of perfeccion by contynens and by stabulnesse of holy conuersacion,
riȝt as þouȝ þay were in profession of religion. And he drewȝ hem not 30
oonly by schewyng of myraclis ne by predicacion, but he drewe hem
by riȝt nobul ensamplis.' And it is seide [of] hym þat he was of so
grete humylite þat he wold haue kutte of his þvmbe for he wold not

EH1GH2A1A2L; E breaks off after 1 *ordre* and resumes at 193 *smyten*   5 write] wri/
ght *changed to* write *with* ght *del.* H1   13 schewid] *on erasure* H1   16 hym] *add* to
be G   20 Seint] sent H1   21 his] *om.* GH1 (*sa* P2)   27 ennoblid] enuolued H1
hym] *om.* G   32 is] 'is' H1   of¹] L, to GH1   33 þvmbe] thumbe *with* th *on
erasure* H1

take on hym the ordre of presthode, but the ordynaunce of God and
þe autorite | of Seint Petir preuaylid þat he was ordeynyd bisshop of
36 Alisaundre. And as sone as he entrid into Alisaundre his shoo brak
sodeynly and was al torente, wherby he vndirstode in spirite and
seide: 'Verily oure Lord hath fulfillid my viage, ne þe fende may not
lette me whom oure Lord hath assoylid fro þe werkis of deth.' And
40 thanne Marke sawe a sowter sowyng olde schone. He toke hym his
shoo to sowe, and as he sowid it he hurt his lifte hond greuously, and
whanne he hadde doon he bigan to crie gretly: 'Oon oonly God is and
no moo.' And whanne Marke hurde þis he seide: 'Trewly God hath
fulfillid my viage.' And þanne he toke a litille erthe and spotille and
45 made a plastir and enoyntid the hond of the man, and he was hole
anoon. And whanne þis man saw3 so grete vertu in hym he ladde hym
to his hous and askid hym what he was and whens he was. He tolde
hym þat he was þe seruant of oure Lord Ihesu Crist. To whom þe
man seide: 'I wold fayne see hym.' And þanne Marke seide to hym: 'I
50 schal schewe hym to the anoon.' And þanne he bigan to preche hym of
Ihesu Crist and baptisid hym with alle his meyne.

      And whanne þe men of þe cite hurd this þyng, þat þer was come a
man [oute] of Galile þat dispisid her goddis, þay lay in awaite of hym,
and whanne he wiste þat, he ordeynyd hym þat he hadde baptisid to
55 be bisshop of þat place and wente hymself into Mentapolyn. And
whanne he hadde be there .ij. 3ere he come a3en into Alisaundre and
fonde good cristen pepul welle ymultiplyed. And þe bisshopis of þe
tempul enforsid hem to take hym, and as Seint Marke halwid þe
solempnyte of Estre, alle þe bisshopis assemblid there and toke hym
60 and putte aboute his nekke a corde and seide: 'Drawe we this bocher
to the bocherie.' And as þay drew3 hym his flessh hangid in the erthe
and his blode we[t]e alle þe stonys. And aftir þat þay enclosid hym in
prison and þere he was comfortid with aungellis, and oure Lord Ihesu
Crist comfortid hym, seying: 'Pees be to Marke my euangeliste.
65 Drede the not, for y am withe the to take þe fro hens.' And þan in [þe]
morowtide þay putte the corde a3en aboute his nekke and drow3 | hym
dispitously here and there and cride: 'Drawe this bocher to the place
of bocherie.' He mekely 3eldid þankyngis to God, seying: 'Y 3elde my
spirite into [thi] hondis.' And in þat seying he putte oute his spirite

38 viage] visage *with* s *erased* H1   41 hurt his lifte] *corrected from* lifte his oon G
43 hurde] hedd *changed to* herd H1   53 oute] *om.* G   55 Mentapolyn] *changed to*
Apentapolyn H1   58 þe] *ins.* G   62 wete] went *with* n *subp.* H1, wente G
65 the²] *ins.* H1   þe²] *om.* G   68 He] ye *changed to* he H1   þankyngis] þonkez H1
69 thi] this G

aboute the ȝere of oure Lord .lvij. vndir Nero. And as the paynymys 70
wold haue brent hym the eyre was sodeynly troblid and bigan to
thundre and to haile and to liȝtne so þat euery creature enforsid h[e]m
to skape and to leue the body there, and þanne þe good cristen pepul
stole the body and buryid it w[orschip]fully in the chirche.

The feturis of hym were siche: he hadde a long nose and bente 75
browis, faire eyen and a long berde, of faire gretnesse, of ripe age,
medlid with hore here, continent by affeccion, ful of þe grace of God.
The blessid Ambrose seith in þis wise of hym: 'So as þe blessid Marke
schynyd by miraclis, it fille þat þe sowter to whom he hadde take his
scho to sowe aȝen perschid his lifte honde in sowyng it aȝen, and 80
[when he] was hurte he cryid there was oon only God. The seruant of
God was glad whanne he hurde þis þyng. He made a litille cleye with
his spotil and with the erthe and anoyntid his hond and helid hym
sodeynly, and he dide his labour. He prechid hym the gospel, and he
was chaungid sodeynly by myracle, and þoo þat were blynd fro her 85
birthe oure Lord ȝaf hem siȝt by his meritis.' Thus seith Ambrose.

In the ȝere of þe incarnacion of oure Lord .iiijC.lxvij. the
Venysiens bere the body of Seint Mark fro Alisaundre into Venyse,
and there þay haue made a chirche of merueylous bewte in the
worschip of hym. Certeynly summe merchauntis of Venyse þat were 90
goon into Alisaundre diden so myche by ȝiftis and by hestis to two
prestis þat kepte the body of Seint Marke þat þay lete hem bere hym
into Venyse. And sewrely whanne þe body was priuyly lifte vp of the
tvmbe so grete a sauour of swetnesse sprong oute þoruȝ alle
Alisaundre þat alle merueylid gretly whens þis sauour myght come 95
þat was so merveylously swote. And whanne þay were in the see
saylyng þay told to her felaschip þat were in [ot]her schippis how þat
þay hadde with hem the holy body of Seint Marke. | And oon of the Gf.115ᵛ
schipmen of anoþir schip that hurde þis answerid and seide: 'Ȝe
perauenture it is summe body of summe Egipcien, and ȝe wene þat it 100
be the body of Seint Mark.' And anoon sodeynly the schippe þat the
body was ynne turnyd hym with grete haste toward the schip þat the
man was ynne [þat] seide þese wordis, and hurtlid with hym so sore
that he rente oute a grete partie of þe side of the schip, and he wold
neuer stynte for no crafte þat eny man couthe doo tille alle the men 105

72 hem] hym G   74 worschipfully] wrongfully G   79 by] *add* vertuys *del.* G
80 lifte] leeft *with second* e *subp. and add* 'hond' H1   honde . . . aȝen] and in sewyng it
ayene *del.* H1   81 when he] L, *om.* GH1   85 chaungid] L, *add* so d *del.* G
92 hem] him H1   97 other] her G   100 þat] *ins.* H1   103 þat] L, and G, and *del.*
'that' H1   105 stynte] stint'te' H1

þat were in þat schippe criden þat þay bileuyd verily þat it was the body of Seint Mark.

Anoþer tyme it fille in a nyght þat as þe schippis saylid faste by tempest and turment of the see þat þe schipmen were so weri and so
110 wrappid in derknesse þat þay wiste not where þay were. Seint Marke apperid to a monke þat kepte his body and seide to hym: 'Goo bidde the schipmen þat þay drowe doun her seylis, for þay be not ferre fro lond.' þay dide so, and in the morowtide thay fonde hemself faste by an yle.

115   And as þay passid by meny dyuerse cuntreis and hidden alwey the body of Seint Marke, the pepul of oon of þe cuntreis þat þay come by come to hem and seide: 'A, how ȝe be blessid þat beren the body of Seint Marke with ȝou. For Goddis loue suffre vs to doo hym worschip and reuerence.'

120   A schipman þat was there leuyd not þat it was the body of Seint Marke, and anoon he was so turmentid with the fende þat he was alle oute of hymself, and so he was brouȝt to þe holy body and anoon the fende lefte hym, and thanne he knowlechid þe blessid body of Seint Marke and þankid God of his dellyueraunce and the precious
125 corseint, and euer aftir he hadde grete deuocion to Seint Marke.

In a tyme it fille þat þe holy body of Seint Marke was closid vp in a piller of marbil [so] þat fewe men knewe þat he was there, and þis was doon for to kepe hym þe more surely and þe more sotilly. And so it happid þat þoo þe wiche hadde knowleche hereof were passid oute of
130 þis world, and no creature hadde knowleche where þis holy body was bicome by no maner of token þat þay couthe perseyue, and for þis
G f. 116ʳ cause þat þay hadde | lost her holy patron, wherfore þay lete ordeyne a solempne fastyng with solempne procession. And þanne þer was a grete complaynte among the clerkis [and] þe lay pepul sorwyng gretly
135 þat þay had loste her holy patron. And the whilis þis solempnyte was adoyng ther fille a wondir þyng, for sodeynly bifore alle þe pepul þe stonys of the same piller wherein the body was lepten oute, þat euery creature myght openly see the schryne wherin the holy body was closid. And whanne the pepul sawȝ þis þay were gretly raueschid and
140 comfortid and ȝauen worthy þankyngis and praysyngis to God, maker of alle þyngis, þat liste of his grace to schewe hem þis grete myracle

108 schippis] shippes *with final* s *erased* H1   113 so] do *changed to* so H1
117 hem] him H1   125 euer] euery ȝere GH1   127 so] L, ʽsecretlyʼ so H1, secretly
G   he] *add* thanne G   128 for] *ins.* H1   and] *add* eke G   134 and] & *on erasure*
H1, þat G   137 theⁱ] ʽþeʼ H1   141 liste of] lift vpp H1

and to graunte hem aȝen the possession of [her] patron. And þanne þe
day was worschipid with so grete solempnyte for þe schewyng of þis
myracle þat it was ordeynyd to be festful euer aftirward.

Ther was a ȝong man þat hadde a canker at his brest the wiche 145
turmentid hym greuously, and so among his grete peynys he prayid
helpe of þis holy seint with grete deuocion. And as þis man sclepte
ther apperid to hym a man in habite of a pilgryme, the wiche hyid
hym faste as þouȝ he hadde a grete iourne to doo. And þis sike man
askid hym what he was þat passid by hym so hastily. He answerid and 150
seide þat he was Seint Marke þat wente in grete haste to helpe a
schippe þat was in poynte to perissh þat hadde hertily and pitously
cryid aftir his helpe. And in þis seying he putte forth his hond and
towchid the sore, and whanne þis man awoke he felte hymself alle
hole. And within a litille while aftir þe schippe come to the porte of 155
Venyse and told what perile he hadde be ynne and þe helpe þat Seint
Mark hadde doon hem. And þanne alle the pepul ȝaf preysyng[is] to
oure Lord for þat one and þat oþir myracle, and þus oure Lord was
glorified in Marke his seynte.

It fille in a tyme þat marchauntis of Venyse weren wente into 160
Alisaundre in a schippe of Saraȝynys, and as þe cristen sawȝ þat þay
were in poynte to perissh þay wente alle into a litille schippe and
smote atwo the cordis, and anoon þe schippe perischid | and alle þe Gf. 116ᵛ
Saraȝynys were drownyd in the wawis of þe see. And oon of þe
Saraȝynys cride to Seint Marke and bihiȝt hym þat if he myght eskape 165
he wold visite his chirche and resseyue bapteme, and anoon a faire
ȝong man ful of briȝtnesse apperid to hym and toke hym oute of þe
wawis and putte hym into [þe] bote among the cristen pepul. And
whanne he come into Alisaundre he toke noon hede to hym that hadde
dellyueryd hym of þis perile, for neythir he visitid his chirche nothir 170
he resseyuyd the sacrament of the feithe. To whom Seint Marke
apperid aȝen [and blamyd hym of that he hadde not holde hys
promyse], and þanne he was conuertid to the faith and come to
Venyse and was cristenyd and callid Marke and leuyd parfitly in God
and endid his lif in good werkis. 175

142 her] the G   143 schewyng] swewing H1   144 aftirward] after H1
145 canker] on erasure H1   153 his'] ins. G   154 hymself] hem selffe with hem changed
to hym H1   155 within] om. H1   156 he] changed to 't'he'i' H1   þe] add he del. H1
156–9 and . . . seynte] twice once del. with 158 oon and þat and 159 'holy' included H1
157 doon] add 'to' H1   preysyngis] preysinges with es erased H1, preysyng G   158 one
and þat] om. H1   159 in] add holy G   160 wente] ins. H1   162 in] add a H1
167 þe] L, a G, þe on erasure H1   172–3 and . . . promyse] L, om. GH1

A man wrou3t an heigh in the stepul of Seint Marke of Venyse and
vnware he fille fro a merveylous heithe, but in his fallyng he for3ate
not to aske the helpe of Seint Marke, wherfore he deseruyd to fynde in
his fallyng a tre, the wiche sustenyd hym tille men gate hym doun by
180 cordis. And so he eskapid withoute hurtyng and turnyd a3en deuoutly
and made an ende of the werke that he hadde bygunne.

The seruaunt of a temperel lord of the prouynce was constreynyd
by avowe to visite the body of Seint Marke, but he myght in no wise
haue leue of his lord, and whanne he saw3 þis he toke more drede of
185 God þanne of man and wente to visite þis seynte with grete deuocion
withoute takyng leue of his lord, the wiche þyng his lord toke so yuel
þat whanne he was turnyd a3en he comaundid þat his eyen schold be
putte oute. The cruel tyrauntis obeyde to her maister anoon and
þrewen hym doun the seruaunt of God to the erthe, he crying to Seint
190 Marke, and with hokis of yren þay wold haue drawe oute his eyen. But
þay couthe not with no strengthe þat þay couthe make, but þese hokis
turnyd a3en and al [to]brasten. And þanne he comaundid þat his þyes
E f. 86ra   schold be | smyten of withe an axe, but whanne thei wolde haue
smiten on hym the iren wexid so softe that in no wise it greued hym.
195 And thanne the lorde comaunded that his tethe shulde be smyten oute
withe hamers of iren, but the iren forgate his naturel kinde of
hardenesse and turned by the vertue of God into gret softenesse.
And whan the lorde seigh all this he asked foryeuenesse and went with
his servaunt with gret deuocion to visite the sepulcre of Seint Marke.

200 A knyght was wounded in a bataile so that his honde was so nye
smiten of that it hangged [but] by a litell skinne of his arme in suche
wise that the leches counsayled hym to smite al of, for there was none
other remedy. But this worthi man hadde grete shame to be one
honded and bade hem sette his honde in his place and binde it vp
205 withe cloutes withoute any medecine and besought hertely the helpe
of Seint Marke, and anone his honde was restored to his furste hele
and ther abode nothing but the dreieng up of the wounde, and in
witnessinge of so gret a myracle and of so gret a benefice he went to
visite the sepulcre of this holy seint.

210 As a knyght rode armed ouer a brigge his hors stombeled and fille
and the knyght fell into the botom of the water, and as he felt that he

176 wrou3t] brought *with* b *changed to* w H1   183 avowe] *add* and *del.* H1
185 wente] *add* to went *del.* H1   188 tyrauntis] T'i'rances H1   191 þat þay couthe]
ins. H1   192 al tobrasten] also brasten G   201 but] *om.* G   205 cloutes]
clothis G

shulde drowne he called to the mercifull helpe of Seint Marke, and
anone the holy seint helde to hym a spere and drewe hym vp of the
water. And than he come to Venise and tolde this miracle and fulfelled
his avowe deuoutely.   215

A man of the citee of Maneue was falsly accused of som enuious |
man so that he was putte in prison, and whanne he hadde be there f. 86rb
fourty daies he was full gretly anoyed, and thanne he beganne to faste
thre dayes and required the helpe of Seint Marke, and anone he
appered to hym and comaunded hym to go oute of [the] prison, for he 220
myght go suerly. This sely man toke no gret hede to his wordes but
fell aslepe of werinesse and went not oute, supposing it hadde bene
but a dreme. And after this Seint Marke appered to hym the secounde
tyme and the thridde tyme and charged hym to go oute, and thanne he
toke beter hede and perceiued the dore of the prisone open, and 225
sodenly his cheines brosten and he went oute of the prisone aboute
mydday before alle [the] kepers and many other, and none of hem alle
sawe hym. And thanne he went to the tombe of Seint Marke and gaue
deuoutely thankinge to God and to the [glorious] seint.

As it fell in a tyme that ther was a gret derthe in Poyle, for al thinge 230
was dreied vp for defauut of reyne, and thanne it was shewed hem that
they hadde that pestilence for they halowed not the feste of Seint
Marke, and as sone as they hadde cried to Seint Marke and behight
hym to halow his feste, he droue oute the pestilence of that contrey
and gaue hem gret abundaunce and good eyre and couenable reyne. 235

Aboute the yere of oure Lord a thousand .CC.xlj.^{ti} there was a frere
of Pauye of the ordre of Frere Prechoures, [that] was holy and of
religious conuersacion. Iulyen was his name, borne of Fauentyne,
yonge in age but auncien in corage, the whi|che was seke vnto the f. 86va
dethe and sent for the priour of his hous and tolde [hym] that his 240
dethe was nighe, and sodenly he appered so full of ioie and gladnesse
that he beganne to streche oute his hondes and to crie: 'Bretheren,
yeue me place, for treuly for the gret abundaunce of ioie that I fele my
soule will oute of my body, so ioifull tidingges I haue herde.' And

215 avowe] *add* ful G   220 the] *om.* E   227 the] L, his EH1G
229 glorious] holy E   230 As] So as H1   a²] *om.* H1G   235 and²] of G   good]
gold G   eyre] ȝire *with* ȝ *on erasure* H1   237 of¹] *add* 'þe cuntrey of' H1, *so* G   of³]
add the G   that] *om.* E   that was] thas *del.* 'þat was a' H1, þat was an G   holy] *add* 'man'
H1, *add* man G   of⁴] a G   238 his] his *changed to* þis *and add* 'Freris', þis Freris G
name] *add* 'and he was' H1, *so* G   239 but] *add* 'he was' H1, *add* he was G
240 and] *add* 'he' H1, *add* he G   for] aftir G   the] his H1   hym] *om.* EH1   241 so]
om. H1   243 fele] *add* 'þat' H1, *so* G   244 my] þe G

245 thanne he lefte up his hondes to heuene ande saide: 'Lorde, take my
soule oute of this prisone. I, wreched man, who shalle deliuer me from
the body of this dedly lyff?' And amonges these saiengges he fell
aslepe of a lyght slomber and seigh Seint Marke comynge to hym and
stode besides his [bed]de, and he herde a vois that saide: 'Marke, what
250 doest thou here?' And he ansuered: 'I am come to this man that
deyethe here for his seruice is agreable to his God.' And thanne the
voys saide ayein: 'Whi art thou rather come hedir thanne other
seintes?' He saide: 'For he hadde to me a speciall deuocion and
hathe devoutly visited the place wher my body rest[ith], and therfor
255 I am come to visite hym atte the houre of his passinge hens.' And
thanne men clothed alle in white fulfelled al the hous, and Marke
saide to hem: 'What do ye here?' And they saide: 'For to present this
soule before oure Lorde.' And thanne the frere awoke and sent for hys
prioure and tolde hym alle these thingges and slepte goodly in oure
260 Lorde Ihesu Crist. And I in myn owne persone herde these thingges
of þe same prioure.

Here endithe the lyff of Seint Marke, and nexst foluithe
the lyff of Seint Marcelline, Capitulum .lvj.

Seint Marcelline gouerned the sege of Rome .ix. yere and [.iiij.]
f. 86ᵛᵇ monthes. | He was take by the comaundement of Dioclician and of
Maximyen and was brought to do sacrifice, and for drede that he
hadde to deye he putte in his sacrifice two greynes of encense. And
5 thanne was ther gret ioye amonge the mesbeleuers, but true cristen
men were fulfelled withe moche sorughe, for her hede was sore smete
and full [s]ike, but the most myghti membres releued and dradde not
the manaces of the princes. And thanne the good cristen peple come
to Marcellyn and vndertoke hym gretly, and whanne he seighe this he
10 submitted hym to the correccion of bisshoppes for to iuge hym as hem
luste. To whom thei saide: 'God defende that euer we iuge oure
souerayn bisshop. Beholde thine owne cause and iuge thiselff with

247 saiengges] seintes *del.* `seiynge' H1   249 bedde] L, hede EH1G   250 thou]
ins. H1   251 for . . . is] `for by cause þat his seruice is ful' H1, *so* G   his seruice is] *ins.*
H1   is] *add* `ful' H1, *so* G      252 hedir] *om.* G    thanne] *add* eny of G      253 He] `and
he answerid' *with* he *ins. within the insertion* H1, and he answerid and G   and] *del. and add*
`bifore oþer and also he' H1, *so* G      254 restith] L, rest E, rest`eth ynne' H1, *add* ynne G
255 am] *add* `now' H1, *add* now G   the] *ins.* H1   260 I] *om.* H1   261 thingges] *add*
þus H1G

EH1GH2A1A2L   1 .iiij.] .viij. E   7 sike] like E, like *changed to* sike H1

thine owne mouthe.' And thanne he repented hym gretly and wepte
heuyly and deposed hymselff, but thei chase hym ayenne. And
whanne the emperour herde this thinge he made take hym ayein 15
and he wolde in no wise sacrifice, and thanne he comaunded that he
shulde haue the hede smete of. And the wodenesse of Goddes
enemyes was so gretly encresed that withinne a monthe .xvij.
thousand were beheded. And whanne Marcellin shulde be byheded
he saide he was not worthy to [be] beried in cristen beriales, and 20
therfor he acursed al tho that wold berie hym, for the whiche cause
the body of hym was vnberied .xxxv.^{ti} dayes. After that Seint Peter
appered to Marcel that was successour to Marcellin and saide:
'Brother Marcell, whi bery ye me not?' He ansuered: 'Lorde, art
thou not beried?' And Seint Peter ansuered ayein: 'I holde me not 25
buried as longe as Marcelline is vnberied.' To whom he saide: 'Lorde,
wost thou not well that | he acursed alle tho that shulde berie hym?' f. 87ra
And thanne Seint Peter said hym: 'Is it not wreten that he that louithe
hymselff shall be enhaunsed, and thow aughtest well to haue
vnderstonde that. And therfor go anone and berie hym atte my 30
fete.' He went anone and fulfelled his comaundement.

Here endithe the lyff of Seint Marcelline, and nexst
foluithe the liff of Seint Vitall, knyght, Cap^m. .lvij.^m

Vitall knyght and consult engendered of Valerie his wyff Gerueyse
and Protaise. And this same Vitall entered into Rauene withe the iuge
Paulyne, and as he seigh there a cristen phisician that hight Vrsin
whiche was comaunded to be byheded after many tormentes, this
Vrsin was in gret drede to deye, wherfor Seint Vitall cried vnto hym 5
and saide: 'Brother Vrsine, leche that were wont to hele other, now
slee not thiselff withe euerlasting dethe. Sethe thou haste had the
victori of many passiones, lese not thi crowne that is araied to the of
oure Lorde.' And whanne Vrsine hadde herde this he was well
comforted and repented hym of his voyde drede and receiued 10
gladly his marterdome. And Seint Vitale beried hym worshipfully
and after that he deyned no more to goo to Paulyn his maister in as

14 heuyly] heuenly *with* n *subp.* H1   19 shulde] shul'd' H1   20 be] *om.* E
21 acursed] *add* hem H1G   23 Marcell] Marcellyn G   26 Lorde] *twice once del.* H1
27 well] *ins.* H1   28 Is it] *trs.* H1   louithe] loued H1   29 aughtest] wotest H1

EH1GH2A1A2L   3 phisician] Phicicion *changed to* Phisicion H1   12 deyned]
d'e'yned H1

moche as he wold verrely be knowen that he was cristen. And thanne
Paulyn comaunded that he shulde be sette in the torment that was
15 called eculee. And thanne Vitall saide: 'Thou art to verray a fool to
thenke that thou woldist deceiue me that haue alwaye be besy to
comfort [other].' And thanne saide Paline to his servauntes: 'Lede
f. 87rb hym | before the palmer, [and] but yef he will do sacrifice, make right
there a depe pitte til ye come to the water and berie hym therinne al
20 quik.' And so thei dede. The blessed Vitalle was beried al quik the
yere of oure Lorde .lvij. And the preste of [the] idoles that hadde geue
his counsell was anone rauished withe the fende and was verray wood
.vij. dayes and cried in the place wher Seint Vitall was buried: 'Allas,
Vitall, how thou brennest me.' And in the .vij.^te day þe fende threwe
25 hym in the riuer wher he deied cursedly.

And as the wiff of Seint Vitall [re]turned ayein to Melan she founde
men that sacrificed to ydoles, the whiche prayed her that she wolde ete
of the thingges that were sacrificed to the idoles. She ansuered and
saide: 'I am a cristen woman. It longethe not to me to ete of youre
30 sacrifices.' And whanne they herde that, they beten her so cruelly that
her men that were with her beren her to Melane as halff dede, and ther
she passed to oure Lorde [debonairly within the thridde day].

Here endithe the liff of Seint Vitall, and nexst foluithe the
lyff of Seint Peter of Melane, Capitulum .lviij.^m

Seint Peter, nwe marter of the Ordre of Prechoures, noble champion
of the faithe, was borne of the citee of Nerone. This same was brought
forthe of the smoke right as a shininge lyght, of thornes as a white
lelye, of breres as a fresshe rede rose, and he come of a blinde kinrede
5 be errour and he was a clere and a no[b]le prechour. Also this same
f. 87va come of virginell beauute fro hem that were woun|ded withe errour in
her mynde and corrupte of her bodies, and loo this glorious marter
stied an hye and come oute of these thornes that were ordeined to
euerlastinge fire, for al his kinrede were heretikes from whos errours
10 he kepte h[y]m euer clene. And as he was of the age of .vij. yere and
come on a day fro scole, his vncle asked hym what he lerned. The
childe ansuered hym ayein that he lerned *Credo in Deum patrem* [et c.].

17 other] L, the EG, the 'kristen' H1   18 and] *om.* EH1   make] made H1
21 the²] *om.* EH1   26 returned] turned EH1   28 sacrificed] sacrafi'c'ed H1
32 debonairly . . . day] *om.* E, *ins.* H1

EH1GH2A1A2L   5 and²] '&' H1   noble] nole E   10 hym] hem E   12 et c.] *om.*
E, *ins.* H1

Thanne he saide to hym: 'Ne saye thou not "maker of heuene", for he was not maker of visible thingges, but the fende was maker of alle thingges that we [see].' And the childe affermed rather to be true as he 15 hadde lerned and as it was wretin. And thanne his vncle enforsed hym to shewe bi auctoritees ayeinst the childe and slowe hymselff withe his owne suerde, so þat he wost not whedir to turne hym, but went his waye al confused to his brother and saide hym alle these thingges betwene hem, and counsailed hym fully to take awaye his sone from 20 scole, and saide hym more: 'I drede me sore lest that Pers, whanne he is fully taught, wille be conuerted to that fals beleue and lest he will destroie and confounde oure lawe, sithe he saithe so moche now and hathe not lerned.' And he prophecied right as Cayphas whanne he saide that Pers shulde destroie the wickednes of heretikes. But for as 25 moche as this thinge was wrought be God, the fader wolde not consent to the [counsel] of his brother, but he hoped that he wolde make hym be drawe to his secte by som maister of heresie whanne he were taught | in the .vij. artes.   f. 87vb

And thanne whan this holy childe seighe that it was not to duelle 30 amonge the scorpions in dispisinge and his kinrede, he entred in al pure into the Ordre of Prechours, in the whiche Ordre he was .xxx.^{ti} wynter, and he liued pesiblye. Innocent the [pope] shewithe in his Epistell sayenge: 'Whanne Seint Peter with good purueaunce was turned from the fals be[gyl]inges of the worlde in his chyldehode he 35 went into the Ordre of Frere Prechoures, in which Ordre he was .xxx.^{ti} wynter made noble by the felawship of vertues, faythe goinge before, hope present, charitee felawe. He ouercome and profited by the defence of the faithe for the which he brende al as in an hote fire of loue, for he hadde continuel striff ayenste his cruel enemyes withe 40 hote corage and stable mynde, and ouercame and w[o]nne his continuel stryff be blessed marterdome. And right as Pers was sadde in the stone of the faithe, atte the laste he was in his passion smiten to the stone and stied vp crowned wor[th]ely to the stone Ihesu Criste.   45

And he kepte always withoute corrupcion virginite of thought and

15 we see] were E, *so changed to* we see H1   rather] rathe`r´ H1         17 auctoritees] auctoritee E        27 counsel] lewdenesse EH1         28 secte] se`c´te H1   he] þay G, he *on erasure* H1   31 and] *paraph del. and* of *on erasure* H1   32 pure] purete G 33 Pope] buschop *on erasure* E   shewithe] shewed H1G   35 begylinges] L, belevingges EH1, bylyngis G   the²] þe *changed to* þis H1, þis G   41 ouercame] *add* `hem´ H1   wonne] whanne E, whan *with* h *marked for deletion* H1   44 worthely] wordely E   46 alwayes] al his wayes E

bodye, and he felt neuer n[o] touch[ing] withe dedly synne, so as it is
well proued by the witnesse of his confessours, and for as moche as a
servaunt deliciously norisched striueth gladly ayeinst his lorde, he
50 spared hymselff fro etinge and drinkinge. And sothely, for he wolde
not suffre by slouthe and ydelnesse the awaytes of his enemye, he
haun[t]ed assiduelly the rightwisnesse of oure Lorde, so that he was so
ocupied in couenable thingges that vncouenable thingges had no place
f. 88ʳᵃ in hym, and he hadde hymselff in suche awaite that he was sure | ynow
55 of the wickednesse of sperites. [And] the silences of the nyght, whiche
bene acounted to mannes reste, he dispen[d]ed hem all in studye and
lesson after a litell reste and ocupied withe wakinge the tyme ordeined
to slepe. And he dispended the day in profite of soules, either in
prechingges, either in heringe of confessions, either [in] confoundinge
60 the venemous techinge of heretikes by right noble resones in whiche
he is knowe to be made noble by yeftes of spirituel grace. He was
agreable by deuocion, light by humylite, plesaunt by obedience, softe
by debonairte, ful of compassion by pitee, stable in pacience, amyable
by charitee, well ordeyned in alle [good maners] of vertues condicions.
65 He drowe other to highe vertues by his vertuous ensaumple. He was a
brennynge louer of the faithe and a noble techer therof. And he this
brennyng fighter had so printed faithe in his mynde that he was al
[yeuen] to her seruise, and the wordes and the werkes of hym were
fulfelled withe the vertue of faithe and that he co[uuei]ted to deye
70 therinne. It was wel proued in þat he hadde praied principaly oure
Lorde many a tyme that he myght deye for the faithe and that he
wolde neuer suffre hym passe oute of this worlde before he hadde take
the chalice of passion for his sake, and atte the laste he was not
deceiued of his desire.
75   And yet in his lyff oure Lorde worshipped hym by many a glorious
myracle. For in a tyme as he examyned a bisshop of eretikes whiche
was take withe the cristen, and many bisshoppes and religious and
grete partie of the citee were assembeled there as wel for to here hym
f. 88ʳᵇ preche as [for] | the examinacion, and ther they abyden longe in

47 felt] lefte H1   no touching] L, ne touched EH1G   it] *twice once erased* H1
48 as²] *ins.* H1   49 norisched] norsheth H1   52 haunted] L, haunsed EH1G
55 And] in EH1   silences] silence E   nyght] *followed by short erased word* H1   56 to]
add in EH1   dispended] dispented E   59 in²] the E   60 in] And H1   61–3 He
was . . . pacience] *twice once del.* H1   63 by²] bi *on erasure* H1   64 good maners]
maner goodly EH1   maners] *illeg. through damage* G   65 by his] *illeg. through damage* G
66 faithe] *illeg. through damage* G   67 fighter] fight'er' *on erasure* H1   68 yeuen]
yeuer E, ʒouen *on erasure* H1   69 couueited] conuerted E, *so changed to* couueited H1
79 for] of E, for *on erasure* H1

brennyn[g] of the sunne þat was right hote so that it t[orment]ed 80
gretly the peple. And thanne this maister of heretikes saide openly
tofore all the peple: 'O thou wicked Pers, [yef thou were] so holy as
these leude peple wenen that thou be and holden þe, whi sufferest
thou hem thus to deye for hete as thou doest? Why praiest thou not thi
god that he wolde ordeyne sum cloude to be bitwene the peple and 85
this hete, that thei perishe not in this wise?' And thanne the blessed
Pers ansuered and saide: 'Yf thou wilt behote me that thou wilt
forsake thine heresies, I shall praie oure Lorde that he do as thou haste
saied.' And than the heretikes crieden anone: 'Behote hym hardely,'
for they trowed verrely that it myght not be done. And the blessed 90
Pers behight verrely that it shulde be do. And than the cristen peple
were gretly abaisshed of this promysse in as moche as ther nas lytell
nor moche cloude that apered in the eyre, dredinge lest the faithe of
holy Chirche shulde be gretly blemisshed therby. And as the heretike
wolde in no wise oblige hym to that, [the] blessed Peter saide: 'To that 95
ende that verrey God be shewed maker of all thingges visible and
invisible, and for the comfort of true cristen men, and confusion to the
heretikes, I praie to oure Lorde that sum cloude arise and putte hym
betwene the sunne and the peple.' And thanne he made the signe of
the crosse, and anone ther come a cloude ouer the peple in maner of a 100
tent that kepte the peple by the space of a gret tyme.

A contracte that hight Acerbe, the | whiche hadde be a contracte the f. 88ᵛᵃ
space of .v. yere and was drawen vpon the erthe in a vessell of tree and
iledde to Seint Peter [in] Melayn, and as sone as Seint Peter hadde
blessed hym withe the signe of the crosse he was al hole and rose and 105
went on his fete. And many other miracles that oure Lorde dede for
hym bene rehersed in the pistell forsaide of Seint Innocent, wherinne
he saiethe that the sone of a noble man hadde right an horrible
swellinge on his knee, whiche greued hym so sore that he myght
nother speke ne brethe. And this holy man lefte up his hondes to 110
heuene and made the signe of the crosse ouer hym and touched the
sore withe hys cope. He was anone hole. And that same man hadde
after suche freting in his bely that he was nyghe dede, and thanne he
sent for the cope whiche he dede kepe right deuoutely, and as sone as

80 brennyng] brennyn E   tormented] turned E, tormentid *with* to *on erasure* H1
82 tofore] byfor *with* by *on erasure* H1   yef thou were] *om.* E   95 the] *om.* E   97 of]
to E   to] to *changed to* of H1   99 the²] this G   102 A contracte] And on *with* on *on*
erasure H1   103 in] *om.* E, *ins.* H1   110 his] *on erasure* H1   114 dede kepe] dede
kepe *changed to* hadde kepte H1, hadde kepte G

115 he hadde leyde it to his breste he caste oute a worme of his mouthe
withe two hedes al rough, and so he was fully deliuered. He putte in a
tyme his fynger in a childes mouthe that was domme, and he speke
anone. Many other miracles oure Lorde dede for hym in his lyff.

Whanne the pestilence of heresie encresed in the province of
120 Lumbardye and hadde entamed al the citees therinne by his malice,
and the [pope] hadde sent many visytours into diuerse parties of
Lumbardye for to haue awaye this fendely mortalitee. But specially
they were in to gret a noumbre in Melane and therto they were
f. 88ᵛᵇ stronge by gret myght of seculers, sharpe [by fals] and | wyly spekinge
125 and fulle of the cunynge of the fende. And whan the souerain bisshop
vnderstode and knewe that the blessed Peter was a man of stronge
corage and that he dradde not the multitude of his enemyes, and also
he knewe the vertue of hym bi the whiche he wolde not obeye to his
aduersaries, and knewe also his faire spekinge by whiche he wolde
130 discouer lightly the wily spekinge of the eretikes, and knewe wel that
he was fully taught in devine scripture by whiche he myght confound
resonably the fals argumentes of the heretykes, he ordeined this noble
champion of the feithe, this worthi fighter of oure Lorde witheoute
werinesse, for to be enquisitour at Melane and in al that erledom and
135 gaue hym his full auctoritee.

He thanne haunted diligentely the office that was enioyned hym
and sought thorughe al the heretikes witheoute yeuinge hem any
reste, but confounded hem mervaylously and putte hem oute
myghtely and ouercome hem wisely so that they myght not withe-
140 stonde his wisdom ne the holy sperit that was in hym. And whanne
the heretikes seigh this they were full of sorugh and begonnen to trete
with her felawship of his dethe, and supposed after that to lyue
pesibly yef thei myght amonge hem destroye so gret a persecutour.
And thanne as this noble prechour that shulde anone be marter went
145 hardely to preche and seke the heretikes atte Melane, he receiued in
that viage peyne of marterdome, so as Innocent the [pope] recordithe
f. 89ʳᵃ in these wordes: 'As he come to Melane | fro the citee of [C]ome wher
he was prioure of the freres of the Ordre for to make inquisicion
ayeinst the heretikes, as it was committed hym by the [se]ge of Rome,
150 lik as he had tolde in open prechinge, one of the heretikes atte the

115 his¹] *so with* s *on erasure* H1   121 pope] L, buschop *on erasure* E, pepul G, pepul
on erasure H1   124 seculers] L, *add* sharpely EH1G   sharpe] Sharppe *subp.* H1
by fals] L, *om.* EH1G   wyly] wylely EH1   126 blessed] *on erasure* H1
136 diligentely] *so with* d *on erasure* H1   146 Pope] buschop *on erasure* E   147 As]
And H1   Come] Rome EH1   149 sege] L, iuge EH1G

request of other corrupte bi yeftes and by praiers arose dedly ayenst
this seint that was in the waye of purpos of helthe. The cruel wolff
arose ayeinst the debonayre lambe, the felon ayeinst the meke, the
wode ayeinst the sobre, the disordeyne ayeinst þe simple durst make
his asaute and proued his strengthe and assaied to yeue hym dethe. 155
And thanne he smote cruelly the hede of the seint withe a knyff and
made hym many woundes and wette his knyff in the blode of the
rightwys man that toke not his hede from the stroke of his enemye.
But he shewed hymselff anone a verrey sacrifice, sustenynge in
pacience the tormentes and the strokes of hym that smote hym. 160
And [in] that same place of his passion he yelded vp the sperit whiche
went to the heuenly place. And that cursed murtherer and sacrilege
doubled his strokes in the seruant of Ihesu Crist. But this holy seruant
neither cried ne gruched but mekely comaunded his sperit to oure
Lorde, saienge: "Lorde, in thine hondes I recomaunde my sperit," 165
and beganne to saie the Crede and lefte not to be a prophete in the
articles therof, so as that cursed whiche þat slowe hym tolde after,
whanne he was taken of good cristen men. And Frere Domynik, that
was felowe of the seint whiche this mortherere smote so that he deyed
after, tolde the same, for as this morthe|rere seigh that the holy blode f. 89ʳᵇ
welled oute, yet witheoute pitee he toke his knyff and cruelly putte 171
hym thorugh the sides.'
      And in that same day he deserued to be a marter, a prophete, a
doctour, and a confessour: a marter in that hc shedde his bloode for to
defende the faithe; prophete in that he was seke in the feuer 175
quarteyne, his felawes saide that he myght not go to Melane, he
ansuered and saide: 'If we mowe not go to the freres we mowe wel
abide atte Seint Symplicien,' and so it fell, for as his body was born
withe freres they myght not that day bringe hym to Melane but abode
atte Seint Symplicien that nyght, for prees of peple was so grete that 180
thei myght not bringe hym no further; he was doctour also in that
whanne he suffered dethe he taught the faithe of holy Chirche withe
hygh voys sayeng: 'Credo in Deum et c.'
      Hys passion is seen to be like the passion of Ihesu Crist, for Ihesu
Criste suffered dethe for trouthe that he preched and Peter suffered 185
dethe for trouthe of the faithe that he defended. Ihesu Criste suffered

    153 felon] folow Hı   154 make] marke E, ma`r′ke Hı   161 in] L, om. EHıG
162 and] of Hı   167 whiche] wich changed to wight Hı   169 mortherere]
m`or′therer Hı   179 abode] add hym G   183 hygh] his Hı   184 Crist] om. Hı
185–6 that . . . trouthe] om. Hı   186–7 faithe . . . and] del. Hı

dethe [of] the vntrue and wicked peple of Iues and Peter [suffered]
dethe of the vntrue peple of heretikes. Ihesu Crist suffered dethe in
the tyme of Paske and Peter suffered dethe in the same tyme. Ihesu
190 Crist whanne he suffered dethe saide: 'Lorde, into thine hondes I
recomende my sperit,' and whanne Peter was slain he saide the same
wordes. Ihesu Crist was solde for .xxx.^{ti} pens and Peter was solde for
.xxx.^{ti} pounde of the money of Pauye. Ihesu Crist brought moche
f. 89va peple to the faithe bi his | passion and Peter conuerted many of the
195 heretikes by his dethe.

Thow it were so that this noble fighter hadde destroied in his lyff
many of the wicked techingges of these eretikes, yet after were they so
destroied by the noble miracles of hym that many lefte her errour and
come to the holy bosom of holy Chirche, so that the citee and þe
200 erledom of Melane wher there hadd be so gret multitude of heretikes
was so purged that there durst none appere there, for e[ith]er they
were conuerted to the feithe or elles chased oute of the cuntre. And
many of hem that were right noble and renomed entred sethe into the
Ordre of Frere Prechoures, the whiche haue be sithen persecutours of
205 heretikes by mervailous brennynge of feithe. And right as Sampson
slowe mo Philistienes in dienge thanne he dede lyvuinge, right so this
greyne of whete fallynge in the erthe and slayne bi the hondes of
vntrue heretykes and he slayn arose ayein into plenteuous whete. And
right as the grape defoul[ed] in the presse reboundethe and yeuithe
210 plenteuous licour, and right as the precious bawme beten withe the
pestell yeuithe his odour more suetely, right so after the glorious
victori of this holy man oure Lorde worshipped hym withe many a
mervaylous myracle, of whiche the souerain bisshop tellithe sum and
saith: 'Surely after the dethe of this holy man many of the laumpes
215 that hing aboute his sepulture were lighted bi hemselff witheoute any
helpe of man, for it was full conable that sethe he hadde be
f. 89vb excel|lentely worshipped by the light of feithe that singuler miracle
of light and of fere appered for hym.'

Also there was a man and as he satte atte the dinere with other he
220 beganne to myssaie of the seint and blamed his miracles, and in that
seyeng he swaloued a morsell and sodeinly he was choked and nye
dede. And he, felinge the gret perill that he stode inne, repented hym
sore and made his avowe withinne hymselff that he shulde neuer

187 of^1] for E   suffered] om. E, ins. H1   189 Paske] Pask`e' H1   201 either] L,
euer EH1G   207 whete] w`h'ete H1   209 defouled] defoulithe E   217 of] add
the H1   222 the] þat H1

more saye no suche wordes, and thanne anone the mussell come oute
and he was deliuered.   225

Another miracle of a woman that hadde the dropsie come to the
place ther he suffered marterdome and made ther her praiers, and
anone she receiued entier helthe by the helpe of God. And some
women that be longe tyme hadde be aseged withe the fende this martir
threwe hem oute by her mouthe with moche blood. He heled feuers   230
and alle other siknesse by his myracles.

And as Innocent the souerain bisshop hadde putte Seint Peter in
the cathologe of holy marteres, the freres assembled in the chapitle of
Melane and wolde haue born the body in more high place, for he hadd
layn more thanne an hole yere vnder erthe al hole and sound   235
witheoute any taste of corrupcion as faire and as hole as thoughe he
hadde be beried the same day. And thanne the freres leyde the holy
body vpon a tapit beside the same place withe gret reuerence, and ther
he was shewed to the peple hole and sounde and was worshipte
deuoute[ly].   240

And witheoute the miracles | that be sette in the letteres of the   f. 90ra
[pope] there were done many other, for upon the place of his passion
many religious and other seighe many tymes brennyng lyghtes
descende fro heuene and stie vp ayen, amonge whiche thei witnessen
to haue sayen two freres in the habite of Prechoures.   245

A yonge man that hight Ge[f]frey of the citee of Come hadde a
litell of the clothe of the cote of Seint Peter. And as an heretik seigh
it he saide to hym by despite that he leued that he were so holy he
shuld thrawe that clothe into the fere and yef it brenne not he wolde
leue that it were holy and receiue the faithe of hym. And anone he 250
threwe the clothe vpon the brennynge coles, but the clothe lepte vp
anone ouer the fire and quenched al the fere. And thanne saide
the heretyke that in þe same wise wolde his cote do. And thanne was
the clothe of the seint leyde vnder quik coles and the clothe of the
heretik in that other partye. And as sone as the clothe of the heretik 255
felt the fere it was brent, and the clothe of the seint ouercome the fire
and quenched it and it was nothinge empeyred. And whanne the
heretik seigh this thinge he turned to the waye of trouthe and
publisshed the miracle.

224 saye no/more] *trs.* E   230 by] of H1   232 And] AN`d´ H1   235 erthe]
add the EH1   239 worshipte] *so with* te *on erased* fully E, worship`t´fully *with* y *del.* H1,
worschipfully G   240 deuoutely] L, deuoute EG, deuoute`li´ H1   241 pope]
changed to buschop E   246 Geffrey] L, Gerfrey EH1G   248 that²] *add* `3if´ H1
251 clothe¹] *ins.* H1   253 ouer] *om.* G

260   At Florence ther was a yong man corrupte withe the wickednesse of
heresye, and as he was in the chirche of the freres atte Florence before
a table in whiche the marterdome of Seint Peter was peinted, and as
he seigh the tormentour smyte withe his naked suerde, he saide: 'A,
f. 90ʳᵇ and I hadde be there, how I wolde haue smite hym more cruel|ly
265   thanne he dede.' And as sone as he hadde saide these wordes he wexe
domme. His felawship axed hym what hym ayled and he myght not
ansuer hem, and so thei ledde hym to his hous, and as thei ledde hym
by the waye he seigh a chirche of Seint Michaell and went oute of her
hondes and entered into the chirche and kneled downe and praied in
270   his herte to Seint Peter that he wolde forgeue hym. And he obliged
hym by a vowe as he myght that yef he wolde forgeue hym and deliuer
hym he wolde confesse his synnes and renye al his heresie. And anone
he recouered his speche and come to the hous of the freres and
confessed his synnes and forsoke alle his heresyes and gaue leue to his
275   confessour to preche þis thinge openly to the peple, and he hymselff
knowlaged this before all the peple.
   A shippe ther was amyddes of the see in point to perisshe withe
cruel betyng of wawes, and the nyght was so hideous and derke that
the shipmen myght nothinge see, and so in grete sorughe and drede
280   eueriche of hem praied to diuerse seintes. But whan they seigh no
token of thaire deliueraunce fro perile one of hem that was born of
Gene bede hcm be still and aresoned hem in this wise: 'Bretheren,
haue ye not herde how a frere of the Ordre of Prechours whiche hight
Peter not longe gone was slayne withe heretikes for the defence of the
285   faithe, and oure Lorde shewithe many a mervaylous myracle for hym?
Wherfor late us alle praie deuoutely to hym and I hope that we shull
f. 90ᵛᵃ not be deceyued [of oure request].' | And alle acorded hereto and
praied to this glorious marter of his helpe. And as thei praied thus
devoutely they sawe the maste of þe shippe hange full of candeles, and
290   of the mervailous shinynge of the lyghtes al the derkenesse was chased
awaye and that right derke nyght was turned into a right clere day.
And therwithe thei sawe a man in the abite of a Frere Prechour
stondinge vpon the sayle, wherof it is no doute but that it was Seint
Peter, and anone the see was apesed and the weder softe and faire.
295   And whanne these shipmen were comen hoole and gladde, they went
alle to the hous of the Frere Prechours and yelded thankynge to God

267 hem] him H1   268 chirche] chi'r'ch H1   278 betyng] betyngges E   279 in]
add a E   285 Lorde] add 'Ihesu' H1, add Ihesu G   shewithe] schewed H1   287 of oure
request] om. EH1   288 this] 't'his H1   295 these] þe G   296 the²] om. G

and to Seint Peter and tolde the freres alle the ordinaunce of this miracle.

A woman of Flaundres whiche hadde [thre] children dede born, wherfor her husbonde hated her, and thanne she praied deuoutely to Seint Peter to be her helpe. And as she was deliuered of the ferthe childe dede born she toke the childe and brought it to the fete of Seint Peter and besought hym deuoutely to graunt her chi[l]de liff by his devoute praiers. And vnnethes she hadde made her praiers but that her childe appered quicke, and as it was born to be cristened it was ordeined to be called Iohn. And thanne sodenly wnwetinge hymselff called hym Pers and so that name he helde alway after in the worship of Seint Peter.

In the prouince of Ceutonyke in the toune of Traret some | women seen how gret plente of peple come to the freres in [the] worship of Seint Peter the Marter as thei were togedre in a place and sponnen. Thei saiden to hem that weren there: 'These Frere Prechoures knowen al [the] maner of wynnynge. They mowe now hepe gret good and make gret paleys for thei haue founde a nwe marter.' And as they saide these thingges and l[ike], al here threde was sodenly blodie and her fyngers [with] whiche they turned her threde were full of blode. And whanne they sene this they mervailed gretly and wiped her fingers curiously leste perauenture they hadde be cutte. And whanne thei seen her fingers hole and her threde so blodie thei saide in trembelinge and in repentynge hem: 'Verrely, bycause we haue detracte the blood of the holy marter this wonderfull myracle is fall to us.' And thanne thei ronne to the hous of the Frere Prechours and tolde to the prioure al this and presented hym the threde blody. The prioure, atte the requeste of many, made [a] predicacion solempne and tolde how it was fall to þe women and shewed the blody threde before alle the peple.

And a maister of the arte of nygromancye was atte that predicacion, and whan he herde this he beganne gretly to despise that dede and saide to hem that were there: 'Se ye not how these freres deceiue the hertes of symple men? For they haue hered these women that bene her loues for to dye her threde in blode, and sithe they sayen that it is done by miracle.' And as sone as he hadde saide this he was smyte

299 thre] two E, iij *on erasure* H1   303 childe] chide E   310 the²] *om*. EG
313 the] *om*. E   315 like] lough E   316 with] in E   317 of] *ins*. H1
322 the²] *om*. G   Frere] *on erasure* H1   324 a] L, *om*. EH1G   325 þe] *om*. G
women] woman H1   the] *add* rede H1   332 he¹] þay G

f. 91ra withe the devyne | vengeaunce and tormented withe so stronge a fever
that he most be born from the prechinge to his hous, and this fever
335 encresed so gretly that he dradde the dethe. Than he sent for the
priour and confessed his synne an [avowed] to God and to Seint Peter
before the prioure that yef he myght haue hele bi his merites he
shulde haue hym allwaye in special deuocion and neuer to saye suche
thingges more. And as sone as he hadde made the said avowe he was
340 perfitely hole.

In a tyme that the prioure of that place ledde right faire sto[n]e in a
shippe by water, sodenly the shippe was so faste asette vpon the
ryuage that they myght not remeue it. And thanne alle the shippemen
went oute and drewe, but thei myght in no wise remeue it. And as
345 they wende that the shippe hadde bene loste, the supprioure come and
bade hem alle goo thennes and withe his only honde he putte a litell
the shippe lightly in sayeng: 'Go thi waye in the name of Seint Peter
the marter, in worship of whom we beren these stones.' And thanne
anone the shippe remeued right hastely and parted fro the ryuage hole
350 and sound, and thanne the shipmen entered witheinne and come
withe gret gladnesse to her propre places.

In the prouince of Fraunce in the citee of Sene it fell that a mayden
passed by a water and fille inne and laye there a gret space of tyme,
and atte the laste she was drawen oute of the water al dede and ther
355 were gret argumentes of her deth, that is to wete shewinge that she
was dede as by longe space of tyme [as] by stiffenesse [and] the
f. 91rb coldenesse | and [the] blaknesse of the body. And thanne she was born
to the chirche [of] Frere Precheours, the which avowed her to Seint
Peter, and anone she recouered lyff and helth.

360 As Frere Iohn [P]olon was atte Boloyne seke on the quartayn, the
whiche shulde make the sermon to the clerkes in the day of the fest of
Seint Peter the Marter, and he abode after the cours naturell to haue
hadde his axes that nyght, wherfor he beganne to drede lest he shulde
haue failed of the sermon that was enioyned hym, and thanne he
365 praied mekely to Seint Peter and besought hym that be his merites he
wolde geue hym helpe sithe he most preche the worship and ioye of
hym. [It was graunted hym] or his fever sesed and neuer toke hym
after.

336 avowed] awoved E   338 hym] *om.* H1G   341 stone] store E   343 alle]
om. H1   348 beren] berien (?) *changed to* beren H1   356 as²] and EH1   by²] *add* þe
H1   and] of EH1   357 the¹] by E   358 the¹] *om.* H1G   of] into the EH1
360 Polon] L, Bolon E, Belon H1, Holon G   365 he] sche G   366 and] *add* the E
367 It . . . hym²] *om.* EH1   or] *changed to* & H1

A ladi that hight Gyrard, þe wiff of Iames of [Valsain], that had be
vexed withe the fende the space of [.xiiij.] yere, come to a preste and 370
saide hym: 'I am tormented withe a wicked sperit and wolde haue
helpe.' The preste hering this fledde into the sextry and toke priuely
his stole and the boke by whiche he wolde coniure the fende and putte
it vnder his cope and [come to] the woman withe good felawship with
hym. And as sone as she seigh hym she saide to hym: 'Thou wicked 375
theef, wher hast thou be? What haste thou hidde vnder thi cope?' And
anone the preste made his coniuracions, but it went not awaye fro her.
But after that she come to Seint Peter whiles he lyued and required
hym to helpe her. He ansuered her by vois of prophecie and saide:
'Doughter, | drede not, but haue good truste in oure Lorde ne f. 91ᵛᵃ
despaire the not though atte this tyme I may not fulfell thi desire, 381
but the tyme shall come that thou shalt pleinly haue thi request of
me.' And so it was done, for after the passion of hym the woman come
to his sepulcre and fully was deliuered of the torment of her enemye.

Another ladi, that hight Effanye, of the strete of Corteyne in the 385
diocise of Melane, was .vij. yere tormented withe the enemye, but
whanne she was brought to the sepulcre of Seint Peter the fendes
beganne more cruelly to torment her and to crie before all the peple:
'Mariable, mariable, perot, perot,' and thanne he went oute and lefte
her as dede. But a litell while after she arose perfitely hole and she 390
tolde how that the fendes tormented her most in Sondayes and other
high festes, and namely whan the masses were saide.

A nonne ther was in Almayne in the cloistre of Combat of the ordre
of Seint Sixte in the diocise of Constancionense, the whiche hadde the
gouute in her knees that her helde sore longe tyme a yere [and] more, 395
so that she myght not be deliuered bi no remedye and she myght not
bodely visite the [sepulcre] of Seint Peter, but bothe she was withholde by obedience and also bi greuous siknesse. Wherfor she
bethought her hou she myght [visite] this holy sepulcre bi ententif
mynde and withe holy deuocion. And she saide withinne herselff hou 400
she myght well go fro thennes to Melane in [.xxxiiij.ᵗⁱ] dayes, and so
she toke deuoutely her iorney in her | mynde. And eueri [day] in stede f. 91ᵛᵇ
of her iorney she said an .C. *Pater noster* in þe worship of Seint Peter,
and right as she dede her iorney by orisones she amended litell and

369 Valsain] L, Alsham EH₁, Alsam G   370 .xiiij.] xiij.E, xiij *changed to* xiijj H₁
374 come] toke *changed to* come H₁   come to] toke E   377 went not] *om.* G
393 A nonne] Anoþer H₁   395 her helde] hire her G   sore] *add* bi EH₁   and] or EH₁
397 sepulcre] body E   399 visite] finde E   401 .xxxiiij.] .xxxiij. E, xxxiii *changed to*
xxxiiij H₁   402 day] *om.* E

405 litell of her sekenesse. And whanne she hadde perfourmed her laste
iorney and that she was come by her mynde to the tombe of the seint,
she sette her doune on her knees as though she hadde be verrely atte
the tombe, and ther withe gret deuocion she saide her hole sauuter,
and by that tyme [that] she hadde al saide she felt so gret alegeaunce
410 that vnnethes she felt any thinge of her siknesse. And thanne she
turned ayein in maner as she was come and bi that tyme that she
hadde al fulfelled her iourneyes homwarde she was perfitely hole.

Atte Florens in the chirche of Ryues ther was a nonne in praihers
the same day that Seint Peter suffered dethe. She seighe the glorious
415 Virgine Marie sitte in her highe trone of ioie and two freres of the
Ordre of Precheours stie on hye to heuene, whiche were sette on eueri
side of this lady. And whanne this nonne asked what they were she
herde a vois þat saide: 'This is Frere Pers that stieth gloriously into
heuene as the smoke of a precious oynement.' And it was sertainly
420 founde that the same day that he deied she seigh that avision. And
thanne as she was falle in a grevous siknesse she sette al her deuocion
to praie to Seint Peter, and anone she receiued perfit helthe.

A scoler that come fro Magalomun bi the mounte of [Pesulen]
brake a veyne as he lepte so þat he myght not goo a pas. He hadde
f. 92ʳᵃ herde preche how that a woman had | be [he]led of the ca[n]cre bi
426 puttinge theron of the erthe that was wete with the blode of the holi
marter, and saide: 'Lorde God, I haue not of the erthe,' and besought
helpe of Seint Peter, 'and bi his merites that God gaue so gret grace to
that erthe thou maist as wel yeue it to this.' And withe that he made
430 the signe of þe crosse vpon the erthe and besought the helpe of Seint
Peter and leide of the erthe on the sike place, and anone he was hole in
the yere of oure Lorde .Mˡ.CC.lix.

Ther was in the citee of Compostele a man that hight Benet whiche
hadde his thies so gretly suolle as the bely of a woman withe childe,
435 and al his body toswolle and his visage [so] horrible with the suellynge
that he was lyke a monstre oute of kinde. And as this man myght
vnnethes be susteyned withe a staffe as he wente, he asked almesse of a
good lady that he mette withe. And she saide to hym that hym neded
moche rather his graue thanne any mete. But yet she saide: 'Do after
440 my counsaile, go to the hous of the Frere Prechours and be confessed

408 the] `þe´ H1   409 that²] om. E   alegeaunce] alengeaunce EH1   411 maner]
add like H1   that²] om. H1   412 al] om. H1G   416 on²] twice H1   423 scoler]
Scloler E   Pesulen] Penulten EH1   425 be heled] besiled E, so changed to beheled H1
cancre] cacre E   434 gretly] grete H1   435 so] to EH1

of thi synnes and aske helpe of Seint Peter the Marter.' And in the
morwtyde as he come to the gate of the freres he founde the gate close.
And thanne he sette hym doune byside the gate and fell aslepe and
hym thought ther come to hym a worshipfull man in abite of a
Precheour, that couered hym withe his cope and brought hym 445
witheinne the chirche. And than this man awoke and founde hymselff
perfitely hole witheinne the chirche, whiche thing gaue gret mervaile
and gret abasshinge to | alle the peple to see a man so nygh dede and so f. 92rb
sodenly deliuered, wherfor alle thanked and worshipped God that of
his souerein goodnesse shewithe so many notable miracles for his 450
seruaunt Seint Peter.

Here endithe the liff of Seint Peter of Melane, and nexst
foluithe the feste of Phelip, Capitulum .lix.^{m}

Whanne Phelip the Apostell hadde preched in Siche .xxj.^{ti} yere he was
take of the panymes and holden and was brought to do sacrifice to the
ydole of Martis and therto constreyned by hem. And thanne anone a
gret dragon went oute of the ydole and slowe the sone of the bisshopp
that mynistred the fere to do sacrifice and slowe two iuges, of whiche 5
the mynistres helde Phelippe bounde in cheynes. And he arraied so all
the other by his blowynge that thei were al nye dede. And than saide
Phelip: 'Take kepe to my wordes. Takithe these fals ymages and
tobrekithe hem and sette in her stede the crosse of oure Lorde and
worship it, and thanne your seke folke shull bene heled and youre 10
dede shull bene rered ayein from dethe to lyff.' Tho that were seke
cried: 'Sire, do so moche that we be made hole and we shull breke
these ydoles.' And Phelip comaunded to the dragon that he shulde
goo into a place of desert so that he shulde neuer anoye to none, and
thanne he parted anone and noyed neuer after to none. And thanne 15
Phelip heled al the seke and gate benefice of lyff to hem that were
dede, and so they leued alle in God, and | he preched to hem after, and f. 92va
ordeyned to hem prestes and [deken]es. And sithe he went into Asie
into the citee of Ia[r]opolyn in the whiche the heresie of Ebronitarum
that saide [that] Ihesu Crist hadde take flesshe fantastik into the 20

441 synnes] synne G   444 hym thought] *om.* H1, *add* how G   449 thanked] *add*
God E   450 shewithe] shewed H1

EH1GH2A1A2L   *Rubric* Phelip] *add* and Iacob EH1   6 the] *om.* H1   8 and]
twice E   9 the crosse] crossis G   10 worship] worschipid G   11 shull] shulde
H1   13 these] the G   17 and he . . . after] *twice at end of folio* E   18 dekenes]
clerkes E   19 Iaropolyn] Ianopolyn E   20 that] *om.* E

Virgine and this the[i] taught [to] the peple he destroied hem. And ther wer two holy virgines by þe whiche oure Lorde conuerted moch peple to the faithe.

And thanne Phelip .viij. dayes before his dethe called alle the
25 bysshoppes and þe prestes of the contre and saide hem: 'Oure Lorde hathe yeue me þe space of .viij. dayes to teche you to rule you to his plesaunce.' And þat tyme he was [of] the age of .iiij.ˣˣ. yere and seuene. And anone the mysbeleuers token hym and fastened hym vpon the crosse in the maner as Ihesu Crist his maister was, the
30 whiche he taught and preched, and so he passid to oure Lorde and fulfellyd his tyme blessidly. And his two doughters weren beried by hym, that one in the right syde and that other in the lefte syde.

Of this Phelip saieth [Isidore] in the boke of the Begynnynge and of the Lyff of Seintes: 'Phelip preched to the Galiens the name of Ihesu
35 Crist, and he brought the peple from the derke see of ignoraunce to the clere lyght of cunnynge and to the port of helthe of feithe. And after in Iaropolyn province of Frise he was crucified and stoned and dede, and there he reste[th] with his two doughters.' This saieth I[sod]ore. Of Phelip that was one of the .vij. dekenes saiethe Seint
40 Ierome in his Marteloge that in the .viij. day of Iuill he rested in Cesar
f. 92ᵛᵇ worshipped with tokenes | and myracles, besides whom his dought-eres be beried in a tombe, for he was beried furst in Ephesim. And the furste Phelip is deferred from this, for he was apostill and this was a deken, and this restithe in Ierapolyn and that other restithe in Cesar,
45 that one hadde two doughters prophetis and that other hadde .iiij., though it be so that the Stori Ecclesiast saiethe that it was Phelip the Apostell that hadd .iiij. doughteres prophetes. But it is more to leue Ierome in this cas.

Here endithe the lyff of Seint Phelip the Apostell, and nexst foluithe the lyff of Seint Iames, Capitulum .lx.

This Iames the Apostell is called Iames Alphey, that is the sone of Alphey, and Iames the brother of oure Lorde, and Iames the Lasse, and Iames the Rightwise. He is called Iames Alphei not only after the

21 thei] the E   to] in EHı   27 of¹] om. E   .iiij.ˣˣ] iij score *changed to* iiijˣˣ score
Hı   33 Isidore] om. EHı   38 resteth] rested E   Isodore] Idosore E
41 doughteres be] doughter he Hı

EHıGH2AıA2L; D resumes at 114 *prestes* and breaks off in a damaged section at 245 *encline thin*; E omits 116 *And þanne* to 157 *more he*

flesshe but after the exposicion of the name, for Alpheus is as moche
to saye as wise or techinge either fleynge or a thousande. He was called 5
wise bi the inspiracion of science, techinge bi techinge of other, fleinge
for he fledde the worlde for to despice it, a thousand bi reputacion of
humilite. He was called brother of oure Lorde for he was like to hym
so that many were deceiued by the lyknesse of hym, wherfor whan the
Iues went to take Ihesu Crist they asked a toke[n] of Iudas that was 10
familyer with hym for to know hym. And also Ignacien witnessith in
his epistell seyinge to Iohn the Euuangelist: 'If it be couenable for me
I wolde come to the into Ierusalem that I myght | see that worshipfull f. 93ra
Iames that is surnamed Iustice, the whiche is right like to Ihesu Crist
as men sayen of visage, of liff and of conuersacion as thow he were his 15
brother iemel and of one wombe. And whan I ha[u]e sene hym [I shall
se] Ihesu Crist after alle the sembelauntes of [the] body.'
    Either he was called brother of oure Lorde, for right as Ihesu Crist
and Iames descended of two susteres, right so men wende that they
hadde come of two bretheren, of Iosephe and of Cleophas. He was not 20
brother of oure Lorde for that he was the sone of Ioseph the husbonde
of oure Lady by another wyff as sum seyne, but for he was the sone of
Mari the doughter of Cleophas, the whiche was brother of Ioseph,
though it be so that Maister Iohn Belett saiethe that Alphe, fader of
that s[ame] Iames, was brother to Ioseph oure Lady husbond, the 25
whiche is not to beleue to be trewe, but the custume of Iues was for to
calle alle the bretheren that aperteyne to two parties of the blood [as]
of fader and moder. And also he may be saide the brother of oure
Lorde for the prerogatiff and the excellence of holynesse for whiche
he was ordeyned bisshopp of Ierusalem before alle. 30
    He was called Iames the Lasse in difference of Zebede, though it so
were that he were furst born, yet he was last called of God. And þe
custume is kepte in many religions that he that enterithe furst into
religion is called the Gretter and he that enterithe after is called the
Lasse though he be gretter of age or more worthi by holinesse. 35
    For after that Seint Ierome saith, he was of so gret reuerence and |
of so gret holinesse to the peple that euery man desired to touche the f. 93rb
frenge of his vestement, and of his holy[n]esse Egisipe saiethe, whiche

    10 a token] L, and toke EG, *so changed to* a token H1   15 of³] *om.* H1G
16 haue] hadde EH1   16–17 I shall se] L, he was euene like EH1, I shall G
17 the²] his EH1   25 same] Seint EH1   26 to beleue] leue H1, to leue G
27–8 as of] of the EH1   30 alle] *om.* H1   31 in] In *starting new sentence* EH1
33 religions] religiouse H1   33, 34 enterithe] entered H1G   37 man] *om.* G
38 holynesse] holymesse E

was neyghebour to the apostelles, and as the Stori of Ecclesiast
40 witnessith that saiethe: 'Iames the brother of oure Lorde Ihesu
Crist surnamed Iustice of Alpheie toke the Chirche fro the tyme of
oure Lorde and dured vnto oure tyme. This same was holy fro the
wombe of his moder. He dranke neuer wyne ne sidre, ne he ete neuer
flesshe, ne iren touched neuer his hede, ne he vsed neuer oyle ne
45 batthe, and he wered neuer lynen. He kneled so ofte in his praiers that
the skynne of his [kneis] was as harde as the soles of his fete. And for
this rightwisse continuaunce witheoute cesinge he was called Iames
the Iuste. And also he was called Abba, that is as moche to saye as a
garnison and defence of the peple. And this same alone amonge alle
50 the aposteles was entered *in Sancta sanctorum*, whiche is the place
wher men sacrified'. And not by cause to sacrifie but for to praie.
   And men saien also that he was the furst that songe masse amonge
the aposteles, for by the excellence of his holinesse the apostilles dede
hym this worship that he shulde be þe furst that after the assencion of
55 oure Lorde shulde halow masse in Ierusalem. And before that he was
ordeyned to be bisshop, for before the ordinacion, as it is saide in
Actibus Apostolorum that the disciples were perseueraunt in the
doctrine of the aposteles in communycacion of the brekyng of brede
which is takin of the halowinge of masse, or elles perauenture he was |
f. 93ᵛᵃ saide that he hadde songe furst for he was the furst that saide [it] *in*
61 *pontificalibus*, right as Peter halowed the furst masse in Antioche and
Marke in Alisaundre.
   This Iames was perduringe in virginite, so as Ierome witnessithe in
the boke that he made Ayeinst Puynyen, and Iosephus in his boke of
65 Good Men, that whan oure Lorde suffered dethe Iames made his
avowe that he wolde neuer ete mete before oure Lorde were rise from
dethe to liff. And in a day of the resureccion oure Lorde apered to
Iames that hadde tasted nothing vnto that tyme and saide to hym and
to tho that were there withe hym: 'Settithe the borde.' And thanne he
70 toke the brede and blessed it and thanne gaue hym, saieng: '[My]
brother, ete on, for the sone of man is risen fro dethe.'
   In the .vij. yere of his bisshopriche, whanne the aposteles were
assembeled in Ierusalem on a Ester Day, Iames asked hem what
thingges oure Lorde hadde do by hem, and thei tolde hym before alle

   41 fro] of Hɪ   44 neᵌ] and Hɪ   46 kneis] fete E, knes *on erasure* Hɪ   the²] his
Hɪ   47 this] this *with* t *erased* Hɪ, his G   48 Iuste] *add and del.* And *or* Ased (?) Hɪ
as a] Abba as G   49 *sanctorum*] *Santorum* E   58 in] `and' in `the' Hɪ, and in the G
58–9 of brede . . . takin] *om.* Hɪ   60 it] *om.* E   65 Men] *add* `seith' Hɪ
70 brede] borde G   My] *om.* EHɪ   74 and . . . hym] *om.* Hɪ

þe peple. And he preched .vij. dayes with other aposteles in the 75
Temple before Caiphas and other of the Iues, and it was nigh brought
that Caiphas wolde haue be cristen, but sodenly ther entered a Iue
into the Temple that beganne to crie: 'Ha, [ye] good men of Israel,
what do ye? Whi suffre ye youreselff to be thus deseiued of these
enchauntours?' And this meued the peple so that thei wolde haue 80
stoned the aposteles. And that wicked man went vp þe degree wher
Iames preched and threwe hym downe from an high so that he halted
euer after.

The blessed Iames suffered dethe in þe .vij. yere after the ascencion
of oure | Lorde. And in the yere of his bisshopriche .xxx.^{ti}, the Iues f. 93vb
seigh that thei myght not sle Paule for that Cesar hadde called hym 86
and that he was sent to Rome, and thei conuerted her cruelte of her
persecucion vpon Iames and sought occasion ayeinst hym. And as
the before [saide] Egysippe that was in the tyme of the aposteles
tellith, af[ter], as it is [founde] in the Stori of Ecclesiast, the Iues 90
assembeled togederes and saide to Iames: 'We praie the that thou
repele the peple, for they erren in Ihesus, wenyng that he be Crist.
Wherfor we require the that thou teche to all tho that shall be gadered
togedre atte this Ester that thei foleye no more in Ihesu Crist, and alle
we will obeie the and bere good witnesse [to] the peple of the that thou 95
[arte] rightwis and acceptest no persone.' And thanne they sette hym
on the hyest place of the Temple and bygonne to crie: 'This is the
most rightwis of men to whom we shull alle obeye, and for that the
peple folyen in Ihesu that was crucified, saie us what ye fele and what
ye seine.' And thanne Iames ansuered hem withe an high vois: 'Aske 100
ye me of the sone of man? He sittethe in heuene in the right side of
[the] souerein vertue and shall come to iuge the quik and the dede.'
And whanne the cristen herde that thei were gretly reioysed and herde
hym more gladly.

And thanne the pharisees and the scribes saide: 'We haue do euell 105
for to take suche a witnesse to Ihesu. Go we vp and thrawe hym
downe fro hye to lowe so that these other be aferde and leue not his
wordes.' And thanne thei cried alle togedre: 'A, loo, the rightwis hathe
folied.' | Alle than wenten up and threwe hym downe, and whanne f. 94ra

78 ye] L, the EH1G   84 .vij.] lxx *on erasure* H1   85 L *punct. as here,* EH1G *end
sentence at* .xxx^{ti}.   89 the before saide] they before EH1G (*le deuant dit* P2)   90 after]
afore E, afore *changed to* after H1   founde] L, tolde EH1G   94 Ester] after H1
95 the¹] þie *changed to* þee H1   to] in E   96 arte] *om.* E, `arte´ H1   99 folyen]
soleyn G   100 hem] him H1   102 the¹] L, his fader and EH1G   109 Alle than]
al`s tanne´ þan *with* þan *changed to* þay H1, als thanne thay G   hym] *add* and drew hym E

110 thei hadde [thro]we hym downe thei [th]rewe stones on hym, saienge:
'St[one] we Iames the rightwis that may not be slain withe the casting
doune fro so hye.' And thanne he turned hym and leide hym on his
knees and saide: 'Lorde, I beseche the foryeue hem þis mysdede, for
thei wote not what þei done.' Thanne one of the prestes that was of
115 the sones of Rechap cried and saide: 'Spare hym, I praie you. What do
G f. 128ʳ ye? He praiethe for you, this rightwis man that ye stonen.' | And
þanne oon of hem toke a grete perche and smote hym on the hede that
þe brayne wente oute. This seith Egisippe, and by siche martirdome
he passed to oure Lord vndir Noyron þat bigan in the ȝere of oure
120 Lord .liij. and was buried there neyȝ the tempul. And as þe pepul
wold haue vengid his deth and taken and punyschid þe wikkid doeris,
thay fledden anoon.

Iosefus tellith þat for the deth [of] Iames the Riȝtwis the distruccion was of Ierusalem and the departicion of the Iewis, but [not] oonly
125 for þe deth of Iamys, but for þe deth specially of Ihesu Crist, and þis
distruccion was doon aftir þat oure Lord seide: 'þay schul not leue |
G f. 128ᵛ stone vpon stone in the, for þou hast not knowe the tyme of þy
visitacion.' But for oure Lord will not the deth of the synful and that
þay hadde noon excusacion, he abode .xl. ȝere her penaunce. And by
130 the apostlis and by Iamys the same brothir of oure Lord þat prechid
contynuelly among hem and callid [hem] to penaunce, and whanne he
myȝt not conuerte [hcm] by techyng he wold calle hem by myraclis.
For in the .xl. ȝere þat was ȝeue hem to penaunce, meny a myracle and
wondir was schewed, as Iosephus seith, for riȝt a clere sterre apperid
135 like a spere and was seyn of alle aboue the cite, and þere ȝit apperid all
the ȝere þoruȝ, and also þer was seyn flambis of fire brennyng. And in
a feste of her azimes in the .ix. houre of þe nyȝt a grete briȝtnes of liȝt
environyd þe tempul and the awtere so þat alle wenden þat it hadde be
clere day, and in þat feste a bole was brouȝt to sacrifise, and in þe
140 hondis of hym þat offrid hym vp he brouȝt forth a lombe all sodeynly.
And anoon aftir as þe sonne wente doun cartis and chariettis were
seyn in the heire thorugh all þat region and hadden with hem
companyes chargid with yren and with armure þat wente rounde
aboute the cite and weren medlid with the clowdis and went aboute
145 vnpouruoiedly.

110 throwe] drawe E   threwe] drewe E   111 Stone] Strew EHı   114 not]
neuer G   117–57 þanne . . . more he²] om. E   119–20 vndir . . . Lord] om. Hı
121 thay] om. Hı   123 of] þat G   124 not] L, om. GHı   128 the²] ins. Hı
131, 132 hem², hem¹] hym, hym G   140 þat] of Hı

And in anothir day þat is callid Pentecost the prestis entridden by
nyght into þe tempul for to fulfille the seruyse aftir her custumys, and
þay felte within þe tempul the erthe quake, thondir and lightnyng,
and þay hurde a vois seying sodeynly: 'Parte we hens fro þis place, for
or fyue ȝere come to ende ther schal be grete bataile.'   150
Also ther was a man þat heiȝt Ihesus the sone of Ananye, bigan to
crie sodeynly the day of the feste of the tabernaclis and seide: 'The
vois of the orient, the vois of the occident, the voice of .iiij. wyndes,
the vois vpon Ierusalem and vpon the Temple, the voice vpon the
spouse and the spousis, the vois vpon all the pepul.' And þanne þis   155
man was take and bete and al tomangled, | but he myght noon oþer   G f. 129ʳ
word seie, and the more he was bete þe more he | cried these wordes. E f. 94ʳᵃ
And atte the laste he was ledde before the iuge and strongely beten
and tormented till his bones appered thorugh the flesshe, but he neuer
wepte ne cried merci but continuelly recorded that he hadde saide   160
before and added more, seyinge: 'Alas, alas verrely vpon Ierusalem.'
And these bene the wordes of Iosephus.
And whanne the Iues wolde not in no wise conuerte hem by
techinges nether by so gret shewingges of mervailes ne thei dradde of
nothing, oure Lorde .xl.ᵗⁱ yere after sent vpon Ierusalem Vaspasien 165
and Tytus, the whiche destroied al the citee, and the cause of her
comyng was this, as it is founde in a storie, though it so be that it be
apocraphum. Pilate seigh that he hadde condempned Ihesu Crist
withoute cause and dredde þe wrathe of Tyberien the emperour and
[sent] to hym a messanger for to excuse hym whiche hight A[l]ben.   170
And in that tyme Vaspasien helde [al] that lordshipp [of] Galacie
vnder Tyberian the emperour, and the messanger hadde contrarie
wyndes, the whiche brought hym into Galacie and so he was brought
to Vaspacien, | and ther was suche a custume that whosoeuer was   f. 94ʳᵇ
brought by torment of the see he shulde be soget to the prince, he and 175
alle his goodes. And thanne Vaspasien asked hym what he was and
whennes he come and whedir he purposed, to whom he ansuered and
saide: 'I come fro Ierusalem and goo towardes Rome.' And thanne
Vaspacien saide: 'Thou comest from the londe of wise men. Canst
thou any crafte of medecine? Thou art a leche, thou shuldest hele me.' 180
For Vaspasien fro his tender age hadde a maner of wormes that come

149 þay] add had del. G   156 noon] not H1   161 more] add to H1G
Ierusalem] add And þese be del. H1   167 though] þer of H1   170 sent] saide E
Alben] L, Abben EH1G   171 al] om. E   of] and E, and changed to of H1
176 thanne] þat G

oute of his nose, and for that cause he was called Vaspasien for men
wende that it hadde bene waspes. And this messangere ansuered hym:
'Sir, I am no leche, and therfor I canne not hele the.' To whom
185 Vaspasien saide: 'But thou hele me thou shalt deye an harde dethe.'
And thanne he saide to Vaspacien: 'He that yeuithe light to the blynde
and arerithe the dede to lyff wote wel that I canne not cure the.' And
thanne Vaspacien saide: 'What is he of whom thou saiest these gret
thingges?' He saide: 'Of Ihesus of Nazareth that the Iues slowen by
190 enuye, and I dare saie it yef thou wilt beleue in hym thou shalt haue
helthe.' And thanne Vaspasien saide: 'I leue verrely, he that arerithe
the de[d]e to lyff may wel deliuer me fro my siknesse.' And in that
saieng the waspes fillen oute of his nose and anone he receiued helthe.
And than was Vaspacien full of gret ioye and saide: 'I am sertayne that
195 he is verrely Goddes sone that hathe heled me.' And thanne he asked
f. 94ᵛᵃ leue of Cesar for to goo into Ierusa|lem withe power of men of armes
and saide: 'I will destroie the traitoures that haue slain hym,' and
hadde leue. And thanne he saide to Albon: 'Go home to thine hous
hole and sounde. I shall [s]aue thi lyff and thi goodes. [Go] surely, y
200 yeue the leue.'
And whanne Vaspacien had be atte Rome and comen ayein he
assembeled by many yeres gret strengthe of peple. And so as the Iues
rebelleden in the tyme of Nero the emperour, wherfor as the cronicle
saiethe he dede not only for the loue of Ihesu Crist but for that they
205 were parted from the lordshippe of Romaynes. And thanne come
Vaspacien into Ierusalem withe gret strengthe and beseged the citee al
aboute myghtely in the Day of Ester and closed witheinne gret
multitude of peple witheoute nombre that were come theder on
Paske Day for the feste. And so bi a sertain space before that
210 Vaspacien come, the good cristen peple hadde be taught by the
holy goste that thei shulde parte from thennes and goo ouer the flom
Iordan into a castell that hight Palan, so that whanne [the] holy m[e]n
were oute of the citee the place of the heuenly vengeaunce were made
of that cursed citee.
215 And thanne Vaspacien assailed furst a citee þat was in Iudee wher
Iosephus was that was named Ionoporam, but Iosephus defended hym
myghtely and alle his men. But whanne he seigh the destruccion of

182 of] atte H1   183 it] þei H1   187 arerithe] `doth´ arere H1   191 that]
ins. H1   192 dede] dethe E   198 hadde] *add* `no´ H1   199 saue] L, haue E
Go] so EH1   204 for²] *om.* G   212 the] an E, *om.* H1   men] man E   213 were¹]
went H1   216 hym] hem G

the citee he entered into a sisterne, he and .ix. Iues, and ther they were
turmented with hunger .iiij. dayes, and maugre Ioseph the Iues hadde
leuer to deye [there] for hunger thanne to submitte hem to the will of 220
Waspa|sian, and so thei purposed to slee eche other and offre her f. 94vb
blood to God in sacrifice. And for that Iosephus was the most worthi
of hem all thei wold slee hym furst, for bi the shedinge of his blood
God shulde be the more plesed and apesed, or ellis as it is saide in the
cronicles, thei wolde slee eche other for thei wolde not be putte in the 225
subieccion of Romaynes.

And thanne Iosephus that was a wise man and lust not to deye, he
ordeyned iuge of the dethe and of the sacrifice and comaunded that
[sorte] were putte be twe[i]ne and twei[n]e whiche shulde deye furst.
And whanne þe sortes were caste thei putte to deth now one now 230
another vnto they come to the laste. And whanne Iosephus seigh that
the sorte moste as well come on hym as on [an]other, he that was a
worthi man and a manly lightly pulled the suerde of that otheres
honde and asked hym whedir he wolde haue lyff or dethe, and
comaunded hym anone to chese withoute any delaye. And he that 235
dredde saide: 'I refuse not to lyue yef it be thi grace my lyff myght be
saued.' And thanne Iosephus spake priuely to one that was nygh
famylier with Vaspacien and besought hym that he wolde gete hym
his lyff of the emperoure. He dede so, and whanne Iosaphus was
brought before Vaspacien, Vaspacien saide to hym: 'Thou ha[dd]est 240
deserued dethe yef thou hadde not be deliuered bi the praiers of this
man here.' And thanne Iosephus saide: 'My lorde, yef anything ha[u]e
be do amisse it may well be turned into beter.' And thanne Vaspacien
saide: 'He that is ouercome, what may he do?' And Iosephus saide: 'I
may do sum thinge wel yef | thou wilt encline thin eeres to my f. 95ra
wordes.' And Vaspasien saide: 'I will well that thou be herde in al that 246
thou wilt wel saie.' And thanne saide Iosephus: 'My lorde, I late the
wete for trouthe that the emperour of Rome is dede and the senatoures
haue chose the to be her emperour.' Thanne saide Vaspasian: 'Yef
tho[u] be a prophete, whi ne haddest thou warned th[is] citee before 250
that she shulde haue be putte in my subieccion?' And thanne Iosephus
saide that he hadde tolde it hem .xl.^ti winter before.

218 a] `a´ H1   219 maugre] in angre H1   Ioseph] *add* seid to H1   220 there]
om. E   221 eche] þe H1   225 eche] þe H1   in the] into H1   229 sorte] *om.* E,
`þer´ H1    putte] *add* `lot´ H1   tweine and tweine] twene and tweie E, twene hem twey
with hem *on erasure* H1   232 another] other E   235 chese] *changed to* tell H1
240 haddest] hast E   242 haue] hadde E, had *changed to* hath H1   248 trouthe]
þou3 G   250 thou¹] tho E   this] the EH1

And in this mene tyme massangers come fro Rome and saide how
Vaspasien was enhaunsed into the empire and so ledde hym to Rome.
255 And Eusebi witnessithe in his Cronicle that Iosephus hadde tolde
before to Vaspasian as wel of the dethe of the emperour as of the
lefting vp of hym into the empire.

And thanne Vaspasien went forthe and lefte his sone Titus to kepe
þe sege of Ierusalem. And whanne Titus herde that his fader was
260 haunsed so into the empire he was fulfelled withe gret ioye so
ferforthely that thorugh the gretnesse of that vnmesurable ioye the
synues of hym were constreined togedre with suche a colde that he
was bynome in his one thye so that he myght not susteyne hym. And
whanne Iosephus herde that Titus was so seke he enquered the cause
265 of his sikenesse and the tyme that it toke hym, and men coude not telle
hym the cause ne what siknesse it was. Wel thei knewe it fell vpon
hym whanne tydingges come of the eleccion of his fader. Iosephus
that was a man purueied of gret wisdom considered of a litell many
f. 95ʳᵇ thingges, so that of the tyme of his siknesse he fonde | the cause of his
270 siknesse and fonde wel that he was seke of gret abundaunce of ioye
and of gladnesse, and he bethought hym that suche thingges bene ofte
cured be her contraries. And he wost well that that thinge whiche is
som tyme goten by loue and bi ioie is loste ofte tyme bi sorugh, and
therfor he enquered yef there were any that were gretly hated of
275 Titus. And thanne thei lete hym wete that ther was one that was so
gretly behated of Titus that he myght not beholde hym witheoute
grete wrathe [ne] in no wyse here hym named in his presence. And
thanne Iosephus went to Titus and saide to hym: 'Yef thou desire to
haue hele of thi siknesse loke that alle that come in my felashippe may
280 come saufly.' To whom Titus saide: 'Who so come in thi felawship
mowe come and go surely.'

And thanne Iosephus comaunded to Titus that he shulde ordeine
a solempne fest, and he ordeined his borde ayeinst [the] borde of
Titus, and he made that servaunt that Titus hated so moche sitte bi
285 hym. And whanne Titus seigh hym he was troubeled with sorugh
and anger so gretly that he trembeled all his body so that he that was
before seke withe ioye enchaufed hym by brennynge of anger so that
al his synues streched oute and was al hole. And after [that] Titus
toke þat servaunt into his grace and Iosephus into his frenshippe.

257 vp] om. Hɪ   258 thanne] on erasure Hɪ   272 that²] om. G   275 so] om.
Hɪ   277 ne] no E, 'ne' Hɪ   283 the] his E   284 that²] of Hɪ   hated] so with ha
on erasure Hɪ   287 enchaufed] enhaunsed Hɪ   288 after that] afterwarde E

But yef this storie apocrifie be lefull to be redde or none I leue it in 290
the will of þe reder.

And thanne was Ierusalem beseged of Titus by two yere, and
amonge alle these euelles that tho that were beseged suffered thei
endu|red so gret famyne that the faders and the moders toke not only f. 95va
the mete oute of her childers hondes but drewe it oute of her mouthe, 295
and so dede the men to the women [and the women to the men], and
þe yonge peple that were strong and lyght[er] of age went aboute the
stretes as madde for hunger and felle downe in the waye as dede
ymages deef and domme witheoute soule. And ofte tymes it fell that
they þat beried the dede fill ofte dede vpon the dede and so thei myght 300
in no wise suffre the [stenc]he of karions but caste hem oute aboute
the walles. And whanne Titus wente aboute the towne he seigh the
walles full of carienes of the citee and he felt al the cuntre corrupte
withe the stenche of hem, and than he lefte vp his hondes to heuene
and saide in wepinge: 'Lorde, thou knowest that I am not cause 305
hereof.' And therwith ther was so gret famyne in the citee that thei ete
her shone and her gerdelys of ledir.

And amonge al this sorugh ther was a lady of noble kinrede and
riche. So as it is redde in the Stori Ecclesiast that theues come to her
hous and toke awaie al her good and lefte her nothinge to ete, and she 310
helde her litell childe in her arme yeuing it souke and saide: 'O thou
most wreched sone of wreched moder. A, thou my sone, to whom
shall I kepe the in this bataile, in this famyne, in this rentinge? Thou
shalt be a praie to moders, wodenesse to robbours, and a fable to the
worlde.' And with that saienge she cutte the throtc of her sone and 315
slewe hym and ete the halff and hidde that other halff. And anone the
theues felt the saueour of the flesshe [soden] and entered | witheinne f. 95vb
the hous and manased her to deye yef she wolde not shewe hem the
flesshe. And thanne she vnhilled the membres of her childe. 'Lo here,'
she saide, 'I haue kept you the beter partie.' And thanne they hadde so 320
gret drede that thei myght not speke a worde, and she saide hem:
'What ailethe you? The childe is myn and the synne is myn, and
therfor etithe on surely, for I haue ete that other partie. Bethe not
more religious thanne I that am his moder, ne more meued with pitee
thanne I that am a woman, and yef pitee ouercome you so that ye dare 325

296 the²] om. H1   and the women to the men] L, om. EH1G   297 lyghter] lyght
EH1   299 deef] dede G   300 they] 'þoo' H1   301 stenche] dethe E
306 hereof] þereof H1   308 And] om. G   311 arme] hond G   souke] so with ke on
erasure H1   317 soden] om. E   321 thei] on erasure H1

not ete hym, I shalle ete this halff as I dede that other.' And thanne
thei went oute trembelyng and quaking for [o]rrour of that sight.

And in the ende of the secounde yere of the emperour Vaspasian,
Titus toke Ierusalem and destroied it, and whanne he hadde take it
330 and the Temple he destroied it vtterly, and as the Iues hadde solde
oure Lorde for .xxx.^{ti} pens, he solde .xxx.^{ti} Iues for a peny. And as
Iosephus tellithe there were solde .iiij^{xx}.xvij.M^l. of Iues, and .xj.
thousande were perished with hunger and with suerde.

And it is redde that whanne Titus entered into Ierusalem he seigh a
335 thicke walle, and he comaunded that it were broken, and whanne the
hole was made they seigh witheinne an auncien and a worshipfull man
faire of coloure and of glad chere, and whanne men asked hym what
he was he ansuered hem and saide: 'I am Ioseph of Aramathie, a citee
of Iudee, that the Iues enclosed and mured here withinne for that I
340 beried Ihesu Crist, and fro þat tyme hedir I haue be fedde withe
heuenly mete and comforted withe [devyne] light.' And yet it is saide
f. 96ra in the | Gospell of Nichodeme that whanne the Iues hadde enclosed
hym hou that oure Lorde Ihesu Crist was risen he toke hym from
thennes and brought hym to Aramathie. And it may wel be that
345 whanne he was take oute thei wold not suffre hym to preche but
closed hym vp ayenne.

And [thanne] after that Vaspasien was dede Titus succeded after
hym in the empire and was a full debonaire prince and of gret bounte,
and he was of so gret [fredom], as Eusebie of Cesarience tellithe in his
350 Cronicle and Ierom tellithe also, that yef ther were any day that he
coude remember hym that he hadde not yeue ne no good done, he
wolde saie anone: 'A, my frendes, this day is foule lost in my partie.'

And longe tyme after that the Iues wolde make ayein Ierusalem. As
thei went oute in the morwtide thei founde many crosses made of
355 deue, bi whiche they were gretly aferde and fledde. And Iosephus
saiethe in his Cronicle they turned ayen the secounde morwtide and
eueriche fonde in his clothinge a crosse of blode, wherof thei were
gretly afraied and fledde ayein, but they turned the .iij.^e tyme and a
fere come oute of the erthe with suche a smoke that thei were alle
360 strangeled and ouercome.

327 orrour] errour EH1   328 Vaspasian] *add* and EG, *so del.* H1   341 devyne]
L, heuenly EH1G   347 thanne] *om.* E   349 fredom] bounte EH1   356 ayen]
add to H1   357 wherof] wherfor H1

Here endithe the lyff of Seint Iames and of the distruccion
of Ierusalem, and next foluithe the Findinge of the Holy
Crosse, Capitulum .lxj.ᵐ

The findinge of the Holi Crosse was .CC. yere and more after the
resureccion of oure Lorde. Men reden in the Gospell of Nichodeme
that whanne Adam was sike Sethe his sone went into the gates of
paradise terrestre and asked piteously of the oyle of mercie for to
anoint | his fader to haue his hele. To whom Michael the archaungell f. 96ʳᵇ
appered and saide: 'Ne trauaile thou not ne wepe not as thou doest for 6
to gete the oyle of the tree of mercie, for thou maist none haue in no
wise by[fore]' that .vMˡ. and .vC. yere be fulfelled,' that is to wete
from Adam vnto the passion of Ihesu Crist, of whiche .v. thousand
and .vC. yere were thanne passed but .CC.xxxiij. yere. And it is redde 10
elliswhere that the aungell toke hym a braunche and comaunded hym
to plante it in the mount of Lyban. And verrely in a stori of the
Grekes, thou it be apocrifie, it is wretin that the aungell toke hym of
the tree of whiche Adam hadde synned and saide hym tha[t] whanne
the tree shuld bere fruit his fader shulde be heled. And whanne Sethe 15
come ayein home he fonde his fader dede, and than he planted this
bowe on his faders tombe, and whanne it was planted it grewe and
become a gret tree and dured vnto the tyme of Salamon. But whedir
these thingges be true or none that leue I in the will of the reder, for
thei be not redde in no cronicle nc in no stori autentik. 20

Salamon thanne seighe this tree so faire he comaunded to smyte
hym doune and putte hym sauf in the hous of Sauxe. And as Iohn
Beleth saiethe, that tree wolde neuer be mete for no manere werke, for
eyther it was to longe or to shorte and therfor the werkemen hadde it
in despite and toke none hede therof but leide it ouer a water as a 25
brigge [for] men to passe ouer. And whanne the Quene of Saba come
to here the wisdom of Salamon, as she shulde passe ouer the water and
ouer the tree, she seigh in sperit | how that the saueoure of the world f. 96ᵛᵃ
shulde deie on that tree, and therfor she wolde not passe therouer but
worshipped that tree. And it is redde in the Maister of Stories that the 30
Quene of Saba seigh that tree in the hous of Saux, and whanne she
was gone home to her owne contrei she sent Salamon worde that a
man shulde be honged on that tree by whos deth the kyngdom of Iues

EH1GH2A1A2L   8 byfore] by E   10 were] om. H1   14 that] L, thanne
EH1G   18 become] begonne H1   23 tree] tre with re on erasure H1   26 for] L,
om. EH1G

shulde be destroied. And thanne Salamon toke awaye that tree and
35 hidde it depe in the erthe, and after that the piscin of probacion was
made there wher men woschen the sacrifices. And men sayen that the
mevinge of the water ne the curacion of the seke peple was not only
done for that the aungell come doun, but by the vertue of that tree.
And whanne the passion neighed it is certaine that the tree flotered
40 aboue, and whanne the Iues seen it thei toke it vp and made the crosse
of oure Lorde. And that crosse of oure Lorde was of .iiij. maner of
trees, that is to saie of palme, of cipresse, of cedre and of oliue, wherof
a vers saiethe: 'The trees of the crosse bene palme, oliue, cedre and
cipresse.'
45   In the crosse there were .iiij. difference, the tree vpright, the tree
ouerthwart, the table that was sette aboue, and the mortays that the
crosse was fastened inne. This difference of trees is sayn to touche þe
apostell Paule whanne he saieth that ye mowe comprehende withe al
the seintes whiche is the lengthe, þe brede, the hight, the depenesse,
50 which wordes Austin the [noble] doctoure expownithe in this manere:
'The brede of the crosse of oure Lorde is saide in the travers wher
f. 96ᵛᵇ oure Lor|des hondes were streched on, the lengthe fro the erthe to
that brede of the armes wher al the bodi was tormented on, the hight
was fro the brede wher the hede cleued on, the dipnesse was that was
55 hidde in the erthe wher the crosse was fastened on, in whiche signes of
the crosse alle cristen mennes dedes bene discriued, that is to saie to
werke well in Crist and to cleue in hym perseuerauntly and to hope in
heuenly sacramentis and not misuse hem.'
     This precious tree of the crosse was hidde witheinne the erthe .CC.
60 yere and more, but it was founde after in this manere by Elyne the
moder of Constantine the emperoure. In that tyme gret multitude of
barbarins witheoute nombre wer assembeled besides the riuer of
Danibe and wolde haue passed ouer and submitted al the regions of
the orient to her lordshippe, and whanne Constantine the emperour
65 wost that, he remeued his oste and come ayeinst hem vpon the
Danibe. These men of Barbari encresed al day and passed ouer the
flode, and thanne Constantine hadd gret drede and seigh that he most
fight withe hem in the morw. In that same nyght the aungell of God
awoke hym and saide to hym þat he sholde loke vpward. And thanne
70 he loked vp to heueneward and seigh the signe of the crosse shinyng

35 hidde it] hidded H1   37 the³] *om.* G   41 And . . . Lorde] `þᵗ´ H1
45 difference] *add* þat `is to sey´ H1, differencis G          vpright . . . tree] `tre and þe´ H1
49 the⁴] and G   50 noble] holy EH1

right clere withe gret light and there was wretin aboue withe lettres of golde: 'Thou shalt ouercome thin enemyes bi this signe.' And thanne he was comforted for that heuenly vision and [thanne] he lete make a crosse and ordeined it to be bore before hym and all his oste, and thanne manly he ranne on his enemyes and putte hem to flight and 75 slew of hem gret multitude.

And after | that Constantine lete calle to hym the bisshops of ydoles f. 97ʳᵃ and enquered of hem diligentely of what god that signe was, and thei tolde hym that thei wost neuer. And thanne ther come some cristen men that tolde pleinly that it was the signe of the holy crosse, and 80 thanne the emperour beleued perfitely in Ihesu Crist and receyued baptime of the pope Eusebye, or after sum other bokes, of the bisshop Cesarience. But many thingges be putte in this stori to whiche the Stori Parted in Thre ayeinsaiethe, and the Maister of Stories also, and the lyff of Seint Siluester and the Gestis of the bisshops of Rome. And 85 after sum other writers this was not that Constantine whiche was baptized of Siluestre the pope like as other stories shewen, but it was Constantine the fader of this Constantine, for this Constantine come otherwise to þe faithe, so as men reden in the stori of Seint Siluestre that tellithe that he was baptized of Seint Siluestre and not of Euseby. 90 For whanne Constantine the fader was dede, Constantine his sone remembered hym of the victorie that his fader hadd bi the signe of the crosse and sent his moder Eline into Ierusalem for to fynde the verrey crosse so [as] it is saide hereafter.

And the Maister of Stories tellithe þat this victorie was done in this 95 wise: he saiethe that whanne Maxence assailed the empire of Rome, Constantine the emperour come besides the brigge of Albynum for to fight with Maxence. He was full of anguisshe and ofte tymes lefte vp his eighen towardes heuene to beseche almyghti God of helpe. And as he slepte he hadde a vision from heuene touard the orient, for he seigh 100 the signe of | the crosse in liknesse of fyre and an aungell after that, f. 97ʳᵇ that saide to hym: 'Constantine, thou shalt ouercome thine enemyes bi this signe.' And as it is saide in the Stori Parted in Thre that as he mervailed hereof what it myght be, the same nyght foluing Ihesu Crist appered to hym with the signe that he hadde sene in heuene and 105 comaunded that he shulde make that figure of that signe and that shulde helpe hym ayenst his enemyes in batayle. Thanne was

75 thanne] *om.* E   79 some] *om.* H1   84 ayeinsaiethe] a yene s`e′ith H1
85 Siluestre] *add* and EH1   89 Seint Siluestre] *trs. and marked for reversal* H1
94 as] L, that EH1G   96 empire] Emperour H1G   101 of¹] *twice* E

Constantine gladde and was al sure to haue the victorie and made a
signe in his forhede, the signe that he hadd sene in heuene and
110 chaunged al his baners of werre and made on hem the signe of the
crosse and bere a crosse of golde in his honde and besought oure
Lorde that he wolde not suffre that right side whiche he had
worshipped withe the signe of h[e]le and sauacion to be bledde
withe þe blood of Romayns, but that of his mercie he wolde graunte
115 hym victorie of the tyrauntes witheoute sheding of blode.

And thanne Maxence comaunded to tho that were withe hym in his
shippes that they shulde go vnder the brigge and þat thei shulde kitle
the brigge for to deceiue her enemyes that shulde passe ouer. And
whanne Maxence seigh that Constantine approched the flode he
120 forgate his werke that he hadd do made and went hastely ayeinst
Constantine withe fewe men and comaunded the remenaunt of the
peple to folw hym anone. And so he went forthe on the brigge and was
deceiued withe the same deceite þat he wolde haue deceiued
Constantine, and so he was drowned in the depe flode. And thanne
f. 97ᵛᵃ was Con|stantine receiued lorde bi the acorde [of alle].
126 And as it is redde in a stori auutentike that Constantine leued not
perfiteli on God that tyme ne hadde not receiued yet [the holy]
bapteme, but witheinne a while after he seigh a vision of Seint Peter
and Seint Paule and thanne he was baptized of Seint Siluester the
130 pope and so he was hcled of the lepore, and after that he beleued in
God perfitely. And thanne he sent his moder Eline into Ierusalem for
to seke the crosse of oure Lorde. Notwitheston[din]g [that] Ambrose
saiethe in his epistell of the dethe of Theodosien, and the Stori
Part[ed] in Thre holt the same, that Constantine abode for to be
135 baptized vnto his laste dayes, and he dede it to that ende that he wolde
be baptized in flume Iordan. And this same saiethe Ierome in his
cronicles, but it is sertayne that he was cristene vnder Siluestre the
pope, but it is a doute whedir he abode to be baptised or none. And so
men doute in the legende of Seint Siluestre many thingges, for this
140 stori of the inuencion of the crosse whiche is founde in the Stori of
Ecclesiast, to whom the cronicle acordithe, semithe more auutentik
thanne that that is recordid in þe Chirche, for ther bene many
thingges witheinne that acordithe not with the trouthe, but yef any

111 and bere a crosse] *ins.* H1   113 hele] hole E, þe hele H1   115 hym] *add* the
EH1   117 brigge] brigges EH1   shulde²] *add* this difference of trees *del.* G
118 brigge] brigges E   125 the acorde of alle] L, alle the acorde EH1G   127 the holy]
om. E   132 Notwithestonding] notwithestong E   that] *om.* E   133 Theodosien]
Theodesien E   134 Parted] partithe E   136 saiethe] s'e'ith H1

perauenture wolde saye so as it is saide ofte aboue, that that same was
not Constantine but Constant his fader, þe whiche is not right 145
auutentike thou it be so that it be redde in stories byyende the see.

And as Eline was come beyende the see she comaunded that all the
wise Iues of that region shulde be brought before her. And this Eline
hadde [be] furst an hostiler, but for the gret beauute of her Con|stant f. 97vb
ioined her to hym, after that Ambrose tellithe by these wordes: 'Men 150
saien,' saithe Seint Ambrose, 'that she was an ostiler, but well I wote
she was wedded to Constaunt the olde that after was emperour. She
was a goode ostiler that so diligently sought the cr[ech]e of oure
Lorde; she was a good ostiler that misknewe not hym that laye in the
stable, a good osteler that acounted al thinge at not sauf the loue of 155
Ihesu Crist, and for to gete þat was al her ioye and al her laboure, and
therfor oure Lorde lefte [her vp] fro this foule place to his endeles
blisse.' And this saieth Ambrose. But other sayne [and] it is redde in a
story autentik that Eline was the doughter of Thoell kynge of
Bretayne, and whanne Constaunt was in Bretayne he toke her to his 160
wyff, and thanne þe ile of Bretayn fell to hym by the dethe of Thoell,
and this the Bretones witnessen.

And thanne the Iues dredden gretly and saide one to another: 'Whi
trowe ye that the quene makithe us to appere before her?' And thanne
one of hem that hight Iudas saide: 'I wote well, she wolde knowe of vs 165
where the tree of the crosse is that Ihesu Crist was hangged on, but
none of you knowlage that to her, for I wote well that oure lawe shall
be destroied and the techingges of oure kinrede a[ni]entised. For
[Z]achee myn graunsere tolde my fader, and my fader told me whanne
he deide and saide: "Sone, I charge the that whanne [the] tyme 170
comithe that men seke the crosse of Crist þat thou shewe it to [none]
tofore thou haue suffered [sum] torment, for after that it shall be
founde the peple of Iues shall haue no kyngdom, but thei shulle haue
it that worshipen the crucified, for he is Crist the sone of God." | And f. 98ra
thanne I saide hym: "Fader, yef youre auncien faders knewen that he 175
was the sone of God, whi henge thei hym in the gibett of the crosse?"
Than saide his fader: "God wote I was neuer of her counsaile but
ayeinsaide hem often, for he was a right wise man and reproued the

149 be] L, om. EH1G   151 saithe] s`e´ith H1   153 creche] L, cribbe EH1G
157 her vp] trs. E   158 and] that EH1   159 that] add that G   161 Thoell]
Koell with k on erasure H1   163 one to] vnto H1   165 saide] om. H1
168 anientised] amentised EH1G (anentised L, aneantis P2)   169 Zachee] Sachee EH1
170 the²] om. E   171 shewe it] shewed H1   none] man EH1   172 sum] to miche
EH1   it] sche G

vices of the pharisees whiche made hym to be crucified, and he arose
180 verrely the thridde day and stied into heuene, seinge his disciples.
And Steuen thi brother beleued in hym, and therfor the wode Iues
stoned hym to dethe. And therfor kepe the, good sone, that thou
blame hym not ne his disciples."' But it is not [right] prouable that
the fader of this Iudas myght haue be in the tyme of the passion of
185 Ihesu Crist, for it was .CC. [yere and] .lxx. fro the passion of Crist
into the comyng of Elyne in whos tyme the crosse was founde but yef
it were perauenture that men liued lenger in tho dayes thanne thei do
now. And thanne saide [the Iues] to [Iudas]: 'We herde neuer of these
thingges, but loke yef the quene enquere of these thingges that thou
190 discouer it not.' And thanne after, whanne thei were all brought
before the quene and she asked hem wher þe place was that Ihesu
Crist was crucified on, thei wolde not telle her in no wise. And thanne
the quene comaunded that thei shulde be alle brent in a fere, so that
thei drede the dethe and deliuered her Iudas, saieng: 'Madame, this is
195 the sone of a rightwys man and a prophete and knewe the lawe right
wel, and he canne shew you alle that ye will aske hym.' And tha[nne]
she lete go alle that other and kept Iudas allone, and thanne she saide
to hym: 'Chese of two thingges, whedir thou wilt deie or lyue. Shewe
f. 98rb   me the place that is called Galgatha wher | Ihesu Crist was crucified so
200 that I may finde the crosse.' Iudas ansuered and saide: 'How may I
knowe the place, sethe it is .CC. hundered yere agoo and more and I
was not in that tyme [borne]?' To whom the quene saide: 'By hym
that was crucified, but thou telle me the trouthe I shall make the deye
for hunger.' And thanne she comaunded that he shulde be caste in a
205 depe pitte and ther to be turmented with hunger, and whanne he
hadde be there .vij. dayes he beesought to come oute and he wolde
shewe the place of the crosse. And whan he was hadde oute he come to
the place, and whanne he hadde made his praiers the place beganne to
move sodenly and men felt a mervailous sauour of swetnesse, so that
210 Iudas mervailed and reioysed and ioyned his hondes togedre and
saide: 'In trouthe, Ihesu Crist, thou arte the saueoure of the world.'
　　And as men rede in the Maister of Stories that the temple of Venus
was in þat place the whiche Adrian the emperoure lete make for that

180 seinge] seying *with* i *subp.* H1
183 right] *om.* EH1   185 yere and] *om.* E
Iues EH1G   189 thou] 3e *on erasure* H1
that E   197 that other] *so on erasure* H1
pepul G   207–8 of the . . . place] *ins.* H1
om. G

181–2 and therfor . . . dethe] *ins.* H1
188 the Iues to Iudas] L, Iudas to the
190 it] 'þys' H1, þis G   196 thanne]
202 borne] L, *om.* EH1G   207 place]
208 whanne he] *om.* G   210 and¹]

cause, [that] yef any cristen man come to worshipp þat place that he
shulde be saye to worship the ydole of Venus, and therfor that place 215
was not haunted but as alle foryeten. And thanne the quene made the
temple to be destroied and that place to be worshipped. And thanne
after that Iudas beganne to digge myghtely and digged .xx.^{ti} pas depe,
and ther he founde th[r]e crosses hidde, the whiche he brought to the
quene, and [w]hanne thei coude not knowe the crosse of Ihesu Crist 220
from the theues crosses, thei leide hem alle thre in the middes of the
citee and abode ther the grace of God. And aboute the oure of none
men bere | a yonge man dede bi the waye, and thanne Iudas toke the f. 98ᵛᵃ
furst crosse and the secounde and leide hem vpon the dede bodie, but
he meued neuer the more. But as sone as he was touched withe the 225
thridde crosse he arose [anone] from dethe to lyff. Men reden [in] the
Stori of Ecclesiast that as a lady whiche was ladi of that cite lay in her
bedde as halff dede, Makari that was bisshop of Ierusalem toke the
furst crosse and the secounde and thei profited her noght, and thanne
he toke the .iij. crosse and touched her therwithe, and she arose anone 230
al hole.

Ambrose saiethe how that thei knewe the crosse of oure Lorde by
þe titel that Pilate hadde sette thervpon that was founde and redde
there. And the fende cried in the eyre and saide: 'O thou Iudas, whi
hast thou do this? Thou hast not folued myn other Iudas but hast 235
done the contrarie, for he dede the treson that I counsailed hym and
thou hast forsake me and hast found the crosse of Ihesu. Bi my Iudas I
haue wonne many a soule and bi the I shall lese tho of the Iues that I
hadde gete. Sumtyme I regned by hym in the peple and bi the I shal
be caste oute of the peple. And therfor verrely yef I may I shall 240
ouercome the, for I shall meue ayeinst the another kinge that shall
leue the lawe of the crucified and make the to renye the crucified;' the
whiche thing the deuel ment by Iulian the apostata the whiche
tormented after the same Iudas with many gret tormentes, for he
was made bisshopp of Ierusalem after and a martir of Ihesu Crist. And 245
whan Iudas herde the deuel so crie he dred hym not but cursed hym
strongly, | saieng: 'Ihesu Crist hathe dampned the depe in hell in f. 98ᵛᵇ
euerlastinge fire.' And after that Iudas was cristened and called
Quiriacus, and he was ordeyned to be bisshop of Ierusalem.

214 that¹] *om*. E   219 thre] the EH₁   220 whanne] thanne EH₁   221 from]
for H₁   226 anone] *om*. E   in] *om*. EH₁   227 was] *add* a G   235 folued]
defouled H₁   236 dede] dredde E   241 kinge] knyght *with* ht *del*.H₁   242 and
. . . crucified] *om*. H₁   244 tormented] *add* and E, *add* and *del*. H₁   246 so crie] to
crie so G   he] and H₁

250 And whanne blessed Eline seigh that she hadde not the nayles of
oure Lorde, she praied Quiriacus that he wolde go to the same place
and seke hem diligentely. And whanne he come thedir and made his
praiers, the nailes of oure Lorde beganne to shine aboue the erthe as
golde. He toke hem and bere hem to the quene. She kneled doune and
255 enclined her hede and worshipped hem with gret reuerence. And
thanne Seint Eline toke one partie of the crosse and that other she
made to be putte in a faire shrine of siluer and bare it into Ierusalem,
and that other partie she bare to her sone. [And also she bare to her
sone] the nayles that oure Lorde was nayled with, of the whiche nayles
260 so as Ce[sar]iens saiethe Constaunt made sette hem in a bridell whiche
he vsed whanne he went into bataile and with the other he arraied his
helme. But many affermen as Gregori of Toures saieth that the[re
were] foure nayles fastened in oure Lorde, of whiche Eline putte two
in her sones bridell, and the thridde was sette in the ymage of
265 Constaunt that is atte Rome and apered aboue all the citee, and the
fourthe she cast in the see of Adrian, the whiche vnto that tyme hadde
be a deluge and destruccion of all tho that come therinne. And she
comaunded that this fest of the Inuencion of the Crosse were euery
yere halowed solempnely.

270 And Ambrose saiethe the same also: 'Elene sought the nayles of
oure Lorde and founde hem, and of that one she made hym a bridell
f. 99ra and of that other a crowne, and she made set|te the nayle right in the
forhede, the crowne in the backe of the hede and the reyne in the
honde, so that the witte appered, the faithe shined, and the myght
275 governed.'

And after that alle these thingges were done, Iulian the apostata
slow Seint Quiriacus the bisshop for that he hadde founde the holy
crosse, and enforsed hym in al that he coude to destroie the holy
crosse. For whanne Iulian went ayeinst the men of Perce he toke
280 Quiriacus and wolde haue made hym to do sacrifice to the idoles, and
whan he hadde deuied it he made cutte of his right honde and saide:
'He hathe wrete to many letteres with his honde bi the whiche he
hathe withedrawe moche peple to sacrifice to oure goddes.' And
Quiriacus saide to hym: 'Thou wode hounde, thou hast do to me a
285 gret profite, for er I was cristen I wrote ofte into the sinagoge of Iewes

250 the] add blessid G   251 to] ins. H1   257 in a faire] ins. followed by a del. H1
258–9 And also . . . sone] L, om. EH1G   260 Cesariens] L, Cerasiens EH1G   sette]
add 'oon of' H1   262–3 there were] these E   271–2 one . . . that] om. H1
273 forhede] add of E   278 and] add he G   278–9 and . . . crosse] twice once del. H1
283 to1] add do E

that none shulde leue in God, and now thou hast caste awaye alle the disclaunder of my body.' And thanne anone Iulian lete melt lede and poure it in his mouthe, and after he made a grediren of yren and made hym to be leide theron and gret fire to be putte vnder of colys and made his woundes to be froted withe salt and grece. And Quiriace 290 helde hym stille witheoute mevinge, and thanne Iulian saide to hym: 'If thou wilt not sacrifice to oure goddes, yet renye that thou art cristen.' And whanne he hadde refused [to do] that in cursinge, Iulyan comaunded to make a depe pitte in the erthe and putte therin Quiriacus and caste vpon hym venemous serpentes, but these 295 serpentes weren dede anone. And thanne Iulian comanded that Quiriace were putte in a caudron of oyle boylinge hote. He blessed | hym and entered inne with his good will and praied to oure Lorde that f. 99rb he wolde baptise hym ayen in the lauatorie of marterdome. And than was Iulian wrothe and comaunded that he were smete thorugh the 300 body with a spere, and so [deserued he to] fulfelle his marterdome.

How miche the vertue of the crosse is it appered in that true notarie that an enchauntour wold haue deceiued and brought hym into a place wher he called the fendes and behight hym that he shulde abounde in al maner richesse. And th[anne] he seigh a gret Ethiope sitte an high 305 vpon a sege and hadde aboute hym many Ethiopes that helden suerdes and staues in her hondes. And thanne he asked of the enchauntour what man that was, and thanne he saide: 'Lorde, it is your servaunt.' And thanne the Ethiope saide: 'Will he worship me and be myne and renye his Crist, and I shall make hym sitte [in] my right side.' And 310 thanne anone this notarie made vpon hym the signe of the crosse and saide that he was servaunt of Ihesu Crist, and anone that multitude of fendes vanisshed awaye. And after that as this notarie in a tyme went with his maister and entered into a chirche of Seint Sophie and stode bothe before the ymage of the saueoure, his maister seigh how that the 315 ymage behelde the notarie verrely and hadde his eyen sette vpon hym ententifly. And whan he seigh this he hadde gret mervaile and made hym turne into the right side of the ymage, and yet he seigh the ymage haue alway [his] eyen vpon hym. And thanne he turned hym to the lefte syde, and the | ymage turned his eyen vpon hym and bihelde f. 99va hym. And thanne his maister coniured hym and praied hym to tell 321

286 none] *on erasure* H1   288 poure] powrid G   289 be²] *om.* H1G
293 cristen] L, a cristen man EGH1   to do] *om.* E   refused to do] do to refuse H1
cursinge] scornynge H1   297 caudron] *add* `ful' H1   301 deserued . . . fulfelle] he
fulfelled E   302 the²] *add* holy E   305 thanne] there E, That *changed to* Than H1
306 a] an heigh G   310 in] on E   319 his] the E   to] vpon G

hym what he hadde deserued towardes God that the ymage behelde
hym so. He saide that he coude not remembre hym of no good dede
that he had done but that he wolde not renye hym afore the fende.

Here endithe of the Holy Crosse, and nexst beginnithe þe
lyff of Seint Iohn the Apostill, Cap^m. .lxij.^m

Whanne Seint Iohn the Apostell and Euuangelist preched in Ephesim
he was take of the prouost and was constreined to sacrifice to the
goddes, and whanne he refused it he was putte in prison. And thanne
the prouost sent a lettre to Domisien the emperour in whiche he
5 witnessithe that Seint Iohn was an enchauntour, a breker of the lawes,
a destroier of þe ydoles and a worshipper of the crucified. And thanne
he was brought to Rome bi the comaundement of Domysien and they
lete shere of the here of his hede for despite and putte hym thanne in a
tonne of boyling oyle and the fere thervnder al brennynge at the yate
10 of the citee that is called Port Latine, but he felt neuer disese therof
[ne peyne, but hole and sounde wente oute therof] witheoute any
hurtinge. And than cristen men made a chirche there in that place,
and that day is made as solempne as the day of [his] marterdome. And
whanne Domisien seigh that he cesed not to preche the name of Ihesu
15 Crist, he sent hym into exile into the ile [of Pathmos].

And the emperour dedc not only pe[r]secucion to the apostell for
[they] preched Ihesu Crist, for [they] refused no god, but for [they]
auctorised Ihesu Crist to be God withoute the licence of the
f. 99vb senatoures of Rome, the whiche thing thei de[u]y|ed not to be done
20 of any. Wherfor men reden in the Stori of Ecclesiast that on a tyme
Pilate sent to Tyberien lettres of Ihesu Crist that he wolde consent
that the faithe of Ihesu Crist myght be receyued of the Romaynes, but
the senatoures refused it atte all for as moche as he hadde not be called
God bi her auctorite.

25 And another cause whi they wolde not receiue hym, as it is
conteined in a cronicle, was for he apered not furst to the Romaines.
And another cause was for he destroied the worship of alle her goddes
that they worshipped. And yet ther was another cause and that was for

324 afore] aftir G

EH1GH2A1A2L   2 to¹] add do E   11 ne . . . therof] L, om. EH1G   13 as¹]
del. H1   as² . . . marterdome] del. H1   his] om. E   15 into¹] `in´ H1   of Pathmos] om.
EH1   16 persecucion] pesecucion E   apostelles] apostell EH1   17 they¹,²,³] he
EH1   no] L, not EH1G   19 deuyed] denyed E

he despised the worlde and the Romains were coueitous of the worlde. And Ihesu Crist wolde not suffre that for as moch as the worlde was 30 made to be soget to mannes pouer. And yet Maister Iohn Belett assignithe another cause whi the emperoures and the senatoures wolde not obeie to Ihesu Crist but pursued hym and his apposteles, for it semed hem that God was to proude and to enuious for that he deined not to haue no felawe. And another cause, as Orose saieth, for 35 that the senatoures hadde despite that Pilate hadde sent lettres of the myracles of Ihesu Crist to Tyberien and not to hem, wherfor thei wolde not suffre that he were sacred amonge men, and for that was Tyberien so wrothe that he slowe many of the senatoures, and sum he sent into exile. 40

And whanne the moder of that Seint Iohn herde that [her sone] was ledde to Rome she was moued by pitee of moderly affeccion and come to Rome to visite hym. And whan she was come and hadde herde that he was sent into exile she turned her ayein, and whanne she come into Compeyne into the citee of Verulane, she | passid to oure Lorde Ihesu f. 100ra Crist, and the bodi of her was beried in a pitte wher she was hidde longe tyme in a sepulcre, and sethe it was shewed to Iohn her sone. And thanne she was born full suete smellinge and shinynge bi many miracles witheinne the citee with gret worship.

Here endithe the lyff of Seint Iohn the Apostell, and nexst beginnithe of the Letanies, Cap^m. .lxiij.^m

The letanies be made two tymes in the yere, that is in the fest of Seint Marke, whiche is called the Gretter Letanie, and another letanie is thre dayes before the Ascencion, whiche is called the Lasse Letanie and is as moche to saie as supplicacion or request.

And the furst letanie is called trebelle for she is called furst þe Gret 5 Letanie; secoundely she is saide procession of .vij. formes; threddely she is called the blacke crosse. She is called the Gret Letanie by .iij. causes, the furst cause for hym that ordeined her furst, whiche was Seint Gregori the pope of Rome. And after for the reson of the place ther she was ordeyned and that was atte Rome, whiche is the hede of 10 the worlde because that ther lieth the prince of apposteles, and also ther is the sege of apostoile, and also bicause of a gret and a greef siknesse,

38 men] hem G   41 her sone] he EH1

EH1GH2A1A2L   11 liethe the] light H1   the²] om. E   12 apostoile] appostels H1   greef] greful H1

for whanne the Romains hadde leued in continence al the Lente and
hadde receiued atte Ester the bodi of oure Lorde, thanne after that
15 thei gauen hemselff to glotenye and to vnclennesse of leving, wherfor
oure Lord was wrothe and sent amonges hem a gret pestilence, the
whiche is called the apostume or suelling in the throte. And this
pestilence was so cruell that men deyde sodenly going by the waye,
f. 100ʳᵇ being at mete, in plaieng and | speking, and in suche wise that whan
20 [a man] fnesed ofte tymes [it] fell [that thei] gaue vp the sperit in
fnesinge, wherof come the custume to saie whanne a man fnes[ed]
'Crist helpe,' whiche good custume is yet used, and also whanne a
man yan[ed] whiche sum callen galpinge thei deied anone. And
therfor as sone as they felt that thei shulde yane they wold make
25 the crosse afore her mouthe, and this custume is yet kept also. And it
is founde in the liff of Seint Gregorie how this pestilence beganne.

Secoundely she is saide procession of .vij. fourmes for that Seint
Gregorie ordeined the processiones that he dede thanne make by .vij.
maner of ordinaunce. For in the furste all the clergie was, in the
30 secounde all the monkes and religio[u]s, in the thridde alle the nonnes
and religious women, in the fourthe were all the children, and in the
fifthe all the laye peple, in the sixte all wedues and continentes, and in
the .vij.ᵗᵉ were alle the maried. But now we mow not ordeine hem so
for the multitude and [the] diuersitee of peple, and that we mowe not
35 fulfell in the nombre of persones we fulfell in the nombre of letanies,
for thei shuld be saide .vij. tymes before that these signes be take
awaye.

Thirdely thei be called the blake crosses in token of the gret
distruccion of men and in token of penaunce and for that men were
40 clothed in blake clothing, or perauenture that men heled or couered
the crosses and the auuteres with blacke couertures or sackes or heires
and toke vpon hemselff clothinge of penaunce.

That other letanie is called the Lasse Letanie, the whiche is thre
f. 100ᵛᵃ dayes before | the Ascension Day. And Seint Mamertine bisshoppe of
45 Viane ordeined it in the tyme of Leon the emperour that beganne the
yere of oure Lorde .iiijC.lviij. and was ordeined before that other, and
it is called Procession, Rogacion and the Lasse Letanie. This is the
cause, for she was ordeined of a lasse bisshop and in a lasse place and

19 that] *om.* H1   whan] *om.* G   20 a man] men EH1   it] thei EH1   that thei]
doune and EH1   21 fnesed] fnesithe EH1   23 yaned] yanithe E   sum] *add* men E
30 and] of H1   religious] religiones E   33 the²] þei H1   34 the²] *om.* E
41 crosses] cros G   and] of H1   or²] of G

for a lasse siknesse, and the cause of the ordinaunce was suche, for that
tyme atte Vyane ther was a gret erthequake and threw downe howses 50
and many chirches and men herde bi nyght gret sownes and dredfull
clamoures, and ther fell a dredfull thinge, for on Ester Day there fill
fere from heuene and brenned the palais of the kinge. And yet ther was
do a more mervaile, for right as pigges and hogges entren into mennes
houses, right so bi the comaundement of God for the sinnes of men 55
wolves and wilde bestes entered into the towne and ronnen comonly
[thorugh] the citee and deuoured men and women and children, yonge
and olde. And whan these sorifull auentures were in þat contre the
bisshop ordeined to faste [thre] dayes and ordeined also the letanye,
and so this tribulacion cesed. And after that it was ordeined and 60
confermed of the Chirche of Rome that this letanie were kept ouer al.

And also it is called Rogacion, þat is as moche to saie as requestes,
for therinne we requere the helpe of all [the] seintes, and bi gret right
it is to [kepe] this ordinaunce in these dayes, for thei were ordeined to
requere these seintes and for to faste these daies bi many gret resones, 65
furst for God will apese the warres that ofte tymes arise in that tyme,
secoundelye that he multeplie the fru|tes that bene in the erthe, f. 100ᵛᵇ
thriddely that he mortefie the flesshely mevingges that meuen more in
that tyme than in any other tyme and the vnordinat steringe[s] that
thanne encresen, ferthely that eueri creature arraie hym and make 70
hym redy to receiue the holy goste honestly and holily and that he
may be the more worthi bi his praiers.

And Maister Guyliam Davenne assignithe thre other resones. The
furst is that the Chirche may þe more trustely requere oure Lorde
Ihesu Crist stienge into heuene whiche saiethe: 'Requere and ye shull 75
haue.' The secounde is that the Chirche fastithe and praiethe for to
haue the lasse flesshe and to make hym lene by fasting and to gete
wingges bi orison, for orison is called the winge of the soule bi whiche
she flyethe to heuene so that she may frely folw oure Lorde stienge up
to heuene and shewithe us the waye before that flye aboue the pennys 80
of wyndes, that is that bridde that aboundithe in flesche and hathe
fewe federes and may well flee; truly none.

And also it is saide Procession for tha[nne] the Chirche makithe a
general procession. [And in that procession] men beren the crosse,

52 on] *add* an EHı   54 entren] entred Hı   57 thorugh] into EHı   59 thre]
foure E, foure *changed to* thre Hı   63 the²] L, *om.* EHıG   64 to kepe] to/ke E
66 the] these E   69 steringes] steringe E   71 holily] holely Hı   77 lene] leue G,
lyue Hı (*amaigrir* P2)   83 thanne] that EHı   84 And in that procession] *om.* EHı

85 thei ringe the belles and beren baners, and in sum chirches thei bere a
dragon with a longe tayle, and in her procession thei asken singuleri
the helpe of all the seintes. Men bere the crosse and ringe the belles
for to chase away the fendes, for right as the kynge in his oste hathe
tokenes of rialte as trompes and baners, right so Ihesu Crist
90 euerlastinge kingge hath in his travelinge chirche bellis in stede of
trompes and the crosse in stede of his baner. For right as a tyraunt
f. 101ʳᵃ that were enemye of a noble kyngge and a myghti and shulde here | the
trumpetis and see the baners in his londe, right so the fendes that be in
derkenesse dreden gretly whanne thei heren the belles ringe of Ihesu
95 Crist and that thei see the signe[s and] baners. And men saien that this
is the reson whi that the chirche ringithe the bellis whanne that she
seithe that any tempest fallithe, to that ende that whanne the fendes
that causen that heren the trumpes of the euerlasting king, thei
withdrawe hem and be aferde and leuen for to meue the tempest.
100 Though it be so that there be another cause, whiche is this, eueri
creature wote whanne bellis be deuoutely ronge it sterithe a good
cristen sowle to be in praiers for the perile that is to come and that is
now present.

And that the baner of [the] euerlastinge kingge is the crosse
105 sheuithe the ympne *Vexilla regis prodeunt*, for the fendes dreden
gretly that baner, after that Crisostemus saiethe, that in what place
that the deuell seith this baner he dredithe it gretly and fleithe the
staffe wherof thei toke so gret a wounde. And this is the reson wherfor
men bere the crosse in sum chirches and sette it evene ayeinst the
110 tempest, for that the fende shulde be aferde and flee whanne he saigh
the baner of the soueraygne kingge. And therfor the crosse is born in
procession and the bellis ringge so that the fendes that be in the [eyre]
shulde be aferde and flee [and leue] to turment the eyre.

And the baner of the cross is born for to represent the victorie of
115 the resureccion and the shewinge of his ascencion, for he stied into
heuene withe a gret praie, and the baner that gothe bi the eyre
betokenithe Ihesu Crist stienge into heuene, for right as a gret
f. 101ʳᵇ multitude of good cristen men foluen these ba|ners, right so a gret
multitude of seintes foluen Ihesu Crist stieng into heue[ne]. And the
120 songe that men singge in the procession betokenithe the song and the

85 in] `in´ H1      90 in¹] and *del.* `in´ H1   95 signes and] signe of the E, signe of
H1   98 that³] *del.* `tempest´ H1   104 the²] *om.* E   108 wherof] wherefor H1
112 eyre] L, citee EH1G   113 and leue] *om.* E   114 cross] crosses EH1
118–19 good . . . of] *om.* H1   119 heuene] heue E

preising of aungels that comen ayeinst Ihesu Crist whanne he stied up and conueied hym withe his felawship into heuene.

Men haue custume in sum chirches, and namely in tho of Fraunce, that men bere before the crosse a dragon with a longe tayle and is full and suollen .ij. the furst dayes, and the .iij. day she is al voide and platte. And that day she is born after the crosse, bi whiche is signified that the furst day the fende was before the lawe, and in the secound day after vnder the lawe, and in the .iij. day after [is] signified that bi the passion of Crist he was putte oute of his kyngdom. And in that procession þe response signifien that we require singulerie the helpe of all the seintes. And ther be many causes whi we praie alle the seintes the whiche bene rehersed before, but ther bene other generall causes whi oure Lorde hathe ordeined that we worshippe the seintes, and that is for oure pouertee and oure nede and for the glorie of seintes and the reuerence of God. For the seintes knowen well the desires of hem [that praien hem], for thei see and vnderstonde it clerely in þe euerlasting mirrour how moche aperteinithe to hem of ioie and of helpe to us. The furst reson is whi we praie hem for oure pouerte and nede, that we myght deserue by oure nede that thei helpe vs, for oure merites suffisen not to that; or for the pouertee that we haue in beholdinge her ioye, sethe we may not beholde the soueraigne | light in hymselff, we mowe atte the leste beholde hym in his seintes; or ellis for defauute that we haue in lovingge, for many tymes an vnperfit man hathe gretter will to praie to a seint thanne to God, and sonner he trowithe to be herde. The secounde reson is for the glorie of seintes, for God wille that we require the seintes so that we haue helpe bi [her] merites that we preise hem and glorifie hem. The .iij. reson is for the reuerence of God, in as moche as the sinfull hathe displesed God he dare not requere [hym in] propre persone and that he makithe menis for hym. And these letanies men shulde syngge the songge of aungels, that is to [wite]: ' Sanctus Deus, sanctus fortis, Holi God, holy strengthe and vndedly, haue merci and pitee on vs.'

Iohn Damacyen tellithe that as men saide the letanie in Constantinople for a gret tribulacion, a childe was rauisshed into heuene in the middes of the peple, and ther this songe was taught hym, and thanne he come ayein to the peple and beganne to singe this songge

128 is] it E   136 that praien hem] *om.* EH1   139 by] *followed by erased ins.* H1
nede] mede *changed to* nede H1   143 lovingge] leuyng H1   146 for . . . seintes] *ins.*
H1   her] L, the EH1G   149 hym in] his EH1   and] but G   151 wite] saie EH1
156 ayein] *on erasure* H1

aungellyk, and thanne anone th[at] tribulacion cesed. In the [Sa]ne of
Calcidoyne this songe was aproued, and Damacien concludith in this
wise this clause: 'We weten well that this songe *Sanctus Deus*
160 restrenithe the fendes and ferithe hem.' The praisinge and the
auctorite of this canticle is praised in .iiij. thingges: furst for the
aungell taught it to the childe; secoundely that whanne it was songe
the tribulacion cessed; thriddely for the Sidon of Calcedoyne hathe
appro[ued] it; ferthely for the fendes dreden it and fleen it.

f. 101vb   Here endithe the stori | of the Letanies, and nexst
beginnithe of the Ascencion, Capitulum .lxiiij.^m

The Ascencion of oure Lord is halowed the .xl.^{ti} day of his
resurreccion, and there[inne] be considere[d] .vij. thingges bi ordre,
furst from whennes he stied vp, secoundely whi he stied vp not anone
as he was arisen but abode the .xl.^{ti} day, thirdely how he stied vp,
5 firthely with whom he stied vp, fiftely bi whos merites [he stied up],
sixtely in what place he stied up, seuenthely wherfor he stied vp.
    In the furst it is to wete that he stied vp from the Mounte of Oliuete
towardes Betanie, he stied into heuene; the whiche hill after another
translacion is called the Hill of Thre Lightes, for bi nyght towarde the
10 partie of the occident it was enlumyned with the light of the Temple,
for ther was euerlastinge fire on the auuter, and in the morutyde it was
lightened toward the orient, for bifore that the sonne arose aboue the
Temple or aboue the citee it receiued the bemes of the sonne, and also
ther was in that mountayne gret habundaunce of oyle that is norsher
15 of light. And Ihesu Crist comaunded his apostelis that thei shulde go
into that mountaine, for the day of his ascencion he appered two
tymes, that one to the .xij. apposteles that were atte her dinere in the
cenaculo, and alle the apposteles with the disciples and the women
duelling in that partie of Ierusalem [that] men called Mello, whiche is
20 in the mount of Syon wher Dauid hadde made a paleys for hymselff,
and the place wher thei dined was a gret froitour wher that Ihesu Crist
hadde comaunded that men shulde dine for his Pasche. And thanne

157 that] L, the EH1G   Sane] L, sone EG, s`id′one *with* i *on erasure* (?) H1
159 this clause] þies wordez H1   160 praisinge] praisinges H1   164 approued it]
approit E, approu`ed it′ H1

EH1GH2A1A2L; D resumes at 80 *and* (*in*) *that* and has been damaged after 358 *chapitle*
by removal of initial beginning the next chapter; H2 breaks off after 206 *that is* and resumes
at 335 *he deuied*   2 therinne] there E   considered] considere E   5 he stied up²]
om. E   8 hill] *om*. H1   11 the²] *om*. G   19 that²] *om*. E   21 the] a H1

the .xj. apostelis duellid ther | in that place and the disciples duellid f. 102ra
here and there bi diuerse houses. And as the .xj. aposteles eten in that
froitour oure Lorde appered to hem and vndertoke hem [of] her 25
misbileue, and whanne thei hadde ete he comaunded hem to goo to
the Mount of Oliuete towardes Bethanie and ther he appered to hem
ayen, and he ansuered hem to her vndiscrete demaundes. And thanne
he leffte vp his hondes and blessed hem and so stied vp to heuene
before hem.   30
   Of that place of his ascencion seithe Supplice bisshoppe of
Ierusalem that after that men edefied a chirche in þat place wher he
stied vp, and in that place the traces of his fete abode long after. And
whanne thei wold haue paued the place ther aboute, the marbill lepte
vp to the visage of hym that wolde haue paued it, and he saithe that it 35
was the shewinge that oure Lorde wolde not suffre the erthe to be
couered ther he hadde stepped in token of his ascencion, and yet the
erthe kepithe the print of his fete.
   To the secound, whanne men aske whi he abode so longe as .xl.^{ti}
dayes and wolde not stie up anone as he was risen, it is to wete that he 40
dede it for thre causes. Furst for the certainte of his resureccion, for it
is a more harder thinge to preue his resureccion than of his passion,
for fro the furste day into the thridde his passion myght be preued,
but for to preue his verrey resureccion was requered longer tyme and
therfor he toke a lenger terme, for it behoued to haue a more space 45
betwene the resureccion and the ascencion thanne betwene the
passion and the resureccion. Of this ascencion saithe Leon the
pope: | 'This day is fulfelled the nombre of .xl.^{ti} dayes that is made f. 102rb
bi the holy ordenaunce and to the profit of oure teching, for in as
moche as the bodely presence of oure Lorde hathe beden and taried 50
for a while, so moche is the faithe [made more stable] and perfit bi
good and profitable techinge, and therfor yelde we thankingges to the
devine ordenaunce and necessari techingges of holy faders and to her
tariengges, for thei taried and dredde for that we shulde not drede.'
   Secoundely he abode for the comfort of the aposteles, for the 55
devine comfortes shulde more abounde than the tribulacion. And the
tyme of the tribulacion of the apostelys was in that tyme of the passion
and therfor the dayes of comfort oughten wel to be more thanne tho of

23 .xj.] L, .xij. EGH1   24 the] om. H1   25 of] and E, and changed to of H1
28 demaundes] `de´maundes H1   41 certainte] certeyn H1   44 to] the H1   his] is
changed to his H1   50 hathe] hade changed to haþe H1   51 made/more stable] trs.
EH1

tribulacion. Thirdely for the debonaire significacion bi whiche it is
60 yeuen to vnderstonde that the devine consolaciones [be] reported to
tribulaciones, right as the day is likened to an oure and the yere to the
day, and that [the] yere be likened to the day is sene bi that men reden
in Ysaie, [in] the .xlj.^{ti} chapitle, wher he saieth: 'I shall preche the
pesible yere to oure Lorde and the day of vengeaunce to oure God.'
65 Loo, here ye may see that for a day of tribulacion he yeldith wel a yere
of comfort. And also that it be likened the day to the oure it shewithe
bi that oure Lorde laye .xl.^{ti} oures dede, wherinne was gret tribulacion, and whanne he was risen from dethe to lyff he appered .xl.^{ti}
dayes to the aposteles, and thereinne was gret consolacion, wherupon
70 the Glose saiethe: 'Thei sene me .xl.^{ti} houres dede,' and therfor he
liued after .xl.^{ti} daies in erthe. |

f. 102va   Fertheli it is to wete that he stied up myghtely, for he stied up bi his
propre myght, so as Ysay saieth in the .xlvj.^{ti} chapitle: 'What is he that
comithe from Edom and gothe in the multitude of his vertue?' And
75 Seint Iohn the Euuangelist saiethe: 'No man [ne] stiethe thedir bi his
propre vertue but he that descended from heuene, whiche is the sone
of man that is in heuene.' Though it be so that he steie up in a cloude,
yet he did it not for that he hadde none nede to the cloude but dede it
for that he wolde shewe that alle creatures be redy to obeye to her
80 creatoure. He stied vp bi the myght of his dyuinite, and [in] that [is]
signified the differencc that is saide in the Maister of Stories of Ihesu
Crist and of Ennok and of Ely, for Ennok was born vp and Ely was
lefte up and Ihesu Crist stied vp by his propre vertue. And after
Gregori[es] saieng, the furst was Ennok, Ennok was engendered and
85 engendered, Ely was engendered and engendered not, the .iij. was
Ihesu Crist whiche was neuer engendered ne engendered not.
Secoundely he stied vp openly for it was before his disciples,
wherof Iohn saiethe that he was lefte up seing hem, and also he
saiethe in the .xvj. chapitle: 'I go to hym that sent me hedir, and none
90 of you askithe whedir I goo.' The Glose saiethe: 'For I goo openly
before you, [wherfor he ought to make no question therof, sithe ye se
it done bodily before you.]' And that was the cause whi he stied vp
before hem, for thei shulde be witnesse of his assencion and that thei
shulde ioye hem in that mankinde was lefte vp gladly into heuene and

59 debonaire] bonaire H1   60 be] bi EH1   62 the¹] L, *om.* EH1G   63 in]
om. EH1   67 laye] seide G   70 dede] *om.* H1   74 in] into E   75 ne] *om.* E
78 that] *add* that G   80 in] *om.* EH1G (*en* P2)   is] *om.* E   84 Gregories] Gregori E
85 engendered and] *om.* H1   91–2 wherfor . . . you] *om.* EH1

desire to folue hym. Thirdely he stied vp gladly for the aungels 95
songen, wherof Dauid sai|ethe: 'God stied vp in ioye,' that is to saye f. 102vb
ioiously, and Austin saiethe: 'Whanne Ihesu Crist stied up alle the
heuenes dredden, the sterres wondered, the companies songen, the
trompes blewen, and the ioious felawship putte forthe her suete
soune.' Ferthely he stied vp hastely, as Dauid saieth: 'He hasted hym 100
as a geaunt for to renne the waye,' he stied vp right hastely for in a
moment he ranne a gret space. And Maister Moises tellithe, whiche
was right a gret philosoph[re], that eueri cercle of heuene and of eueri
planete hathe of space the viage of .vC. yere, that is to saie as moche
space of way as a man myght goo in pleyne way in .vC. yere, and as the 105
same saiethe, ther is as moche distaunce bitwene one heuene fro that
other. And for as moche as ther be .vij. heuenes he saiethe that ther is
as moche space from the erthe to the heuene of Saturne, whiche is the
.vij. heuene, as a man myght goo in .vijM^l. yere, and vnto the
concauete, that is to saye the [.viij. fro that heuene the space of the 110
goyng is] .vijM^l. and .vijC. yere, yef a man myght lyue so longe and
euery yere ordeined of .CCC.lxv. dayes and in eueri day that a man
myght goo .xl. myle and that eueri myle were of .ijM^l. paces; and this
saith Raby Moyses. And whedir this be true God wote that knowithe
wel the mesure of the sonne and of the mone as he that made al by 115
nombre and by wight and bi mesure. That was a grete lepe that God
made fro erthe to heuene. Of that lepe and of other thingges of Ihesu
Crist saiethe Seint Ambrose in this wise: 'Ihesu Crist come withe a
lepe into this worlde, he was withe his fader and come into the
Virgine, and fro the Virgine he lepte into the crach | and descended f. 103ra
into the flome Iordan and stied vp into the crosse and descended into 121
the sepulture and arose and stied vp into the right side of his fader.
  The .iiij. thingge is with whom he stied vp, that is to wete that he
stied vp withe gret praie [of men and gret multitude of aungels. And
that he stied vp withe gret praie [of men] it shewithe by the psalme 125
that saiethe: 'Thou stiedest on high and tokest with the tho that were
in chetiuison.' And that he stied vp withe gret multitude of aungeles it
shewithe by the demaundes of the lasse aungels maden to the gretter
aungels, for whanne oure Lorde stied vp into heuene, so as it is saide
in Ysaie in the .xliij. chapitle: 'What is he that comithe from Edom, 130

103 philosophre] philisophie E   cercle] cerkil *on erasure* H1   109 vnto] into H1
110 .viij.] hight E, viij *on erasure* H1   110–11 fro þat heuen the space of the goyng is]
om. E   112 yere] 'ʒier' H1   and^1] *om.* H1   113 paces] spaces E   120 crach]
erth H1   122 and^1] he G   128 maden] mayden E, maiden *with* i *subp.* H1
129 saide] *om.* H1G

his clothis died in coloure?' And ther saieth the Glose that sum
aungels that knewen not pleinly the misterie of the incarnacion and of
the passion, whan thei seigh oure Lorde stie vp to heuene withe gret
multitude of aungels and of holy men bi his propre vertue, the misteri
135 of the incarnacion and of the passion was ministred to hem, and
thanne thei saide to the aungels that feloushipped oure Lorde: 'What
is this he that comithe from Edom?' And in the [ps]alme he saiethe:
'What is this kyng of ioye?'

Seint Denyse saiethe in the boke of the Gerarchie of Aungels that
140 whanne Ihesu Crist stied vp into heuene th[r]e questiones were made
of aungels, and the grettest aungels made the furst togederes betwene
hemselff, and so deden the secounde to the gretter making question in
Cristes stieng vp, the .iij. degre of aungels to the gretter aboue hem.
f. 103rb The grettest asked among hemselff and saide: 'What is he that | is
145 come from Edom, his clothes died in Bosra?' Edom is as moche to saie
as 'blodi' and Bosra is to saie 'aduersarie' or ellis 'araied', as though
thei saide: 'What is he this that comithe fro the worlde blody by sinne
and araied by malice ayeinst oure Lorde?' And thanne oure Lorde
ansuered: 'I am he that speke rightwisnesse.' And Seint Denise
150 saiethe it in this wise: 'I am he that ordeine iustice and rightwisnesse
of hele.' In redempcion of mankinde he was [verray] rightwise as wel
as maker, for he brought his creature ayenne fro the lordeshipp of a
straunger, and he was iugement in as moche as he ouercome the fende
that assailed anothers right and toke myghtly man from hym [which
155 he helde]. But Seint Denise makithe a question vpon this thing and
saiethe: 'Hou is [it], that sethe the souereyne aungels be nexst to God
and be enlumyned withe God withoute any mene, whi made thei this
question that one to that other?' But he hymselff assoilithe this
question, and the gloser expounithe it also, and seyne in that that
160 thei asked thei signified to coueite and aske the science, and in that
thei counsailed togederes thei shewed that they durst not goo before
in hemselff the devine precognicion, so that thei asked before eche to
other lest perauenture thei myght distourbe bi to hasty a demaunde þe
enlumyninge that was made to hem of God.
165   The secounde question that thei made to Ihesu Crist, that is to saye
the lasse aungels, is: 'Whi is thi clothinge rede and thi clothinge is alle

136 aungels] aungel E   137 psalme] spalme E   140 thre] the E
144 that is] þis þat H1G   145 Bosra] Besra EH1   146 is] add as moche EH1
saie] add as EH1   149 rightwisnesse] rightwis'nes' H1   150 it] om. H1
151 verray] high EH1   154-5 which he helde] om. E   156 it] L, this EH1G
164 to hem of] of hem to H1

defouled in a pressure?' For it is saide that oure Lorde hadde a clothinge
whiche was his bodie al rede | and blodie, for whanne he stied up into f. 103ᵛᵃ
heuene he hadde al his fresshe blody woundes. And after that Bede
saiethe, he wolde kepe his woundes for .v. causes, and he saiethe in this 170
wise: 'Oure Lorde wolde kepe his woundes in his bodie and shall kepe
hem into the day of iugement for to preve the faithe of the resureccion,
for to present hem to his fader whan he shall praie for his peple, for that
the good shulde see hou piteously þei bene bought ayein, and that the
wicked shul knowe how rightwisly thei be condempned, and also for 175
that he will shewe certaine tokenes of his perpetuel victorie.' And to that
question oure Lorde ansuerid in this wise: 'I haue alone bene defouled
in the presse, and of alle men not one withe me.' The crosse may wel be
likened to a presse [in] whiche he was so sore pressed that his precious
blode went oute largely of alle the parties of hym. And also the deuell 180
is called a presse, the whiche wrappe[th] so mankinde withe the cordes
of synne and streinithe hem so sore that al spirituel goodes he pressithe
oute and leuithe nothinge withoute the man but vice. But this noble
fighter defouled so the presse that he breke all the bondes of synne and
stied into heuene, and after that he opened the taverne of heuene and 185
poured oute the wine of the holy goste.

The thridde question that the lasse aungels made to the gretter was
this: 'What is this king of ioye?' Thei ansuered and saide: 'The Lorde
of vertues, he is king of ioie.' Of this question and of other questiones
of aungels that comen saieth Seint Austin: 'Alle the [eyre] was halued 190
by the devine felawship, and alle þe | tourbe of fendes that were in the f. 103ᵛᵇ
[eyre] fledde in his ascencion. And the aungels that come ayeinst hem
enquered of hem what it was, saienge: "What is this kinge of ioye?"
And they ansuered and saide: "This is of rede and white coloure that
had neither beaute ne fairenesse, feble and sike on the crosse, stronge 195
in dispoiled, vile in the body, armed in the bataile, stin[k]ynge in the
dethe, faire in his resureccion, white born of the Virgine, rede in the
crosse, blewe in reproues, clere in heuene."'

Fiftely it is [to] knowe bi whos merites he stied up. It is trewe that
he stied up by trebel merites, wherof Ierom saiethe: 'It was for to 200
shewe the trouthe that he hathe fu[l]felled whiche he hadde behight

169–70 And . . . woundes] *om.* H1   172 for] for *untidily on erasure repeated in
margin* H1   173 for²] how H1   179 in] the EH1   181 wrappeth] L, wrapped
EH1G   184 defouled] 'de'fouleth H1   the²] thre E, þe *on erasure* H1   190 saieth]
sithe G   eyre] erthe EH1G (*air* P2)   192 eyre] L, erthe EH1G   hem] him H1
196 stinkynge] stingynge EH1G (*puant* P2)   199 to] *om.* EH1   201 fulfelled]
fufelled E

[by] the prophetes and sethe for his debonairte, for he was brought to
sacrifice for liff of the peple and for rightwisnesse, for he deliuered not
only man bi strengthe but bi rightwisnesse, for his myght and his
205 vertue ledde hym to heuene.

Sixtely that is to wete wher he stied vp. It is to knowe that he stied
vp aboue all heuenes that he myght fulfell all, for ther be many
heuenes and he stied aboue hem alle. Ther is heuene materiall, heuene
resonable, heuene entendible, heuene supersubstancial, *ignium, side-*
210 *rium, christallinum et [empi]rium.* The heuene resonable is eueri
rightwise man, and he is called so by reson of the devine habitacion.
For right as heuene is the sege of God, after that Ysay seith, 'The
heuene is my sege;' right so is the soule of [the] rightwisse man, like as
it is wrete in the Boke of Wisdom: 'The soule of the rightwisse man is
215 the sege of wisdom.' By reson of holy conuersacion and be desire they
f. 104ra   duell alway in heuene, | like as the apostill saiethe: 'Oure conuersacion
is in heuene.' Also it is called resonable bi continuel werkes, for right
as heuene meuithe continuelly, right so God bi his good werkes
continuelly mevithe.

220   The intellectual heuene is aungels. Thei bene saide aungels for thei
be in heuene most high of reson, of dignite, of excellence. Of the
dignite and of the excellence of hem saiethe Seint Denys in the boke
of Devine Names in the ferthe chapitle: 'Aboue all other thingges thei
liven of the devine thought, thei vnderstonde and knowe aboue al
225 other thingges levinge and aboue witte and reson and moche more
thanne any soule that may be, and thei desire well and be parteners of
beauute and of goodnesse.' Thei be made [by] reson of nature and of
glorie. Of the beauute Seint Denys saiethe in the same boke: 'Aungel
is the shewing of an hidde light and is a faire and a clere mirrour
230 witheoute spotte or filthe, and yef it apperteinith to be saide he is
resseiuour of the beauute of gode fourme, the fourme of God.'
Thirdely thei bene right strong bi reson of her vertue, of her myght
and of her strengthe, wherof Damacien saiethe in the secound boke
[in] the .iij. chapitle: 'Thei bene strong and arraied to fulfell the will of
235 God, and thei be founde in eueri place wher oure Lorde sent hem bi
the twynkelinge of an yghe.' The heuene hathe beauute, highnesse
and strengthe. Of two the furst saiethe Ecclesiast in the [.xliij.]

202 by] *om.* E   210 *christallinum*] *Cristalinum* H1   *empirium*] *imperium* H1G, *illeg.*
E (*emperium* P2, *empirium* LgA)   213 the²] a EH1   214 man] *ins.* H1   220 is]
his E   221 dignite] add 'and' H1, add and G   224 of the] by G   227 by] of EH1
229 hidde] heigh G   231 gode fourme] god H1, *add* to E   234 in] of EH1
237 .xliij.] .xlij. E, xlij *changed to* xliij H1

chapitle of the highenesse of the firmament and c., and Iob saieth in the .xvij. chapitell: 'Thou hast perauenture forged thre thingges with hym.'

240

The heuene substancial is the qualite of the devine ex|cellence fro f. 104ʳᵇ whiche heuene Ihesu Crist come and stied ayen thedir, wherof Dauid the prophete saiethe: 'The goinge oute of hym was fro the souerain heuene and his recours ayein vnto the highest heuene.' And oure Lorde stied vp aboue alle these heuenes vnto this substancial heuene, 245 and that he stied aboue alle these material heuenes it is seyn by that that Dauid saiethe in the Sauter: 'Thi glorie and thi preisinge is lefte vp aboue all the heuenes.' And than oure Lorde stied vp aboue alle the material heuenes vnto the [imp]erial heuene, but not as Ely [that] stied vp [upon] a cha[re] of fyre vnto the high region. In that imperial 250 heuene is the propre and most special duellyng place of oure Lorde Ihesu Crist and of aungels and of other seintes. And this is a couenable duelling place for the duellers witheinne, for this heuene is more noble thanne the other bi dignitee, by furste being, bi the stonding, and by the compas aboute, and therfor it is a couenable duelling place 255 to Ihesu Crist whiche pass[ed] all other heuenes resonables and intellectuel by dignite, by perdurabilite, by vnmeuable stondinge, bi largesse of myght. Also it is conable habitacion of seintes, for that heuene is called a beauute of a perfit lyght and vnmeuable and of gret capacite, and therfor aungels and seintes, that bene and weren of one 260 manere of worchinge, wrought rightwisly and bene vnmeuable in the loue of God and enlumyned in the faithe and plenteuously takinge in the receiuinge of the holy goste.

And it shewithe wel that the seintes stied vp aboue alle the heuenes reso|nables in the Canticles that saien: 'Lo, here the same that comithe f. 104ᵛᵃ leping in the hilles and thorugh persinge the mountaynes, the hilles be 266 called the aungels and the mountaynes the holy men.' And it shewithe well that ther steien vp aboue alle heuenes intellectuels, that be the aungeles, bi that Dauid saieth in the Sauter: '*Qui ponis nubem ascensum tuum, qui ambulas super pennas ventorum,*' þat is to saye: 'He that 270 puttithe the cloude in his stienge vp and went aboue the pennes [of wyndes].' And ouer this he saiethe he stied vp aboue cherubin and flye aboue the pennes of wyndes.

239 forged] forgete H1G   245 this] his H1   249 imperial] L, material EG, substanciall *above del. previous attempted correction* H1   that] L, *om.* EH1G   250 vpon] L, aboue EH1G   chare] chaier E, chaaer *with second a changed to* i H1   256 passed] passithe E   258 is] *add* 'a' H1   259 a perfit . . . of] right G   261 of] *changed to* in H1, in G   265 the²] this G   271–2 of wyndes] *om.* E, *ins.* H1

Also it apperithe that he stied vp aboue the substancial heuene, that
275 is to knowe vnto the qualite of God as it shewithe bi that þat Seint
Matheu saiethe: 'Oure Lorde Ihesu Crist whanne he hadde spoke with
his disciples he was take vp into heuene and sittithe in the right side of
his fader.' The right side of his fader is called the qualite of God. And
Bernarde saiethe: 'Mi Lorde is saide singuleri of God and it is yeue
280 hym to sitte in the right side of his ioie, that is to saie in his glorie
sembelable and in escence of sembelable substaunce for likly generacion and in mageste not disperpeled and in euerlastinge sembelable.'
And it may be saide that Ihesu Crist in his ascencion was so haunsed
bi foure haunsyngges and that was by remuneracion of the place bi
285 knowlache of vertuous guerdon. Of the furst saiethe the apostell to the
Ephesiens *quarto*: 'He that descended is he that stied vp aboue all the
heuenes.' And the secound he saiethe also to the Ephesiens: 'He is
f. 104vb made obedient [vnto the dethe].' Wherof Au|stin saiethe this:
'Humilite is desert of clerenesse and clerenesse is guerdon of
290 humilite.' And of the thridde saieth the psalme: 'He stied aboue
cherubin,' that is to saie aboue all the plente of science. And of the
ferthe he stied up as the apostell saiethe aboue cherubin and aboue
seraphin, which bene as aboue alle science.
    Seuenthely whanne he asked whi he stied into heuene [it] is to
295 answer that for .ix. profitez whiche come by his ascencion. The furst
profite is the habitacion of the dcvine loue, wherof saiethe Seint Iohn
the Euuangelist: 'But yef I goo the holy goste may not come to you.'
And ther saiethe Austine: 'Yef ye be carnally ioyned to me ye shull not
receiue the holy goste.'
300   The secounde [profite] is gretter [knowlage] of God. Seint Iohn the
Euuangelist saiethe of this thinge: 'Yef ye haue loued me truly ye shull
reioyse you, for I goo to my fader.' And ther saiethe Seint Austine: 'I
shall withdrawe from you this forme of servaunt in whiche my fader is
gretter thanne I as God that ye mowe spiritually see hym as God.'
305   The .iij. profite is merit of feithe, and of that saiethe Leon the pope
in a sermon of the ascencion: 'Thanne it behouith that faithe and
beleue teche us the sone to be egall withe the fader by steppes of
thought, and that Ihesu Crist be submitted [to] the fader bi the
lightnesse of bodely substaunce. And that is a thinge of perfite
310 thought and of a gret vigour for to liue withoute serchinge that that

281 sembelable²] *add* of sembelable E   282 mageste] *add* and EH1   288 vnto
the dethe] *om.* EH1   294 it] that EH1   300 profite, knowlage] L, *trs.* EH1G
308 to] in EH1   310 that that] þat H1

may not be saie withe bodely yee, and for to fasten ther his desire wher
he may not putte his sight.' And Austine saiethe in the boke of
Confessiones: 'He arose as a geaunt to renne in his waye, he taried |
not in the waye but ranne crienge by worde, [by dede], bi dethe, by   f. 105ʳᵃ
lyff, bi comynge doune, bi steyenge vp, crienge that we shulde turne   315
to hym, and parted hym from oure eyen to that ende þat we shulde
turne to oure herte and that we see hym there.'

The .iiij. profite is oure seurete, for he stied vp for to be oure
aduocate towardes his fader. And we aught to be full sure whanne we
considre to haue suche an aduocate to his fader, and therof saieth   320
Seint Iohn the Euuangelist in the secounde chapitle: 'We haue Ihesu
Crist the rightwis aduocate towardes his fader to praie for us and for
oure synnes.' And of th[is] surete saiethe Seint Bernard: 'Man, thou
haste a sure goinge before God as the moder before her sone and the
sone before the fader. The moder shewithe her brestes, the sone   325
shewithe to the fader his open side and his woundes, so that
ayensaienge may [not] be there as so many tokenes bene.'

The .v.ᵗᵉ profite is oure [right] gret dignite, that is [oure dignite]
whanne oure nature is lefte vp vnto the right side of God, for whan
the aungeles hadde considered this dignite in man, anone they deuied   330
to be worshipped of men, as it is saide in the Apocalipes: 'I fill,' he
saide, 'before the fete of hym for to haue worshipped hym, and he
saide to me: "Loke that thou do it not to me, for I am thi conservaunt
and of thi bretheren."' And ther saiethe the Glose: 'In the olde lawe
he deuied not to be worshipped, but after the ascencion, whanne he   335
seigh man lefte up aboue, thanne he dredde to be worshipped of man.'
And so saiethe the pope Leon in the sermon of the Ascencion: 'The
nature of oure humanite is this day born vp ouer þe | highnesse of al   f. 105ʳᵇ
myghtes into the right side of God the fader bi his consentinge, so that
the grace of God were made more mervailous, so that feithe ne   340
mistruste not, hope ne drede not, and charite wexe not colde, with the
thingges remeued in the regard of men the whiche bi her desert felten
to shewe her reuerence.'

The .vj.ᵗᵉ profite is the stabelnesse of oure beleue, so as Poule
saiethe to the Ebrewes: 'Ye haue a gret bisshopp Ihesu Crist, the sone   345
of God, that hath persed the heuene holdinge the hope of confession.'

313 Confessiones] confessouris G   314 by dede] om. E   dethe] defe H1
315 comynge] connynge H1   323 this] the EH1   326 the] his G   that] L, add men
EH1G   327 not] L, om. EH1G   328 right] L, om. EH1G   oure dignite] L, om. EH1G
330 deuied] denied (?) E   334 saiethe] with H1   335 deuied] denied (?) E
345 gret] gretter H1   Ihesu Crist] twice once del. H1   346 the²] om. H1

And of this assencion saiethe yet the pope Leon: 'The ascension of Ihesu Crist is oure haunsinge, and ther as he went before us is the ioie of oure hede [*etc.*].'

350   The .vij.^{te} profite is [the] shewinge of the waye, wherof Michee saiethe: 'He shall stie vp to shewe the waye before hem.' And Austin saiethe: 'This saueoure hathe made the waye; arise vp and goo, thou [ha]st well whedir, forslouthe it not.'

The .viij.^{te} profite is the openinge of the gate of heuene. Right as 355 the furst Adam opened the gates of hell, right so the secound of paradise, wherof the Chirche singethe: 'Whanne thou haste ouercome the prik of dethe thou shalt vndo the gates of heuene.'

The .ix.^{te} profite is the reperacion of the place, and therof saiethe Seint Iohn in the .xiiij.^e chapitle: 'I goo to araie to you a place.' And 360 Seint Austin saiethe: 'Lorde, araie that thou haste made redi, araye vs to the and the to us. And the place that thou araiest to the witheinne vs, araye it witheinne the to us.'

Here endithe the fest of the Ascencion of oure Lorde, and nexst foluithe the fest of Pentecoste, Capitulum [.lxv.] |

f. 105va So as the storie of the Dedes of the Aposteles witnessen that is holy, the holy goste was this day sent to the aposteles in tongges of fire, and this comynge [or] sendynge of the holy goste is to be considered .viij. thingges, furste from whom he was sent, the secounde in how many 5 maners he was sent, the .iij. in what tyme he was sent, the .iiij. how many tymes he was sent, the .v. how he was sent, the .vj. wherfor he was sent, the .vij. bi whom he was sent.

The furst is to knowe from whom he was sent, that is to saie that the fader sent the holy goste and the sonne sent hym, and that same 10 holy goste gaue hymselff and sent hymselff. And of the furste saiethe Seint Iohn in the .xiiij.^e chapitle: 'The holy goste my fader [shall sende] to you in my name.' Of the secounde Seint Iohn saiethe in the .xvj. chapitle: 'Yef I were gone I shulde sende hym to you.' Sendyng in these lowe thingges hathe comparison to her sender in thre wises, 15 þat is to saye as to hym that yeuithe hym being, and so is sent the

349 *etc.*] L, *om.* EH1G   350 the¹] *om.* E   353 hast] L, wost EH1G   well] *om.* H1   358 therof] therefore H1   360 Seint] *om.* G

EH1GDH2A2L; D has damage through loss of initial and ornament from beginning to 65; A1 has lost five folios, part of one of which, containing fragments of nos. 68–71, has been re-inserted back to front   *Rubric* .lxv.] .lxiiij. E   3 or] and E, and *changed to* or H1 6 wherfor] by whom H1   7 bi] to *on erasure* H1   10 and . . . hymselff] *om.* H1 11 goste] *add* 'fro' H1   11–12 shall sende] was sent EH1

beme from the sonne, and as he yeuithe vertue and so is sent the darte
fro hym that castithe it, or as to the yeuer of vertue or of auctorite, and
so is the massage sent fro the sender. And so after this trebel maner
the sendinge may be likened to the holy goste, for he is sent fro the
fader and fro the sone as that same that hathe of hem beinge and 20
vertue [and auctorite]. And so this holy goste gaue hymselff, as Seint
Iohn the Euuangelist saithe: 'Whanne that the sperit of trouthe shall
come he shall repro|ue the worlde of synne.' For as Leon the pope f. 105vb
saiethe in a sermon of Whitsontide: 'The godhede of the Trinite is
vnmeuable, oo substaunce and vndevided, acordinge in werke and in 25
will, pareile in myght, egal in glorie. The merci of the Trinite lefte to
h[y]mselff the werke of oure redempcion, bicause the fader shulde be
to us debonayre and that the sone shulde make hym debonayre and
that the holy goste shulde enchaufe vs in his loue. And for that the
holy goste is God, therfor he is saide [that] he gaue most rightwisly 30
hymselff.'

Ambrose shewithe that the holy goste [is God, in the boke of the
Hoy Goste], wher he saiethe that the glori of þe diuinite of hym is
openly proued bi .iiij. thingges. 'He is knowen to be God bi that he is
witheoute synne, and by that he foryeuithe synnes, and by that he is 35
not creature but creatoure, and also [by] that he worshippithe none
but is worshipped.' And in that it is shewed vs how the blessed
Trinite gaue hym al to us. The fader gaue us all that he hadde, for as
Seint Austine saiethe, he sent his sone for to be pris of oure
redempcion, the holi goste in priuilege of oure adopcion, and he 40
reserued alle hymselff to be heritage to his sones of adopcion. In the
same wise the sone hymselff gaue all to vs, for as Seint Bernard
saiethe: 'He was shepard and pasture, and he was redemptour'. He
gaue vs his soule in pris, his blode [in] drinke, his flesshe in mete, and
his diuinite in guerdon. In the same wise the holy goste gaue all his 45
geftes to us and geuithe hem continuelly, as the apostell saithe to the
Corinthees: 'He gaue to sum wisdom, to sum the word of science after
that spirit, to another | feithe in that sperit.' And Leon the pope f. 106ra
saiethe: 'The holy goste is the enspirer of feithe, doctour of science,
welle of loue, the signacle of chastite and cause of al hele. 50

18 sender] sondre *or* soudre H1   21 and auctorite] *om.* E   24 Whitsontide]
Whitsonday H1   27 hymselff] hemselff EH1   30 that] *om.* EH1   32–3 is God
. . . Goste] *om.* EH1   36 by] L, *om.* EH1G   40–1 and . . . adopcion] *om.* G
43 was] *add* shepe E, *add* the H1   shepard, pasture] L, pasture, shepard EG *with*
shepasture *for* pasture G   44 in^1] to EH1   46 the^2] *om.* G   50 of^3] *ins.* H1

In the secound it is to wete in how many maners he is sent. It is to knowe that the holy goste is sent in [two] maners, visibly and vnvisibl[y], visibly whanne he was shewed in any token visible, and vnvisibl[y] whanne he enterith into chaste thoughtes. Of that he was
55 sent invisible saiethe Seint Iohan the Euuangelist: 'The holy goste inspirithe ther as he will and men heren his vois, but men wote not whennes it comithe ne whider he gothe.' And that is [no] mervayle, as Bernard saiethe of the worde invisible: 'She enterithe not by the eyen for it is not coloured, [ne] by the eeris for it sownithe not, ne bi the
60 nose for it [is] not medeli[d] withe the eyre but withe the mynde, and she ne brekithe not the eyre but makithe it, ne she enterith not by the lyppes for it is not mete ne drinke, ne be touchinge of the body for it is no[t] fel[able]. And how it be so that the waies of this thinge be not enquirable thou askest perauenture how I knowe that is true, and I
65 ansuer and saye truly, I haue vnderstonde bi the mevinge of my herte the presence of hym, and I haue perceiued bi the fleinge of vice[s] the myght of the vertue of hym, and by discussivn [and] serchinge of myn inwarde mynde I haue mervailed the gretnesse and the dipnesse of his wisdom, and bi the mendinge of my maners I haue experience of the
70 goodnesse and of the suetnesse of hym, and by the reformacion and
f. 106rᵇ renouacion of the sperit of my myn|de I haue perceiued how faire the beauute of hym is. And of beholding of alle these thingges togeders I haue mervailed and be aferde of þe multitude and of the gretnesse of hym.' And this saiethe Bernarde.
75   The sendinge of the holi goste visibly is whanne he is shewed by sum token visible, and it is to know that the holi goste is shewed visibly in .v. maners. Furst in liknesse of a dovue vpon Ihesu Crist whanne he was baptised, and that saieth Luke in the .iij. chapitlee: 'The holy goste descended in bodely liknesse in hym right as a dovue.'
80 Secoundely in lyknesse of a clere cloude vpon Ihesu Crist whanne he was transfigured, and of that saiethe Seint Mathew the Euuangelist: 'Right as he speke the cloude shadued hym.' And the Glose saiethe that right as oure Lorde was baptised the holy goste shewi[d] the mysterie of the holy Trinite in forme of a dovue, right in the same

51 to¹] `to´ Hɪ   51–3 It . . . sent] *ins.* Hɪ   52 in two] into E   visibly] visible Hɪ
53 vnvisibly] vnvisible EHɪ   54 vnvisibly] vnvisible EHɪ   enterith] entrid G   into]
in G   57 he] it Hɪ   no] to E, to *changed to* no Hɪ   59 ne¹] *om.* E   60 is not
medelid] not medelithe E   eyre] eyer *on erasure* Hɪ   61 ne she] nesshe EHɪ
63 not felable] L, no felawe EHɪG   66 vices] vice EHɪ   67 and²] of EHɪ
68 his] this E   69 my] L, many EHɪG   78 chapitlee] *add* `also´ Hɪ   79–80 in²
. . . lyknesse] *om.* Hɪ   80 clere] clerere EHɪ   83 shewid] shewithe EHɪ

wise he shewed hym whanne he was glorified in a bright shining 85
cloude. Thirdely he shewed hym in lyknesse of a brethinge, so as Iohn
saiethe in the .xx.^{ti} chapitle: 'He blewe in hem and saide: "Receiuethe
the holy goste."' Ferthely he shewed hym in liknesse of fire, and
fiftely in liknesse of tunges, and in this double lyknesse he apered this
day to the apostelis.   90

And for that cause he sheued hym in these .v. maners bycause that
he wolde geve to vnderstonde that he myght be likened to the
propertees of these thingges in the hertes of hem in whiche he
enterithe. The douve hathe a compleint in stede of songe, she hathe
no galle, she dwellithe | in holes of stone. Right so as the holi goste   f. 106va
fulfellith he makithe h[e]m plein for her synnes, of whiche Ysaie   96
saithe: 'We shull rore as beres and we shull pleyne as dovues.' And the
apostell saithe in the .viij. chapitle to the Romaynes: 'This holy goste
requirithe of vs weylingges and pleintes witheoute nombre.' [Also]
she is withoute galle or bitternesse, wherof it is saide in the boke of 100
Sapience: 'Lorde, how thi sperit is suete and good in vs.' And in that
same boke he saithe that he is suete, debonaire and lovinge, swete for
that he makithe us suete in wordes, benigne for that he makithe vs
benigne and debonaire and louynge in oure werkes. Thirdely he
duellithe in the holes of stones, that is to saye in the woundes of oure 105
Lorde that be colde. And of that it is sa[i]de in the Canticles: 'Arise
up, my faire spouse, my dovue.' Wherof the Glose saiethe 'that
norisshithe my checonys,' that is to wete 'withe the infusion of the
holy goste;' 'in the holis of my woundes.' And elliswher it is saide:
'The sperit of oure mouthc, Ihesu Crist oure [Lorde], is take for oure 110
synnes, and in [the] shadwe of the we lyue amonge the peple,' as
though he saide: 'The sperit that is of oure mouthe, that is to saye that
Ihesu Crist oure Lorde is oure mowthe, and oure flesshe makithe vs to
saie to Ihesu Crist: "In the shadue of the," [that is to saye in the
shadue of thi] passion, in the whiche thou were derke and despised, 115
"we lyuen by gret mynde amonge the peple."'

Secoundely he was shewed in maner of a cloude. The cloude is lefte
vp fro the erthe and engenderithe reyne and yeuithe re|fresshinge.   f. 106vb
Right so the holy goste leftithe fro the erthe tho that he fulfellithe [f]or
to despise erthely thingges. And of that saiethe Ezechie .vij.°: 'Thi   120

93 propertees] propertes *with* es *on erasure* H1, prophetis G   96 hem] hym E
99 Also] And EH1   100 or] of H1   102 for] *on erasure* H1   106 saide] sade E
110 Lorde] *om.* E   111 the^r] a E, *om.* H1   114–15 that . . . thi] *om.* E   119 for]
or EH1

sperit hathe lefte me vp betwene the heuene and the erthe.' Also
Ezechiel *primo*: 'Whersoeuer the sperit went in the same wise the whelis
were lefte vp and folowed hym, the sperit of lyff was in the whelys.' Also
Seint Bernard saiethe: 'Whanne a man hathe tasted of the sperit al
125 flesshely thingges be vnsaueri to hym.' Secoundely he yeuithe refres-
shinge ayeinst al enbrasinge of vices, wherof it [was] saide [to] the
blessed Virgine Marie: 'The holy goste shal come [in] the and the vertue
of the right high shall shadowe the,' that is to saye shall refreshe the and
make the colde from al the hete of synne. Wherfor the holy goste is
130 called water, the which refressheth al synne bi his strengthe. And of that
saiethe Seint Iohn the Euuangelist: 'The flodes of the holy goste that
renne from his wombe bene quik waters.' And therwith as she
engenderith water of teres, wherof Dauid saieth in the Sawter: 'The
sperit of hym shal blowe and wateres shull renne,' that is to saie of teres.
135 Thirdely he was sheued in maner of brethinge or blowynge. Brethinge
is swifte, it is hote, light and necessarie to respire. Right so the holy
goste is light, that is to say suyfte to shede hymselff, and he is the most
meuable of all meuable thingges. The Glose saithe vpon that: 'A sowne
was made sodenly in heuene and c.,' he canne do nothing tariengly.
140   The holy goste secoundely is hote for to enflaume, and therof saieth
f. 107ra Seint Luke the | Euuangelist: 'I am come to sende fire into the erthe to
brenne tho þat I will.' Wherof he is lykened to þe wynde of Austro
that is hote. And of that is saide in the Canticles: 'Arise up Aquilo and
come Auster and blowe.' Thirdely he is lyghtly to apese, and for to
145 shewe his lyghtnesse he is called vnccion, *Iohannis tercio*: 'The
vnccion of hym techithe vs alle thingges.' Also he is called a dewe,
wherof the Chirche singeth, and [h]is most inwarde dewe shedde in vs
fulfellith oure entrailes. Also he is called a softe wynde, .xix.: 'And
after the fire ther blewe a softe wynde and ther oure Lorde.' Ferthely
150 he is necessarie to respire. What meruaile, he is so necessarie that yef
[he] were take away fro man the man shulde deye anone, and in the
same wise it farithe bi þe holi goste. And therof saieth Dauid: 'Take
away the sperit of hem and they shull faile and turne to pouder.' And
also it is saide elliswhere: 'Sende thi sperit and they shull bee made.'
155 And Seint Iohn the Euuangelist saieth: 'The sperit is he that
quikenithe.' Ferthely he was shewed in the fourme of fire, as it
shall be saide after whi he apered in [t]his double maner.

123 were . . . whelys] *ins.* H1   124 Seint . . . saiethe] seith Bernard G   126 was] is
EH1   to] in E, *in changed to* to H1   127 in] to EH1   144 lyghtly] light G   to²] `to' H1
147 his] is EH1   151 he] we EG   157 this] his EG, his *changed to* þis H1

The .iij. that he saiethe [is] in what tyme he was sent. It is to knowe
that he was sent the .l. day after Ester, and he was sent in that day for
it shulde be vnderstonde that in þat day was the perfeccion of the lawe 160
by the holi goste and the euerlastinge guerdon and the remission of
sinnes. The perfeccion of the lawe after the Chirche was made for that
fro the .l. day that the [lambe] withoute spotte was sacrified the lawe
was yeuen to Moyses in a brennynge fire, and therfor in the | Nwe f. 107rb
Testament in the .l. daye of Pasche Ihesu Crist the holy goste 165
descended in the fire in the Mount of Syon, and the lawe was yeue
in þe Mount of Synay, the holy goste in the Mount of Syon, the lawe
in þe highest partie of the hille, and the holi goste was yeue there as
the disciples supped; and so is it shewid by these thingges, that the
holy gost is perfeccion of alle the lawe, for the fulfellinge of the law [is] 170
dileccion, that is to saie verrey loue. Secoundely he is perdurable
guerdon, and therof saiethe the Glose that right as after his resureccion he conuersed .xl. dayes withe his disciples, whiche signifiethe the
Chirche present, right so the holi goste that [was] yeue in the .l. daye
betokenithe the peni of euerlastinge rewarde.   175

Thirdely he was remission of synnes, wherof the Glose saithe in
that place: 'Therfor it was in the .l. daye that right as in the .l. yere
ther is a yere of ioie that comune indulgence was made atte Rome and
synnes be foryeue bi þe holy goste;' and as the Glose saieth: 'In that
day of spirituel ioye the prisoners be vnbounde, that were in dette 180
were quite, tho that were exiled were reconsiled to her owne contre
and her heritages bene yolden ayein, the seruauntes be deliuered of
her seruages, tho that were gilti of dethe be vnbounde and lete goo.'
Wherof the apostell saith to the Romaynes: 'The lawe of the sperit of
lyff Ihesu Crist hathe deliuered me fro the lawe of synne and of dethe, 185
for charite couerithe the multitude of synnes.' Thoo that were in exile
be brought ayein, wherof Dauid saiethe in the Sauuter: 'Thi | good f. 107va
sperit shall lede me into the right contre', wherof the apostell saithe to
the Romaynes: 'That sperit yeuithe witnesse to oure sperit that we be
his sones; and yef we be his sones, and his heyres.' The servauntes shull 190
be deliuered of synne, wherof the apostell saiethe to the Corinthiens:
'Ther where the sperit of oure Lorde is, ther is oure heritage.'

158 is¹] om. E   160 perfeccion] profescion G   163 lambe] lond E, lond changed
to lombe H1   166 the³] L, add same EH1G   169 is] om. H1G   170 law is] lawes
E, lawe 'is' H1   172 after] so with af on erasure H1   173 conuersed] conuersand with
an on erasure H1   174 was] om. E   yeue in] 3euen G   176 remission] remissiones
EH1   177 Therfor] there of H1   180 spirituel] spiruel H1   184 the³] þi H1
187 brought] bought H1   191 the²] om. G

To the fourthe, it is to wete how many tymes he was sent to the
apostelis, therto the Glose saieth that the holy goste was yeue to hem
195 thre tymes, and that was before the passion, after the resureccion and
after the ascencion. He was yeue to hem furst whanne he sent hem to
preche. He gaue hem also pouer to chase away fendes and for to cure
al maner siknesse. And these miracles be done bi the holy goste after
that Seint Mathew saieth: 'For I chace the fendes bi the sperit of
200 God.' But for that yet it is not conuenient that though a man haue the
sperit of God that he do miracles, for as Seint Gregorie saieth that
miracles make not a man holy but shewithe hym holy, and also all tho
that do miracles haue not the holy goste, for the wicked shul afferme
that they haue do miracles and saie: 'Lorde, haue we not prophecied
205 in thi name?' God dothe miracles bi auctorite, the aungels by abilite of
mater, the deuel bi naturell vertue ymped in thingges, the enchauntour makithe hem bi secrete contracte betwene the fende and hym, the
good cristen by comune rightwis[nes]se, the wicked by signe of
comune rightwisnesse.

210 Secoundely he gaue hem the holy goste whanne he blewe in hem
f. 107vb and saide: 'Receiuithe the holy gost, and tho that ye forye|ue, her
synnes shul be foryeue,' notwithstondinge that eueri prest may not
foryeue synne as to the spotte of the soule or as to the gilte bi whiche
he is bound to euerlastinge paine or as to the offence of God, the
215 whiche ben onli foryeuen bi the infusion of the holi goste and bi vertu
of contricion. And allwayes say men that the preste assoileth in as
moche as he shewithe to be assoiled of the gilt sithe he chaungi[th] the
peyne of purgatorie into peyne temporall, and for that he relesithe a
party of the temporall peyne.

220 Thirdely he gaue to hem this day whanne he conserued so [her]
hertes that thei dredde no torment, wherof Dauid saiethe in the
Sauuter: 'The sperit of the mouthe of hym is their vertue.' And Seint
Austine saiethe: 'Suche is the grace of the holy goste that yef she finde
sorugh [or] heuinesse she brekithe it, if she finde wicked desire she
225 wastithe it, yef she finde drede she chasithe it away.' Leon the pope
saiethe: 'The aposteles hadde thanne good hope for to haue the holi
goste, but not as thanne duellinge furste in hem but in that he shulde
enchauf the holy brestes of hem and fulfell more abundauntly in
encresinge his thingges, not in beginnynge ne it was not nwe in

werkinge, but thei were made more riche bi largesse and plente 230
therof.'

To the .v. thinge, hou thei were sent, it is to knowe þat thei were
sent in tongges of fire with a soune, and these tungges apered to the
[disciples] in sittinge, and the soune was sodeyn, heuenly and hasti
and [ful]fillinge. He was sodein for the holy gost hathe no tarienge 235
mevinges; it was heuenly for he made the disciples heuenly; he was
hasti and dredfull for he putte in hem a sones drede and | toke away f. 108ra
the euerlastinge drede and caried her mynde from al flessheli loue;
and also he was fulfellinge for he fulfelled alle the aposteles, wherfor it
is saide: 'Thei bene alle fulfelled with the holy goste'. Ther be .iij. 240
tokenes for to be full, the whiche were in the aposteles. The furst
signe is whan the thinge full withholdith not, wherof Iob saiethe:
'Whanne the oxe is ful before the creche he criethe not,' as though he
wolde saie that whanne the creche of the hert is full of grace crieng
hathe no place of inpacience. This token hadde the aposteles in her 245
tribulacions, for thei were so full of the holi goste that thei withehelde
no parte of inpacience but wenten ioiusly before hem that tormented
hem. The secounde token is that they mow no more receiue whanne
thei be full, for a vessell whanne it is full of any licour [it] may receyue
none other; right so the seintes whanne thei were fulfelled withe grace 250
thei myght receiue none other licour of erthely delectaciones. And of
that saieth Isaye: 'I am full and therfor I coueite no more the
sacrifises.' And right so whanne the seintes hadde tasted the heuenly
sauoure [thei] coueyted no more erthely delite. And of that saieth Seint
Austin, that whoso hadde dronke ones of that flode of paradys, wherof 255
one drope is gretter thanne alle the Grete [See], it appertenithe that
alle the thruste of this worlde be quenched in hym. And this signe
hadde the aposteles that wold haue nothinge propre but departed al in
comune. The .iij. signe is to go or renne [ouer] so as it apperithe in a
riuer whanne it is so full that it rennithe [o]uer, wherof Ecclesiast 260
saieth that it is that fulfellithe withe wisdom | right so [as Fyson] f. 108rb
properly after the letter: 'This flode Phison hathe his properte in
[ouer] aboundinge and rennithe alwayes and waterithe or d[ewi]the
the contre aboute hym.' And right so the aposteles begonne to renne

232 .v.] furste G   234 disciples] aposteles EH1   sodeyn] sodenli H1
235 fulfillinge] fillinge E, fal/filling H1   238 caried] taried G   249 it²] and E
254 thei] om. EH1   256 Grete See] see is grete E, se grete H1   259 ouer] L, either
EH1, other G   260 ouer] euer EG   wherof] wherfore G   261 as Fyson] L, Affyson
EG, a Fison H1   263 ouer] eueri EH1   or] and H1   dewithe] L, driuthe E, driuith
H1G

265 abrode afore to watre alle the contreies aboute hem, for thei beganne
to speke mani diuerse langages, wherof the Glose saiethe: 'The
grettest token of fulnesse is whanne that the vessell is so full that it
gothe ouer. Also fere in a bosum may not be hidde, so these aposteles
were shedde oute ouer all. Wherof anone Seint Peter beganne to
270 preche and conuerted .iiij. thousand men.'
    Secoundely thei were sent in tongges of fire, and vpon that is to
considre thre thingges, furst whi he was sent in tongges of fire,
secoundely whi he was more sent in tongges thanne in any other
membre, thirdely whi he was more sent in fire thanne in any other
275 element. Of the furst it is to wete that he appered in tongges of fire for
thre causes, the furst that thei shulde bringe forthe firi wordes, the
secounde that thei shuld preche the firi lawe, that is to saye the lawe of
loue. Of these two saiethe Seint Bernard: 'The holy [goste] come in
tongges of fire, for that the tongges of al peple shulde speke wordes of
280 fire, and that firi tonges shulde preche the firi lawe.' The .iij. that the
holi goste, that is fire, were knowe by hem and that thei shuld not
mystruste ne sette the conuersion of none other to her owne merites
and that thei shulde here her wordes as thei come fro God. Of the
secound it is to knowe that he was sent in fourme of fire by many
f. 108ᵛᵃ resones. The furst reson is take bi | his grace, the whiche is multeplied
286 in .vij. yeftes of the holi goste in maner of fire makinge meke [hye]
thingges bi the yefte of drede; he makith softe harde thingges bi the
yefte of pite; he lightenith the blinde bi þe yefte of [conn]inge; he
restreinithe tho that rennen oute by vices by the yefte of counsaile; he
290 comfortith tho that be to softe bi the yefte of strength; he clerithe
[thingges] in doing away the ruste of synne bi the yefte of vnderstondinge; he makithe creatures to draw vpwarde bi the yefte of
wisdom. The secounde reson is take for dignite and excellence of
hymselff, for fire is the most noble of all elementes bi beauute, by
295 order and bi vertue. Bi beauute for the reson of [the] beauute that she
hath in yeuinge of her lyght; by ordre for the reson of the shewinge of
her hinesse; by vertue [for] the reson of vigorosite that he hathe in his
werkinge. Right so the holy goste surmountithe all these thingges. As
to the furste it is saide in what thing is the holy goste defiled; in the
300 secounde that comprehend[ithe] all the spirites intendibles; [as] to the

    277 that² . . . lawe] om. H₁   278 goste] om. E   282 conuersion] L, conuersacion
EH₁G   286 hye] bi E, `hy´ replacing bi del. H₁   288 connynge] knowinge E
291 thingges] L, om. EH₁G   295 the²] om. E   297 for] of EH₁
300 comprehendith] L, comprehended EH₁G   as] and EH₁

.iij. that is he that hathe alle the vertu of wisdom. The .iij. reson is take
ayenst the multeplienge swiftenesse of hym.

And Raben assignith .iiij. resones, saienge in this wise: 'þe fire
hathe foure natures, it brennith, it purgithe, [it warmith, it lightenithe.
In the same wise the holy goste brennith synne, it purgithe] the herte 305
and puttithe slouthe away and [he] enlumynithe þe vncunnynge.' Her
Rab[a]nes. He brennithe the synnes, wherof Zakarie saieth: 'Brenne
hem bi fire right as the siluer is brent.' And with that fire the prophite
desiri[d] to be brent whanne he saide: 'Lorde, broyle me my reynes
[etc.].' He purgithe the hertis, | wherof Ysay seithe: 'If thou wasshe þe f. 108ᵛᵇ
synnes of Ierusalem in the sperit of iugement and in spirit of 311
brennynge fire.' Thou shalt take awaye the slouthe and coldenesse
of hem, wherof also saithe the aposteles to the Romaynes of hem that
the holy goste fulfellithe: 'The holy goste apperithe in fire, for that he
take oute [of] alle hertes the slouthe of coldenesse so that he maye stie 315
vp into the desire of his perdurabilite.' He enluminethe the vncu-
ninge, wherof it is saide in the Boke of Wisdom: 'Lorde, who shall
knowe thi wisdom and thou yeue us not wisdom and sende thi sperit
fro the hiest thingges?' And the apostell saiethe to the Corinthiens:
'To vs God hathe shewed his wisdom bi his holy goste.' The .iiij. 320
reson is take in the nature of his loue, for bi .iij. resones loue is
signified to fire. Furst for that fire is alway meving, right so the loue of
the holy goste makithe a man to meve alwaies in good werkes, and
namely tho that he fulfellith, and of that Seint Gregorie saieth that the
loue of God is neuer idell but dothe alwaye gret thingges ther as she is. 325
And she werke not it is not loue. Secoundely for afore all other
elementis fire is a formable thinge and hathe of mater and moche of
fourme and of beaute. Right so the loue of the holy goste dothe withe
hem that he fulfellith withe his grace to haue litell loue to erthely
thingges and gret loue to spirituel thingges, so that he loue not 330
fleschely thingges [but spirituel thingges]. Bernarde puttithe foure
maner of lovingges, that is to saye to loue carnally, and the spirit
carnaliter, the flesshe spirituelly and the spirit | spirituelly. The .iij. f. 109ʳᵃ
hathe fire, bouithe doune [hye] thingges and strechithe vp to high

303 Raben] so changed to Raven repeated in margin H1   304–5 it warmithe . . .
purgithe] om. EH1   306 puttithe] purgith G   he] om. E   307 Rabanys] Rabynes EH1
He] om. G   308 right] twice EH1   309 desirid] desirithe E   310 etc.] L, om. EH1G
þe] þe tho E, twice once subp. H1, the þe G (the thy L, le P2)   311 iugement . . . of] om. H1
313 aposteles] so with es subp. H1   315 of¹] L, om. EG, ins. H1   alle] L, add oure EH1G
318 sende thi] send þi with n and i on erasures H1   324 he] ins. H1   325 is] ins. H1
331 but . . . thingges] om. E   334 hye] L, by EG, by 'low' H1

335 thingges, and thingges that flowen abrode he gaderithe togedre and
ouneth hem. And bi [these] .iij. thingges be vnderstonde the treble
strengthe of loue. For as Seint Denis saiethe in the boke of Names:
'The devine loue hathe treble strengthe, enclining, ordening and
lefting: enclynyng for she enclinethe the souerayne thingges [to lowe
340 thingges], ordenyng for she ordeineth egal thinge [to] equality, lifting
for she leftith [the] lowe thinggez to the souerein thingges.' And this
trebell loue makithe the holy goste in hem that he fulfellith with his
grace, for he enclinithe hem by humilite in despisinge hemselff, he
lefte hem vp in desire of souereyne godes and makithe hem ordinat by
345 vniformyte of maners.

Of [the] .iij. thing it is to wete whi he appered in liknesse of a tunge
more thanne of any other membre, it is by .iij. resones. For the tonge
is a membre enflamed withe euerlasting fire, str[o]nge for to governe
and profitable whanne he is well governed, and for she was enflaumed
350 with the fire of hell it was nedefull to her to be enflaumed withe the
fire of the holy goste. And for that the tunge is harde to be gouerned,
therfor hadde she nede of the grace of the holy goste before alle other
membres. And for as moche as she is profitable yef she be well ruled
and gouernid, ther it was nede that she hadde the holy goste to her
355 gouernour. And he appered in the tongge for to shewe that was
necessarie to the prechour gretly, for he made hem preche feruently
f. 109ʳᵇ witheoute any drede, and | therfor he was sent into the sperit of fire.
And of that saiethe Seint Bernard: 'The holi goste come in tongges of
fire vpon the disciples for that thei shulde speke firi wordes and that
360 thei shulde preche the brennyng lawe withe tongges of fire sadde and
witheoute any drede.' And of þat saithe the boke of the Dedes of [the]
Aposteles: 'Alle were fulfelled withe the holi goste an beganne to
speke the worde of God withe gret faithe and sadnesse multiplyingly
after the capacite of the diuersite of peple that herde hem.' And
365 therfor it is saide in Actes .ij.° that thei begonne to speke diuerse
tongges to profite and edificacion of the [herers]. And therfor saiethe
Ysay .lxij.: 'The spirit of oure Lorde is vpon me for that he hath
anointed me.'

Thirdely these tongges appered in sittyng for to signifie that he
370 shuld be necessarie to presidentis, that is to saye to hem that sitte in

336 these] om. E, þe H1   339–40 to lowe thingges] om. E   340 to] in EH1
341 the¹] om. E   346 the .iij. thing] .iij. thingges E   appered] appereth H1
348 stronge] straunge EH1   353 as²] om. G   357 into] in G   361 the²] om.
EH1   366 herers] eres E

highnesse and in worshippes as lordes and iuges of the peple, for he
yeuithe auctorite to foryeue synne. And of that saieth Seint Iohn the
Euuangelist: 'Receiuithe the holy goste, for tho that ye foryeue her
synnes shull be foryeue.' He yeuithe wisdom, and of that saiethe Isay:
'He shall putte [my] sperit vpon the iugement of peple for to supporte 375
hem by debonayrte and suetnesse.' And it is saide in the Boke of
Nombres: 'I shal yeue hem of the sperit that is in the that thou may
bere the charge of the peple withe the.' The sperit of Moyses was the
spirit of debonairte and suetnesse, as it shewithe *Numeri* .xij.°:
'Moyses was a man most benygne.' He yeuithe ournement [also] of 380
holy | Chirche for to enfourme. And therof saiethe Iob: 'The sperit of f. 109ᵛᵃ
oure Lorde hathe ourned the heuenes.'

The .vj. thingge is to knowe in whom thei were sent. It is sertaine
that thei were sent to the disciples, for they were pure and clene to
receiue hym after that [as] it is songe of hem, whiche saiethe that thei 385
were clene, pure and meke to receiue the holi goste for .vij. thingges
that were in hem. Furste thei were pesible in all thingges, whiche is
noted in that [that] is said of hem: 'Whanne the day of Pentecoste was
fulfelled', that is to saye the day of reste, [for this fest was acounted to
a day of reste,] wherof Isay seiethe: 'Vpon whom shall my sperit rest 390
but vpon the humble and the pesiblee?' Secoundely thei were
assembeled by loue, and that shewithe in that he saiethe: 'Thei
were togeders', for thei were al one herte and one will. Right as the
sperit of man quikenith not the membres but yef thei be togederes,
right so neither the holy goste the spirituel membres. And right as fire 395
[is] quenched by diuision of the wode, right so the holy goste is by
discorde of men. And therfor singgen men of the aposteles: 'He fond
hem alle in one acorde of charitee, and for that he enlumyned hem
withe the godhede of his charite habundauntly.' Thirdely thei were in
secrete place, that is to saye in the senacle, that is in the place wher 400
thei ete. And of that saiethe Osee: 'I shall lede hem into a secrete place
and speke to the hertes of hem.' Ferthely thei were in orison
continuelly, wherof it was saide atte the begynnyng: 'Thei were
perseueraunt in orison all withe one wille,' wherfor the Chirche
singithe of the apostelys that whan the holy goste come he founde 405
hem | alle in orison togederes. And to that þat orison be necessari for f. 109ᵛᵇ

---

371 and²] in H1   374 shull] shuld H1   and] as G   375 my] L, in her EH1G
380 ournement also] and also ournement EH1G (*aornement* P2)   385 as] *om.* E   thei]
we H1   388 that²] L, *om.* EH1G   389–90 for . . . reste] *om.* E   390 sperit]
spiritis G   392 and] `&´ H1   393 will] *add* right as the spirite G   396 is¹] *om.* E

to receyue the holy goste it is shewed in the Boke of Wysdom that
saiethe: 'I haue called and þe spirit of wisdom come in me.' And also
Seint Iohn saieth: 'I shall praie my fader and he shall geve you ayein
410 the holy goste.' Fiftely they were arraied withe humilite and is
signified in that he saieth that thei satte, wherof the psalme saiethe:
'He that sendithe the wellys into valeyes,' that is to saye [that] the holy
goste yeuithe grace to tho that bene meke and humble, like as he
saiethe [before]: 'Vpon whom shall my sperit rest [but vpon the
415 humble of spirit]?' Sixtely thei were ioyned togedres by pees, and that
is betokened in that that he saieth in Ierusalem, for Ierusalem is
named vision of pees, and oure Lorde shewithe that reste and pees is
necessarie to receiue the holy goste, and Iohn the Euuangelist saiethe
that he sayde furst to hem: 'Pees be with you.' And anone he was
420 amonges hem and saide: 'Receiuithe the holy goste.' Seventely thei
were lefte vp in contemplacion, and that is signified bi that that thei
receiued the holy goste in the souerein parte of the senacle, wherof the
Glose saieth: 'Whoso desirethe to receyue the holy goste, [he] most
defoule in surmountynge the hous of his flesshe by contemplacion of
425 mynde.'

The .vij. in that he saiethe whi was he sent, it is to wete that he was
sent for .vj. causes that be signified in this auctorite: 'The holy goste
that my fader shall sende in my name.' And furst he was sent to
comfort the sorifull, the whiche thinge is signified in that he saiethe
430 'the holy goste' is as moche to saye as comfortour. Wherof Isay seieth:
f. 110ra 'The sperit of oure | Lorde be vpon me,' and it foluithe after 'and
bringithe consalacion to hem that wepe in Syon.' And Gregorie
saiethe: 'The comfortable sperit is called he that arraiethe and
ordeinithe hope to tho that wepen and waylen for the filth of her
435 synnes and releuen her mynde fro the affliccion of sorw.' Secoundely
he was sent to quicken the dede, and that is signified whanne he saieth
for the sperit is he that quikenith. And Ezechiell saieth: 'O ye drie
bones, herithe the worde of oure Lorde and I shall sende to you my
sperit and ye shull lyue.' Thirdely to signifie hem that were not clene,
440 and that is signified bi that he saiethe 'holy,' for right as the spirit
quikenithe, right so the holy halowithe and clensithe. For the holy is
clene, wherof the psalme saieth: 'The comynge of the flode reioysith
and gladith,' that is to saye the comynge of the flode ouer aboundynge,

407 is] erased H1   412 that³] om. E   414 before] lyff E, life del. H1
414–15 but . . . sperit] om. E   423 he] in EH1   426 .vij.] .viij. E   435 fro] to G
441 holy¹] add gost G   the²] he del. H1

'gladithe the citee of God', that is the Chirche, and by this flood
halowed the right high Lorde his tabernacle. Firthely it was to 445
conferme loue betwene the discordinge and hatefull, the whiche
thinge is signified in that he saide: 'Fader', for that thei shulde loue
you kindely. And that saiethe Iohn the Euuangelist: 'That same fader
louithe vs,' and we be his bretheren and his sones togederes, and perfit
frendshipp perseuerithe betwene bretheren. Fifetly he was sent to 450
saue the rightwisse men, and that [is] signi[fi]ed in that he saide:
'I[n] my name', that is Ihesu Crist, [and Ihesu Crist] is as moch to saye
as saucoure. And so in the name of Ihesu Crist, that is saueoure, the
fader sent the holy goste for to shewe that he was come to saue the
peple. Sixtely he was sent to teche the vncunynge and that is signified 455
[in] | that he saide: 'He shalle teche you alle thingges.'   f. 110rb
    And [as] to the .vij. thingge that he was sent or yeue in the furst
chirche and bi orison wher he saiethe: 'And the aposteles praieng.' And
Luke the Euuangelist saieth: 'Ihesu praied and the holy goste come
downe.' Secoundely he was sent bi deuoute and ententif reson herde of 460
the word of God, and that saiethe he in the Dedis of Apostelis, and that
is signified in that he saide: '[Piers] spake yet and the holy goste fill
[in] hem.' Thirdely it is signified bi assiduell werke, and that is signified
in the touchinge of her hondes wher he saieth: 'Thei leide her hondes
vpon hem and they receiued the holy goste.' And this leyeng of the 465
hondes signifieth the absolucion that is made in confession.

Here endithe the feste of Whitsonday, and nexst foluithe
the liff of Seint Ierom doctour, Capitulum [.lxvj.]m

Seint Ierom saiethe that whoso will here or tell holy scripture he
ought wel laboure to kepe it in his mynde and to folue the werkes
therof, wherof Seint Ierom shewith vs ensaumple that many one taken
grete hede of. And in this ensaumple he saieth that he was in a tyme in
a towne that was .xxx.ti myle from Antioche, and this towne was called 5
Maromas and was but a litell towne. And in that towne ther was
travailinge an olde man that gretly was broken by age and semed full
nigh his dethe.
    'This man was called Mal[c]us, and it semed wel that he was of the

451 is signified] signied E   452 In] I E   and Ihesu Crist] om. E   456 in] hem E,
be H1   457 as] om. E   460 ententif] entent H1   462 Piers] L, praiers EH1G
463 in] to EH1

EH1GDH2L   Rubric liff] story on erasure H1   .lxvj.] .lxv. E   3 wherof]
wherfore G   8 Malcus] Malus EH1

10 same contre of birthe and by his langage. A woman ther was also with
hym of right gret age. This olde man and this olde woman liued in

f. 110va suche wise that | thei were alway in the chirche in her praiers, and thus
as I telle you thei ledde her lyff togeders in right gret deuocion. And
whanne I seigh hem lyue in suche deuocion, I asked of hem that were

15 there in what wise they were assembeled togedre, whedir it [were] be
rage other bi waye of mariage either be wille of oure Lorde that he
hadde ordeyned hem in that wise that thei shulde lyue so holyli
togeders. And alle thei ansuered with one voys that thei were blessed
creatures and plesaunt to oure Lorde and begonnen to telle of many

20 mervailes, and I levinge her talkinge went myselff to this olde man and
asked hym of his liff and conuersacion. He ansuered me that he was
born in Athenes: "And my fader and my moder hadde no mo children
but me only, and for that cause thei wolde make me her heyre of alle
her goodes, londes and possessiones and also mary me, but I wolde not

25 in no wise but ansuered hem whanne thei speke to me therof that I
hadde leuer to be a monke and serue oure Lorde continuelly thanne
for to haue a wyff. And whanne my fader herde me he was full of
sorugh and beganne to rebuke me gretly and saide þat in any wise I
shulde haue a wyff. But for al that I wolde not folow his entent but

30 lefte the hous of my fader and forsoke my moder and al that they
hadde and fledde me into another cuntre for to be a monke.

' "I myght not go into the parties of the orient ne into the londe of
Egipte for periles that were betwene of wicked peple that wolde suffre
none to passe, and therfor I turned into the occident and bere

f. 110vb no|thinge withe me but a litell mete. And so fer I went til I come
36 into the hermitage of Calcedoce, whiche is a grete and a stronge
desert, and ther I fonde holi men that lyued vnder the rule of monkes
and ther I duelled withe hem, and bi the trauayle of my hondes I gate
my livelode, and thus withe fastinge and withe praiers I daunted the

40 will of my flessh. A gret tyme I ledde thus my liff til a grete will come
to my mynde for to turne ayen into my contre for to see my fader and
my moder and for to comforte her in her widuhode, for my fader was
nwly dede as I herd saye, and thanne I thought that I wolde [selle my]
possession and devide it in two parties and yeue that one partie to the

45 pore and withe that other part I wolde store a selle ther as I lerned,

15 it] *subp.* H1   were] *om.* EH1   20 talkinge] tales *changed to* talkyng H1
22 in] of G   25 ansuered] answere H1   26 continuelly] *om.* G   27 a] eny G
34 into] towardes G   35 til] þat G   43 selle my] *om.* E   my] *om.* H1
44 devide it] devided H1

and the remenaunt I wolde kepe to my lyvinge. And whanne I hadd thought al this I come to the abbot that I hadde duellyd withe so longe and tolde hym all this thinge, and the abbot saide that I shulde not do it in no wise, for certainly it was temptacion of the fende that wolde I shuld take vpon me this thinge, wherfor he charged me to abide stille 50 and serue oure Lorde as I hadde purposed. And thanne he beganne to shewe me many faire ensaumples of scriptures, but what therfor alle that availed me not, for I was so ferforthely sette in the contrari that I toke none hede of none ensaumples, and whanne myn abbot seigh that he myght not ouercome me by no wordes that he coude saye he felle 55 downe atte my fete and besought me sore wepinge that I wolde not forsake hym. But I wreche wolde nothinge do atte his requeste, for I | wende that he wolde [more haue] withholde me for his felawshippe f. 111ʳᵃ thanne for my profit.

'"And thanne I went oute of the abbey, and the abbot and alle the 60 bretheren went with me a gret waye, sore wepinge and waylinge withe so gret lamentacion as though thei hadde brought me to my graue. And atte the laste I praied hem to abide and go no further that I m[i]ght take my leue of hem, and so I dede as the custume was. And thanne the abbot saide to me: 'Sone, I see well that the fende hathe 65 aspied the. Oure Lorde defende the and bringe the oute of his bondes.' But of tho wordes toke I none hede but parted fro hem and helde my waye.

'"Thanne I went on so longe that I come into a comune desert that is of Berre a citee and another citee fast by that is called Edise, and in 70 that desert ther duelled often tymes Sarisenes that there durst none passe bi hem but yef thei were of gret felawship, and I abode ther so longe til that we were in gret felawship, mo thanne .lx.ᵗⁱ persones. And thanne we toke the streites of the waye, and whanne we were entered the Sarisenes come vpon vs on hors and on cameles, bering gret 75 crestes on her hedes and bendes, and fro the gerdell downe thei wered no clothe but a clothe that hinge fro her shuldre doune to the erthe, and they bere gret cases full of arues and longe dartes, and so thei ronnen vpon us [not] for to sle vs [but] for to take us, and whanne thei hadde taken us they departed amonge [hem] oure goodes. 80 Thanne I repented me gretly that I hadde not leued myn abbot, but

48 that] om. H1   53 ferforthely] ferthforthli with first th subpunct. H1
54 none²] hys L, om. H1   58 more haue] trs. E   63 that] on erasure H1
64 might] mght E   69 on] om. H1   71 Sarisenes] Sazarynes changed to Sarazynes
H1   73 mo thanne] om. G   75 vpon] vpp del. vppon H1   78 arues] `a´rowes H1
79 not] om. E   but] and E   80 departed] add vs EH1   hem] om. E

f. 111rb it was to late. Bitwene a woman and me we were ledde into serua|ge
      not on fote but vpon a gret hors and camelys, and as we went thorugh
      the desert we were so aferde of fallinge that we wost not what to do,
   85 for us semed that we hangged and not rode, in suche peyne we were
      for to holde oure bestes withe oure armes and hondes aboute her
      neckes. Oure mete was flesshe halff rawe and we hadde no drinke but
      the melke of cameles, and suche was not oure custume before.
          ' "So long we went that we passid a riuere and thanne we come into
   90 the gret desert, [and] ther we founde the wiff and the children of hym
      that ledde us into seruage. Thanne chaunged I myn abite for I most go
      naked as alle other dede, and sauf only for shame it was none other
      greuaunce for the eyre was so attempre that ther neded no clothing.
      Than was I comaunded to kepe bestis, and in comparison of that euell
   95 that I hadde, that semed to me gret comfort that I shulde see selden
      my lorde and his meyne, and ther as I was in [the waste] desert with
      my bestis I recorded witheinne myselff how Iacob and Moyses were
      kepers of bestes in desert. I ete none other mete but melke and softe
      chese that was made of the bestes þat I kepte, and I was alwaye in my
  100 praiers towardes oure Lorde and saide suche psalmes as I hadde
      lerned in the abbey, and in this lyff I delited me gretly sithe I myght
      none otherwise do. But good Lord God litel tyme [l]asted myn ese, for
      the fende that hadde awayted my litell rest of his olde malice hadd
      gret enuye therto, as I shall tell you.
f. 111va   ' "The lorde whos bestes I | kepte seigh that his bestes multeplied
  106 and that I kepte hem witheoute gile, rememberinge me vpon þe wordes
      of the apostell that saiethe that a man shulde as truly serue his lorde as
      God in rightwisnesse, and for I dede so he purposed to guerdon me
      the seruise that I hadde do to hym so that I shulde be the beter willed
  110 to do hym good seruise after. Thanne he gaue me that woman whiche
      was take in oure felawshipp, and her husbonde also, but her husbonde
      fille in lotte to another maister that held hym in prison. And this
      woman he wolde for any thinge that she duelled as my wiff withe me,
      and whan I tolde hym that I hadde liued chastely al my liff and
  115 purposed for to do so forthe, he in grete wrathe drow his suerde and
      ranne on me and swore al that he myght suere that yef I toke not this
      woman anone and vsed her as my wiff he wolde slee me anone. The

      84 so] *add* sore E   86 holde] L, beholde EG, be hold *with* be *subp*. H1   withe oure]
withoute G   90 the¹] a H1   and] thanne EH1   93 greuaunce] greuanaunce H1
94 euell] yuellis G   96 the waste] *om*. EH1   97 witheinne] in G   102 lasted]
hasted E   108 he] I *changed to* he H1   115 for] so H1   so] *om*. H1

dethe methought was right nye by his wordes, and I was in the gret
desert and was sore aferde to lese my liff and tolde hym that I wolde
do alle his wille, and thus I toke my nwe wyff and ledde her withe me 120
into the caue wher I duelled full of sorugh, and thanne perceiued I
furst the wrechidnesse that I was inne. I fell downe to the erthe and
beganne to pleyne and to wayle the order of monke that I shulde lese
and saide to myselff: "O thou wreche, into this tyme thou haste bene
kepte, but my foly and my outrage hathe brought me hereto that I 125
haue take a wiff in myn age that wolde in no wise none haue whanne I
was yong. What availleth it to me or profiteth that I lefte my contre for
oure Lorde | and my fader and my moder yef I do now that werke that f. 111ᵛᵇ
I haue euer refused to do? And this cas is falle me now for I desired to
go ayein into my contre." And thanne I beganne to wepe bitterly and 130
saide to my soule: "What shal we do now? Shulle we be loste or ellis
ouercome? Biholde we and abide the helpe of oure Lorde or ellis deye
bi oure owne will. Take hede how thi dethe is more to drede thanne
bodely dethe, and though thi body deye thou shalt be kept pure
witnesse of Crist, that though I be here vnberied in this wildernesse I 135
shall be bothe pursuer and marter."

' "And thus I fole drowe me into a derke place and drew oute my
suerde and sette the point ayenst my breste and said to my wyfe:
'Farewell now, wyff, for thou shalt rather haue me a marter thanne an
husbonde.' Thanne she fille doune to my fete and coniured me bi the 140
name of Ihesu, seyeng: 'Shede not thi blode in my gilte, but yef thou
wilt deye sle me furst so that I bere the felawship, for truste well,
though myn husbond repayred ayein to me, that I wolde kepe my
chastite fro hennes forward or ellis I wolde deye, and truste fully that
though thou woldest lie withe me bi thi will that I hadde leuer dye. 145
And thanne whi wilt thou deye for suche cause? Do as I shall
counsayle the, holde me as a chaste wyff and loue more the
matrimonye of the soule thanne of the body, and the lorde that we
be with shal wene that we be togedre as [a] man and his wiff, and oure
Lorde the verrey God wote that we be togedre as brother and suster, 150
and thus we shull deceiue hem that shall see vs thus loue togedre.'
And I knowlage with hert and with mouthe that I was abasshed and
hadde gret | mervayle whanne I seigh and herde the gret [sadnesse] f. 112ʳᵃ

118 the] *om.* H1   119 desert] drede *on erasure* H1   122 and] *add* y G
129 desired] desire`d' H1   131 Shulle] schold G   138 wyfe] self H1
145 withe] by H1 bi] with H1   148 the¹] thy G   149 a] *om.* EH1   151 that]
twice E   153, 154 sadnesse, vertu] *trs.* EH1

and [vertu] of this woman. And thanne I beganne to loue her more
155 thanne I was wont and graunt her alle her desire, and trustith well that
I neuer behelde her naked body ne touched her neuer, dredinge lest I
shulde [lese] in pese that I hadde kept in sore batayle. And thus the
tyme passed forthe a gret while and the lorde that we were with loued
vs well and hadde no suspecion of vs but that we lyued as we hadde be
160 maried. And suche tyme ther fill that I was with my bestis a monthe
togeders witheoute repayringe home ayein.

' "And so after that I [hadde] ladde [this] lyff longe tyme, it fell on a
day that I was allone in the desert and seigh nothinge but heuene and
erthe, and thanne I beganne to thenke me in this wise and to recorde
165 the holy lyff and conuersacion of monkes [with] whom I hadde
duelled before in felawship, and also I remembered me of my fader
and of my moder and how I hadde al loste hem by my wrechidnesse.
And as I bethought me of alle this in suche wise, I behelde and seigh a
gret hill of emptes before me, and ther I seigh hem laboure
170 mervaylously. That one bere a grette[r] burdon thanne al the body
was, that other drewe after hym I wote not what maner of sedes, some
digged the erth oute of her pittes for that the reyne of wynter that was
to come shulde not gre[u]e hem, some bere the dede eyre[n]. It was
gret mervayle that in so gret felawship as ther was that tho that went
175 oute lete not the comers inne, but yef it happed that yef one were so
charged that his burdon fell fro hym for gret wyght, that other of his
felawshipp wolde turne ayein and helpe hym. What shall I saye of
f. 112rb this? | Alle the day longe I delited me in this biholdinge, and thanne I
remembred me of that Salamon saithe how men shulde take hede of
180 the besinesse and continuel labour of emptis and by that consideracion
put abacke slowe thoughtes, and thanne I beganne to lothe my seruage
and to desire the sellis of monasteries.

' "The nyght I retorned ayein and the woman come ayeinst me, and
I myght not dissimule the wille of my corage, for she asked me whi I
185 was so hevy. I tolde her the cause and I saide her I wolde fayne stele
away yef she wolde graunte therto. She refused it not, and I required
her that she wolde ensure me, for I leued her not, and she dede it
gladly. And thanne hadde I amonge my bestes two fatte oxen, and tho
I slowe and araied the flessh for to bere it with me to ete by the waye,

157 lese] L, *om.* EG, `kepe' H1   in pese] unpese *or* impese G   159 as] has *with* h
erased H1   162 hadde] *om.* E   this] my EH1G   165 with] by EH1   167 al
loste] allost *with second* l *erased* H1   170 gretter] grette E   171 wote not] not H1
173 greue] grede E, greue *with* u *on erasure* H1   eyren] eyre E   was] *add* `a' H1
181 slowe] *add* thingges and EH1   182 the] *ins.* H1   188–9 tho I slowe] þay saw3 G

and the skynnes I arraied in suche wise that they myght well holde 190
water. Whanne alle this was done we went priuely oure way in an
euentyde whanne oure lorde wende that we hadde be stille in pees,
and we bere withe vs the skynnes of the oxen and some of the flessh.
So longe we went that we come to the ryuere that was ten myle fro
thennes that we remeued. Thanne we filled the skynnes with wynde 195
and entered into the water, eueriche of vs vpon an hide, and stered it
with oure fete to we come ouer. But we myght haue come to the same
place by londe, but it was fer aboute. And also we were gladde that yef
any folued vs that they myght sone lese the trace of vs. Oure flesshe
that we bere to susteyne oure lyues with was so wete withe the water 200
that it dured us but thre dayes. Thanne | we dranke inow of the ryuere f. 112ᵛᵃ
for we wost not whanne we shulde fynde more therafter, and thus we
parted fro the ryuere and went [on] faste on oure waye, alway lokyng
behinde us as tho that were euer in drede, and euer we went more by
nyght thanne by day. O cause was for the grete hete of the sonne, 205
another was for fere of the Sarizenes leste they hadde founde us.

  ' "And yet now I am aferde ther as I am to tell the auenture that byfell
us thanne, for in the thridde day as we hadde gret drede and loked
behinde us we seigh .ij. men on horsebacke vpon two cameles comyng
after us a gret pase. Thanne thought I wel and woste certainly that it 210
was he that hadde be oure lorde, and yef he myght ouertake vs he
wolde slee us. Thanne was the sonne so lowe that he wente doune, and
he neyghed faste, and as we went togeders we we[r]e in so gret drede
that vnnethes we lyued for drede, for we wost wel that we were
pursued. Thanne we behelde on the right syde [of] the waye, and we 215
seigh a gret caue and a longge. Anone we drow to that way, and
whanne we come thedyr we dredd to entre lest any serpent were
entered before vs, for the scorpiones and other bestes that beren
venyme seken gladly the colde places whanne the grete hete of the
sonne brennythe hem. But for al that, we entered into the caue for the 220
ouer gret drede that we hadde of oure maister whanne we herde hym,
for moche more greued vs the dethe that we abode though we hadde
suffered it. I hadde so gret drede that though I wolde haue spoke I |
myght not, for though my lorde hadd called me I myght not one f. 112ᵛᵇ
worde haue ansuered hym. And thanne he made his servaunt alyght 225

  193 and²] L, add the EH1G   195 Thanne] þat G   196 an hide] his hede G
197 But] add if subp. ʒit' H1   201 the] add water of the E   203 on] oute E
207 the] add þe H1   auenture] auenturis G   213 were] wepe E   214 we³] ins. H1
215 of] on E   222 that] þanne ꞌþat' G   abode] add þanne G, add and changed to as H1
224 for . . . not] om. H1

and go into the caue for to drawe vs oute, and he hymselff helde the
cameles allone and hadde his suerde drawe and abode oure comynge.
The servaunt entered into the caue and ouerpassed vs wel .iiij. cubites
and seigh no sight of vs, but we seigh hym behynde his backe. We
230 helde us stille, and he cried and called: 'Ye theues that be witheinne,
comithe oute, for youre ende is come. My lorde callithe you. Comythe
oute, not so hardy that ye tarie lenger.' And as he spake in this wise we
seigh a gret lyonesse that come fro witheinne and strangelid hym
anone and drow hym withe her into the caue al alowe.

235   ' "And what trowe ye than," saide this olde man that al this tolde to
Seint Ierom, "how we hadde gret fere and [grete] ioye togederes? And
thus we seigh oure enemye before us and oure lorde woste no worde
therof. And whanne he seigh that he taried so longe he wende that for
as moche as we were tweyne that we wolde not haue come oute of the
240 caue for hym allone and was right angry and come into the caue withe
his suerde drawe naked, and he beganne to chide his servaunt for he
taried so longe. But he was vnnethes entered whanne the lyonesse that
hadd slayne his servaunt come ayeinst hym and strangeled hym
anone. But [who] coude leue that I saye that thilke wilde beste
245 faught for us, we were in gret fere as reson and right wold, but for
al that we were more sure to abide the rage of the lyonesse than the
cruelte of the man. Gret drede we hadde, but stere we durst not but |
f. 113ʳᵃ abode al that nyght in drede til on the morw. Thanne the lyonesse,
that hadde fere lest she hadde be awaited, toke her faune in her
250 mouthe and went her waye and lefte us th[at] hous al quite. But
though she were go we durst not go oute a gret while but abode longe
tyme dredynge the lyonesse, and in this drede we abode all that day
into the nyght, and [thanne we went oute and] founde the cameles
that thei that were dede hadde riden on. We were sore anhungered
255 and we founde but litell to refreshe us, but atte the hardest we lepte
vpon the cameles that were swifte and dede the beste that we coude,
and on the .xiiij. day we come by the desert to a castell of Romayne.
      ' "And as it was befalle us there we tolde it to the tribunal, and thanne
[we] were sent to Sabyny[en] duke of Mesopotanye for to shewe hym
260 this auenture, and to hym we solde oure cameles and he gaue us right

226 into] to G   230 he] *so corrected from* we G   231 Comythe] com//cometh
H1   232 we] he *erased* H1   235 what] þat *changed to* what H1   236 we] he H1
grete] *om.* E   237 us] *add* slayn & *on erasure* H1   worde] þing H1   244 who] so E
thilke] *om.* G   245 faught] fa'ȝ'te H1   250 that] the EH1   253 thanne . . . and]
om. EGH1   259 we] *om.* E   to¹] into *with* in *erased* H1   Sabynyen] Sabyny E
260 he] þay G

well as they were worthe. Thanne was myn abbot dede that I was
parted fro, but yet I come to that place and duellyd withe the monkes.
And this is that same olde woman," quod the olde man, "that was
withe me in chetiuyson, and we haue euer continued oure lyues sithe
we come togedre in chastite. And wetithe well now that I haue tolde 265
you al the manere of my chetivyte and of my lyff." '

Now saiethe Seint Ierom that this auenture hathe drawe oute to us
like as he herde it of the olde Malcus. He saiethe: 'Ye that heren and
vnderstonden this that I haue tolde al by ordre like as he tolde me, and
I tell it you for to expounde to olde chaste men the storie of chastite. 270
And I exhorte virgines to kepe virginite | and tell to tho that comen f. 113rb
after you that purete and clennesse may neuer be chetyue amonge
wilde bestes neyther in desert, for he that yeuithe hym al to oure
Lordes seruise and will do his comaundementis, he may well dye of
bodely dethe but he may in no wise be disseuered fro God ne fro his 275
endeles ioye that foluith, to the whiche ioye bringe us he that lyuithe
and regnithe in the worlde of worldes witheoute ende. Amen.'

Here endithe the lyff of Seint Ierom, and nexst foluithe the
lyff of Seint Gordian whiche was vicare to Iulian, Capitulum [.lxvij.]^m

Gordian was vicare to Iulyan the emperour, and as he constreyned in a
day a cristen man that hight Ianyver to do sacrifice, [the] same Ianyver
by oure Lordes grace conuerted hym and his wyff and .lij. men. And
whanne Iulyan herde that, he comaunded þat Ianyuere were sent into
exile, and that yef Gordian wolde not do sacrifice that he shulde haue 5
his hede smyte of. And so it was done and his body was caste vnto
houndes, and ther it laye amonge hem .vij. dayes and neuer none
touched hym. And thanne atte the laste he was stole of his mayne and
beried with Seint Epimache that Iulian hadde a gret while before
slayn, and þat was nygh the cite of Rome aboute a myle, and this felle 10
in the yere of oure Lorde .CCC.lx.^ti

263 woman] man G   quod . . . man] *om.* H1   265 now] *om.* G, not H1
270 to²] þe H1   274 of] a H1

EH1GDH2A2L   *Rubric* .lxvij.] .lxvj. E   1 Iulyan] *add* to H1   2 the] *om.* E
7 .vij.] .viij. H1G

Here endith the lyff of Seint Gordian, and nexst beginnithe the lyff of the Seintes Nerey and Achilley, Capitulum
[.lxviij.]ᵐ

f. 113ᵛᵃ Neryn and Achilley were chaste and full | of vertue, and they were
chamberleyns to Domycelle that was nece to the emperoure Domycien, the whiche Seint Peter the Apostell baptised. And whanne
Domycell was maried to Aurelyen the sone of a consult and was
5 clothed with purpure and precious stones, Nerine and Achille
preched to her the faithe and comended to her gretly virginite,
shewinge to her how that virginite was nye to God, suster to aungelis
and cosin to seintes, and how that the woman that is soget to man is
ofte tyme bete withe fe[t]e and with hondes, and ofte tyme with suche
10 betingges they be made to caste her chyldren. And they shewed her
how that she coude vnnethes suffre þe softe techingges of her moder,
but now [she] moste nedes suffre the grete and bitter chidyngges of
her husbonde. And thanne she ansuered and saide to hem: 'I wote wel
that my fader was ielouse and that my moder suffered moche sorugh
15 with hym, but myn husbonde will be no such.' And thanne they saide
to her: 'Thenke fully, the fayrer that they speke and the more they
s[em]e debonayre, whan they haue her entent and bene maried þey
take anone vpon hem lordship more cruelly, and many tymes they
putte the chambereres before her wyues. And alle holynesse loste may
20 be recouered by penaunce, but virginite onys loste may neuer be
brought to his furste estate. Alle synnes may be putte away by
penaunce but only virginite loste may not be recouered that euer
she come to her furst estate of holynesse.' And so bi these wordes
Domycell beleued in oure Lorde and avowed chastite and was
f. 113ᵛᵇ halowed | and veyled of Seint Clement.
26 And whan her husbond herde that, he asked leue of Domycien to
sende the virgine with Nerin and Achillee into the ile of Poncyen and
supposed that therby he shulde chaunge her purpos. And so withinne
a litell tyme after he went into that ile, wenyng bi his yeftes to haue
30 made the seintes to haue remeued the virgine of her purpose. And thei
refused it in al wise and comforte[d] her more in oure Lorde, for

EH1GDH2A2L; A1 resumes, at top of f. 114ᵛᵃ, a half folio re-inserted back to front, at
35 .iiij̇ˣˣ. and her bodies and continues for about 18 lines of text, mostly illegible.   Rubric
of²] twice E   .lxviij.] .lxvij. E   6 comended] comaundid G   9 fete] fere E
12 she] ye E, she with sh on erasure H1   15 no] 'non' H1   17 seme] sayne E
19 alle] add the EH1G (om. L, toute P2)   22 only] 'oonli' H1   23 bi] with G
31 comforted] comforte E

whiche thinge they were constreyned to do sacrifise, and thei saide
how they were baptized of Seint Petre and that þei wolde in no wise
do sacrifice. And þan her hedes were smete of aboute the yere of oure
Lorde .CCC.iiij^xx. and her bodies were beried besides the sepulture of 35
Seint Pernell.

And other seintes, that is to saye Eu[tich]e, Victorien and Marro,
whiche were aboute Domycell as servauntes, they made euery day to
laboure as bonde servauntes [in] her londes, and in the euentyde for
her lyuelode they gaue hem hogges mete. And after that he 40
comaunded that Eu[tich]e were so sore beten that he gaue vp the
sperit, and Victorien he made to be drowned in stinking water, and he
comaunded that Marro were al tobroste withe a grete roche. [And
than thei cast vpon hym a grete roche] that .lxx. men vnnethes myght
meue, and he toke that stone vpon his shuldres and bere it as lyghtly 45
as it hadde ben a strawe two myle thennes, and for this miracle many
leued in God. And thanne the consult made hym be slayn.

And after, Aurelian brought ayein Domycell fro her exile and
ordeyned to her two virgines to serue her, that one hight Eufrodice
and that other Theodore, for to teche her and to counsayle her to 50
obeye to hym, the whiche she conuerted both | to the faithe. And f. 114ra
thanne Aurelius and the husbondes of the two virgines comen to
Domycele withe .iij. iogelours to make her weddingges either for to
take hem withe force. And as oure Lord wolde, Domycele conuerted
the two yong men to the faithe. And whanne Aurelian seigh that, he 55
ledde Domycelle with hym vnto the chaumbre, and ther he made the
iogelours to daunce and to syngge and made other to daunce and to
syngge with hem, and he purposed after that to haue defouled her.
And whanne alle other were so wery that they myght no more daunce
ne syngge, Aurelien cesed neuer to daunce nor to singge in two dayes, 60
and atte the last he deyed in daunsynge. And thanne Luxymyen his
brother asked leue of the emperour and slew alle tho þat beleuid in
oure Lorde Ihesu Crist, and sithen he sette fire in the chaumbre wher
the virgines were, and so they passed to oure Lorde in holy praiers.
And Seint Cesarien founde the bodies in the morw al hole and 65
vntamed and beried hem.

---

35 .CCC.] .CCCC. *with final* C *erased* H1   37 Eutiche] Eustace EH1, Eustice G
(Eusteche L, *eutiche* P2)   39 in^1] *om.* E   41 Eutiche] Eustace E, Euthice G
(Eusteche L, *eutiche* P2)   43–4 And . . . roche] *om.* E   44 than] L, þat H1G
53 her] *add* dw *del.* H1   54 take] make H1

Here endithe the lyff of Seintes Nerin and Achille, and
nexst foluithe the liff of Seint Pancrace, Capitulum
.lx[ix].^m

Pancrace was born of right noble kinrede, and as he was orphenyne of
fader and of moder in Fryse vnder the governaunce of Denys his vncle
they commen bothe to Rome wher they hadde gret heritages, and in
the strete wher they duelled the pope Cornelyen was hidde withe
5 other good cristen men, and that Denys and Pancrace receyued the
faithe of Ihesu Crist of Cornelyen. And so Denys was lefte in pees and
Pancras was take and presented to the kynge Cesar, and Pancras was |
f. 114rb that tyme of the age of .xiiij. yere. And thanne Dyoclician sayde to
hym: 'Childe, I counsaile the that thou do not so moche that thou
10 deye of [euel] dethe, for thou art but a childe and maist lyghtly be
deceyued, and for thou art noble and sone of a ryght dere frende of
myn I praie the leue this madnesse and I shall holde the and cherisshe
the as myne owne sone.' To whom this holy childe Pancrace ansuered:
'Though I be a childe of body I haue an hert of gret age, and therfor
15 by vertue of my Lorde Ihesu Crist youre thretyngges is as moche to
me as this peinture that I beholde, for th[y] goddes that thou woldest I
shulde worshipp they were deceyuours and corumpours of her owne
susteres and spared not her owne kynne, and yef thou wist atte this
day that any of thi servauntes were suche, thou haddest leuer sle hem
20 thanne haue hem [of] suche governaunce. And therfor I mervayle me
gretly that thou haste no shame to worship suche goddes.' And thanne
the emperoure, dradde that he shulde be ouercome of suche a child,
comaunded that he shulde be biheded in the hygh waye aboute the
yere of oure Lorde .CC. and .iiij^{xx}., and Octavile the wyff of a
25 senatoure beried the body withe gret diligence. And Gregori de Tours
saithe þat yef any will come to his sepulture for to suere any fals othe,
or euer he come into the chauncell either he is rauisshed with a fende
or ellys he fallithe anone vpon the pament and endithe his lyff.

Ther was a discorde betwene .ij. men, and the iuge wist well whiche
30 was gilty, but for loue to shewe rightwisnesse the iuge brought these
f. 114va .ij. men to the auuter | of Seint Peter and constreined hym that was
gilty to [ex]cuse hymselff and to preue by his othe his innocence, and

EH1GH2A2L; A1 has two passages on f.114vb and ^{ra}, from 5 *receyued* for about 18 lines
of text, mostly illegible, and from 41 ⟨*ta*⟩*ke it ayen* to end, continuing into 70 Urban.
Rubric .lxix.] .lxviij. E   6 was] *so with* s *on erasure* H1   10 euel] will E, wille *changed
to* ville H1   16 thy] the EH1   20 of] in EH1   26 þat] *om.* H1   32 excuse]
L, accuse EG, *so changed to* ascuse H1

praied the apostell that by sum token he wolde shewe the trouthe of
the dede. And whanne he hadde suore and the iuge seighe þat he
suffered no harme for his fals oth, the iuge al ful of madnesse that wost 35
wel the dede cried and saide: 'I dar saye that this Seint Peter is [to]
debonaire [or] he hathe commytted th[is] werke to a yongger thanne
he is. Go we to Seint Pancrace the yonge and require we hym that he
discouer the trouthe.' And whan they come to the auuter of Seint
Pancrace and he that was gilti wolde haue sworn a fals othe, he leyde 40
forthe his honde but he myght neuer take it ayen, and sone after that
he deyed. And yet atte this day it is kept that men maken her othes for
gret causes vpon the reliques of Seint Pancrace.

Here endithe the liff of Seint Pancrace, and nexst foluithe
the lyff [of] Seint Vrban pope, Cap^m. .lxx.

Vrban was Pope after Calixt, and in his tyme ther was grete
persecucion vpon the cristen. And in the ende Alisaundre was
emperour and his moder hight Bamea and was cristen, for Origene
hadde conuerted her. And that same his moder demened hym so by
praiers that he sesed of the persecucion of cristen, and alway for al that 5
Dalmacien the prouost of þe citee of Rome, whiche hadde beheded
Seint Cecile, engroged gretly ayeinst the cristen, and he made seke
curiously Seint Vrban, and | he was founde in a pitte withe .iij. prestes f. 114vb
and .iij. dekenes and Karpesien her mynistre and comaunded that
they were putte in prisone. And after that he comaunded that they 10
were brought before hym, and he saide that [þat] same cursed man
had conuerted .vM^l. men withe Seint Cecile and the [noble] men
Tiburce and Valerien, and also he asked hym the tresour of the
chirche. And thanne saide Vrban to hym: 'I se well that coueitise
makithe the rather wexe madde ayeinst [the] cristen peple thanne the 15
worship of thi goddes, but I telle the that the tresour of Cecile is stied
up into heuene bi the hondes of pore men.' And thanne he made to
bete Seint Vrban and his felawes withe plometis of lede, and thanne
Seint Vrban called the name of oure Lorde Helyon, and thanne the
prouost saide: 'This olde felawe wolde be holde wise, and therfor he 20

36 to] *om.* E   37 or] L, and EH1G   this] the E   41 that] *om.* G

EH1GH2A2L; A1 continues from 69 Pancras on restored half folio, f. 114ra, to Urban 15
rather, and on f. 114rb from 34 *the fende* to end, continuing into 71 Petronilla   *Rubric del.*
but legible E   of²] *om.* E   .lxx.] .lxix. E   1 Pope] *del. and* 'bushop' *substituted* E
4 same] was G   7 engroged] engregged H1G   11 þat] the EH1   12 noble] holy
EH1   13 hym] *changed to* hem H1   15 the²] *om.* E

saiethe vnknowen wordes.' And whanne they myght not ouercome
hym thei putte hym ayen in prisone, and thanne there come to hym
.iij. iuges, the whiche he conuerted withe Anelo that was keper of the
prisone and baptised [hem]. And whanne the prouost wost that Anelo
25　was cristen he made hym come before hym, and whanne he wolde not
do sacrifise he was beheded, and Seint Vrban with his felawshipp was
brought to the ydole and was constreined to encense hym, and thanne
Seint Vrban praied and the ydole fell downe and slowe .xxij. prestes
that mynistred the fire. And they were greuously bete and brought
30　ayen to another ydole, and they spette ayeinst [hem] and made the
signe of the crosse vpon he[r] forhedes and kessed togedres and |
f. 115ʳᵃ　weren beheded by sentence vnder Alisaundre that beganne the yere of
oure Lorde .CC. and .xx.ᵗⁱ And anone Carpace and Almaciene were
rauisshed of the fende and blamyng her goddes and preising the
35　cristen maugre hem they were strangeled of the fende, and whanne
Marmenye and his wiff seighen this thei receiued holy bapteme withe
her doughter and her meyni of Seint Fortunat the prest, and after that
she beried deuoutely and worshipfully the holy bodyes [of] the
seintes.

Here endithe the liff of Seint Vrban, and nexst foluithe the
lyff of Seint Pernell, Capitulum .lxx[j].ᵐ

Pernell, of whiche Seint Marcell wrote the liff, she was the doughter
of Seint Peter the Apostell. She was right fayre and so bi the will of
her fader she was seke of feuers, and as the disciples dyned withe hym
Titus saide to hym: 'Syr, thou hast heled this day alle the seke that
5　come to the. Whi leuest thou Pernell seke?' And thanne Seint Petre
saide: 'For it is spedefull so for her, but notwithstondinge, for ye shull
wel wete that it is not inpossible to me to make her hole, I comaunde
the, Pernell, arise up and serue [vs].' And anone she arose vp al hole
and serued hym. And whan her seruise was fulfelled he ⟨saide⟩ to her:
10　'Pernell, turne ayein t⟨o thi⟩ bedde.' She went anone and b⟨ega⟩nne to
trauaile withe the feuers right as she dede before, but as sone as she
beganne to be perfit in the loue of God she was perfitly heled.
　　The erle Flactus come to her and wolde haue her to his wiff for her

21　they] þe H1　　30　hem] L, hym EH1G　　31　her] hem E　　34　goddes]
goodez *changed to* goddez H1　　preising] pre˙i˙sing H1　　38　of] and EH1

EH1GH2A2L; A1 on re-inserted damaged folio f. 114ʳᵇ breaks off after 11 *trauaile withe
the* ⟨*feuers*⟩　　*Rubric* .lxxj.] .lxx. E　　8　vs] L, *om.* EH1, anoon G

beauute, to whom she saide: 'Yef thou wilt haue me to thi wyff, comaunde that | the virgines come to me to bere me felawship into thin hous.' And whiles he made redy the virgines and the feste [for] Pernell, she putte herselff in fastinge and in praier and receiued the body of oure Lorde and leide her downe in her bedde and passed to oure Lorde the .iij. day. And whanne Flactus seigh that he was deceiued, he turned towardes Felicule the felaw of Pernell and comaunded her aither to be his wyff either to do sacrifice to the idoles. She refused bothe that one and that other, and thanne he putte her in prison and made her to be meteles [and drinkeles .vij. dayes], and sethe he made her to be tormented vpon the turment that is called eculee, and sithe he dede her to be slayne and her body to be caste in a prevy. And Seint Nichodemus toke her up and beried her, and thanne was Nichodeme called before the erle Flactus and for that he wolde not do sacrifice he was bete with plommes of lede and so deyed, and his body was caste in Tybre of Rome, that is a riuer called so, but Iuste his clerke toke hym up and beried hym worshipfully.

f. 115rb

16

20

25

30

Here endithe the liff of Seint Pernell, and nexst foluithe
the liff of Seint Petre the Deken, Capitulum .lxx[i]j.

Petre the Deken was holde in prisone bi Archiuyen prouost, of whiche the doughter was tormented withe a fende and therfor her fader wepte ofte and sore, to whom Petre sayde: 'Yef thou woldest beleue in God thi doughter shulde sone receyue helthe.' To whom Archiuyen saide: 'I mervayle me gretly bi what reson thi god myght deliuer | my doughter that may not deliuer the that sufferest so moche for hym.' And thanne Peter saide to hym: 'My God is almyghtty to deliuer me, but he will that bi passion that is transitorie we come to the ioie that is euerlastinge.' And thanne Archiuien saide: 'I shall putte the in double cheynes, and yef thi god deliuer the I shall anone beleue in hym.' And thanne it was done atte the request of Seint Petre, and than Seint Peter was cloded with white vestementis and helde in his honde the signe of the crosse, and the holi goste appered vpon hym, and thanne he fell doune to his fete and his doughter anone was heled. And thanne he and all his meyne were baptised and suffred tho that were in

f. 115va

6

10

15

---

16 for] of E   23 and drinkeles/.vij. dayes] L, trs. EH1G   25 slayne] flayne G
28 plommes] plometis G

EH1GH2A2L   Rubric .lxxij.] .lxxj. E   1 of] add 'þe' H1   6 sufferest]
suffredist G

prison went atte large wher they wolde al quite, and tho that wolde be
made cristen and many other that beleued in God were baptised of
Seint Marcellyn the prest.

And whanne the prouost comaunded that alle shulde be brought
20 before hym, thanne Archeuyen called hem all and kissed her hondes
and saide to hem that yef they wolde come to marterdome that they
shuld come withoute drede, 'and whoso will not, late hym go al quite.'
And whanne the iuge wost that Marcelline and Peter hadde baptised
hem, he toke hem and putte hem in prison eueriche by hymselff, and
25 thanne Marcelline was al naked leide vpon peces of broken glas and
Petre was putte in a streite prison, and thanne the aungell of oure
Lorde clothed Marcelline and vnbond hym and sette hym withe Petre
in the hous of Archeuyen for to comforte the peple .viij. dayes hole,
f. 115vb and | thanne he comaunded hem that after that they shulde present
30 hem to the iuge. And thanne as the iuge founde hem not in prison he
made calle Archevien, and whanne he seigh that he wold not sacrifice
he made hym and his wiff to be enmured in erthe.

And whanne Seint Petre and Seint Marcelline herd that thei went
thedir and Seint Marcelline songe his masse before .vijC. cristen
35 peple that were withinne that pitte wher Archivien was. And thanne
the seintes saide to the misbeleuers: 'We myght well haue deliuered
Archevien and we wolde haue hidde vs, but we will nother do that one
ne that other.' And whan the paynimes herde this thinge thei slowe
Archevien and stoned his wiff and his doughter, and thei ledde
40 Marcelline and Petre to be biheded in the Blacke Forest that now is
called the White Forest for her marterdom. And this was in the tyme
of Diocliciane that beganne aboute the yere of oure Lorde .CC. and
.iiij^xx., and Doroth that beheded hem seigh her soules bore up into
heuene [with] aungels, clothed with shy[n]yng clothes and araied
45 withe precious stones, and for that sight he become cristen and rested
after that in oure Lorde.

16 prison] L, *add* and EG, *so subp.* H1   33 herd] L, *add* whanne EG, *so subp.* H1
40 now is] *trs.* G   41 White] whight *changed to* whit H1   44 with'] and EH1
shynyng] shymyng E

Here endithe the liff of Seint Petre the Deken, and nexst
foluithe the lyues of Seintes Prime and Feliciane, Capitulum .lxx[i]ij.

Prime and Feliciane weren accused to Dioclucian of the bisshoppes of
[the] ydoles, and they saide hym that but he wolde [make hem do]
sacrifice he shulde no benifice haue of his go[d]des. And thanne they
were putte into prison bi the comaundement of the emperour, but thei
were deliuered bi the aungell, and sithe thei were ayein presented | 5
before the emperour, and for that thei helde hem stedfast in the faithe, f. 116ra
her bodies were cruelli torent. And thanne saide the iuge to Feliciane:
'Sp[a]re thine olde age and do sacrifice to oure goddes.' To whom
Feliciane saide: 'I haue now .iiij^{xx}. yere, and .xxx.^{ti} winter therof [ben
that] I haue knowen the trouthe and chosen that God that may deliuer 10
me fro thi hondes.' And thanne the iuge comaunded that he shulde be
bounde and nayled faste honde and fote and saide to hym: 'Thus thou
shalt stonde till thou consent to us.' And whanne he seigh that he
stode so merily he made to bete hym and forbede that no man shulde
mynistre to hym neither mete ne drinke. 15

And after that he made Seint Prime to be brought afore hym and
saied to hym: 'Loo here thi brother consentithe to the ordenaunce of
prince[s] and therfor he is gretly worshipped in the paleys, and therfor
do thou as he dothe.' To whom Prime saide: 'Thou it be so that thou art
the sone of the fende, yet saiest thou sothe in partie, for my brother 20
consentith to the ordnaunce of the emperour of heuene.' And than was
the iuge wrothe and comaunded that his sides were bete withe firi
brondes brennynge and that boylinge lede were yote in his mouthe, the
whiche he dranke as esely as it hadde be colde water. And thanne the
iuge was nygh madde for angger and comaunded that two lyones shulde 25
be brought to deuoure hem, the whiche leyde hem doune anone atte her
fete and layen ther as mekely as two lambes. And after that thei brought
two wilde beres, and thei leide hem downe withe the lyones debo-
nayrely, and for to beholde this ther were mo thanne .CC.M^l. men, of
whiche ther beleued in God .vC. And thanne | the iuge made hem to be f. 116rb
biheded and lete caste her bodies vnto houndes and vnto briddes, but 31
they touched it not, and thanne they were beried of cristen men al hole.
And they suffered dethe aboute the yere of oure Lorde .CC.iiij^{xx}.vij.

EH1GH2A2L   *Rubric* .lxxiij.] .lxxij. E   1 bisshoppes] bisshop G   2 the]
om. E   make hem/do] L, *trs*. EH1G   3 goddes] L, goodes EH1G   5 aungell]
angells H1G   8 Spare] spire E   9–10 ben that] *om*. E   18 princes] prince E

Here endithe the liff of the holy Seintes Prime and
Felician, and nexst foluithe the lyff of Seint Barnabe the
Apostell, Cap^m. .lxxii[i]j.^{m}

Seint Barnabe, Leuyte, was of the kinrede of Cipre, and he was one of
the [.lxxij.] disciples of oure Lorde, and he is praised in many wises
and lefte vp by gret commendacion in the Dedes of Aposteles, for he
was right well enformed and right well demened bothe to God and to
5 hymselff and to his neygheboure.

A[s] to hymselff he was ordinat in th[r]e strengthes, that is to wete
resonable, coueytous and irous. He was enlumyned withe the light of
knowlage, wher[of] it is saide in the .xiiij. chapitle of *Actus Apostolorum*: 'Thei were in Antioche prophetis and doctours, among the
10 whiche ther was Barnabe and Symon.' Secoundely he hadde coueitise
purged from alle wordely affeccion, wherof it is saide in the Dedes of
the Aposteles that Ioseph that was surnamed Barnabe hadde a felde
that he solde and brought the price tofore the fete of the aposteles,
there the Glose saiethe: 'In ordeynynge he preued that he eschewed to
15 touche it, and he taught that gold was to be trode vnder fote, the
whiche he made sogette to the fete of the aposteles.' Also he hadde a
wreth enforsed bi the gretnesse of worthinesse, and that was in
f. 116va assaylinge strongely the gret thingges either | in doying stronge
thingges perseuerauntly or in sufferinge sadly and stably the contrary
20 thingges. So as it shewithe, that is to saye whanne he toke vpon hym
to conuerte that grete citee of Antioche, as it is sayde in the Dedes of
the Aposteles. For after the conuersion of Paule he come into
Ierusalem and wolde haue medeled hym with the disciples, but þei
fledde hym as the lambes done the wolff, but Barnaba toke hym
25 hardely and ledde hym to the aposteles opinly in doyng gret thingges,
for he tormented his body by fastingges, wherof the boke of the Dedes
of þe Aposteles saiethe that Barnabe and sum other serued to oure
Lorde and fasted and suffered stably aduersitee, so as the apostelles
witnessin [it] in sayeng that were oure right dere frendes and token
30 her soules to men for the name of oure Lorde Ihesu Crist.

Secoundely thei were ordeyned as to God in obeyenge [to] the
auctorite, to the mageste and to the bounte of God. To the auctorite,

EH1GH2A2L; D resumes at 44 *withedrawe*   *Rubric* .lxxiiij.] .lxxiij. E   2 .lxxij.
disciples] L, disciples of .lxxij. EH1G   6 As] And EH1   thre] the EH1   8 wherof]
L, wher EH1G   12 the] *om.* G   29 it] *om.* E, *ins.* H1   30 the] to *del.* 'þe' H1
31 to^2] *om.* E   32 auctorite^2] *add* 'of god' H1

so [as] it apperithe whanne he wold not take vpon hymselff the office
of predicacion but wolde take it by [the] auctorite of God, so as it is
saide in the Dedes of the Aposteles wher the holy goste saide: 35
'Departe Barnabe from Paule and hem in that office that I hadde
hem for.' Also they were ordinat as to the mageste of God, so as it is
saide in the same boke of the Dedis of the Apostelis: 'For there were
[some] that wolde haue done hem worshipp as goddes and wolde haue
do sacrifice to hem.' And they called Barnabe Iupiter so as the furst, 40
and Paule Mercury right as wise and well spekyng. And thanne
Barnabe and Paule | torent her clothinge and cried and sayden: 'Men, f. 116ᵛᵇ
what do ye? We ben dedly men as ye be, shewinge you and techinge
you that ye shulde withedrawe you fro suche vanitees and conuerte
you to God.' Also thei wer ordinat to the bounte of God, so as it is 45
saide in the boke aforesayd wher he saide the bounte of the grace of
God bi the whiche we be saued and not bi the lawe, and sum of the
Iues wolde haue amenused or lassed that bounte, sayenge that she
myght not suffice [withoute] circumsicion. Poule and Barnabe withe-
stode hem myghtely and shewed hem that the bounte of the grace of 50
God suffisi[d] witheoute the lawe, and yet thei brought that question
to the aposteles and praied hem to haue her pisteles ayeinst that
errour.

Also thei were gretly ordinat ayeinst her neyghboures, for they
fedde her flocke by worde, by ensaumple and be benefice. By worde, 55
for they preched bysily the worde of God, so as it is saide in the Dedys
of the Apostelys: 'Paule and Barnabe duelled in Antioche techinge and
prechinge the worde of God withe many other.' Also it semithe by the
gret multitude that they conuerted to God in Antioche that þei were
furst called cristen disciples. Also by ensaumple, for his lyff was to alle 60
a byholdinge of holinesse and an ensaumple of religion. And he was
also in all thingges strong, noble and shynynge in all vertues, full of
grace of the holy goste, and he was clere in all the faithe and vertue.
And of these .iiij. it is saide in the Dedes of the Apostelis: 'They sent
Barnabe into Antioche,' and 'he taught hem alle for to abide in | oure f. 117ʳᵃ
Lorde in purpose of herte for he was a good man and full of the holy 66
goste and of faithe'. Also bi benefice in double manere. Ther is double
benifice or almesse temperell and spirituell. The temperell is in

33 as] that E   34 the] om. E   36 hadde] haue G   39 some] L, om. EH1G
42 Paule] Poule on erasure H1   and²] om. G   43 We ben] be we not G   46 he] she
with s erased H1   48 lassed] lassyng G   49 withoute] L, om. EG, ins. H1
51 suffisid] suffisithe EH1   59 þei] L, add that EH1, add þat þay G   60 cristen]
cristes with second s on erasure H1   67 bi benefice] beneficis G   68 in] add the G

admynistracion [of] necessite[s], þe spirituel in remission of synnes.
70 Seint Barnabe hadde the furst whan he bare the almesse to the
bretheren that were in Ierusalem, for as it is saide in the Dedis of the
Apostelis how that ther was a gret famyne vnder [C]laudyen, the
whiche famyne Agalus hadde prophesied, so that the disciples
purposed that euery, after that they hadde, shulde sende to the
75 bretheren that were in Iudee, and so they deden, for they sent to
the olde men that they myght spare by the hondes of Barnabe and of
Paule. And he hadde the secound thinge whanne he foryaue Iohn þat
was surnamed Marke the mysdede that he hadde done. For that
disciple forsoke Barnabe and Paule, but whanne he repented hym and
80 turned ayein Barnabe forgaue hym and toke hym ayein to his disciple,
and Paule refused hym, and therfor ther was made a departie betwene
hem. And yet euery of hem dede it for good cause and good entent, for
whanne Barnabe toke hym he dede it for gret suetnesse of mercye, and
in that Paule wolde not receyue hym [it] was be gret brennynge of
85 rightwisnesse. For as the Glose saiethe: 'For that he hadde be made to
colde f[ro] the hete of charite as it apperi[d] in his visage, Paule
refused hym withe good right for that the vertue of other shulde not
corumpe bi the ensaumple of hym'. This departinge was not meued |
f. 117rb be no [vice] ne synne, but only by the stering of the holy goste for that
90 they shulde preche in diuerse places to many, and so it was done
afterwarde. [For] whanne Barnabe was in Iconye the cite, a man gretly
shynyng appered to that Iohn his cosin in a visyon and saide hym:
'Iohn, be stable, for fro hennes forwarde thou shalt not be called Iohn
but so haunsed.' And whanne he tolde this to Barnabe he saide [hym]:
95 'Loke thou open this to none that thou seest, for [also] this nyght oure
Lorde [hathe] appered to me and saide: "Be sadde and stable,
Barnabe, for thou shalt haue euerlastinge guerdon for that thou
haste lefte thi peple and thi frendes and thiselff for my name."'
   As Paule and Barnabe hadde longe preched in Antioche the aungell
100 of oure Lorde appered to Paule and saide hym: 'Haste the to come
into Ierusalem, for sum of thi bretheren abide thi comynge.' And
Barnabe wolde go into Cipre for to see his kynne, and Paule hasted

69 of¹] L, in the EH1, of þe G   necessites] L, necessite EH1G   70 Barnabe]
add seith he H1   almesse] on erasure H1   72 Claudyen] Olaudyen or Olandyen E
74 that²] add þat G   hadde] om. H1   78 mysdede] add The mysdede H1, so del. G
84 it] and E, And del. 'It' H1   86 fro] for E   apperid] apperithe E
88 ensaumple] ensaumples EH1   89 vice] L, wise EH1G   91 For] And EH1
94 hym] om. EH1   95 also] L, om. EH1G   96 hathe] L, om. EH1G
100 the] 3e G

hym to go to Ierusalem, and also by steringe of the holy goste they
departed ech from other. And whanne Paule hadde [tolde] to Barnabe
that the aungell of oure Lorde hadde saide to hym, Barnabe ansuered: 105
'The wille of God be done, for I goo into Cipre now, and ther I shall
ende my lyff and see the no more.' And thanne he wepte and wolde
haue leyde hymselff doune to Poule is fete, and Paule hadde pitee of
hym and saide to hym: 'Wepe not, for this is the will of oure Lorde,
for this nyght oure Lorde appered to me sayenge: "Distourbe not 110
Barnabe to goo into Cipre, for he shalle enlumyne there moche peple
and ful|fille ther his marterdome."' And than went Barnabe into f. 117ᵛᵃ
Cipre withe Iohn and bare withe hym the gospell of Seint Mathew
and leide it vpon the seke and heled many bi the vertue of God.

And as thei wente oute of Cipre they founde Helman an 115
enchauntour, whiche Paule hadde take away his sight for a tyme,
the which they founde contrarie and withsaid hem the entre into the
ile of Paphos. In a day Barnabe seigh men and women [renne] al naked
and made her festes. [He] hadde abhomynacion therof and cursed the
temple wher they duelled inne, and sodenly ther fille doune a gret 120
partie that slow moch peple. And atte the laste he come into Salamyn,
and thanne that enchauntour meued gret discorde ayeinst hym. And
thanne the Iues toke Barnabe and dede to hym gret iniuries and
drowen hym and hasted hym gretly to deliuer hym to the iuge of the
citee for to ponisshe hym, and thanne thei herde that Eusebe, a gret 125
man of Neroes kynne, was come into the citee. Thei dredde leste he
wolde haue take hym oute of her [h]ondes and lete hym go alle quite,
and therfor they bounde a [corde] aboute his necke and drow hym
oute of the gates of the citee and al torent hym. And yet the [felon]
Iues were not fulfelled withe this but token alle hys membres and 130
closed hem in a vessell of lede for to caste hem into the see, and Iohn
his disciple and .ij. other rauisshed hym by nyght and beried hym
priuely in a pitte. And ther they laye, soo as Sychebert saiethe, into
the tyme of Zenon emperour and of Gelase the pope that were in the
yere of oure Lorde .v. hundered. And the blessed Dorothe | saiethe, f. 117ᵛᵇ
but thanne he hymselff re[uel]ed wher he was, and was founde. 136
Barnabe preched furst Ihesu Crist atte Rome and was made bisshop of
Melan.

103 they] the`y' H1   104 tolde] take E   Barnabe] Bernabe *with* abe *on erasure* H1
107 wepte] wente G   107–8 wolde haue] *om.* G   110 Distourbe] Bestourb`le' H1
114 seke] *changed to* sike H1   118 renne] *om.* E   119 He] and EH1
127 hondes] bondes E   128 corde] L, rope EH1G   129 felon] L, *om.* EH1G
136 reueled] releued E

Here endithe the lyff of Seint Barnabe, and nexst foluithe
the lyff of Seint Victe, Capitulum .lxx[v].^m

Victe was a noble childe and a true and he hadde but .xij. yere of age,
and he suffered marterdom in Secile. This blessed childe was ofte
tymes sore bete of his fader for he despised the ydoles and wolde not
worship hem. And whanne Valerian the prouost herde that he was in
5 suche plite he sent hym that he shulde do sacrifice, and he wolde not
do it in no wise. And thanne he comaunded that he shulde be al tobete
with staues, and anone the prouostes hondes and his armes dried vp,
and also tho that beten hym. Thanne cried the prouost: 'Alas, I haue
loste bothe armes and hondes.' Thanne saide the blessed childe Victe:
10 'Now make thi goddes come and helpe the yef they mowe.' 'But
mayest thou helpe me?' saide the prouost. [And thanne Victe saide:] 'I
maye helpe the in the name of my Lorde and my God.' And anone he
praied for hym and he was hole forthwithe. Thanne saide the prouost
to his fader: 'Chastise thi sone that he perishe not wickedly.'
15 And thanne the fader ledde hym to his hous and entermeted hym to
reme[u]e the corage of the childe by diuerse songes of musyk and be
playes and delites of maydenes. And whanne he hadde closed hym in a
chaumbre there come oute mervailous sauour of suetnesse, the whiche
fulfelled the fader and the moder and al her meyni with right suete
20 sauour. And thanne the fader loked inne atte the dore and seighe .vij. |
f. 118ra aungels going aboute the childe, and thanne he saide: 'The goddes
bene come to myn hous.' And anone he was blynde, and he beganne to
crye so loude þat alle the citee of Luke was meued therwithe. And
whanne Valerian herde it he come rennynge to hym to wete what hym
25 ayled, and he ansuered and saide: 'I seigh the goddes that were so clere
that I myght not susteyne her brightnesse, and thorugh that I haue
loste my sight.'
And thanne was he brought to the temple of Iouis and behight hym
a bole withe hornes of golde so that he myght recouer his sight, and
30 whanne this profited hym not he requered his sone to hele hym, and
thanne he recouered his sight by the praier of the blessid childe. And
whanne the fader wolde not leue this errour for alle these benefices
but thought to sle his sone, the aungel of God appered to Modeste
that was maister to that blessed childe and comaunded hym to entre

EH1GDH2A2L   *Rubric* .lxxv.] .lxxiiij. E   10 the] þe *changed to* the H1
11 And . . . saide] *om.* E   16 remeue] L, remedye EG, remeue *with* u *on erasure* H1
of¹] and *subp.* 'of' H1   23 loude] L, *so* (?) *with* g *changed to* d E, longe H1G

into a shipp and that he shulde lede the childe into another contrey, 35
and whanne thei hadde so done, eueri day an [egle] brought hem her
mete, and ther thei dede gret myracles.

And aboute this same tyme the sone of the emperoure Dioclician
was rauisshed withe a fende, and the fende spake in hym and saide
that he wolde not go oute of hym but yef Victe of Luke came to putte 40
hym oute. And thanne was he sought and founde and brought to the
emperour, to whom Dyoclician saide: 'Mayst thou hele my sone?'
And thanne he ansuered and saide: '[Not] I, but oure Lorde Ihesu
Crist.' And as he sette his honde vpon hym the deuel vanisshed away.
And thanne saide Dyoclician: 'Childe, take good counsell to the and 45
sacrifice to oure goddes that | thou perisshe not of euell dethe.' And f. 118rb
whanne he refused to do it he was sette in a stronge prison withe
Modest, and sodenly the whightes of iren that were sette vpon hem
fell away and the prison was lightened with gret lyght. And whanne
this was saide to the emperour he was lete oute and putte in an ovene 50
brenning hote, but he went oute and none harme hadde. And thanne a
wode lyon was made renne to hym for to deuoure hym, but he was
sone pesible bi the vertue of his faithe, and than it was comaunded
that he shulde be hangged in the turment that is called eculee withe
Modeste and Crescence his norice that folued hym oueral wher he 55
went, but the eyre was sodenly troubled [and the erthe trembeled] and
thundres come, and the temples of [the] ydoles fell doune and slowe
moche peple.

And the emperour fledde foule afraied, sayenge: 'Alas, I am
ouercome with a childe.' Thanne the seintes were anone vnbounde 60
bi an aungell and founde hemselff besyde a flode, and there thei rested
and praied and yald up her soules to God, and her bodies were kepte
withe aungeles. And thanne the holy childe sheued hym to a lady of
Florence whiche fonde hem and toke hem up and beryed hem
worshipfully. Thei suffered dethe vnder Dioclician that [beganne] 65
aboute the yere of oure Lorde .CC.iiij^{xx}.vij.

36 egle] L., aungelle EH1G   38 tyme] tide H1   43 Not] I note E, I *erased* not
H1   52 hym²] *om.* H1   56 and the erthe trembeled] *om.* E   57 the²] *om.* E
63 holy] *om.* H1   64 and toke hem] *ins.* H1   65 beganne] L, was EH1G

Here endithe the lyff of Seint Victe and his felawshipp,
and nexst foluith the lyff of Seint Quiryne, Capitulum
.lxxv[j].^m

Quiryni was sone of a noble lady of Yconye, the whiche lady wold flee
f. 118va the persecucion and went withe Quir[yn]e her sone which | was but
thre yere olde into Tarce, a citee of Cesile, and notwithestonding she
was presented to the prouost Alisaundre and bere [her] childe in her
5   armes, and [whanne] her two chaumbreres seigh this thinge thei
fledde anone and lefte her allone. And thanne the iuge toke the child
in his armes and constreined Iulit to do sacrifice, and she refused it
atte alle, and thanne he [comaund]ed that she shulde be bete withe
rawe synues, and whanne the childe seigh his moder bete he wepte
10 bitterly and cried pitously. The prouost toke the childe in his armes
and vpon hys knees and wolde haue pleased the childe withe
cussingges and with faire wordes, and þe childe behelde his moder
and hadd abhominacion of the prouostes cussinge and turned awaye
his hede by gret despite and scratte hym in the visage and gaue a voys
15 acordinge to his moder as though he saide: 'I am cristen,' and
continuelly he faught withe the prouost, and atte the laste he bote
hym by the ere and raced it fro his hede. And thanne the prouost was
[so] cursidly meued withe anger and withe payne that he [th]rewe the
childe doune [the] degrees that the tender brayne was shedde. And
20 whanne that Iulit seigh that her sone was goo before her to the
kingdom of [God] she was glad and gaue thankyngges to God. And
thanne it was comaunded that Iulyt were flayne and thanne her body
wasshe with boylinge piche and after that to haue her hede smyte of.

It is founde in another legende that Quir[yn]e disp[i]sed the tyraunt
f. 118vb as wel whanne he glosed hym as | whanne he blamed hym, and
26 confessid that he was cristen. And after þe tyme that he was a childe
and witheoute speche, yet the holy goste was in hym. And whanne the
prouost asked hym who hadde taught hym so he saide: 'O thou
prouost, I meruaile of thi folye. Sithe thou seest me so yonge a childe
30 whi enquerest thou of me who hathe taught me? Ner thi blinde malice

EH1GDH2A2L; A1 resumes at 14 *by*   *Rubric* .lxxvj.] .lxxv. E   2 Quiryne]
Quirice EH1   4 her¹] their E, theire *with* t *and* i *erased* H1   5 whanne] *om.* EH1G
(*quant* P2)   7 and²] but G   8 he] she *with* s *erased* H1   comaunded] graunted E,
comaund`id´ *on erasure* H1          14 by] *ins.* H1          16 faught] fau`ȝ´te H1   17 ere]
here *with* h *del.* H1   18 so] *om.* EH1   threwe] drewe E   19 the¹] *om.* EH1
21 God¹] heuene E   22 body] *add* `was´ H1   24 Quiryne] L, Quirice EH1G
dispised] disposed E

thou myght clerely see that the devine wisdom of God techithe me.'
And whanne he was bete he cried: 'I am cristen,' and euer as he cried
so he recouered more strength and more amonge his tormentes. And
the iuge made dismembre the moder and the childe membre fro
membre and comaunded that thei shulde be caste here and there to 35
þat ende that thei shulde not be beried of cristen men. But for al that
the aungel of oure Lorde God gadered hem togedre and thei were
beried bi nyght of cristen men. In the tyme of Constantine the gret
whanne pes was yolde to the Chirche thei were shewed by one of the
chaumbreres tha[nne yet lyuinge] and the[i] be holde in gret deuocion 40
of al peple. And they suffered dethe in the yere of oure Lorde .ijC. and
.xxx.^{ti} vnder Alisaundre.

Here endithe the liff of Seint Qu⟨irin⟩e, and nexst foluithe
the liff of Seint Maurine, Capitulum .lxxv[i]j.^m

Seint Maurine was a noble virgine and was only withe her fader
witheoute brother or suster, and her fader after the deth of her moder
entered into a monasterie of monkes and chaunged the clothinge of his
doughter so that me[n] wende that she hadde be his sone. And thanne
the fader praied the | abbot of the hous and the monkes that thei wolde f. 119ra
receiue his sone as a monke for [he] hadde no mo children, and they 6
graunted hym goodly and was called amonge hem Brother Mauryne,
and she beganne to liue right religiously and was atte al obedience.
And whanne she was of the age of .xxvij.^{ti} yere her fader felt hym sike
nye to the dethe. He called his doughter to hym and confermed her 10
in good purpos ande charged her vpon his blessinge that she shulde
neuer discouer to no creature that she was a woman. And so he deied
and she abode in her holy purpos and contynued her lyff as an holy
monke vnknouynge to alle creatures that she was a woman.
    And thanne it fel so that she went ofte tymes withe other monkes to 15
the wode withe her carte and her oxen for to bringe home wode to her
monasterie, and her custume was whanne he went so to herburgh hym
in a frankeleyne his hous whiche hadde a doughter that hadde
conceyued a childe by a knyght, and whanne it was perceiued and

31 myght] add not erased H1   40 thanne yet lyuinge] L, that lyued E, þat þan lyued
with erasure after þan H1, thanne þat lyuyd G   thei] ther E   be holde] one word E

H1GDH2A1A2L   Rubric .lxxvij.] .lxxvj. E   4 men] me E   6 he] om. E
8 she] he G   11 in] add hir G   12 discouer] add it EH1   creature] add And subp.
H1   17 he] þay G   hym] hem G

20 that she was aresoned who was the fader, she saide suerly that it was
the monke Maryn whiche hadde gote her withe childe. Whanne the
fader and the moder herde this thei went to the abbot and made an
[horrible] clamour vpon hym for his monke. The abbot, hauynge gret
shame and sorugh for this foule clamoure, sent for Maurin and asked
25 hym whi he hadde do so horrible a synne. He mekely ansuered and
saide: 'Holy fader, I aske oure Lorde mercye, for I haue synned.' The
abbot hering this was oute of hymselff for sorugh and shame and |
f. 119ʳᵇ comaunded that he shulde shamfully be putte oute of her monasterie.
He paciently abode witheoute and duelled still atte the gate .iij. yere,
30 and vnnethis thei [th]rewe hym a morsell of brede in a day.
     And whanne the child was born it was sent to the abbot, and he sent
it anone to Maurine and bade hym kepe suche tresoure as he hadde
brought forthe. Than this sely Maurine mekely and paciently toke this
childe and cussed it and wepte sore and kepte it tenderly to her pouere
35 and thanked God of all in gret pacience, and so she kepte it .ij. yere.
And so atte the laste her bretheren hadde gret pite and compassion of
her humilite and of her pacience and preied the abbot that he wolde
haue pitee on hym her brother, consideringe the gret punisshinge and
the shame that he hadde receyued and also the gret mekenesse and
40 obedience that thei seigh in hym, besechinge hym that he wolde atte
þe reuerence of God foryeue hym and that he myght be receiued into
her m[o]nasterie ayein. And so atte the laste the abbot withe gret
instaunce graunted therto, charginge that he shulde be in warde to all
the foule ocupaciones that were to do in that monasterie. He mekely
45 and paciently dede all seruise gladly and deuoutely, and thus endured
his lyff in holy werkes til she passed to oure Lorde.
     Than the bretheren come to the abbot to aske wher they shulde
berie þe body. He ansuered and saide in the vilest place that they
coude finde witheoute the cimytarie, sayenge that he that hadde
f. 119ᵛᵃ defouled hymselff so horribly shulde not [lye] | amonge his bretheren
51 in none holy place. And thanne thei went to wasshe this body as the
custume was, and as the[i] wosshe her thei pe[r]ceyued that she was a
woman, and in that sight thei were hougely abaysshed and ronnen in
gret haste after the abbot, sayenge to hym: 'Fader, come, come and se
55 the mervailes of God.' And he, mervaylenge gretly what they ment,

     23 horrible] opin E   25 a] *om.* H1   30 threwe] drewe E   33 this²] his H1,
þe G   38 on hym] of G   38–9 and the] of G   42 monasterie] manasterie E
43 be] do G   to] *om.* G   48 vilest] wildest H1   50 lye] be EH1   52 and as . . .
was] *ins.* H1   thei¹] the E   perceyued] peceyued E   54 Fader come come] come
Fadir G   55 And] *om.* G

went withe hem, and whanne he seigh that she was a woman he fell
downe to the grounde, askinge mercie and grace of þat rigour that he
hadde shewed her, coniuringe her that she wolde take no vengeaunce
vpon hym for his ignoraunce and mysdede, saienge to the body withe
gret wepingges and sighingges: 'A, holy chaumbrere of oure Lorde, 60
what wronges haue y do to the? A, holy virgine, foryeue me, for I haue
to sore offended God and the. Thou saidest in thi gret mekenesse:
"*Pater, peccaui,*" but I may saie for my gret wickednesse: "*Mater et
soror,* I haue greuously synned to God and to the and saide in my
malice that thou shuldest be beried in a vile place, but, holy virgine, 65
thou hast deserued a precious place of clennesse and therfor thou shalt
lie in the worshipfullest place of oure monasterie, for thou art oure
worship and oure ioye."'

Thus withe gret sorugh and lamentacion thei wosshen vp the body
and toke it vp withe gret reuerence to bere it to the chirche, and with 70
that the belles of the monasterie begonne to rynge witheoute mannes
honde solempnely, and so thei contynued till this blessed body was
beryed. And that woman that defamed this holy Maryn was vexed
withe | a fende and confessed her felonye and come to the sepulture of f. 119vb
this virgine and was heled, and alle the peple assembeled aboute her 75
tombe and preised God for his virgine, and many notable myracles
bene done there continuelly. And she passed to oure Lorde the .xiiij.
day of Iulitt.

Here endithe the liff of Seint Maryn, and nexst foluithe
the lyves of the Seintes Geruase and Prothase, Capitulum
.lxxv[i]ij.^{m}

Geruase and Prothase were bretheren gemelles, that is born atte one
tyme, and sones of [Seint] Vitale and of the blessed Valerie, whiche
gaue her good to pore men and duelled hemselff with Seint Nazarien.
And Seint Nazarien made an oritarie at Hebredirnense and a childe
that hight Celisus mynistred hym [the] stones therto. But where 5
Nazarien hadde Celse with hym at that tyme I wote neuer, for the
stori of Nazarien tellithe that Celse come to hym longe after. And as
they alle were ladde to Nero the emperour the childe Celce folued

57 þat] *add* grete G   59 mysdede] mi`s´dede H1   61 the] teche H1

EH1GDH2A1A2L; G breaks off after 73 *gret* (catchword *felauschip*)   *Rubric* .lxxviij.]
.lxxvij. E   1 were bretheren] *on erasure* H1   2 sones] sone E   Seint] *om.* E, *ins.* H1
4 Seint] *om.* G   5 the] *om.* E

hem wepinge, and one of the knyghtes bofetid the childe and
10 Nazarien blamed hym therfor, wherfor all the knyghtes in gret
angre bete Nazarien and defouled hym vnder [her] fete, and they
putte Celce with the other in prisone, and after that thei caste hym
into þe see. Makary was deliuered by miracle and come to Melane.
    In that tyme come vpon hem the erle Astace that went to bataile
15 ayeinst hem of Maresne, and the kepers of the idoles come ayeinst
hym and saide that her goddes wolde geue none ansuere to hem
onlasse that Geruase and Prothase sacrified to hem before. And
f. 120ʳᵃ thanne anone they were take | and brought to sacrifice, and thanne
Geruase saide that alle the ydoles were deeff and dovme and that thei
20 shulde require victori of God almyghti. And thanne was the erle
wrothe and comaunded that he shulde be bete vnto the tyme he yelde
vp the sperit. And thanne he called Prothase and saide to hym: 'Thou
cursed wreche, stody now to lyve and perisshe not withe thi brother
with wicked dethe.' Thanne Prothase sayde: 'Thou that art cursed, I
25 drede the not, but thou, cursed, dredest me.' To whom Ascacien
saide: 'Thou wicked man, how shulde I drede the?' To whom
Prothase saide: 'Thou shewest the to be aferde of me in that thou
thenkest thou shuldest be hurte by me yef y dede not sacrifice to thi
goddes.' And thanne the erle comaunded that he shulde be hangged in
30 the torment that is called eculee. Thanne saide Prothase to the erle: 'I
am not wrothe withe the for that I see the eyen of thin herte blynde,
but I haue gret pitee of the for thou wost not what thou doest. And
therfor do as thou haste begonne, so [that] this day I be worthi to
come to the blessidnesse of my brother.' Thanne the erle comaunded
35 that he shulde be biheded. Thanne one Phelip, the seruaunt of Ihesu
Crist, rauisshed the bodies of hem, and he and his sone beried hem
priuely in his hous in a tombe of stone and leyde a boke atte her hede
that conteyned her birthe, her lyff and her ende.
    Thei suffered dethe vnder Nero that beganne aboute the yere of
40 oure Lorde .lvij. and her bodies were hidde longe tyme. But in the
tyme of Seint Ambrose bisshopp of Melane they were found in this
f. 120ʳᵇ manere. Seint Ambrose was in his praiers in the chirche of | Seint
Nabor and of Seint Felice. He was neither verrely slepinge ne
wakynge and hym thought that two yonge men clothed in one
45 clothinge of cote and mantel and hosen appered withe hym and
praied withe hym withe hondes streched vp to heuene, and thanne

11 her] om. E   17 that] þanne G   19 deeff] dede G   22 the] his G
33 that] as E   36 and¹] om. G   43 of] om. H1   46 streched] strechinge H1

Ambrose praied that yef this were illusion that it myght vanisshe away, and yef it were a true vision that he myght knowe what it ment. And thanne whanne the cocke hadde crowed the yonge [men] appered praienge withe hym in lyk manere. And the thridde nyght he appered 50 whanne he hadde fasted and waked and was nye ouercome withe laboure and slepte not, and withe hem appered a persone that semed hym Seint Petre the Apostell as he hadde sayne hym peinted, and thei helde her pees. And thanne the apostell saide: 'These be tho that desired none erthely thinge but they haue folowed my techingges, and 55 these bene tho of whom thou shalt fynde the bodyes in this place. And thou shalt fynde an arch of stone keuered withe .xij. peces of erthe, and also thou shalt fynde at her hede a boke wherinne is conteyned her birthe, her lyff and her ende.'

Thanne Ambrose called the neygheboures aboute and made hem to 60 digge the erthe and founde al as the apostell hadde sayde hym, and thou it were .CCC. yere passed her bodyes were founde as hole as they were that oure thei were beried, and a mervailous and a suete sauour come fro hem. Thanne a blynde man come to the bere and touched it and anone he receiued his sighte, and many other were cured by the 65 merites of hem.

And in her solempnite | pees was refourmed bytwene þe Lum- f. 120ᵛᵃ bardes and the emperour of Rome, and therfor Seint Gregorie the pope ordeined that the office of her masse shulde begynne in this wise: '*Loquetur Dominus pacem.*' And this office in sum wise aperteinithe to 70 the seintes and in sum wise to the auentures that felle that tyme.

Seint Austin tellithe in the boke of the Citee of God that he hymselff was present and the emperour and a gret felawship whanne a blynde man receiued his sight atte Melane atte the bodies of Geruase and Prothase. Also he saiethe in the same boke that a yonge man 75 wosshe his hors in a flode that rennithe by a towne that hight Victorien and anone the fende strangeled hym and threwe hym in the riuer dede. And as men songe Euesonge in a chirche of Seint Geruase and Prothase that was [there] nye, this dede man was [as he hadde be] smiten withe her voyces. He sterte vp alyue and come vp to 80 the chirche withe a gret fray, and he toke the auuter and helde it so that he myght not be take thennes. And as the deuel was wroth that he

49 men] *om.* E   52 not] *del.* H1   54–7 And thanne . . . peces] *twice once del.* H1
62 were¹] *add* so that it were G   71 wise] *om.* H1   77 and²] and & E   78 men]
þei D   79 there] the E   79–80 as . . . be] L, *om.* EH1D   80 voyces] *add* and
anone D   alyue] 'as' a lion H1   82 as] than D   deuel] Fende D

shulde go thennes he manaced hym that yef he went thennes that he
wolde cutte of his membres. And whanne he went thennes by
85 coniurement they seighe his eye hange downe bi the cheke by lytell
veynes lyke thredes, and thanne thei putte his ye into his place as they
myght and witheinne fewe dayes by the merites of Geruase and
Prothase the holy marteres he was fully heled.

   Seint Ambrose saiethe of hem in his Preface: 'These ben tho that |
f. 120ᵛᵇ bi the heuenly baner token the armes of the apostill, and thei hauynge
91 the victorie be assoiled fro the snares of this worlde, and thei distroied
the felawshipp of the fende and folued frely witheoute [enp]echement
oure Lorde Ihesu Crist. A, hou debonayre a brethered is that [þat
g]aue hemselff [so] to holy wordes that no felthe was medeled amonge.
95 A, hou that was a glorious cause of striff that be now crowned togedre
right as the striff of a wombe at one tyme putte hem oute togedre.'

   Here endithe the liff of Seintes Geruase and Prothase, and
   nexst foluithe the liff of Seint Albone marter, Capitulum
   .lxx[ix].ᵐ

After that Iulius Cesar the furst emperour of Rome hadde so
[subdued] the lond of Fraunce, he made [an armee] to Bretayn
whiche is now called Englond in the tyme of Cassobolan, and after
many batailes withe grete difficulte he hadd the victorie and putte the
5 londe vnder tribute. He ordeined than statutes whiche were longe
tyme kept in the ile, amonge whiche he ordeined that none of that
londe shulde receiue the ordre of knyghthode but only bi the hondes
of the emperour of Rome, lest perauenture the [r]ude peple and
vnworthi wolde take vpon hem that ordre and vnworship so gret a

     83 go] *om.* D   he¹] and D   that¹] *add* h *del. and subp.* Hı   84 thennes] *om.* Hı
85 coniurement] conuenimentis D   86 thredes] þrede D   ye] eyen aȝen D   his] her
D   as] *add* wel as D   87 dayes] *add* after D   91 snares] snayres *changed to* snares
Hı   this] the D   92 enpechement] L, any prechement E, ony pechement HıD
93 þat] *om.* EHı   94 gaue] haue E   so] *see* E   96 striff] str`i´fe Hı, streene D

     EHıDH2AıA2L; G resumes at 711 *voys;* D breaks off after 106 *duke,* resumes at 356
(*vn*)*to Albones,* breaks off again after 483 *fastne that* and resumes at 606 *thei toke the knyght;* D
is also damaged in lines 979–983 by the excision of an initial on the verso; Hı originally
omitted from 634 *atte his fete* to 651 *from the bodye,* but a folio supplying this passage written
by Stephen Dodesham was later inserted.   *Rubric* .lxxix.] .lxxviij. E   1 subdued] L,
deliuered EHı, devidid D   2 an armee] L, arivan E, an arivan *with second* n *erased* Hı, a
ryvage D   to] into D   Bretayn] Brethayne *with* ayne *on erasure* Hı   3 Cassobolan] *add*
kynge D   5 ordeined] ordeyne D   statutes] *add* þe D   were] *add* a D   in the] aftir in
þat D   6 that¹] *ins.* Hı   7 knyghthode] kinghode Hı   8 rude] Iude E
9 and unworship] vnwortheli þat is of D

dignite. And for as moche as the[se] knyghtes shulde neuer arise 10
ayeinst the emperoure of Rome thei shulde make an open othe neuer
to bere armes ayeinst the emperoure, the whiche statutes were not
only kept of the kyngges of that londe but of alle | kingges thanne f. 121ra
being vnder the subieccion of Rome vnto the tyme of kyng Seuerus,
king of Bretaigne, whiche was after emperour of Rome. 15
Also he ordeined that in euery londe there shulde be a prince of
knyghtes an another, a stuard, the whiche shulde rule the peple and
[do to] hem rightwisnesse and restreine hem fro all conspiraciones
ayeinst the empire of Rome. And right as a diademe other a crowne is
the ornament of a kinge, right so he wolde that a pilyon shulde be 20
ornament of a prince and a clothe frenged withe golde shulde be the
clothinge of the stuarde, the which bothe degrees shulde be yeue of
the emperour, that whiles the prince of knyghtes and the stuarde were
one with the emperour ther shulde be none in eny rewme that durst
presume hem to disasent ayeinst hym. 25
Regninge thanne in that londe King Seuere, the whiche for to plese
the emperour Dioclisian sent his sone that hight Bassian with many
other lordes sones, withe alle the noble of Cornewaile, of Wales, of
Scotlond and of Irlond vnto the nombre of a thousand fyve hundred
and sixty, amonge the whiche ther was a princes sone of Wales in gret 30
arraye that hight Amphiball, a goodly yong man and well taught in the
langage of Latyne, of Frenshe, Greke and Ebrewe. Also ther was in
that felawship a lordes sone of the citee of Verolamye, a semely yonge
man of body and wel avysed in his gouernaunce whiche was called
Albon. Alle this felawship come to Rome in prosperite and were 35
receyued of the emperoure withe gret worship.
In that same tyme was Se[i]nt Ze|pherinus [pope] of Rome, the f. 121rb
whiche seinge so moche beauute of yougthe laboured in al that he
myght to conuerte hem to the faithe of Crist. And amonge other he
conuerted the sone of the prince of Walis secretely and taught hym 40
the faithe and sone after baptised hym, the whiche castinge away al

10 these] the E   11 an] and *with* d *erased* H1   13 alle] *add* the   14 being]
add as *erased* H1   the²] *om.* D   17 the¹] *om.* D   18 do to] *trs.* E   19 empire]
emperoure D   other] or D   20 be] *add* the D   22 the¹] a D   23 prince]
princis D   24 eny] euery H1, no D   25 hem to disasent] to offende D   hym] H1D
punct. after hym   26 Regninge thanne] *trs.* D   that] the D   londe] *add* of Bretaigne D
28 Wales] *add* and D   32 Frensche] *add* of D   and] *add* of D   35 Albon] *add* and D
36 worship] *add* And D   37 Seint L] sent E, *om.* D   pope] *erased with* bushop *ins.* E
Rome] *add* in prosperite and were receyued of þe emperoure with grete worshipp *del.* H1
38 seinge] þat sawe D   39 of] *add* Ihesu D   40 Walis] *add* whiche hyȝte
Amphiabel D   41 castinge] caste D

wordely pride toke vpon hym wylfull pouerte for the loue of Crist and
continued his lyff in al perfeccion. And there were many other of that
felawship conuerted in tho dayes, wherfor Dyoclician, whanne he
45 hadde knowlage therof, he was gretly meued and comaunded that they
shulde be sought thorugh the londe and the see and brought to his
presence, but they myght in no wise be founde. Thanne Dyoclician
lefte the sekinge of hem and ordeined a day in whiche these yonge
knyghtes shulde receiue her ordre bi his hondes and he hymselff gerte
50 her suerdes aboute hem withe his owne hondes, enfourmyng hem of
the estate and gouernaunce of th[is] ordre, comaundinge that amonge
all thinges thei shulde be perfite men and kepe her bodies fro all folye
and inordinat delectaciones, takinge vpon hem hardinesse, and in al
wise eschewe cowardise, redy to fight for rightwisnesse and yef
55 necessite fell to offre hemselff gladly to deye therfor, and also that
thei shulde neuer bere armes ayeinst hym that hadde yeue hem so gret
a worshipp, and for nothinge in erthe they shulde do no wronge [ne]
harme to [no] creature.

Whanne alle was fulfelled that longed to othe of knyghthode,
60 Bassianus the sone of kinge Seuerus, beynge that tyme .xxx.^{ti}
f. 121va wynter, be|sought the emperoure that they might dedyen the furst
fruites of her ordre by iustes or other knyghtely excercises atte Rome
in his presence. Dyoclician graunted hym frely, approvinge and
commendynge gretly the manly desire of that yonge lorde, sayenge
65 to hym: 'I canne you gret thanke of youre desire, and al this woke ye
shull iuste and turneye withe my knyghtes that bene here present.
And in the mene tyme I shall sende aboute and calle other from ferre
contreyes to fulfell youre manly desire.' So all that weke Basianus
with his Bretones deden so worthely in armes that they deserued to be
70 gretly preysed of the emperoure and of alle Romaynes. In this mene
tyme that this turnament was co[n]tinued by Basian and his felawshipp and by the Romaynes, the Ficulues, the Spaynardes and the
Sardynes, withe knyghtes of Almayne, of Cipre and of Cretence

42 pride] *add* and D of] *add* Ihesu D and] *add* so D   43 And] Also D   44 tho]
two *del.* `þo´ H1   49 bi] *add* the emperoure D   50 hem^1] him D   51 the] *om.* D
this] the E   53 hardinesse] harnesse H1   54 cowardise] *add* And D   55 gladly/to
deye] *trs.* H1D   therfor] þere for *with* for *on erasure* H1   also] *om.* D   57 erthe] *add* that
D   ne] in E   58 no] *om.* E, *ins.* H1   creature] *add* and D   59 to] *add* the H1D
61 wynter] *add* of age D   dedyen] edifie D   62 or other] or elle3 H1, othir by othir D
63 presence] *add* Than D   hym] hem D   64 desire] desiring H1   65 gret] gretli D
68 desire] *add* And D   weke] werke H1   69 they] the D   69–70 to be/gretly] *trs.* D
70 alle] *add* the D   Romaynes] *add* And D   71 continued] cotinued E
72 Spaynardes] Speyners H1   and^2] *om.* D   73 Sardynes] *changed to* hardynes H1

comen and deden in armes worthely, but the victori was continuelly
graunted to the Bretones, and aboue all other of the Bretones hadde 75
Albon the price of knyghtly strengthe in whom abode the souerein
name of victori, whos armes as it is saide was of asure withe a sawter of
golde, the whiche armes after hym bere the noble and worthi kinge
Offa, the foundour of this monasterie, either casuelly or myraculously,
vnder whiche armes he hadde euer glorious victories. After his dethe 80
he lefte the armes in the monasterie of Seint Albone rather yeldinge
hem ayein [than biquethe hem ayein]. And in this wise thorugh all
Ytalye the fame of þe Bretones encresed gretly, but specially the
emperour hadde ioye of her worthinesse.

Whanne alle these | knyghtly dedes were ended Bassianus asked f. 121ᵛᵇ
leue of the emperour to turne ayenne to his owne contre withe all his 86
felawshipp. The emperoure, hauynge special loue to Albone before
alle other for his semelyhede of persone and for his worthinesse of
armes, saide: 'Ye shull withe oure most fauoure go ayein whanne ye
wyll, sauf only Albone shall abide in oure seruise and be one of the 90
kepers of oure body.' And in this wise Bassiane withe alle his Bretones
and all other that come with hym turned ayein to her owne contre,
sauf only Albone abode in the seruise of the emperoure .vij. yere.

In this mene tyme ther was a knyght that hight Caransius, the
whiche by sufferaunce of the senatoures was made keper of the 95
Bretisshe See, the which knyght traytourly slowe Bassiane that
hadde receyued the kyngdom after his fader Se[ue]rus. And
whanne he hadde slayne hym he vsurped the londe of Bretaygne,
and ayeinst her furst oth he denyed to paie the tribute that was thanne
yeven to the emperoures of Rome, and he gaue duellynge places to the 100
Pi[c]tes in Albanye, the whiche is now called Scotlonde. And for this
cause ther was sent fro Rome into Bretaigne a gret senatour whiche
was called Allectus ayeinst Caransien [with .iij. legions of knyghtes for
to sle Caransien] and to putte hym oute of mynde, the whiche slayne
the Romaynes gretly opressed the Bretones, for whiche cause they 105

76 knyghtly] knyghti H1   79 or] othir D   80 victories] victorie. And D
82 than . . . ayein] L, *om.* EH1   And] *add* þus D   82–3 thorough all Ytalye/the fame
of þe Bretones] *trs.* D   82 thorough] *add* oute D   83 Ytalye] *add* and D   Bretones]
add arose D   but] and D   specially] principalli D   84 hadde] *add* gret D
worthinesse] *add* And D   86 leue] licence D   89 oure] youre H1   93 the¹]
om. D   yere] *add* and D   95 by] *add* the D   96 knyght] *om.* H1   97 Severus]
Serus E, Seʼueʼrus H1   99 and] *om.* H1   99–100 thanne yeuen] *trs.* D
100 emperoures] Emperoure D   101 Pictes] pittes E   103–4 with . . . Caransien]
om. E   103 legions] religions *with* re *erased and first* i *subp.* H1   104 slayne] syth D

[haue chose] amonge hem the duke of Cornewayle, the whiche hight
Asclepeodot, for to resiste the Romaynes, the whiche slewe Allectus in
the felde and putte his felaw that hight Gallum to flyght, and they
slowe so many atte London vpon the riuere that of his name they
f. 122ra   called it Walbroke that tyme. Thanne | withe one wille the Bretones
111   haue chose Asclepeodot duke of Cornewaile to be her kynge, the
whiche, though he agreed to the eleccion, he wolde not bere the
crowne witheoute þe fauoure of the emperoure of Rome. And whanne
the emperoure Dioclician vnderstode that the Romaynes were slayne
115   [for] the depo[pula]cion of Bretones and other vnrightfull causes, he
sent Maximian his felawe for to crowne Asclepeodotte.

And so atte þat tyme the emperoure Dyoclician hathe remembered
hym of the no[ta]ble seruise and trouthe of Albone and hath ordeyned
hym prince of knyghtes thorugh all Bretaigne and stewarde of the
120   same ile, and so he sent hym home ayein into the soile of his birthe,
that he myght be withe Maximien atte the coronacion of the nwe
kynge, and also for he shulde make his othe to Maximyen after the
custume by reson of the dignite that was yeuen to hym. Whan alle
these thingges were fulfelled, Maximien turned ayein to Rome with
125   .iij. thousand pounde owynge of the tyme of Carensius the tyraunt
with many other precious iuelles for to plese the emperour.

And so in that tyme Seint Poncian satte in the sege of Rome, the
whiche bi hymselff and other of his sesed not, what by prechinge and
doinge of miracles, for to conuerte the Romaynes to the faithe of
130   Crist. And so ferforthly he profited in his werchinge that in the citee
of Rome there were conuerted to the right faithe .xlvjM^l., the whiche
whanne the emperoure hadde knowlage of he was troubled not a lytell
and comaunded that all the senatoures and the worthi of the kingdom
f. 122rb   shulde | come before hym for to here what þei felt and what was to do
135   in so streite a nede that touched hem alle. And whanne they were
come they gaue her avys that the [pope] shulde be called oute openly
amonge alle the peple and ther he shulde be dampned withe alle his
cristen peple, and not only in the cite of Rome but oueralle in euery

106 haue] gaue *changed to* haue H1   haue chose] gaue choyse E   109 that] *om.* H1
they] *om.* H2   110 it] *om.* H1   that tyme] L, om. EH1H2   113–14 of Rome . . .
emperoure] *om.* H1   114 the emperoure] *om.* H2   115 for] L, bi EH1
depopulacion] depolucion EH1   117 the emperoure] *om.* H2   118 notable] H2L,
noble EH1 (*not in* Tractatus)   and trouthe] *om.* H2   123 the] *om.* H2   hym] *add* And
H2   126 plese] pees H1   129 of] *add* Ihesu H2   130 so] *om.* H2   131 .xlvj.]
.xlvjˈjˈ. H1   132 of] therof H2   not a lytell] gretli H2   133 of] *add* alle H2
134 hym] *om.* H2   136 gaue] seide H2   pope] *erased with* bushop *ins.* E   137 alle
the peple] hem alle H2

londe [thei] haue ordeyned to seke the cristen and to ponisshe hem
withe diuerse tormentes. And ouer that he ordeined that alle the bokes 140
of cristen men shuld be brent and withholders slayne and the chirches
to be ouerthrawe and men of holy Chirche to be slayn in euery place.
The whiche ordenaunce whanne it was knowe amonge the cristen that
were atte Rome of diuerse parties of the world thei toke her waye into
her owne contreyes, amonge the whiche Seint Amphiball that be 145
many yeres hadde duelled atte Rome in holy places towarde the soyle
of his birthe he dressed his waye, and by the ledinge of oure Lorde he
come to the noble citee of Verolamye, wher ther was none that wolde
receyue hym into her hous, and so he walked aboute the stretes
abydinge the comfort of God. 150

So it happed that he mette withe Albon, which was lorde of the
citee and prince of knyghtes and senescal of alle the prouince, withe
multitude aboute hym of seruauntes, clothed richely withe clothes
frenged with golde, to whom alle the citezeines and other straungers
beren grete worship. And as sone as Amphiball seigh hym he knewe 155
hym anone, but Albon knewe not Amphiball, notwithstondinge that
they hadd | passed the see towarde Rome in one felawship. Thanne f. 122ᵛᵃ
Amphiball, that hadde fo[r]sake all wordely armes and toke vpon hym
the signe of a clerk, besought Albone of herburgh for the loue of God,
the whiche Albone witheoute any fayle hadde euer bene a louer of 160
hospitalite gladly graunted to this clerke and receyued hym benygnely
and mynistred to hym his necessarie levinge.

And whanne he was parted from his servauntes he went priuely to
this pilgrime and spake to hym in this wise: 'Hou is it,' he saide, 'sithe
ye be a cristen man, that ye durst parte or passe thorughe the parties 165
of the genteles and come to this citee vnhurte?' To whom Seint
Amphiball saide: 'Mi Lorde Ihesu Crist, the sone of God lyvinge,
hathe be my sure guyde and kepte me amonge the periles bi his might,
and that same Lorde hathe sent me into this prouince for I shulde
preche and anounce the faithe of Crist to the genteles that thei be to 170
hym acceptable peple.' And thanne Albone sayde: 'What is he that is

139 thei] to E   and] for H2   140 he] thei H2   141 men] *om.* H2   and²] *add*
alle H2   141-2 and the . . . slayn] *om.* H1   142 ouerthrawe] throwe down H2
145 contreyes] cuntre H2   146 places] *add* wente than H2   towarde] *so with* w *on*
erasure H1   147 he¹] and H2   and] *add* so H2   the] *om.* H1   149 so] And so H2
154 frenged] frenchid H2   and] *add* alle H2   156 not Amphiball] him not H2
158 forsake] fosake E   160 the whiche] *twice* H2   161 this] *twice* H2   163 he¹]
Albon H2   parted] departid H2   164 it] yt *on erasure* H1   sithe] þat *changed to* sith
H1   165 durst] *add* parte or E H1   passe] parte H2   167 Amphiball] Amphi`b'all
H1   168 kepte] kepe`th' H1   170 of] *add* Ihesu H2   thei] *add* sholde H2

the sone of God? What is that ye afferme that God shulde be bore?
These be nwe thingges, for I herde hem neuer before. I wolde fayne
wete what ye cristen men fele therof.' Thanne Amphiball [entred
175 into] the disputacion of the gospell and saide to hym: 'The afferminge
of oure faithe that is that we saye God þe fader and God the sone to
be, the whiche God the sone for the hele of mankinde toke vpon hym
oure kynde of his gret benignite, and thus he procured that he that
made man shulde become man, and he that is maker of virgines shuld |
f. 122ᵛᵇ mervailously be made of a virgine. And whanne the tyme was come
181 þat this nouelte shulde be shewed, an heuenly massage was sent to a
virgine, the whiche whanne he was entered to her he saide: "Haile,
full of grace, oure Lorde is withe the, iblessed be thou amonge all
women." The whiche whanne she herde this salutacion [she] was
185 troubeled in his wordes. Thanne the aungell saide to her: "Drede the
not, Mary, for the holy gost shall come in the and thou shalt bere a
sone, and thou shalt calle hym Ihesu." Thanne saide Mari to the
aungell: "How may this be, sithe I knewe neuer man?" The aungell
ansuered: "þe holy goste shall come in the and the vertu of the almighty
190 shall shadu the. Therfor [he] that shal be born of the shall be holy and
called the sone of God." Thanne saide Mari to the aungell: "Lo me
here, the seruaunt of God, be it [do] to me after thi worde." In this
wise the Virgine to God, the servaunt to the Lorde, the doughter
deserued to be[re] her fader, the Virgyne is made a moder and lefte
195 not the nobelnesse of her virginite. This thinge was longe tyme before
[talk]ed of bi the prophetis, wherfor, my good oste, yef thou wilt
beleue these thingges to be trwe, alle thingges that longen to the faithe
may worthely be fulfelled anentes the, for sothely yef thou be made
cristen thou shalt mowe hele withe the namynge [the name] of Crist
200 the blynde, the lame and all manere siknesse. Ther nys none
aduersitee that shall noye the, dethe may not neygh the but yef it
be the wille of the creatour, but atte the laste thou shalt ende this lyff
f. 123ʳᵃ by marterdome. Holy and blessed is thi partinge | hennes that shall

172 What is] and what is he H2   God] Ihesu Criste H2   bore] add of a virgyne H2
173 thingges] tydingez H1, add to me H2   174–5 entred into] L, saide vnto EH1H2
176 that¹] om. H2   180 of] om. H2   182 he²] om. H2   184 she²] he E
185 aungell] add that was massinger H2   188 man] add and and H2   aungell] om. H2
189 ansuered] add and seide H2   the almyghty] almyghty god H2   190 he] om. EH1
192 do] om. EH1   worde] add And H2   194 bere] L, be EH2, be're' H1   195 her] the
H2   virginite] add And H2   before] om. H2   196 talked] called EH2, so changed to talked
H1   oste] frende H2   197 alle] add these H2   198 anentes] ayenst H2   199 the¹]
om. H2   the name] om. E   of] add Ihesu H2   201 the¹] add ne no H2   not neygh] noye
H2   202 the²] thi H2   203 marterdome] add and H2   thi] þe H1, this H2

passe fro the worlde to God. The benigne Lorde will recompence
withe heuenly lyff the charitable office that thou vsest.' Than saide 205
Albon: 'What reuerence or worshipp shulde I geue to Crist yef it so
were that I receiued the faithe?' He ansuered: 'Beleue that oure Lorde
Ihesu Crist withe the fader and the holy goste to be one God, and
thanne thou doest a gret thingge in his sight.' Thanne saide Seint
Albone: 'What is this that thou spekest, thou mad man? What talkest 210
thou? Ther is no reson in thi talkinge that may admitte thine
affermyngges, ne the vnderstondynge takethe it not. If it were
knowe in this citee that thou spekest suche thingges of Crist, thou
shuldest be punisshed as for blasfeme and haue thi hede smete of. I
am full sore aferde lest anye aduersite take the or thou go oute of this 215
place.' And withe that he rose up and went oute al meued withe anger,
notwithestondinge that he hadde full paciently herde al that he hadde
saide, but he wolde not shew by his visage that he was plesed with the
techinge.

Amphiball abode all that nyght allone in his praieres and Albon in 220
his chaumbre restinge, to whom mervailous thingges of þe dyuinite
was shewed that nyght. And as he was gretly affraied and trouble[d]
withe this newe vncouthe sight he rose anone and went downe to his
oste and saide: 'My frende, yef it be true that thou prechest of Crist, I
praie the that thou drede not to shewe me the trouthe of my dreme. I 225
dremed that I behelde and seigh a man come fro heuene [whiche]
innumerable multitude of men haue taken and dispended in hym
di|uerse [maners of] tormentes. They haue bounde his hondes withe f. 123ʳᵇ
cordes and rent his bodye withe scourges. His holy body thei hangged
on a crosse. This man that was thus tormented was al naked and 230
hadde no shone on his fete. His hondes and his fete was harde
fastened withe nayles and his side opened withe a spere, of the whiche
wounde of his syde ther come oute a large streme of blood and water,
as me semed. They putte a rede in his honde and crowned his hede

205 withe] add the H2   206 it] om. H1   207 He] Than Amphiabel H2
ansuered] add and seide H2   209 Seint] om. H2   212 affermyngges] affermynge H2
the] om. H1, in thi H2   takethe] takeþe changed to ta`l´keþ H1, wherfore talke H2   not]
add for H2   it²] thou H2   214 blasfeme] a blasphemer H2   215 lest anye] þat some
H1   216 he] Albon H2   rose up and] om. H2   withe] add grete H2   217 he²]
Amphiabel H2   218 shew] add hit H2   the] that H2   219 techinge] add Than H2
220 allone] om. H2   221 þe] om. H2   222 troubled] trouble E   223 newe] now
H2   224 oste] add Amphiabel H2   226 whiche] L, with EH1H2   227 men]
add that H2   hym] criste H2   228 maners of] L, om. EH1H2   229 scourges] add
and H2   230 crosse] add and H2   231 fete¹] add but H2   was] were H2
233 and] add of H2   water] add And H2

235 withe a crowne of sharpe thornes and fulfelled all that mannes cruelte
coude putte vpon hym. Thei scorned hym withe wordes, sayenge to
hym: "*Aue, rex Iudeorum*, yef thou be Goddes sone descende doune of
the crosse and we shull beleue in the." And in all these despites that
goodly yonge man ansuered nothinge to her wordes, and whanne they
240 hadde sayde and done al that they wolde, atte the laste he cried withe
an hygh voys and saide: "*Pater, in manus tuas commendo spiritum
meum*." And thus saide he and yalde up the sperit. The body
witheoute [the soule] was take doune of the crosse, the blode of the
woundes yet largely flowynge oute. They putte the body in a
245 sepulture and enseled the stone and ordeined kepers to kepe the
sepulture. A wonder thinge that the dede bodi turned ayein to lyff.
Takynge his myghtes he went oute of the close monument, and how
he arose fro dethe to lyff I behelde withe my propre eyen. Thanne
come ther men from heuene clothed in white clothing and toke this
250 man with hem and ladde hym up fro whennes he come. And syngers
f. 123va witheloute nombre folowed hym that by al the way songgen witheoute
stintinge and I wote not what [fader] and [what sone] continuelly
blessed, sayenge: "*Benedictus sit Deus pater, Deus filiusque vnigenit[u]s*."
This ioie amonge hem was grete an vnspekable, so ferforthe that none
255 erthely ioye may be likened therto. These thingges and many other
that is not lefull for none erthely man to telle were shewed to me this
nyght in a vision, but what it betokenithe I praie the shewe me the
trouthe and drede not.'

Whan Amphiball hadde herde al this he ioyed in oure Lorde more
260 thanne any man coude thenke, knowing wel that he was specially
visited of God. Thanne anone he brought forthe þe crosse that he
hadde withe hym and saide: 'Lo in this signe thou maist openly knowe
what thi nyghtes [vision] betokenithe. The man that thou seest come
from aboue is my Lorde Ihesu Crist, the whiche denyed not to obeye

235 cruelte] *add* that thei H2   238 beleue] leve H2   in²] to H2   239 whanne]
add that H2   240 and done] al and do H2   wolde] couthe *followed by add* atte laste he
cried with 'an' hie vois and seid and done all þat þei wolde *del.* H1   242 up] *om.* H1
sperit] *add* and than H2   243 the soule] Saule E   the²] his H2   244 largely/
flowynge oute] *trs.* H2   flowynge] folowinge *with first* o *subp.* H1   oute] *add* and than H2
the] and H2   in] into H1   245 the¹] that H2   246 thinge] *add* to me H2   the] this
H2   247 myghtes] *add* and H2   251 songgen] songine *with* o *on erasure* H1
252 and¹] *om.* H2   fader . . . sone] L, and sum EH1, and euer H2   253 sayenge]
singing H1   vnigenitus] vnigenitas E   254 This] The H1H2   was] *add* a E
vnspekable] vnspectabil H2   255 other] *add* mo H2   256 not] *om.* H1   for] to H2
to²] *om.* H1   259 al] *om.* H2   in oure Lorde/more] *trs.* H1   263 nyghtes] *so with* s
on erasure H1   vision] L, dreme EH1H2   seest] sawist H2   264 the] *twice* H2   not]
add himselfe H2   264–5 to obeye/hymselff] *trs. and add* him H2

hymselff to the torment of the crosse for that he wold deliuer us by his 265
blood [fro] the gilte that we were streytely holden inne bi the defauute
of oure furste fader. Tho that ye sawe sette hondes on hym and
torment hym withe diuerse paynes beto[ke]nithe the peple of the
Iwes, the which hadden by byheste that God shuld sende his sone to
hem fro heuene, and atte the laste he come that they hadde all longe 270
abide, but neyther thei receyued hym whan he come ne they knewe
not the auctour of thayre helthe, but in all thinge they withesayde
hym and euer dede hym euel for good, and yelde hym hate for loue.
And atte the laste they were so ladde | be enuye ayeinst hym that they f. 123vb
breke oute withe [so] gret wickednesse that thei toke that man inne in 275
whom they founde no cause of dethe. They crucified hym and slewe
hym thus that benigne Lorde bought us withe his precious blood, and
so in deyeng he was victor and he, lefte up on the crosse, drewe to
hym alle thingges, descendynge be his fre will to þe cloister of hell and
vnbounde his owne that were holde ther and bound the fende withe 280
euerlastinge bondes and threwe hym downe into the lowest place of
derkenesse.'

Thanne Albon gretly mervayleng vpon these wordes breke oute
with a gret sperit and saide: 'Thei bene verrely true, tho thingges that
thou haste saide of Crist, ne they mowe not in no wise argue any 285
falsenesse, for myself this nyght knewe it euydently how Crist
ouercome the fende and threwe hym doune into the depe mowthe
of helle. With my propre eyen I behelde how that blacke fende laye al
forwrapped in euerlastinge bondes, and bi this I knowe that al that
thou haste saide is verray trewe. Fro hennes forward I offre me to be 290
most true herer to þat thou shalt teche me. Tell me, I praie the now
that knowest alle, what longithe to me to do to the fader and [what] to
the holy goste. How shall I neygh to the seruise of the sone?' The
whiche wordes Amphiball heringe withe soueraigne ioye he saide: 'I
yeue thankinge to my Lorde Ihesu Crist that thou canst shewe these 295

266 fro] for EH1H2   267 fader] add Adam and H2   268 torment] turmentid
H2   betokenithe] betonithe E   the^{2}] om. H2   269 by] om. H2   270 all] om. H2
273 hate] followed by one or two erased letters H1   275 so] the EH1   inne] om. H2
276 They] and H2   277 Lorde] L, add that EH1H2   278 in] add his H2   lefte]
liftinge H2   up] vppon H2   280 and] add he H2   281 into] to H1H2
283 Thanne] And than H2   284 verrely] veri H2   tho] alle these H2   285 they
mowe not] no man may H2   286 falsenesse] falnesse H2   287 and] add howe he H2
288 eyen] add and H2   fende] om. H2   290 verray] vereli H1   hennes] this tyme H2
forward] add and H2   be] add þe H1   291 me^{1}] add Wherfore H2   Tell me/I praie
the] trs. H2   292 to^{1}] om. H1H2   to the fader] add to the father to the sone E   what]
om. E   293 goste] add and H2   I] om. H2   294 he] om. H2

.iij. names by thiselff allone. Therfor these thre persones, the whiche
openly thou haste tolde her names, beleue only on God, sadly and
truly knowlage hym.' Albon ansuered and sayde: 'I beleue fully and
f. 124ra this | is my faithe, that ther nys no God but my Lorde Ihesu Crist that
300 for the redempcion of man wolde take vpon hym mankinde and
sustene the passion of the crosse. He withe the fader and þe holy goste
is one God and besydes hym is none other.'

Thus sayde he ofte tymes, and fell downe before the crosse and
behelde oure Lorde as though he hadde hangged in the crosse, and
305 mekely the blessed penitaunt asked foryeuenesse. And so thanne
continuelly he kessed the hondes and the fete as though he hadde be
verrely atte the same place wher oure Lorde was crucified and seigh
alle his passion. Withe blode medeled the teres ranne doune
plentevously bi his mouthe that thilke worshipfull crosse was al
310 bewette. 'Here,' he said, 'I forsake the deuell and hate all the enemyes
of Crist, in hym only beleving, and to hym only I committe me þe
whiche thou affermest that rose fro dethe to lyue on the thridde day.'
Thanne saide Amphiball: 'Be strong of faithe, for oure Lorde is withe
the and his grace will not fayle the, for faithe that hathe be taught to
315 other [of] men before this tyme thou hast not only lerned of man but bi
reuelacion of Ihesu Crist. Wherfor, sethe I am sure of the, I most goo
[to] further contreyes to shewe the way of trouthe to the paynimes.'

Thannc saide Albon: 'I beseche the, maister, abide withe me one
weke, and in þe mene tyme whiles thou shalt laboure to shewe to me
320 the true doctrine of the faithe that I may know and be more pleinly
taught of þe worshippe that longithe to cristen religion.' Amphiball,
feling than that his partinge shulde be heuely take of Albon,
f. 124rb consented. And so | euery day as sone as it drowe to night the maister
and the disciple, eschewinge the haunt of men, drewe hem to a ferre
325 place wherinne was a litell hous that was called Tugurium, and ther
alle the nightes they were in the praisingges of God. And this dede

297 only on] that tho .iij. be oo H2   298 hym] hem H2   Albon ansuered and] Than
Albon H2   301 sustene] suffre H2   303 Thus sayde he] And thus Albon seide H2
and²] add he H1H2   304 in] on H1H2   305 the] this H2   penitaunt] add Albon H2
306 fete] add of that ymage H2   307 place] om. H2   308 passion] add Than H2
308–9 doune plentevously] trs. H1   310 bewette] bywepte H2   deuell] fende H2
311 of] add Ihesu H2   312 on] om. H2   313 Amphiball] add to him H2
316 sethe] add that H2   317 to¹] L, om. EH1H2   further] add into othir H2   to²] om.
H1   the²] om. H2   318 abide] add her H2   319 whiles] om. H2   320 that] om.
H1   322 feling] felingng with ing on erasure and ng subp. H1   heuely] heuenly EH1
Albon] add and H2   323 consented] add to him H2   to] add the H2
326 praisingges] preisinge H2

they that her counsaile shulde not be knowe to vntreue lyuers whiche
wolde not folowe þe faithe [but pursue hem for the faithe].

And so in this tyme ther was a paynim that hadde espied hem, the
whiche toke his waye to the iuge and boldely shewed hym alle that he   330
hadde herde, and lefte vntamed nothinge that myght noye the
innocentis either compell the iuge to wodenesse. And whan it was
knowe to the iuge, anone he was sette afere in gret wodenesse and
comaunded that Albone and his maister shulde be brought to his
presens, that they withe thoo that were worthi of reuerence thei   335
shulde offre her sacrifices to her goddes, and yef thei wolde not þan
thei shulde be take withe violence and streitelye bounde and leide
vpon the auuter of her goddes [and] ther to be slayne in stede of
sacrifice. This iugement was not hidde fro Albon, the whiche
coueytinge to go before the malice of [þe] princes he made Amphiball   340
to go oute of the towne and dede caste vpon hym a clothe of golde that
he myght the more suerly be kept fro his enemyes, for the dignite of
that clothinge was so gret in that tyme and of so gret reuerence that
whoso that wered it myght passe thorughe an oste of men vndesesed.
And Albone withehelde to hymselff his maister slaven, knowinge   345
certainly that his cruell | enemyes couthe not beholde hym paciently   f. 124ᵛᵃ
withe that clothinge. Amphiball, doing by Albones counsaile, toke his
waye erly or the day rose, drawinge the waye oute of þe citee towarde
the northe, and Albon ledde hym on his waye as longe as hym thought
nedefull. But whanne thei shulde departe and euery toke leue of other,   350
who myght witheoute teres talke of the piteous teeres thei shedde?
And so Amphiball highed hym to his marterdome into Walis, and
Albone to the citee of Verolamye clothed in his maister clothinge so
that in that wise he myght prouoke the paynimes hertes ayeinst hym
the more lyghtly.   355

Whan the day was spronge, sodenly vnware ther come to Albones
place horsemen withe a gret power of fotemen, and as wode men
withe gret crie and noyse they sought alle the hidde places in his hous,
and atte the laste they come to that Tigurium wher þei founde this
noble man Albone in a pilgrime clothingge kneling, bare the fete,   360

327 they] add for H2   to] add the H2   lyuers] leuers H1   328 but . . . faithe] L,
om. EH1H2   329 hadde] om. H1   331 hadde] om. H2   335 thei] om. H2
336 þan] that H2   338 and] in E   340 þe] her E   344 that] om. H2   of men]
om. H2   345 to hymselff] with him H2   347 clothinge] add Than H2   348 the¹]
om. H2   rose . . . waye] om. H1   the²] his H2   351 thei shedde] that shewid H2
356 spronge] add and H2   357 place] house D   and] add so D   359 that] om. D
wher] add ynne D   360 bare the fete] barfoote D

before the crosse of oure Lorde. Thanne anone þat cursed felawship
rennynge inne and asked wher was that clerk that he hadde receiued.
To whom Albone saide: 'He is with God, by whos helpe he is
susteined that he dredithe not the thretingges of men. Wherto seke
365 ye hym?' And whanne they coude not fynde hym that they sought, the
mynistres of wickednesse turned vpon Seint Albon al her cruelte.
They toke hym, they drewe hym, thei bounde hym withe harde
f. 124ᵛᵇ cheynes, and som drew hym | bi the clothes, sum by the here, and
tre[t]ed hym in the most cruell wise withe many iniuries, and so thei
370 brought hym to her idole where al the citee were togedre gadered
togederes withe the iuge Asclepiodote.

But for Albon wolde be knowen verrely the servaunt of the crosse
he bere openly the signe of oure Lorde in his honde. The peinymes,
beholding this nwe vnknowen signe, were gretly troubled and aferde,
375 but the iuge that went before alle tho of the citee bihelde that signe
and that blessed man with cruell visage and threting eyen, whos
wrathe it is saide that Albon despised so ferforthe that hym luste not
to tell hym of what kinrede he was come ne whos servaunt he hadde
bene, but amonge many questiones that were asked hym he ansuered
380 that his name was Albone and that he was f[re]ly a cristen man.
Thanne the iuge beganne to speke to hym in these wordes: 'Albon,
wher is that clerke that is entred into oure citee now nwly speking of
Crist I note what for to begile and beiape oure citezenes? Knowe it wel
that he wolde frely haue come before oure sight but yef his gilti
385 conscience hadde remorded hym and that he hadde mistruste the
qualite of his cause, and as a worthi maister aleged hym for his
disciple. Sothely how moche gile and falsnesse is hidde in his doctrine
he hathe shewed wel bi this ensaumple whanne hym that he shuld
defende in his cause he hathe forsake and fledde fro hym for drede. Be
390 the whiche in dede thou maist evidentely vnderstonde to how folische
f. 125ʳᵃ a man thou hast yeue thi con|sent, that now sodenly art wrapped in so
gret madnesse that alle that is in this worlde thou woldest forsake

361 Lorde] add Ihesu Criste D   þat] þis D   362 and] om. D   clerk] add þe
whiche D   365 that they sought] thei þat were D   the] add wicked D   366 of
wickednesse] om. D   Albon] add with D   cruelte] add for D   367 drewe, bounde] trs.
D   thei] and D   369 treted] L, treded E, þretened H1, þretid D   370 idole] ydollis
D   togedre] del. H1   372 But for] And for þat D   the crosse] the on erasure god and
crosse del. H1   374 nwe] add and D   and] om. D   375 bihelde] biholdinge D
379 ansuered] saide D   380 frely] L, fully EH1D   381 in] om. D   383 what]
wherfore but D   beiape] iape D   384 frely/haue ..sight] trs. D   385 remorded]
remotid D   that] þan D   387 disciple] disciplis D   how] om. D   in] vndir D
389 defende] haue diffendid D   hathe] add nowe D   391 now] add so D

anone and dredest not to despise oure gret goddes. Wherfor that we
be not sayne to ouerpasse lightly the iniurie done to oure goddes it
likithe us to revenge the despisinge of hem be dethe of hym that 395
despisethe hem. But for as moch as ther is none but that may be
begiled, with penaunce and forthinkinge thou mayst bowe away fro
her indignacion, the grace of whom thou maist deserue so gretly in
this manere, yef thou wilt be departed fro that most wicked secte and
do be holsum counsaile and deferre not to do sacrifice to oure goddes, 400
and thanne thou shalt not only haue forye[ue]nesse of synne but
moreouer townes and men, golde, prouinces and al maner power shal
lyghtly folowe the.'

Thanne Albone, witheoute any drede of his thretingges or ioye of
his promisse, ansuered in this wise to the iuge: 'O thou iuge, thi 405
wordes in whiche thou haste sore laboured, hou thei bene veyn and
superflue is openly knowe. That clerke, yef it hadde thought hym
good and profitable, and yef bothe oure hertes hadde acorded therto,
he hadde come to thyne audience. But I wolde not assent therto in no
wise, knowing well that this peple is euer redy to euel, for that iuge 410
plesed neuer to hem that wolde do rightwisnesse in dome. His
doctrine I knowlage that I haue receyued, and that me repentithe
nothinge, and that I haue not yeue faithe to the wordes of an vnwise
m[a]n ne to none of the comune peple pera|uenture ye shull knowe by f. 125rb
that that shall folowe after. The feithe that I haue receiued, the feble 415
and the seke restorithe to her furst hele. This to be true preuithe the
witnesse of her hele. This faithe is more dere to me thanne alle the
richesse that thou behightest me, more precious thanne alle the
worship that thou purposest, for though he hadde all the richesse
that euer was, yet shall he deye, will he nyl he, ne that golde that is 420
kepte with so gret diligen[c]e may not calle ayein his keper fro dethe.
But whereto shal I drawe my wordes alonge? Shortely, youre [goddes]
fals and faylinge I will not sacrifise to, the whiche haue norisshed alle
my kynrede in veyne hope, for whiles they besely serued hem they
most wrechidly deceyue[d] hem.' 425

393 that] *om.* D   394 goddes] *add* for D   397 fro] for D   398 grace] L,
graces EH1D   thou] thou//þu H1   401 shalt] maist D   only haue] *trs.* H1
foryeuenesse] foryenesse E   402 golde] grete D   407 superflue] *add* and D   That]
that þis D   408 and²] *add* also D   411 neuer to hem] hem neuer D   412 that²]
þerof D   413 the wordes of] *om.* D   414 man] men E   peple] *add* for D
415 shall] *om.* H1   416 hele] *add* and D   418 richesse] *so with* hesse *on erasure* H1
that] *ins.* H1   me] *add* and is D   419 purposest] purposed *changed to* purposest H1
420 that²] *om.* H1   421 diligence] diligenge E   422 goddes] is EH1, *add* ben D
423 faylinge] *add* wherfore D   not] no't' H1   425 deceyued] deceyue EH1

This sayde, sodenly ther was made gret sorugh in the peple, here
wepinge, ther clamour, and multitude of noyse is spronggen vp, but
this most blessed marter dredde not the thretingges of the iuge ne the
wodenesse of men that stode aboute hym. Thanne anone ther come
430 forthe a gret tourbe of paynymes and withe strengthe wolde haue
compelled this holy man to do sacrifice, comaundynge hym that anone
he shulde offre to her goddes, but the mynde of one man a gret
multitude myght not breke that he wolde in any wise consent to her
most cursed rightes. Than by the comaundement of the iuge he was
435 take and streched oute to scourges, and [as] he was greuously bete he
turned hym to oure Lorde with a gladde visage and saide: 'My Lord
f. 125ᵛᵃ Ihesu Crist, I beseche the kepe my mynde | that it me[ue] not ne that
she falle not awaye [fro] the state that thou haste yeue her, for, Lorde,
with all myn herte y offre my soule to the in verrey sacrifice, and y
440 desire to be made thi witnesse be shedinge of blood.'

These wordes amonges his betingges he sowned, and as the hondes
of the tormentours waxen wery and yet thei hadde not the effecte of
that they desired, the peple, hopinge yet in sum other wise the mynde
of þe marter to reuoke [fro] his purpos, made hym be putte vnder
445 gouernaunce of the iuge, and ther he was .vj. wokes and more. And
thanne anone the elementis bare witnesse of the iniurie do to the
marter, for fro the tyme of his takinge into the tyme þat he was
assoiled fro the bondes of his flesshe, ther come neuer dewe ne reyne
vpon the erthe [but euer] brennynge hete of the sone and the nighttes
450 were vnsufferably hote, so that neither the trees ne the feldes brought
forthe fruite in any wise. Alle the elementes foughten for the
rightwisse man ayeinst the wicked m[e]n, but the iuge Asclepeodot
dredde gretly to slee hym for the gret familiarite that he hadde withe
Dioclucian and for the reuerence of [his] dignite and for the power of
455 his kynne vnto the tyme that he hadde enfourmed pleinly Dioclucian
of his conuersion.

And whanne Deoclician hadde sene the lettres of Asclepiodot he

426 This . . . sodenly] And than D   427 ther] her D   428 most] om. D
430–1 haue compelled] compelle D   433 any] no D   435 as] om. E   437 meue]
me E   not] add me H1   438 fro] for EH1   439 herte] add and al my mynde D
442 waxen] weren changed to wexen H1, were D   yet] om. D   443 wise] add to turne D
444 marter] mater E, ma'r'tere with final e erased H1   fro] for E, Fro on erasure H1
purpos] add and D   447 þat] om. D   449 but euer] ne neuer EDL, but euer on
erasure H1 (sed W)   and] add also D   451 fruite . . . wise] no frute And D
452 men] man EH1   but] And D   453 withe] add þe emperoure D   454 his] the
EH1   the²] om. H1   455 vnto the] add into þe del. H1   456 conuersion] L,
conuersacion EH1D   457 Deoclician] the emperoure D   the] this H1

anone sent his felawe Maximian Hercule, yeuynge hym power
thorugh alle Bretaigne for to do dome to the peple and to destroye
the faithe of the cristen and alle her chirches, comaundynge no cristen 460
shulde be spared sauf only Albone. For wh[om] he ocupied hym |
sayenge: 'Loke ye assaye to bringe in Albon be alle fayre promisses, f. 125vb
and make hym aferde withe thretyngges and compellithe hym to turne
ayen to oure secte, and yef he will agree to oure praiers, moniciones
and comaundementes in this partie, wher that euer he will in al the 465
worlde I shal make hym gret and worshipfull. And yef he will not be
conuerted in no wise, late hym be sharpely scourged, and yef he be not
thanne corrected, lede hym to the iugement that shall be suche: late
hym be beheueded by sum knyght that is worshipfull in the ord[r]e of
knyghthode, and the clerke that hathe conuerted hym late hym be 470
slayne withe the most foulest dethe that canne be imagened, that the
beholders therof mowe haue drede and horrour.'
    Whanne Maximianus come into Bretayne he toke withe hym the
kinge Asclepeodot and went streite into Verolamy for to fulfell the
comaundement of Cesar. Thanne anone Albon was brought oute of 475
prison, and be alle the wayes that thei coude imagine they tempte hym
to peruerte hym. But as the seruaunt of God hadd no cure neither to
here hem ne to do hem reuerence, they hauynge indignacion therof
anone thei ordeyned a day of iustice, the whiche day come they hadde
iuged that Amphiball whereuer he may be founde shall be take and 480
cruelly scourged and after that al naked be bounde to a stake fastened
in the erthe, and than his nauell to be opened and drawe oute [a]
bowell of his body and fastne that bowell faste to the stake, and thanne
withe speres ande suerdes and knyues compell hym to go aboute till
alle his bowelles | hange aboute the stake, and whan this is do to haue f. 126ra
his hede smite of. These were the iugementes yeuen in wrytinge 486
ayeinst Albone and Amphiball be Maxymien and Asclepeadot.
    Thanne alle the burgeys of Verolomye, of London and of alle the
townes aboute were somened that thei shuld come the nexste
Thou[r]sday foluinge for to here the iugement and execucion yeuen 490

459 the] *om.* H1   460 chirches comaundynge] clerkis and commaundid that D
461 whom] whanne EH1   463 hym¹] *add* also D   withe] bi D   thretyngges] þre
thinges H1   465 and] or D   467 be] wyl D   468 thanne] *add* be D   suche]
this D   469 is] he be D   ordre] orde E   470 hathe] *om.* D   hym] *om.* H1
471 withe] in D   472 horrour] *add* And D   474 into] to D   475 Cesar] *add*
emperoure H1   478 therof] *om.* D   479 day²] *om.* H1   480 whereuer] *add* þat D
482 a] L, eueri EH1H2   483 faste] *om.* H2   484 withe] *om.* H1   485 is] were
H2   488 the²] *om.* H2   489 townes] *add* there H2   490 Thoursday] thousday E

be Maximian and Asclepeodot ayeinste Albone prince of knyghtes and
sumtyme lorde of Verolamye and senescal of all Bretayne, and atte
that day sette there come peple withoute nombre for to here and see
the noueltee of so gret a thingge. Thanne was Albon brought oute of
495 prison and monisshed for to offre encense to Iubiter and Apolyn, the
principall goddes of the citee, the whiche holy martir willynge in no
wise to do it, but ouer that he preched so that he conuerted m[any] to
the faithe of Crist, and many of hem douted whiche faithe they myght
cleue to.

500   Thanne Maximianus and Asclepeodot gave sentence vpon hym
vnder these wordes: 'In the tyme of the emperour Dioclician, Albon
the lorde of the citee of Verolamy, prince of knyghtes and senescall of
alle Bretayne terme of his lyff, hathe despised Iubiter and Apolyn and
hem haue do derogacion and vnworshippe, for the whiche cause bi the
505 law he is iuged to be dede bi the honde of sum knyght [for he is a
knyght]. His hede shall be smyte from the body and that his body be
beried in the same place wher he loste his hede, the sepulcre of whom
be worshipfull for worshippe of knyghthode wherof he was prince.
The crosse that he bere [and] the sclavyne [that] he dede [were be]
f. 126rb beryed withe hym in the | erthe, his body that it be wrapped in a
511 cheste of lede and leyde in a sepulcre. This sentence the lawe hathe
ordeyned for he hathe renied the principall goddes.' Thanne gret
murmur arose amonge the peple and saiden that they myght not esely
suffre the iniuries of so noble and of so good a man, and namely his
515 kynne and his frendes whiche laboured sore for his deliueraunce.
        This maner of merci Albon toke hevily lest he shulde haue be
deferred fro his marterdome. Stondinge in myddes of all the peple
withe grete waylynge behelde to heuene and drewe forthe the crosse
of oure Lorde and saide: 'Lorde Ihesu Crist, I beseche the that thou
520 suffre not the fende to preuayle ayeinst me be his wyles and that the
acord of thi[s] peple lette not my marterdom. Her enforsing I beseche
the, Lorde, to make feble, represse her boldenesse.' And thanne he,

497 many] mo EH1   499 cleue] enclyne H2   500 hym] hem H1H2
502 the citee of] om. H2   Verolamy] add and H2   503 of] add al H2   505–6 for
he is a knyght] L, om. EH1, add and therfore H2   507 wher] add that H2   loste]
lefte H2   hede] add and that H2   whom] him H2   508 for] add the H2   wherof]
w'h'er of H1   prince] add And that H2   509 and] in E, in on erasure H1   that] om.
E   dede] de'e'd H1, om. H2   were be] L, om. E, 'were' H1, werid be H2
510 erthe] add And also that H2   that it] om. H2   511 hathe] late H1   512 the]
oure H2   Thanne] add a H2   514 iniuries] iniurie H2   of¹] om. H1   518 to]
towarde H2   521 this] thi E, 't'his H2   521–2 I beseche the/Lorde] trs. H2
522 feble] add and H2

turnynge to the peple, saide: 'What abide ye? Whom [susteyne] ye?
See ye not well that the tyme passithe faste awaye? If ye will not
encline to [t]his sentence, gothe, takithe counsell of youre lawes, 525
sechithe the statutes of youre citee and that will teche you what ye
aught to do. What suffre ye so long abydinge? Wetith wel [alle] that I
am a stronge enemy to youre goddes, whedir [thei] be worthy any
dignite, the whiche is knowe nothinge to haue in [hem] of the
dyuinite. Ye youreself be her witnesse that neither they here ne see 530
ne vnderstonde. Desirithe any of you so to here or to see as youre
goddes that ye worshipp? Nay, hardely. What shull we saye of suche
goddes whanne the worshippers of hem wolde holde hem | despised to f. 126ᵛᵃ
be like hem? O vanite, how moche thou art de[te]stable that hopest liff
of hem that neuer hadd lyff, to offre praiers to hem that neuer herde, 535
to seke hele [of hem] that felt neuer wele. Wherfor I anounce pleinly
that whoso worshippeth suche goddes is wors thanne madde. I praie
you, what is more wreched thanne that man of whom his hondewerke
hathe [lordeshippe]? Therfor wo to ydoles. What semethe you these
thingges?'   540
   Thanne all the paynimes speke togedre and by one will they haue
assented to [the sentence of] his dethe, and þat be done they haue
chose anone a place whiche was called Holmeherst. But thanne arose a
gret contencion amonge the peple, not fyndyng by what manere of
dethe thei myght slee her enemye. Sum wold haue hym crucifyed as 545
the disciple of hym [that] was crucified, other wold that he shulde be
beried quik in þe erthe for he was enemy to her goddes, but the
iuge and alle the peple of the citee be the comaundement of the
emperoure wolde haue his hede smite of. Thanne by the iugement
Albon was drawe to his marterdom. And alle the peple, leuinge the 550
iuge in the towne, ronne oute to beholde this meruayle, the whiche
besely folued this holy man withe chydingges and gret rebukinges,
sayeng forthe: 'Oute, thou enemye of this citee and of oure goddes,
go on faste, for thi wickednesse callithe the that thou may receiue

523 susteyne] suffre E   525 this] his E   gothe] add and H2   lawes] add and H2
527 What] wherfore H2   alle] om. EH1   528 thei] he EH2, ye H1   529 hem] hym
EH1H2   529–30 the dyuinite] eny dignite at al for H2   530 neither they] they may
nothir H2   ne] no H2   532 goddes] add doo H2   we] ye H1   533 wolde] wil H2
despised] dispisable H2   534 like] add vn to H2   detestable] destable E   liff] to lyue
H2   536 of hem] om. E   537 worshippeth] worshiped E   goddes] so with g on
erasure H1   538 that] add a H2   539 lordeshippe] L, mercy EH1H2   541 will]
assent H2   542 the sentence of] om. EH1   þat] add to H1   545 as] twice H2
546 that¹] L, om. EH1H2   other] and some H2   547 beried] add al H2   549 the]
om. H2   553 sayeng] add Goo H2   this] on erasure H1, the H   554 on] oute H1

555 [wor]thy mede for thi merites.' But the blessed marter ansuered no
worde to [hem].

So moche multitude of peple come to beholde this sight that the
f. 126ᵛᵇ place, whiche was large and brode by|fore, now for thiknesse of men
semed wonder narow. And therwithe the strengthe of the sonne was
560 so gret þat withe the gret brennynge of her the erthe scalded the fete
of hem that went theron. And so they ledde hym tille atte the laste
they come to a swifte riuere, atte the whiche riuere the peple
stondinge myght not lightly passe ouer for gret pres, but as they
passinge ouer vnordinatly many one were shoft ouer and were
565 drowned pitously. Thanne many of þe peple that myght not suffre
this delayenge dede of her clothes and swomen ouer the riuere. Other
that coude not swymmen presumed to do the same and wrechidly
ended her lyues in the water, wherfor ther was gret wepinge and gret
sorugh in the peple.

570 And whanne Albone perceiued this he wayled and wepte the harme
of the peple perisshing and was gretly meued with mercye vpon the
peple. He kneled downe and lefte vp his [eyen] to heuene and dressed
his mynde to Crist and saide: 'Lorde Ihesu Crist, of whos most holy
side I behelde bothe blode and water come oute, I beseche the that this
575 water may be lassed and that the flode withdrawe so that alle this
peple mow be withe me atte my passion.' A wonder thinge, as Albon
bowed downe his knee the water was anonc dried up, the whiles Seint
Albone shed oute teres ther lefte no water in the riuere. His orison
drewe up the vertue of the riuere and shewed a way to the peple. Than
580 miracles beganne to encrese and the merites of Seint Albone were
more clerely shewed be the myght of Crist, for th[o] creatoures that a
f. 127ʳᵃ litell before were rauisshed and loste be strength | of the riuere bene
now founde in the depenesse of the riuere havinge none harme ne no
token of dethe shewed vpon hem.

585 Thanne one of the knyghtes that drowe Albone to his torment

555 worthy] thy EH1   556 hem] hym EH1   557 to] twice E   this sight] him H2
558 byfore now] but H2   560 gret] om. H1   her] 'þe' eyr on erasure H1, hete H2
564 passinge] passid H2   were²] om. H2   566 the] that H2   riuere] add and also H2
567 swymmen] s⟨...⟩om on erasure H1   570 this] add thinge H2   571 peple] peples
H2   572 peple] add than H2   eyen] hondes EH1   to] add Ihesu H2   573 Crist]
om. H2   574 side] sides H2   575 lassed] blessid H2   flode] add may be H2   alle]
om. H1   576 passion] add than anone H2   thinge] add fel H   577 the¹] om. H2
the²] om. H2   whiles] add that H2   578 teres] add so that H2   riuere] add for H2
579 vertue] add of the water EH1   579 a way] al way EH2L, alway with l del. H1 (viam
W)   Than] add the H2   580 to] add wexe and H2   581 myght] m'y'ght H1   tho]
the EH1   582 be] add the H2

deserued to come to his sauacion by Seint Albon, for whanne he
seighe these glorious miracles þat God dede for hym he threwe away
his swerde and fille downe to the grounde and saide: 'I knowlage myn
errour and aske foryeuenesse,' and with gret wepinge saide ayein: 'O
Albon, the servaunt of God, verrily thi God is almyghty God and 590
none but he, and therfor I knowlage fro hennes forwarde me to be his
servaunt, for this flode that be thi praiers be turned to not berithe
witnesse that there nis none like to hym of might and of doinge
meruayles vpon the erthe.' This herde, anone wodenesse encresed in
[the] servauntes of wickidnesse fersely turnynge to hym and saide: 'It 595
is not as thou sayest ne as thow affermest that by Albone this ryuere is
so sone vanisshed away, but we to whom the secrete thingges of
science be yeuen bi the benignite of oure goddes canne shew whi this
thinge is falle. We only worshippen oure goddes, and aboue alle
thingges we do hem gret reuerence, and they, hauynge mynde of oure 600
deuocion and for oure ease, thei haue take up the water bi the
strengthe of this gret hete so that alle this multitude al hole and
sounde mowe withe gladde eyen beholde the dethe of oure enemye.
But sothely thou that presumest þe to turne the benefices of oure
goddes to other wicked interpretacion hast deserued the payne that 605
longethe to blaspheme.' Whanne thei | [had] saide [this] thei toke the f. 127rb
knyght and drow oute his tethe, and that holy mowth that [had] bare
witnesse of the trouthe was greuously bete withe wicked men. But as
so many hondes might not suffice to peyne that one membre of the
bodye, thei went to alle the body and braste alle his bones and lefte 610
nothinge on hym vnhurte sauf only faithe, whiche was so feruent in
hys breste that they might in no wise hurte it and [so alle] his body is
al torent. Thei lefte hym halff dede vpon the sondes.

   But who might withe[oute] teres recorde hou this most holy man
was ledde thorugh harde breres and thornes and amonge the sharpe 615
stones so that the precious blode of his fete coloured þe waye that he
went inne and the stones were al blodye. Thanne atte the laste thei

   592 flode] ryuere H2   that] om. H2   thi] þe H1   be²] is H2   berithe] wherfore I ber
H2   593 and] ne H2   594 This] And whan this was H2   anone] add the H2
595 the] her EH1   wickidnesse] add encresed H1   597 we] add seie H2
598 goddes] on erasure H1   599 falle] add And H2   600 hauynge] haue H2
602 multitude al] peple H2   603 the] that H2   604 But] And H2   presumest] add
þe E   benefices] benefice H1H2   606 blaspheme] add and H2   had saide this] thus
saide E, seid þus H1   thei toke] to D   607 and¹] thei D   had] om. E   608–9 as so]
also D   609 hondes] houndes EH1   610 thei] but D   thei . . . body] ins. H1
611 on] of D   612 so alle] L, om. EH1, so D   is] was D   613 Thei] and D
614 witheoute] withe EH1   615 harde] om. D

come to the hille wher that this holy Goddes knight is for to ende the
cours of his bataile. Ther laye in that place a companie witheoute
620 nombre that with hete of the sonne were nye stuffed and dede for hete
and thruste, the whiche whanne thei seigh Albon they g[ryn]ted her
tethe vpon hym, sayeng: 'O thou most wicked man, hou thi
wickednesse is so grete þat thou makest us deye witheoute remedye,
for bi the arte magike that Albon stintithe not to werke oure dayes be
625 do and we be perisshed.' The wrechidnesse of whom Seint Albone
sorued withe gret affeccion, and withe feruent herte of charite to yeue
up praiers for his persecutours he stinted not. 'Lorde,' he saide, 'that
madest man of erthe, I beseche the suffre not thi creatoures in any
wise to perisshe in [my] cause. The eyre, blessed Lorde, make it
f. 127va tempre | and sende plente of waters, the wynde beg[y]nne to blowe
631 more fresshely, and that this thruste and hete that this peple is
laboured withe by thi mercifull yefte be sone restreyned.'
And in the mene tyme that he praied in this wise, sodenly ther
sprange up a welle atte his fete and the peple stondinge al aboute. A,
635 merueilous vertu of Crist! The erthe was gretly brent withe the sonne,
and yet fro the coppe of the hille and fro the poudry erthe a colde
welle sprang vp anone, flowinge al aboute with large stremes rennynge
doune to þe lowest partie of the hill. Than rannen the peple to the
water and dronken and were gretly refresshed, and thus bi the merites
640 of this holy man al her [thrustes] were quenched, but yet for al this
they thrested continuelly mannes blode. Thei were relesed of thruste
of the bodye, but the feruour of her cruelte was not lassed, hele was
goten to the seke, but thei wolde not knowe the auctur of helthe,
wherfor in blasphemynge Crist thei saide: 'Worshippe and preisinge
645 be to the grete god Venus that hathe vouched sauf to prouide remedye
to his servauntes that were so harde bestadde in yevinge vs plente of

619 bataile] add And also D   620 with] add þe D   621 whiche] add peple D
grynted] gneisted E, gneyssed H1   623 us] add to D   624 for] om. D   the] thyne D
that] add þu D   stintithe] styntist D   not] non H1   werke] add wherfore D   625 The
wrechidnesse of] þoru3 thi wickidnesse for D   626 herte] hete H1D
627 persecutours] add for D   not] followed by short erasure E   629 my] any EH1D
(mei W)   it] add in good D   630 waters] add Than anone D   begynne] L, beganne ED, so
subþ. H1   631 and^1] Also lorde D   thruste, hete] trs. D   and^2] add this D   633 that]
om. D   634 welle] below this next after this shuld folow þat is þe begynnyng of þe next lefe
saue oone at this sign and the text continues on f. 164ra at a similar sign with atte his fete H1
and] om. D   al aboute] aboute him D   635 vertu] add hit was D   of] add oure lorde Ihu D
Crist] add for D   639 and dronken] om. D   640 holy man] blessid Albon D   thrustes]
L, merites EH1, þurst D   were] was D   641 continuelly] add this holi D   Thei] þe H1
of] add the D   642 lassed] add Also D   643 helthe] her hele D   644 Crist] Ihu
Criste D   645 prouide] proue D   646 vs] vp D

water in oure gret nede.' This saide, anone they toke this blessed
marter and bound hym to a stake aboute, [and his hede to a bowe], and
sought amonge the peple who shulde do this dede. One was redy
anone and toke a swerde and withe gret cruelte he smote so the holy 650
marter in the necke that his hede was parted from the bodye atte one
stroke, þe body fallynge doune to the ground, the holy soule redy to
heuene. The hede hanged on the bowe by his | here that was wrapped f. 127ᵛᵇ
aboute, the crosse that he hadde in his honde al blody fille vpon the
erthe oute of his honde, the whiche one that was priuely cristen, 655
vnwetinge [to] the panymes, toke and hidde it. And as the tormentour
that slowe hym hadde smite that stroke, bothe his eyen sterte oute of
his hede. But this wreche might in no wise be restored to his helthe,
wherfor many of þe paynimes sputinge togedre saide that this
vengeaunce come of gret rightwisnesse. 660
Whanne this was done, sodenly that knight that was lefte halff dede
a litell before in the sondes bynethe and forsaken of the paynymes as
for dede, enforsinge hymselff as he myght he crepte vp on his hondes
to the crosse of the hill wher Seint Albone was beheded. Thanne the
iuge seigh hym and beganne to scorne the miracles that were do there 665
by Seint Albone, and saide: 'O thou lame and croked, now praie thin
Albone that he restore the to thin furst helthe. Renne and hye the
faste, leue the bodye and take the hede that thou maist be hym receiue
hele. Wherto tariest thou? Go bery the dede and do hym seruise.'
Thanne he, sette all afere withe charitee, saide: 'I beleue stedfastely 670
that the blessed Albone bi his merites may gete me perfite hele, and he
may bringge oure saueoure to suche mercy that it may lyghtly be
fulfellyd in me that ye saye now in scorne.' And whanne he hadde
saide this the holy [man] byclipped the hede [of the holy marter] and
reuerently vnlosed that holy relique. Than that feble knyght brought 675
it to the body and sette it therto withe his hondes, and thanne anone

647 This] And whan this was D   anone/they toke] *trs.* D   648 and² . . . bowe] L,
om. EH1, and sith hynge him vppon a bowe bi his heer of his hede D   649 this] the D
dede] *add* Than D   653 hanged] hanging H1   654 that] the whiche D   655 the
whiche] And D   priuely] privey D   656 to] *om.* EH1   it] þat crosse D   as] also D
tormentour] *add* þe whiche D   658 helthe] siȝte aȝen D   661 Whanne] Than whan
D   that¹] the D   662 a . . . before/in . . . sondes] *trs.* D   in] vppon D   bynethe] *add*
in the valey D   forsaken] was forsake D   663 he²] *om.* D   vp on] on D
664 crosse] coppe H1, toppe D   665 iuge] iuges E   seigh] seynge D   and] *om.* D
beganne] *add* for D   the] him and the D   667 hye] hyre D   668 receiue] *add*
thyne D   669 thou] *add* so D   Go] *add* and D   670 he] þis knyȝte D
671 perfite] parfiȝtli D   674 man] marter EH1   of the holy marter] *om.* EH1
675 vnlosed] vnclosed E, vnsesid H1   676 it¹] the heed D

ther fille a gret meruaile, for this knight beganne to recouer al his
myghtes and was restored to his furst hele, the whiche a|none stinte
not to preche to alle the peple the might of oure Lorde Ihesu Crist and
680 the merites of Seint Albone, and thanne he was more strengger to
laboure withe his owne handes.

He yelded due seruise to the holy seint. He beried the body in the
erthe and leyde a tombe ouer hym. And whanne the paynimes seigh
what he dede thei were fulfelled withe zele and spoken togederes and
685 saide: 'What shul we do? This man may not be slayne withe none iren.
We hadde al tobrost his bones and he is restored to hys furste
strengthe and his flesshe is [as] hole and as fayre as euer it was.
What shull we more do to hym? Ordeyne we a counsaile what we
aught do.' Thanne one of hem stode vp amonges hem and saide: 'This
690 man,' quod he, 'ther may no suerde slee hym but yef he were
dismembred [before] membre fro membre, for he is an enchauntour
and bi his art magike ther may none iren noye hym.' The whiche
thingge herde, anone the knyght was comaunded to be take and
bounden withe iren cheynes, and thanne his body was al torent and
695 atte the laste they smote of his hede. And so this blessed knyght,
perseueringe in the faithe of Crist vnto the ende, deserued to be lefte
vp bi croune of marterdome that same day only withe most blessed
Seint Albone, and he that was made felawe of passiones lefte not the
felawship of consolaciones. Whanne this marterdome was fulfelled the
700 iuge gaue lycence to alle the peple for to go home ayein, and as the
peple went they despised and lothed the cruelte of the iuge and
sayden: 'Woo to that iuge in whom is none equite, and wo to that iuge
in whos dome wodenesse hathe lordeshipp and not | rightwisnesse and
that endithe his sentence only bi will witheoute reson.'
705 The night foluynge oure Lorde Ihesu Criste hathe declared by
euident tokenis the merites of his servaunte Seint Albon. For whanne
night come ther was sene a clere beme come fro heuene strechinge

678 restored] *add* aȝen D   679 not] *add* for D   and] *add* of D   682 He yelded]
to ȝelde D   the¹] þat H1D   seint] martir D   He²] and D   the body] *twice* H1
683 And] *om.* H1   684 zele] stele H1   685 iren] *add* for D   686 restored] *add*
aȝen D   687 as¹] L, alle EH1D   was] *add* bifore D   689 aught] *add* to D
691 before] *om.* E   fro] for D   692–3 The . . . herde] and than D   693 herde
anone] *trs.* H1   694 thanne] after D   696 of Crist] *om.* D   the²] his laste D
697 most blessed] *om.* D   699 consolaciones] *add* and D   700 alle] *om.* D   go/
home ayein] *trs.* D   701 went] *add* homward H1   and¹] *add* gretly H1   the¹] *add* iuge
and the D   the iuge] hym D   703 and²] *add* he D   704 witheoute] and not by D
reson] *add* Than D   705 The] *add* next H1   Criste] *om.* H1   706 servaunte]
servauntes EH1   whanne] *add* the D   707 come] *om.* D   fro] *twice* E

right downe vpon the sepulcre of Seint Albone, and aungels alle the
night descendinge and goinge vp ayein with ympnes and praisingges
driving forthe that nyght, and amonge other songges that thei songge 710
this voys was most continuelly herde: 'Albon the glorious man is a
noble marter.' And as the concours of peple come to þis spectacle
more and more the nomb[re] encresed of the biholders, the which
peple stondinge and wonderinge were troubled withe vncustumable
light, and the nouelte of this thinge they turned into a myracle. 715
Thanne one of hem whiche seigh the peple stonde so astonyed and
afrayed saide: 'This mervayle that we beholde is openli wrought be
Crist the sone of God, and the fals goddes that we haue worshipped
vnto this tyme be rather proued fendes thanne havynge any godhede
withe hem. Oure werkes haue be vnprofitable werkes and oure dayes 720
haue [flow]ed oute in idelnesse. Lo, the derkenesse of the nyght is
couered with the lyght of heuene, and the citezenis of heuene gone
and comen continuelly praisinge the holynesse of Seint Albone.
Allas,' he saide, 'the worlde is all now [wrapped] in derkenesse, but
the clerenesse of Albone sufferithe no derkenesse, for his merites 725
mowe not be derked. [Therfore] we [that] haue vsed an vnprofitable
religion vnto this tyme, late vs now dampne the olde errour and turne
we fro | falsenesse to trouthe and fro a fals faithe to a true faithe, and f. 128ᵛᵃ
go we seke that blessed man of God the whiche conuerted Albone [as
ye knowe] bi his predicacion. Hou trewe it is that he spe[k]ith of Crist 730
ye mow opinly see bi these mervayles that bene shewed by Albone, for
the werkes that bene done bi the disciple witheouten fayle bere
witnesse of the wordes of the maister.'
    And as this man hadde spoke these wordes all tho that herde hym
receiued his praisable sentence withe fauour, and anone thei forsoke 735
her furst errour and the faithe of Crist is preched of alle. And as sone
as they myght they dressed her waye towarde Walys, where they
hoped to fynde Amphiball the servaunt of God. And thei were not
deceyued of her opinion, for witheinne a while after, thei hadde
knowlage wher he was by the fame of his holinesse, and whanne they 740
come into Walys they founde hym prechinge the worde of God to alle
þe men of that region. And whanne thei hadde tolde hym the cause of

708 the¹ . . . Albone] his sepulcre D   710 forthe] add all H₁   that¹] al D   amonge]
add alle D   713 nombre] nombes E   714 withe] add þe G   716 and] add so E
719 tyme] add thei H₁   721 flowed] L, folued EH₁G   724 wrapped] dropped E
726 Therfore] om. E   that] om. E   728 a¹] all H₁   729–30 as ye knowe] om. E
730 spekith] spellith EH₁   739 of] for H₁   740 knowlage] add aftir G

her comynge they offered to hym the crosse that he hadde sumtyme
taken to Albone, whiche was al rede of fressh blode that was shedde
745 vpon hym of the marter, whiche was an euident token to Amphiball of
his marterdom. Thanne anone this holy man, yeuyng souereigne
thankingges to God for alle these thingges, bowed hym adowne and
worshipped the crosse withe dieu reuerence and deuocion, and thanne
he made a solempne sermon to these nwe herers. Thanne anone all
750 they consented to the faithe, casting away the super[sticion] of her
f. 128vb vanite, and receyued gladly of his holy hondes the sacre|ment of
bapteme.

And as many dayes passed, the fame of this dede is talked of in al
that region, the whiche by processe of tyme came atte the laste worde
755 hereof to the citee of Verolamye, affermynge that diuerse men of that
citee haue folwed a straunge man and by hys steringe they haue withe
alle her hertes caste awaye the worship of her goddes and the lawes of
her contree, whiche thinge herd, alle the citee was meued and
troubled. Thanne they sought who went and thei founde that ther
760 lacked a .M¹. men of the citee, whos names were anone wretin.
Thanne þei arrayed hem for the werre and with gret noise they go to
batayle warde. Heringe thanne the holy name of Amphiball, witheinne fewe dayes they come where he was and hem that they sought
[they] founde aboute hym intendynge to his sermones, the whiche
765 sayne, anone one of hem withe gret cruelte hathe aresoned þat holy
man and saide: 'O thou deceiuour and most wicked of alle men, whi
hast thou thus withe thi begylinge wordes deseyue[d] this vnwyse
peple that coude not be ware of thi wyles? What haste thou do? Thy
stering hathe made hem to forsake her lawes and presumed hem to
770 forsake her goddes. How is [it] that thou dredest not to wrethe oure
goddes? Thou shalt in no wyse fele ease therby, for yef hem luste to
revenge the iniurie that ye haue do to hem, wetithe it well that ye shull
all perisshe. But yef thou wilt apere vngilty withe these that thou haste
brought in bondes of thine errour, comaunde hem that they departe
775 from her nwe errour and turne ayein withe vs into oure contre. And
f. 129ra yef so be that they | be so presumptuouse in [her] errour that they will
not consent to turne ayein, there shalle not one leue on lyue of hem,
but they shull be slayne. This sentence shall stonde.'

743 they] and H₁G   747 thankingges] þankis G   750 supersticion]
superfeccion EH₁   755 to] ins. H₁   759 ther] thei H₁   764 they] and E
766 most] om. G   767 deseyued] L, deseyuest EH₁, disseyuyth G   770 her] her
del. with oure ins. G   it] om. E   772 it] om. G   773 But] add ʒit G   776 her]
that E

Thanne one of the cristen that was all sette afere withe the hete of
faithe ansuered for the clerke, sayenge: 'This man that [ye] behold- 780
ithe, perauenture this same day ye shull preue that he is a verray
servaunt of God, for we truste that in [youre] sight he shall restore
sum sike man to his furst hele by the name of Crist. And wete it well
that we be come to his holynesse and alle that longithe to the faithe of
Crist is fulfelled in vs, hopinge that he shalle make vs partiners of 785
euerlastynge liff. God defende that euer that wickednesse be founde in
vs that we forsake the steppes of this holy man and folowe you ayein in
youre veyn super[sticions]. But we will counsayle you to take the
faithe of Crist, prouoked bi oure ensaumple, and leue youre striff that
ye may come withe vs to endeles ioye, for as touchinge vs we be all 790
redy for the loue of Crist gladly to suffre dethe. God and oure Lorde
ordeyne for his servauntes as hym luste. Wherto enforce ye you to
reuoke us [fro] a good and a profitable purpos? Wetithe wel that [that]
we left onys for Crist we shul neuer turne ayein therto, and therfor
this sentence shall holde.' Whanne the paynymes herde this, thanne 795
anone þei were sette all afire withe anger and ronnen to armes and
shedden the blode of the innocentis. Allas, what pitee it was to see hou
cruelly the wicked mynistres demened hem, for the fader spared not
to slee the sone, the brother his brother, the sone the fader. Ther was
no reuerence | yeu[en] to age ne mercy to kinrede. Sothely the holy f. 129rb
marteres obeyed hem frely and gladly to the cruelte of þe swerdes of 801
[the] tyrauntes.

Seint Amphiball all beclipped withe dede bodyes on eueri syde
recomaunded the soules to God withe speciall ioie of her victorie. And
thanne these wicked mansleers turned al her wrethe vpon Amphiball 805
and sworen that they shulde neuer ete vnto the tyme that they hadde
brought hym quik or dede to her citee. Thei bounden his hondes
togedre with harde cordes and droue hym forthe before her hors, for
they were all on her hye horses but only Amphiball went barefote. But
the nere that he neighed Albon, the more esely he felt his iniurie and 810
his laboure in þe waye. And as they laboured in her waye, thei founde
a seke man whiche was come fro Verolamye touarde Amphiball. By
fortune he fell so seke by the waye that he myght no further withe his
felawshipp, and as the sike man perceiued that Amphiball passed by

780 ye¹] the EH1   782 youre] L, oure EH1G   788 supersticions] superficience
EH1   791 and] erased H1   793 fro] L, to EG, to changed to fro ʿaʾ H1   Wetithe]
with G   that²] L, om. EH1G   794 shul] shulde E   800 yeuen] yeuinge EH1
802 the] thi EH1   808 hors] horsis G   810 and] add in EH1

815 hym he beganne to calle and saye: 'Seruaunt of þe hye God, helpe me,
that I whiche am depressed withe gret siknesse may be releued be thi
praiers, for I beleue that yef thou wilt name ouer me the name of Crist
that thou maiste lyghtly get me hele.' These turmentours not movinge
bere the inportunite of this clamour laughed hym to scorne, but
820 witheoute any tarienge vnder her scornefull yen the syk man arose and
by vertue of hym that was streitely bounde his sore bondes of siknesse
were losed, and this done thei went forthe in her waye. But that
f. 129ᵛᵃ miracle done myght be no[t] co[nseled], but anone | it was spredde
abrode [bi] alle that region. Also the same turmentours toke hede
825 therof so ferforthely that sum of hem glorified God, sayenge: 'A, hou
the God of cristen men is gret and myghti and full of vertue.'

Thanne atte laste thei come to the soile of her birthe so nye that thei
might se her citee, and they were nye ouercome withe [hunger] and
laboure. They rested a while and refresshed hem and sette her speres
830 and her suerdes by hem and dede of her sheldes, and whiles alle other
rested only Amphiball streitely bounde hadde no reste. And though
he were harde constreined with bondes, yet he stinte not to preche the
worde of God to his persecutoures, for the worde of God might not be
bounde. In this mene tyme tydingges come to the citee that the
835 citesenes of that citee were turned ayen and the maister of Albone
withe hem for to do solempne and acceptable sacrifice to the goddes.
And whanne this was herde gret ioie and gladnesse was thorugh the
citee, for they trowed that they hadde brought withe hem tho that
[they] went after.

840 But whiles this gret ioie was amonge hem sodenly there come to the
citee [on] of the turmentours and saide: 'Alle oure laboure is loste, for
tho that we hoped to haue brought ayein bene alle [perished] withe
suerdes.' And whan they herde this, all her ioye and gladnesse was
turned into sorugh and wepinge, the fader for the sone, the brother
845 for [his] brother, cosin for cosin, neighebour for neighebour. They
rent her clothes and thorugh the citee was clamour and sorugh, here
wepinge, there waylinge, and sayenge amonge: 'Woo to vs. Whi
f. 129ᵛᵇ comen these sorwes vpon vs? Vndedly God, | we praie the yf euer we

815 to] *ins.* H₁   817 that] *om.* H₁   822 were] *add* so H₁G   823 be not
conseled] be no counsaile EH₁GL (*celari non potuit* W)   824 bi] *om.* EA₁, 'bi' H₁
region] *add* and G   828 hunger] anger EH₁   829 and²] *om.* G   836 withe hem/
for to ... sacrifice] *trs.* G   838 trowed] *so with* row *on erasure* H₁   839 they] *om.* E
840 come] *add* 'in' H₁   841 on] *om.* EGL, *ins.* H₁ (*quidam* W)   842 perished]
opressid E   843 suerdes] swerde H₁G   845 his] the EH₁   847 there] here H₁
and] *om.* G

dede the seruise, distroie this man and reuenge oure sorwes and oure
iniuries in hym.' Whanne these tormentours perceiued the vntoller- 850
able sorugh that the peple made, [thei] went amonge hem and saide:
'O ye citesenes, wepithe not thus ouer mesure, restreine youre teres,
receiuethe comfort that ye be not seen to haue enuye of the ioye of
youre children. It is no nede for to make ouer gret sorugh vpon the
dede, whos deth is lyff and of whom ioye foluithe þe sorwe. We knowe 855
well that ther nys no sorwe gretter thanne the departinge of frendes by
dethe and namely among us wher no hope of comfort comithe after,
but [these] that be thus passed be rather for to make ioye for hem than
for to sorugh for hem, the whiche blessidly regnen withe Crist. Ne we
shulde in no wise make sorugh but gretly yeue thankingges to Crist 860
that vouche[d] sauf of his especial grace to take so gret a multitude of
this toune and lede hem with hym to his blisse. Herithe furste what
was done aboute [the] dede and ye shull knowe that youre wepinge is
in veyne.'

And they suore thanne that thei wolde in no wise medle her tale 865
with any falsenesse, and thanne they beganne her tale in this wise: 'We
went oute as ye knowe to seke oure kynne and oure frendes into
Walys, wher we founde this clerke prechinge and exortinge the
Walshemen and the Pictys, and oure citezenis we founde alle
amonge hem. And thanne we withoute any noise disseuered oure 870
frendes from other, desiringe to bringe hem with vs home ayein by
monicions, bi prayers, by thretingges and bi all that we coude
thenkke. But so gret sadnesse was in hem that it was in no mannes |
pouer to disseuer hem fro that man one hole oure, and we, seinge that, f. 130ra
in gret anger ronne to armes and revenged the iniurie of oure 875
contemptes in slaughter of hem of oure citee. And verrely eche of
hem striued with other who myght sonnest come vnder the swerde,
and withe gret gladnesse they toke her dethe for Crist, and it was a
piteous sight to see how the fader slowe the sone, ther was no merci ne
no reuerence was yeue to age. Allas, for sorugh we mowe not reherce 880
this witheoute gret waylinge and sorugh.

Whanne all this wofull iorney was done, lo, that Ihesu for whom
thei hadde geue her lyues behelde fro heuene and saide withe a clere

851 thei] he EH1GL (*inquiunt* W)   854 vpon] *add* hem G   858 these] *om.* EH1
861 vouched sauf] vouches sauf EG, vouchesaueþe H1   863 the] this EH1
868 we] we *with* w *on erasure* H1   868–70 exortinge . . . thanne] *om.* H1
871–4 desiringe . . . oure] *om.* H1   872 prayers] *add* and G   873 in no] not in G
877 striued] sty *subp.* stryuyd G   881 this] *add* deth H1   witheoute] *so with* te *on
erasure* H1

voys: "Comithe to me, my knyghtes, for the gate of heuene is open to
885 you, that blisse that neuer shall lesse is ordeined to you and the ioie
that neuer shall faile is redy to you," the which thinge herde of vs we
were fulfilled withe more ioie thanne any man may thenke, vnderstondinge that oure frendes and oure kynne wenten fro deth to heuene
and duellen withe Crist. And vs thought that we were blessed that we
890 hadde suche kinrede that were citezenis withe aungels and þat Crist
luste to come and mete withe hem. But notwithestondinge oure ioye
we were gretly troubeled and aferde with this devine heringe.
[Thanne] we desired to knowe how many hadde falle by þat slaughter,
and we acounted the dede bodies and founde .ixC. and .xxx.^{ti}, and all
895 suffered dethe for the loue of Crist, and there the bodyes laye all trode
with hors fete [that] we might not knowe one from another. But
whiles þis holy man offered vp hys praiers to God for grace to this
f. 130rb nede, sodenly all the woundes of the dede bodies were | woxen hole
and her blode is turned into liknesse of melke and her flesshe is turned
900 ayein to her furste fourme so ferforthe that no token of woundes was
sene in hem. This is the trouthe that [þe] knowlage of the fourme of
man whiche we hadde take awaye be oure cruelte was [resto]red ayein
by the praier of the rightwys man.'
      Thanne the peple, turninge the benefice of Crist to the worse parte,
905 ayeinsaide the vertues of Crist in alle thinge and denyed the bodies
her sepulture in alle wise. But the grace of oure Lorde was nye,
whiche wolde glorifie his servauntes after her deth and yelde her
enemyes more mercifull to hem. He sent sodenly an egle and a wolff to
kepe the dede bodyes, the wolff [for] to kepe hem fro wilde bestes and
910 the egle fro alle maner foules of raueyn, and whanne this was sayne the
peple perceiued anone þat thei were sent for her kepinge. And thanne
was there a gret mervaile. The Walshemen wondred, þe Pictes were
aferde, the wodenesse of man cesed ayeinst hem that the devine power
defended. Thanne shuld ye see of alle parties the peple with gret
915 concours comynge aboute hem and withe gret reuerence beclippinge
the reliques of the ma[rte]res, and tho that they hadde a litell before in
gret scorne and despite, now thei were gladde to yeue hem due seruise
in her berienge, and gauen souerayne thankingges to the high God

      893 Thanne] L, That EGH1   slaughter] slaundre H1   896 that] and EA1, and
changed to þat H1   899 of] to H1   901 þe] ye E, ye *changed to* we H1
902 restored] stered E, 're'stored H1   905 Crist] *add* to þe worse parte þe vertuose of
crist *del.* H1   bodies] *add* of E   909 for] *om.* EG   910 whanne] 'wan' H1
911 for] fro G   913 the^1] þe *on erasure* H1   916 marteres] L, maistres EH1G
917 seruise] *changed to* seruice H1

that wolde vouchesauf to halow the region with the blood of so many
worthi men. Alle this multitude that went oute togedre haue sene and 920
herde alle that we haue tolde and of alle these thingges we be verrey
witnesse. Whanne these turmentours hadd | saide that thei wolde of f. 130ᵛᵃ
these mervailes, the peple beganne to stinte of wepinge and lesse her
sorugh, and many that herden it preised the might of Criste, and of
her frendes ioie thei ioyeden and saide: 'The God of cristen men is 925
gret and myghti that yeldith his servauntes so glorious yeftes. A
sinfull man myght not hele the woundes of dede bodyes. Soþely he is
a good leche that so sodenly canne calle ayein the furst hele to his
servauntes woundes. Of this it may lightly be gadered hou grete the
merites of this clerke is afore God and hou good it is to beclippe his 930
sermones that bi his only praiers might gete all tho thingges that we
haue herde of you.'

Thanne the iuge heringe these wordes, for to please the paynimes
breke oute in a wode maner, sayenge these wordes: 'Hou longe shull
we suffre this disclaundre? This man may not be of God, that bi his 935
wordes hathe slayne so many innocentes. This clerke canne deceyue
withe his wordes the eyen of hem that beholde hym, and that that is
fals he makithe hem deme that it is true. Be his deceyuinge wordes the
worthiest of oure citee be perisshed, and therfor we comaunde that
whosoeuer folue this man or magnifie the wordes of these bochers, 940
whereuer thei be founde, that thei be punisshed withe suerde.' Than
he sent for all the peple and saide to hem: 'Go we oute ayeinst oure
enemye and that [he] may knowe that he hathe offended vs alle, and
we shull shewe oure vengeaunce vpon hym.' And this saide, al the
peple ranne and toke in her hondes what they founde of wepen and 945
thei cried eche to other: 'Go to faste.' | And so thei drewe oute of the f. 130ᵛᵇ
citee touarde the northe. The peple that went oute of the citee was so
gret a multitude that thei might not be nombered, and so thei lefte her
citee al voyde.

In this mene tyme one of hem thought that they taried to longe. He 950
toke a by pathe and longe or his felawes come he was wher this holy
man stode [harde] bounde. Than anone cruelly he dispoiled hym and
opened his nauel and drowe oute a bowel and stiked a stake faste in the
erthe and tied the bowel therto and withe scourges droue this holy

919 the¹] her G   921 of] in G   922 saide] *add* all H1G   923 of] her G
924 preised] prei`s′ed H1   the] þei *changed to* þe H1   926 gret] *add* ne *subp.* G
929 it] If I H1   936 clerke] werke *changed to* clerke H1   943 enemye] enemyis G
he¹] we EH1   946 to] go *changed to* to H1   948 nombered] remembred H1   so] *ins.*
above deletion H1   952 harde] faste E   953 stake] staff *changed to* stake H1

955 man aboute the stake. And as this holy marter amonge al these
turmentes by þe yefte of God gaue no token of sorugh ne disese, the
turmentours, seinge this, more and more sette afere withe wodenesse
they ronnen on hym withe suerdes and speres and compelled hym
continuelly to renne aboute tille alle [his] bowels henge vpon the
960 stake. This holy man stode stably withe a gladde visage as thow he
hadde suffered none harme, and the token of his marterdom he
shewed in al his body, for he was a mervaile to alle the peple
wonderinge that amonge so many diuerse tormentes þat he myght
lyue, wherfor many of þe peple bi the touchinge of grace weren
965 compuncte and forsoke her idoles and obeied hem to cristen faithe,
praieng the marter that by his holy praiers thei might deserue to be
partiners of that endeles blisse that God hath ordeyned for hym, for
getinge of whiche blisse thei dredde not to forsake her bodely lyff.

Whanne the princes knewe this, anone thei called turmentours and
970 comaunded hem to sle alle tho that hadde forsake the worshippe of
f. 131ʳᵃ her goddes and folowed | the techinge of the clerke. They anone
fulfelled this comaundement and haue slayne of that felawship a .Ml.
men, the whiche slaughter blessed Amphiball behelde and withe gret
ioye recomaunded her soules to God. Thanne one that was bolder
975 thanne another spake to this holy man and saide: 'O thou most wicked
of alle men, whi haste thou with thi begylinge wordes deceiued this
symple and vnwise peple? What hath oure cite offended the that thou
so cruelly dispoiled the peple? Thou art cause of the dethe of this
peple, wherfor thou stondest as thou seest alle forwounded and art
980 besette with thine enemyes rounde aboute that thou maist in no wise
fle, and yet, though thou haue prou[ok]ed bothe God and man to
wrethe aboue al mesure, thou maist deserue her grace bi sorowe and
forthenkinge. And this shalle be the shewinge of thi penaunce, that
thou forsake thi secte and worship oure goddes that thou haste
985 offended, and be not sori for that is done, for oure goddes mowe
restore the to thi furste hele and make alle thi woundes full hole of thi
bodie.'

Thanne saide Seint Amphiball: 'O thou paynime, wete it welle that
thou offendest gretly in that thou enforsest the to lefte vp thi goddes

958 suerdes, speres] *trs.* G   959 tille] to H1   his] the EH1   960 stode] toke *del with* stode *ins.* G   965 to] *add* þe H1   966 his] *on erasure* H1   972 that] *so on erasure* H1   973 slaughter] sclachter *on erasure* H1, *add* the D   974 bolder] helder *with* h *erased* H1   979 thou stondest] *twice* E   980 with thine] withinne *changed to* with þine H1   981 prouoked] proued EH1   984 thi] this E, þe H1 986–7 woundes . . . bodie] wofull body hole G

by fals preisinge. Only my Lorde Ihesu Crist areisithe the dede and 990
yeuithe [hem] lyff, and sothely [tho] goddes that ye worshippe and
deme hem mighti in heuene sufferen full migthi tormentis in helle, for
there is þe mynde [and] euerlastinge duellynge places of hem, for ther
is wepinge and g[ryn]tinge of tethe, ther be the wormes that shall
neuer deye and the fere that neuer shall quenche. The | vnrightwisse f. 131ʳᵇ
men, the auoutreres, þe cursed, shull be made her felawes and 996
partiners withe hem in turment, and alle other whiche while they
lyued here yalde hemselff to the fende by reprouable werkes, the wille
of whom they folwed bi acorde of vices, thei shull not faile her
felawship in sufferinge of turmentis. Therfor, thou paynime, withe 1000
other that bene here [of] fals worshipers of ydoles, but yef ye forsake
the sonner [the] errour of youre fals secte and thenkithe that the merci
of God is grete, and despeire you not and be conuerted to the faithe of
Crist leste ye falle in alle these sorwes, thanne arisethe fro youre
wikked wayes and comithe to the grace of bapteme. Rennithe withe 1005
most haste, for what bapteme yeuithe take hede diligently. In
receiuynge of the sacrement of bapteme synnes be fo[r]yeue and
heuene is opened to man and it makithe in maner a nwe creature, and
tho that were furst by her gilte the sonis of the fende be made after
that by grace the sonis of God. To this grace I counsaile you to flee in 1010
haste that ye mowe eschewe the euerlastinge peyne.'
   Whanne they herde this thei ronnen anone on hym and withe her
cruel hondes thei stoned hym. The wicked were feruent in the dethe
of the innocent and laboured withe all her myghtes to putte oute his
blessed sperit, but though this glorious marter were greuously smiten 1015
withe [harde] stonis in eueri syde, yet he abode continuelly in his
praiers sadly withoute mevinge in any parte or bowinge asyde. Atte
the laste whanne his holy sperit shulde be yolde to God, | he lefte up f. 131ᵛᵃ
his eyen and seigh oure Lorde Ihesu Crist stonde in the right side of
his fader and he herde the songe of aungels in heuene, and amonge 1020
hem he knewe his Seint Albone, the which he called vnto his helpe
and saide: 'O holi Seint Albon, I beseche the that thou praie to oure
Lorde for me, that he sende me his good aungell to lede me suerly that
I be not lette in my waye be that cursed enemie the fende.' Vnnethis

991 hem] L, hym EH₁G   tho] the E   ye] ʒe *on erasure* H₁   992 sufferen] *add* a
litill *del.* G   993 and] of EH₁   994 gryntinge] gnaistinge EH₁   996 þe] þei H₁
1001 of¹] withe EH₁   1002 the¹] youre EH₁   1007 foryeue] foyeue E
1008 heuene] *above erasure* H₁   it] *om.* G   1015 though] þouʒt H₁   1016 harde]
hande E, *so changed to* harde H₁   1021 his¹] *om.* H₁   Albone] *add* in G   1024 be²]
but G

1025 he hadde ended this worde but sodenly ther come to hym fro heuene
two bright shininge aungels and sayd to hym withe heuenly vois: 'We
saye to the truly that this [day] thou shalt be withe Albon in paradys.'
Whanne the paynimes herde this heuenly voys [thei] stode al
abaisshed. Thanne these aungels toke this blessed soule and withe
1030 songes and preisingges they bere it up to heuene.

But the soules of men stered to wikkednesse cesed not yet to thrawe
stones atte the body witheoute soule. Thei might yeue none helpe to
the dede ne deliuer hym fro the [h]ondes of cruelte. Her dukes and
her erles weren nigh ouercome withe fastinge and laboure. Thanne
1035 rose there a grete debate and striff amonge þe paynimes and eueri
faught withe other ouer that holy bodi. But almighti God wolde not
suffre the enemyes of trouthe to be sothesaiers in that thei hadde
sworn that thei wolde bringe the blessed marter to her citee quik or
dede, for a cristin man stale priuely the body of the marter and hidde
1040 it vnder þe erthe, and whanne God wille, as we truste, that blessed
tresour shall be shewed forthe. Whanne alle this was done the
f. 131ᵛᵇ vengeaunce of oure Lorde beganne to be shewed up|on the peple,
for her visages begonne to be disfigured, her handes, her armes and all
her membres dried vp, and mani other diuerse turmentis they
1045 suffered. The iuge hathe loste his reson and vnderstondinge and is
woxse madde. There nys none that might reioyse hem of the dispite
that thei hadde do to God and to Seint Amphiball, for he that will
lefte vp his honde ayeinst God is worthi to resseiue vengeaunce for his
merites of the rightfull iuge.

L f. 154ᵛᵇ   This thinge [doone] might not longe be | [hidde] ne helyd, for as
1051 soone as thys rumour was goone abrode alle that cyte hadde resseyved
crysten feythe and preysed owre lorde in hys ryghtwysse domes, and
many were steryd by devyne grace, lefte alle that they hadde and
wente to Rome for to wayle theyre defautes. And soo fro that day
1055 forwarde alle the pepull of that cyte knewen welle that they hadde
worschypped veyne and false goddys, and nowe with all theyre
studyes and wyttes they study to loue and worschyp Crist the
E f. 131ᵛᵇ sonne of God. Thys] | and many other thingges that the goodnesse
of oure Lorde wolde not shuld be hidde, I haue diligentely putte it in
1060 writinge.

1027 day] night EH1   1028 thei] the E   1029 this] his H1   1032 atte] to G
1033 hondes] bondes E   1036 other] add euery del. followed by day þ subp. G
1038 the] this G   her] þe G   1039–40 hidde it] hiddid H1, it is G   1045 and¹] in
G   1046 nys] is H1, was G   1050 doone] L, om. EH1G   1050–8 hidde . . .
Thys] L, om. EH1G

Blessed be God, alle [that] vntrewe felawship be gone that gaue
sentence in the dethe of Albone, but the mynde of Seint Albon
abidethe endelesly. The tyme shall come, we truste, that religious
men shall come and preche the faithe of Criste amonge the panymes
in Bretaigne. Thanne, the trouthe knowen, that ile shall reioyse and 1065
the bondes of the errour of paynimes shull be vnbounde and thei shull
be fulfelled with multeplyenge ioye. But this saide tyme of grace of
visitacion that is to come, for I am not sure whanne it comithe, I loke
not after that gretnesse of ioie. But yef any desire to knowe my name,
wete they wele that yef they will call me a true man and a true name 1070
thei moste call me most wreched and most sinfull. To Rome I went to
putte fro me þe errour of paynimes, and ther I resseiued bapteme and
for to haue remission of my synnes. This boke I brought in my hondes
to be examined of þe Romaynes, that yef it were not as it shulde be,
thei to correcte it into beter. Be oure Lorde Ihesu Crist that liueth | 1075
and regnithe worlde witheoute ende, Amen.   f. 132ra

Here endithe the liff of Seint Albon and of worthi Amphiball, and nexst foluithe the natiuite of Seint Iohn the
Baptiste, Capitulum .lxxx.

The natiuite of Seint Iohan the Baptist [was] denounsed of the aungell
Gabriel in this wise. The kinge Dauid, as it is redde in the Maister of
Stories, wolde encrese the worship of God and ordeyned .xxiiij.
souerein prestes, of which alwayes one is the grettest and is called the
prince of prestes. So than he ordeyned .xvj. of the kinrede of Eleazar 5
and [eight] of the kinrede of Itamar, and after the sorte he gaue to
eueri to do his woke in þe Temple so that Abias hadde the .viij. woke.
Zakarias was of the kynrede of hym, and Zakarie and his wyff were
olde and witheoute children. As Zakarie entred into the Temple of
oure Lorde for to yeue encence, the aungel Gabriel appered to hym 10
and saide: 'Drede the not, Zakarie, for thou haste founde grace before
oure Lorde, for thou shalt haue a sone whos name shalle be Iohn, and
he shall be halowed witheinne the wombe of his moder. Wyne ne

1061 that¹] L, om. EH1G   1066 and] al H1   1068 sure] suffre H1
1074 not] it H1   1076 worlde] twice E

EH1T1GDH2A1A2L; D breaks off after 20 whanne that; T1 has corner torn off affecting
from 49 satte to 56 erthe and from 74 Nazarethe to 83 to hem, 158 ayein to 167 tell you in, 178
and lepte to 192 wey, 217 proue to 244 prosperite   Rubric .lxxx.] .lxxix. E   1 was] om. E,
ins. H1   6 eight] Eilche EG, erasure H1   of the] add good EH1   9 As] And G

syder shall he none drinke, and he shall come before oure Lorde in the
15 sperit and in the vertue of Ely.' Zakarie than heringe this, considered
the age of his wiff, [and] how she was bareyn, and dradde hym sore of
this promys and beganne to aske a signe in the maner of Iwes. Thanne
saide the aungell to Zakarie: 'In as moche as thou levest not the promis
of oure Lorde witheoute a sygne, oure Lorde will that thou be domme
f. 132ʳᵇ till the tyme come that the childe shall be bore.' And | whanne that
21 Zakarie come oute to the peple and thei seen that he might not speke,
thei knewe be tokenes þat he shewed hem that he hadde sene a vision
in the Temple.

And whanne the woke of his office was fulfelled he went to his hous
25 and Elizabeth conceiued and hidde her .v. monthes for, as Seint
Ambrose saiethe in that place, she was ashamed that she shuld geue
her consent in that age to conceiue a childe, and yet in that other syde
she hadde gret ioye to forgo the name of a barein woman, for in that
tyme it was the grettest repref that might falle to a woman for to be
30 barein. Thanne in the .vj. monthe the blessed Virgine Marie, that
hadde tho conceiued oure Lord Ihesu Crist, ioyed gretly that her
cosin was withe childe. Withe gret haste she went to her into the
mountaine and entered into the hous of Zakarie and grette her cosin
mekely and said: 'Worship and thanke be to oure most souerayne
35 Lorde that hathe do his gret mercye to you, my dere cosin.' And
anone as Elizabeth herde the salutacion of Marie, the childe in her
wombe beganne to make ioye, and Elizabeth anone was fulfelled withe
the holy goste and braste oute withe an high voys and saide: 'Blessed
be thou aboue alle women and the fruit of thi wombe. How and in
40 what manere is it that my Lordes moder is come to me? For as sone as
thi worde entered into myn ere the childe reioysed in my wombe.
Blessed art thou that hast lyued, wherfor it is perfitely fulfelled in the
that was sayd to the of oure Lorde.' Than saide oure blessed Lady:
'My soule magnifiethe God and my sperit hath ioied in God my
45 saueoure.'
f. 132ᵛᵃ   Than | Elizabeth toke oure blessed Lady and sette hem downe and
asked of her the maner of her conceyuinge, and she mekely tolde her
al by ordre. And than oure blessed Lady desired of Elizabeth the
same, and she tolde her diligentely, and thus thei satte togedre

14 and] ne *erased* H1   16 and¹] *om.* EH1   and²] *om.* G   17 this] his G
21 not] *ins.* H1   26 place] *erased* H1   31 ioyed] ioyned *with* n *subp.* H1
42 lyued] `bi´leued H1   43 Than] And G   oure] *om.* G   44 God] god *changed to*
our `lord´ H1   46 hem] her H1

talkinge withe gret gostely ioye. Than Elizabeth praied the holy 50
Virgine oure blessed Lady that she wolde vouchesauf to do her that
worshipp and ioie to duell withe her till she were deliuered, and she
mekely and benignely graunted her, and so she duelled withe her .iij.
monthes. Whanne tyme was come Elizabeth brought forthe her
blessed sone, and oure Lady was full diligent aboute her to do her 55
seruise in that gret nede and lefte up her litell sone fro the erthe and
wosshe hym and dight hym withe gret ioye, and þe litell babe, whiche
was fulfelled withe the holy goste, knowinge his Lorde witheinne her,
behelde on her withe gret ioye and wolde neuer haue parted from her,
for whan she wolde take hym [to] his moder he wryed euer the hede to 60
her, castinge al his sight vpon her, and she goodly cussed hym many a
tyme and blessed hym and toke hym to his moder.

Whanne the .viij. daye was come [that] the childe shulde be
circumsised, they come to the moder and asked her what men
shuld calle hym. She saide that he shuld hight Iohn, and thei saide 65
ayein that ther was neuer none of her kinrede that hight that name.
Thanne thei asked Zakarie the fader, and he toke penne and ynke and
wrote: '*Iohannes est nomen eius*.' And anone by vertue of the namynge
of that name his voys | was geue ayein to hym, and he with gret ioye f. 132ᵛᵇ
prophecied, sayenge: '*Benedictus Dominus Deus Israel quia uisitauit et* 70
fecit redempcionem plebis sue,' and so forthe. He made alle that blessid
canticle, and so in that hous were made the blessed canticles
Magnificat and *Benedictus*. After the circumcision of this blessed
childe, oure Lady went home ayein into Nazarethe to her pore hous
and ther mekely abode her blessed tyme, and this blessid childe Seint 75
Iohn abode with his moder till he was .v. yere olde. And thanne, as
Bonauenture tellith, he went into wildernesse and beganne to do
penaunce, notwithestondinge he was euer witheoute spotte of synne,
and ther he duelled till he come to a perfite age and lyued by herbes
and locustes and drank water and wered no clothinge but the skynne 80
of a camell gert withe a lederin gerdill. Whanne the peple seigh the
gret holinesse of Seint Iohn they drowe to hym, and he mekely
preched to hem and taught [them] þat they shulde do penaunce. And
than the worde of God was made vpon Iohn the sone of Zakarie, and
he come in al the region of Iordan, prechinge bapteme and penaunce 85

51 do] *ins.* H1   57 dight] di'ȝ'te H1   60 to¹] from E, from *subp.* to H1
63 that] L, *om.* EH1G   69 his] *om.* G   ayein to] *om.* G   71 And so forthe *begins
next sentence in* EH1L *and probably* GT1   72 the] þoo G   77 Bonauenture] Bona
Auenture H1   78 euer] *ins.* H1   79 till] to *changed to* tyl H1   he²] a H1   a] 'a' H1
85 and] of *subp.* '&' H1

in remission of synnes, as it is wrete in the boke of sermones of Ysay the prophete: '*Vox clamantys in deserto, parate viam Domini, rectas facite semitas eius.*'

90   This holy man and blessed forgoer Seint Iohn fulfelled the comaundement of his Lorde and baptised the peple whiche come to hym by gret multitude. And amonge alle other come that moste innocent lambe of God oure Lorde Ihesu mekely to his servaunt as he f. 133ʳᵃ hadde be another of the peple, and as sone as Seint | Iohn seigh hym he knewe hym and withe gret reuerence and dredde saide to hym: 'A, 95 my Lorde, I shulde be baptised of the, and thou comest to me.' Thanne oure Lorde mekely ansuered and saide: 'Suffre a while and discouer me not, for my tyme is not yet come. Thus me behouith to fulfell al rightwisnesse, and therfor baptise me, for now is tyme of humilite and not of mageste.' And whanne Seint Iohn seigh the will of 100 his Lorde he obeied to hym and baptised hym.

    Now takithe good hede how the Lorde of mageste dispoiled hymselff as he were another simple man of the peple, stondinge in the colde water in tyme of gret colde for oure loue, werchinge oure hele, ordeninge the sacrement of bapteme in wasshinge oure synnes. 105 He hathe wedded to hym alle holy Chirche and singulerye he hathe wedded to hym alle trwe soules, for whi in the faithe of bapteme we be wedded to oure Lorde Ihesu Crist, as the prophete saieth, in the persone of Crist: '*Desponsabo te in fide michi*,' that is to saie: 'I shall wedde the in faithe to me.' And also the Chirch singithe: '*Hodie et c.*,' 110 'This day the heuenly spouse is ioyned to the Chirche, for Crist hathe wassh his synnes in the flode of Iordan.' Of this mervailous werke alle the Trinite beren witnesse in shewinge hem, for the holy goste light downe on the sone and reste on hym in likenesse of a dovue, and the voys of the fader was herde, sayenge: 'This is my beloued sone in 115 whom I am well plesed.'

    Whanne oure blessed Lorde was baptised of Seint Iohn, Seint Iohn f. 133ʳᵇ withe gret reuerence shewed hym to the peple withe | his fingre and saide: '*Ecce agnus Dei qui tollit peccata mundi.*' Thanne he went into the hille, where he fasted .xl.ᵗⁱ dayes, and Seint Iohn abidinge still 120 prechinge and baptysinge the peple, whos lyff and gouernaunce appered so holy and so perfite that sum of the peple said that he was Crist, sum sayde that he was Hely, and sum saide he was a

    93 as sone] anoon G   94 dredde] *add* and E   101 dispoiled] dispoyleth Hı
103 in tyme] *om.* Hı   loue] lorde Hı   118 into] vp to G, vnto Hı   119 Seint]
seide G   122 that] *om.* Hı

prophete. The Iues, heringe the mervailes of [his] lyff and gouernaunce, sent to hym prestes and Levites of her lawe, and whanne they
come to hym thei asked: 'What art thou that takest vpon the suche 125
maner governaunce? Art thou Crist?' He ansuered: 'I am not Crist.'
'Art thou thanne Ely?' He saide: 'Nay.' 'Art thou thanne a prophete?'
'Nay,' he saide. 'What ansuer,' saide thei thanne, 'shull we yeue to
hem that sent vs, what [thou saiest] of thiselff?' Thanne saide Iohn: 'I
am a voys in desert crienge to alle, "Makethe redy the wayes of oure 130
Lorde," as Isaie the prophete saide.' Than saide they that were sent:
'Why baptisiste thou, sethe thou art not Criste nother Ely ne
prophete?' Than ansuered Seint Iohn: 'I baptise in water. In the
middes of you ther is one that ye knowe not. He it is that shall come
after me, that was made before me, the whiche I am not worthi to 135
vndo the lace of his shone.' And whanne they hadde herde this thei
parted fro hym wonderinge gretly on his wordes.

   In this mene tyme Seint Iohn herd how that Kynge Herodes helde
his brotheres wyff wrongfully, and anone for zele of rightwisnesse he
come to hym and argued hym and blamyd hym gretly, saieng | to hym f. 133va
that it was not liefull to hym to holde his brotheris wyff, and for this 141
cause Herodes hated hym gretly, but specially his cursed wyff, seking
al the menys that she coude to destroie this blessed forgoer of oure
Lorde Ihesu, Seint Iohn. And atte the laste they [bere hym on honde
that] he was a deceiuour of the peple and thei putte hym in prison, 145
and whan this holy man was in prison he desired that his disciples
shulde go to oure Lorde Ihesu Crist and see the mervailous werkes of
hym and so to be drawe to his loue. And so he called two of his
disciples to hym and saide to hem: 'Gothe to Ihesu Crist and askethe
hym yef it be he that is to come, or that we shull abide any other.' And 150
whanne the disciples come to oure Lorde Ihesu he hadde a gret
multitude of peple tofore hym, and they seinge hym deden her
message mekely. And whanne oure Lord hadde herde hem he
ansuered hem gladly and saide: 'Gothe and saieth to Iohn that ye
haue herde and sene. The blinde haue sight, the lame gone, lepres ben 155
clensed, the deef heren, the dede arisen, the pore men and symple
prechen, and he ys blessed that hathe not be sclaundred in me.'
Whanne thei hadde herde this thei turned ayein to report to her

   123 his] oure E, hys *on erasure* H1   125 asked] *add* hym E   127–8 Art².
. . .saide'] *ins.* H1   129 thou saiest] *trs.* E   131 Isaie] I saie E   133 in] *add* þe H1
137 on] ouer *changed to* on H1   140 argued] angered H1   144–5 bere hym on
honde that] said EH1

maister these tydingges, and whan they were parted oure Lorde Ihesu
160 turned hym and saide to the tourbe of peple in praysinge of Seint
Iohn: 'What trowe ye that ye see in desert, a rede that wawithe withe
eueri wynde? But what trowe ye to see, a man clothed in so[fte]
clothes? Lo, [ay] suche men that vsen softe clothes bene in kyngges
houses. But what wene ye that ye see, a prophite? Ye, I tell you
f. 133vb pleinly, and more thanne a pro|phete, for truly it is he of whom it is
166 wrete wher he saiethe: "I shall sende myn aungell before the [that
shall make redy the way before the]." Wherfor I tell you in trouthe
that amonge alle the children that bene born of women shall not arise
a gretter of vertue and of dignite than Iohn the Baptist.'
170   Now turne we to the blessed Seint Iohn þat liethe in sore prison.
Whanne his disciples come to hym fro oure Lorde Ihesu withe the
massage beforesayd, he was fulfelled withe gret ioye, notwithestondinge that he knewe full well before what he was, but thus he dede for
the prophete of his disciples for to make hem knowe the might and the
175 goodnesse of oure Lorde Ihesu Crist, that they myght turne to hym
and duelle withe hym. In this mene tyme this wreched kynge Herodes
helde a gret feste of his natiuite, and the whiles he satte atte his mete
the cursed quenes doughter come before hym and daunsed and lepte,
tumbeled and dede hym so gret plesaunce therin that he bade her aske
180 of hym what she wolde haue, ye though she asked halff his reawme.
The cursed quene her moder heringe this bade her that she shulde
aske the hede of Seint Iohn the Baptist. And whanne she dede so the
kynge feyned hym as though he hadde be sori of her askynge, but þat
he sayde he must nedys fulfell his othe and graunte, and so he
185 comaunded that he shulde be byheded ande marter for loue of
rightwisnesse. Of whom Crisostome saiethe: 'O thou blessed martir
Seint Iohn, the scole of vertues, maister of lyff, the renome of
holynesse, the rule of rightwisnesse, mirrour of virginite, cure of
chastite, ensaumple of clennesse, waye of penaunce, pardon of synnes,
f. 134ra discipline of faithe. Iohn is gretter thanne man, | euene withe aungels,
191 souerayne of the gospels, light of the worlde, message of the iuge,
mene of al the Trinite, sawer of faithe, wey of the aposteles, stintinge
of the prophetis.' Thus worthi and thus gret a man was putte to
marterdom and his blessed hede was yeue to the doughter [of] a

161 wawithe] wagged H1, waggith G   162 softe] solf E   163 clothes] clothingez
E   ay] om. EH1   that] as H1   166–7 that . . . the²] om. E   180 asked] wolde aske
H1   his] my H1   184 graunte] graunted EH1   185 for] of H1   194–5 of a
cursed] and acursed E, and a cursed H1

cursed auouuterere. Herodes was not punisshed for this gilte, but he 195
was dampned [of] another after and bothe he and his wiff deuoured
withe wilde bestis, as the Maister of Stories tellithe.

Whanne this blessed prophete had ended his holy lyff bi glorious
marterdom, his disciples toke his body that was so holy and bare it
into the citee of Sebaste in Palastine and beried hym betwene Helser 200
and Abdias. And for there were many a glorious miracle done atte his
sepulture, Iulian the apostata, that was a cursed tyraunt, made
[de]parte his bones, and yet the miracles cessed not, ande whanne
he seigh that, he made the bones to be gadered togedre and brent hem,
and whanne thei were turned to asshen he lete wenw þe pouudre in 205
the wynde. But as Bede tellithe in his Cronicles that, whiles men
gadered togedre these blessed bones to brenne, ther come of auenture
amonge hem monkes that come fro Ierusalem, and priuely thei
gadered amonge hem a gret parti of the holy bones and bare hem to
Phelip that was bisshopp of Ierusalem, and he sent hem after to 210
Athanasie bisshopp of Alisaundre. And longe tyme after Th[e]ophile
bisshopp of that citee fonde hem in the temple of Sarapis whan he
purged it from filthe and dedied | it, and thanne he sacred there a f. 134ʳᵇ
chirche of Seint Iohn the Baptist. Thus is that the Maister of Stories
tellithe, and now thei be worshipped deuoutely and arraied withe 215
precious stonis, so as Alisaundre the fourthe and Innocent the fourthe
that knewe the trouthe proue it bi her priuileges. And right as
Herodes that made hym to be byheded was punisshed for his
cursed dede, right so Iulian the apostata that made his bonis to be
brent was smiten withe the devine vengeaunce. And that persecusion 220
is conteyned in þe storie of Seint Iulian that is after the Conuersion of
Seint Paule.

And of the findinge of the blessed hede of this holy marter it is
wretin in the Storie of Ecclesiast that saiethe in this wise. Seint Iohn
was bounde and his hede smite of in a castell of Arabie that hight 225
Mathe Rouche. Herodyen made [bere] þe hede into Ierusalem and
lete b[ery]e it priuely besydes the habitacion of Herode, for she
dredde her leste the profit wolde haue risen ayein if the hede hadde
bene beried withe the bodye. And as it is wretin in the Maister of

196 of] to EHɪ   197 of] *add* the HɪG   200 Helser] Hel'ï'see Hɪ, Helisee G
203 departe] to parte EHɪ   bones] *add* to be gadered EG, *so del.* Hɪ   211 Theophile]
Thophile EHɪ   211 temple] m *has four minims* E   213 dedied] dedi'fi'ed E
217 proue it] proue Hɪ, prouyd G   223 And] As G   226 bere þe hede] þe hede be
bore E   227 berye] L, brenne E, berie *on erasure* Hɪ, purye G

230 Stories, in the tyme of Marce prince that beganne the yere .CCC.liij.
Iohn re[uel]ed his hede to .iij. monkes that were come into Ierusalem,
and thanne they went to the paleys that was Herodes and founde the
hede of Seint Iohn wrapped in an olde sacke of here, and as I trowe it
was the [same] vestement that he wered in deserte, and thanne thei
235 toke the blessed hede withe hem and thei turned ayein to her owne
propre places.

f. 134ᵛᵃ   And as they went by the waye a pore man, that was | a maker of erthin
pottis and bere one withe hym to sell, mette with these monkes a litell
from the citee of Misse and fill in felawshipp with hem, and thanne
240 anone they toke hym the skrippe to bere withe this holy hede. The
same night Seint Iohn appered to this pore man and taught hym that he
shulde parte from hem, and anone the same night he turned ayein to
the citee of Misse and bere it to his pore hous and hidde it in a pitte, and
eueri day he worshipped it and as longe as he liued he hadde gret
245 prosperite. And whanne he shuld deye he tolde it to his suster and toke
the [blessid] hede to her vnder gret assuraunce and as longe as she
lyued she keped it. Longe tyme after this, Seint Iohn reueled his hede
to Seint Marcell, a monke that duellid in that pitte, in this manere: it
semed hym in his slepe that a gret felawshippe of syngers went ther and
250 saide: 'Lo here Seint Iohn the Baptist that commithe.' And thanne
Seint Iohn come worshipfully ledde betwene two and blessed alle tho
that come to hym. And thanne Marcell asked hym and saide: 'Mi lorde,
from whennis art thou come?' He saide: 'I am come from Sebaste.' And
thanne Marcell went nye hym and Seint Iohn toke hym by the chynne
255 and cussed hym, and whanne Marcell was awaked he mervailed gretly
of this vision. The nexst night as he slepte ther come a man to hym and
awoke hym, and whanne he was waked he seigh a sterre shine in the
middes of the selle thorugh the dore. And he arose for to haue touched
f. 134ᵛᵇ it, and it turned sodenly to that | other syde, and he ranne after into the
260 tyme that the sterre rested upon the place where the hede of Seint Iohn
was hidde, and thanne he digged there and founde a potte and the holy
tresour witheinne. Another monke that wolde not leue it putte his
honde to the potte and anone his honde cleued faste therto, and thanne
his felawes praied for hym and he withedrowe his honde, but it was
265 witheoute strengthe. And thanne Seint Iohn appered to hym and
saide: 'Whanne my hede shalle be sette in the chirche thou shalt
touche the potte and receiue hele.' And so it was done and he perfitely

hole. Thanne Marcell shewed this thinge to Iulio[r]en bisshopp of
that citee so that they lefte it vp and brought it to the citee, and fro þat
tyme forthe the decollacion of Seint Iohn beganne to be halowed in 270
þat citee. And after that it was born into Constantinenople, and as it is
saide in the Storie Parted in Thre, Valent the emperour comaunded
that this holy hede shulde be sette in a chayere and ledde into
Constantinenople, and whanne they come nye Calcedoyne the
chayer wolde in no wise go further for aught that bestes and men 275
myght drawe. After that Theodesyen the emperour wolde take hym
from thennes and ther he founde a noble lady that was ordeyned to
kepe the hede. He praied her þat she wolde suffre hym to take awaye
the hede. She consented, wenynge that as he hadde done in the tyme
of Valent that he wolde haue done [at] this tyme, and thanne the 280
devoute emperour enbrased the hede witheinne | his purpure and bere f. 135ra
it into Constantinople and edefied there a faire chirche. After that in
the tyme that Pepyn regned in Fraunce that blessed hede was brought
into Fraunce, and ther bi his merites many a glorious miracle is done.
And right as Herode and Herodien were punisshed that beheded 285
hym, and Iulian the apostata that brent his bones, right so the
wreched doughter was for she asked the hede of hym, for as she
walked on a tyme the erthe opened and swaloued her inne and so she
deied wrechidly.

Also this day is halowed for the translacion of his fynger and the 290
dedicacion of this chirche, for as men saine that finger that he hadde
shewed oure Lorde withe whanne he saide: '*Ecce agnus Dei qui tollit
peccata mundi*' wolde neuer brenne, and that same finger was founde
of the monkes tofore saide. But Seint Tecle brought it after ouer the
mountaynes and sette it in the chirche of Seint Martin, and that 295
witnessithe Iohn Beleth hou that Seint Tecle brought that finger into
Normandye and dede make there a faire chirch in the worship of Seint
Iohn, and thanne was it ordeyned of the pope that this day shulde be
halowed thorugh al the worlde.

268 Iulioren] Iuliozen E   273 chayere] *changed to* chare H1   276 myght] *add*
be G   280 at] as EH1   this] þat G   the] `þe' H1   290 this] his G   294 But]
And G

Here endithe the liff of Seint Iohn the Baptist, and nexst
foluithe the liff of Seint Iohn and Paule,¹ Cap^m. .iiij^xx.j.

Seint Iohn and Paule were prouostes and maisters to Constance
doughter of Constantine emperoure of Rome, and in that tyme the
men of Siche hadde ocupied the londe of Dacye and of Trace. And |

f. 135rb Gallican that was duke of the oste of Rome shulde be sent ayeinst that
5   mayne, and thanne he asked of that emperour that he might haue his
doughter in guerdon of his labour and payne, and alle the princes of
Rome requered the emperour of the same. Thanne was the emperour
right hevye, for he wost wel that sethe his doughter was heled of Seint
Anneis she was in suche purpos that she wolde rather deye thanne she
10   wolde consent to the felawship of man. This virgine, trustinge in God,
counsailed her fader that he shulde promisse hym to haue her after he
come home ayein and hadde the victorie, and thanne Gallican, content
herewithe, sent two of his doughters that he hadde by his wiff the
whiche was dede to duelle with Constaunce to enfourme her of his
15   condiciones and maners, and in hope of gretter surete he desired of
[her] .ij. prouostes Iohn and Paule. And she graunted hym gladly,
praienge full deuoutely to oure Lorde that bi his grace she myght
conuerte hym and his doughters to Ihesu Crist. This praier plesed
oure Lorde and therfor she was herde.
20   Thanne Gallican toke Iohn and Paule withe hym and a meruailous
gret hoste and went ayeinst his enemyes, but for al that his hoste was
ouercome of his enemyes, the men of Chichens, and was beseged of
hem in a cite of Trace. And thanne Iohn and Paule come to hym and
saide: 'Makithe youre avowe to God of heuene and ye shull spede
25   beter thanne ye haue do.' And as sone as he hadde made his avowe a
yonge man appered to hym that bare [a] crosse vpon his shuldre and

f. 135va saide to hym: 'Take | thi spere and folowe me.' He toke it and went
thorughe the tentes of all his enemies witheoute sleynge any and come
euene to the kinge, and alle submitted hem to hym by gret drede and
30   he putte hem vnder the truage of Rome. And .ij. knyghtes armed
appered to hym and comforted hym, that one here, that other there,
so that [he] receiued cristendom and turned ayen to Rome and was
receiued withe gret worshipp. And thanne he besought the emperoure
that he wolde not be displesed though he wedded not his doughter,

EH1GH2A1A2L; D resumes at 84 *to be*   5 that¹] the G   10 man] men G
13 two of] of *del*. two 'of' H1, *trs.* G   16 her] he E   26 a] the EH1   32 he] L,
they EH1, *om.* G

for he purposed from thennes forward to lyue in continence to Ihesu 35
Crist. This liked welle to the emperour because of his doughter and
also for his doughters were conuerted by Constaunce. And thanne this
Gallican lefte his ducherie and gaue his good to pore folke and serued
only Ihesu Crist [with other seruauntes of Ihesu Crist]. And his
conuersacion was so holy that he dede many miracles, for only by his 40
beholdynge he chased oute fendes of the bodyes that they were inne,
and the renome of his gode conuersacion encresed so gretly thorugh
alle that londe that moch peple come to beholde this holy man and to
here hym, wonderinge that he that hadde be a paynyme how he now
wisshe the fete of pore men and leide her bordes and gaue hem water 45
to her hondes and ministred to hem her lyvinge and curiously kepte
seke folke and dede al lowly seruise.

And whanne Constantine was dede his sone Constancience, whiche
was a stronge heretyk, held the empire after hym, sothely as
Constancience the brother of Constantine hadde .ij. sones lefte 50
hym, | Gallum and Iulian. This emperour Constancience made his f. 135vb
vncle ys sone Gallum cesarien and sent hym into Iudee for to fight
withe hem in as moche as they rebelled ayeinst hym. And atte the laste
whanne he hadde done alle his laboure the emperoure slowe hym, and
Iulian his brother seynge þat dredde leste the emperoure wolde serue 55
hym of the same, and entered into an abbaye and feyned hym to be
vnder religious. And so he was made lectour and he counsailed withe
the fende and hadde ansuere of hym that he shulde be lefte vp [aft]er
that vnto the empire of Rome. And so witheinne a while after,
Constancien, for as moche as he hadde nede to cheueteynes, he 60
made Iulian cesarien, and thanne he sent hym into Fraunce and he
dede there wonder nobly. And thanne whanne Constancien was dede
Iulian the apostata was chosen emperoure.

Thanne anone he comaunded that Gallican shulde do sacrifice to her
goddes or ellys go oute of the contre, for he durst not slee so gret a man 65
as he was, and thanne Gallican went into Alisaundre and there he was
perced thorugh the herte and receyued marterdome. Thanne this
Iulyan, that was ouertake withe couetise, confermed and enforced his
cursed couetise by witnesse of the gospell, for in takinge aweye the
goodes fro cristen peple he sayde: 'Youre Crist saiethe in the gospell 70
that whoso renounsithe not al that he hathe he may not be my disciple.'

37 for] om. H1   38 ducherie] doucherie changed to doughtres H1   39 with . . .
Crist] om. E   42 gode] om. G   43 this] þat G   57 lectour] collectour EH1
58 after] vnder EH1   65 the] þat G   67 perced] perischid G   70 fro] of G

And whanne he herde that Iohn and Paule susteyned the pore withe
the goodes and richesse that Constanc[e had] lefte, he sent hem worde
f. 136ʳᵃ that they aught as well to be withe hym as with | Constantyne. Thei
75 ansuered and saide: 'Whanne the glorious emperour[es] Constantine
and Constancien his sone hadde ioie to be cristen we serued hem
gladly, and for that thou hast lefte the religion full of vertue we be
departed from the and will not obeie the.' Thanne Iulian sent hem
worde ayein: 'I haue holde my clergie in the chirche, and yef I wolde I
80 coude haue come to the hyest degree therinne, but I haue concidered
that it is a veyne thing to folowe slouthe and idelnesse, and therfor I
haue yeue my corage to knyghthode and in sacrifienge to goddes I
haue the empire be her helpe. And therfor ye that haue be norisshed
in the palays riall shulde not fayle to be withe me so that ye myght be
85 my princes in my palays, and yef I be dispised of you I shall do so
moch that I shall not longe.' And they ansuered: 'We putte God
before the and therfor we drede not thi thretinge[s] ne thi manaces,
for we will not fall in the enmyte of God euerlastinge.' To that
ansuered Iulian: 'Yef ye despise to come to me witheinne these .x.
90 dayes, ye shull be constreyned to that ye will not do now with youre
good will.' Thanne the seintes ansuered: 'Imagine in thine herte that
[tho] .x. dayes be passed and do this same day that thou manacest.' To
whom Iulyan ansuered: 'Wene ye that [the] cristen will make you
marteres? But yeſ ye conscnt to me I shalle ponisshe you as comune
95 enemyes and not as marteres.' Iohn and Paule were all tho .x. dayes in
praiers and in almesse dedys and gauen all her good to the pore. And
thanne the .x. day Terencien was sent to hem and sayde: 'Oure lorde
f. 136ʳᵇ Iulian hathe sent you here | a litell image of Iubiter, that ye do sacrifice
to hym or ellis ye shull perisshe bothe togeders.' To whom the seintes
100 sayde: 'Yef Iulyan be thi lord kepe well his pees, for we haue none
other lorde but Ihesu Crist.' Ande thanne Iulyan comaunded priuely
that they shulde be beheded and made hem be beried in an hous in a
depe pitte, and he saide to alle the peple that he hadde sent hem into
exile for her renome. And after that the sone of Terenciene was
105 rauisshed withe the fende and beganne to crie witheinne the hous that
he was al brende withe the fende, and whanne Terencien seigh this
thinge he was cristened and confessed his felonye, and his sone was

73 Constance had] Constancien E   75 saide] *add* þat H1G   emperoures] emperour
EH1   86 longe] *add* 'suffer yowe' H1   87 thretinges] thretinge EH1   92 tho]
the EH1   93 the] L, ye EH1G   103 the] þoo G   104 Terenciene] Geroncience
with G *changed to* T H1

deliuered atte the sepulture of the seintes, and he wrote her passion. And they suffered dethe aboute the yere of oure Lorde .iiij^{xx}. and .xiij.

Seint Gregorie tellithe in his omely vpon the gospell *Si quis uult* 110 *uenire post me* hou ther was a lady and ofte tymes she haunted the chirche of these marteres, and as she come from the chirche in a daye she mette two monkes stonding in abite of pilgrimes and she wende that they hadde be pilgrimes and comaunded hem almesse, but er the aumener myght come to hem withe almesse thei come to her and saide 115 her: 'Thou doest visite vs now and atte the day of iugement we shull seke the and yeue the that we may.' And whanne they hadde saide th[i]s they vanisshed away from her sight.

Seint Ambrose saiethe of hem in his Preface: 'þe blessed marteres Iohn and Paule fulfelled verrely that Dauid sayde: "Loo how good 120 and ioyfull it is bre|theren to duelle togedre." They duellyd togedre f. 136va by lawe of nature of birthe, felawes of one faithe, ioyned by likly felawshipp, be equalite of passion, and alleway glorious in oure Lorde Ihesu Crist.'

Here endithe the lyff of Iohn and Paule, and nexst beginnithe the liff of Seint Leon the [pope], Cap^m. .iiij^{xx}.ij.

As it is redde in the Miracles of the Blessed Virgine, Leon the [pope] halowed [the] masse on Ester Day in the chirche of Oure Lady the Maior, and as he houseled the peple a lady kessed hys honde, and anone a gret temptacion of his flesshe toke hym, and thanne this holy man was a cruel vengeour of hymselff and priuely the same day he 5 kitte of his honde bi whiche he was hurt and threw yt away. And thanne withein a while after ther felle a gret murmure in the peple for that the souerayne bisshop sange not his masse as he was wont. Thanne the [pope] turned hym all to the blessid Virgine Marie and committed hym in [all] to her purueaunce, and than she come anone 10 and restabeled hym his honde ayein withe her holy hondes and comaunded hym that he shulde go and do sacrifice to her sone. And thanne Seint Leon preched to alle the peple and tolde hem as it was befalle and shewed his honde before alle hou it was restabled ayein.

110 Seint] And seint G   111 *me*] *add et c.* EH1   114 er] bifore G   116 her] Here *beginning speech* H1G   doest visite] visitist G   117 they] he *changed to* they H1 118 this] thus EH1

EH1GDH2A1A2L   *Pope* is changed to *buschop* throughout in E and ineffectively erased in L.   2 the^r] his EH1   10 in all to] into E   14 restabled] restablisshed H1

15   And thanne the Counsayle was celebred in Calcidoyne, and ther he
ordeyned that ther shulde no woman be veyled in ordre but yef she
were a virgine, and also it was ordeyned in þat Counsaile that the
f. 136vb Virgine Marie | shulde be called Goddes moder.

And in that tyme Attile waste[d] Italy and Seint Leon was .iij. dayes
20 and .iij. nightes in orison in the chirche of Seint Petre and Seint Paule,
and thanne he saide to his men: 'Whoso luste to folue me, [folowe].'
And thanne he went his waye, and as sone as he neighed to Attile he
light downe of his horse anone and leyde hym downe atte his fete and
praied hym to comaunde hym as hym luste, and Seint Leon bade hym
25 that he shuld go oute of Italye and relese alle tho that he hadde
brought in prison. And whanne this lorde was vndertake of hys men
that he that was a lorde and one of the conquerours of the worlde
shulde be ouercome of a preste, he ansuered and saide: 'I haue bothe
spared myselff and you, for I seigh in the right honde of hym a right
30 stronge knight that hadde his suerde drawe and sayde to me: "But
thou obeye to hym thou shalt deye withe alle thine meyni."'

And whanne the blessed Leon hadde wretin a pistell to Fabyan
bisshopp of Constantinople ayeinst Eutiche and Vescorin, he leyde it
on the sepulture of Seint Petre the Apostell, and was in fastinge and in
35 orison and sayde: 'That I haue erred in this pistell as man, thou [that]
the cure of the Chirche is committed to, correcte it and amend it.'
.xl.^ti dayes after, Seint Peter apperd to hym in his prayers, sayeng: 'I
haue redde thi pistell [and amended it].' And thanne Leon toke the
letter ande founde it corrected and amended by the aposteles hondes.
40   Another tyme Seint Leon was fourti dayes in fastinge and in praiers
f. 137ra atte þe sepulture of Seint Peter, preyeng | hym to gete hym
foryeuenesse of hys synnes, to whom Seint Peter appered and saide
to hym: 'I praied oure Lorde for the and alle thi synnes bene foryeue
the, excepte of the imposicion of honde: thou shalt be enquered for to
45 wete yef thou haste sette any honde in any creature in wele or in euell.'
He passed to oure Lorde aboute the yere [of oure Lorde] .CCCC.
and .xl.

---

15 ther] þan H1   19 wasted] L, wastes EH1G   21 to²] del. H1   folowe] om.
EH1   22 as sone] anoon G   23 leyde] seide G   35 thou that] L, though E,
þoughe subþ. H1, þou3 þat G   36 committed] add 'to þe' H1   38 thi] the H1   and
amended it] om. EH1   40 Leon] add þe Pope H1   46 of oure Lord] om. E, ins. H1

Here endithe the lyff of Seint Leon the [pope], and nexst
foluithe the lyff of Seint Petre the Apostell and marter of
oure Lorde, Capitulum .iiij^{xx}.iij.

Seint Petre the apostell amonge alle other and aboue all other he was
the moste feruent in brennynge loue, for he wold haue knowe the
[traytour] of Ihesu Crist, and so Austin saiethe, if he hadde knowe
hym he hadde alle torent hym withe his tethe, and therfor oure Lorde
wolde not tell hym hys name. He went vpon the see. He was chosen of 5
God to be atte his transfiguracion and he rered the mayde from dethe
to lyff. He founde the balaunce in the wombe of the fysche. He
receyued of oure Lorde the kayes of the kingdom of heuene. He toke
vpon hym to fede the shepe of oure Lorde Ihesu Crist. He conuerted
atte Whitsontide thre thousand men by his predicacion. He saide to 10
Ananye and to Saphire her dethe before. He cured Enee that hadde
the palsye. He baptised Cornelyen. [He] arered from dethe to lyff
Tabite. The shadowe of hys body heled the seke. He was putte in
prison by Herodes but he was deliuered by the aungell.

What hys cloth[inge] and hys mete was he wetenessithe it in the 15
boke of Seint | Clement, for he saiethe: 'The brede only withe olyues f. 137rb
and full selde with wortes is myn vsage, and I haue suche clothinge as
thou seyst, a cote and a mantell, [and] whanne I haue it I desire none
other thinge.' It is saide that he bare alwaye a kerchef in hys bosom
wherewith he wiped awaye ofte tymes the teres that he wepte, for 20
whanne he bethought hym of the swete wordes and of the presence of
oure Lorde hc might not restreine his teres for the right gret suetnesse
of loue. And whanne he remembered hym of that he hadde renied
hym, he wepte so habundauntly that by continuell custume of
wepinge his visage was alle forscalded withe teres. This saiethe 25
Clement. And he saiethe also that on nyghtes whanne he herde the
cok crowe he custumed to arise and praie and wepe also. And after
that it is founde in the Storie of Ecclesiast that whanne the wiff of Pers
was ledde to his passion he had right a gret ioie and called her by her
name and bade her to remembre her of oure Lorde. 30

In a tyme whanne Seint Peter the Apostell hadd sent two of hys
disciples for to preche and whan they hadde go fourty dayes that one

EH₁T₁GDH2A₁A2L; T₁ starts at 282 *saiethe*   3 traytour] trayton E   knowe]
knowed *with* ed *subp.* H₁   12 He²] L, and EH₁G   13 body] *add* he E
15 clothinge] clothes EH₁   16 saiethe] seith *with* th *on erasure* H₁   18 and²] *om.*
EH₁   25 saiethe] seint G

of hem deied and that other turned ayein to Seint Peter and tolde hym
how it was falle. And som sayne that it was blessed Marciall, and after
35 sum other it was Seint Mertinus, and it is redde ellyswhere that the
furst was Seint Franke and hys felawe that [was] dede was Gorge the
preste. And thanne Seint Petre toke hym his staffe and comaunded
f. 137ᵛᵃ hym that | he shulde go to hys felawe and ley it vpon hym, and
whanne he hadd do so he that hadde laye dede .xl.ᵗⁱ dayes arose hym
40 vp al quik.

     And in that tyme ther was in Ierusalem Simon the enchauntour
that sayde that [he] was the furst trouthe, and he affermed that whoso
leued in hym [he wolde make hym] perpetuel, and he sayde there was
nothinge inpossible to hym. And as it is redde in the boke of Seint
45 Clement that he saide that he shulde be worshipped of alle men as
God and that he might do alle that he wolde. And he saide more:
'Whanne my moder Rac[h]el comaunded me that I shulde go gadre
whete in the felde and I seigh the [sithe sette], I comaunded to the
sithe that she shuld gadre, and she gadered tho double more thanne
50 any other.' And yet he putte [more] therto and saide: 'I am the worde
of God. I am right faire. [I am a spouse.] I am the holy gost. I am
almighti. I am the soule of God.' He made the serpentes of iren to
meve, and he made ymages of iren to laughe, and he made houndes
for to syngge.
55   And as Lyne saiethe, he wolde dispute withe Seint Petre and shewe
that he was God, and a daye was sette and Peter come to the place of
this striff and saide: 'Pees be to you bretheren that louen trouthe.'
Thanne Simon saide: 'We haue no nede of thi pees, for yef pees and
acorde were made we shulde not profite to fynde the trouthe. For
60 theues haue pees amonge hemselff, and therfor I will haue no pees but
batayle, for whanne two fighten thanne is the pees [w]hanne one is
ouercome.' Thanne Seint Peter saide: 'Whi dredest thou to here of
f. 137ᵛᵇ pees? For debates bringe forth synnes, and there as synne ys is | no
pees, and trouthe is in dispitosons and rightwisnesse is in werkes.'
65 And thanne Simon saide: 'It is not as thou saiest, but I shall shewe the
the might of my divinite. I am the [furste vertu], and I may flee bi the
eyre and make nwe trees and turne stones into brede and abide in the

35 other] add seiþ H1   36 was²] is EH1   42 he¹] om. E, 'he' H1   43 he
wolde make hym] om. E   45 that²] om. H1   47 Rachel] Racel E   48 sithe] sight
EH1   sette] L, om. EH1G   50 more] L, om. EH1G   51 I am a spouse] L, om.
EH1G   52 soule] changed to sonne H1   55 shewe] L, add hym EH1G
61 fighten] fiʒten H1   whanne²] thanne E, add þat G   63 ys] add there G   64 in²]
add the EH1G   66 furste vertu] L, trs. EH1G   67 nwe trees] nowe ste'r'res H1

fire witheoute brennynge, [and I do all that I wille].' Thanne Seint
Peter disputed ayeinst hym and discouered al his malice[s]. And
thanne Simon seygh that he might not resiste ayeinst Peter [and] caste 70
alle his bokes into the see that were of art magike by cause that Seint
Petre shulde not preue by his bokes to the peple that he was an
enchauntour, and thanne he went to Rome.

And whanne Seint Petre woste it he folued hym to Rome and come
to Rome in the fourthe yere of Claudyan the emperour, and there he 75
satte .xxv. yere, and he ordeined two for to helpe hym, and that was
Lyne and Clete, and as Iohn Belett saiethe he ordeyned one withoute
the wallys and that other witheinne and entended to predicacion and
conuerted moche peple to the faithe and heled many of the seke. And
in [his] predicacion he preised gretly chastite, and he conuerted .iiij. 80
maydenes of the prouost Ag[r]ippe whiche wolde no more come to
hym, wherfor the prouoste was wrothe withe hym and sought
occasion ayeinst Seint Peter. And thanne oure Lorde appered to
hym and sayde: 'Simon and Nero purposen ayeinste the, but drede
the not, for I am with the and I shall geue the Paule my servaunt to thi 85
comfort that tomorw shall entre into Rome.' And thanne Seint Petre
knewe þat he shulde be hastely take oute of this world; he made
assemble of his | bretheren and toke Clement and ordeyned hym in f. 138ʳᵃ
bisshoppe and made hym sitte in the chaier in hys place in stede of
hym. Thanne after that come Paule to Rome as oure Lorde hadde 90
saide and beganne to preche of Ihesu Criste withe Seint Peter.

And Simond was so well beloued withe Nero that withoute faile he
went he hadde be keper of his lyff and of his hele and of al the citee.
And as Leon the pope tellithe that in a day whanne Simon was before
Nero he chaunged sodenly hymselff and it semed to Nero that one 95
tyme he seigh hym right yonge and another tyme right olde, and
therfor Nero wende that he hadde be Goddes sone. And thanne saide
Simon to Nero: 'Emperour, for that thou shalt knowe that I am verrey
Goddes sone, comaunde that I be byheded, and I shall rise ayein the
thridde day.' And thanne Nero comaunded that hys hede shulde be 100
smete of, and whan the bocher wende to haue smiten Simon he
beheded a shepe, and tha[n] Simon be hys art magike escaped and
gadered the membres of the moton and hydde hem, and so he dede
hymselff thre dayes, and the blode of the shepe laye vpon the pament

68 and . . . wille] om. EH1   69 malices] malice EH1   70 and] om. EH1
80 his] om. EH1   81 Agrippe] Agippe E, Ag`r´ippe H1   93 went] add þat H1
95 Nero] on erasure H1   102 than] L, that EH1G

105 in gret foyson. And the thridde day he appered to Nero and bade hym
wype awaye the blode that was shedde, 'for lo me here that haue be
byheded, and now I am arise the .iij. day like as I behight the.' Ande
whanne Nero seigh hym he was al abaisshed and wened verrely that
he hadde be Goddes sone. And Leon saiethe that sumtyme whanne he
110 was secretely withe Nero the fende was witheoute in hys lykenesse
and spake withe the peple, and atte þe laste the Romaynes helde hym
f. 138rb in | so gret worshipp that thei made an image of hym and wrote the
titell of þis image: 'þe Simon the holy God.'

And as Leon berithe witnesse, Seint Petre and Seint Paule went to
115 Nero and discouered to hym alle his enchauntementz, and Seint Petre
saide ouer that: 'Right as ther be in Ihesu Crist two substaunces, God
and man, [right] so ther be in th[is] enchauntour man and fende.' And
than saide Simon, as Leon and Marcell beren witnesse: 'For that I will
not longe suffre this enemye, I comaunde myn aungellys that thei
120 revenge me of hym.' To whom Petre saide: 'I drede not thine
aungelles, but they drede me.' And thanne saide Nero: 'Dredeste
thou not Simon, that shewithe his diuinite in gret thingges?' And
Petre saide: 'Yef he haue diuinite in hym, late hym telle me what I
thenke now [or] what I do, and to that ende that I lye not I shall tell
125 the in thine ere what I thenke.' Thanne saide Nero: 'Come hedir and
telle me in myn eere what thou thenkest.' And Seint Petre went to
hym and saide: 'Comaunde sumbody to bringe me a barly loef
priuely.' And whanne it was take hym he blessed it and putte it in
hys sleue and saide: 'Now saye, Simon, what I haue thought, saide and
130 done.' Thanne saide Simon: 'I comaunde that gret dogges come and
deuoure the.' And thanne come ther forthe horrib[l]e dogges and
made a saute vpon Seint Peter, and anone he offered to hem the
brede that he hadde blessed and, [as sone] as they seigh it, thei fledde
awaye. Thanne saide Seint Petre to Nero: 'I haue shewed you that I
135 knewe welle what he [th]ought ayeinst me not only bi wordes but be
f. 138va dede, for the aungeles that he comaunded [to] come | ayeinst me, he
shewed hem in fourme of houndes, and so it is shewed that he hathe
none aungelles but fendes.' Thanne saide Simon: 'Vnderstonde, Peter
and Paule, thou y may do nothinge to you here, ye shull come there
140 [as] I shall iuge you bothe, but atte this tyme I spare you bothe.'

113 image] *add* the E   117 right] *om.* E   this] that EH1   124 or] and EH1
125 ere] here E   129 saye] *om.* H1   I haue] I *subp.* haue 'I' H1   131 horrible]
horribbe E   133 as sone] anone EH1   135 he] ye H1   thought] wrought EH1G
(*pensoit* P2)   136 to] L, *om.* EH1G   shewed] sheued *with* u *changed to* w H1
139 as] *om.* EH1

And as Egisippe saieth, Simon durste avaunte hym that he arered
dede bodyes, and thanne it felle that a yonge man deyed and thanne
was called forthe Petre and Simonde the enchauntour, and bi the wille
of Simon this sentence was confermed of alle, that he shulde be slayne
that might not arere the body from dethe to lyff. And whanne Simon 145
hadde made hys enchauntementes vpon the dede body, he enforced
hym to make hym meue his hede, and it semed to alle that there were
that the dede body meued hym. And thanne cried alle and wolde haue
stoned Seint Petre, and thanne Seint Peter withe gret peyne made
[hem] holde her pees and sayde: 'Yef the dede body be releued, late 150
hym arise and goo and speke. It is but fantasye of þat ye see his hede
meue. Late Simon be putte away from his bedde and thanne shull ye
see pleinly the falsenesse of the fende.' Thanne was Simon
d[isseuer]ed from the bedde and the childe abode witheoute any
mevinge. And thanne Seint Petre þat stode aferre made his praier and 155
cried to the childe and saide: 'Arise vp, thou childe, in the name of
Ihesu of Nazareth that was crucified.' And anone the childe arose ande
went. Thanne alle the peple wolde haue stoned Simonde, and Seint
Petre saide: 'It is payne inow | to hym that he knowlage hymselff to be f. 138ᵛᵇ
ouercome in his arte, for oure maister techithe us that we shulde yelde 160
good for euel.' And thanne saide Simon to Petre and Paule: 'It is not
falle to you as ye desired, for ye be not worthy marterdome.' The
whiche ansuered hym: 'That we coueite come to us, and neuer be
thou wele, for thou lyeste in alle that thou sayest.'

And than, as Seint Marcell saiethe, Simon went to the hous of 165
Marcell and teyed a gret dogge atte the dore of the hous and saide:
'Now shall I see yef Peter, that is wont come to the, will come.' And a
litell while after come Seint Peter and Seint Paule, and than Seint
Peter made the signe of the crosse and losed the dogge, and the dogge
was pesible to alle saue only to Simon whom he ranne vpon and 170
threwe hym downe to the erth and wolde haue strangeled hym.
Thanne ranne Seint Petre and cried to the hounde that he shulde do
hym none harme in the body, but he rent so his clothes that into lytell
he lefte hym alle naked. And thanne the peple withe the children
ranne after hym withe the hound that they droue hym oute of the 175
towne as a wolff, and thanne he might not endure the shame of þis
reproef and hidde hym alle a yere togederes. And Marcell, that was

141 avaunte] auaunte *del.* 'auante' H1   149 and . . . Peter] *ins. followed by* wyth grete
peyne *erased* H1   150 hem] *om.* EH1   154 disseuered] L, deceiued EG, deceuered
on erasure H1   173 in] to G

thanne disciple to Simon, whan he seigh this mervayle he ioyned hym
to Petre.

180   After that Simon come ayein and was receyued to the frenship of
Nero. And than, as Leon saiethe, Simon assembeled the peple and
sheued hem how he hadde be gretly wrethed withe the Galylees and
f. 139ʳᵃ therfor he wold leue the citee that he was wont | to kepe and defende,
and he wolde ordeyne a day in whiche he wolde stie up to heuene, for
185   hym luste no lengger abyde in erthe. And thanne in a day that he
hadde ordeyned, as Leon sayethe, he went vp into an highe toure that
was in the capitaille and caste hymselff from pilour to pilour and
beganne to flee. And thanne saide Paule to Seint Petre: 'It apertey-
nithe to me for to praie and the for to gete.' Thanne sayde Nero: 'þis
190   man is verrey God and ye be traitours.' Thanne saide Petre to Paule:
'Dresse up thine hede and loke.' Ande whanne he hadde lefte up his
hede [and] seigh Simon fleinge, [he] saide: 'Petre, what abydest thou?
Perfourme that thou haste begonne. Oure Lord callithe vs now.' And
thanne saide Petre: 'I coniure you, aungeles of hell that beren [hym]
195   vp in the eyre, in the name of Ihesu Crist that ye bere hym no lengger
but that ye late hym falle to the erthe.' And anone they lefte hym and
he fell to the erthe and breke hys necke and deied.

And whanne Nero knewe that he hadde loste suche a man, he
sorued gretly and saide to the aposteles: 'Ye haue done this in despite
200   of me, and therfor I shalle destroyc you,' and toke hem to Paulyn, a
full noble man, and toke hem into the kepinge of Mamentyn that was
vnder the cure of knyghtes Processe and Martynien, the whiche
knyghtes [Seint] Petre conuerted. And thanne thei opened the prison
and lete hem goo all frely, for whiche thinge Paulyn appeled Processe
205   and Martynien and he fond that they were cristened, and they hadde
her hedys smite of.

And the bretheren praied Seint Petre that he wolde go thennes, but
f. 139ʳᵇ he | wolde [not] in no wise, and atte the laste he was ouercome by
praiers and went his way, and, as Lyne and Leon witnessen, whanne
210   he come to the gate that is now called Seint Mary a Pas he seigh Ihesu
Crist comynge ayeinst hym and saide to hym: 'Lorde, whedir goest
thou?' He saide: 'I go to Rome ayein to be crucified.' And thanne
Seint Petre asked hym: 'Lorde, shalt thou be crucified ayein?' And he
saide: 'Ye.' And thanne saide Petre: 'Lorde, I shalle turne ayein to be

192 and] L, he EH1G   he] thanne EH1   194 hym] L, om. EH1G   200 hem]
þanne G   201 Mamentyn] mamertine H1   203 Seint] sayn E, seyn't' H1
208 not] om. EH1   212 to Rome/ayein] trs. G

crucifyed withe the,' and these thingges saied, oure Lorde stied up 215
into heuene. Petre seynge this wepte full sore for his departinge, and
whanne he vnderstode that it was saide to hym for his passion, thanne
he retorned ayein, and whanne he tolde this to his bretheren he was
take of the ministres of Nero and deliuered to the prouost Agrippe,
and his visage was [as] bryght as the sonne, so as Lyne saiethe. Than 220
sayd Agrippe to hym: 'Thou art he that glorifyest thiselff in the peple
and in women whiche thou partest from the beddes of her husbondes.' The whiche man the apostel blamed and sayde that he
glorified hym in the crosse of oure Lorde. And thanne was Seint Petre
comaunded to be crucified as a straunger, and for that Paule was a 225
citezein of Rome he was comaunded to haue hys hede smiten of.

And of yeuinge of this sentence saiethe Seint Denys in a pistell to
Timothee in these wordes: 'O Tymothee my brother, yef thou seigh
the batayles of the ende of hem thou shuldeste defaille withe wepinge
and sorughe. Who is that wolde not wepe whanne the comaundement 230
of the sentence | was geue ayeinst hem, that Seint Peter shulde be f. 139ᵛᵃ
crucified and Paule byheded? Thou shulde se thanne the felawshippe
of Iwes and of paynimes [that] smeten hem and spitte in her visagez.
And whanne the orible tyme come of the ende of hem that they were
departed that one from that other, they bounden the pilers of the 235
worlde and that was not witheoute crie and wepinge of the bretheren.
And thanne Seint Paule saide to [Seint] Petre: "This is a grete
wonderinge to see the thus demened that art the fundement of the
Chirche and sheparde to the shepe and lambe of Ihesu Crist." Thanne
Peter saide to hym: "Go in pees, prechour of goodnesse, mediatour 240
and leder of þe hele of rightwisse men." And they departed that one
from that other; I folued my maister, for thei were not slayne bothe in
one strete.' And thus saiethe Denys.

And, as Leon and Marcell wytnessen, that whanne Seint Petre
come to the crosse he saide: 'Whan my Lorde come from heuene into 245
erthe he was lefte up in the crosse vpright, and me that the crosse
shuld calle fro the erthe to heuene ought putte myn hede towardes the
erthe and dresse myn fete to heuene. And for I am not worthi to be
sette so in the crosse as my Lorde was, late the crosse be turned to
me.' And thanne they turned the crosse and fastened hys fete vpwarde 250

217 thanne] þat G   220 as¹] om. E   223 blamed] blames changed to blamed H1
226 to haue] ins. H1   228 Tymothee] thy mouth G   230 is] add þis H1
233 that] and E, and del. ʼþatʼ H1   235 they] þeʼiʼ H1   237 Seint²] om. EH1
grete] L, gretter EH1G   246 me] L, men EH1G   the crosse] del. and subp. H1

and his hede do[u]nwarde. And thanne alle the peple were so wood
that they wolde haue slayne Nero and the prouost also and deliuer the
apostell, and he praied hem that they wolde not lette hys passion. And
as Leon and Lyne tellen, oure Lorde opened the eyen of hem that
f. 139vb were there and wepten, so that they seigh the aungelles | crowned
  256 withe roses and lelyes besides Seint Petre [that was on the cross and
oure Lorde with the aungelles, and Seint Petre] as he was on the
crosse toke a boke of oure Lorde Ihesu Crist, and þe wordes that he
saide he redde in that boke in this wyse: 'Lorde, I haue coueyted to
  260 folw the, but I wolde not be crucified vpright. Thou art alway [right]
and souerayne, and we be sones of the furst fader that hadde his hede
enclined towardes the erthe, of whom þe falle signifiethe the fourme
and condicion of mankinde, and so we be born that we be sayn
bowynge to the erth by effecte, and the condicion is chaunged, for the
  265 worlde wenithe that suche thinge is good that is right [eu]ell. Lorde,
thou art alle thinge to me, thou art alle to me and nothinge is to me but
thou allone. I haue yeue þe thankyngges, Lorde, withe alle the sperites
lyue by whiche I vnderstonde the, by whiche I vndertake the gret
thingges of the.' And ther be other two causes wherfor he wolde not
  270 be crucified vpright. And whanne Seint Peter seigh that the good
peple seyen his glorie, in yeldinge thankingges to God and in
recomaundynge the good to God he yelded up the sperit, and
thanne Marcell [and] Apuleus his brother, that were his disciples,
toke hym downe of the crosse and anoynted hym withe diuerse
  275 oynementes and beried hym.

Isodore saiethe in the boke of the Natiuite and of the Dethe of
Seintes that whanne Seint Petre hadde founded the chirche of
Antioch vnder Claudien the emperour he went to Rome ayeinst
Simon the enchauntour, and there he preched the gospell and helde
  280 the bisshoprich .xv. wynter, and in the .xxxvj. yere after the passion of
oure Lorde he was crucified of Nero the hede douneward as he
f. 140ra desired; and this saiethe Ysodore. | And after that, as Seint Denis
saiethe in the forsayd pistell to Timothee, in the same day he apered
to Seint Denis, wherfor Denis saiethe: 'Brother Timothee, vnder-
  285 stonde the miracle and the token of the day of her sacrifice, for I was
present atte the day of her seperacion of this worlde, and after her

251 dounwarde] don/warde E   256–7 that . . . Petre] om. E, ins. H1
259 redde] hurde G   260 right] L, Crist EH1G   265 euell] well E
267 the] þi H1   273 and] om. E, `&' H1   274 toke] to kepe with þe erased H1
280 the²] om. G

dethe I seigh hem, [honde in honde] enteringe into the citee of Rome
araied withe vestementis, withe baners and withe crownes of shininge
brightnesse.' This saiethe Seint Denis.

Nero abode not vnponisshed, but for this wickednesse and many 290
other that he hadde done he slowe hymselff withe his owne honde, of
whos felonies we shull w[ri]te here some of hem shortely. Senek his
maister techithe in a storie, thou it be apocraphum, that as Senek
loked and abode to haue [hadde] his guerdon for the payne and the
labour that he hadde in techinge hym, Nero bede hym chese the bowe 295
in whiche he wolde be hangged, for other guerdon gete he none of
hym for his laboure. And whanne Senec asked whi he hadde deserued
this turment of dethe, thanne Nero made one take a sharpe naked
suerde and bade hym shake it faste ouer hys hede, and Senec turned
his hede hedire and thedir for to flee the stroke and dredde gretly this 300
perell of dethe. And than Nero saide to hym: 'Maister, why turne ye
awaye so [the] hede from the suerde that manasithe you?' Senec
ansuered: 'I am a man and therfor I drede the dethe.' And thanne
Nero saide: 'Right so I drede the yet, as I was custumed in my yougthe
whanne I was a childe, wherfor I may not lyue suerly as long as thou 305
lyuest.' And thanne saide Senec: 'Sethe I shall nedes deye, late me
chese of | what dethe I shall deye.' Thanne Nero saide: 'But yef thou f. 140ʳᵇ
chese hastely I shall make the to deye anone.' And thanne Senec lete
make hym an hote batthe and lete hym blode witheinne the bathe, and
so in lesinge of all his blode he ended his lyff. And therfor be sum 310
token he might well hight Senek, that is as moche to saye as sleinge
hymselff, for though it were so that he was constreined therto, yet he
slowe hymselff withe his owne honde. This Senec hadde two
bretheren, that one was Gylyan, a noble doctour that slewe hymselff
withe his propre honde, and that other was called Mela, fader of 315
Lucan the poete, the whiche Lucan hadde hys veynes cutte by the
comaundement of Nero, and so he deyed.

And after that as it is redde in the stori of Nero ledde withe hys
wickednesse and madnesse comaunded to slee his moder and open her
wombe for to see where he hadde layne in her wombe. And thanne the 320
physicianes vndertoke hym of the dethe of his moder and saide to hym

---

287 honde in honde] how they EH1G (*main a main* P2)   enteringe] entered H1
292 write] wete EG, wr`i'te H1   here some] *trs.* H1   294 hadde] *om.* E   296 he²]
add ther EH1   299 it faste] his fest H1G   hys] þe *subp.* his H1   299–300 and Senec
. . . hede] `& than senec bowed his heed' H1   302 the¹] youre EH1   315 his] *add*
owne EH1   319 his] *add* owne EH1   open] opned H1   320 thanne] the G

that alle right de[u]iethe suche thinge and reson defendithe it that the
sone shuld not slee the moder whiche she brought forthe withe so gret
trauaile and payne. And thanne Nero saide: 'Make me to conceyue a
325　childe and bringe it forthe that I may knowe what sorugh my moder
suffered for me.' He hadde conceyued this will to bringe forthe a
childe as he hadde herde a woman that trauailed of childe as he went
by the [towne].

　　The phisiciens saide it was not possible to be do, for it was ayeinst
330　kynde, and thanne Nero saide: 'Makithe me to conceyue and bere a
childe or ellys I shall make you deye a cruell dethe.' And thanne they
f. 140va　gaue hym to drinke priuely a yonge | frogge and made it encrese in his
bely bi [her] crafte, and anone his bely that might not susteine
contrarie thingges swolle soo that Nero wende he had be withe
335　childe, and thei made hym be of suche dyete as they knewe that
shulde norisshe the frogge, and they saide that thei moste do suche
thingges nedes for his conceyvinge. And so atte the laste he sayde that
he was so trauailed withe sorugh and payne that he bade his
phisicianes in al haste to deliuer hym, for he might not endure [the]
340　payne of that labour, and thanne they gaue hym poisones for to make
hym brake, and so he brought forthe that frogge alle forwrapped in
blody humours foule and horrible to beholde. And whanne Nero seigh
his childe he hadde abhominacion therof and mervailed gretly of that
monstre. Thanne the phisicianes saide that he hadde brought forthe
345　so horrible a childe for he hadde not abidde the dieu tyme. And than
saide he: 'Was I suche one in my moders wombe?' They saide: 'Ye.'
And than he comaunded that his fruit were norisshed, and so it was
putte to norissh in the creueis of a stone. Thise thingges be well redde
in the cronicles, but thei be apocraphum.

350　　　After that he beganne to mervaile and to thenke how gret the
distruccion of Troye was and lete sette fire in Rome .viij. dayes and
.viij. nyghtes, and he behelde it from an highe toure and hadde gret
[ioie] of the [beaute] of the flawme and songe in a solempne garnement
[the s]onge of the Holyade. And as it is sayde in a cronicle he fysshed
355　withe nettis of golde; he was so ententyf in synginge that he
surmounted alle harpes and all tragedies, þat is to saye the maners
f. 140vb　of syngingges; | he wedded a man for a woman, and the man toke hym

322　deuiethe] deniethe E　　　326　me] *add* 'and whan' H1　　　328　towne] waye EH1
332　to] a H1　　　333　bely'] bodie H1　　　her] L, *om.* EH1G　　　335　suche] *add* 'a' H1
337　sayde] seid *with* d *erased* H1　　　338　bade] hadde G　　　339　the] in EH1
343　his] this EH1　　　348　creueis] Greues H1　　　353　ioie, beaute] *trs.* EH1
354　the songe] L, so longe EH1G　　　Holyade] L, holy Ade EH1G

for husbonde, a[s] Orose saiethe. The Romaynes myght not suffre his
cursidnesse and made a risinge ayeinst hym and droue hym oute of
the towne, and whanne he seighe that he myght not escape he toke a 360
sticke and sharped it withe his tethe and stiked hymselff thorugh the
body, and so he ended his cursed lyff. And in an other place it is redde
that he was devoured with wolves. And whan the Romaynes retorned
they founde the frogge in an hole of a walle and caste hym oute of the
citee and brent hym, and thanne th[at] partye of the citee toke name of 365
the frogge that was soked there and is called Lateren.

In the tyme of Seint Cornelyen [the pope] the Grekes hadde stole
the bodies of the apposteles, but the fendes that duelled in the idoles
were constreyned by the diuine vertu and cried: 'Ye men of Rome,
socour youre goddes that men take away from you.' For whiche thinge 370
the good cristen men vnderstode that it were the apposteles, and the
paynimes that they hadde [be] her goddes. And thanne there
assembeled gret multitude of cristen and of paynimes and pursued
hem, and thanne the Grekes dredden and [threwe] the bodyes in a
pitte at Catacombes, but they were after take away of good cristen 375
men. And Seint Gregore saiethe in his Regestre that so gret thundre
and lyteninge felle vpon hem that they were so afraied that they lefte
hem at Catecombes and went her waye, but as they went they were in
doute whiche bones were of Seint Petre and whiche of Seint Paule.
They toke hem to fastinge and praiers, and thanne it was | ansuered f. 141ra
[hem] from heuene that the gretter were of the prechour and the lasse 381
of the fyssher, and so they deseuered þe bones and putte eche of hem
in the chirche that was edefied for hem. And another sayenge is that
Seint Siluester the pope wolde blesse the chyrches, and he wayed the
bones litell and moche withe gret reuerence and dede putte the halff in 385
þat one chirche and that other halff in that other chirche.

Gregorie tellithe in his Dyaloge that in the chirche of Seint Petre
wher hys body restith ther was a man that hight Agencien and was a
man of gret humilite and of gret holynesse. And ther was a mayde that
was longe in the chirche and she hadde loste bothe body and fete and 390
drewe her body after her vpon her hondes, and whanne she hadde
longe praied to Seint Petre he apered to her in a vision and said to her:
'Go to Agencien my servaunt and he shall restable the to helþe.' And

358 as] a E, A`s′ H1   As begins new sentence in G   365 that] L, the EH1G
367 the pope] L, om. EH1G   372 be] by E   373 paynimes] add that they hadde E
374 threwe] putte EH1   380 and¹] add `to′ H1   381 hem] om. E   385 litell]
lite H1   386 þat] þe changed to þᵗ H1   one] `oo′ H1   388 body] bones H1
392 to¹] om. G   he] om. G   388 restable] restablisshe G   to²] thyne G

thanne she beganne to drawe her here and there thorugh the chirche
395 and enquered who was Agencien. He that she sought come ayeinst her
and thanne she saide to hym: 'Oure sheparde,' quod she, 'and oure
norissher the blessed apostell Seint Petre sent me to the that thou
shuldest deliuer me of myn infirmite.' He ansuered [her]: 'Yef thou
art sent by hym, arise up.' And he toke her by the honde and lefte her
400 up and she was perfitely heled.

And in that same Dialoge saiethe Seint Gregore that a right noble
mayde of Rome that hight G[o]lye that was doughter to Semake
consult and was yeuen in mariage to Patricien of Rome, and in a lytell
f. 141ʳᵇ space of tyme she was made wedowe. And after | that her frendes
405 purposed to ordeyne her another husbond as most was acordinge to
her age and to her rychesse, but she chase rather to be ioyned to the
spirituel weddinge of oure Lorde, that beginnithe withe wepinge and
endithe withe euerlastinge ioye, thanne to flesshely mariage þat
beginnithe withe ioye and endith withe sorugh. And after that, for
410 it appered in her that she was hote of complexcion, the phisiciens
tolde her but yef she hadde mannes felawshypp that she shulde haue a
berde ayeinst kynde, whiche thinge fell after, but she dredde nothinge
the foulenesse v[t]warde for she desired to haue her beauute witheinne, and for that she deserued to be byloued of the heuenly spouse
415 of heuene [that] rewardethe not the vtwarde beauute but only the
beauute of the soule. And thanne she caste of her seculer clothinge
and gaue herselff alle to the chirche of Seint Petre, and there she
serued God many yeres in symplenesse, almesse and orisones. And
atte the laste she was smete in the breste withe a cancre, and always
420 two [chaundelers were] brenninge before her bedde as she that was
alwaye the louer of lyght, and she hadde not only the gostely
derkenesse but also the bodely. And so in a nyght she seigh Seint
Peter the Apostell stonde betwene the two [chaundelers], and than she
by hard[i]nesse of loue spake to hym and sayde: 'Good lorde, what is
425 that? Be my synnes foryeue me?' To whom he that was of right
debonayre chere graunted her with hede enclined and saide: 'Come
on, for they bene fully foryeue the.' And thanne she sayde: 'I beseche
f. 141ᵛᵃ you that | my suster Benet may come with me.' And he saide: 'Nay,

394 her . . . and] here del. here self with self on erasure H1   there] add she yede E
398 her] om. EH1   402 Golye] Glye E   413 vtwarde] vpwarde E, so changed to
vtwarde H1   415 that] and EH1   418 in symplenesse] twice once del. H1
420 chaundelers] candelles E   were] L, om. EH1G   421–2 gostely derkenesse] so
changed to 'bodeli' li3t H1   422 bodely] goostli H1   423 chaundelers] candelles E
424 hardinesse] hardenesse E   425 foryeue] L, add hem EH1G

shall she not, but suche one shall come withe the.' And she denounsed
that to her abbesse and in the .iij. daye she deyed withe her.   430

In the same boke saiethe Seint Gregore that as a preste of gret
holynesse was brought to the terme of hys ende he beganne to crie
withe gret gladnesse: 'Welcome be ye, welcome be ye, my lordes,
whan ye luste to come to so pore a servaunt of youres. I come to you
and yelde you thankingges.' And whan tho that were there asked hym   435
what they were to whom he sayde such wordes, and he ansuered hym
mervaylinge and sayde: 'Haue ye not sayne to come hedyr the
apposteles Peter and Paule?' And as he cried ayein the holy soule
parted from the body.

Some maken doute for to wete wher Petre and Paule suffered dethe   440
in one day, and some saye that [it was that same] day .xij. monthe, but
Ierom and all the seintes that treten [of] this mater accorden that it
was in one yere and in one daye, and it is conteyned in a pistell of
Seint Denis, and as Leon sayethe in a sermon wher he saieth: 'We
suppose not that it is do witheoute cause that in one day and in one   445
place they suffered the sentence of one tyraunt. Thei suffered deth in
one day so that thei myght come togedre to Ihesu Crist, in one place
þat neyther the one ne that other shulde fayle to Rome, vnder one
persecutour [so that] egal cruelte shulde constreine eueriche of hem.
The day was for her merite, the place for her glorie, and the   450
persecucion was ouercome by vertue.' And this saith Leon. And
though it were so that they suffered dethe in one houre | and in one   f. 141ᵛᵇ
day, yet it was not in one place but in dyuerse, and that Leon saiethe
that it was in one place he saicthe for that they were bothe dede atte
Rome. And therof saiethe a versifiour in hys vers: 455

Ense coronatus Paulus, cruce Petrus, eodem
Sub duce, luce, loco, dux Nero, Roma locus.

This is to saye: 'Poule was crowned with a suerde, Petre was crucified
a trauers, and Nero was the duke, and the place was the citee of
Rome.' And though it were [that they deide] in one day, yet Seint   460
Gregore ordeyned that speciall[y this] day shulde be ordeyned the
sollempnite of the Office of Seint Petre and the day foluynge the
rememberaunce of Seint Paule, in so moche as that the chirche in that

---

431 Seint] *om.* HIG   441 it . . . same] L, *om.* EHIG   442 of] on EHI
443 conteyned] *so with second* n *on erasure* HI   449 so that] L, *trs.* EHIG   451 this]
thus G   454 place] *add* but in diuerse HI   455 therof] þerfore G   456 *Ense*] *ence*
G   457 *Nero*] *vere* G   460 that they deide] *om.* EHI   461 specially this] speciall E

day was dedi[ed] of Seint Petre, and also for he was gretter of dignite
465 and was the furst in conuersion and helde furste the principalite of
Rome.

Here endithe the lyff of Seint Petre, and nexst foluithe the
commemoracion of Seint Paule, Capitulum .iiij^{xx}.iv.

Poule the Apostell after his conuersion suffered many persecuciones,
the whiche the blessed Hillary tellithe shortely, sayenge: 'Seint Paule
the Apostell was bete withe yerdes of Philip, he was putte in prison
and hys fete sette faste in stockes, he was stened in Listre, he was
5 pursued of felons in Ico[nyk] and in Thessalony, he was deliuered in
Ephesim to wilde bestes, and in Damaske he was caste oute ouer the
wallys, in Ierusalem he was arested and bounde and bete and espied to
be slayne, in Cesarie he was enclosed and defamed. He come into
f. 142ra Itaille be water wher he | was in perill, and from thennes he come to
10 Rome and was iuged vnder Nero, and there he ended.' And this
saiethe Hillarie.

He toke vpon hym to be apostell amonge the paynymes. In Listre
ther was a contracte the whiche he redressed, and he arered a yonge man
from dethe to lyff and dede many miracles. In the ile of Milite a serpent
15 assailled hym and he toke hym in his honde, but she misdede hym not
and he threwe her in the fyre, and men sayn that alle the men of that
[kynrede] that receyued Paule into hys hous mow not be hurt withe no
venemous beest, and whanne her children be born the faders of hem
putten serpentes in her cradeles for to proue whedir it be her childe.

464 dedied] L, dedicat EH1G

EH1T1GDH2A1A2L; D breaks off after 202 *ioyned* and resumes at 452 *whan*
Rubric endith . . . And] *om.* L   Petre] *add* the Apostle L, *add* the apostle and of the
indulgence of alle the churchis in Rome and whate pardon avayleth to man A2   nexst
foluithe] bygynnyth GDH2A2L   commemoracion] lyfe L, *add* and þe lyfe H1T1   Paule]
add the holye doctoure A2   2 the^2] *om.* DH2   4 hys] by the A2   in^1] *add* the A2
stockes] *add* and A2   5 Iconyke] Icombe EH1T1DH2A1A2   in^2] *om.* A1
Thessalony] Thessalonyque L   6 oute] *om.* T1   7 arested and] *om.* A1   espied]
add for L   8 defamed] *add* and DH2A2   10 ended] *add* his lyfe DH2A2   this] thus
DH2A2   saiethe] *add* seint A2   12 the] *om.* A2   paynymes] *add* and A2   13 he^1]
add losid and A2   and] & *on erasure* H1, *add* there A2   arered] rerid A2   14 lyff] live
A1   dede] *add* þer A2   15 she misdede] he hurt A1, she hurte A2   16 and^1] *add*
then A2   men] som A2   sayn] saide A2   alle] *add* that alle D   alle . . . that] who so euer
A2   the^2] *om.* T1   men of that] *om.* A1   17 kynrede] contre E   hys] hir T1DH2A2,
his *changed to* hir H1   hous] housis A2   withe] by A2   18 beest] bestes A1A2   and]
add yet A2   be] were H1T1A1   the faders] frendes A1   the faders . . . hem] thaye A2
faders] fadir GDH2   19 in her] into the A2   childe] *add* or no A2

It was shewed sum tyme that he was lasse thanne Seint Petre, sum 20
tyme gretter in predicacion and egal in holynesse. Aymon tellithe that
fro the cok crowynge into the houre of .v.ᵉ Paule laboured withe his
hondes, and after that he entended to prechinge, and the remenaunt
of the tyme was inow necessarie to ete, slepe and praie. He came to
Rome in þat tyme that Nero was not confermed in the empire, and not 25
for that Nero herde ther was question made betwene Paule and the
Iwes of the lawe of Iewes and of the faithe of cristen, and he raught not
gretly, and so Paule went suerly wher he wold and preched f[re]ly
ouerall. I[e]rom in the Lyves of Good Men tellithe þat .xxv.ᵗⁱ yere
after the passion of oure Lorde, whiche was the secounde yere of 30
Nero, Paule was take and putte in cheynes and sent to Rome, and .ij.
yere he was in fre holde he preched and disputed ayeinst the Iwes, and
after that he was late go be Nero | and preched the gospell in the f. 142ʳᵇ
parties of the occident, and thanne in þe .xiiij. yere of Nero in the day
that Petre was crucified he hadde the hede smete of. 35
The wisdom and the relegion of hym was publisshed ouerall, and
he was mervailous to alle and made hym many frendes in the hous of
Nero and conuerted hem to the faythe of Ihesu Crist. And sum of his
writingges were redde before Nero, and they were merueylously
preised of alle, and the senate hymselff helde gretly withe hys 40
auctoritees. It felle in a day that Paule preched in a soler, and a
yonge man that was boteler of the emperour and gretly beloued [of]
hym, for the multitude of men and for to here more profitably Paule,
he went up into a wyndow, and atte the laste he beganne to slombre
[a litell] and fell downe to the erthe and deyed. And whan Nero herde 45
it he was wonder sori of his dethe and putte another in his stede. And

20 that] add þu that A1   Petre] add and DH2A2   21 gretter] om. A1   22 fro]
fore H1   into] vnto D   .v.ᵉ] lyfe L   23 that] om. A2   24 the] om. A1   inow] add
and DH2A2   ete] add and GDH2   and²] add to L   25–7 not for that] neuerthelese A2
26 herde] add þat DH2A2   question] questions A1A2   27 of the . . . Iewes] om. A1
lawe of Iewes, faithe of cristen] trs. and add men to cristen A2   28 frely] firly E
29 Ierom] Igrom E   Lyves] lif GDH2A2   tellithe] sayeth A2   yere] wynter DH2
32 fre holde] freholde E, add and A2   33 that] om. A2   and] add he A2   34 .xiiij.]
.xxiiij. DH2A2   35 that] add seinte DH2A2   he] Poule DH2A2   the] his T1DH2A2
36 ouerall] end of paragraph DH2   37 and] add he DH2A2   39 writingges] writyng
A1   were¹] was A1   before] afore GDH2L   they were] hit was A1   meruelousy]
meruelous T1   40 senate] Senator A1A2   41 day] tyme A1   and] om. A2L
42 of¹] to A1A2   of²] withe EH1T1A1   43 hym] add went A2   for¹] add to see
DH2A2   men] peple DH2, the people A2   here] add the DH2A2   profitably] profitable
A1   44 up into] vppon H1T1A1   45 a litell] om. E, a lite H1   whan] þan H1T1
46 wonder] vndir DH2, very A2   of] for A2   and] add then he A2

thanne Paule knewe th[is] thinge in sperit and bade hem that were
there that they shuld bringe hym Patrok the frende of Nero that was
dede, and whanne he was brought Paule releued hym and sent hym to
50 Nero that was dede to hys felawes, and as Nero compleyned hym of
the dethe of hym, Patrok come and was come euene to his gate.

And whanne he herde that Patrok was alyue that he wende hadde
be dede he was gretly aferde and refused hym the entre to hym, and
atte the laste be amonastinge of his frendes he lete hym come, to
55 whom he saide: 'Patrok, lyuest thou?' He saide: 'I lyve verrely.' And
f. 142ᵛᵃ　thanne saide Nero: | 'Who made the liue?' Thanne Patrok saide: 'My
Lorde Ihesu Crist, kinge of al the worlde[s].' And thanne was Nero
wrothe an saide: 'Thanne shall he regne in worldes and destroie alle
the kingdomes of the worlde?' To whom Patrok saide: 'That is verrey
60 trwe.' And thanne Nero gaue hym a bofet, seyenge: 'Go, ride forthe
with hym.' And he saide: 'Sikerly I am fully withe hym, for he hathe
reised me from dethe to lyff.' And thanne five of the ministres of Nero
saide to hym: 'Emperour, whi smitest thou this yonge man that is wys
and well ansueringe? Truste truly that we will folwe that same kinge
65 almighty.'

And whanne Nero herde þat, he made hem to be putte in prison for
to turment hem strongely that he hadde gretly loued before. Than he
made seke alle the cristen and witheoute any demaunde he made hem
to be punisshed withe greuous tormentes. And thanne amonge other
70 Paule was brought bound before Nero, to whom Nero saide: 'O thou
man, servaunt of the gret kinge, that art brought bounden before me,

47 thanne] when A2　this] the EH1T1, tho A1　and] he A2　47–8 were there] trs.
DH2　48 bringe] add vnto A1, add to A2　Patrok] Patrik GDH2A2 passim　was] add
þer A2　49 whanne] assone as A2　hym¹] add aȝen to lyfe DH2A2　50 that] and
H1T1A1　that . . . felawes] wenynge to Nero and alle his meyne þat he was ded DH2, and
he and alle his men wende verelye þat he had ben dede A2　felawes] add sight A1　hym]
om. A2　51 come and] om. DH2A1A2　euene] om. A2　his gate] þe ȝate of Nero
DH2A2　52 was] add come DH2　that²] þe which DH2A2　wende] add that DH2A2
53 the] thee E, for to A2　to] into DH2A2　54 be] add the T1　amonastinge] mevinge
DH2A2　he] om. G　come] add in A2　55 he] Nero DH2A2　lyuest] leuest A1A2
thou] add and DH2A2　lyve] leue A1A2　56 saide Nero] trs. DH2A2　Who] ho⟨.⟩
with who in margin in smaller hand A1　liue] lyfe T1, leue A1, lefe A2　Patrok saide] trs. A1
57 worldes] L, worlde EH1T1GDH2A1A2　Nero] add full L　58 shall he] trs. GL
in] add the DH2A2　59 the¹] om. DH2A2　To . . . saide] than seide Patrik DH2A2
verrey] verryly A1　60 seyenge] and saide A2　62 five] v or Arabic 6 H1, .vj. T1
64 truly] verrili DH2A2, fully A1　same] om. A1　67 gretly] fulle welle A2　gretly
loued] wel bilovid DH2　before] add and A2　68 made¹] add to DH2A1A2　the] om.
H1T1A1　demaunde] demandyng ending sentence A1　69 greuous] gret DH2, om. A1
other] add pepul GDH2　70 Paule] pepul G　bound] om. T1　Nero²] he DH2A2
71 brought] om. GDH2A2

whi withedrawest thou my knightes from me and makest hem to folwe
thi foly?' Thanne Paule saide to hym: 'Wetithe wel that I gader not
hem only fro thine corner here, but I gadre hem fro alle the parties of
the worlde to whom oure kinge may yeue the yeftes that shull neuer 75
fayle. And yef thou wilt be soget to hym thou shalt be sauff, for he is of
so gret might that he shall come and iuge alle the world and destroie
the figure of this world [by fire].'

And whanne Nero herde this he was so sette afire withe wrathe
that, for he saide that the world | shulde be destroied by fire, he f. 142vb
comaunded alle his knyghtes to be brent in the fire and comaunded 81
that Paule shulde haue his hede smite of as gilty of his mageste. And
thanne [so] gret [a] company of cristen were slayne that the peple of
Rome breke the paleys withe strengthe and enforced hem to m[eu]e
contecte ayeinst Nero, whanne the goode cristen begonne to crie and 85
the trwe men that were withe Nero: 'Cesar, amende thi maners,
attempre thi comaundementes, these bene oure peple that thou
destroiest, they defended the empire of Rome.'

And thanne the emperour dradde and chaunged his ordinaunce and
comaunded that no man touche [eny] cristen before that he hadde 90
ordeyned more pleinly, for whiche thinge Paule was brought ayein to
Nero, and whanne Nero seigh hym he cried and sayde: 'Take oute of
my sight this wicked man, behede hym anone and late not this traitour
leve upon the erthe, take hym oute of this worlde, the deceiuour of
wittes, the chaunger and the strangeler of thoughtes.' [To whom 95
Paule saide:] 'Nero, I shall suffre dethe in short tyme, but I shall

72 withedrawest] drawist DH2A2   73 foly] add And A2   Paule saide] trs. DH2A2
Wetithe] wete ye A2   74 fro¹] for G   corner] court A1   here] om. H2   hem²] to my
lorde A2   75 worlde] wor'l'de H1   shull] may A1   76 hym] add þan H1T1   thou
shalt] shalt `þu' H1, trs. T1   77 and] add he shalle A2   78 by fire] om. E
79 Nero] add the emperoure A2   this] that A1A2   so] sore A2   80 that¹] om. DH2A2
that for] trs. A1   that²] om. A1   81 to] sholde DH2A2   82 haue ... of¹] be bihedid
DH2A2   83 thanne so gret a] L, so thanne a gret EH1T1GDH2A1A2   of²] add the
A1DH2   cristen] add people A2   that] and then A2   84 breke] add vp the gatis of A2
meue] make EH1T1A1   85 contecte] contempt A1, debate A2   ayeinst] add the
emperoure A2   whanne] whan changed to than H1, than T1DH2, and then A2   and] add
then A2   86 withe] aboute A2   Nero] add saide A2   maners] add and A2
87 comaundementes] add for DH2A2   88 they] the G   they defended] wherfore we
diffende the DH2A2   defended] defende H1T1A1   empire] Emperowr L   89 the
emperour] Nero DH2A2   90 man] add schulde A1   touche] hurte A2   eny] no EA1
cristen] add man A1A2   before that] to A1   91 pleinly] add his lawis A2   ayein] om.
A1   92 Nero²] he DH2A2   92–3 oute ... sight] aweie DH2A2   93 man] add
and DH2A2   94 level] lyve H1T1GA1, add no lenger A2   the¹] om. A1A2
95 chaunger] strang A2   the²] om. T1A1   95–6 To ... saide] om. EH1T1G, Then
Poule seyde L, Than said Paule to A1

lyue euerlastingly in oure Lorde Ihesu Crist.' And thanne saide Nero:
'Smyte of his hede that he may knowe þat I am strengger thanne his
kinge that I haue ouercome, and thanne we shulle see whedyr he shall
100 alwaye lyue.' To whom Paule saide: 'For that thou shalt wete that I
shalle leue endelesly whanne my hede shall be smete of, I shalle apere
to the alle quicke, and thanne maist thou knowe that oure Lorde is
lorde of lyff and not of dethe.'

f. 143ʳᵃ   And thanne he was ledde to the | place of his torment, and as men
105 ledde hym, .iiij. knyghtes that were there saide to hym: 'Telle us,
Paule, what is he that is youre kinge that ye loue so moche that ye
hadde leuer deye for hym thanne lyue? What guerdon shull ye haue?'
And thanne Paule preched to hem the kingdom of heuene and the
peynes of helle in suche wise that he conuerted hem to the faithe. And
110 thanne thei praied hym that he shulde go al quite wher he wolde, and
he said ayein to hem: 'God defende, my bretheren, that I flee. I am not
fleinge but abidinge, a true knyght of Ihesu Crist, for I knowe well
that bi þis transitori lyff I shall passe to the euerlastinge lyff, and as
sone as y shall be biheded the good cristen will take my body and berie
115 it. And comithe to that same place tomorwe and ye shull fynde two
men bysides my sepulcre, that is to wete Titus and Lucas, praieng,
and ye shull tell the cause whi I haue sent you to hem and thei shull
baptise you and make you heyres of the kingdom of heuene.'
And thanne as thei spake togederes Nero sent two of his knyghtez

97 lyue] leue H₁A₁GA₂, beleue T₁   euerlastingly] euerlastinge H₁T₁   And] om. A₁
99 that] add he dwellyth with whan A₂   ouercome] add hym A₂   we shulle] trs. GDH₂A₂
whedyr] where H₁T₁L, add we sch del. G, if A₁   100 alwaye] euermore DH₂, euer A₂
lyue] add or noo L, add ayen as he sayeth A₂   101 shalle] add euer A₂   of] add sone
after A₂   apere] add ayen A₂   102 oure] my DH₂A₂   is] add the A₂   103 not]
om. A₁   104 he] Poule DH₂A₂   his] the A₂   men] the turmentours A₂
105 hym] add ther of ET₁G, add þere of with þ on erasure H₁, add þere were DH₂A₂, add
ther to A₁   .iij.] add of the L   were there] om. DH₂A₂   us] vp G   106 youre] thy A₂
ye¹] he L   ye loue] thou louyst A₂   106–7 ye hadde] thou haddist A₂   107 thanne]
add for to DH₂   lyue] for to leue but A₂   guerdon . . . haue] rewarde shalte thou haue
therefore of hym that thou louyst so welle A₂   108 preched] teched A₁   heuene] add to
hem G, add 3e shal haue and to hem that be contrarie to þe feithe of 3hu crist DH₂, add that
ye shalle haue and alle tho that ben contrary to the feithe of ihu cryste thaye shalle haue A₂
and] om. DH₂A₂   109 peynes] peyne A₂   in . . . that] add in this wyse DH₂A₂   hem]
tho .iij. knyghtis A₂   faithe] add of ihu cryste A₂   110 praied] desirid A₂   that he
shulde] to A₂   wher] add that DH₂A₂   and] om. GL, add then DH₂A₂   111 ayein]
om. A₂   hem] him H₁   my] add dere A₂   flee] add for DH₂, add awaye for A₂
112 abidinge] add as A₁   a] om. L   113 lyff] add þat A₂   the] om. DH₂A₂   and] for
A₂   114 cristen] add men A₂   will] wolde A₂   115 that same] this DH₂, the A₂
and] an`d´ H₁   116 men] me A₁   sepulcre] sepulture H₁T₁A₁   wete] seie DH₂A₂
praieng] add þere A₂   117 ye] þei changed to ye H₁   tell] add them A₂   to] vnto L
119 thanne] om. DH₂   spake] add this A₂

to wete whedir he were beheded, and whanne Seint Paule [wolde 120
haue] conuerted hem they saide to hym: 'Whanne thou shalt be dede
and arise ayein, thanne shulle we leue that thou sayest. Come on
anone and receiue that thou hast wonne.' And as he was ledde to the
place of his passion ther mette hym atte the gate a lady that hight
Plancille whiche was his disciple, and after Seint Deny[s] she hight 125
Lemobye, and perauenture she hadde two names, the whiche wepte
sore and | recomaunded her to his praiers. And thanne Paule saide to f. 143rb
her: 'Goo in pees, Plancely, doughter of euerlastinge hele, and take me
youre kerchief þat ye binde youre hede withe and I shall binde myn
eyen therwithe and sethe take it ayein to you.' And whanne she hadde 130
taken it [to hym] the bochers scorned her, sayenge: 'Whi hast thou
take so precious a clothe to this wicked enchauntour to lese it?'

And whanne he come to the place of his passion he turned towarde
the orient and dressed his hondes towarde heuene and praied right
longe and yelded thankingges in the tonge of the contreye withe 135
teeres, and thanne he comaunded his bretheren to God and bounde
his eyen withe Planciles kercheff and sette his knees to the grounde
and streched forth his necke, and so he was beheded. And as sone as
the hede was departed from the body she beganne to name in Ebrewe
withe a clere voys Ihesu Crist that hadde be so suete to hym in his lyff 140
and had named it so ofte, for it is saide that he named it in his pisteles
.vC. tymes. And of the wounde ther come oute a gret streme of mylke
that lepte vpon the clothe of a knight, and sethe come blood and gret

120 whedir] where L   were] om. DH2   beheded] add or no A2   Seint] om. DH2
120-1 wolde haue] hadde EH1T1A1, haue DH2   121 hem] add to the feythe of cryste
A2   thou shalt] trs. T1   122 and arise] aryse vp L   arise] risen GDH2, rise H1T1A1
ayein] add to lyfe A2   shulle we] trs. A2   leue] lyve H1, beleue T1DH2A2   that] add þat
A2   on] om. H1T1A1   123 that] what H1T1, add þat A1A2   as] add that L
125 Plancille] Pantille H1T1A1   disciple] disciples H1A1A2   after] as A2   Denys]
Denye E, add sayeth A2   126 Lemobye] lemovy T1   and] for A2   names] add after
hir .ij. husbondis A2   whiche] add ladie DH2A2   wepte] add fulle A2   127 and] add
she A2   recomaunded] commaunded H1T1A1   praiers] prayere H2   128 Plancely]
plancylle LDH2A2, Plancily G, Planteli H1T1, Plantille A1   me] om. A2   130 sethe]
siþ'e' H1, than DH2A2   131 to hym] om. EH1T1G   132 a] om. H1T1   this] hym
A1   enchauntour] add for DH2A2L   133 passion] add then A2   turned] add hym A2
134 hondes] add vp L   135 and] add he A2   thankingges] add to god A2   the¹] om.
A1   the²] that L   136 bretheren] brothir DH2   and] add then he A2
137 Planciles] Plantiles H1A1, Pantylles T1, Plancyles G   kercheff] clothe A2   and] add
than DH2   sette . . . knees] he knelid downe A2   to] vn to L   139 departed] parted
H1A1GDH2L   she] Plancille DH2A2   140 hadde be] he louyd A1   141 had . . .
it³] she namyd that name ihu so ofte to hym forhe vsid it fulle ofte A2   141 named¹]
namened H1   it¹] om. H1T1A1   pisteles] pistil DH2, add as it is redde of hym more þan
A2   142 And] add owte A2L   the] Poules DH2A2   come] ranne A2   oute] om. L
143 lepte] sprange A2   the] a A2   sethe] after A2

shinynge lyght in the heyre and right suete smelle come oute of his
145 body.

Seint Denys in hys epistell to Timothee saiethe in suche wise of
Paule: 'In that hour full of sorugh, right dere brother and frende, that
the bochers saide: "Make redy thi necke," the blessed apostell beheld
f. 143ᵛᵃ into heuene and arayed his forhede and hys breste withe the | token of
150 the crosse and saide: "Lorde, into thine hondes I recomaunde my
sperit." And thanne witheoute any sorugh he streched forthe his
necke and receiued crowne of marterdome, and whanne the bochers
smote of the hede of Paule, the right blessed man toke the kercheef
and plied it withe the stroke and gadered the blode and lapped it
155 withinne the kerchief and yelde it ayein to the woman. And whanne
the bochers were returned Pancile saide to the bocher: "Wher haste
thou lefte my maister Paule?" And one of the knightes saide: "Yender
he lyethe witheoute the citee with a felawe of his, and his visage is
couered withe thi kercheef." And she ansuered and saide: "Lo here
160 that Petre and Paule entered right now into the citee clothed withe
right noble vestementis and hadde crounes on her hedes more
brighter thanne the sonne and haue brought me ayein my kercheef
al bewette withe blood." For whiche thinge many leued in oure Lorde
and were cristened.' And this saiethe Seint Denys.
165   And whanne Nero herde this that was befall he dredde hym gretly
and beganne to speke of alle these thingges withe philisofers and
withe [his] frendes, and as they speke of this thinge Paule come

144 lyght] *add* was A2   and] *add* a A2   146 in . . . Timothee/saiethe] *trs.*
DH2A2   hys epistell] a pistil DH2A1A2   suche] this A1   147 sorugh] *add* saide
A2   brother, frende] *trs.* A2   that²] *om.* A2   148 saide] *add* to poule A2   necke]
add and DH2A2   149 token] tokenesse EH1T1   150 recomaunde] comende A1
151 his] þe GL   152 receiued] *add* the T1A1DH2A2L   bochers] bocher A1A2
153 the hede of Paule] his hede H1T1A1A2   the³] his H1T1A1   154 it¹] *om.* H2
blode] *add* to geder L   lapped] wrappid GDH2A2L   it²] *om.* GA1   155 to] vn
to L   156 were] *om.* A2   returned] *add* homwarde A2   Pancile] Plancile
GDH2A2L, Pantile H1T1, Pantille A1   the bocher] hym A2   haste] hat A1
156-7 lefte/my . . . Paule] *trs.* DH2   159 thi] *add* visage *subp.* H1   And] *add* than
H2A2   ansuered . . . saide] saide to hym A2   here] *add* is A2   that] *add* here T1
159-60 that/Petre and Paule] *trs.* DH2A2   160 right now/into the citee] *trs.* A2
withe] in A2   161 vestementis] clothyng A2   hadde] haue A2   on] vppon DH2,
of A1   hedes] *add* that shyne A2   162 and] *add* Poule A2   haue] hath A2
bewette] wette T1   withe] in A2   163 thinge many] grete myracle moche people
A2   leued] beleuyd T1DH2A2   Lorde] *add* Ihu criste DH2A2   164 cristened]
baptyzed A2   this] thus T1   saiethe/Seint Denys] *trs.* L   165 that . . . befall] *om.*
A2   166 and¹] *add* then he A2   166-7 of . . . frendes] with his frendis and he
askid councelle of philosophyers in this mater A2   167 his] *om.* EH1T1GA1   this
thinge] þese þyngis A2   come] *add* anon H1T1A1, *add* in A2

amonge hem and the gates shette and stode euene before Nero and
saide: 'Thou emperour, see here Paule the knyght of the euerlastinge
kinge and not ouercome. Now leue that y am not dede but that I leue, 170
but thou, wreche, shal[t] deye of wicked dethe for that thou hast
slayne withe wronge the seintes of God.' And whanne he hadde so |
saide he vanisshed awaye, and than was Nero of that gret afraye oute f. 143ᵛᵇ
of hymselff and wyst not what to do, and thanne be counsell of his
frendes he vnbounde Patrok and Barnabe withe many other and lete 175
hem goo where they wolde. And the tother knightes Longis and
Acestus come in the morwtyde to the sepulture of Paule. And whanne
Titus and Lucas see hem they were gretly affraied and beganne to flee,
and thanne the knyghtes cried after them and sayde: 'Turnithe ayein,
for we pursue you not as ye wene, but we wold be baptised of you as 180
Paule bade us, the whiche we sawe right now praienge withe you.'
And whanne they herde that they turned ayein withe gret ioye and
baptized hem.

    The hede of Paule was caste in a vale, and for the multitude of other
hedes that hadden be slayne and caste there they myght not fynde it. 185
Men rede in that same pistell of Seint Denis that in a tyme as that
valey was clensed and that hede was caste oute withe other thingges
that men putte oute, but a sheparde [lefte] it up withe his rodde and
pight it be his folde of his shepe. And thanne he and his maister sawen
.iij. nightes togedre continuelly gret lyght shyninge vpon that hede, 190
and whanne he hadde tolde it to the bisshopp and to other good

168 amonge] amonges DH2   hem] add alle A2   gates] add fast A2   and³] ins. H1, add he
A2   169 the¹] om. T1   169–70 cuerlastinge kinge] trs. L   170 kinge] kingges H1
and] add 3it DH2, add yet I am A2   leue¹] beleue T1DH2, thou mayste knowe A2
171 but] and A2   shalt] shall EH1A1   of] om. DH2, a A2   172 so] this A2   173 of]
for A1DH2   afraye] add ny3he DH2   173–4 of that . . . hymselff] nye madde for fere A2
174 and¹] `&´ H1   what] add for D   175 many other] oþer many mo A2   176 where]
add that A2   And] add than DH2, add to subþ. H1   the] to þat G, two the A1   tother] .ij.
othir DH2A2, other T1GA1   Longis] Longius DH2A2   177 Acestus] a Cestius G, a
Cestus L, Cestus DH2A2   morwtyde] moren tide H1, morow tyde T1A1, mornyng A2
178 hem] him H1   180 you not] trs. A2   we²] om. L   you²] add as Poule del. H1, add lyke
A2   183 hem] add And DH2A2   184 was] add sette del. G   caste] om. DH2   in] in to
A2L   vale] valeye L, valeye amonge oþer heddis A2   for] om. A1   the] add grete A2   other]
om. DH2A2   185 hadden . . . caste] laye A2   slayne and] om. T1   there] add that L
myght] coude A2   it] the hed of seint poule A2   186 rede] redde E, add that L   that¹] the
DH2A1A2L   that³] `þᵗ/ H1, the A1A2   187 valey] valeye with ye erased H1, vale T1A1,
valerie G   188 men putte] was caste A2   but a] and A1   sheparde] schepe hede herde
with hede del. G   lefte] pight EH1T1, put A1, toke A2   up withe his] vpon a A1   withe] add
a croke del. G   withe . . . rodde] apon a pole A2   189 his¹] the A2   folde of] L, felde A1
shepe] add to fraye awaye wolfys and doggis fro his shepe there wyth A2   he] the shepeherde
A2   sawen] se there A2   190 togedre continuelly] trs. A1A2   191 he] they DH2A2
to²] add the T1

cristen men, they sayde: 'Verrely that is the hede of Seint Paule.'And
than went the bysshop oute with gret multitude of cristen peple and
brought the hede inne withe hem and leyde it in a table of golde and
195 wolde haue assaied to ioyne it to the body. To whom the patriarke
f. 144ra saide: 'We wote well that many good | cristen men be slayn and that
her hedes be disperpled, wherfor I drede to sette this hede to Paule as
his hede, but late us sette it to hys fete, and than praie we to oure
Lorde almighty that yef it be his hede that the body may turne and
200 ioyne hym to hys hede.' And thanne they sette [the] hede atte the fete
of Paule and as they praied they were alle abaisshed, for the body
turned and ioyned hym to hys hede, and than alle they thanked God
and knewen verrely it was the hede of Paule.

Gregori tellithe that ther was a man that fell in dispeyre and
205 ordeyned a corde to hange hymselff, and alway he called the name of
Seint Paule and saide: 'Seint Paule, helpe me.' And thanne there come
a derke shadowe and sayde: 'Good man, do on in haste as thou haste
purposed.' And whanne þe corde was redy there came another
shadowe as though it hadde be the shadowe of a man, sayenge to
210 hym that hasted the man: 'Flee hennes, thou cursed, for Paule that is
called comithe.' And thanne the derke shadowe vanisshed and the
man come ayenne to hymselff and dede caste aweye the corde and
dede worthy penaunce.

In the Regestre of Scint Gregorie bene shewed many miracles of
215 the cheynes of Seint Paule. Sum comen and aske[n] some of the
fylinge of the cheynes. The prestes comen [with] the file and whanne
they asken in faithe, as sone as the file touchithe ther fallithe therof

192 that] add it EH1T1A1A2   is] was A2   193 of] add gret E   cristen] om. A1
cristen peple] marked for trs. H1   194 inne] om. L, reuerentlye A2   195 assaied] saied
H1T1   196 that²] at A1, om. A2   197 disperpled] disparkeled H1T1, disperblid A2
to¹] on erasure H1   as] at A1   198 to¹] vn to L   198–9 than ... almighty] lete vs praye to
almyghtye god A2   199 almighty] add god DH2, Ihu crist A1   200 the¹] his E
200–1 the fete . . . Paule] Poulys fete and made þer prayers A2   201 praied] add
devoutelye to god A2   202 turned] add him H1T1A1A2   hys] the A1   alle they] trs.
H2A2   203 and] add then thaye A2   verrely] add that H2A2L   the . . . Paule] his hed and
A2   hede] body A1   of] add seynt L   204 and] add he A2   205 hymselff] add with
A1A2   and] but A2   207 on] om. A1   in haste] om. H2A2   as] that L   208 redy]
aboute his necke A2   209 as . . . be] lyke A2   as . . . shadowe] om. T1   though] thought A1
210 that hasted] haste A2   cursed] add enemye A2   211 comithe] add anone A1
vanisshed] add aweie H2A2   and] add than H2   the²] when this A2   212 ayenne/to
hymselff] trs. H2   and dede] then he A2   the] his A2   213 penaunce] add for his grete
trespace A2   215 Paule] add for A2   and asken] and asked EH1T1A1, to aske A2   some
of] of H2, for A2   216 cheynes] add and A2   comen] comethe H1   with] om.
EH1T1A1G   the²] to A1, ins. H1   whanne] when with en on erasure H1   217 they] add
that A1   asken] askid GL, add þerof A1A2   in] haue A1, with very A2   touchithe] towchid
GL, is touchid H2A2   therof] add as smalle as powdre A2

withoute laboure, and whanne sum other comen witheoute faithe, they sette to the file but thei canne no[ne] gete.

In a pistell of Seint Denys he wepithe the dethe of Paule his maister 220 be right debonayre wordes, sayenge: 'Who shall yeue water to myn eyen and a well | of teeres to my prunelles so that we wepe night and f. 144rb day for the lyght of the Chirche is queint? Who is he that shulde not wepe and weille and clothe hym in vyle clothes and be abaysshed of gret abasshement? Lo here Petre, the foundement of the Chirch and 225 the ioye of holy aposteles, is departed from us and hathe lefte vs orphelions, and Paule the debonayre comfortour of peple is failed vs and shalle no more be founde, the whiche was fader of faders, doctour of doctours, sheparde of shepardes, the depenesse of wisdom, an harpe hygh sowninge, a prechour of trouthe, I saye Paule that was a 230 right noble apostell and neuer wery, an heuenly man, an aungell vpon erth, ymage and similitude of the diuinite, and he hathe lefte alle the spirites of foule fourme and us nedy and vnworthi he hathe lefte in þis worlde despised and wicked and is gone to Ihesu Crist his God, his Lorde and al hys loue. Alas, brother Timothee, the loue of my soule, 235 wher is thi maister, thi fader, and alle thi loue? Wher shall he salue the any more? Thou art lefte orphanyn and alon, that right holy honde shalle write to the no more in sayenge to þe "right dere sone." Alas to me, brother Timothee, how moche is falle to me of sorugh, of derkenesse and of harme for we be made orphanies? The episteles 240

218 withoute^1] *add* anye A2   whanne . . . comen] thaye that come theder A2   other] *om.* H2   witheoute^2] *add* verye A2   219 file] *add* and laboure A2   but] *add* with all the labour that they can do A1   canne] cowthe L, may A1   none] not EH1T1G, nought H2A2   gete] *add* þerof and A2   220 Denys] *add* where A2   of^2] *add* seint GH2A2
221 be . . . debonayre] mekely saying þese A2   sayenge] nowe A2   water] teerys A2
222 and . . . prunelles] *om.* A2   we] I maye A2   223 queinte] quenchede A1A2, *add* and A2   224 be] to be gretely A2   224–5 of . . . here] for to se A2
225 abasshement] abasshementez H1T1GA1, basshementis H2   here] he A1   Petre] *add* that is A2   226 of] *add* alle the A2   227 orphelions] orphanynes T1, orpheynes A1   the] *om.* A1   debonayre] meke A2   of] *add* the A2   is failed] hath fayleth A1
228 faders] *add* and A2   229 of^1] *add* alle A2   doctours] *add* and A2   of^2] *add* alle A2   shepardes] *add* and A2   the] *om.* H1T1A1, *add* very A2   an] and ET1, and the A2
230 sowninge] *add* and A2   a^1] *add* and G   Paule that] *trs.* H2A2   231 wery] very *changed to* wery H1, lyer A1, *add* of prechyng þe worde of god A2   heuenly] holy A1   man] *add* and E   232 vpon] *add* the A1   the] *om.* A2   diuinite] dignyte T1   lefte] *om.* A2
233 spirites . . . fourme] fourme of foule spirite clene forsakyn A2   hathe] *om.* A2
234 wicked] *add* thynges A1   and^2] *add* he A2   234–5 God, Lorde] *trs.* A2
235 loue^1] lyfe T1   236 salue] grete A2L   237 more] *add* for A2   orphanyn] orphalyn A2L   right] *om.* T1   238 write . . . in] no more write A2   to the/no more] *trs.* H2   239 me^1] my H2A2   of^1] *add* synne and A2   240 orphanies] orphanyne H1, orphanynys T1H2, orphanys G, orphayne A1, orphalyns for A2, orphelyn L

of hym shull no more come to the in whiche he was wonte to saye:
"Paule litell and right lytell servaunt of Criste." He shalle no more
write to the cytes sayenge of the: "Receyuethe my right dere sone."
Brother, ply the bokes of the prophetis and sele hem aboue, for we
haue no man that canne ex|poune hem. Dauid the prophete wept his
sone and saide: "Allas to me, sone, for the." And I saye thanne: "Alas
to me for the, maister, verely alas to me," for from hennes forwarde
cessithe and defailethe the assemble of the disciples comynge to Rome
to seke the. Shal ther neuer none saye from hennes forwarde: "Go we
and see we the noble doctours and aske we hem how we shall gouerne
the chirches commy[tt]ed to us, and praie we hem to expowne us the
wordes of oure Lorde Ihesu Crist and the wordes of God by the
prophetis." Sothely, wo to those children, my brother, that be
depriued from her spirituell fader. Alas to us, brother, that be
depriued of oure spirituell maister, the whiche hadde gadered
togederes the vnderstondinge and the cunnynge of the olde lawe
and of the nwe and ioyned hem togederes in her pisteles. Wher is now
the c[ours] of Paule and the labour of his holy fete? Wher is the
mouthe spekinge and the tonge counsellynge and the sperit well
plesinge to God? Who is that that ne wepithe ne criethe to behold that
tho whiche deserued glori and ioye and worship toward God be putte
to dethe as wicked doers? Alas to me, for I behelde in that oure that
holy body alle bewrappcd in hys bloode. Alas, my fader and my
maister and my doctour, thou were not gilty of suche a dethe. Where
shalle y seke the nowe, ioye of cristen men and the praysinge of good
men. Who made stinte th[i] shrill voys that sovned so high and so

f. 144va
246
250
255
260
265

241 wonte] vsid A2   242 of] *add* ihesu A2L   shalle] *add* here after A2
243 write] *om.* L   write/to the] *trs. and add his* epystlis A2   the²] *add in praysing the* A2
Receyuethe] restreyne A2   right dere] dere right *marked for trs.* H1   sone] *add* and A2
244 ply] loke ye applye to rede A2   the²] *om.* A2   245 wept] *add* vnto A2   246 I
saye] ysaie A2   thanne] *add* saide A2   246–7 the . . . the] thy T1   And . . . the] *om.*
H1A1   247 verely] of verye doctryne is gone A2   248 Rome] *add* for A2
249 the] *add* And A2   Shal ther] *trs.* A2   neuer none] *trs.* G   250 we¹] wele L   we²]
om. L   251 chirches] chirche GA1L   commytted] commyned E   we] *om.* L, *add to*
H2A2   expowne] *add to* A1   252 God] *add* trulye saide A2   253 Sothely] *om.* A2
wo] *add* be A2   those] þise H1T1A1   brother] Brethere H1T1   254 from] for H2
255 of] from A1, also fro A2   256 cunnynge] *add* bothe A2   257 nwe] *add* law A2
and²] *add* haue A2   her] hys T1   258 cours] cure ET1, coure H1, toure A1
259 and¹] *om.* A2   counsellynge] conceylinge H2   260 to¹] vnto A2   that¹] *om.*
H1T1GH2A1L   ne wepithe ne criethe] canne not wepe and crye A2   261 tho] þe
A2L   and¹ . . . God] *om.* H2   putte] *add* nowe A2   262 to] *add* the L   as] of L
263 bewrapped] wrappyd A1   hys] *add* owne L   264 and] *add* also L   dethe] *add*
nowe A2   265 nowe] newe H2A2   and] *add* also L   266 made] maye A2   thi] tho
E, þe *with* 'i' *above* H1, the T1A1A2   shrill] schille GH2, *add of* H1A1

greuously in the Chirche, and who made stinte þe sawtry of .x. cordes? Thou [art] entred to thi God that thou hast desired and coueited withe alle thi wille. Ierusalem | and Rome bene two euell f. 144ᵛᵇ frendes, for thei bene made egal in euel, Ierusalem crucified oure 270 Lorde Ihesu Crist, and Rome hathe slayne the aposteles of that same, Ierusalem serued hym þat he crucified, and Rome glorifie[th] in solempnisinge hem that he hathe slayne. And now, my brother Timothee, these bene tho that thou louedest and desiredest withe alle thi herte. Saul the kinge and Ionathan were neuer departed in her 275 lyff ne in her dethe, and no more am I parted from my lorde and my maister but in as moche as the wicked men hathe departed us, and this tyme of departinge shall not alway endure, for the soule of hym knowithe alway his frendes though thei speke not to hym, and tho that be ferre fro hym now shul fle to gret sorugh [to] be departed from 280 hym atte the day of the resureccion.' And this saiethe Denis.

Iohn Crisostome saiethe in the boke of Preisingges of Seint Paule: 'What t[u]nge is founde suffisaunt in commendacion of hym, sithe alle the goodnesse that is in man [one] only saule posseded and hadde pleinly alle togederes in hym, and not only of man but more yet of 285 aungels, and in what manere we shull telle you after. Abel offered sacrifice and of that he was preised, but we shewe the sacrifice of Paule it will appere gretter as myche as heuene is hygher thanne the erthe, for he sacrifised hymselff eueri day and offered double sacrifice in hert and in body, the whiche he mortefied. He offered not shepe ne nete 290 but sacrifised hymselff in double wise, and yet that suffised hym not but that he stodied to offre to God alle the worlde, for he enviround | alle the world that is vnder the heuene and made aungelles of men, f. 145ʳᵃ

267 greuously] gloriously GT₁H₂A₂L, *so with* glo *on erasure* H₁   who] so L   made] to H₂, did to A₂   268 cordes] *add* for A₂   art] *om.* E   270 crucified] crucyfying A₂ 271 of . . . same] that seruyd at A₂   272 serued . . . crucified] the same ihu cryste A₂ he] that they T₁, be A₁   glorifieth] glorified E   274 Timothee] Thimothe *changed to* Thymothe H₁   louedest] louest A₁A₂   desiredest] desirest A₁A₂   275 neuer] not L 276 ne] nor GH₂, neyther L   parted] departed H₁T₁A₁A₂   and] nor fro my A₂ 278 of¹] *om.* H₂   soule] soulis A₂   hym] them A₂   279 his] there A₂   hym] þem A₂ 280 hym] them A₂   to¹] *add* the A₁   to²] and EH₁T₁A₁   281 the²] *om.* A₁   saiethe] *add* seynt A₁A₂L   Denis] *add* And A₂   282 Preisingges] preching A₁, praysing A₂ 283 tunge] thinge EH₁T₁A₁, is that þat A₂   284 is] be L   one] L, *om.* EH₁T₁GH₂A₁A₂   only] *add* the A₂   saule] soule *changed to* Poule H₁, poule T₁ posseded] possedith G   hadde] hath A₂   285 pleinly] plannely H₁   more] *om.* A₁ of²] *add* the H₂A₂   286 telle] offre to A₂   you] *add* here A₂   287 shewe the] that L Paule] *add* ant A₂   288 will appere] well appereth H₁T₁A₁   gretter] *add* in A₂ hygher] *om.* L   289 he] Paule A₂   291 but] *add* he A₂L   292 that] *om.* A₂ 292–3 for . . . world] that ys vnderstonde all L   293 the²] *om.* T₁A₂

and yet moreouer the men that were lyke fendes he chaunged hem to
295 aungeles. Who is he that is founde paraile vnto this sacrifice, the
whiche Paule withe the suerde of the holy goste offered up to the
auuter that is aboue heuene? Abel was slaine [by the] treson of his
brother, but Paule was slayne by tho that he wolde withedrawe from
wicked werkes. And vnnethes a man may shewe his dethes, for he
300 hadde as many dethes as he lyued dayes.

'Noe as it is redde kepte in the arche hym and his children alonly,
but Paule in a more perilous flode that surmounted be the [deluge]
deliuered fro the waters that pershed in al the worlde, not in an arke
that was ioyned of bordes but in makinge episteles for tables. This
305 shippe that he made environde a place that comprehended alle the
[endes] of the worlde, ne she was not anointed withe no piche ne
withe glewe, but thei were anointed withe the grace of the holy goost.
In this doinge he made tho that were more foles thanne bestes
witheoute reson to folue aungels in conuersacion. And he ouercome
310 that ship [in] that þat Noe hadde the ravin witheinne the shippe and
he putte hym oute witheoute comynge ayenne. He hadde also a wolfe
and he might neuer chaunge his cruelte, but this Paule made the
faucones, the egles and the kytes become doues and toke awaye al her
cruelte.

315   'Some folke mervaile of Abraham for that atte the comaundement of
f. 145ʳᵇ God he lefte his contrey and his kinrede, but how may he be lyke|ned
to this Paule that lefte not only his contre [and his kindrede] but he
lefte alle the worlde and hymselff to, and in dispisinge al erthely
thinge he toke hym to Ihesu Crist and required one thinge aboue alle
320 other thinge[s] and that was the charite of Ihesu Crist, for he saide: "I

294 he] *om.* H1T1A1   to] in to L   295 vnto] to A2   296 up to] vnto H1T1A1
297 is] it may be A1   by the] L, withe EH1T1A1, by GH2A2   298 wolde] *add* haue
A2   withedrawe] with with drawe H2   299 may shewe] *trs.* H2   dethes] dedes T1A2
299–300 for . . . dethes] *om.* H1T1A1   300 dethes] dedis A2   lyued] lyved *changed to*
lyvyd H1, leueth A1, *add* 'in' his T1   301 hym] hymselfe his wyffe A2   302 Paule]
om. L   a more] another A1   surmounted] surounded H2   deluge] diluvie EH1T1A1,
dealyng for he A2   303 in²] *om.* A2   304 of] with L   in] *add* a G   makinge] *add* of
A1A2   305 that²] *add* is L   306 endes] places E   not] *om.* A2   no] *om.* A2L   ne]
nor G, neyþer L   306–7 ne withe] neither A2   307 withe²] *add* no T1   of] *add* god
A2   308 In] and *subp.* 'in' G   that were] *om.* A1   310 in] and EH1T1A1   hadde]
add in H1T1A1   311 witheoute] *om.* H1T1A1   312 and] '&' G   he] *add* ne L
313 and¹] *om.* A1   kytes] *add* to A1   314 cruelte] *add* And A2   315 that] *add* that
H2, *om.* T1, he A2   the] *om.* A1   317 and his kynrede] *om.* EH1T1A1   he] *om.* A1
318 dispisinge] displesyng A1   al] of H1T1A1   319 thinge¹] thinges A1A2   hym]
add fullye A2   hym to] *trs.* L   and] *add* he A2   required] *add* to haue A2
320 thinges] thinge EH1

will not tho thingges that be present ne tho thingges that be to come."
Also Abraham putte hym in perile and deliuered his brother from his
enemyes, and Paule deliuered alle the worlde fro the pouer of the
fende and suffered gret nombre of periles ande bought to other gret
suerte withe his propre dethe. Abraham wolde haue sacrifised his 325
sone, but Paule sacrifised hymselff a .M^l. tymes.

'And sum mervaylen of the pacience of Isaak for that he suffered to
stoppe the well that he hadde made, Paule not beholdinge the welle
filled vp withe stones ne his owne body alonly beten but he stodied to
bringe to heuene tho that he suffered paynes by. And so moche more 330
as the w[ell]e was stopped, so moche ouerflowed more the stremes of
hym in shedynge his water al aboute. The scripture meruailethe of the
debonairte and of the pacience of Iacob, and what is that pacience that
might folowe the pacience of Paule? For she endured not be .vij. yere,
but be space of alle his lyff he dede seruise for the spouse of [Crist]. 335
He was not only brent withe the sonne of the day and withe the colde
of the nyght, but he suffered moche tempest, for now he was bete,
now he was stoned, now with staues smiten. He lepte amonge these
batayles and drewe oute of the hondes of the fende and of hys |
mouthe the shepe that he hadde rauisshed. Ioseph was ennobelisshed f. 145va
withe the vertue of chastite, and I drede me not but that Paule 341
surmounted in chastite merueilously, [as] he that crucified hymselff
and despised not only the beauute of bodyes of mankinde but of alle
th[e] thinggez that he seigh clere and faire to the eye right as we
despise filthe and asshes, and who was witheoute eny stiringe as the 345
dede body to the dede.

'Alle meruaylen of Iob for þat he was a mervaylous champion, but

321 ne] nor A2   322 hym] hymselfe A2   322–3 his^l . . . deliuered] om. A2
323 and] add he A2   324 bought] b`r´ought H1, brought T1A1   to other] togidre
H1T1A1   325 dethe] add For A2   326 sone] add to god A2   hymselff] add to god
A2   a] om. H2   327 mervaylen] merveyled L   329 filled] fillyng A1   ne] nor A2
330 he] add had A2   331 welle] witte ET1A1L, wit changed to wel H1   was] add
stonyd and L   more] om. L   stremes] stremyd G   332 shedynge] add of H2A2   the]
ins. in margin A1   333 debonairte] mekenes A2   of the] om. A2   that^l] this H2A2
334 not] add in hym A2   be] om. T1   335 be] the T1, add the A1A2   he] And A1
of^2] subp. H1, om. T1   Crist] om. EH1T1, manys soule A1   338 smiten] add and A2
amonge] add alle A2   339 batayles] peryllis A2   oute] om. A2   fende] fendys A1
of^3] he drewe fro A2   340 hadde] dud G   ennobelisshed] enneblisshed H1,
anneblysshyd T1   341 of] add the A2   and] but L   but] om. A2   342 chastite] add
and in Chastite G   as] and E   343 and] add he A2   beauute] bewties A2   of^l] add the
A2   of^2] om. H1T1A1A2   344 the^l] tho EH1T1A1, om. H2A2   clere, faire] trs. T1
345 and^l] om. A1   who] he A2L   346 body] om. L   to] of A1   dede^2] add and A2
347 of] to subp. `of´ G

Paule was not only be monthes but dured many yeres in gret agonye
till he appered bright and clere. He shoue not away the rotenesse of
350 [his] flesshe withe a shelle, but he ranne euery day ayeinste þe mouthe
of the lyon ententifly and faught ayeinst alle the temptaciones and alle
the iniuries of wicked companies, wher he was founde more sufferable
thanne any stone, and he susteined not the iniurie of thre or foure
frendes but of alle vntrue beleuers, and also of his bretheren he
355 susteined reproves and he was chidde and cursed of alle. Iob was a
gret hospitaler and hadde gret besinesse aboute the pore, but that
good that he dispended was to susteine the filthe of the flesche, and
this Paule laboured aboute the seke corages and hys hous was open to
alle that wolde come and his soule was redy for al the worlde. Iob
360 hadde oxen and bestes witheoute nombre and was liberall to the pore,
and Paule posseded nothinge but his bodie and of that he amynistred
sufficiauntly to the nedes, and as he saiethe hymselff in sum place of
f. 145ᵛᵇ his | writinge: "These hondes here serued to my necessitees and to tho
that were with me." Also wormes and r[o]tones made sorugh and
365 a[k]inge in the woundes of Iob, but yef thou wilt considre than the
betingges of Paule, the honger, þe cheynes, the prisone, the periles
that he suffered of his knowlage, and of straungers, as moche for the
Chirche as for the sclaundre of other, thou shuldest see that he were
harder thanne any stone, his soule surmounted al hardenesse of iren
370 and of ademond. And tho thingges that Iob sustened in [body, Paule
sustened in] thought, [tristesse,] that is sorugh, whiche is more

348 but] troublid but his trouble A2   in] *add* fulle A2   349 till] *add* that A2
350 his] the EH1T1A1   351 the¹] *add* wode A2   lyon] *add* fulle A2   the²] þoo G, *om.*
A1A2   352 the] *om.* L   of] *add* the A2   wicked] *om.* A1   companies] *add* of men and
of feendis A2   wher] wherefore A2   353 not] *add* only A2   or] *add* of L
354 frendis] feendis A2   but] *add* also A2   alle] *om.* T1   vntrue beleuers] mysbelevers
and vntrewe and wickid people A2   beleuers] leuers H1A1, lyuers T1   355 susteined]
add manye A2   alle] *add* tho that were yvylle disposid but euer he toke it mekely and
thonkid god at alle lymes and A2   356 hadde . . . aboute] fulle grete besynes he had
among A2   pore] *add* people A2   357 dispended] spendid G   358 was] *add* euer A2
359 alle] whom A2   was] *add* euerA2   for] to A2   worlde] *add* in gode councelle yevyng
to theyme A2   361 nothinge] no þis þinge *with* þis *del.* G   he] the L   amynistrid]
ministrid H2A2, admynystred T1A1   362 place] placis A2   363 writinge] writhing
A1, wrytingis A2   hondes] bondis H2   364 rotones] ratones E   and²] *om.* G
365 akinge] a thinge EA1, *so changed to* akinge H1, akynges G   366 betingges] bitinges
H1T1A1   the¹] to H1A1, to *changed to* the T1, *add* grete A2   368 other] *add* wherefore
A2   shuldest] maiste welle A2   were] *add* and was L, was GH2A2   369 any] þe L
stone] *add* for A2   his soule] *om.* A1   hardenesse] harnesse H1   370 of] *add* þe A2
ademond] ayemant L   And tho] stone. Tho A2   370–1 body . . . in] *om.* E
371 tristesse] trustisse E, thirstesse A1, trystesly L   tristesse . . . sorugh] hevynesse and
sorowe for the deth of synners the A2   is¹] his E   is²] *add* a L

hardefull thanne any worme, wasted Paule, and suete wellys of teeres
went oute of Paule not only by dayes but be nyghtes. He was more
tormented thanne woman travelinge of childe in euery creature,
wherfor he sayde: "My children that I haue bore ayein."   375
'Moyses wolde haue be defaced oute of the boke of lyff for the
saluacion of Iues and offered hymselff to perisshe withe other, but
Paule wolde not only perisshe withe his kynne, but so that alle other
might be saued he wolde be caste downe fro euerlastinge ioie. And
Moyses faught withe Pharao and Paule faught with the deuell, and   380
that one faught for one peple and Paule faught for al the worlde, and
not only be suetinge but be shedinge of his blood. Seint Iohn ete
locustes and wilde hony, but Paule gouerned hymselff in the middes
of the worlde as Seint Iohn dede in deserte, but he ete not locustes ne
hony but he was susteined withe more vile lyvinge and withe many   385
other necessitees, for he lefte many tymes his mete for feruent stody
of prechinge. Iohn | appered verrely withe gret sadnesse of corage   f. 146ʳᵃ
before Herodiane, but this Paule ne correcte[d] not only .ij. ne .iiij. but
he corrected witheoute nombre that were right gret and in right high
myght and moche more cruel tyrauntes thanne was Herodes.   390
'Than now it aperteinithe to vs that we liken Paule to aungeles of
whiche we preche gret thingges, for they obeyen to God withe al her
cure. Of whom Dauid mervaylenge saiethe: "They be myghty in
vertue and done the comaundement of hym." And for that the profete
hym mervailithe of aungeles, he sayde: "He that made his aungeles   395
spirites and his ministres fire brennynge." But al that mowe we fynde
in Paule, that right as fire and a sperit he ranne thorugh the worlde,

372 hardefull] hardir A2   wasted . . . and] or rotenes of flesh and poule had fulle ofte A2
teeres] add that A2   373 Paule] his eyen for þe synnes of the people A2   but] add also A2
374 thanne] add a H2A2   travelinge . . . childe] with chylde in traveylyng L   of] withe H2
in] his petye was so grete to the helthe of A2   375 ayein] add I praye euer for them A2
376 wolde] twice once del. H1   377 and] add he A2   378 so] also A2   that] as H1T1A1
380 deuell] feend A2   381 that one] moyses A2   for] add þat G   382 his] om. L
Iohn] add the baptist A2   383 hony] add sowks A2   hymselff] hym A1   the] om. A1
384 of] om. A1   as] and L   in] add the L   he] poule A2L   not] no T1   384–5 ne hony]
nor wilde hony sowks A2   385 but] bothe H2   he] om. H2L   vile] vi followed by two
erased letters H1   vile lyvinge] be/leuyng T1, byle/uyng A1   388 this] om. A2   ne¹] he
A1, om. A2   corrected] correcte E   ne²] or H2A1A2L   389 corrected] conuertyd A1, add
evylle doers A2   nombre] nomble H2   389–90 and in . . . myght] cruelle and high of
estate and myghty A2   390 more] om. A1   cruel] add tormentez subp. H1, om. A2
thanne] add were del. G   was] om. A1   Herodes] herodyan And A2   391 now/it
aperteinithe] trs. A2   392 obeyen] obeying GH2L, be obeying alwaye A2   393 saiethe]
add that A2   394 done] do euer A2   comaundement] commaundementes H1T1A1A2
hym] god H2A2   395 hym mervailithe] trs. A2   his] om. A2   396 But] and A2
397 a] om. G, as A2   thorugh] add alle A2

and in hys rennynge he purged it, and yet he was not in heuene, and
that is in alle wyse mervailous that s[uc]he one shulde duelle in erthe
400 and enviround withe dedely flesshe. A, Lorde, how be we thanne
worthi gret dampnacion whanne we see al goodes to be assembeled in
one man and we stodye not to folowe the leste partie of hem. Ne he
hadde in this worlde none other thinge, ne none other nature, ne none
disse[mbl]able soule to us, ne he was of none other worlde, [but in this
405 same worlde] he was norisshed and vnder the same lawes and in his
maners and condiciones he surmounted alle the men that bene and
hauc bene [by] the corage of nature. Ne this thinge is not to mervayle
in hym only, for by the habundaunce of deuocion that was in hym he
felt not in a maner the sorwes that he hadde for vertue, but he
410 recompensed in hym that vertue for his guerdon. And whanne he |
f. 146rb seigh that his dethe neighed he called other to [the] delite of his ioie,
seyinge: "Makithe ioye and reioyse you with me." And certainly he
hasted more to go to harmes and iniuries that he susteined for grace of
prechinge than he dede to a gret feste full of ioye, he coueited more
415 the desire of dethe thanne of lyff and of pouerte more thanne richesse,
and also he coueyted more trauayle thanne other done reste, and [in]
hys reste he chase rather wepinge thanne [the] delyte of rest. He used
to praie more gladly for his enemyes thanne other for her frendes.
And aboue al thinge he dradde the wratthe of God, ne he hadde desire
420 of none other thinge but only to plese God. And I sayc not only that
he forsoke all present thingges, but alle thingges that be to come he
refused atte onys, that is to saye, alle the prosperitees that euer were or
euer shall be in erthe. But yef we shulde speke of thingges that be
behyght of heuene, than shalt thou see the loue of hym in Ihesu Crist,

398 he] ne *changed to* he H1   399 suche] sithe EH1T1A1   duelle] dwell *with* d *on*
erasure H1   in] *add* the EH1T1A1   400 enviround] vnvirond H1T1   thanne] *om.*
401 to] *om.* L   402 hem] hym L   Ne, ne] nor, nor A2   403 ne[1,2]] nor, nor A2
none[1]] *add* other EA1A2   404 dissemblable] dissensable EH1A1   404–5 but . . .
worlde] *om.* EH1T1A1   405 the] thys L   his] thes A1   407 by] *om.* E   the] *om.*
H1T1A1   Ne] *om.* A2   409 sorwes] sorow T1   409–10 but . . . vertue] *om.* A1
410 guerdon] rewarde A2   411 the] *om.* E   412 Makithe] make ye A2   you] ye A2
413 go] good *with* d *erased* H1, god A1   go to] *om.* A2   and] *add* to A2   iniuries] *add* and
A2   414 than . . . dede] and was more gladder there of than though he shulde go A2
a] *om.* M   feste] festes A1   ioye] *add* for A2   coueited] conuertid GH2   415 of[2]] *add*
bodely A2   of[3]] he desirid A2   pouerte more] *trs.* A2   thanne] *add* of T1
416 coueyted] conuertid GH2   other] *add* men A2   and[2]] for A2   in] *om.* EH1T1A1
417 the] *om.* E, *ins.* H1   used] *add* also A2   418 other] *add* doone L, *add* men done A2
her] *add* goode L   419 And] *om.* A1   al] *add* oþer A2   thinge] thinges A1   ne] and
A2   420 of] to A2   thinge] thinges A1   only] *add* for A2   421 thingges[2]] *om.* L
422 refused] suffred L   423 in] *add* the H2   we] *ins.* H1, I A1   shulde] schul G, shul
H1T1GA2   424 shalt] shall H1T1A1   the] by H1T1A1   of] *add* heven L

for truly for the loue of hym he desired not the dignite of aungell ne of 425
archaungell ne of no like thingges, but tho thingges that were gretter
he vsed, that was of the loue of Ihesu Crist, and withe þis loue he
bethought hymselff blessed of alle, and witheoute that he coueited not
to be felawe withe dominaciones ne princes ne aungeles [ne arch-
aungelles], but he coueited more withe that loue to be leste man of tho 430
that be ponisshed thanne witheoute that to be amonge the souerayne
worshippes. And that was to hym most souerayne turment for to
departe fro this charitee, for that departinge was to hym an helle, that
only was | to hym, and torment witheoute ende, and on that other side f. 146ᵛᵃ
to use the charitee of Ihesu Crist was to hym lyff, worlde and rewme 435
and alle goodes witheoute nombre.

'And so alle thingez that we dreden here as men dispised a welked
leef. The tyrauntes [and] the peple full of wodenesse thei were not to
hym as in greuaunce but as flees, and he acounted tormentes and
dethe as game of children whanne he susteined hem for Ihesu Crist, 440
hym thought hymselff more worshipped withe a cheyne fastened to
hym thanne though he hadde be crowned withe a crowne, and whanne
he was constreined in prison, he duelled in heuene and receyued
gladlyer woundes and betingges thanne other done victories, and he
loued not lasse sorues thanne medes. And he helde the sorwes in stede 445
of guerdones, and þe anguisshes that he suffered he called hem grace,
and tho thingges that be to us cause of tristesse were to hym gret
delyte. He was enbraced withe right gret wepinges, wherfor he saide:

425 aungell] angels A2   ne] nor A2   426 archaungell] archaungels A2   ne] nor A2
tho] the A1   427 vsed] add and A2   of'] om. H2A2   þis] his H1T1A1   loue²] and A1
427–8 he bethought] hym þou3t GH2, he thought A2   428 coueited] couth A1
429 withe] add the ordre A2   ne princes] nor with principites A2   ne²] nor with A2
429–30 ne archaungelles] om. EH1T1A1   430 that loue] the love of god A2   be] add þe
H1T1GH2A1L   tho] om. L   431 be] add bi del. G   433 this] his A2   that] add the
H1T1A1GH2L   departinge] partinge H1T1GH2L   434–5 that only] and it A2
434 and'] a H1T1A1A2   on] that L   side] add for L   435 Crist] add the which A2
436 goodes] goodnes A1   437 thingez] the kynges A1   we] were with re subp. G, were A2
dreden] dredyng L   as men] he A2   men] add he A1   despised] dispise GH2, add as A1A2
welked] wikkid GA1A2   438 leef] lyfe A1   The] add turmentis of A2   and] of
EH1T1A1, add of A2   thei] om. A2   439 as²] add byting of A2   tormentes] turment A2
440 as] add the A2   hem] hym L   for] of H2   441 hym] he LA2   cheyne] thefe A1
442 thanne] om. A2   crowned] add lyke a kyng A2   443 prison] add and fulle sore bounde
with chaynes hethought þat A2   and] add he A2   444 gladlyer] more gladly A2L, gladder
A1   betingges] bitingez H1T1   other] add men A2   he] corr. from be in same hand A1
445 sorues] add in stede of guardons del. followed by space for 4 letters A1   thanne . . . helde]
ins. in margin in later hand A1   the] his A2   in] add the A2   446 guerdones] medis G,
rewardis A2   þe] his A2   anguisshes] anguisshe E   grace] gracis A2   447 tho] the A1
tristesse] sorowes A1A2   to²] vnto A2   448 delyte] add and A2   was] add euer A2
wepinges] wepyng A1   saide] add that A2

"[Who] is desc[l]aundred and I am not brent?" And he canne saye
450 that any delite be in wepinge, and yet many a man is wounded full
sore withe the dethe of his childe and takithe his comfort in that he
may wepe ynough, and it is his moste greuaunce whan he is restreined
of his [sorw]inge. Right so Paule toke night and day comfort of teres,
for there coud none wepe so moche his propre defauutes as he wepte
455 for the defauutes of other, as well of straungers as of familiers, for
f. 146ᵛᵇ right as thou woldest wene that he were tormented as he that wep|te
his pershinge for her synnes, the whiche coueited to be forclosed fro
the ioye of heuene so that other myght be saued, for he felt no more
esely the pershinge of other thanne hys owne dampnacion.

460 'And to what thynge thanne shull we lyken hym, to what iren, to
what ademond? Some may calle hym the soule gilte or ellys that is
mo[re] of ademond, for she is strengger thanne any ademonde and
more precious thanne any golde or any precious stone, and of alle
other materes she surmounted the strengthes bi sadnesse and by
465 preciouste. And thanne we may saye that Paule is more worthi and
more precious thanne the worlde and alle the thingges that bene
therinne, for he fleigh as thow he hadde winges thorugh the worlde in
techinge, and dispis[ed] alle trauayles and periles as though thei hadde
be one body, and right as he possedithe now the heuene he dispised
470 alle erthely thingges. And right as iren whanne it is leyde in the fire is
made alle fire, right so Paule enbrased with charite was made al
charitee. And right as he hadde be a comune fader of alle the worlde,
he loue[d] alle men and he surmounted alle other faders bodely and

449 Who] He EA1H2A2, he *changed to* who H1   desclaundred] deschaundred E   and]
om. L   he] who GA1L   450 that any] I canne A2   any] oonely T1   be] *om.* A2   many]
may L, mana A1   is] be L   451 his²] *om.* A2L   453 sorwinge] wepinge E, sorw
H1T1A1   toke] *add* euery A2   comfort] *add* in shedyng A2   454 for there] other L   his
propre] ther L   455 for] *om.* A1   other] *add* men A2   of³] *add* frendis and of A2
456 as²] and A1   457 her] his A2L   forclosed] sore closyd A1   fro] for A1   458 that]
add all GDH2A2L   458–9 no … esely] asmoche A2   459 esely] *om.* L   thanne] saules
as he felte A2   460 And] *om.* A2   shull] schulde A1L   hym] *add* or A2   what] *om.* A1
iren] ire L   460–1 to what] or A2   461–2 Some … ademond] *om.* A2   461 soule]
Saule H1T1   that] *add* he A1   is] his DH2   462 more] L, moder EH1T1A1GDH2
ademond] *add* and more precyous L   she] *om.* H1, he T1   for … ademonde] *om.* A1
463 golde] *add* or syluer A2   any²] *om.* A1, *add* other A2   stone] stones A1   464 materes
she] martyrs he T1   she] she *with* s *erased* H1   surmounted] surmownteth A1   strengthes]
strengest T1   465 preciouste] precioust H1, precyosnesse T1   we] Whe H2
466 thanne] *add* all A1   467 thorugh] *add* alle A2   468 techinge] prechyng A1, *add* for
he set at nought A2   dispised] dispisinge EH1T1A1   trauayles] trauayleris G   periles] *add*
and A1   as] and H1T1, and as A1   469 he¹ … the] nowe he possedid A2   now] *add* to
EH1T1A1   heuene] *add* so A2   471 with] *add* þe H1T1   472 he] hit DH2A2
worlde] *add* so A2   473 loued] louethe E   he²] *om.* A1

gostely by curiosite and bi pitee, and he coueyted and hasted hym to
yelde alle men to God and to his kingdom as though he hadde 475
engendered hem alle.

'This man that was so simple and haunted [the] crafte to make
basketis come to so gret vertue that in space of .xxx.^{ti} yere he dede so
moche that he drowe to the state of trouth the Perses, the Parties, the
Medes, þe Iudayes, the Scites, the Ethiopes, þe Sa[romat]es and the 480
Sarisenes, and | that more is, alle maner of men, and right as fere putte f. 147ra
in haye or in tough wastithe alle, right so wast[ed] he alle the [werkes]
of the fende. And whanne he was ledde thorugh the Gret See he ioyed
hym as gretly as though he hadde be ledde to see an empire, and
whanne he was entered into Rome it suffised hym not to be there but 485
ranne hym into Spayne, ne he passed neuer [oo] day idell ne in rest,
but was more brenninge thanne fire in the brenninge of prechinge, for
he dradde no periles ne he hadde no shame of despites. And that was
also gretter meruaile, for he was worthi and hardy and euer redy in
bataile, and anone he shewed hymselff pesible and amiable. And whan 490
his disciples seyen hym bounde in cheines, notwithestondinge that he
preched in prison, thei sayen hym also wounded and bete al day withe
wordes, and yet thei gadered gretter truste and techinge of hym.
Wherfor in shewinge this thinge he sayde: "Some of our bretheren,
seinge and consideringe oure techinge and [spek]inge witheoute drede 495
the word of God in prison bounden, token in hem more strengthe and
were more hastely b[orn] ayenst her enemies."

'Right as fire that is take in diuerse maneres and withe diuerse
materes encrese[th] the more and is more hote, right so the tonge of

474 bi] *om.* DH2A2   475 to²] vn to L   as] and A1   477 the] this EH1T1A1
478 basketis] *add* and after A2   in] *add* the A2   .xxx^{ti}.] *on erasure* H1   479 to] *om.*
H1T1   Perses] *add* and A2   the Parties] the persyes L, *om.* T1A1   the⁴] of A2
480 Medes] modis G, modes A1   Iudayes] yndes A2   Scites] Tretes T1, sates A1
Saromates] Samaritanes EH1T1A1   481 that . . . is] more ouer A2   fere] *add* that is A1
482 haye] hey D, heth H2   wasted] wastithe ET1   he] Poule A2   werkes] rightes ET1,
rightes *with -gh- subp. and del.* H1, thinges A1   483 ioyed] ioyned L   484 hym] *om.*
T1   485 hym not] *trs.* T1   486 ranne hym] he ranne A2   ne¹] and A2   oo] a E,
om. H1T1A1   day] *add* idid *subp.* G, *add* in DH2   idell ne] in ydylnes and A2   487 was]
add alwaye A2   the] *om.* L   488 ne he] ne DH2A1, nor A2   of] ne H2   that] yet it A2
489 also] *om.* A2   gretter] gret A1   in] to GDH2L, vnto A2   490 and¹] but A2
491 cheines] *add* and L   491-2 notwithestondinge . . . preched] but for alle that he
cessid not to preche while he was A2   492 in] *add* the L   prison] *add* and A2   al] *add*
the A2   day] wey H1T1A1   493 and¹] but A2   gadered] *add* the A2   and²] in A2
494 thinge] *om.* A1   495 spekinge] prechinge E   drede] *add* of A2   496 in²] vnto
A2   hem] hym A1L, *add* the A2   497 were] *add* the A2   born] beringe EH1T1A1
498 maneres] materis GDH2A2L   499 materes] wordes L   encreseth] encresed E
is] hys L   more] moost A2   hote] *add* þerby A2   of] *add* the blessid A2

500 Paule to what thinge that she was meued she was anone transported to
the same thing, and that she vndertoke were made spirituel pastoure
to his fire, for the flambe of the gospell encresed hem more and more.'
And this saiethe Crisostome.

Here endithe the liff of Seint Paule, and nexst foluithe the

f. 147rb   lyff of the .vij. bretheren whos names | be rehersed
hereafter, Cap^m. .iiij^{xx}.v^m

The .vij. bretheren weren of the blessed Felice, and the names of hem
bene these: Phelip, Aluanie, Alexander, Vitall, Ianiver and Marcial.
Alle these withe her moder were called bi the comaundement [of] the
emperour Antoigne before Publien that was prouoste, and thanne he
5 counsailed the moder that she wolde haue pitee [of] herselff and [of]
her sones, the whiche ansuered in this wise: 'Neither withe thi
blandisshinge wordes ne withe thi thretinge thou shalt not betraie
me, ne be thi merites thou maist not breke me. I am sure by the holy
goste that is withe me that I lyuinge shalle ouercome the, and yet
10 moche beter whanne I am dede.' And than she turned her to her sones
and said to hem: 'My dere sones, bethe sadde and beholdethe up to
heuenewarde, for Ihesu Crist abidethe us. Fighttithe strongly for his
loue and shew you true knightes to hym.' And whan the prouost herde
her speke in this wise he comaunded that she shulde be bete withe
15 pa[um]es, and as the moder and the sones abode right stable in the
faithe the moder comforted hem alle, and so in her presence thei were
slayne alle withe diuerse tormentes.

And Seint Gregori [ca]llithe this blessed Felice more thanne
marter, for she suffered .vij. dethes in her .vij. sones and the .viij.
20 in her [owne persone]. And he saiethe in his omely that 'the blessed
Felice in beleuinge was made the seruaunt of oure Lorde, and in
prechinge she was made the marter of oure Lorde Ihesu Crist, and her

f. 147va   .vij. sones that she | dredde in suche wise to leue hem behinde her in
prison, like as worldely frendes vsen to drede lest thei shuld deye in
25 prison. She hadde born hem by the holy goste tho that she hadde born
of her flesshe, and now by prechinge she brought to God the sones

500 to] in H1T1   that] om. H1T1A1   she¹] hit T1, he A2   she²] hit T1
transported] transposid A2   to] in H1T1A1   501 she] hit T1   vndertoke] vnder L
were] was T1   503 And] om. G   this] thus T1

EH1GDH2A1A2L   3 of] be EH1   5 of^{1,2}] on E   6 Neither] Ne þere H1
12 abidethe] abieth H1   15 paumes] pannes EH1G (paumees P2)   the²] om. H1
18 callithe] tellithe EH1   20 her owne persone] herselff EH1

that she hadde born to the worlde, and tho that she seigh that were
come of her flesshe she might not se deye witheoute sorugh, but ther
was a strengthe of loue witheinne her that ouercome th[e] sorugh of
the flesshe. And therfor I haue saide rightwisely that this woman is 30
more thanne marter that so ofte desired dethe desiringly in her sones,
whan she hadde in that multeplied marterdome, and she ouercome
the victorie of marterdome whanne for the loue of God her only dethe
suffised her not.' And they suffered dethe aboute the yere of oure
Lord .C.l. and .x.   35

Here endithe the liues of the .vij. bretheren, and nexst
fol⟨ui⟩the the liff of Seint Theodore marter, Cap^m. .iiij^{xx}.vj.

Theodore was a noble woman and a faire in Alisaundre in the tyme of
the emperoure Zenonys and hadde a riche man to her husbonde
dredinge God. And the fende, whiche hadde envie to her holynesse,
meued a riche man to loue her and hasted her gretly be yeftes and be
messages and required her that she wolde consent to hym. But she 5
refused the massages and despised the yeftes, and he continued his
besinesse aboute her that she might haue no tyme of reste but was
almoste ouercome. And sithe he sent to her an enchauntoure that
praied her to haue pitee of that man | and consent to hym, and whanne f. 147vb
she tolde hym that she wolde not do so gret a synne in the sight of 10
God he ioyned withe her wordes and saide to her: 'I wote well that as
moche as is done by day God knowithe, but whanne it is euene and
the sonne is downe God seithe nothyng that is done.' And thanne
saide Theodore to the enchauntour: 'Thou saieste not trewe.' And he
saide to her: 'Sekirly I saie trouthe.' And thanne Theodore was 15
deceiued bi the wordes of the enchauntour and saide to hym whanne
it is euene that he shulde make hym come and she wolde fulfell his
wille. And whanne he hadd tolde this to the man he was fulfelled
withe moche ioie and come atte his houre assigned and laye withe her
and thanne went his waye.   20
    And thanne whanne Theodore was come to herselff she wepte
bitterly and bete her visage, sayinge: 'Alas to me, alas to me, for I haue
loste my soule and destroied the beauute of my name.' Thanne her
husbond come fro witheoute and seigh his wiff so discomforted and

28 not] *changed to* now H1   29 the] that E   30 therfor] thereof H1
EH1GDH2A1A2L   2 Zenonys] Szenonys E   3 holynesse] *add* of Theodore G
12 knowithe] L, *add* ande seithe EH1G   16 whanne] what G

25 wepinge and knewe not the cause. He enforsed hym to comforte her
[but] she wolde take no comforte, but on the morwe she went to an
abbey of nonnes and asked of the abbesse yef God might knowe a gret
synne that was done by night, and she saide her ayein that nothinge
might be hydde fro Godde, for Godde seithe and knowithe alle that is
30 done in what oure that it be. And thanne she saide withe wepinge
bitterly: 'Yeue me the boke of the gospelles so that sum lotte falle to
me.' Than she opened the boke and founde wretin witheinne: '*Quod*
f. 148ra *scripsi scripsi.*' And thanne she turned ayenne to her | hous.

And in a tyme whanne her husbonde was oute she toke the
35 clothinge of a man and went to a chirche of monkes that was fro
thennes [.xviij.] myle and required that she might be receyued withe
the monkes. And thei graunted her and asked her name, and she saide
her name was Theodore. And thanne she dede humblye alle the
offices and her seruise was agreable to alle. And witheinne [fewe] yeres
40 after, the abbot bade hym that he shulde couple the oxen and go to the
towne and bringe hem oyle. And in that other syde her husbond gretly
dredinge leste she hadde be go awaye withe sum other man. And
thanne the aungell of oure Lorde said to hym: 'Arise erly in the
morwtyde and holde the in the waye of [the] marteres Petre and
45 Paule, and she that thou shalt mete is thi wyff.' And thanne Theodore
came withe the cameles and seigh her husbonde and knewe hym and
saide to herselff: 'Alas, my good husbonde, how trauaile I to bringe me
oute of the synne that I dede ayeinste the.' And whanne he neighed to
her she salued hym and sayde: 'Oure Lorde yeue the ioye, my lorde.'
50 And he knewe her nothinge, and whanne he hadde longe abidde her
there he helde hym deceiued. Thanne a voys saide to hym: 'That same
that salued the in the morwtyde was thi wiff.'

And Seint Theodore was of so gret holinesse that she dede many
miracles, for she toke away fro wilde bestes a man al torent withe hem
55 and areised hym from dethe to lyff by her praiers, and she folowed
that beste and cursed it and anone he fell dede. And the fend, hauinge
envie to her holinesse that he might not suffre her, apper[ed] to her
f. 148rb sayenge: 'Thou wicked woman | aboue alle other and avouterere, thou
hast lefte thine husbonde for to come hedir to dispise me. [By] my
60 vertues that be dredfull [and tremble] I shall ar[e]ise ayeinst the suche

26 but¹] and EH1   36 .xviij.] .viij. EH1   37 her²] *add* hir G   39 witheinne]
add 'a' H1   fewe] L, *om.* EH1G   44 the²] L, *om.* EH1G   49 yeue] if *on erasure* H1
50 longe abidde] *trs. and marked for reversal* H1   55 hym] 'hem' H1   57 appered]
apperinge EH1   59 By] L, for EH1G   60 and tremble] L, *om.* EH1G   areise]
arise E

batayle that yef I make the not renye the crucified, saye not that it am
I.' And anone she made the signe of the crosse and the fende
vanisshed away.

In a tyme as she come fro the towne withe the cameles and was
herborued in an ostrie, a mayde come to hym and saide to hym: 'Slepe 65
withe me this night.' And whanne he hadde refused her she went and
laye withe another that gete her withe childe. And whanne her bely
arose they asked her who hadde brought her withe childe, and she
saide the monke Theodore hadde layne withe her. And whanne the
childe was bore they sent it to the abbot of the chyrche there 70
Theodore was, and the abbot blamed gretly Theodore and she
praied mekely of foryeuenesse. Than the abbot toke her the childe
and shoued her oute of the gates and bade her kepe withe sorugh that
she hadde gete in so gret synne and shamc, and .vij. yere she norisshed
that childe withe melke of bestes. And the fende hadde enuye [of] her 75
pacience and transfigured hymselff in lykenesse of her husbonde and
saide to her: 'What doist thou here, my wyff? I languisshe for the and I
haue no comfort. Come with me that art al my ioie, for though thou
haue leye withe another man I shall foryeue it the.' She wende that he
hadde be her husbonde and sayde to hym: 'I shalle no lengger be 80
withe the, for the sone of Sir Iohn the knight hathe laye withe me, and
I will do my penaunce for I haue | synned ayeinst the.' And thanne she f. 148ᵛᵃ
went to her praier and the fende vanisshed away, and thanne she
knewe that it was the fende.

Another tyme the fende wolde make her afrayed and come to her in 85
likenesse of wilde beestis, and a man saide to hem: 'Etithe this wicked
woman.' And thanne she praied and thei vanisshed away. Another
tyme gret multitude of knightes come to her and her prince went
before and eueriche of hem worshipped her. And thanne one of the
knightes saide to her: 'Theodore, arise up and worshippe oure prince.' 90
And thanne she saide: 'I worshippe only God almighty.' And whanne
thei hadde tolde this to her prince he comaunded that she were
brought forthe and so moche tormented that men deme her dede, and
thanne al that companye vanisshed awaye. Зet another tyme she come
thedir and ther she founde a gret hepe of golde, and thanne she 95
blessed her and recomaunded her to God and fledde away. Another
tyme she seigh a panier full of diuerse metes of alle maners that a man

61 it] Y G   67 gete] brouзt G   73 of] at G   75 of²] to EH1   86 of] add
and del. H1   88 tyme] ins. H1   89 before] add hem E   90 saide] seyde with ey
on erasure H1

bare and saide to her: 'Oure prince that bete the sent the this and
bidde the take it and ete it, for thou dedest that be vnconninge.' And
100 she than blessed her and he vanisshed awey.

And whanne the .vij. yere were comen oute the abbot considered
the pacience of that brother and reconsiled hym and putte hym in the
chirche withe hys bretherin and his sone withe hym. And whanne she
hadde fulfelled .ij. yere praisably she toke her childe and closed hym
f. 148ᵛᵇ withe her in her selle, and whanne it was tolde to | the abbot he sent
106 sum of his monkes priuely to wete what she wolde saie to hym, and
thanne she toke and cleped the childe and kissed hym and saide: 'Mi
right dere sone, the tyme of my lyff is come, and therfor I leue the to
God that he be thi fader and thine helper. Sone, loke [that] thou abide
110 in fastinge and in orison and serue thi bretheren deuoutely.' And in
that sayenge she yelde up the sperit and slepte in oure Lorde aboute
the yere of oure Lorde .iiijC.lxx. And whanne the childe seighe this
thinge he beganne greuously to wepe.

And that night a vision was shewed to the abbot in this wise. Hym
115 thought a gret weddinge was ordeyned and thedir come ordres of
aungeles and of prophetis, of marteres and of alle seintes, and in the
middel of hem there was a woman besette with so gret ioye that no
tonge might tell it, and she come right to the weddinge and sette her
vpon the bedde, and alle tho that were aboute her dede her worshipp.
120 And thanne ther come a voys to the abbot that sayd: 'This is
Theodore, that was falsly accused of the childe. The tymes be
chaunged withe her, for she is chastised for she hadde defouled the
bed of her husbonde.' And thanne the abbotte awoke and went alle
meued to her selle withe his bretheren and founde her dede, and than
125 he entered inne and vncouered her and fonde her a woman. And
thanne the abbot sent to seke the fader of her that hadde defamed her
and saide to hym: 'Lo, the man that thi doughter defamed is dede.'
And thanne they toke awaye the clothe and sayen that she was a
f. 149ʳᵃ woman, and thanne there was | gret drede to alle tho that seen or herde
130 this thinge.

And thanne the aungell of oure Lorde spake vnto the abbot and
saide: 'Arise hastely and light upon thine horse and ride into the citee,
and yef thou metest any man take and bringe hym hedyr.' And as the
abbot went he mette withe a man rennynge, and the abbot asked hym
135 whedir he ranne and he saide: 'I goo to see my wyff that is dede.' And

100 he] she E, she *changed to* he H1   107 hym] it G   109 that²] *om.* E   116
alle] *add* oþere H1   118 tonge] thinge H1G   133 metest] *add* with G

thanne the abbot toke the husbond of Theodore upon his hors and brought hym thedir, and ther he wepte gretly and they beried the body with gret deuocion. And thanne the husbonde of Theodore toke his wyves celle and duelled there and atte [the] ende slepte in oure Lorde. And thanne the childe of Theodore folued his norice in alle 140 vertu[ou]s werkes and encresed so gretly in name of goodnesse that whanne the abbot was dede he was chose of alle to be abbot.

Here endithe the lyff of Seint Theodore, and nexst foluithe the blessed lyff of Seint Margarete, Capitulum .iiij^{xx}.vij.

Seint Margarete was of the citee of Antioch, doughter of Theod[o]sien a painime patriark, and she was deliuered to a norise, and whanne she come to a perfite age she was baptised, and therfor she was gretly hated of her fader. And in a day whanne she was .xv. yere she kepte her norise shepe in the feld amonge other maydenes. The prouost 5 Olibrius passed therby and concidered the beauute of this virgine and was take withe her loue and, alle meued, sent massangeres anone and saide to hem: 'Gothe and takithe that mayde, and yef she | be free I f. 149rb shall take her to my wiff, and yef she be bounde I shalle make her my concubine.' 10

And whanne she was presented before hym he enquered her of her name and of her kinrede and of her religion, and she ansuered that her name was Margarete and that she was noble of kynne and of cristen religion. Thanne the prouost saide to her: 'The two furst thingges perteynen to the rightfully, for thou art amyable and noble and art 15 prouide to be right a faire margarete, but the .iij. thinge apertenithe not so fayre and so noble a mayde to worship a god that was crucified.' To whom she sayde: 'Wost thou thanne that God was crucified?' And he saide: 'Ye, by the bokes of cristen men.' And than saide she to hym: 'A, what shame is th[is] to you, whanne ye rede there the might and 20 the glorie of hym, that ye beleue [that one] and renye that other.' And thanne as she affermed that he hadde be crucified of his owne propre will for the redempcion of mankinde, thanne the prouost comaunded

139 the] his EH1   141 vertuous] vertues and EH1

EH1GDH2A1A2LK   1 Theodosien] Theodesien E   3 a] *om.* H1   4 yere] wynter of age L, *add* old K   5 other] `o'thir G   maydenes] *add* Then K   6 therby] by her L   7 alle meued] meved so sore that he L   9 make her] haue her to L   11–12 her^1 . . . kinrede] of her what was her name and of what kynne L   12 and^1] *om.* G   13 that] *om.* K   noble of] of riche L   15 perteynen] apperteynyng K   17 not] *add* to be K   was] ys L   20 this] that E   21 that one] not on hym E   renye] reyne G

that she were putte in prison, and the day foluinge he made her to be
25 called before hym and saide to her: 'Thou voyde and veyne made,
haue pitee of th[i] beauute and worshippe oure goddes.' To whom she
sayd: 'I worship hym to whom the erthe trembelithe, the see dredithe,
the wynde and alle creatoures obeyen.' To whom the prouost sayde:
'Yef thou wilt not consent to me I shal make thi body to be alle torent.'
30 To whom Margrete saide: 'My Lord Ihesu Crist deliuered hymselff
[to] dethe for me, and therfor I drede not to deye for the loue of Ihesu
Criste.' |

f. 149va　　And thanne the prouoste comaunded that she were so strongely
bete that the blode shulde renne of her as plenteuously as of a welle,
35 and þan that she shulde be streched oute to the turment of eculee.
And tho that were there wepten and saiden: 'Margarete, verrely we
playne the gretly for that we se the so pitously [to]rent and totorn.
Allas, what beaute hast thou loste withe thy beleue; yet haue pitee on
thiselff so that thou maist leue.' To whom she sayd: 'A, ye wicked
40 counsellours, parte you from me and gothe hennes, for this turment of
the flesshe is sauinge of my soule.' And thanne she turned her to the
prouoste and saide: 'Thou shameles hounde that canst not be
fulfelled, thou maist haue power of my flesshe but God kepithe my
saule.' And the prouoste couered his visage withe his mantell for that
45 he wolde not see so gret shedinge of blood. And after that he made her
be enclosed in the prison and mervailous brightnesse of light shyned
witheinne.

And whan she was in prison she praied oure Lorde that he wolde
shewe her visibly hym that so cruelly vexed her and faught withe her,
50 and than come there forthe a gret dragon and appered to her, and as
he assailed her for to deuoure her she made a signe of the crosse and
he vanisshed awaye, or, as it is redde ellyswhere, he opened hys
mouthe and sualued her, and by the vertue of the crosse that she
hadde made the dragon breke anone and the virgine went oute of hym
55 al hole and sounde. And than the fende come ayein to her and
f. 149vb transfigured hym in forme of a | man for to deceiue her, and whanne

25 made] m'y'ade H1　　26 thi] the E, þe changed to þi H1　　beauute] selfe L
28 alle] add þe K　　31 to¹] L, fro EGK, to þe on erasure H1　　34 her] add downe L
of²] om. K　　35 þan] om. L　　that] om. K　　37 torent] rent EH1　　38 on] of LK
41 thanne] om. L　　42 that canst] kanst thowe L　　43 thou] þat K　　45 shedinge]
chidinge changed to shedinge H1　　46 enclosed] changed to vnclosed and then v del. and 'e'
superposed H1　　and] add then L　　47 witheinne] add that preson L　　50 there forthe]
om. L　　51 he] she with s erased H1　　52 he] she E, she with s erased H1, then he L
awaye] add from her L　　or] for changed to or H1, for G, add ellis K　　or as] om. L
54 dragon] drakon changed to dragon H1　　56 forme] fygure L

she seigh hym she went to her prayer, and whanne she arose the fende
come to her and toke her by the hond and saide: 'Sese now as to my
person and suffise the that thou haste done.' And thanne she toke hym
by the here and threwe hym to the erthe and sette her right fote upon 60
his necke and saide to hym: 'Lye stille, thou enemye, under the fote of
a woman,' and bete hym. And the fende cried and saide: 'A, blessed
virgine Margarete, I am ouercome. Yef a yonge man hadde bete me I
hadde not rought, but I am ouercome of a yonge tender mayde, and
that I may moste sorugh, for her fader and her moder haue be my 65
good frendes.'

And thanne she constreined hym so sore that he shulde tell her whi
he tempted the cristen peple so ofte, and he ansuered her for he hadde
kindely haterede to hem and to alle vertues, and though he were ofte
tymes putte abacke by hem and deposed of hem, yet he pursued hem 70
withe continuel desire for to deceyue hem, and for that he hathe envye
to the wele of man for the blisse that he loste that he may neuer
recouer ayein, but he hopithe to exclude hem therfro. And thanne he
tolde her how Salamon hadde enclosed in a vessell of glas right gret
multitude of fendes, but after his deth the fendes putte oute fire of the 75
vessell so that men wende that ther hadde be gret tresoure therinne
and breke the vessell, and thanne the fendes went oute and fulfelled
the eyre. And whanne he hadd saide al this the virgine lefte vp her fote
and sayde: 'Flee, thou wreched caytef.' And anone the fende
vanisshed away. 80

And thanne was | she sure, for [who]so hathe ouercome the prince f. 150ʳᵃ
witheoute faile may lightly ouercome the ministre. And the daye
foluinge the peple assembeled ande she was presented to the iuge, but
she wolde in no wise sacrifice to her goddes, and thanne was her tendir
body broyled withe brondes of fire so that alle meruayled how so 85
tendre a maide might suffre so many turmentes. And after that they
putte her in a vessell full of water faste ibounde so that bi the
chaungynge of peynes the strengthe of the payne shulde encrese, and
anone sodenly þe erthe trembeled and the eyre waxe right hideous and

60 here] Eere K   to the erthe] downe to her feet K   62 and¹] add sche LK
65 I may] ys to me L   66 good] most K   68 her] add in þis wise K
70 deposed] dispisid GLK   71 continuel] contynuesse L   72 that²] then L
73 recouer] add yt L   but] yit K, that L   hopithe] hopyd L   therfro] there of L
76 men] add that wente there L   be] add right L   79 And] om. K   81 whoso] he
so E, he del. 'who' so H1   82 may] ins. H1   may lightly] he may sone K   ministre]
mynystris G   84 wise] add do LK   86 many] moche H1, add divers K   89 the
eyre] there L   hideous] add weder L

90 the virgine went oute witheoute any harme. And than .vM^l. men
beleued in God and were beheded for the name of Ihesu Criste, and
thanne the prouost dradde hym leste other wolde haue do the same
and comaunded hastely that the blessed virgine Margarete shulde be
beheded. And thanne she besought a tyme for to praie for herselff and
95 for her persecutours and for alle tho that maden any mynde of her or
asked her helpe deuoutely, and she praied full deuoutely and sayde
that what women asked her helpe in trauelinge of childe that she
might be deliuered withoute perill of woman or of childe so that bothe
might be saued, the woman to lyff, the childe to cristendom. And as
100 sone as she hadde praied a voys come from heuene that saide that she
was herde of her prayers, and than she thanked oure Lorde and saide
to the turmentour: 'Brother, take thin suerde and smite.' And thanne
he smote of her hede atte one stroke, and so she receiued a croune of
marterdome. And she suffered dethe the .xij. kl. of Iuill.

f. 150rb And an holy man saiethe in this | wise of this virgine: 'The blessed
106 Margarete was sadde and stable in the loue and dredde of God,
worshiped with relygion, araied withe compunccion, environde
withe praisable pacience, and th[er]e was no contrarie thing founde
in her, she was hatefull to her fader and frende and loue to oure Lorde
110 Ihesu Criste.

        Here endithe the lyff of that blessed virgine Seint Margarete,
        and nexst foluithe the liff of Seint Calixte, Capitulum
        .iiij^{xx}.viij.

Calixte was sone of a right noble man that hight Eufemyen and was
the furst of the emperoures halle and hadde under hym .iij. thousande
yonge men that were gerte withe gerdeles of golde and clothed withe
clothes of golde and of sylke. And this Eufemyen was right piteous to
5 eueriche and euery day he hadde in his hous .iij. tables for pore
orphenyns, [for pilgrimes] and pore wedues the whiche he serued
nobly, and atte the oure of none he toke his mete withe the relygious

---

94 besought . . . praie] prayed L   95 that] *add* in any tyme L   or] and G
96 and she . . . deuoutely] *om.* L   she . . . sayde] in her praier she desired K   98 or]
and K   100 that^1] and H1   102 turmentour] tormentoures L   thin] þe H1
108 there] L, thanne EH1GK

    EH1GDH2A1A2L   For details of MS spellings of Calixt/Alexis, see note
Rubric Margarete] Katery *subp.* Margrete G   1 Calixte] *changed to* Alexis *with* Alexus *in
margin* H1   a] *om.* H1   2–3 E *has an illegible erasure in margin*   5 for] of H1
6 for pilgrimes] *om.* E

in the drede of God. And hys wyff þat he hadde hight Aglas and was
of the same relygion, and as they were witheoute children oure Lorde
gaue hem a sone by her prayers, and thanne they behight to lyue 10
after[ward] in continence and chastite. And the childe was sette to
scole and was taught in alle the artes of philysofye and come to his
perfite age. And thanne was there chosen to hym a mayde of the
emperoures hous and was yeue hym to his wyff, and whanne the night
came that they were pesibl[i] togeders he beganne in priue wyse to 15
teche his wiff in the loue and in the drede of God and to drawe her to
the worshippe [and] chas|tite of virgines, and toke her his ring to kepe f. 150va
and all the goodes that he hadde, and saide to her: 'Take these thingges
and kepe hem as longe as it plesithe the, [and oure Lorde be with the].'
And thanne he toke parte of his goodes and went priuely into a shippe 20
and sailed into Loadice, and fro thennes he come into [the] citee of
Adice in Surri, ther the ymage of oure Lorde is made in a clothe
witheoute werke of mannes honde. And whanne he come thedir he
solde alle the good that he hadd brought withe hym and gaue it to the
pore and toke vile clothinge upon hym and went withe other pore men 25
and satte in the porche of the chirche of the blessed Virgine Marie
moder of God, and of the almes that men gaue hym for the loue of
God he lyued, and the ouerplus he gaue for the loue of God.

The fader was wonder sori of the departinge of his sone and sent
messengers thorugh the worlde to seke hym diligentely, and sum of 30
hem come into Edice. Thei were well knowen of hym and they in no
wyse knewe hym but gaue hym almes withe other pore men, and he
toke it and gaue thankinge to God and sayde: 'Lorde, I yelde the
thankingges that thou haste [made] me resseyue for thi loue the almes
of my seruauntes.' And thanne the messangers retorned ayein and 35
sayde that they coude in no wyse finde hym. And the moder, fro the
tyme that her sone parted from her, she putte a sacke in stede of a
bedde vpon the pament wheron she wepte and cried, sayenge: 'Here
shall I abyde in sorugh and wepinge till I haue recouerid my sone.'
And hys wyf saide to his fader: 'I shall abide withe the | allone till I f. 150vb
here tydingges of my husbonde.' 41

And whanne Calex hadde be there .xv. yere in the citee aforesayd in
the seruice of God in the porche witheoute, atte the laste the ymage of

10 sone] *add* Sceynt Alexis *above column* H1   11 afterward] after E   15 pesibli]
pesible E   17 and¹] L, of EH1G   19 and oure . . . the] *om.* E   21 the] a EH1
21–2 and fro . . . Adice] *twice once del.* H1   22 ther] where G   34 made] *om.* E,
'made' H1   resseyue] resseyued E   37–8 a bedde] Avell *with* vell *on erasure* H1
42 Calex] *with* C *del.* H1

oure Lady saide to hym that kepte the chirche: 'Do entre,' she sayde,
45 'the seruaunt of God witheinne, for he is worthi the kyngdom of
heuene and the sperit of God restithe in hym, for hys praiers styen up
before God right as encence.' [And] he asked the ymage of whom she
ment, for he knewe hym not, and thanne she saide to hym: 'That same
that sitte witheoute the porche.' Thanne he went oute hastely and
50 brought hym witheinne the chirche. And whanne this was knowe
amonge the peple he was worshipped [of] alle the peple, and whanne
he perceiued this he purposed to flee mannes praysinge and parted
from thennes and come [in]to Loadice and toke a shippe and wend to
haue goo into Tarce of Cili[ci]e, and by the will of God the wynde
55 droue hym into the port of Rome.

And whan Calixt seigh that, he sayde: 'I shalle duelle vnknowe in
the hous of my fader. I will seke no further.' And thanne he mette his
fader comynge fro the palays withe multitude of seruauntes aboute
hym, and thanne he beganne to crye after hym and sayde: 'Seruaunt
60 of God, I beseche the that I may be receyued into thine hous for the
loue of God and susteyned as a pilgryme and straunger withe the
crommes that comen fro thi borde.' And whanne hys fader herde hym
he comaunded that he were receyued for the loue of his sone and
ordeyned hym a place in his hous and euery day ordeyned hym mete
f. 151ra   from hys owne borde. And | he perseuered in orisones and amentised
66 hymselff by wakingges and fastingges, and ofte tymes the servauntes
of the hous scorned hym and threwe water upon hym many a tyme in
scorne, but he was full pacient in all, in so moche that he duelled
vnknowe in his faderis hous .xviij. yere.

70   And thanne whanne he knewe in sperit that the tyme of his ende
neighed he asked to haue parchemyn and inke and wrote be order al
his lyff. And thanne in a Sonday after the solempnite of [the] masses a
voys was herde that come from heuene whiche sayde: 'Comithe to me,
alle ye that labouren and be charged and I shalle refresshe you.' And
75 whanne they herde this they were alle afrayed and fellen flat to the
erthe. And thanne [the] voys sayde the seconde tyme: 'Praiethe the
servaunt of God þat he praie for Rome.' And thanne they sought hym
but they founde hym not. And thanne it was saide hem ayein bi the
voys: 'Seke hym in the hous of Effemyen.' And thanne the seruaunt

---

47 And] *om.* E, *ins.* H1   51 of] amonge EH1   53 into] to E, 'in'to H1
54 Cilicie] Ciline EH1   droue] drowe H1   56 Calixt] Calex *with* C *del.* H1
62 crommes] crounes H1   65 from] fro *on erasure* H1, for G   68 all] L, *add* and to
alle EH1G   72 the²] L, *om.* EH1G   76 the¹] a EH1

that ministred to Calixt come to his lorde and saide: 'My lorde, truly I 80
suppose that it be youre pilgrime, for he is a man of good lyff and of
gret pacience.'

And thanne Eufemyen ranne to hym and founde hym dede, and the
visage of hym was as clere as of an aungell. And than Eufemyen wolde
haue take the wrytinge oute of his honde, but he might not haue it. 85
And thanne he parted thennes and tolde this thinge to the pope and to
the emperoure and anone they went thedir and sayde: 'Thou it be so
that we be synfull, alwayes haue we the gouernaunce of the kingdom,
and oure holy fader hathe the cure of the gouernaunce of [the] pe|ple f. 151ʳᵇ
as oure shepard, wherfor take us this scrowe so that we may knowe þat 90
is witheinne.' And thanne went þe pope and toke the skrowe out of
hys honde, and he lefte it anone, and than he made it b[e] redde before
alle the peple. And whanne Eufemyen herde this he hadde right grete
drede and was so abasshed and ouercome that he loste al hys strengthe
and felle to the erthe, and whanne he was come ayein to hymselff, he 95
rent hys clothes and todrewe his here of his hede and of his berde and
cried upon his sone and saide: 'Allas, sone, why hast thou so gretly
heuied me and hast made [me haue] so moche sorugh and wepinge
this longe tyme? Allas, sorifull wreche that I am, now I see the lye
dede before me and thou were the ioye and keper of myn age, and now 100
maist thou not speke to me. Allas, what counsaill shall I take from
hennes forwarde?'

And whanne the moder herde of this thinge, right as a madde
woman she ferde withe herselff and lefte up her hondes to heuene and
saide: 'Allas, men, yeue me entre that I may goo to my sone and see 105
hym that was the comfort of my soule, whiche I norisshed withe my
brestes.' And whan she came to the body she felle downe therupon
and cried and saide: 'Alas, my right dere sone, the light of myn eyen,
whi hast thou be so cruell towardes me? For many a tyme hast thou
sene me and thi fader full of sorugh and full of wepinge for the, and 110
thou woldest neuer shewe the to us. Allas, thi seruauntes haue done
the many a gret wronge and alle thou haste susteined full mekely.'
And as she talked to the body, euer she cussed | hym and cried and f. 151ᵛᵃ
wepte pitously, sayenge: 'For Goddes loue wepithe all withe me that
be here, for alas I haue hadde my dere sone this .xvij. yere in my hous 115
and neuer knewe that he was my childe. Oure servauntes haue many a

80 Calixt] Calix *with* C *del.* H1   85 oute] *om.* G   88 synfull] simple H1
89 the³] *om.* E   91 out] *om.* H1G   92 he¹] *om.* G, *ins.* H1   be] b E   97 gretly]
grete῾li´ H1   98 me haue] *om.* E, ῾me´ hadde H1   112 full] *om.* G

tyme rebuked hym, scorned hym and smiten hym. Alas, who shall
yeue me to myn eyen a welle of teeres so that I neuer stinte of wepinge
night nor day?' And thanne his wyff, that was clothed withe clothes of
120 mournynge, ranne thedir cryenge and sayenge: 'Alas to me, for I am
departed this day and in the state of a wedowe. Alas, now haue I none
that I dare beholde ne that I dare lefte up myn eyen to. Now is my
mirrour broken and alle my hope loste. Now is to me sorw begonne
that shall neuer ende whiles that I leue.' And the peple that herde alle
125 these thingges wepten doune right. And thanne the pope and the
emperour putte the body in a bere worshipfully and brought it to the
middes of the citee and tolde to the peple that the seruaunt of God
was founde whiche alle the citee [sought], and thanne alle went
ayeinst hym. And yef any seke body touched the bere he was anone
130 made hole, the blynde receyued her sight, tho that were vexed withe
fendes were deliuered, and all seke of what siknesse that thei hadd, as
some as they touched the holy body, they were heled.
　　And thanne the pope and the emperour that seen so many
meruayles beganne to bere the beere hemselff so that they might be
135 halowed withe that holy body, and they comaunded that men shuld
caste thorugh the place gret habundaunce of golde and siluer so that
f. 151vb the peple might tende to gade|ringe of [the] golde and [of the] siluer
and suffre the body to be bore to [the] chirche. But the peple lefte the
loue of the golde and of the syluer and comen more and more to
140 touche the holy body, and so withe gret payne they brought hym to
the chirche of Seint Boneface the marter, and they were .vij. dayes in
[the] praisinge[s] of God, and they dede make a shrine of golde and of
precious stones wherinne thei putte the holy body withe gret
worshippe in the .xvij. day of Iulet. And so gret swetnesse [of]
145 sauoure come oute of the shrine that it semed to alle that it was
fulle of precious oynementes. And he passed oute of this worlde in the
.xvij. kl. of August in the yere of oure Lorde .iiijC.iiij^{xx}. and .xviij.

118 of] om. G   119 his] þis changed to his H1   121 in] om. H1   122 my] `þe´
H1   128 sought] wost EH1   134 be] ins. H1   135 men] ins. above þay subp. G
137 to] add the EH1   the¹] om. E   of the²] om. E   138 the²] L, om. EH1G
142 the] L, om. EH1G   praisinges] praisinge E   144 of²] and EH1   145 it²] is del.
H1, sche G

Here endithe the lyff of Seint Calixt, and nexst foluithe the lyff of Seint Praxedes, Cap. .iiij^{xx}.ix.

Seint Praxedes was suster of Seint Potencian and were bothe susteres of Seint Timothee, [that] was taught of the aposteles in the faithe. And whanne the persecucion was of the cristen thei beried the body`es´ of [the] cristen and gauen al her goodes to the pore, and in the ende they slepte in pees in oure Lorde [in] the yere .C.lx. vnder 5 Marke Antoyne.

Here endithe the liff of Seint Praxedes, and nexst foluith the liff of the blessed Mari Magdalene, Cap. .iiij^{xx}.x.

Mari Maudeleyn was surnamed of Magdalon the castell, and she was born of the kinrede þat were descended of reall [lingne], and her fader hight Syrus and her moder Eucharie. And she and Lazar her brother and Martha her suster helden the castell that ys .ij. myle fro Genazarethe, and Betanye | that ys nighe [to] Ierusalem, and gret f. 152ra party of Ierusalem, and thei devided these thingges betwene hem in 6 suche wise that Mari hadd Maudeleyn wherof she was surnamed, and Lazar hadd the party of Ierusalem, and Martha hadd Bethanie. And whanne the Maudeleyn was yeuen al to [the] delytes of the body and her brother Lazar enten[d]ed most to knyghthode, Martha that was 10 wyse gouerned [right nobly] the parti of her brother and of her suster and minystred to knightes and to seruauntes and to pore men her necessitees. And they solde alle these thingges after the assencion of oure Lorde and brought al the money therof to the aposteles feet.

And Mari Maudeleyne abounded gretly in richesse, and for that 15 delite is felawe [to] habundaunce of thingges and in as moche as she shined more in beauute and richesse, so moche more she [ma]de her body sogette to delites, and therfor she loste her propre name and was of custume called the sinfull woman. And whanne oure Lorde

EH1GDH2A1A2L   *Rubric* Calixt] *so with* C *and* t *del.* H1   2 that] and EH1
4 the¹] *om.* E   5 in³] *om.* E, *ins.* H1

EH1T1GDH2A1A2LDu; D breaks off after 151 *litell*; Du breaks off after 307 *withe*
2 the] *om.* G   lingne] L, kingges EH1G, kynne Du   3 moder] *add* highte Du
5 to] *om.* E   and²] *add* a Du   8 the] *om.* Du   9 whanne the] thanne Mary Du
the²] *om.* E   10 entended] entented E   11 wyse] L, wyseli EG, *so changed to* wyse &
H1, *add* and Du   right nobly] L, chase E, *om.* H1GDu   12 and¹] she Du   to¹,²,³] two
H1   16 delite] *add* she Du   is] his *with* h *erased* H1   to] in EH1   of] *add* other Du
17 made] L, hadde EH1GDu

20 preched here in erthe she was enspired withe grace and went to the
hous of Simond the lepre whanne oure Lorde dyned there, but she
durst not apere amonge the rightwisse men for she was sinfull, but she
came to the fete of oure Lorde and there she wosshe hem withe her
teeres and wyped hem withe her here and anoynted hem withe
25 precious oynementes, for the duellers of that londe vsed bathes and
oynementes for the right gret hete of that londe. And for that Simond
thought in hymself that yef oure Lorde were a verrey prophete he
wolde not haue suffered þat a synfull woman shulde haue touched
hym, and therfor oure Lorde vndertoke hym of verrey pride and
30 forgaue the woman al her synnes.

f. 152ʳᵇ   And | this is Mari Mauudeleyn to whiche oure Lorde gaue so many
gret geftes and shewed so many gret tokenes of loue that he deliuered
her of fendes. [He] sette her al afere in his loue and made her right
familyer withe hym. He wolde that she were his ostesse and hys
35 procuresse, he wolde that she were with hym in his v[i]age, he excused
her alway suetly. He excused her ayeinst the Pharis[ien] that sayde
that she was not clene, and ayeinst her suster that she was idell, and
ayeinst Iudas that saide þat sche was a wastour of goodes, and whanne
he seigh her wepe he might not kepe his teeres, and for her loue he
40 reysed Lazar fro dethe to lyff which hadde leye .iiij. dayes dede, and
he heled her suster of the blody flixe that had holde her .vij. yere, and
by the merites of her he made Marcell the chaumbrere of Martha to be
worthi to saye these suete wordes: 'Blessed be the wombe that bare the
and the brestes that gaue the sucke.' But Ambrose saiethe it was Martha
45 that sayde these wordes and [this was] her chaumbrere. 'This Mari,'
saiethe he, 'is she that wisshe the fete of oure Lorde and wyped hem
withe her here and anointed hem withe precious oynementes and dede
solempne penaunce in tyme of grace and was the furste that chase the
beste partye, that satte atte the fete of oure Lorde and herde his wordes.
50 This is she that anointed his hede, that atte the passion was besyde the
crosse, that made redy the oynementes and wolde anointe hys body and
parted not fro the sepulcre, to whom Ihesu Crist appered furst whan he
arose from dethe to lyff, and she was felawe to the aposteles.'

32 many²] om. GDu   33 He] and EHı, and he Du   35 viage] Du, vsage EHı,
visage G (voiage P2)   36 Pharisien] L, Pharisees EGDu, so with final s subp. Hı
37 that²] om. Du   38 þat] om. Du   39 he¹] she with s erased Hı   41 and] add
also Du   44 saiethe] add that Du   45 this was] L, they were the wordes of EHı,
þese wordis were GDu   chaumbrere] chambreris GDu   This] add is Du   46 saiethe
. . . she] om. Du   47 her here] hir her heere Du   51 wolde] add haue Hı
52 parted] parte Du

Tha[nne] after the ascension of oure Lorde in the .xiiij. yere of his
passion, after that the | Iues hadde slayne Steven and hadde dreuen f. 152ᵛᵃ
oute the other disciples of that contre and thei were disperbled abrode 56
amonge the genteles and sawed the worde of God, thanne was Seint
Maximye amonge the aposteles [one] of the .lxxij. disciples of oure
Lorde, to whom Mari Mauudelein hadde be recomaunded [of]
blessed Seint Petre. And thanne whanne the disciples were departed, 60
Seint Maximye, Mari Mauudelein, the Lazar her brother and Martha
her suster and Marcell chambrere of Martha and Seint Cenodyne that
was bore blynde but oure Lorde gaue hym sight, alle these togedre
and many other cristen were take of the mysbeleuers and putte in
[a] shippe and sette in the see witheoute gouern[aunce] to that ende 65
that they shuld alle be drowned, but by the wille of God they come to
Marcell, and ther thei founde none that wolde receyue hem into her
hous, but they duelled in a porche that was before a temple of the
peple of þat contre. And whanne the blessed Mari Mauudelein seigh
the peple assemble to that temple for to sacrifice to [the] ydoles she 70
arose her up pesibly withe a glad visage and a discrete tunge and well
spekinge and beganne to preche Ihesu Crist and to withedrawe the
peple from the worshippinge of idoles. And than alle hadde gret
meruayle of the beauute and of the reson that was in her and of her
faire spekinge, and it was no wonder though the mouth that so 75
debonairly and so goodly had kussed the fete of oure Lorde were more
enspired withe the worde of God thanne other.

And after that it befell that the prince of the pro|vince dede sacrefye f. 152ᵛᵇ
to the idoles he and his wyff for to haue a childe, and Mari
Mauudelein preched of Ihesu Crist to hym and reproued his sacrifice. 80
And witheinne a while after, Mari Mauudelein appered to the lady in
a visyon sayenge: 'How is it, sethe thou hast so gret plente of richesse,
that thou durst leve the pore seruauntes of oure Lorde dye for hunger
and for [threst and for] colde?' And she was aferde to shewe this vision
to her lorde. And the secounde night she appered to her ayein and 85
saide to her the same and manaced her gretly that but yef she wolde
stere her husbond for to refresshe the pore seruauntes of oure Lorde
she shulde repent her, but yet wolde she not saie it to her husbonde.

54 Thanne] That EH1   57 sawed] shewed H1   58 one] LDu, *om.* EH1G   .lxxij.]
so with lx *subp.* E   59 of] and E, of *on erased and* H1   61 the] þe *erased* H1, *om.* Du
62 Marcell] *add* the Du   65 a] the E   gouernaunce] gouernours EH1   68 but] *add*
than Du   70 assemble] assembled H1   to²] *add* do Du   the²] LDu, *om.* EH1G
72 preche] *add* of GDu   79 idoles] *add* bothe Du   80 hym] hem Du   84 threst
and for] *om.* E   86 that] *om.* Du

And thanne the thridd night she appered to hem bothe as they were in
90 bedde togedre and sayd withe an angri visage: 'Slepest thou, tyraunt
and membre of thi fader þe fende, withe thi wiff, the serpent þat luste
not to telle the my wordes? Rest[est thou] now, thou enemye of the
crosse, that hast the glotenye of th[y] wombe full and thou sufferist to
perisshe the seintes of God? Thou lyest in thy paleis wrapped withe
95 clothes of silke and thou seest hem witheoute hous alle discomforted
and takest none hede. Thou shalt not ascape so lyghtly, thou felon, ne
thou shalt not parte witheoute ponisshinge that thou hast abidde so
longe.' And whanne she hadde thus sayde she parted, and the lady
awoke and sighed and the husbonde sighed also for that same cause
100 and trembeled, and thanne she saide: 'Syr, haue ye seen the dreme
that I see?' 'I haue sene it,' he sayde, 'and haue gret meruayle and am
f. 153ra sore aferde.' And thanne his wyff sayde | hym: 'It is more profitable to
us to obeye her thanne for to renne in the wrethe of her God that she
prechithe.' For whiche cause thei receiued hem into her hous and
105 ministred to hem [her] necessitees.

   In a tyme as Mari Mauudelein preched to the forsaid prince, and
[than] the prince saide to her: 'Wenest thou that thou might defende
the lawe that thou prechest?' And she saide: 'Seker I am redy to
defende it as she that is confermed euery day by miracles and by the
110 predicacion of oure maister Seint Petre that sittithe in the se[g]e of
Rome.' To whom the prince saide: 'I and my wiff be redy to obeye the
in alle thingges yef thou wilt be thi prayere gete us a sone of thi God
that thou prechest.' And thanne the Mauudelein saide: 'For that it
shall not abide.' And thanne the blessed Mari Mauudelein praied to
115 oure Lorde for hem that he wolde of hys merci graunte hem a childe,
and oure Lorde herde her praiere[s] and that ladi conceyued.

   And thanne the husbonde wold goo to Seint Petre to preue whedir
the merite were suche of Ihesu Crist as Mari preched, and thanne his
wyff saide to hym: 'Sire, wene ye to goo witheoute me? Nay, in no
120 wyse, for whanne ye goo I will goo and come ayenne, yef God will,
whanne ye come.' To whom her husbonde said: 'Wyff, it may not be
so, for ye be with childe and the periles of the see be witheoute

91 and membre] remembre the Du   92 Restest thou] L, Rest EH1GDu   thou²]
om. Du   93 thy] L, the EH1GDu   95 witheoute] add the E   97 parte] skape
GDu   ponisshinge] pershinge Du   98 parted] add thens Du   99 the] hir Du
sighed] om. Du   104 prechithe] prechid G   105 her] LDu, the EH1G
106 and] om. Du   107 than] om. E   110 sege] L, see EH1GDu   113 the] Mary
Du   114 Mari] om. Du   116 praieres] praiere EH1Du   118 Mari] add
Magdeleyn Du   119 to²] om. H1   121 may] wil Du   122 so] om. Du

nombre and ye might lightly perisshe. Ye shull abide atte home and
take hede of oure possessiones.' And the lady stroue as a woman and
wolde not chaunge her womanly maners and felle doune on her knees 125
to his fete we|pinge, and atte the laste he graunted hir her request. f. 153rb
And thanne Mari Mauudelein marked hem on her shuldres withe the
crosse for that the wicked enemye shulde not lette hem of her way,
and so they charged a shippe withe gret habundaunce of good of alle
thingges that were necessarie to hem and lefte alle her other thingges 130
in the kepinge of Mari Mauudelein and went her waye.

And whanne they hadde sailed the cours of a day and a night, the see
beganne to suelle and the wynde to encrece so that alle were full sore
aferde, and namely the lady that was withe childe and feble were full
of anguisshe of so grete wawes and trouble of the see, and for 135
anguisshe the lady beganne to trauaile sodeinly, and bctwene the
gret turment of her trauaile and the strengthe of the tyme she brought
forthe a sone and the lady deyed. And whanne the childe was born it
cried for to haue hadde the breste of his moder and made a pitous
noyse. Alas, in what sorugh the childe was born and was made sleer of 140
his moder, and he most nedis deye for ther was not that might
norisshe hym. Alas, what shall this pilgrime do that seigh his wyff
dede and his childe br[ay]inge withe wepinge voys sekinge the brestes
of his moder? The pilgrime wepte pitously and said: 'Allas, I wreche,
what shall I do? I desired to haue hadde a sone and now I haue l[os]te 145
bothe the moder and the sone.' And the shipmen cryed on that other
side sayenge: 'Caste we this dede body into the see lest we perisshe
alle, for as longe as it is | withe us this tempest will neuer cese.' And f. 153va
whanne they hadde take the body for to caste it into the see, þe
pilgrime saide: 'Sufferithe a while, sufferithe, and though ye will not 150
spare me ne my wiff, yet sparithe atte the leste this litell babe that
wepithe and criethe. Abidethe a while for to wete perauenture yef the
woman be in a swoun withe wo and paine and may, yef God will,
awake ayenne.'

And thanne an hille appered not fer from the shippe, and whanne 155
he seigh it hym thought it more goodly to bere the body and the childe
thedir thanne for to caste it in the see for to be deuoured in the see.
And thanne he dede so moche by praiers and be yeftes that they sette

126 to] tofore Du   128 for] *ins.* H1   134 and²] *add* was Du   were] and Du
140 born . . . was] *om.* Du   143 brayinge] brethinge E   145 loste] lefte E
147 sayenge] and seide Du   149 they] the shipmen Du   to] *add* haue Du   152 yef]
om. GDu   153 a swoun] swounde H1   yef] and Du   156 he] the housbonde Du

her shippe towardes the hille and bare the body thedir, and whanne
160 they seen that they might not digge the erthe for hardenesse of the
roche, thei leide the body in the most secrete place in the mountayne
and couered it withe a mantell, and thanne þe fader leide the childe
atte the brest of the moder and saide withe sore wepinge: 'O Mari
Mauudelein, how thou come to Marcell to myn euel auenture. Alas, I
165 wreche, whi toke I this iorney vpon me be thi techinge? Hast thou
required of thi God that my wiff shulde conceyue to perisshe, her and
the childe? This is that that I haue resseiued be thi praiers. I
recomaunde her now to the [to] whom I haue comaunded alle myn
other [thingges], and I recomaunde her to thi God, that yef he be
170 mighty that he helpe the soule of the moder and that be thi praier he
haue pitee on the childe that it perisshe not.' And thanne he couered
f. 153vb all the body of the moder and the childe with | his mantell and went
ayenne to the shippe.

    And whanne he was come to Seint Peter, Seint Peter come ayeinst
175 hym and seigh the token of the crosse upon his shuldre and asked hym
what he was and whennes he come, and he tolde hym alle the maner
by ordre. Thanne saide Seint Petre: 'Pees be withe the. Thou art
welcome for thou haste leued good counsayle. Be not sori ne hevy
thoughe that thi wyff slepe and thi litell sone restithe withe her, for
180 oure Lorde Ihesu Crist is almighty to yeue lyff to whom he will and to
take ayein whom h[ym] luste that he hathe youe and for to turne al
wepinge into ioye.'

    And thanne Seint Peter ledde hym into Ierusalem, and there he
shewed hym al the places wher Ihesu Crist hadde preched and the
185 places wher he suffered dethe and wher he stied into heuene. And
whanne he was wel taught of Seint Petre in the faithe and that two
yere were passed he toke his leue of Seint Petre and went into a shippe
for to retorne into his contrey. And as they sayled they come by the
ordenaunce of God besydes the roche wher the body of his wyff and of
190 his childe hadde be putte, and thanne he dede so moche by prayer and
by yefte that they sette the shippe thedir. And the childe hadde alway
be kepte al that tyme by Mari Mauudeleyn and went often tyme,
whanne he coude goo, to the see syde, and as [a] childe played with

159 the¹] that GDu   163 O] om. GDu   164 how] om. Du   168 to²] L, om.
EH1G   169 thingges] goodes E   170 praier] prayers Du   171 on] of H2
172 and¹] add of Du   174 Seint Peter²] he Du   175 and²] add he Du
181 whom] whanne GDu   hym] he E   youe] add the Du   al] add thi Du
185 places] place Du   189 the¹] that Du   190 prayer] prayers Du   191 yefte]
yiftys Du   192 al] into Du   193 a] the EH1Du

the litell stones that he fonde [vpon] the ryuage, and whanne they
come thedir they founde the childe playenge upon the see syde as it 195
was wonte, and he mervailed gretly what it might be and come thedir.
And whanne the childe seigh hym whiche | hadde neuer see no suche f. 154ʳᵃ
thinge before he was aferde and fledde priuely vnto the brestes of his
moder and hidde hym vnder the mantell. And thanne the pylgrime
went for to see more clerely this thinge and se[igh] the childe that was 200
right faire sukkinge the breste of his moder, and thanne he toke the
childe and sayd: 'O blessed Mari Mauudelein, how I were blessed and
alle thingges wel happed me yef my wyff turne ayenne to lyff and
come withe me home into my contre. I wote verrely and beleue
witheouten any drede that thou that hast yeue me the childe and hast 205
fedde hym .ij. yere in this roche myghtest well be thi praier restore the
moder to [her] furst helth.'
    And withe tho wordes the moder respired and saide right as though
she hadde awaked from an harde slepe: 'Blessed Mari Mauudeleine,
how thou art of gret merite and glorious in the sight of God, for in al 210
my gret sorugh of my trauaile of childe thou were to me a mydwiff,
and in al my necessytees thou hast benignely serued me.' And whanne
the pilgrime herde this thinge he meruayled hym and sayde: 'Lyuest
thou, my right dere wyff?' To whom she saide: 'Ye, suerly I lyve and
am right now come from the pilgrimage that ye come fro, and right as 215
the blessed Seint Peter ledde þe aboute Ierusalem and shewed the alle
the places wher oure Lorde suffered dethe and was beried and many
other places, I was withe you, and Mari Mauudeleyn was my felaw
and my leder, and I seigh alle the places there and haue hem well in
my minde.' And thanne [she tolde pleinly] alle the places and alle the 220
myracles that her hus|bonde hadde sene and went neuer oute of the f. 154ʳᵇ
way in none article.
    And thanne the pilgrime resseiued his wyff and his childe and went
full of ioye into the shippe, and within a while after they aryved atte
the port of Marcellys and founde the blessed Mari Mauudelein 225
prechinge withe her disciples, and thanne they kneled downe to her
and tolde her al that was befalle hem and receyued bapteme of Seint
Maximyen. And thanne they destroied alle the temples of ydoles in

194 vpon] aboute EH1   196 wonte] *add* to doo Du   and¹] *add* than Du
197 hym] hem Du   see] segh *with* gh *subp.* H1   suche] sight *changed to* sighe (?) H1
200 and] *add* come and Du   seigh] see E   that was] *om.* Du   203 wyff] *add*
myght GDu   207 her] the EH1   216 Seint] *om.* Du   þe, the] yow, yow Du
220 my] *om.* H1Du   thanne] *om.* Du   she tolde pleinly] L, *om.* EH1G, tolde Du
alle²] *om.* Du

the citee of Marcellys and made chirches of Ihesu Crist and chosen by
230 one acorde the blessed La[zar] for to be bisshop of that citee. And in
the ende they come by the will of God to the citee of Days and by
many myracles thei brought the peple to the faithe of God, and ther
was Maxymien made bisshop.

In this mene tyme the blessed Mari Mauudeleyn was so coueitous
235 of the souerayne loue that [she] chase right a sharpe place in [the]
desert and was in a place that was ordeyned to her by the hondes of
aungellez, and ther she duelled .xxx.^{ti} wynter withoute knowlage of
any creature. In whiche place ther was neuer cours of water ne
comfort of trees ne of herbes, and it was done for this cause, that it
240 shulde be clerely shewed that oure Lorde wolde fede her withe
heuenly metis and not with erthely metis. And euery day atte eueri
Houre of the day she was lefte up an hyghe withe aungelles and herde
the glorious songge of the heuenly felawship withe bodely eeres,
wherwithe she was euery day fedd withe these right suete metes, and
245 thanne was she born withe these aungelles to her propre place so that |
f. 154va she hadde no nede of bodely norisshing.

So it fell in a tyme that a prest that desired to lyue a solitarie lyff
toke a celle for hymselff even .xij. bowshotes from her place. And in a
day oure Lorde opened the eyen of that preste, that he seigh withe his
250 bodely eyen in whiche maner[e] the aungeles descended to the forsaid
place where Mari Mauudelein duelled and how they lefte her up into
the eyre, and thanne after by the space of an houre they brought her
ayenne withe diuine praysingges to the same place. And than the
preest desired to knowe the trouthe of th[at] mervailous uision and
255 recomaunded hymselff by his prayers to oure Lorde his maker and
went suerly withe gret deuocion to the forsaid place. And whan he
neyghed ny by a stones caste, his thighes begonne to wexse so stiff as
though they hadde be harde bounde and alle his inward lymes
beganne to tremble for fere. And whanne he turned hym to haue go
260 fro thennes, his thies and his fete were redy to goo, but whanne he
enforced hym to go to that place al his body was in langoure and
myght not meue hym.

And thanne he vnderstode witheoute any fayle that it was sum

230 one] om. Du   Lazar] lady EH1   be] L, add thaire EH1, add there GDu
235 loue] add of God Du   she] L, om. EGDu, `che´ H1   the^2] om. E   236 to] for Du
241 heuenly] hevenli with venli on erasure H1   242–3 herde the] here H1   245 place]
placis Du   247 fell] befil Du   249 Lorde] om. Du   250 manere] maners EH1
descended] add doun Du   254 that] this E, þe changed to þat H1   258 harde] fast Du
259 fere] drede GDu   haue] om. Du   260 fro thennes] then Du

secrete heuenly place that none erthely man might come to, ande
thanne he called the name of Ihesu Crist and cried: 'I coniure the by   265
the vertue of oure Lorde that yef thou be man or any other resonable
creature that duellest in that pitte that thou ansuer me and telle me
the trouthe of the.' And whanne he hadde saide [so] | thre tymes, the   f. 154vb
blessed Mary Mauudelein ansuered and saide: 'Co[m]e nere, and thou
shalt knowe the trouthe of thi desire.' And thanne he come   270
trembelinge halff waye to [her] warde, and thanne she saide to hym:
'Hast thou naught minde of the gospell that makithe minde of that
right named sinfull woman that wette and wosshe the fete of oure
saueoure withe her teeres and wyped hem withe her here and
deserued foryeuenesse of her synnes?' And thanne the preste sayde: 275
'I remembre me well and it is more thanne .xxx.^{ti} wynter passed that
holy Chirche leuithe and confessithe that it was done.' And than she
saide: 'It am I that by the space of .xxx.^{ti} wynter haue be here withoute
any worldly felawship, and as it was yesterday suffered the to see,
right so I am euery day lefte up by the handes of aungeles into the eyre   280
and haue deserued to here withe my bodely eeres euery day .vij. tymes
the right suete songe of the heuenly felawshippe. And for it is shewed
me þat I shall passe oute of this worlde, go to Seint Maximian and
saye to hym that the nexst day after the resurection of oure Lorde, in
þe same tyme that he is wont to go to Mateins, that he entre allone   285
into his oratori and there he shall finde me by the misterie and seruice
of aungeles.' And the preeste herde the uoys of her right as þe voys of
an aungell, but he seigh nothinge.

And thanne he went anone to Seint Maximien and tolde hym al by
ordre, and than was Maximian fulfelled withe gret ioye and yolde   290
grete thankyngez | to oure Lorde, and in the day and houre that was   f. 155ra
saide hym he entered into his oratorie and seigh the blessed Mari
Mauudelein that was in the quere in the felawshippe of aungeles that
hadde brought her thedir. And she was lefte up from the erthe .ij.
cubites of hyght and praied and hadde her hondes streite vp to oure   295
Lorde. And Seinte Maximian dredde for to go to her, she turned her
towardes hym and sayde: 'Come hedyr, myn owne fader, and fle not
thi doughter.' And thanne whan he neighed her, as it is redde in the
bokes of Maximien, he seigh that by the continuel vision of aungelles

264 heuenly] L, *add* thinge and EH1G, *add* thing and a Du   268 so] *om.* EH1
tymes] *add* so EH1   269 Come] cone E   nere] nerer H1   271 to her warde]
towarde EH1   272 minde] mencyon Du   279 as] *om.* Du   the] 'þe' H1   see] *add*
and Du   282 right] *add* and E, *add* 'mere' and þe H1   295 vp] *add* to heuene E
299 the] *om.* Du

300 euery day, the visage of this holy lady shined as it hadde be a bright
beme of the sonne. And thanne alle the prestes were called, and
blessed Mari resseiued the body of oure Lord of the bisshop withe
gret abundaunce of teres, and after that she streched her body before
the auuter and her right holy soule passed to oure Lorde. And after
305 the passinge of her holy sperit, so gret a sauour of suetnesse abode
there that it was felt by the space of .vij. dayes among hem. And Seint
Maximien anointed the body of her withe diuerse oynementes and
beried her worshipfully, and sithe he ordeined to be beried withe her
afore his dethe.

310   Egisipe, after sum bokes, and Iosephus acorden well withe this
forsaid story, for Iosephus saieth in a tracte that he made that Mari
Mauudelein after the ascencion of oure Lorde was so sette afire withe
the charitee of Ihesu Crist that for sorugh and noye that she felt she
f. 155rb wolde haue sene no man, and therfor whanne she come into | the
315 londe of Ayes she went into desert and duelled there .xxx.^ti yere
withoute knowlage of any creature, and he saiethe that euery day in
euery Houre canonike she was lefte up into the eyre withe aungeles.
But he saiethe that whanne the preest come to her he fonde her
enclosed in her celle, and she asked of hym a clothe and he toke her
320 one, and thanne she went withe hym to the chirche, and ther she
resseiued her hosyll and thanne went to her praier the hondes ioyned
to oure Lorde, and so she rested in pees.

In the tyme of the kinge Charles the Grete, in the yere of oure
Lorde .lxxj., the duke of Burgoyne might haue no childe be his wyff,
325 wherfor he gaue his goodes largely to the pore peple and founded
many chirches. And whanne he hadde made the abbey of Seliazense,
he and the abbotte of that chirche sent to Ayse, for to bringe thennes
yef they might of the relyques of Mari Mauudelein, a monke withe
sufficiaunt suerte. And this monke come to this forsaide citee and
330 founde it al destroyed withe paynimes. And thanne be auenture he
founde the sepulture of marble shewed that the blessed body of Mari
Mauudelein rested inne, and the stori of her was merveilously
entailled in that sepulcre. And thanne the monke opened it be night
and toke the reliques and bare hem withe hym to his hous. And that
335 same night Mari Mauudelein appered to hym sayenge: 'Drede the

300 shined] shynynge Du   301 and] add the Du   302 Mari] add Magdeleyne
Du   the^1] add holy Du   of^2] add Maxymyen Du   303 streched] add up Du
313 of] add oure lorde E   316 withoute] with'oute' H1   319 enclosed] closed H1
328 of^1] fore subp. H1   329 citee] Crete (?) on erasure H1

not, but performe thi werke.' And thanne he come but halff a myle
from his monasterie, but he might in no wise remeue the reliques
thennes till the abbot | and the monkes come withe procession and f. 155ᵛᵃ
receiued h[e]m worshipfully.

A knight that eueri yere hadde in custume to visite the body of 340
Mari Mauudelein was slayne in batayle, and as his frendes wepte for
hym atte his bere they sayden in suete compleyninge wyse to Mari
Mauudelein: 'A, good lady, whi hast thou suffered thi devouute
seruaunt to deye witheoute shrifte and penaunce?' And thanne he that
was dede arose sodenly before hem alle and lete call a preest to hym 345
and shroue hym with gret deuocion and receiued the sacrement, and
thanne anone he rest in pees.

Ther was a shippe that was charged with men and women that were
adrowninge in the see, and amonge hem ther was a woman [grete]
withe childe that was in drowninge, and as moche as she myght in her 350
minde she called Mari Mauudelein and besought her that be her
merites she might escape, and yef she hadde a sone she wolde ye[u]e
hym to her chirche. And as sone as she hadde avowed this vowe a
woman of gret beauute and in worshipfull clothinge appered to her
and toke her by the chynne and brought her to londe al hole, and alle 355
the other were perisshed. And after that she brought forthe a sone and
fulfelled her avowe goodly.

Sum sayen that Mari Mauudeleyn was wedded to Seint Iohn the
Euuangeliste and that oure Lorde called hym from the weddynge and
she, for despite that oure Lorde hadde take awaye her husbond, gaue 360
her bodye to alle delite of the flesshe. But for it was not conable that
the callynge of Seint Iohn shulde be occasion of dedly synne and for
dampnacion | of her, oure Lorde conuerted her pitously to penaunce, f. 155ᵛᵇ
and for that he hadde take her fro the flesshely delite, he fulfelled her
withe souerayne heuenly delite that was withe his owne loue. And thei 365
seyn that he worshipped hym before other withe suetnesse of his
familyarite in as moche as he hadde take hym fro the forsayd delite.

A man that was blynde made hym be ledde to the chirche of Mari
Mauudelein be way of pilgrimage for to visite her body, and as thei
walked his leder saide to hym that he seighe the chirche, and thanne 370
the blynde man cried withe high voys and sayde: 'A, blessed Mari

339 hem] L, hym EHɪ, it G   340 in] add his G   341 in] add a G
342 suete] changed to swete Hɪ   344 shrifte] schrifte del. strif G   349 grete] L, om.
EHɪG   351 that] add he del. Hɪ   352 yeue] yelde EHɪ   354 and] ins. Hɪ
361 alle] add the E   366 he] they EG, he on erasure Hɪ   368 A] And a Hɪ   be] to
changed to be Hɪ

Mauudelein, that I might deserue one tyme to see youre chirche.' And
anone his eyen were opened and he seigh clerely.

A man wrote his synnes in a scrowe and leide it vnder the hillinge of
375 the auutere of Mari Mauudelein, praienge her of goodnesse to aske
grace for hym. And withe that withein a while after he toke the scrowe
and fonde alle hys synnes [ef]faced.

Ther was a man that was holde in prison for money, and he called
in hys helpe the blessed Mari Mauudelein often tymes. In a night
380 there appered to hym a right fayre woman that brake his irnes and
vndede his dore and bade hym go faste his waye. And whanne he felt
hymselff vnbounde he fledde faste.

A clerke of Flaundres that hight Steven was fall in so gret
wrechidnesse that he haunted alle maner of synnes, and that [that]
385 longed to his gostely hele he wolde in no wise here. Notwithestondinge that, he hadde allewaye gret deuocion to Mari Mauudelein and
f. 156ʳᵃ fasted her Even and wor|shipped her Feste. And in a tyme as he
visited her tombe, betwene slepinge and wakingge, Mari Mauudelein
appered to hym in lyknesse of a faire woman susteined withe two
390 aungeles in eueri syde of her, and she saide to hym withe a dispitous
loke: '[Steven], why acountes thou the dedes of my merites vnworthi?
Why maist thou not by the instaunce of my merites be meued to no
repentaunce? For s[i]the thou begannest to haue deuocion to me I
haue euer stedfastely praied for the, and therfor arise up and repent
395 the and I will not leue the till thou be reconsiled to God.' And withe
that he felt so gret grace comen in hym that he forsoke the worlde and
entered into religion and was of right perfit lyff. And atte his dethe
Mari Mauudelein was saye stonde besides his bere withe aungelles
and bere withe hem the soule of hym in lyknesse of a [white] douve.

Here endithe the liff of the blessed Mauudelein, and nexst
foluithe the lyff of Seint Apolinare, Cap. .iiij^xx.xj.

Apolinare was disciple of Seint Petre the Apostell and was sent fro
Rome into Ravene, and ther he heled the wyff of the iuge and baptised
her withe her husbonde and alle her meyne. And thanne it was tolde

---

376 the scrowe] `þe´ *with* scrowe *on erasure* H1   377 effaced] L, defaced EH1G
379 tymes] *add* and G   384 that³] L, *om.* EH1G   387 her²] hir *changed to* her H1
390 dispitous] depitous H1   391 Steven] *om.* E   393 For sithe] L, Forsothe EH1
399 white] *om.* EH1

EH1GDH2A1A2L; D resumes at 26 *dede*   2 he] *om.* H1

to the prouost, and anone he sent for Apolinare and wolde haue made
hym to do sacrifice to Iupiter, and he saide to the preest of the ydoles 5
that the golde and syluer that was in the ydoles were moche beter to be
sette to yeue to the pore thanne for to be dispended tofore the
[deuels]. And thanne he was take and so sore beten | that he was lefte f. 156rb
for dede, and hys disciples toke hym up and kepte hym till he was
hole, and thus he was kepte .vj. monthes in a wedues hous.   10
    And fro thennes he come into the citee of Classe, and ther he heled
a noble man that was deef. And as [he] entered into the hous of a
mayden, a man that hadde the wicked sperit in hym cried and sayde:
'Go hennes, thou servaunt of God, or ellys I shall make the to be
drawe by the fete thorugh the towne.' And Apolinare blamed hym and 15
comaunded hym to go oute of that creature. And whanne he called the
name of oure Lorde ayeinst this enemye, mo thanne .vM^l. persones
leueden in God. And the paynimes bete hym withe staues and
de[u]yed hym that he shulde not name Ihesu Crist, and ther as he
laye vpon the ground he cried: 'That is for he is verraye God.' And 20
thanne they made hym al barefote to goo on brennynge colys, and
whanne they sene that he wold neuer stinte to preche Ihesu Crist they
drove hym oute of the citee.
    And in that tyme [Rufus] patricien, duke of Rauene, hadde a
doughter seke and he lete calle Apolinare to hele her, and as sone as he 25
entered into the hous she was dede. And thanne saide Rufus to hym:
'I wolde that thou ha[dde]st neuer entered into myn hous, for the gret
goddes be wroth and luste not hele my doughter. How shuldest thou
thanne do it?' And Apolinare saide: 'Drede the not, but behote me
pleinly that yef thi mayde be releued ayein from dethe to lyff that thou 30
shalt not de[u]ye her to folowe her creatoure.' And whanne he hadde
ensured hym, Apolynare made hys orison and the maydene arose anone
and con|fessed the name of Ihesu Crist and receiued baptyme, she and f. 156va
her moder and a gret foyson of peple, and she abode still virgine.
    And whan Cesar herde this thinge, he wrote to the prouost of the 35
iugement that he shulde make Apolinare to do sacrifice or ellys that he
shulde sende hym into exile. And whanne he wolde not do sacrifice
the prouost made hym to be bete withe staues, and sethe he made hym
to be hangged in the torment of eculee, and as he preched the name of

7 sette] besette EH1   yeue] *changed to* yeve H1   to^2] *add* refute of EH1   8 deuels]
ydoles EH1   9 was] *add* al E   12 he] *om.* E   19 deuyed] denyed (?) E
20 is^1] *add* he E   24 patricien] Pleratricien G   Rufus] L, Rophis EH1, Ruphis G
27 haddest] hast E   31 deuye] denye (?) E   35 whan] *add* he wolde not do sacrifice
or ellys that he shulde sende hym into exile EG, *so del.* H1

40 God right stably, he comaunded that men shulde caste vpon his
woundes hote scaldinge water, and they bound hym in stronge irnes
and wolde haue sent hym into exile. Ande whanne the cristen seen
[so] gret felonye they were meued in her corage and ronnen vpon the
paynimes and slowen mo thanne .ijC. of hem. And the pr[o]uoste
45 hidde hym and putte Apolinare in a streite prison, and after that he
bounde hym faste in cheynes and sette hym in a shippe and sent hym
into exile withe .iij. clerkes withe hym, and ther he escaped only the
tempest of the see and the clerkes withe hym and .CC. knightes, [and]
baptised [the .CC. knightes].

50   And after that he retorned into Rauen and was take withe paynimes
and brought to the temple of Apolyn, and whanne he seigh that fals
god he cursed it and it felle downe anone. And whanne the bysshopes
seen that, they presented hym to Thaure her iuge. And he gaue sight
to hem that were blynde, and the iuge beleued in God and made hym |
f. 156ᵛᵇ foure yere to duelle in his kepinge. And thanne the bisshop[e]s of
56 [the] ydoles accused hym to Vaspasyen, and he comaunded whosoeuer dede iniurie to the goddes that anone he shulde sacrifice
witheoute any abydingge or ellys be depriued oute of the citee; 'For it
is right,' he sayde, '[that we] venge us of oure goddes, and hemselff,
60 yef hem luste, mowe wel venge hem of her enemyes.'

   And thanne Domestenis, whanne he wolde not sacrifice, he
deliucred hym to a cristen knight, and by the praier of hym they
went into a strete of lepres for to hyde hem fro the wodenesse of Iewes
and of paynimes, and yet thei were folowed of the paynimes. And
65 Apolinere was bete to the dethe and .viij. dayes he lyued techinge his
disciples, and sethe he deyed and was beried worshipfully of cristen
men aboute the yere of oure Lorde .lxx. vnder Vaspasyen.

   And of this ma[r]ter saithe Seint Ambrose in his Preface: 'The right
worthi bisshop was sent into Raven from Petre the Apostell for to
70 denounce the name of Ihesu Crist to the mysbeleuers, and as he
shewed hem mervaylous tokenes of vertues he was ofte trauayled
withe cruel tormentes, but he, [perfite] in the loue of Ihesu Crist,
shewed gret miracles. For after his tormentes he arered a mayde fro
dethe to lyff and he gaue lyght to the blynde and [restabled] speche to
75 the doume and he deliuered men that were vexed with the fende and

   43 so] L, the EH₁G   44 prouoste] pruoste E   45 streite] stronge G
48–9 and³ . . . knightes] L, were baptised EH₁G   55 bisshopes] bisshop E   56 the]
om. E   comaunded] *add* And H₁   59 that we] L, to EH₁G   68 marter] mater EH₁
72 perfite] profited EH₁   Crist] *add* and E   74 restabled] L, *om.* EH₁G

clensed lepres, he heled al manere of infirmitees, he destroyed the ydole withe the temple. O thou worthy bisshopp of meruaylous praisinge, th[at] deseruedest to haue dignite and p[o]este of the aposteles withe the dignite of a bisshopp. | O right stronge champion f. 157ʳᵃ of oure Lorde, that continuelly in thi gret tormentis thou prechedest 80 sadly Ihesu Crist the saueoure of the worlde.'

Here endithe the lyff of Seint Apolinare, and nexst foluithe the lyff of that holy virgine Seint Cristin, Cᵐ. .iiijˣˣ.xij.ᵐ

Cristine was borun of right noble kinrede of Tiry in Itaile, and her fader putte her in a toure withe .xij. chaumbreres, and also she hadde with her the goddes of golde and of syluer. And for she was right fayre she was desyred of many to haue hadd her to wyff, and her fader wolde graunte her to none, but he wolde that she shulde abyde and 5 worshipp her goddes. She that was taught by the holy goste dredde the sacrifice of ydoles and hydde the encence wherewithe thei sacrifised in a wyndow.

And whanne her fader come thedir in a tyme her chaumbreres saide hym: 'Thi doughter that is oure lady will not do sacrifice to [oure] 10 goddes and she saiethe that she is cristen.' And than her fader flatered her and plesed her for to make her sacrifice. [To whom she saide: 'Calle me not thy doughter, but doughter of hym to whom sacrifice] of preisinge belongithe, for I offre sacrifice to God of heuene and not to dedly goddes.' And thanne the fader saide to her: 'My doughter, ne 15 offre not sacrifice to one god [alone] lest that other goddes wratthe hem withe the.' And thanne she saide to hym: 'Thou hast wisely spoken that art vncunynge. [For] I offre to God the fader, to God the sone, to God the holy goste, thre persones and one God.' Ande thanne her fader saide: 'Yef thou worship thre goddes, why worshipest thou 20 not other as wel?' To whom she saide: 'For these .iij. that | I worshipp f. 157ʳᵇ is one Godhede.' And than her fader went thennes, and Cristine toke al his goddes and brake hem and gaue the golde and [the] syluer to pore men. And thanne after that þe fader come ayen for to worshippe hys goddes, but he founde hem not, and the chaumbreres tolde hym 25

78 that] thou EH1   poeste] preste EH1   of] and H1   80 prechedest] prechest H1
EH1GDH2A1A2L   5 shulde] wolde H1   10 oure²] L, *om*. EH1G   12 her³]
add `do' H1   12–13 To . . . sacrifice] *om*. EH1   14 of¹] þem *on erasure* `she seid to
him' H1   16 alone] aboue EH1   18 For] *om*. E   God the fader to] *ins*. H1
20 her] þe G   23 the²] *om*. EH1

what Cristine hadde do, and thanne her fader comaunded that she
shuld be dispuled and beten withe .xij. men till they were al wery.
And thanne saide Cristen to her fader: 'O thou witheoute worshipp or
shame and abhominable to God, seest thou not hou they faylen? Praie
30 thi goddes that [they] yeue hem vertu and strength.' And thanne he
comaunded that she shulde be faste icheyned and putte in prison.
      And whanne the moder of the virgine vnderstode this thinge she
rent her clothes and ranne to the prison and felle downe to the fete of
her doughter and saide: 'A, doughter, Cristin, the lyght of myn eyen,
35 haue pite on me.' And thanne she saide to her: 'Whi callest thou me
thi doughter? Wost thou not well that I haue the name of my God?'
And whanne it wolde none otherwise be, she come ayenne to her
husbonde and tolde hym how she hadde ansuered. And thanne the
fader comaunded that she shuld be brought tofore hym in iugement,
40 and so she was. And thanne he sayde to her: 'Sacrifice to oure goddes
or elles thou shalt suffre diuerse tormentes and thou shalt no more be
called my doughter.' And Cristin ansuered hym and saide: 'Now hast
thou do me a gret grace sithe I shall no more be called the deuel ys
f. 157va doughter, for he that is born of the deuel is the | deuel, and thou art
45 fader of the same Sathanas.'
      And thanne he comaunded that her tendre flesshe shulde be al
torent withe hokes and alle her membres tore from other. And thanne
Cristine toke an handfull of her flesshe and threw it to her fader and
saide: 'Holde, thou tyraunt, and ete the flesshe that þou hast gote.'
50 And thanne her fader sette her on a whele and putte under fire and
oyle, but suche a flawme come oute therof that it slowe a .M^l. and .vC.
men. And her fader acounted al this but [to] art magike and made her
ayein to be putte in prison and comaunded [his seruauntes] that as
sone as it were night that they shulde bynde a gret stone aboute her
55 necke and caste her into the see. And whanne thei hadde so done,
anone the aungeles toke her and Ihesu Crist descended downe to her
and baptized her in the see, sayenge: 'I baptise the in the name of God
my fader, and in my name Ihesu Crist his sone, and of the holy goste.'
And sethe he com[mitt]ed her to Seint Mighell the archaungell, that
60 brought her to londe. And whanne [her] fader herde this he smote
hymselff in þe forhede and sayde: 'Be what wychcrafte dest thou these
thinges that doest suche wichecrafte in the see?' And she ansuered and

      27 be] add þanne G   30 they] om. EH1   he] þay G   49 the] thi H1   52 to]
om. E   53 his seruauntes] om. EH1   59 committed] L, comaunded EH1G
60 her²] the EH1

sayde: 'Thou cursed wreche, I haue this grace of Ihesu Crist.' And
thanne he putte her ayein into prison and saide that she shulde be
byheded in the morw. And that same night Vrban her fader was 65
[founde dede].

And thanne after hym come a felon iuge that hight Zien, the whiche
ordeined a tonne of iren and putte therinne piche and oyle and terre,
and whanne all | was brenninge he made caste Cristine in the middes f. 157vb
therof and made .iiij. men to meue the tonne for to make her al 70
towasted therinne. And thanne Cristein preysed Ihesu Crist by whom
she hadd be newly cristened, and now he wold that she shulde be
rocked in a cradell as a childe. And [thanne] the iuge made for to
shaue her hede and made her to be ledde al naked thorugh the citee
vnto the temple of Apoline, and ther [s]he comaunded to the idole 75
that he shulde falle, and the idole fell and become pouuder. And
whanne the iuge herde it he was aferde and deyed.

And to this succeded Iuliane, and he made to enbrace a furneys and
made Cristine to be caste therinne, and ther she was .v. dayes
synginge with aungelles and went oute witheoute any harme. And 80
whanne Iulian knewe this thinge he helde [it] all done by enchaunte-
mente and lete go to her tw[o] adderes, two serpentes and .ij. aspides;
[but these serpentes licked here fete, and the .ij. aspides] hangged atte
her brestes and dede her none harme, and the adders wounde hem
aboute her necke and licked up her suete. And thanne saide Iulian to 85
his enchauntour: 'Art thou not k[onn]inge to meve these serpentes?'
And thanne as sone as he stered hem they made a saute to hym and
slow hym anone. And than Cristine comaunded to the serpentez to go
into desert places and she areysed the dede man from dethe to lyff.

And thanne Iulian comaunded that she shulde haue her brestes 90
cutte of, and oute of hem come melke in stede of blood. And after that
he made her tungge [to] be cutte of, but she lost neuer her speche
therfor, but she toke the pece of her tungge that was cutte of and
threwe it in the iugez visage and smote oute bothe hys | eyen f. 158ra
therwithe. And thanne was Iulian wrothe and made two arowes to 95
be shotte towardes her hert and one towardes her syde, and whanne
she was smetin she yelded up the sperit to oure Lorde aboute the yere
of oure Lorde .CC.iiij^{xx}.vij. vnder Deoclician. And the holy body

64 shulde] wolde *changed to* sholde H1   66 founde dede] *trs.* E   70 therof]
ther'of' H1   73 thanne] *om.* E, *ins.* H1   74 shaue] saue G   al] *ins.* H1   75 she]
he E, `s'he H1   81 it] *om.* E, *ins.* H1   82 two] tw E   83 but . . . aspides] *om.* E,
ins. H1   85 suete] snotte H1   86 konninge] knowinge E   92 to] *om.* E
96 one towardes] vnto G

reste[th] in a castell that is called Buffennim betwene Orbenice and
100 Viterbe. And Tyre that is besyde the castell was ano[ne] distroied.

Here endithe the liff of Seint Cristen, and nexst foluithe
the lyff of Seint Iames, Cap^m. .iiij^{xx}.xiij.^m

Iames the Apostell, [the] sone of Zebede, [as] he preched the
resureccion of oure Lorde thorugh Iudee and [thorugh] Samarie, in
the ende he was sent into Spayne for to sowe there the worde of Ihesu
Criste. But whanne he seigh that he profited not and hadde goten
5 there but .xj. disciples, he lefte there tweyne be cause of prechinge
and the other .ix. he toke withe hym and come ayenne into Iudee. And
Maister Iohn Belet saiethe that he conuerted there but only one.

And whanne he preched in Iudee the worde of oure Lord, an
enchauntour that hyght Hermogenys was withe the Pharisees and his
10 disciple Philette [came to Iames for that Philete] shulde ouercome
hym before alle and to shewe that hys predicacion was fals. But the
apostell ouercome hym before alle and dede gret miracles before hym.
Thanne Philete turned to Hermogynes and comaunded gretly the
doctrine of Iames and tolde hym of hys miracles and sayde that he
15 wolde be his disciple and counsailed hym to do the same. And thanne
Hermogynes was wrothe withe Philete and brought hym in suche
estate be hys enchauntementes that he might not meue hym in no
f. 158rb wyse and sayd: | 'Now shull we see whedyr thi Iames shall helpe the.'
And whanne Philet hadde sent to Seint Iames be a childe, Seint Iames
20 sent [hym] a couer of hys hede and sayde: 'O Lorde, lefte up tho that
be hurt, and vnbynde tho that be bounde.' And anone as he hadde
sayde, he was vnbounde of al the wichecrafte of Hermogenes and went
anone to Seint Iames and was full gladde.

And thanne Hermogenes called the fendes to hym and comaunded
25 hem that they shulde bringe to hym Iames and Philette for to be
revenged of hem so that hys disciples fro hennes forwarde durst no
more dresse hem ayeinst hym. And the fendes come to Seint Iames

99 resteth] L, rested EH1G   100 anone] ano *at end of line* E

EH1GDH2A1A2T2L; the main hand of G ends at 332 *body*, and the last few words are
written below in a small cursive hand.   1 Apostell] *add* Iames T2   the²] *om.* E   as]
om. E   2 thorugh²] *om.* E, throweth T2   Samarie] *add* and EH1T2   3 sowe] showe
H1T2   worde] wordis G   4 But . . . not] *om.* T2   5 .xj.] .xj. *changed to* .ix. H1
6 .ix.] .vij. H1GT2   into] *add* the T2   9 the] *om.* T2   10 disciple] disciplis T2
came . . . Philette] *om.* EH1T2   came] L, *om.* G   16 in] 'in' H1, suche *del.* T2
20 hym] *om.* ET2, *ins.* H1   O] O'wr' H1   21 And anone] *twice* T2

and begonne to howle and to cryen in þe e[yr]e sayenge: 'Iames, apostell of Ihesu Crist, haue pitee of us, for we brenne tofore oure tyme come.' To whom Seint Iames saide: 'Whi be ye come to me?' 30 And thei saide: 'Hermogenes sent us to the and to Philette for to bringe you to hym, and as sone as we were come [to the], the aungel of God bounde vs withe cheynes of fyre, and so he holdethe us in greuous turment.'

And thanne saide Iames: 'The aungell of God shall vnbynde you. 35 Gothe and bringethe hym to me vnhurt.' And thanne they went and toke Hermogenes and bounde his hondes behynde hym and brought hym to Iames and sayden to Hermogenes: 'Thou hast sent us ther as we haue be cruelly bounde and tormented.' And thanne the fende[s] saide to Iames: 'Yeue us power ouer hym so that we may reuenge oure 40 iniuries and oure brennynges.' And thanne Iames saide: 'See ye not Philette before you? Whi take ye not hym?' Than sayde the fendes: 'We mow no more | touche hym thanne though we hadd neuer knowe f. 158ᵛᵃ hym.' And thanne said Iames to Philette: 'For that thou shalt yelde good for euel, like as Ihesu Crist techithe us, go and vnbynde hym.' 45 And thanne Hermogenes helde hym al confused. Thanne Iames said to hym: 'Now go thi waye wher thou wilt al quite, for it longithe not to oure discipl[in]e that any be conuerted ayeinst his wille.' Thanne Hermogenes saide: 'I knowe so well the wrethe of the fendes that, but yef thou geue me sum thinge of thine that I may haue aboute me, they 50 will slee me.' And thanne Seint Iame gaue hym hys staffe. And than he went and brought to the apostell alle his bokes of enchauntementez for to brenne hem. But lest perauenture the sauoure of [the] brennynge shuld in any wise noye to any foles, he lete caste hem into the see, and whan he hadde so do he turned to the apostell and 55 fell downe to his fete and saide: 'Delyuerere of sowles, receyue me repentaunt.' And so he beganne to be perfit in the drede of God, that many gret vertues were after shewed by hym. And whanne the Iues sayen that Hermogenes was conuerted, they were gretly meued withe enuye and went to Iames and gretly blamed hym for that he preched 60 Ihesu Crist crucified. And he proued [hem clerely] by her scriptures the comynge and the passion of Ihesu Crist so that many leued theron.

Abiathar, þat was bisshop that yere, meued the peple gretly ayeinst
hym, and thanne they teyed a corde aboute the necke of Seint Iames
65 and ledde hym to Herodes Agrippe, and by the comaundement of
f. 158vb Agrippe he was ledde to be byheded. A man that was | smiten withe
the palasye laye in the waye and cried to hym that he shuld yeue hym
helthe. And Iames sayde to hym: 'In the name of Ihesu Crist, for whos
loue I am ledde to be byheded, arise al hole and blesse thi maker.' And
70 anone he arose al hole and blessed oure Lorde. And whanne one of the
scribes that hight Iosias whiche helde the corde aboute his necke seigh
this thingge, he fell downe atte hys fete and asked hym foryeuenesse
and praied hym to make hym cristen. And whanne Abiachar seigh
that, he made to take hym and saide: 'Yef thou corse not the name of
75 Crist thou shalt be byheded withe Iames.' To whom Iosias sayde:
'Cursed be thou and cursed be alle thy goddes, and the name of oure
Lorde Ihesu Crist be blessed witheouten ende.' And than Abiachar
comaunded that hys mouth shulde be bete withe festes, and sent a
massengere to Herodes that he might be byheded withe Iames, and it
80 was graunted hym. And whanne they shuld be byheded, Iames asked
of hym that shulde behede h[y]m a litell potte with water, and withe
that same he baptised Iosias, and anone they fulfelled her marterdome, bothe that one and that other be crowne of marterdome. The
blessed Seint Iames was beheded the .viij. kalend of Auerell and was
85 born in[to] Constantinenople in the [.viij.] kalendes of August and he
was beried in the .viij. kalend of Ianiuer, for his sepulcre was a
makinge fro August to Ianiuer, and therfor the Chirche hathe
ordeyned that his fest be halowed the .viij. kalend of August for the
most conable tyme.
90 And as Iohn Belet saiethe, that made this translacion diligently,
whanne Iames was beheded his disciples stale hys body by night for
f. 159ra drede of Iwes | and putte it in a shippe and committed it to the devine
gouernaile, and as the aungel of oure Lorde gided hem they ariued in
Galice in the rewme of Louue, for in Spayne was a quene that tyme
95 that by her name and by her desert of lyvinge hight Louue, that is as
moche to saye as a wolff. And than thei toke oute the body of the
shippe and leide it vpon a gret stone, ande thanne anone the stone
gaue place to the body as though it hadde be wex and ordeyned hym

---

64 a corde] acorde EH1   67 the²] a T2   79–80 withe . . . byheded] ins. and add
And H1, and T2   81 hym²] hem EG   83 bothe . . . marterdome] ins. H1, om. T2
85 into] L, in ET2, in changed to to H1, to G   .viij.] om. ET2, ins. H1   87 therfor] om.
T2   93 aungel] aungellis G   95 that¹] twice T2   96 as] om. H1T2

to the body merveylously right as a sepulcre. And than the disciples
went to Louue the quene and saide to her: 'Oure Lord Ihesu Crist 100
hathe sent to the the body of hys disciple, so that thou shuldest
receiue hym dede whom thou wold not receiue quyk.' And thanne
they tolde her the miracle how they were come thedyr witheoute
gouernayle and requered her of a couenable place for hys sepulture.

And whanne the quene herde this, she sent hem to a right cruel 105
man by trecherye, and as sum men writen, to the kinge of Spayne for
to haue hys acorde upon this thingge, and he toke hem and putte hem
in prison. And as he was atte hys dinere, the aungell of God opened
the prisone and lete hem go oute al frely. And whanne he wost this he
sent hastely after hem knyghtz for to take hem, and as the knyghtez 110
passed a brigge, the brigge brake vnder hem and thei fell in the ryuere
and were drowned. And whanne the kinge herde that, he was
repentaunt and dradde for hym and for hys peple and sent for hem
ande praied hem that they wolde turne ayenne and do in that contrey
as hem luste. And thanne they turned ayein and conuerted the peple 115
of that citee | to the faithe of oure Lorde. And whan the quene Louue f. 159rb
herde that she sorwed gretly, and whanne they come to her and tolde
her the acorde of the kinge she ansuered hem and sayde: 'Take the
oxen that I haue in that mountayne and ioynithe hem to my chare, and
bringgethe the body of youre maister and edefiethe hym a place after 120
youre desyre.' And thus sayde she of verray cursednesse, wetinge wel
that they were wylde boles and they myght not be ioyned to no chare
by no mannes powere, and yef they were, yet thei wolde todrawe the
holy body and slee hem alle. But ther ys no wyle ayeinst God, and tho
that thought not her wyckednesse went up to the mountayne and they 125
founde a dragon þat caste fyre ayeinst hem and ronne on hem, and
they made the signe of þe crosse ayeinst hym and he departed euene
atweyne. And after that they made the signe of the crosse vpon the
wylde boles and anone they were as meke as lambes, and than they
ioyned hem to her chare and putte witheinne the body of Seint Iames 130
withe the stone where[on] they leyde hym, and these wylde bestes

100 Louue] add to E   101 thou] 'þou' H1   101–2 shuldest receiue] schold haue
resseyuyd G   102 hym] hem T2   hym . . . whom] hem wiche G   103 miracle]
miracles T2   thedyr] there T2   104 her] here on erasure H1   hys] hire changed to his
H1, here T2   105 this] om. T2   106 men] om. T2   107 to] he wolde T2
109 hem] him H1   he'] þay G   112 whanne] þan H1   114 contrey] curteyne G
123 todrawe] not drawe H1T2   124 hem] him changed to hem H1   wyle] w/hill with
wh del. and w written over h H1, while T2   128 crosse] add ayenes del. T2   129 as']
all G, al changed to as H1   131 wheron] whereinne EH1T2   leyde hym] laidd (?) 'him'
H1, lithe T2

witheoute any gouernynge brought the body into the myddes of the
paleis of Louue the quene. And whanne she seygh that, she was gretly
abaysshed and beleued and become cristen and deliuered hem alle that
135 they asked, and dedied her paleys into a chirche and endowed it
gretly. And sithe she lyued and ended in good werkes.

Bernard, a man of the bysshopriche of Modre, so as Calixte the
pope tellithe, was taken and bounden in yren and thrawen in a depe
f. 159va prison and called | alwaies after the helpe of Seint Iames, and atte the
140 laste Seint Iames appered to hym and saide: 'Folowe me and come
withe me into Galice.' And anone hys irnes tobrast and Seint Iame
vanisshed away. And thanne he went up an high into the toure [with
his fetres on his necke] and lepte doune of the toure witheoute any
hurte, and yet the toure was .lx. cubites of highthe.

145   And as Seint [Bede] saiethe, ther was a man that hadde do right an
orrible synne wherof the bisshop dredde to assoyle hym, wherfor he
sent this man to Seint Iames withe a scrowe wherinne that synne was
wretin. And whanne he hadde leyde the scrowe vpon the auuter in the
day of the fest of Seint Iame, he praied to Seint Iame that by his
150 merites that synne might be effaced, and thanne he opened the scrowe
and founde al clene witheinne, and thanne he gaue thankingges to
God and to Seint Iame and publisshed this miracle [al] aboute.

.xxx.^ti men of Loreine went to Seint Iames aboute the yere of grace
a .M^l.lxxiij., and alle they ensured hem eche to other to serue eche
155 other and kepe hem truly in al astates, excepte one that wolde not
make no co[u]enaunt. And so it happed that one of hem felle sik, and
his felawship abode hym .xv. dayes, and atte the laste thei lefte hym,
alle sauf he that hadde made no co[u]enaunt, the whiche abode still
withe hym and kepte hym atte þe fote of the mount of Seint Michell.
160 And for it was night, the quicke man dredde gretly for the place that
was solitarie and for the presens of the dede body and for the cruelte
of the straunge peple and the derkenesse of the night. But anone
f. 159vb sodenly | Seint Iames appered to hym in liknesse of a trauelinge man
and comforted hym and sayde: 'Take me the dede body before me and
165 lyght thiselff up behynde me upon myn horse.' And so he rode al that

---

132 gouernynge] houernynge T2   137 as] that as a T2   138 a] om. H1T2
142-3 with . . . necke] om. EH1T2   143 doune] add out T2   144 of highthe] hie
H1G, hie and his fetirs in his nek T2   145 And] gap in G, om. T2   Bede] gap in EG,
Calixt ins. in gap H1, Iames T2 (bede P2)   150 be] ins. H1, om. T2   152 al] om.
EH1T2   156 couenaunt] comenaunt E   157 lefte] felte G   158 hadde made] trs.
and marked for correction H1   couenaunt] comenaunt E, conne T2   160 for^1] add that T2
162 But] And T2   163 trauelinge] trave'i'lyng H1   165 up] del. and ins. H1

night till [they] come to the mountayne that is but a myle from Seint
Iames, and ther the seint sette hem to the erthe and comaunded to the
quik man that he shulde assemble the chanones of Seint Iames to bery
this dede man, and that he shulde saye to hys felawes that for her
faithe that they hadde broken her pilgrymage was not. And he dede 170
his comaundement, and whanne his felawes wondered [how] he hadde
goo so gret a way in so shorte tyme he tolde hem [all] as Seint Iame
hadde tolde hym.

As the pope Calixte tellithe, a man of Almayn and hys sone went to
Seint Iames in the yere of grace .M^l. .iiij^{xx}.iij., and so they come to 175
Tolouse for to haue herborughe and were made dronke withe her oste,
and thanne the osteler putte a cuppe of siluer in thayre male. And in
the morwtyde whanne they went oute he folued hem as theues and
bare upon hem that they hadde stole the cuppe, and tolde hem that yef
he might fynde the cuppe vpon hem þat they shulde be punisshed 180
after the lawe. And thanne thei sought and it was founde in the male,
and anone they were brought to iugement. And thanne the sentence
was yeuen that all that thei hadde shulde be yeue to the oste and that
one of hem shulde be hangged. And as the sone profered to deye
before the fader and the fader before the sone, at the last the sone was 185
hangged and the fader went wepinge and soruinge towardes Seint
Iame, and retorned | ayein to that place the .xxxvj.^{ti} day after, and f. 160ra
thanne he turned to that place ther his sone was hangged for to
beholde hym and cried and wepte pitously. But anone the sone that
was hangged beganne to comfort hys fader and saide: 'Right dere 190
fader, wepe not, for it was neuer so well with me, for Seint Iames
hathe susteyned me and fedde me euer sethe withe heuenly mete.'
And whanne the fader herde that, he was fulfelled withe right gret
ioye and ranne to the citee and dede so moche that the peple come and
see this miracle, and thanne they toke doune the sone and hangged the 195
oste.

Hugh [de] Seint Victor tellithe that the fende come and appered in
the fourme of Seint Iame to a pilgrime and recorded to hym many
wrechidnessez of the worlde, and saide to hym that he shulde be

166 they] L, he EH1GT2   but] om. T2   168 assemble] L, add alle EH1T2, add
to G   170 they] he G   171 how] that E   172 hem] him changed to hem H1
all] om. E   173 hadde] om.   175 .iij.] iij changed to ij H1, .ij. G   176 Tolouse]
'To'louse H1   179 cuppe] add Thei seid nay H1T2   179–80 that yef he] if þat and
þei changed to he H1, if that thei T2   181 and] add þan T2   187–8 the ... place] om.
T2   189 wepte] went T2   190 hangged] add for to bihold him and cried subp. and
del. H1   193 right] om. T2   gret] ins. H1   197 de] of EH1T2

200 blessed yef he wolde slee hymselff in the worshyppe of hym. And
anone this pilgryme toke a kniff and slow hymselff. And thanne his
oste that he was herborued with was hadd in suspesyon and dredde to
deye, but anone he that was dede arose fro dethe to lyff and tolde hou
that the fende that hadde taught hym to slee hymselff and wolde haue
205 ledde hym to turment, but anone Seint Iame come to the sege of the
iuge wher the fendes accused hym and ledde hym withe hym ayenne.

An abbot of [Clyni] witnessithe how that a yonge man of the contre
of Lyon was wont to goo to Seint Iames, and so in a tyme as he wolde
go, the night before he shulde remowe, he fell in fornicacion and in
210 the morw he went. And thanne in a night the fende apered to hym in
f. 160rb the [forme] of Seint Iame and sayde to hym: 'Whost | thou what I am?'
And he ansuered: 'Nay.' And thanne he sai[de]: 'I am Iame þe apostell
that thou art custumed to visite euery yere, and I reioyse me gretly of
thi deuocion. But now late or thou wentest oute of thine hous thou
215 fillest in fornicacion and tokest vpon the to come to me witheoute
confession, wherfor thi pilgrimage may n[ot] plese God ne me. For
whoso will come to me in pilgrymage shuld putte away his synnes by
confession and contricion.' And whanne he hadd so sayde he
vanisshed away. And thanne this yonge man was full of sorugh and
220 wolde haue gone to hys hous to haue be shriuen and sithe to go his
[vi]age, but thanne the fende apered ayein to hym in likenesse of the
apostell and forbade hym that in any wyse and tolde hym that [that]
synne might in no wise be foryeuen but yef he cutte [of] hys membres,
and yet he saide he shulde be moche more blessed yef he wolde slee
225 hymselff and be marter for his loue. And thanne he the same night
whanne his felawes were aslepe toke a suerde and cutte of his
membres and withe the same suerde he slow hymselff. And whan
his felawes were awaked and [they] seen this thei were gretly aferde
ande fledde anone. And thanne as men ordeined for his pitte he
230 releued, and thanne alle were abaysshed and fledde and he beganne
to tell how it was befalle hym. 'Whanne', he saide, 'that [I] hadde
slayne [my]selff atte the fendes request, the fendes toke [me] and

204 that²] om. T2   205 but] And T2   207 Clyni] Olym E, Olyny H1
211 forme] lykenesse EH1T2   212 saide] saiethe EH1   213 art] haste G
214 of¹] for T2   now] ins. H1, om. T2   215 witheoute] add any E   216 not] L,
neuer EH1T2, neythir G   219 of] ins. H1   220 go] add to T2   221 viage]
pilgrimage E   thanne] þat G   the²] om. H1T2   222 that that] L, that EH1GT2
223 of] oute EH1, on T2   225 marter] martered EH1T2   226 felawes were] Felaw
was H1, fellawes was T2   228 they] om. EH1T2   230 beganne] gan T2
231 hym] add And EH1T2   that] om. T2   I] he EH1T2   232 myselff] hymselff
EH1T2   me] hym ET2, me on erasure H1

ledde [me] towardes Rome, but anone Seint Iame come after and
blamed the fendes gretly of her fals wyles, and whanne thei hadde
longe striuen | togedre, Seint Iame constreined hem withe me to come f. 160va
into a medowe wher that the blessed Virgine Mari was spekinge withe 236
many seintes. And thanne Seint Iame pleyned hym gretly to her for
me, and she blamed gretly the fendes and comaunded þat I shulde
turne ayenne to lyff. And thanne Seint Iames toke me and gaue me liff
as ye see.' And there apered thre dayes after in his woundes but the 240
traces, and he toke ayein his viage and founde his felawship and tolde
hem al be ordre.

So as Calixt the pope tellithe how ther was a Frenshe man aboute
the yere of oure Lorde a thousande an hundred whiche wolde eschewe
the mortalite that was in Fraunce and went in pilgrimage to Seint 245
Iames, hymselff, his wyff, and his children. And whanne thei come to
Pampilion hys wyff deyed, and his oste toke awaye al his moneye and
his hors wheron he caried his children. And thanne he went al full of
sorugh and discomforted, beringe his children vpon his shuldres, and
one he ledde after hym, and mette with a man ridinge on an asse, 250
whiche man hadde pitee of hym and lent hym his asse for to bere his
children. And whanne he come to Seint Iames, as he woke and praied,
Seint Iame apered to hym and asked hym yef he knewe hym, and he
sayde: 'Nay.' And thanne he saide: 'I am Iames the apostell that haue
lent the myn asse, and yet I lene it the atte thy goinge ayenne, and 255
wete thou wele that thine oste is falle downe of a solere and is dede,
and thou shalt haue ayenne alle that he toke fro the.' And whanne all
this was fulfelled he turned ayenne, | he and his children, glad and f. 160vb
mery towarde his hous. And whanne he was come home and toke his
children downe fro the asse, the asse vanisshed away and no man 260
woste where she become.

Ther was a marchaunt whiche a tyraunt hadde robbed withe
wrongge and putte hym in prison, the whiche called devoutely
Seint Iame to his helpe, and Seint Iame apered to hym before tho
that kepte hym and woke hym and ledde hym into the hyest parte of 265
the towre, and anone the towre enclined and bowed so lowe that the
highthe of the toure was euene withe the erthe, and he went out esely

233 me] hym ET2, me *on erasure* H1   Rome] *with* Ro *over-written by* Pa (?) H1
239 gaue] *om.* T2   240 as ye see] *twice* T2   apered] *add* to him T2   241 viage]
visage *changed to* viage H1, visage T2   243 pope] *add* of Rome EH1T2   246 thei]
he G   253 Seint Iame] *twice* T2   255 it] *om.* GT2   256 thou] it G   258 he
and] he and // he and E   and'] an'd' H1   260 the asse²] *twice* T2   263 prison] L,
add to EH1GT2   267 highthe] heighist G

witheoute any lepinge frely wher he wolde. And thanne his kepers
folowed hym and went euen by hym and they might in no wise see
270 hym.

Thre knightes of the diesise of Lyon went to Seint Iames, and one
of hem was required of a pore woman that for the loue of Seint Iame
he wolde bere her vpon his hors, and anone he toke her and sette her
on his hors. And after that he fonde a seke man and leide hym on his
275 hors a[lso] and toke the b[urdo]n of the man and the sacke of the
woman and folowed hem afote, but what by the brennynge hete of the
sonne and his laboure of his fete he was right wery. And whanne he
come into Galice he felle strongely seke, and his felawshippe sene but
dethe upon hym and counsailed hym goodly to take kepe to his soule,
280 but he might no worde saye to hem for he laye thre dayes witheoute
speche. In the .iij. day he woke and sighed sore and sayde: 'I yelde
f. 161ra thankyngges to God and | to Seint Iame, for I am deliuered be his
desert. For whanne I wolde [full] fayne haue done as ye counsailed
me, the fendes come to me and streyned me so greuously that in no
285 wyse I might saye no worde that was for the sauacion of my soule, and
I herde you well but I might in no wise ansuere. And [than] the
blessed Seint Iame came and bare in his right honde the sacke of the
pore woman, and in his lefte honde he bare the burdon of the pore
man to whom I hadde holpe in the way, and helde the burdon for a
290 spere and the sacke for a sheld and assailed the fendes in grete anger
and afraied hem so that he putte hem to flyght. And in this wise the
blessed Seint Iame hathe deliuered me and geue me ayenne my
speche, wherfor I praie you calle to me a preste, for I may not longe
abide in this lyff.' And thanne he turned to one of his felawes and
295 saide to hym: 'My frende, ride no more with thi lorde, for sekirly he
ys dampned and shall hastely deye an euel dethe.' And thanne he was
shriuen and deyed, and whanne he was beried his felawes retorned
ayein into her contre, and thanne one of hem tolde his lorde as it was
saide to hym, and he made but a iape therof and hadde despite to
300 amende hym. And thanne anone he was smite withe a spere in a
bataile and deyed.

269 and¹] om. G   they] om. T2   271 Seint] 'S' H1   275 also] L, ars EH1GT2
burdon] L, birthen EH1GT2   277 of] on G   he was . . . and] om. G   278 sene]
seenge T2   283 full] om. E   ye] he changed to ye H1, he T2   285 for] om. H1T2
286 than] om. ET2, ins. H1   287 came and] om. H1T2   288 burdon] burthen GT2
289 in] in // In T2   290 assailed] he railed T2   in] add a E   291 afraied] a raied
T2   in] om. T2   295 sekirly] om. H1T2   296 an] in T2   298 thanne] þat G
300 a²] om. T2

Seint Calixt the pope tellith that a man of Viriliak went to Seint
Iames, and his money fayled hym by the waye and he was sore
ashamed to begge. And so for sorughe and shame he leyde hym vnder
a tre to rest, and in hys slepe he dremed þat Seint Iame fedde hym. 305
And whanne he was awaked he founde a loef | bake in the asshes atte f. 161rb
his hede, and withe that loef he lyued .xv. dayes tille he come ayenne
till his propre place. And he ete .ij. tymes [on the day] sufficiauntly of
that brede, and on the morw he founde it hole in his bagge.

Calixt the pope tellithe that a burgeys of the citee of Barseloigne 310
went to Seint Iames, and his praier was only that he shulde neuer be
take of his enemyes. And as he come by Sisile he was taken in the see
with Sarisenes, and many tyme was he ledde to fayeres to be solde, but
alwaye the cheynes that he was bounde with were vnbounde. Ande
whanne he hadde bene solde .xiij. tymes he was bounde withe double 315
cheynes, and thanne he called Seint Iame to his helpe, and Seint Iame
appered to hym and saide: 'For that thou were in my chirche and
roughtest nothinge of the helthe of thi soule, but requiredest alway
helthe of body, therfor thou art fall in this perell. But for oure Lorde
is mercifull he hathe sent me to [by the].' And anone the cheynes 320
brasten, and he went his waye and bere a partye of the cheynes withe
hym, and passed thorugh the lond of Sarisenes and come into his
contre before alle the peple, that were gretly abasshed of this miracle.

It was in the yere of oure Lorde a thousand two hundered .xxxviij.
in the Vigile of Seint Iame in a castell that hight P[r]ate betwene 325
Florence and Pistore, ther was a yonge man the whiche was deceyued
by sympelnesse [by] counsayle of an olde shrewe and sette fire in the
cornes of his maister, whiche he shulde haue kept, for that he wolde
haue away his | heritage. And thanne he was take and confessed the f. 161va
dede and was iuged to be drawe and brent. And thanne he vowed hym 330
to Seint Iames, and whanne he hadde longe be drawe by stoni wayes
he felt neuer hurt in his body ne in his sherte. And after he was
bounde to a stake and wode sette rounde aboute hym and fere sette
theron, his bondes were brent and he called alway Seint Iame, but ther
was neuer founde harme in his body ne in his shert. And yet thei caste 335
hym in the fyre, and anone he was deliuered by the apostell, and so

305 Iame] om. G   308 on the day] L, om. EH1GT2   309 it] om. T2
311 was] add euer T2   312 And as] twice T2   313 many tyme] þe mene tyme T2
ledde] add with Sarazynys G   fayeres] Fe'i'res H1   318 the] om. G   helthe] helpe T2
requiredest] requirest H1T2   320 by the] L, be thin helpe EH1GT2   325 Prate]
Poate EH1T2   327 by²] of EH1T2   328 cornes] corners EH1T2   maister]
maisters hous EH1T2   336 so] om. T2

oure Lorde was glorified in his apostell and this pore man was deliuered.